The Psychologist as Detective

An Introduction to Conducting Research in Psychology

THIRD EDITION

RANDOLPH A. SMITH
Ouachita Baptist University

STEPHEN F. DAVIS
Emporia State University

PEARSON

Prentice Hall

Upper Saddle River, New Jersey 07458

Library of Congress Cataloging-in-Publication Data

Smith, Randolph A., 1951–
    The psychologist as detective : an introduction to conducting research in psychology /
Randolph A. Smith, Stephen F. Davis.—3rd ed.
        p. cm.
    Includes bibliographical references and index.
    ISBN 0-13-111764-5
    1. Psychology—Research. 2. Psychology—Research—Methodology. 3. Psychology,
Experimental.   I. Davis, Stephen F.   II. Title.

BF76.5.S54 2003
150'.7'2—dc21   2002045049

VP/Editorial Director: *Leah Jewell*
Senior Acquistions Editor: *Jayne Heffler*
Editorial Assistant: *Kevin Doughten*
AVP/Director of Production
   and Manufacturing: *Barbara Kittle*
Managing Editor: *Joanne Riker*
Production Editor: *Maureen Richardson*
Manufacturing Manager: *Nick Sklitsis*
Prepress and Manufacturing Buyer: *Tricia Kenny*
Cover Design: *Kathy Mystkowska*
Cover Art: *Todd Davidson/Stock Illustration Source, Inc.*
Cover Image Specialist: *Karen Sanatar*

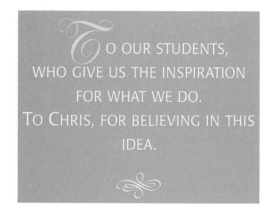

To our students,
who give us the inspiration
for what we do.
To Chris, for believing in this
idea.

This book was set in 9/12 Poppl-Laudatio Light by comp and was printed
and bound by R.R. Donnelly & Sons Company. The cover was printed by Bradford & Bigelow.

ISBN: 0-13-111764-5

Pearson Education LTD., London
Pearson Education Australia PTY, Limited, Sydney
Pearson Education Singapore, Pte. Ltd
Pearson Education North Asia Ltd, Hong Kong
Pearson Education Canada, Ltd., Toronto
Pearson Educación de Mexico, S. A. de C. V.
Pearson Education—Japan, Tokyo
Pearson Education Malaysia, Pte. Ltd
Pearson Education, Upper Saddle River, New Jersey

Contents

Chapter Two

Research Ideas and Hypotheses 23

Chapter Three

Ethics in Psychological Research 48

Chapter Four

Nonexperimental Methods I: Descriptive Methods, Qualitative Research, and Correlational Studies 68

Chapter Five

Nonexperimental Methods II: Ex Post Facto Studies, Surveys and Questionnaires, Sampling, and Basic Research Strategies 86

Chapter Six

The Basics of Experimentation I: Variables and Control 104

Chapter Seven

The Basics of Experimentation II: Final Considerations, Unanticipated Influences, and Cross-Cultural Issues 142

Chapter Eight

Chapter Nine

Chapter Ten

Designing, Conducting, Analyzing, and Interpreting Experiments with More Than Two Groups 229

Chapter Eleven

Designing, Conducting, Analyzing, and Interpreting Experiments with Multiple Independent Variables 258

Chapter Twelve

Chapter Thirteen

Chapter Fourteen

Preface

Because our objectives and goals and the special features we've included in *The Psychologist as Detective* remain unchanged in this third edition, our original Preface follows.

Note to the Instructor

Margery Franklin (1990) quoted former Clark University professor and chair Heinz Werner's views on psychological research. Werner indicated:

> I got rather apprehensive at finding that students were frequently taught that there was only one acceptable way of conduct in the laboratory—there has to be an hypothesis set up, or a set of hypotheses, and the main job of the experimenter is to prove or disprove the hypothesis. What is missed here is the function of the scientist as a discoverer and explorer of unknown lands. . . . Hypotheses . . . are essential elements of inquiry, but they are so, not as rigid propositions but as flexible parts of the process of searching; by the same token, conclusions drawn from the results are as much an end as a beginning. . . . Now . . . academic psychologists [are beginning] to see research not as a rigid exercise of rules of a game but as a problem-solving procedure, a probing into unknown lands with plans which are not fixed but modifiable, with progress and retreat, with branching out into various directions or concentration on one.

Clearly Werner's views are as applicable in the twenty-first century as they were during the heyday of behaviorism; they reflect perfectly the intent of this text.

From our vantage point, research in psychology is like a detective case; hence the title we have chosen, *The Psychologist as Detective*. A problem presents itself; we discover clues; we must evaluate bits of evidence that compete for our attention and accept or discard them; and finally, we prepare a report or summary of the case (research) for consideration by our peers.

When presented in this light, the research process in psychology will, we believe, be an interesting and stimulating endeavor for students. In short, our goal is to attract students to psychological research because of its inherent interest.

To accomplish this goal, we have incorporated several pedagogical features in this text:

1. To provide a sense of relevance and continuity, the theme of "psychologist as detective" runs throughout the text.

2. **Interactive Style of Writing.** Because we believe that the experimental psychology/research methods text should be lively and engaging, we employ an interactive, conversational style of writing that we hope will help draw students into the material.

3. **The Psychological Detective Feature.** The questions or situations posed by these sections that appear throughout each chapter will encourage students to engage in critical thinking exercises. These sections also serve as excellent stimulants for productive class discussions.

4. **Marginal Definitions.** Key definitions appear in the margin, close to the introduction of the term in the text.

5. **Review Summaries.** To help students master smaller chunks of material, each chapter contains one or more review summaries.

6. **Check Your Progress.** A Check Your Progress feature follows each Review Summary. Students can use these sections to test their mastery of the material they have just completed. These study breaks should be especially helpful to your students when they prepare for quizzes and examinations.

We hope that these special features will provide your students with a positive experience as they learn the fundamentals of research methodology in psychology.

Note to the Student

Welcome to the world of psychological research! Because the two of us have taught this course for over 50 years (combined!), we have seen the excitement that research can generate in student after student. As you will learn, conducting psychological research is very much like being a detective on a case.

Throughout this text we have tried to make it clear that research is something that you can (and should) become involved in. We hope you will enjoy reading about the student projects that we use as research examples throughout this text. Student research projects are making valuable contributions to our field. We hope to see your name among those making such contributions!

At this point we encourage you to stop immediately to review the list of pedagogical features highlighted in the "Note to the Instructor."

Did you humor us by actually looking at that list? If not, please do so now. To make full use of this text, you need to become actively involved; these pedagogical features will help you. Active involvement means that you need to stop to think about **The Psychological Detective** sections immediately when you encounter them, refer to figures and tables when directed to do so, and complete the **Check Your Progress** sections when they appear. Becoming actively involved in this course helps the material come alive; your grade and your future involvement in psychology will thank you.

What's New for the Third Edition?

Without hesitation, we're excited about the changes and new features of the third edition of *The Psychologist as Detective.* Here's a sampling of the changes we've made. We

- Changed all of the student research examples throughout the entire book. To ensure that the Third Edition is as current as possible, these new research examples carry 2000 (or more recent) publication dates.
- Added a section on a "new view of hypothesis testing." (Chapter 2, page 43)
- Added new material on qualitative research methods. (Chapter 4)
- Replaced the single chapter on nonexperimental research methods with two separate, shorter chapters (chapter 4 and 5). This change will allow instructors to pick and choose more effectively the material they wish to cover.
- Added relevant Sherlock Holmes quotes throughout the book. Holmes's views are as relevant to experimental psychology as they are to detective work.
- Completely updated the chapter on APA format (Chapter 14) to include material from the fifth edition of the *Publication Manual.*
- Included a new checklist so students can evaluate their adherence to APA format before submitting their reports. (Chapter 14, pages 402- 404)
- Expanded the Instructor's Manual under the guidance of Steve Seidal, Texas A&M University, Corpus Christi. (Electronic Test Item File also available. Please contact your local Prentice Hall representative).
- New Website www.prenhall.com/smith
  Developed by Brian Pope, Andrew College. This website included helpful study tools such as chapter objectives, study guide, flashcards, and much more! Also available on the website are Powerpoint presentation slides.

Acknowledgments

We express our appreciation to the consultants who suggested improvements for this text: Chris Spatz, Hendrix College; Beth Dietz Uhler, Miami University (Ohio); Janet Larson, John Carroll University; Doreen Arcus, University of Massachusetts, Lowell; Lynette Zeleny, California State University, Fresno; Robert Batsell, Kalamazoo College; Scott Gronlund, University of Oklahoma; Laura Bowman, Central Connecticut State University; Celia Brownell, University of Pittsburgh; Lee Fernandez, Yosemite Community College; Michael Brannick, University of Southern Florida; Maureen McCarthy, Austin Peay State University; Elizabeth Yost Hammer, Loyola University; Terry Pettijohn, Mercyhurst College; Gina Grimshaw, California State University, San Marcos. Their comments were especially helpful.

In many ways the final preparation of a text is only as good as the publisher. Special thanks to our editor, Jayme Heffler, and her assistant, Kevin Doughten, and our hard-working production editor, Maureen Richardson. Thanks, folks—it would not have worked without your concern and support!

We also thank our families (Corliss, Tyler, and Ben—RAS; Kathleen and Jennifer—SFD) for putting up with us during the preparation of this text. True friends and real supporters are few and far between!

R. A. S.
S. F. D.

The Science of Psychology

Welcome to the world of psychological research! Because the two of us have taught this course for over 50 years (combined!), we have seen the excitement that research can generate in student after student. Throughout this text we have tried to make it perfectly clear that research is something that you can (and should) become involved in. We hope you will enjoy reading about the student projects that we use as research examples throughout this text. Student research projects are making valuable contributions to our field, and we hope to see your name among those making such contributions!

To make full use of this text, you need to become actively involved. Active involvement means that you need to

1. Stop and think about **The Psychological Detective** sections immediately when you encounter them. Each of these sections asks you to think about a question concerning psychological research. Take full advantage of these sections; we designed them to help you think critically about psychological research. Critical thinking is vital to good detectives; we want you to become the best psychological detective possible.
2. Refer to figures and tables when directed to do so.
3. Complete the **Check Your Progress** features when they appear.

Becoming actively involved in this course helps the material come alive; your grade and your future involvement in psychology will thank you.

We purposely titled our text *The Psychologist as Detective* to convey the excitement and thrill that researchers have when they investigate questions that are at the core of what it means to be a psychologist. To make the third edition of *The Psychologist as Detective* as lively as possible, we've included several quotations from the world's most famous detective, Sherlock Holmes. For example, Holmes reflected his passion for his work when he said, "I swear that another day shall not have passed before I have done all that man can do to reach the heart of the mystery" (Doyle, 1927, p. 732). Psychological researchers are just as passionate in their pursuit of the truth as Sherlock Holmes.

The parallels between conducting psychological research and working on a detective case are striking. The detective has to know the boundaries of the case (the experimenter develops a research question). The detective eliminates suspects (the researcher exercises control over unwanted factors), gathers evidence (the researcher conducts the experiment and makes observations), proposes a solution (the researcher analyzes research results and offers an interpretation), and offers a solution to the jury (researchers share their results and interpretations with their peers).

Our examination of psychological research begins by considering a research project that would intrigue even the best psychological detective:

> You have been receiving junk e-mails inviting you to try out the many online dating services for several months. Your typical response is to click the "delete" key; however, you finally start to wonder about online dating services. What characteristics do people look for in a potential date? Are there differences in the characteristics that men and women look for?

Such questions prompted Kim Driggers and Tasha Helms, students at Oklahoma State University, to conduct a research project that involved an evaluation of salary as a factor in dating. Driggers and Helms (2000) reported, "Male and female college students viewed pictures of the opposite sex and rated the target's attractiveness and their own willingness to

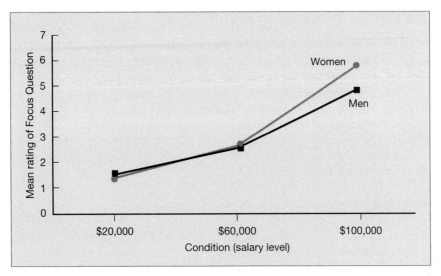

FIGURE 1-1 The mean rating of male and female participants for each condition ($20,000, $60,000, $100,000) on the focus question ("How willing would you be to go on a date with this person?").

Source: Figure 1 from Driggers, K. J., & Helms, T. (2000). The effects of salary on willingness to date. *Psi Chi Journal of Undergraduate Research, 5,* 76–80. Used with permission.

date the target" (p. 76). As you can see from Figure 1-1, they found that willingness to date increased as salary increased. Moreover, the female participants seemed to be more influenced than the male participants by the highest salary level.

For the time being we will not concern ourselves with exactly how Driggers and Helms gathered their information concerning willingness to date. Our concern at present is why they gathered this information. The answer really is quite straightforward—they had an interesting question that needed an answer. Asking and then attempting to answer questions are at the heart of what psychologists do. In short, psychologists are in the business of acquiring new knowledge.

Ways to Acquire Knowledge

Although the task of acquiring new knowledge may sound simple, it is actually more difficult than it appears. The difficulty comes about because there is more than one way to acquire knowledge and because once knowledge is acquired, you need to ensure its *truthfulness.* Let's examine several methods that have been used to increase our store of knowledge. These techniques were suggested by the philosopher-scientist Charles S. Peirce, who helped to establish psychology in the United States in the 1880s. As you will see, the **validity** of the knowledge produced by some of these methods is doubtful.

Validity The degree to which a knowledge claim is accurate.

Tenacity

Tenacity Acceptance of knowledge or information simply because it has been presented repeatedly.

When we hear a statement repeated a sufficient number of times, we have a tendency to accept it as being true. Thus, **tenacity** refers to the continued presentation of a particular bit of information; no matter which way you turn, the same information seems to be present and you begin to believe it. According to the tenacity view of acquiring knowledge, you should accept this repeated message as being true. For example, consider a young child whose older brother has repeatedly said, "A witch lives in the old brown house on Maple Street." Because this is the only message that is presented concerning the old brown house on Maple Street, the child accepts it as fact.

Authority

Much of our daily behavior relies on the acceptance of knowledge from authorities. For example, do you *personally* know that exposure to the sun results in skin cancer, or do you put on lotion with a high sun protection factor (e.g., SPF 25) simply because you have taken the word of an authority? How many other authorities, such as ministers, automobile mechanics, stockbrokers, lawyers, and teachers, influence your daily life?

Authority also depends on another factor—the credibility of the person presenting the information. The detective knows that the knowledge you acquire is only as good as the credibility of the authority who presents it. Any time of day or night you can see "authorities" dispensing great amounts of information as they try to convince you to buy any number of different products on television commercials. What credentials do these "authorities" have? How accurate is the information they are providing?

From watching television commercials you should now be aware that tenacity and authority may not be completely independent of each other. Think of how many times (tenacity) you saw one specific commercial where 'NSync (authority) was selling Chili's baby back ribs or the commercial where Tiger Woods (authority) is selling Buick automobiles. The combination of these two factors may be stronger than either one alone.

Clearly, we are able to acquire new knowledge through tenacity and authority. However, this newly acquired knowledge may not be as valid as we would like. What problems can you identify with acquiring knowledge through tenacity and authority?

Tenacity and authority share two problems. First, you have no way of knowing whether the knowledge you have gained is true. Merely repeating that the moon is made of green cheese does not make this statement true. The second problem concerns the inability (or unwillingness) of tenacity and authority to change in the face of contradictory evidence. When they hear conflicting evidence, individuals who have accepted knowledge based on tenacity or authority either ignore the evidence or find some way to discount it. For example, if you really believe the moon is made of green cheese, and an astronaut reports bringing back a rock from the moon, you might decide that the astronaut had never been to the moon and that the claim that this rock came from the moon was an elaborate hoax.

Experience

Another way to gain knowledge is through direct experience. Surely if you experience something firsthand, there is no better or more accurate method for acquiring new information. Right? Unfortunately, this assumption is not always true. If you are color-blind or tone-deaf, your perception of the world is altered and your knowledge base may not be accurate. Likewise, a theory developed under the effects of a hallucinogenic drug may not conform to reality very well. Even normal individuals under normal conditions may see the world differently. Ask 10 people to describe a situation and you will likely get 10 different descriptions; we all see the world differently. Our past experiences and culture may make some events and behaviors seem more important than others. For example, a person from an Arab culture would expect interactions with other people, even casual acquaintances, to take place in very close proximity. Americans, on the other hand, are comfortable interacting with casual acquaintances at greater distances (e.g., 4 to 5 feet; Matsumoto, 1997). Hence, Americans would vividly recall close-proximity interactions because they are atypical occurrences.

Reason and Logic

This approach is based on the premise that we can apply reason and logic to a situation in order to gain knowledge and understanding. Typically, we start with an assumption and then logically deduce consequences based on this assumption. This process is frequently called a **logical syllogism**. For example, we may start with the assumption that "beautiful people are good." Then when we met Claudia, who is an attractive person, we would think, "Beautiful people are good (major premise). Claudia is a beautiful person (minor premise). Therefore, Claudia is a good person (conclusion)." The fallacy of this deduction should be apparent. We have no proof to support our original assumption that "beautiful people are good." Without such proof, we cannot trust our conclusion about Claudia. Before you say you are sure you would never fall prey to such faulty logic, we would like to point out that the "beautiful is good" stereotype is a thoroughly researched topic of social psychology (Dion, Berscheid, & Walster, 1972); it is a bias that many people fall prey to. For example, attractiveness affects first impressions when viewing photos on résumés (Mack & Rainey, 1990); attractive people created more favorable first impressions.

> **Logical syllogism**   A scheme of formal logic or argument consisting of a major premise, a minor premise, and a conclusion.

Science

Each of the techniques for acquiring knowledge that we have discussed so far has had a major problem or problems associated with it. Hence, although psychologists may use these methods to generate hypotheses and stimulate research ideas, these methods are not likely to add to our store of psychological knowledge. What method do psychologists prefer?

The year 1879 marks the beginning of modern psychological study. Although numerous other dates could be used to mark the founding of psychology, most historians select 1879 because it marked the establishment of a research laboratory at the University of Leipzig, Germany, by Wilhelm Wundt. Wundt used the scientific method to gather new information. Over 100 years later, psychologists continue to believe the scientific approach is best suited for adding to our knowledge of psychological processes.

The key elements in the scientific approach are

1. objective measurements of the phenomenon under consideration
2. the ability to verify or confirm the measurements made by other individuals
3. self-correction of errors and faulty reasoning
4. exercising control to rule out the influence of unwanted factors

We will discuss each of these characteristics in the next section. For now, we will simply say the scientific method attempts to provide objective information that anyone who wishes to repeat the observation in question can verify.

Review the methods for acquiring knowledge that we presented. How does the scientific method avoid the problems associated with tenacity, authority, experience, and reason and logic?

When scientists use the scientific method, they make observations and gather new information. However, we don't have to accept the scientists' knowledge claims on faith (authority) or merely because they are repeatedly discussed and presented (tenacity). The methods and procedures the scientist uses to acquire knowledge are open to public scrutiny, and should individuals decide to question the scientist's information, they are able to test the conclusions themselves. Thus, the possibility of individual experiences also can be ruled out. In short, researchers can verify the knowledge claims made by science; the other methods do not afford us this opportunity.

Components of the Scientific Method

We describe the features that characterize the scientific method in this section. We will have much more to say about these characteristics in subsequent chapters.

Objectivity

In conducting a research project, the psychologist, like the good detective, strives to be objective. For example, psychologists select research participants in such a manner as to avoid biasing factors (e.g., age or sex). Researchers frequently make their measurements with instruments in order to be as objective as possible. We describe such measurements as being **empirical** because they are based on objectively quantifiable observations.

> **Empirical**   Objectively quantifiable observations.

Confirmation of Findings

Because the procedures and measurements are objective, we should be able to repeat them and *confirm* the original results. Confirmation of findings is important for establishing the validity of research. Psychologists use the term **replication** to refer to a research study that is conducted in exactly the same manner as a previous study. By conducting a replication study, the scientist hopes to confirm previous findings. Other studies may constitute *replication with extension,* in which scientists generate new information at the same time as they confirm previous findings. For example, Matisha Montgomery, a student at the University of Central Oklahoma in Edmond, and her faculty advisor, Kathleen Donovan, replicated and extended the conditions reported to be responsible for the "Mozart effect" (the finding that participants' cognitive and spatial performance was better after they listened to music by Mozart). Their results indicated that students actually performed worse after listening to the classical music by Mozart (Montgomery & Donovan, 2002).

> **Replication**   An additional scientific study that is conducted in exactly the same manner as the original research project.

Self-Correction

Because scientific findings are open to public scrutiny and replication, errors and faulty reasoning that become apparent should lead to a change in the conclusions we reach. For example, some early American psychologists, such as James McKeen Cattell, once believed that intelligence was directly related to the quality of one's nervous system; the better the nervous system, the higher the intelligence (see Goodwin, 1999). To verify this predicted relation, Cattell attempted to demonstrate that college students with faster reaction times (therefore, having better nervous systems) earned higher grades in college (had higher levels of intelligence). However, his observations failed to support the predicted relation, and Cattell changed his view of intelligence and how to measure it.

Control

Probably no single term characterizes science better than **control**. Scientists go to great lengths to make sure their conclusions accurately reflect the way nature operates.

Imagine that an industrial psychologist wants to determine whether providing new, brighter lighting will increase worker productivity. The new lighting is installed, and the industrial psychologist arrives at the plant to monitor production and determine whether productivity increases.

> **Control**   Two meanings: directly manipulating (1) a factor of interest in a research study to determine its effects or (2) other, unwanted variables that could influence the results of a research project.

There is a problem with this research project that needs to be controlled. What is the nature of this problem, and how can it be corrected?

The main problem with this research project concerns the presence of the psychologist to check on production after installation of the new lighting. If the researcher was not present to observe production before the lighting changes were made, then he or she should not be present following the implementation of these changes. If production increases following the lighting changes, is the increase due to the new lighting or to the presence of the researcher who is monitoring production? Unfortunately, there is no way of knowing. The psychologist must exercise control to make sure that the only factor that could influence productivity is the change in lighting; other factors should not be allowed to exert an influence by varying also.

This example of research on the effects of lighting on worker productivity (which is an actual research study) also illustrates another use of the term *control*. In addition to accounting for the effects of unwanted factors, *control* can refer to the direct manipulation of the factor of major interest in the research project. Because the industrial psychologist was interested in the effects of lighting on productivity, a change in lighting was purposely created (control or direct manipulation of factors of major interest), whereas other, potentially influential but undesirable factors, such as the presence of the psychologist, were not allowed to change (control of unwanted factors).

When researchers implement control by directly manipulating the factor that is the central focus of their research, we say that an experiment has been performed. Because most psychologists believe that our most valid knowledge is produced by conducting an experiment, we will give this topic additional coverage in the next section.

The Psychological Experiment

In many respects you can view an **experiment** as an attempt to determine the cause-and-effect relations that exist in nature. Researchers are interested in determining those factors that result in or cause predictable events. In its most basic form, the psychological experiment consists of three related factors: the independent variable, the dependent variable, and extraneous variables.

Independent Variable

The factor that is the major focus of the research and that the researcher directly manipulates is known as the **independent variable (IV)**: *independent* because it can be directly manipulated by the investigator and *variable* because it is able to assume two or more values (often called *levels*). The IV is the causal part of the relation we seek to establish. Lighting, the IV in our previous example, had two values: the original level and the new, brighter level. *Manipulation of the IV corresponds to one use of the term* control.

Experiment An attempt to determine the cause-and-effect relations that exist in nature. Involves the manipulation of an independent variable (IV) recording of changes in a dependent variable (DV) and control of extraneous variables.

Independent variable (IV) A stimulus or aspect of the environment that the experimenter directly manipulates to determine its influences on behavior.

Dependent Variable

The **dependent variable (DV)** consists of the recorded information or results (frequently called *data;* the singular is *datum*) of the experiment. The DV is the effect half of the cause-and-effect relation we are examining. In our example, level of productivity was the DV; the researcher measured it under the two conditions of the IV (original and brighter lighting). The term *dependent* is used because if the experiment is conducted properly, changes in DV scores will result from (depend on) the manipulation of the IV; the level of productivity will depend on the changes in lighting.

> **Dependent variable (DV)** A response or behavior that the experimenter measures. Changes in the DV should be caused by manipulation of the independent variable (IV).

Extraneous Variables

Extraneous variables are those factors, other than the IV, that can influence the DV and change the results of your experiment. Suppose an experimenter has her participants complete several tasks. At the conclusion of the experiment, she compares performance on the tasks and finds there is a large performance difference among the groups. Was the difference caused by the different tasks (the IV) or by the sequence of performing the tasks (an extraneous variable)? Unfortunately, when an extraneous variable is present we have no way of knowing whether the extraneous variable or the IV caused the effect we observe. Robyn Scali, a student at Catawba College in Salisbury, North Carolina, and her faculty advisor, Sheila Brownlow, were faced with just this problem; they had their participants complete three tasks. How did they deal with this potential extraneous variable? They stated, "Because any given task may have influenced performance on subsequent tasks, we presented tasks in one of six different orders, with each task appearing first, second, and third, exactly two times" (Scali & Brownlow, 2001, p. 7). Obviously, attention to extraneous variables is very important; it represents another use of the term *control.*

> **Extraneous variable** Undesired variables that may operate to influence the dependent variable (DV) and, thus, invalidate an experiment.

Establishing Cause-and-Effect Relations

Why do psychologists hold experimental research in such high regard? The answer to this question involves the type of information that we gain. Although we might be very objective in making our observations and even though these observations are repeatable, unless we have directly manipulated an IV, we cannot really learn anything about cause and effect in our research project. Only when we manipulate an IV and control potential extraneous variables are we able to infer a cause-and-effect relation. Please do not equate these comments with the idea that experimental research is the only way to gather good research data; it is not. As you will see in Chapter 4, there are numerous excellent nonexperimental research techniques.

What is so important about establishing a cause-and-effect relation? Although objective, repeatable observations can tell you about an interesting phenomenon, these observations cannot tell you why that phenomenon occurred. Only when we can give a cause-and-effect explanation do we begin to answer the *why* question.

For example, Naomi Freeman, a student at Earlham College in Richmond, Indiana, and her faculty advisor, Diana Punzo, wondered whether jurors were more persuaded by eyewitness testimony or by DNA evidence. To answer this research question, they conducted an experiment (Freeman & Punzo, 2001) in which college students served as mock jurors. The student participants read one of two excerpts from a court transcript of a first-degree murder trial. A practicing attorney assisted in the preparation of the excerpts. In one excerpt the prosecution produced evidence from an eyewitness. In a second excerpt the prosecution presented DNA evidence. After the participants completed reading their particular excerpt, they indicated whether they thought the defendant was guilty.

The IV (or *cause* in the cause-and-effect relation that they were examining) was the type of evidence the prosecution presented in the transcript: eyewitness testimony or DNA evidence. At the outset of the experiment, Freeman and Punzo hypothesized that the eyewitness testimony condition would result in more guilty verdicts than the DNA condition. Why? On the basis of previous research, they believed that "although DNA evidence is extremely reliable, it is often ignored by jurors" (p. 110).

Review the experiment we have just described. What extraneous variables did the researchers control? Should they have controlled any other extraneous variables? What was their DV?

Freeman and Punzo used several controls when they conducted this research. First, they randomly determined which transcript a participant read. Second, in order to create an equivalent sense of reality for the court transcript excerpts, they asked an attorney to assist in their preparation. The type of evidence should be the only difference between the excerpts.

What other controls have you thought of? How about what happens to the excerpt when a participant finishes reading it? Should the participant be allowed to keep it? Unlike the case in a real courtroom, if the excerpt is retained, the participant could refer to it when making a decision of guilty or not guilty. In order to control for this potential problem, all participants returned their excerpt before answering any questions. Further, even though they tested the participants in small groups as they completed the experiment, the experimenters made sure that each participant answered all questions independently; collaboration with other participants would nullify our confidence in the cause-and-effect relation the researchers were trying to establish.

The participants' guilty or not guilty verdict was the DV. By comparing the number of guilty verdicts between the groups, Freeman and Punzo (2001) hoped to show that the type of evidence (cause) resulted in differences in guilty verdicts (effect); recall that they believed there would be more guilty verdicts from the participants who read the eyewitness excerpt.

Just as if you were concluding a detective case, you now want to know what happened. Contrary to the initial predictions, the results showed that participants who read the DNA transcript produced significantly more guilty verdicts than did the participants who read the eyewitness transcript. By controlling extraneous variables, Freeman and Punzo (2001) estab-

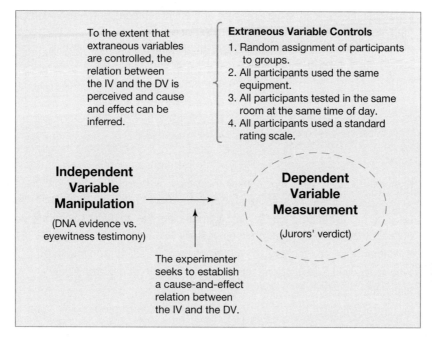

To the extent that extraneous variables are controlled, the relation between the IV and the DV is perceived and cause and effect can be inferred.

Extraneous Variable Controls
1. Random assignment of participants to groups.
2. All participants used the same equipment.
3. All participants tested in the same room at the same time of day.
4. All participants used a standard rating scale.

Independent Variable Manipulation
(DNA evidence vs. eyewitness testimony)

Dependent Variable Measurement
(Jurors' verdict)

The experimenter seeks to establish a cause-and-effect relation between the IV and the DV.

FIGURE 1-2   Diagram of the Relation of the IV, DV, and Extraneous Variable Controls in an Experiment on the Effect of DNA Evidence and Eyewitness Testimony on Jurors' Verdicts.

lished a cause-and-effect relation between type of evidence presented to mock jurors (independent variable) and number of guilty verdicts (dependent variable). The greater our control of extraneous variables, the clearer our view of the cause-and-effect relation between the IV and the DV becomes. This arrangement of IV, DV, and control of extraneous variables in Freeman and Punzo's experiment is diagrammed in Figure 1-2.

REVIEW SUMMARY

1. Psychologists engage in the process of acquiring new knowledge. Although knowledge can be gained through **tenacity** (repetition), from an authority, from experience, or by reason and logic, science is the preferred method.

2. Three characteristics of the scientific method are the use of (a) objective **(empirical)** findings that can be (b) confirmed by others and (c) corrected, if necessary, by subsequent research.

3. **Control** also is a distinguishing characteristic of science. Control can refer to (a) procedures for dealing with undesired factors in an experiment and/or (b) manipulation of the factor of main interest in an experiment.

4. Experimenters seek to establish cause-and-effect relations between variables they manipulate (**independent variables** or **IVs**) and behavioral changes (**dependent variables** or **DVs**) that result from those manipulations. Control also is exercised over **extraneous variables** (unwanted factors) that can influence the dependent variable.

CHECK YOUR PROGRESS

1. Radio announcers who repeat their messages over and over rely on the method of _____ to impart new knowledge to their listeners.
2. Because her astronomy teacher said that Sirius is the brightest star in the sky, Eleanor believes that Sirius is brighter than other stars. Eleanor has acquired knowledge through
   a. authority   b. tenacity   c. experience   d. reason and logic
3. Why is personal experience not always a valid source of new knowledge?
4. Matching

   1. logical syllogism   A. conducting a research project over again
   2. empiricism   B. factor of central interest in an experiment
   3. replication   C. can contain a faulty assumption
   4. independent variable   D. objective measurements
   5. dependent variable   E. results of an experiment

5. Explain what is meant by the "self-correcting nature of science."
6. A researcher conducts a study to confirm the effects of a previously tested drug. This is an example of
   a. objectivity   b. replication   c. control   d. repeated measures
7. Explain the nature of the cause-and-effect relations that psychological research attempts to establish.
8. Leo conducts a study that examines the effects of extracurricular involvement on levels of self-esteem. In this study, extracurricular involvement serves as the
   a. dependent variable   b. independent variable
   c. extraneous variable   d. intrinsic variable

The Research Process

Although conducting experiments is a crucial aspect of research, it is not the only activity that is involved. A number of interrelated activities make up the research process. These activities appear in Table 1-1. As you can see, one activity leads to the next one until we share our research information with others and the process starts all over again. We will now briefly describe each of these steps but will cover them in greater detail in the following chapters.

TABLE 1-1	**Components of the Research Process**

Each component builds on the previous components until a new problem is developed and the process starts over again.

Problem	You detect a gap in the knowledge base or wonder about a relation.
Literature Review	Consulting previous reports determines what has been found in the research area of interest.
Theoretical Considerations	The literature review highlights theories that point to relevant research projects.
Hypothesis	The literature review also highlights hypotheses (statements of the relation between variables in more restricted domains of the research area). Such hypotheses will assist in the development of the experimental hypothesis—the predicted outcome of your research project.
Research Design	You develop the general plan for conducting the research project.
Conducting the Experiment	You conduct the research project according to the research design.
Data Analysis and Statistical Decisions	Based on the statistical analysis, you decide whether the IV exerted a significant effect on the DV.
Decisions in Terms of Past Research and Theory	The statistical results guide decisions concerning the relation of the present research project to past research and theoretical considerations.
Preparation of the Research Report	You write a research report describing the rationale, conduct, and results of the experiment according to accepted American Psychological Association (APA) format.
Sharing Your Results: Presentation and Publication	You share your research report with colleagues at a professional society meeting and/or by publication in a professional journal.
Finding a New Problem	Your research results highlight another gap in our knowledge base, and the research process begins again.

Finding a Problem

Each research project begins as a problem or a question for which we are seeking an answer. Driggers and Helms (2000) wanted to know whether a person's salary affected the willingness of others to date that person; Freeman and Punzo (2001) wanted to know whether the type of evidence presented in a trial affected the number of guilty verdicts.

Reviewing the Literature

Once you have chosen the problem you plan to research, you must discover what psychologists already know about the problem. Thus, the next step is to find out what research studies already exist in this area. You may find that the exact experiment you have in mind has been conducted many times before. Hence, a modification of your idea, not a replication, may be more informative.

Theoretical Considerations

Theory A formal statement of the relations among the IVs and DVs in a given area of research.

In the course of your literature review you will undoubtedly come across theories that researchers have developed in the area you have chosen to research. A **theory** is a formal statement of the relation among the relevant variables in a particular research area. Leon Festinger's (1957) cognitive dissonance theory is a good example of a psychological theory that has generated considerable research. Festinger proposed that tension is aroused when two beliefs, thoughts, or behaviors are psychologically inconsistent (dissonant). In turn, we are motivated to reduce this cognitive dissonance by altering our thoughts or behaviors to make them more compatible. For example, (1) believing that high cholesterol is bad for your health and (2) eating pizza (which raises cholesterol) almost every day are inconsistent. The dissonance created by having this incompatible belief and behavior might be reduced by deciding that the reports on the harmful effects of cholesterol really are not correct or by eating pizza less often. Many researchers have tested predictions from Festinger's theory over the years.

All good theories share two common properties. First, they represent an attempt to organize a given body of scientific data. If a theory has not been developed in a particular area of research, we are faced with the task of having to consider the results of many separate experiments and decide how these results are related to each other.

The second property shared by theories is their ability to point the way to new research. By illuminating the relations among relevant variables, a good (i.e., testable) theory also suggests what might logically happen if researchers manipulate these variables in certain ways. You can think of a theory as being like a road map of your home state. The roads organize and show the relations among the towns and cities. By using this map and a bit of logic, you should be able to get from point A to point B. Thus, theories that you encounter while conducting a literature review will help point you to a relevant research project.

Hypothesis

Hypothesis An attempt to organize certain data and specific IV–DV relation within a specific portion of a larger, more comprehensive theory.

If a theory is like a road map of your home state, then you can think of a hypothesis as being like the map of a specific town in your state. The **hypothesis** attempts to state specific IV–DV relations within a selected portion of a larger, more comprehensive research area or theory. Within the general domain of cognitive dissonance theory, a number of studies have been concerned with just the finding that cognitive dissonance results in arousal. The hypothesized arousal occurs through increases in such physiological reactions as perspiration and heart rate (Losch & Cacioppo, 1990). Just as the map of your hometown may show you several ways to arrive at your destination, researchers may find that there is more than one route to their research objective. Hence, researchers may develop several hypotheses to answer the research question. For example, you might predict that a reduction in arousal would result in a decrease in cognitive dissonance. This prediction has been tested; one experiment showed that participants who consumed alcohol (arousal reduction) had reduced levels of cognitive dissonance (Steele, Southwick, & Critchlow, 1981).

As your research project takes shape, you will develop a specific hypothesis. This hypothesis, frequently called the **research** or **experimental hypothesis**, will be the predicted outcome of your research project. In stating this hypothesis you are stating a testable prediction about the relations between the IVs and DVs in your experiment. Based on the scientific literature you have reviewed, your experimental hypothesis will be influenced by other hypotheses and theories that researchers have proposed in your area of interest. For example, your hypothesis might be "If potential customers dress in old, worn-out clothes, then they will not be waited on as quickly as customers dressed in better clothing."

> **Research** or **experimental hypothesis**   The experimenter's predicted outcome of a research project.

It is important that you be able to directly test the experimental hypothesis you propose. This requirement means that you must be able to objectively define all the variables you will manipulate (IVs), record (DVs), and control (extraneous variables).

Research Design

Once you have formulated your hypothesis, you need a general plan for conducting your research. This plan is called a **research design**; it specifies how you will select your participants and assign them to groups, the type of extraneous variable control(s) you will use, and how you will gather your data.

> **Research design**   The general plan for selecting participants, assigning participants to experimental conditions, controlling extraneous variables, and gathering data.

Conducting the Experiment

The next step is to actually conduct the experiment. It is not a foregone conclusion that you will conduct your research in a laboratory. You may find yourself gathering research data in a shopping mall, an animal observation station, an archive, or hundreds of other possible locations. You will put all your preparations and controls to the test as you gather your research data.

Data Analysis and Statistical Decisions

Our experiment is not complete when we have gathered the data; the next step is to analyze the data that we gathered. Based on the results of our data analysis, we will decide whether manipulating the IV had a significant effect on the DV. In short, our statistical decisions will tell us whether we have found a cause-and-effect relation. If our statistical test indicates that a significant difference exists between the groups we tested, then we can infer that, if we have conducted a well-designed experiment, our IV manipulation was the cause of the DV effect we recorded. We will have more to say about statistical significance later.

Decisions in Terms of Past Research and Theory

Once we make our statistical decisions, then we must interpret our results in light of past research and theory. Was our experimental hypothesis supported? Do our results agree with past research? How do they fit into the current theoretical structure in this research area? If our results do not fit perfectly, what changes need to be made in our interpretation or existing theory to accommodate them? Does lack of support for our hypothesis disconfirm the theory? We will have more to say about hypothesis testing and theories in subsequent chapters.

Experimenters want to be able to extend or generalize their experimental results as widely as they legitimately can. Would Driggers and Helms's (2000) experimental results on the effect of salary level and willingness to date also generalize to other types of participants besides college students? Would Freeman and Punzo's (2001) data showing more guilty verdicts when college student mock jurors receive DNA evidence generalize to other types of participants and a real courtroom? These are the types of issues with which generalization deals.

Preparing the Research Report

Before you share the results of your research with the scientific community, you must prepare a written research report. You will prepare this research report according to the format prescribed by the American Psychological Association (APA). This format, often called APA format, is detailed in the *Publication Manual of the American Psychological Association* (2001).

Although many specific details of APA format have evolved over the years, the basic structure of the research report was originally proposed by University of Wisconsin psychologist Joseph Jastrow in the early part of this century (Blumenthal, 1991). Jastrow's purpose in suggesting a standard format for all psychological papers was to make the communication of research results easier and more consistent. Using a standard form, researchers knew exactly what to include in their papers and readers knew where to look for specific experimental details, procedures, and results. We will discuss APA format in detail in Chapter 14. We encourage you to look at that chapter now and refer to it throughout the course; the more familiar you are with this format, the easier it will be for you to prepare your own report.

Sharing Your Results: Presentation and Publication

Once you have conducted the experiment, analyzed the data, and prepared the research report, it is time to share your results. The two most popular ways to accomplish this objective are to (1) make an oral presentation or present a poster at a psychological convention and (2) publish an article in a professional journal.

Even though many of you may be shaking your heads and saying, "I could never do that in a million years," we believe (and know, from experience) such accomplishments are within the grasp of most motivated undergraduate psychology students. In fact, such opportunities, especially for presenting papers and posters at psychological conventions, have increased dramatically in recent years. Paramount among these opportunities are a growing number of state and regional student psychology conventions. These events, summarized in Table 1-2, feature student presentations exclusively.

If there is not a student convention in your area, you can consider presenting a paper in one of the Psi Chi (National Honor Society in Psychology) sessions at a regional convention. One of the six regional association meetings held each year (Eastern, Midwestern, Rocky Mountain, Southeastern, Southwestern, and Western Psychological Associations) should be

TABLE 1-2	Opportunities for Undergraduates to Present and Publish Their Research

State and Regional Conferences

Southeastern Undergraduate Psychology Research Conference

Arkansas Symposium for Psychology Students

ILLOWA Undergraduate Psychology Conference

Mid-America Undergraduate Psychology Research Conference

Great Plains Students' Psychology Convention

Joint Meeting of the Association for Psychological and Educational Research in Kansas and the Nebraska Psychological Society

Michigan Undergraduate Psychology Paper Reading Conference

Minnesota Undergraduate Psychology Conference

Carolinas Psychology Conference

Delaware Valley Undergraduate Research Conference

Lehigh Valley Undergraduate Psychology Research Conference

University of Winnipeg Undergraduate Psychology Research Conference

Information concerning these conferences appears regularly in the *APA Monitor.* Faculty members who are APA members automatically receive the *APA Monitor;* ask them to loan you the issue that has this listing. The journal *Teaching of Psychology* also carries a listing of undergraduate student conferences. For additional information you also might want to try the Society for the Teaching of Psychology Web page, which features an excellent list (http://teachpsych.lemoyne.edu/teachpsych/div/conferences undergraduate.html).

close enough to offer a potential forum for your research (see Table 1-3). In addition to the sessions at these regional meetings, Psi Chi sponsors student paper sessions at the national meetings of the American Psychological Association and the American Psychological Society. Finally, if none of these options is a viable opportunity for you to present your research, then you should consider starting a paper-reading or poster presentation session on your own campus. Very successful annual events of this nature occur at several schools.

Although the opportunities for students to publish a journal article may be a bit more difficult to find than opportunities to present a paper at a convention, such opportunities do exist. For example, *Modern Psychological Studies,* the *Journal of Psychological Inquiry,* and the *Psi Chi Journal of Undergraduate Research* (see Table 1-4) are journals devoted to the publication of research conducted and reported only by undergraduate students. If your faculty advisor has made a significant contribution to the design and conduct of your project, then you can consider including him or her as a coauthor. *The Journal of Psychology and the Behavioral Sciences* is an annual journal that solicits manuscripts by students and faculty. Your faculty advisor also will be able to suggest other journals to which you can submit your

TABLE 1-3   **Student Sessions Sponsored by Psi Chi (National Honor Society in Psychology)**

Psi Chi routinely features paper and/or poster sessions at regional and national conferences.

Eastern Psychological Association	Rocky Mountain Psychological Association
Southeastern Psychological Association	Western Psychological Association
Midwestern Psychological Association	American Psychological Association
Southwestern Psychological Association	American Psychological Society

For information on Psi Chi and these sessions contact

Psi Chi National Office
P.O. Box 709
Chattanooga, TN 37043-0709
423-756-2044
psichi@psichi.org

The dates and locations of these conferences are routinely published in the *American Psychologist* (faculty members who belong to the APA receive copies of this journal) and *Teaching of Psychology.*

TABLE 1-4   **Publication Opportunities for Students**

Several journals publish papers authored by students. Contact each journal to determine specific submission procedures.

1. *The Journal of Psychology and the Behavioral Sciences*
Professor John Brandi, Faculty Editor
Department of Psychology
Fairleigh Dickinson University
Madison, NJ 07904

2. *Modern Psychological Studies*
Department of Psychology
University of Tennessee at Chattanooga
Chattanooga, TN 37043-2598

3. *Journal of Undergraduate Studies*
Department of Psychology
Pace University
861 Bedford Rd.
Pleasantville, NY 10570

4. *Psi Chi Journal of Undergraduate Research*
Psi Chi National Office
P. O. Box 709
Chattanooga, TN 37043-0709
423-756-2044

5. *Journal of Psychological Inquiry*
Dr. Mark E. Ware
Department of Psychology
Creighton University
Omaha, NE 68178
402-280-3193

S. Gross, 1994 *The New Yorker Magazine, Inc.*

"Well, you don't look like an experimental psychologist to me."

Attending a psychological convention will convince you that experimental psychologists are a most diverse group. Although you may not feel like an experimental psychologist now, completing a research project or two will change that situation.

paper. Although undergraduates typically do not publish by themselves in the professional journals, collaborative papers featuring student and faculty authors are not uncommon.

The main point of this discussion is to encourage you to take advantage of the opportunities to share your research results with others. Much of the research you will read about in this book was conducted by students and then presented at conventions or published in journals such as the *Psi Chi Journal of Undergraduate Research* and *Journal of Psychological Inquiry.* If they can do it, so can you! Once you are involved in the research process, you will quickly find that it is a highly stimulating endeavor that never seems to end. There are always new problems to investigate.

Finding a New Problem

As you consider the relation of your experimental results to past research and theory and share your results with others who give you feedback, new research ideas will present themselves (see Horvat & Davis, 1998). Why didn't the results turn out exactly as predicted? Did you leave some extraneous variable uncontrolled? What would happen if you manipulated this or that variable in a different manner? The more deeply you immerse yourself in a research area, the more questions and problems you will find to research. As you can see from Table 1-1, we have now come full circle to the start of a new research project.

Why Is the Research Methods Course Important?

When students are asked, "Why are you taking a course in research methods (or experimental psychology)?" typical responses might be these:

"It's required for the major."

"I really don't know; I'll never conduct any research after this course."

As we go through this text, we hope to convince you that an understanding of research methods and data analysis can give you some real advantages in the field of psychology. Here are a few of those advantages:

1. ***Assisting You in Other Psychology Classes.*** Because psychology's knowledge base rests on a foundation of research, it makes sense that much of what you will cover in your other psychology classes will consist of research examples. The more completely you understand research methodology, the better you will be able to master the material in your other classes. Although this point might make sense to you for courses such as learning or perception, even courses such as personality and abnormal psychology are based on research.

2. ***Conducting a Research Project After Graduation.*** Your authors learned a long time ago that it is smart to "never say never." This caution also applies to you as students of psychology. Consider the following example: Several years ago, a very bright student took the research methods course with one of your authors. Although this student found the class sessions interesting and intellectually stimulating, she disliked the material and vowed that she would never think about research in psychology after the class was over. How wrong she was—her first job following graduation was conducting research for the Medical College of Virginia! If your career plans even remotely relate to the field of psychology, then the chances are quite good that you may have to conduct some type of research project as part of your job. Clearly, a course in research methods will provide a good understanding of what you will need to do in such instances. Even students who go into nonpsychological fields may use their training on the job to conduct research on nonpsychological topics.

3. ***Getting into Graduate School.*** There is no getting around the fact that psychology graduate admissions committees view a course in research methods or experimental psychology very positively (Keith-Spiegel & Wiederman, 2000; Landrum & Davis, 2004). Your having completed such a course tells the admissions committee that you have a good grasp of basic research methodology. Graduate programs in psychology value such knowledge.

   Frequently the research methods course includes or is followed by conducting an original student research project. If you have such an opportunity, take advantage of it and then plan to present and publish your research findings (refer to our earlier discussion of the research process). Having presented or published a research report is also rated very highly by graduate school admissions committees (Landrum & Davis, 2004; Thomas, Rewey, & Davis, 2002).

4. ***Becoming a Knowledgeable Consumer of Research.*** Our society is flooded with knowledge claims. Many of these claims deal with psychological research and phenomena, such as the claims that a particular type of diet will improve your disposition, IQ tests are good (or bad), scientific tests have proved that this brand of cola tastes best of all, or that this toothpaste fights cavities better than the rest. How do you know which of these claims to believe?

   If you understand the research on which these claims are based and the "facts" presented as supporting evidence (or that there is no supporting evidence), then you are in a position to make a more educated decision concerning such knowledge claims. The research methods course will give you the basic foundation from which you can make educated decisions concerning knowledge claims you encounter in your everyday life.

REVIEW SUMMARY

1. The research process consists of several interrelated, sequential steps: finding the problem, doing a literature review, taking theoretical considerations into account, making a hypothesis, choosing a research design, conducting the experiment, doing the data analysis and making statistical decisions, reviewing decisions in terms of past research and theory, preparing the research report, sharing your results, and finding a new problem.

2. A **theory** is a formal statement of relations among variables in a particular research area, whereas a **hypothesis** attempts to state predicted relations among variables in a selected portion of a theory.

3. The **research** or **experimental hypothesis** is the experimenter's predicted outcome of a to-be-conducted experiment.

4. The **research design** specifies how the experimenter will (a) select participants, (b) form groups, (c) control extraneous variables, and (d) gather data.

5. We encourage students to submit their research reports for presentation at professional society meetings and for publication in journals.

6. The research methods course can (a) assist you in understanding research in other courses, (b) prepare you to conduct research after graduation, (c) increase your chances of being accepted to graduate school, and (d) make you a knowledgeable consumer of the results of psychological research.

CHECK YOUR PROGRESS

1. Briefly describe the steps involved in the research process.

2. "A formal statement of the relation among relevant variables in a research area" best describes
   a. a logical syllogism   b. acquisition of knowledge by authority
   c. acquisition of knowledge by experience   d. a theory

3. You believe that giving rats a dose of vitamin C will improve their learning ability. This statement represents your
   a. theory   b. experimental design   c. problem   d. hypothesis

4. Which of the following is a method of sharing your results with the scientific community?
   a. presenting a paper at an undergraduate research conference
   b. presenting a paper or poster at a psychological convention
   c. publishing an article in a professional journal
   d. any of the above

5. Other than fulfilling a requirement, what are the reasons for taking a research methods or experimental psychology course? Describe them.

KEY TERMS

Validity, 3
Tenacity, 4
Logical syllogism, 5
Empirical, 7
Replication, 7

Control, 7
Experiment, 8
Independent variable (IV), 8
Dependent variable (DV), 9
Extraneous variable, 9

Theory, 14
Hypothesis, 14
Research or experimental
   hypothesis, 15
Research design, 15

LOOKING AHEAD

In this chapter we provided you a general introduction to how psychologists gather data. Subsequent chapters will build on and expand this general introduction. In Chapter 2 we will examine how you can find a researchable problem. Once we have identified the sources of research problems, then we will discuss the formulation of a good research hypothesis.

CHAPTER 2

Research Ideas and Hypotheses

The Research Idea

Research idea
Identification of a gap in
the knowledge base or an
unanswered question in
an area of interest.

The starting point for your project is a research idea or problem. You find a **research idea** when you identify a gap in the current knowledge base or an unanswered question that interests you. For example, in Chapter 1 we saw that Kim Driggers and Tasha Helms were interested in whether salary level was related to willingness to date. They found this information was not available and conducted research to correct this deficiency. In this section we will examine the characteristics of good research ideas and then explore several sources for research ideas.

Characteristics of Good Research Ideas

All possible solutions to a detective case are not equally likely. Likewise, not all research ideas are equally good. Good ideas have certain characteristics that set them apart from less acceptable ideas and problems.

Testable   The most important characteristic of a good research idea is that it is testable. Can you imagine trying to conduct research on a phenomenon or topic that you cannot measure or test? This situation would be like trying to answer the old question "How many angels can dance on the head of a pin?" For many years people have seen this question as unanswerable because we have no way to measure the behavior of an angel. Although you may be chuckling to yourself and saying, "I would never ask that kind of question," remember our caution in Chapter 1 about never saying never.

Suppose, for example, you became interested in cognitive processes in animals. Although humans can describe their thoughts, a research project designed to measure cognitive abilities in animals *directly* is doomed to failure before it starts. At present, the best one can do in this situation is to provide an indirect measure of animal cognition. Consider, for example, the research conducted by Irene Pepperberg on an African gray parrot named Alex. Pepperberg (1994) reported that Alex was able to acquire the concept of "blue key," and when asked "How many blue keys?" Alex was able to examine a group of 10 to 14 items and answer how many blue keys were present. Certainly, Alex appears to have excellent cognitive abilities. The point we are making is that although some research problems, such as the number of angels dancing on the head of a pin, may never be testable, others such as animal cognition may lend themselves to evaluation through indirect tests. Moreover, just because a problem is not presently testable does not mean it will always remain in that category. You may have to wait for technology to catch up with your ideas. For example, scientists proposed synapses and neurotransmitters in the nervous system long before they were directly seen and verified.

Likelihood of Success   If you stop to think about it, each research project is a contest to unlock the secrets of nature. (If we already knew all of nature's secrets, there would be no need for research.) Given that our view of nature is not complete, we must try to arrange our research project to be as close to reality as possible (Medewar, 1979). The closer our project comes to approximating reality, the greater the likelihood of successfully unlocking some of the secrets of nature. Sometimes our view of nature is not very clear and our research does not work very well; consider the following example.

In the 1980s researchers claimed that a new chemical compound, denatonium saccharide, was the most bitter substance in existence. Because denatonium saccharide offered intriguing practical applications, such as being an additive for plastic telephone and computer cable coverings and garbage bags to discourage animal pests, one of your authors and several of his students began to conduct research on this noxious chemical. Our view of nature was that denatonium saccharide was incredibly bitter and that all creatures great and small would react to this substance in the same manner. To verify this prediction, we began testing the aversiveness of denatonium saccharide with a variety of animals, ranging from rats, grasshopper mice, and gerbils to prairie dogs. Test after test yielded the same results: Our test animals did not behave toward denatonium saccharide as especially bitter or aversive (Davis, Grover, Erickson, Miller, & Bowman, 1987; Langley, Theis, Davis, Richard, & Grover, 1987). Following an experiment in which human participants rated denatonium saccharide as significantly more bitter than a comparable solution of quinine (Davis, Grover, & Erickson, 1987), our view changed. Denatonium saccharide is very bitter as far as humans are concerned; when testing animals, however, it does not have the same effect. Had we not changed our view of nature, we might still be conducting experiment after experiment wondering why our test animals were not behaving as they were "supposed" to.

Hence, in addition to testability, a second characteristic of the good research idea is that your chances for success are increased when your view of nature approximates reality as closely as possible.

Other than by direct trial-and-error investigation, how can we determine the relevant factors in our chosen research area?

Examining past research is your best bet. Those variables that were effective in previous studies are likely to be the ones that will work in your experiment. We will have more to say about that topic presently.

Sources of Research Ideas

There are two general sources of research ideas: nonsystematic and systematic. We will discuss each source in some detail.

Nonsystematic Sources   **Nonsystematic sources** include those occurrences that give us the illusion that a research idea has dropped out of the sky. These sources are nonsystematic in that we have not made any concerted effort to locate researchable ideas; they present themselves to us in a somewhat unpredictable manner. Although we refer to these sources as nonsystematic, we are not implying that the researcher is unfamiliar with the research area. Good researchers are fa-

> **Nonsystematic sources**
> Sources for research ideas that present themselves in an unpredictable manner; a concerted attempt to locate researchable ideas has not been made.

miliar with the published literature and previous research findings. We do not seem to generate meaningful research ideas in areas with which we are not familiar.

Among the major nonsystematic sources of research ideas are inspiration, serendipity, and everyday occurrences.

Inspiration Some research ideas may appear to be the product of a blind flash of genius; in the twinkle of an eye an inspired research idea is born. Perhaps the most famous example of inspiration in science is Albert Einstein (Koestler, 1964). Ideas just seemed to pop into his mind, especially when he was sailing. Although such ideas just seem to appear, it is often the case that the researcher has been thinking about this research area for some time. We see only the end product, the idea, not the thinking that preceded its appearance.

Serendipity ***Serendipity*** refers to those situations where we look for one phenomenon but find another. Serendipity often serves as an excellent source for research ideas. According to B. F. Skinner (1961), "When you run onto something interesting, drop everything else and study it" (p. 81).

> **Serendipity** Situations in which we look for one phenomenon but find something else.

Consider the following scenario in which B. F. Skinner described his reaction to the malfunctioning of a pellet dispenser in an operant conditioning chamber (commonly called a Skinner box):

> As you begin to complicate an apparatus, you necessarily invoke a fourth principle of scientific practice: Apparatuses sometimes break down. I had only to wait for the food magazine to jam to get an extinction curve. At first I treated this as a defect and hastened to remedy the difficulty. But eventually, of course, I deliberately disconnected the magazine. I can easily recall the excitement of that first complete extinction curve. I had made contact with Pavlov at last! . . . I am not saying that I would have not got around to extinction curves without a breakdown in the apparatus. . . . But it is no exaggeration to say that some of the most interesting and surprising results have turned up first because of similar accidents. (Skinner, 1961, p. 86)

His initial reaction was predictable; he saw the malfunction as a nuisance and wanted to eliminate it. However, with the eyes of an insightful researcher, he saw beyond his temporary frustration with the broken equipment to a more important possibility. By disconnecting the pellet dispenser he could study extinction. All of the subsequent research conducted on extinction and the various schedules of reinforcement that were developed indicate that Skinner capitalized on this chance happening. It was truly a serendipitous occurrence.

Everyday Occurrences You do not have to be working in a laboratory to come in contact with good research ideas. Frequently, our daily encounters provide some of the best possibilities for research. Another incident from the life of B. F. Skinner provides an excellent example of this source for a research project:

> When we decided to have another child, my wife and I decided that it was time to apply a little labor-saving invention and design to the problems of the nursery. We began by going over the disheartening schedule of the young mother, step by step. We asked only one question: Is this practice important for the physical and psychological health of the baby? When it was not, we marked it for elimination. Then the "gadgeteering" began. . . . We tackled first the problem of warmth. The usual solution is to wrap the baby in half-a-dozen layers of cloth—shirt, nightdress, sheet, blankets. This is never completely successful. Why not, we thought, dispense with clothing altogether—except for the diaper, which serves another purpose—and warm the space in which the baby lives? This should be a simple technical problem in the modern home. Our solution is a closed compartment about as spacious as a standard crib [see Figure 2-1]. The walls are insulated, and one side, which can be raised like a window, is a large pane of safety

FIGURE 2-1   Skinner's Air Crib.

glass. . . . Our baby daughter has now been living [in this apparatus] for eleven months. Her re-markable good health and happiness and my wife's welcome leisure have exceeded our most optimistic predictions. (Skinner, 1961, p. 420)

This description of the original Air Crib appeared in 1945. Subsequently, the Air Crib was commercially produced and several hundred infants were raised in them. Thus, an everyday problem led to an interesting, if not unusual, research project for B. F. Skinner.

It also is clear that your ability to see a potential research project as you go through your daily activities depends on some knowledge of your field of interest. Because B. F. Skinner was knowledgeable in the techniques of behavior control, he was able to conceptualize and develop the Air Crib. Because your authors are not well versed in archaeology, we do not see possible sites for excavations and discoveries. Conversely, an archaeologist would find it difficult to propose meaningful research problems in psychology.

Systematic Sources   Study and knowledge of a specific topic are the basis of **systematic sources** of research ideas. Research ideas developed from systematic sources tend to be carefully organized and logically thought out. The results of past research, theories, and classroom lectures are the most common examples of systematic sources for research ideas.

> **Systematic sources**
> Thoroughly examined, carefully thought-out sources for research topics.

Past Research   As you read the results of past research, you gradually form a picture of the knowledge that has accumulated in a research area. Perhaps this picture will highlight our lack of knowledge, such as the influence of clothing on eyewitness credibility. On the other hand, you may find that there are contradictory reports in the literature; one research project supports the occurrence of a particular phenomenon, whereas other reports cast doubt on its validity. Perhaps your research project will be the one that isolates the variable(s) responsible for these discrepant findings! Your consideration of past research may also indicate that a particular experiment has been conducted only

"The curse of mad scientist's block."

Unlike this poor fellow, psychologists find potential research
ideas all around them.

once and is in need of replication, or you may find that a particular project has been
conducted numerous times and needs not replication but new research. In each of these
instances our review of past research prompts a research project.

One specific type of past research that can serve as an excellent source of research ideas
deserves special mention. The *failure to replicate* a previous finding creates an intriguing situation for the psychological detective. What features of the initial research resulted in the
occurrence of the phenomenon under investigation? What was different about the replication that caused the results to be different? Only continued research will answer these questions. As Sherlock Holmes would say, "Data! Data! Data! I can't make bricks without clay!"
(Doyle, 1927, p. 318).

Theory   As we noted in Chapter 1, the two main functions of a theory are to organize
data and to guide further research. The guidance function of a theory provides an endless
panorama of projects for researchers who take the time and trouble to master the theory
and understand its implications.

Consider, for example, *social facilitation theory*. According to Robert Zajonc (1965), the
presence of other people serves to arouse a person's performance. In turn, this increased

arousal energizes the most dominant response. If you are a skilled pianist, then the presence of others at a recital will likely yield a stellar performance; playing well is the dominant response in this situation. If you are just learning to play the piano, mistakes may be your dominant response and the presence of others may result in an embarrassing performance. Based on this theory, researchers have conducted over 300 social facilitation studies involving thousands of participants (Guerin, 1986). Theory truly does guide research!

Classroom Lectures Many excellent research projects are the result of a classroom lecture. Your instructor describes research in an area that sparks your interest, and ultimately this interest leads you to develop and conduct a research project. Although lectures may not seem to be strictly nonsystematic or strictly systematic sources of research ideas, we chose to include them as systematic sources because they often include an organized review of relevant literature.

For example, after hearing a lecture on conditioned taste aversion, one of our students, Susan Nash, became interested in the topic. Subsequently, she did a term paper and conducted her senior research project in this area. Moreover, several of the research projects she conducted as a graduate student dealt with the process by which animals acquire taste aversions. Yes, one lecture can contain a wealth of potential research ideas; it will pay rich dividends to pay close attention to lectures and keep careful notes when you see potential topics for research.

Developing a Research Question

Regardless of the source of your research idea, your first goal should be to turn your idea into a question. Having a question in mind will guide you during the activities that we summarize in the remainder of the chapter. With little effort, you can probably recall instances in which a question has guided your research efforts in the past. For example, you may have had a chemistry set as a child. Like most children with chemistry sets, you probably wondered to yourself, "What will happen if I mix this chemical with that chemical?" Again, like most children, you probably proceeded to mix the chemicals and find out! In the examples we cited previously, don't you imagine that B. F. Skinner thought to himself, "I wonder why the rat quit pressing the bar when the food magazine jammed?" or "I wonder if I can make taking care of a baby easier?" Those questions guided his research.

Likewise, we hope you remember times in classes when, after a particularly interesting point, you asked the instructor, "What would happen if they . . ." or "Has anyone ever tried to do that experiment this way?" Those are great examples of questions that could guide a research project for you. Once you have a question, all you need to do is find out how much psychologists already know about that question—you need to survey the literature.

Surveying the Psychological Literature

We have already mentioned the importance of being aware of past research several times in this chapter. However, simply telling someone to go look up the past research in an area may seem to be an insurmountable task. Michael Mahoney summarized the state of affairs as follows:

> The modern scientist sometimes feels overwhelmed by the size and growth rate of the technical literatures relevant to his or her work. It has been estimated, for example, that there are over 40,000 current scientific journals publishing 2 new articles per minute (2,880 per day and over one million per year). . . . These figures—which are, indeed, overwhelming—do not include books, newsletters, or technical monographs.
>
>   Given the sizeable and growing number of active journals, one should not be surprised by the emergence and popularity of services that summarize, abstract, scan, and otherwise condense the literature into more feasible dimensions. No one would be able to "keep up" without the aid of such services. (Mahoney, 1987, p. 165)

Mahoney reflected the state of affairs in the later 1980s. There is no doubt that technological advances, such as online journals, have led to an even greater increase in the number of psychological publications currently being produced.

Given the vast amount of literature we may be dealing with, we need an organized strategy. Table 2-1 summarizes the procedures you should follow in reviewing the literature in a particular area. The steps are as follows:

1. ***Selection of Index Terms.***   The key to conducting a search of the literature is to begin with terms that will help you access the relevant articles in your chosen area. Whether you are working with a computer database (see Step 2 in Table 2-1) or going through printed abstracts (see Step 3), the terms you choose will be your guides. You need to find the psychological terms for the concepts you included in your research question. Psychologists may use different terms than the words you used in your question.

   An excellent starting place for selecting terms is the APA'S *Thesaurus of Psychological Index Terms* (2001). The first edition of the *Thesaurus* was based on the 800 terms used in *Psychological Abstracts* prior to 1973. These terms were expanded to include those that describe interrelationships and related categories, which is how you can find your question's concepts. Each edition of the *Thesaurus* is updated to include new terms.

   Let's return to the investigation of salary as a factor in dating that we introduced via the Driggers and Helms (2000) study in Chapter 1. Our research assistant, Casey Hadsall, a student at Emporia State University in Emporia, Kansas, conducted the following search of the literature. She began her literature review with the *Thesaurus*. Figure 2-2 shows a

---

TABLE 2-1   **Steps in Conducting a Search of the Literature**

1. **Selection of Index Terms.** Select relevant terms for your area of interest from the *Thesaurus of Psychological Index Terms*.
2. **Computerized Search of the Literature.** Use the selected index terms to access a computerized database, such as PsycINFO.
3. **Manual Search of the Literature (If Needed).** Use index terms to access publications in *Psychological Abstracts*.
4. **Obtaining Relevant Publications.** Use a combination of reading and notetaking, photocopying, interlibrary loan, and writing or e-mailing for reprints to obtain needed materials.
5. **Integrating the Results of the Literature Search.** Develop a plan that will facilitate the integration and usefulness of the results of the literature search.

page from the *Thesaurus* that contains relevant terms for the general topic of social dating. She selected "social dating" as her key term.

2. ***Computerized Searches of the Literature.*** Once she selected her key term, the next step was to use it to access a database. Currently, most colleges and universities turn to the American Psychological Association's (APA) PsycINFO to search the published literature. Because the scope and nature of the database services that APA offers can vary widely, you should familiarize yourself with the services offered at your college or university. For example, your school may not have online access to abstracts of all articles published from 1887 to the present. If your online database is not complete, you will need to consult *Psychological Abstracts* (see the following section) for abstracts of earlier journal articles. In short, you cannot be sure your search is complete unless you know what your database covers. It is important to make your review of the literature as thorough as possible in order to avoid repeating previous mistakes and needlessly replicating research that has already been conducted time and again. Your computer search provides the author(s), title, journal, volume, and page numbers and an abstract of each article. All you need to do is enter your index term(s) from the *Thesaurus* and let the computer do the rest. (An example of a PsycINFO printout that Casey Hadsall obtained appears in Figure 2-3.)

Once you have determined the number of publications in your chosen area, you can limit or expand your choices as you see fit. Because easy-to-follow instructions are provided, running the PsycINFO computer should pose no problems for you. If you are interested in just the most recent literature, you might also ask your librarian about PsycFIRST. PsycFIRST maintains only the last three years of entries and is handy for a quick scan of the most current literature.

If your library does not yet have such a computerized system, do not despair. Your librarian should be able to help you find a nearby library that can (for a minimal fee) accommodate your needs. As we will see, you can also conduct a manual search of the literature.

And what about the Internet? The amount of information that is available on the Internet staggers the imagination. Can this vast storehouse be tapped for the literature review? The answer is yes, but just as the good detective carefully evaluates the credibility of each witness and each piece of information, you must be very cautious. Let's see what the Internet can contribute on the topic of the effects of salary on dating. First, we selected a search engine, such as *Overture*, and asked it to search for "dating." This search yielded 240 hits! A quick perusal indicates that the vast majority of these entries are not appropriate to our task and can be disregarded. For example, sites such as *Amazing Love, Starmatch, Date-a-Doc,* and *Free Thinkers Match* deal with dating *services* and are not in line with our goal of gathering information on the effects of salary on dating. Likewise, the three sites that deal with "radioactive dating" are not appropriate to our research topic. The Internet did not assist us in this instance. However, many reputable journals and scientific groups publish quality material on the Internet, and it *can* be an excellent tool for the researcher.

Remember that you must be very careful in selecting information from the Internet to use in your literature review. There are no quality controls on the Internet; anyone can create a Web site with any type of information. What criteria should you use to evaluate

| Social Control | RELATIONSHIP SECTION | Social Interaction |

Social Control — (cont'd)
B Social Processes 1967
R ↓ Emotional Control 1973
↓ Social Influences 1967

Social Dating 1973
PN 1280   SC 48150
UF Dating (Social)
B Human Courtship 1973
Interpersonal Interaction 1967
R Acquaintance Rape 1991
Couples 1982
Friendship 1967
Male Female Relations 1988
Premarital Intercourse 1973
↓ Relationship Termination 1997
Romance 1997

Social Demonstrations 1973
PN 76   SC 48160
UF Demonstrations (Social)
Picketing
B Social Behavior 1967
R ↓ Collective Behavior 1967
↓ Political Participation 1988
↓ Social Movements 1967
Student Activism 1973

Social Density 1978
PN 497   SC 48165
SN Number of animals or humans per given space unit. For specifically high density conditions use CROWDING.
UF Density (Social)
Population Density
R Crowding 1978
Overpopulation 1973
Personal Space 1973
↓ Population 1973
↓ Social Environments 1973

Social Deprivation 1973
PN 291   SC 48170
SN Limited access to society's resources due to poverty, neglect, social discrimination, or other disadvantage. For a lack of social contact use SOCIAL ISOLATION. Consider also CULTURAL DEPRIVATION.
B Social Processes 1967
Stimulus Deprivation 1973
N ↓ Social Isolation 1967
R Cultural Deprivation 1973
Disadvantaged 1967
↓ Homeless 1988

Social Desirability 1967
PN 1417   SC 48180
UF Desirability (Social)
B Social Influences 1967
R Need for Approval 1997

Social Development
Use Psychosocial Development

Social Discrimination 1982
PN 1071   SC 48185
SN Prejudiced and differential treatment based on religion, sex, race, ethnicity, disability, or other personal characteristics rather than on the basis of merit. Use a more specific term if possible.
UF Discrimination (Social)
B Discrimination 1967
Social Issues 1991
N Age Discrimination 1994

Social Discrimination — (cont'd)
N Disability Discrimination 1997
Employment Discrimination 1994
Race and Ethnic Discrimination 1994
Sex Discrimination 1978
R Affirmative Action 1985
↓ Civil Rights 1978
Racial and Ethnic Relations 1982
Racism 1973
↓ Social Integration 1982
Stereotyped Attitudes 1967
Stigma 1991

Social Drinking 1973
PN 496   SC 48190
SN Consumption of alcoholic beverages in social settings.
B Alcohol Drinking Patterns 1967
Social Behavior 1967

Social Environments 1973
PN 2507   SC 48200
B Environment 1967
N ↓ Academic Environment 1973
↓ Animal Environments 1967
↓ Communities 1973
Home Environment 1973
Poverty Areas 1973
Rural Environments 1967
Suburban Environments 1967
Towns 1973
↓ Urban Environments 1967
↓ Working Conditions 1973
R Cultural Deprivation 1973
Social Density 1978

Social Equality 1973
PN 851   SC 48210
UF Equality (Social)
B Social Issues 1991
R Affirmative Action 1985
↓ Civil Rights 1978
Equal Education 1978
↓ Human Rights 1978
↓ Justice 1973
Racial and Ethnic Relations 1982
↓ Social Integration 1982

Social Facilitation 1973
PN 443   SC 48220
UF Facilitation (Social)
B Social Behavior 1967
R ↓ Social Influences 1967

Social Groups 1973
PN 1160   SC 48230
UF Cadres
Cliques
Groups (Social)
N Dyads 1973
Ingroup Outgroup 1997
Minority Groups 1967
Reference Groups 1994
R ↓ Social Networks 1994

Social Identity 1988
PN 1980   SC 48235
SN An aspect of self image based on in-group preference or ethnocentrism and a perception of belonging to a social or cultural group.
N Professional Identity 1991
R Ethnic Identity 1973
Ethnocentrism 1973

Social Identity — (cont'd)
R Ingroup Outgroup 1997
Minority Groups 1967
Reference Groups 1994
↓ Self Concept 1967

Social Immobility
Use Social Mobility

Social Influences 1967
PN 5700   SC 48250
UF Influences (Social)
N Coercion 1994
Criticism 1973
Enabling 1997
Ethnic Values 1973
↓ Interpersonal Influences 1967
↓ Power 1967
↓ Prejudice 1967
Propaganda 1973
Social Approval 1967
Social Desirability 1967
Social Norms 1985
Social Values 1973
Superstitions 1973
Taboos 1973
R Authority 1967
↓ Ethics 1967
Mentor 1985
Popularity 1988
Psychosocial Factors 1988
Reference Groups 1994
Role Models 1982
↓ Social Behavior 1967
Social Change 1967
Social Comparison 1985
Social Control 1988
Social Facilitation 1973
↓ Social Movements 1967
↓ Social Reinforcement 1967

Social Integration 1982
PN 1110   SC 48258
SN Process of uniting diverse groups (e.g., racial, ethnic, religious, or disabled) of a society or organization. In 1982, this term was created to replace the discontinued term RACIAL INTEGRATION. In 2000, RACIAL INTEGRATION was stripped from all records and replaced with SOCIAL INTEGRATION.
UF Desegregation
Integration (Racial)
Racial Integration
Segregation (Racial)
B Social Issues 1991
Social Processes 1967
N School Integration 1982
R ↓ Activist Movements 1973
↓ Civil Rights 1978
↓ Mainstreaming 1991
Racial and Ethnic Relations 1982
↓ Social Discrimination 1982
Social Equality 1973

Social Interaction 1967
PN 7584   SC 48260
UF Interaction (Social)
B Social Behavior 1967
N Encouragement 1973
↓ Interpersonal Interaction 1967
Nonviolence 1991
Peace 1988
Physical Contact 1982
Victimization 1973
R ↓ Aggressive Behavior 1967

FIGURE 2-2   A Page from the *Thesaurus of Psychological Index Terms*.

PsycINFO

Journal of Youth & Adolescence, 1986 Dec Vol 15(6) 487-496

Characteristics of married and unmarried adolescent mothers and their partners.
Lamb, Michael E.; Elster, Arthur B.; Peters, Laura J.; Kahn, James S.; et al (U Utah, Salt Lake City, USA)

Summary: Studied a middle-class, urban-clinic sample of 275 mostly Caucasian adolescent mothers (aged 12-29 yrs) and their partners (aged 14-36 yrs). Couples married at the time of conception (n = 22) enjoyed more positive responses from prospective grandparents and earned more than couples not married at the time of conception, but they were more likely to be high-school dropouts, suggesting limits in their lifetime earning capacities and less likelihood in identifying one another as sources of emotional support. Couples who married between conception and delivery (n = 110) reported that prospective grandparents responded less favorably to the pregnancy, but while their current salaries were lower, they were more likely to be continuing with their education. Those married after conception had fewer antisocial and conduct disorders than Ss who chose to continue in a dating relationship. Overall, the couples who married after conception appeared to face less severe problems than either initially-married couples or steady daters. ((c) 1999 APA/PsycINFO, all rights reserved)

Key Phrase(s)	parental approval & salary level & educational status, 12-19 yr old unmarried vs married before conception vs delivery, mothers & their 14-36 yr old partners
Maj Subject(s)	Adolescent Fathers, Adolescent Mothers, Marital Status
Min Subject(s)	Adolescence, Adulthood, Childhood, Couples, Educational Background, Family Relations, Income Level, Parental Attitudes, Unwed Mothers
Class. Code	2840
Classification	Psychosocial & Personality Development
Population	Human, Male, Female
Age	Childhood (birth-12 yrs), Adolescence (13-17 yrs), Adulthood (18 yrs & older)
Language	English
ISSN	0047-2891
Document Type	Journal Article
Form/Content Type	Empirical Study

FIGURE 2-3   A Printout from PsycINFO.

sites? At present there are no universally accepted guidelines for evaluating Internet sites. However, we have found the following criteria to be useful. We hope these guidelines will be helpful as you surf the Web (see Table 2-2).

3. *Manual Searches of the Literature.* If your school does not have access to the complete PsycINFO database, you will need to conduct a manual search in order to make your literature review as thorough as possible. A manual search will involve searching through *Psychological Abstracts,* a monthly journal that provides essentially the same information that the PsycINFO computer searches yield. Because the index terms used in the *Thesaurus* were taken from *Psychological Abstracts,* it will be an easy task to use this resource to locate relevant articles.

TABLE 2-2   Evaluating Internet Resources

The WWW is a self-publishing medium in which anyone with the appropriate computer and software and an Internet connection can create and disperse information. Web pages should be evaluated carefully using some of the same criteria used to evaluate a print source. Be aware, however, that Web pages present additional evaluation challenges.

Authority	Who is the author? Is the author's name clearly visible? Is there a link to the author's e-mail address?
	What are the author's qualifications, education, and occupation?
	Has the author written articles or books other than Web pages? Check journal databases, such as Psyc INFO.
	Is there a link to additional information about the author? A personal home page?
	Is the source peer-reviewed or edited? If so, by whom?
	Does the author belong to an organization? If the page is authored by an organization, what additional information about that organization is available?
	Check the domain name of the URL (.gov, .edu, .com, .org, .net, .mil).
Accuracy	Are there clues to tell you that the information on the page is true?
	Does the author list sources? Is there a bibliography on the page?
	Can the information be verified elsewhere—perhaps in a print source?
	Are there obvious errors (spelling, grammar, etc.)?
Objectivity	Does the page reflect a particular bias or viewpoint? Does the author use inflammatory or provocative language?
	What is the purpose of the page? To inform? To sell or market a product or an idea? To entertain? To persuade?
	Why was this page written and for whom? (The Web can be a "soapbox" for organizations or people.)
	Is there advertising on the page? If there is advertising, can it be differentiated from the informational content?
Currency	When was the page first published and last updated?
	Are the facts on the page current?
	When was the information gathered?
	Are the links current?
Coverage	Is the page a complete document or an abstract/summary?
	Does the author adequately cover the topic? What time period is covered?
	Are there links to additional coverage?
	Does the page contain information that is pertinent to your research topic? How can you use this information?

(continued)

TABLE 2-2	Evaluating Internet Resources (continued)
Navigation/Design	Is the page easy to read? Does the background interfere with the page's content? Is the color "easy on the eyes"?
	Is the material presented in an orderly format?
	Do the graphics and images add to the presentation of the page?
	Are links appropriate to the topic of the page? Do they work?
	Is there a link at the bottom of the page to go back to the top?
	Is there a link on each supporting page to go back to the main page?
	Is there a comment link at the bottom of the main page?
	Do you need special software to view the information? Is there a fee to obtain the information?

Source: Binghamton University (http://library.lib.binghamton.edu/search/evaluation.html).

For example, Casey Hadsall looked at the May–June, 1998, issue of *Psychological Abstracts* and located her index term, "dating (social)." She found several numbers identifying abstracts in that issue that might be of interest; among these numbers was 14134. She found the page that contained abstract 14134 and located it (see Figure 2-4).

4. ***Obtaining the Relevant Publications.*** Once you have assembled a listing of books and journal articles relevant to your area of interest, it is time to acquire copies. There are several techniques for going about this task; you will probably use a combination of these strategies. First, find out what is available in your own library and plan to spend time reading this material and making photocopies for later use.

There are two options for obtaining items that are not available in your library. First, you can order them through the *interlibrary loan* department of your library. Most interlibrary loan services are reasonably fast and efficient. However, there may be a small fee for providing copies of journal articles. Second, for journal articles, you can write directly to the author to request a reprint (authors typically receive a supply of copies of each article they publish).

Writing for a reprint has an added advantage: It allows you to request additional, related articles that the author may have published. With the advent of e-mail and the Internet, the task of communicating with researchers in your area of interest has become fast and convenient. Most authors are pleased to comply with such requests, and there is no charge for reprints. Your literature search is likely to uncover publications that are several years, even decades, old. Because authors receive a large number of reprints when they publish an article, the chances are good they will have copies of even their older articles; don't hesitate to ask. Concerned about addresses for authors? The computer search or the abstract in *Psychological Abstracts* lists the institutional affiliation of the author(s). Hence, you should be able to look up the institutional address in any number of the guidebooks to colleges and universities that are in your library. If you have only the author's name, consult your faculty members to see if they have a membership directory for the American Psychological Association (APA) or the American Psychological Society (APS). There is a good chance that an actions in a manner different from common stereotypes. —*Journal abstract.*

14134. Katz, Jennifer; Anderson, Page & Beach, Steven R. H. (U Georgia, Athens, GA) **Dating relationship quality: Effect of global self-verification and self-enhancement.** *Journal of Social & Personal Relationships,* 1997(Dec), Vol 14(6), 829–842. —Explored the effects of self-verification and self-enhancement on dating relationship quality. It was predicted that dating persons should be more intimate, satisfied, and committed when they perceive that their partners evaluate them in ways that are either consistent with or more positive than their own self-evaluations. A survey of 317 dating undergraduate women involved in stable dating relationships tested these predictions, using global and specific measures of self-evaluations and perceived partner evaluations of the self. Global self-verification and self-enhancement each accounted for unique variance in measures of intimacy and satisfaction. Parallel findings emerged with regard to self-verification and self-enhancement based upon specific self-attributes, although these findings were less robust.

14135. Keys, J. Bernard. (Georgia Southern U, Ctr Managerial Learning, Statesboro, GA) **Strategic management games: A review.** *Simulation & Gaming,* 1997(Dec), Vol 28(4), 395–422. —This article describes seven currently available management games commonly used in the strategic management course within colleges and universities. The games reviewed have had sustained use through several editions. All are now scored by a microcomputer and use up-to-date computer technology. Five tables are included summarizing the dimensions of the games reviewed. The tables summarize for the seven games the factors categorized as the external environment and industry factors, marketing variables, production variables, and financial variables. Variables included by all of the seven games are first reviewed in each table, then unique variables are itemized for each game This review suggests that management games are becoming much more robust and much more strategic since the author's last review (B. Keys, 1987) of games.

14136. Knox, David; Gibson, Laurin; Zusman, Marty & Gallmeier, Charles. (East Carolina U, Greenville, NC) **Why college students end relationships.** *College Student Journal,* 1997(Dec), Vol 31(4), 449–452. —185 students (64% female) at a large southeastern university reported why they ended their last relationship—involvement with someone else was a major reason. Women were significantly more likely to report involvement with someone new and to end relationships in which their partner was violent/abusive or used drugs. Implications suggest the value of fidelity, nonviolent conflict resolution, and being drug free for relationship stability.

14137. Knox, David; Zusman, Marty & Nieves, Wandy. (East Carolina U, Greenville, NC) **College students' homogamous preferences for a date and mate.** *College Student Journal,* 1997(Dec), Vol 31(4), 445–448. —278 undergraduates (72% female) at a large southeastern university reported the degree to which they preferred selecting a dating and marriage partner who was similar to them in each of 10 background characteristics. Females preferred to date a man who was similar to them in education and occupation and preferred to marry a man who had these similarities as well as religious values, and desire for children. Only men emphasized physical appearance in both dating and marital partners. Both sexes believed that homogamy is associated with happy and lasting relationships. Previous research supports their beliefs.

14138. Levine, Sara Pollak & Feldman, Robert S. (U Massachusetts, Dept of Psychology, Amherst, MA) **Self-presentational goals, self-monitoring, and nonverbal behavior.** *Basic & Applied Social Psychology,* 1997(Dec), Vol 19(4), 505–518. —Examined how particular interpersonal goals relate to the expression of emotions during social interaction for 172 pairs of same-sex undergraduates rated as high vs low in self-monitoring needs. Before interacting with a partner, Ss were assigned a goal of either self-promotion (appearing competent), ingratiation (appearing likable), or were assigned no specific goal. Naive judges viewed 15-sec segments of these interactions and rated Ss regarding the emotions displayed. Results indicate that displays of positive and negative emotion are differentially affected by an individual's self-monitoring status, self-presentational goal, and

gender. Overall, high self-monitors and women expressed less negative emotion and more positive emotion than low self-monitors and men. Furthermore, although women showed little variability in their displays of negative emotion due to goal, men's displays of negative emotion were affected by self-presentational goals.

14139. Llanos, Raimundo Abello; Orozco, Camilo Madariaga & Hoyos de los Ríos, Olga Lucía. (U Norte, Barranquilla, Colombia) **Redes sociales como mecanismo de supervivencia: Un estudio de casos en sectores de extrema pobreza. [Social networks as a survival mechanism: A case study in sectors of extreme poverty.]** *Revista Latinoamericana de Psicología,* 1997, Vol 29(1), 115–137. —Examined family social networks which belong to economically and socially disadvantaged persons in the city of Barranquilla, Colombia, where social networks are described as survival mechanisms used by disadvantaged communities. The scheme used was a descriptive design. The information was collected based on a sample of 162 families through combinations of qualitative and quantitative techniques, and the results were managed by a percentage analysis of their frequency. Results indicate that the social network potential is an alternative for social development from the local contexts that guarantees active social participation in the process of political, social, and economical transformation.

14140. Martínez, José Luis. (U de Salamanca, Escuela Universitaria de Magisterio, Zamora, Spain) **Desarrollo personal, ambiente familiar y relaciones de pareja en la adolescencia. [Personal development, family environment and dating in adolescence]** (Spanish) *Revista de Psicología Social,* 1997, Vol 12(1), 59–78. —Examined the relationship between several personal factors (i.e., identity and emotional autonomy) and family factors (i.e., environment and parental support), and the experience of dating relationships (i.e., dating status, duration, intimacy and sexual experience) among 600 17–20 yr olds. Gender differences are emphasized. The results show that females were involved in more long-lasting and intimate relationships. Furthermore, the female Ss involved in dating relationships, relative to those not involved in them, showed more identity achievement. Finally, the identity was positively associated with intimacy for females, and with sexual experience for males. These results are discussed in terms of the connection between adolescents' personal and social development.

14141. Morgan, David; Carder, Paula & Neal, Margaret. (Portland State U, Inst on Aging, Portland, OR) **Are some relationships more useful than others? The value of similar others in the networks of recent widows.** *Journal of Social & Personal Relationships,* 1997(Dec), Vol 14(6), 745–759. —Contacts with other widows are often seen as having particular value for those who are coping with bereavement. Both the benefits of associating with other widows and the difficulties of maintaining ties with married friends make it likely that recent widows' friendship networks will show increasing homophily, based on substituting widowed friends for married friends. We investigated these issues in a year of longitudinal interviewing with 321 recently widowed women (aged 59–85 yrs), who provided data about their social support networks. Results indicate that these widows did shift their networks toward greater association with others who had experienced this life event. We did not, however, find evidence that this was due to the amount or quality of the support they received from widowed rather than married friends. One possible explanation is that widows' preference for associating with their similar others has more to do with the nature of the companionship they share in such relationships, rather than with the provision of social support.

14142. Murstein, Bernard I. (Connecticut Coll, New London, CT) **On exchange theory, androcentrism and sex stereotypy.** *Psychological Reports,* 1997(Dec), Vol 81(3, Pt 2), 1151–1162. —J. T. Wood's article (see record 82:29092) was evaluated for its comments on exchange theory and male–female differences in relationships. The author, in disagreement with Wood, believes that despite its androcentric origins, exchange theory, of itself, is not androcentric. Moreover, it is neither necessarily oriented toward personal gain nor lacking in process, as Wood claims. Last, the research literature does not warrant talking about men and women as having basically different ways of relating.

FIGURE 2-4   A Page from *Psychological Abstracts.*

author you are trying to locate will be a member of one or both associations. If so, you can get the institutional and e-mail addresses from a current membership directory.

5. ***Integrating the Results of the Literature Search.*** Once you have assembled the journal articles, book chapters, and books relevant to your research area, you will need to make sense of this material. This task can be formidable indeed; it will help if you have a plan.

Our students have found the following procedure to be quite effective. You also may find it useful in organizing the results of your literature search. As you read each article, keep good but succinct notes. Because most journal articles appear in the following sequence, your task will not be difficult. We will have more to say about how you actually write the results of your research in Chapter 14. For now, you need to master the task of summarizing what others have already written and published.

> ***Reference Information.*** List the complete citation (in APA format; see Chapter 14) for the article you are abstracting. This information will facilitate completing the reference section of your research report.
>
> ***Introduction.*** Why did the researchers conduct this experiment? What theory does this research seek to support?
>
> ***Method.*** Use the following sections to describe how the project was conducted:
>
>> ***Participants.*** Describe the participants of the experiment. List such specifics as species, number, age, and sex.
>>
>> ***Apparatus.*** Describe the equipment that the researcher used. Note any deviations from the standard apparatus, as well as any unusual features.
>>
>> ***Procedure.*** Describe the conditions under which the participants were tested.
>
> ***Results.*** Which statistical tests did the author use? What were the results of these statistical tests?
>
> ***Discussion and Evaluation.*** What conclusions did the author reach? How do these conclusions relate to theory and past research? Describe any criticisms of the research that occurred to you as you read the article. (See the guidelines for critiquing research publications in Chapter 13.)

Once you have completed taking notes on these sections, you should condense them so all this information will fit on one side of a sheet of paper. As you prepare these single sheets, be sure always to use the same sequence of headings that you followed in making your notes. An example of a completed sheet appears in Figure 2-5.

Once you have prepared all your relevant literature in this manner, it is an easy task to lay out the pages on a table and make comparisons and contrasts between research projects. Because you put the same type of information in the same location on each page, it is easy to make comparisons of the various aspects and details. Additionally, using a single sheet for each reference allows you to arrange and rearrange the references to suit your various needs: alphabetically to create a reference list, into separate stacks to represent positive and negative findings, and so forth.

As you have probably realized, the format we are suggesting is modeled after the accepted APA format for preparing papers (see Chapter 14). The experience you get in summarizing the results of your literature search will help you as you prepare a full-length APA-format paper. At this point, we are now ready to do something with the results of our literature survey.

Wann, D. L., & Dolan, T. J. (1994). Spectators' evaluations of rival and fellow fans. *The Psychological Record, 44*, 351-358.

Introduction

Even though "sports fans are biased in their evaluations and attributions concerning their team" (p. 351), no research has examined the evaluations spectators make of other spectators. Hence the present experiment was conducted to examine spectators' evaluations of home team and rival fans.

Method

Participants - One hundred three undergraduate psychology students received extra credit for participation.

Instruments - A questionnaire packet consisting of an information sheet, Sports Spectator Identification Scale, a five-paragraph scenario describing the behavior of a home team or rival spectator at an important basketball game, and several questions concerning the general behavior of the spectator described in the scenario was given to each participant.

Procedure - The questionnaire packet was completed after an informed consent document was completed and returned. One-half of the participants read the home team fan scenario, while the remainder of the participants read the rival team fan scenario. The determination of which scenario was read was determined randomly.

Results

Analysis of variance was used to analyze the data. The results of these analyses indicated the home team fan was rated more positively than the rival team fan by participants who were highly identified with the home team. This pattern of results was not shown by lesser identified fans. Of particular note was the finding that the highly identified participants did not rate the rival team fan more negatively than did the lesser identified participants; they just rated the home team fan positively.

Discussion and Evaluation

These results support the authors' initial predictions that participants would give more positive evaluations of fans rooting for the same team and more negative evaluations of fans rooting for a different team. Wann and Dolan's prediction that such evaluations would be shown only by fans who were highly identified with their team also was supported. These predictions were seen to be in accord with social identity theory. The study appeared to be well conducted. The fact that the study was not conducted at a sporting event limits its applicability.

FIGURE 2-5 Sample of a Summary of a Journal Article.

Formulating the Research Hypothesis

Once you have completed your literature review, your own research begins to take shape. The next task is to develop a *research hypothesis*—a formal statement of your research question—taking into account what you learned from searching the literature.

Recall from Chapter 1 that the hypothesis is an attempt to organize data and IV–DV relations within a specific portion of a larger, more comprehensive research area or theory. Thus, hypotheses that have been supported by experimental research can make important contributions to our knowledge base.

Because you have yet to conduct your research project, the **research or experimental hypothesis** is your *prediction* about the relation that exists between the IV that you are going to manipulate and the DV that you will record. If the results of your experiment support the research hypothesis, then it has the potential to make a contribution to theory; you have some grounds on which to infer a cause-and-effect relation. In order to understand the nature of the research hypothesis, we will examine some of its general characteristics.

> **Research** or **experimental hypothesis** The experimenter's predicted outcome of a research project.

Characteristics of the Research Hypothesis

For the detective and the psychologist, all acceptable research hypotheses share certain characteristics—they are stated in a certain manner, they involve a certain type of reasoning, and they are presented in a certain format.

Types of Statements   Because our research hypothesis is nothing more than a statement of what we believe will occur when we conduct an experiment, we must carefully consider the statements used in constructing it.

Synthetic, Analytic, and Contradictory Statements   A statement can be one of three types: synthetic, analytic, or contradictory.

Synthetic statements are those statements that can be *either true or false*. The statement "Abused children have lower self-esteem" is synthetic because although there is a chance that it is true, there also is a chance that it is false.

> **Synthetic statement** Statements that can be either true or false.

Analytic statements are those statements that are *always true*. For example, "I am making an *A* or I am not making an *A*" is an analytic statement; it is always true. You are either making an *A or* you are not making an *A*; no other possibilities exist.

> **Analytic statement** Statements that are always true.

Contradictory statements are those statements that are *always false*. For example, "I am making an *A and* I am not making an *A*" is a contradictory statement; it is always false. You cannot make an *A* and not make an *A* at the same time.

> **Contradictory statement** Statements that are always false.

Review the three types of statements that we just presented. Which one is best suited for use in a research hypothesis?

When we conduct an experiment, we are attempting to establish the existence of a cause-and-effect relation. At the outset of the experiment we do not know whether our prediction is correct or not. Therefore, synthetic statements, which can be true or false, must constitute our research hypothesis. If our research hypothesis is an analytic or contradictory statement, there is no need (or way) to conduct research on that topic. We already know what the outcome will be by merely reading the statements.

General implication form   Statement of the research hypothesis in an "if . . . then" form.

General Implication Form   You must be able to state the research hypothesis in **general implication form** ("if . . . then" form). The "if" portion of such a statement refers to the IV manipulation we are going to make, and the "then" portion refers to the DV changes we expect to observe. An example of a general implication form statement would be the following:

> If students in one group of third-graders receive an M&M each time they spell a word correctly, then their spelling performance will be better than that of a group of third-graders who do not receive an M&M for each correctly spelled word.

If you have read articles in psychological journals, you are probably saying to yourself, "I don't recall seeing many statements in general implication form." You are probably correct; most researchers do not formally state their research hypothesis in strict general implication form. For example, the hypothesis about the third-graders and their spelling performance might have been stated like this:

> Third-graders who receive an M&M each time they spell a word correctly will spell better than third-graders who do not receive an M&M for each correctly spelled word.

Regardless of how the research hypothesis is stated, it must be restateable in general implication form. If it cannot be stated in this manner, then there is a problem with either our IV manipulation or the DV we have chosen to measure.

Read the last general implication statement again, starting with "If students in one group of third-graders . . . ." What IV is the researcher manipulating? What is the DV? In addition to being stated in general implication form, is this statement synthetic, analytic, or contradictory?

Whether the students receive an M&M after correctly spelling a word is the IV. The spelling performance of the two groups of third-graders is the DV. Because this statement has the potential to be true or false, it is synthetic.

The use of synthetic statements presented in general implication form highlights two additional, but related, characteristics of the research hypothesis. The **principle of falsifiability**, the first characteristic, means that when an experiment does not turn out as you predicted, this result is seen as evidence that your hypothesis is false. If, after the experiment, the two groups of third-graders do not differ in spelling ability, then you must conclude you made a bad prediction; your research hypothesis was not an accurate portrayal of nature. Even though you do not want such results to occur, your research must be capable of producing results that do not support your experimental hypothesis.

Principle of falsifiability   Results not in accord with the research hypothesis are taken as evidence that this hypothesis is false.

Because we use a synthetic statement for our research hypothesis, our results will never prove its truth absolutely; this is the second characteristic of the research hypothesis. Assume we did find that third-graders who received M&Ms spelled better than third-graders who did not receive M&Ms. Later we decide to replicate our experiment. The fact that we obtained positive results the first time we conducted the experiment does not prove that our research hypothesis is unquestionably true and that we will always obtain positive results. When we conduct a replication, or any experiment for that matter, our hypothesis contains a synthetic statement that is either true or false. Thus, we can never absolutely prove a research hypothesis; we simply cannot yet disprove it. Certainly, as the number of experiments that support the research hypothesis increases, our confidence in the research hypothesis increases.

Types of Reasoning   In stating our research hypothesis, we also amust be aware of the type of reasoning or logic we use. As we will see, inductive and deductive reasoning involve different processes.

Inductive Logic   **Inductive logic** involves reasoning from specific cases to general principles. Inductive logic is the process that is involved in the construction of theories; the results of several independent experiments are considered simultaneously, and general theoretical principles designed to account for the behavior in question are derived.

> **Inductive logic**
> Reasoning that proceeds from specific cases to general conclusions or theories.

For example, John Darley and Bibb Latané (1968) were intrigued by a famous incident that occurred in 1964 in the Queens section of New York; a young woman named Kitty Genovese was stabbed to death. Given the number of murders that take place each year in any large city, this event may not seem especially noteworthy. However, an especially horrifying aspect of this murder was that the killer attacked the young woman *three separate times* in the course of half an hour and that 38 people saw the attacks or heard the young woman's screams. The killer was frightened off twice when people turned their lights on or called from their windows. However, both times he resumed his attack. None of the people who witnessed the attack came to the victim's aid, and no one called the police while she was being attacked. Why?

Darley and Latané reported the results of several experiments they conducted. On the basis of their results, they theorized that individuals are more likely to give assistance if they are alone than if others are present. The finding that groups of bystanders are less likely than individuals to aid a person in trouble is known as the *bystander effect*. The development of this principle is an example of the use of inductive reasoning; several specific results were combined to formulate a more general principle.

Deductive Logic   **Deductive logic** is the converse of inductive logic; we reason from general principles to specific conclusions or predictions. Deductive logic is the reasoning process we use in formulating our research hypothesis. By conducting a search of the literature, we have assembled a large amount of data and considered several theories.

> **Deductive logic**
> Reasoning that proceeds from general theories to specific cases.

From this *general* pool of information we seek to develop our research hypothesis, a statement about the relation between a *specific* IV and a *specific* DV. For example, on the basis of previous research on the bystander effect, a social psychologist might make the following deductive statement:

If an experimenter increases the number of bystanders who are present during a feigned seizure on a subway, then the likelihood that a specific research participant will offer assistance will decrease.

Read the preceding statement once again. Is this statement acceptable as a research hypothesis?

Yes, this statement would appear to be acceptable as a research hypothesis. It is a synthetic statement (it can be true or false) presented in general implication form ("if . . . then"). Moreover, deductive logic is involved: we have gone from a general body of knowledge (about the bystander effect) to make a specific prediction concerning a specific IV (number of bystanders present) and a specific DV (receiving assistance).

Certainly we are not maintaining that deductive and inductive reasoning are totally separate processes. They can, and do, interact with each other. As you can see from Figure 2-6, the results of several initial experiments in a particular research area may lead to the development of a theory in that area (inductive reasoning).

In turn, an examination of that theory and past research may suggest a specific research project (deductive reasoning) that needs to be conducted. The results of that project may result in modification of the theory (inductive reasoning), which prompts the idea for several additional research projects (deductive reasoning), and so forth. Clearly, the research process we described in Chapter 1 is based on the interplay between these two types of logical reasoning.

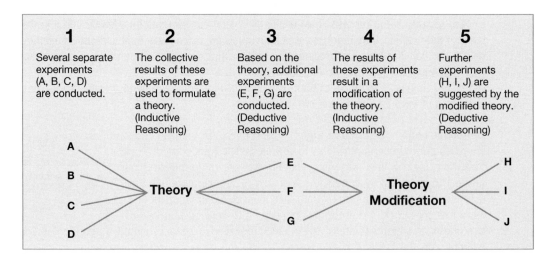

FIGURE 2-6   The Relations between Deductive and Inductive Reasoning.

A New View of Hypothesis Testing   Robert Proctor and John Capaldi, psychologists at Purdue University, have presented a new view of hypothesis testing that warrants considerable thought. They based their comments on the premise that research methodology is not a static, finished process; it is constantly in a state of change and flux. Principles may be rejected or modified. The data that researchers gather really determine the methods that are accepted and continue to be used.

They contend that hypothesis testing is not a simple affair; it "is a great deal more complicated than it seems on the surface" (Proctor & Capaldi, 2001, p. 179). Several factors can determine what the researcher does when an experimental hypothesis is confirmed (or disconfirmed). For example, the *importance* of the research problem may determine whether a researcher sticks with the problem, even if a specific hypothesis is disconfirmed. Likewise, the *promise* of the research program to answer theoretical questions may determine whether that research program flourishes.

Early in the developmental stages of a theory, hypothesis testing actually may be harmful. Because the researchers do not know all of the relevant variables (IVs, DVs, and, especially, extraneous variables), it may be very easy to disconfirm an experimental hypothesis and thereby disconfirm the theory. Proctor and Capaldi also argued that researchers are never really able to achieve a clear-cut test of a hypothesis. Why? No hypothesis is ever tested in complete isolation; we are always testing other things at the same time. For example, the adequacy of our research equipment is tested at the same time as we test a hypothesis. If the hypothesis was disconfirmed, was it due to an incorrect hypothesis or inadequate equipment? Likewise, we always make auxiliary assumptions, such as the effectiveness of randomization as a control technique, when we test a hypothesis. If these auxiliary assumptions are incorrect, we may reject a valid experimental hypothesis.

What should researchers do? Proctor and Capaldi suggested that researchers should use more inductive logic when a research area is new, because there is a high probability of disconfirming hypotheses when they might be true. Their suggestion would be to let the data be your guide. Sherlock Holmes made this point quite eloquently when he said, "I make a point of never having any prejudices, and of following docilely wherever fact may lead me" (Doyle, 1927, p. 407). The empirical results of your research will help reveal important relations. Hypothesis testing is important and valuable when it works. However, researchers must be sensitive to the drawbacks associated with it.

Directional versus Nondirectional Research Hypotheses   Finally, we must consider whether we are going to predict the direction of the outcome of our experiment in our research hypothesis. In a **directional research hypothesis** we specify the outcome of the experiment. For example, if we test two groups, we could entertain *one* of the following directional hypotheses:

> **Directional research hypothesis**   Prediction of the specific outcome of an experiment.

Group A will score significantly higher than Group B.

or

Group B will score significantly higher than Group A.

In either case, we are directly specifying the direction we predict for the outcome of our experiment. (Note that although we can entertain either of these directional hypotheses, we cannot consider both of them at the same time.)

On the other hand, a **nondirectional research hypothesis** does not predict the exact directional outcome of an experiment; it simply predicts that the groups we are testing will differ. Using our two-group example once again, a nondirectional hypothesis would indicate that

> Group A's scores will differ significantly from Group B's.

For this hypothesis to be supported, Group A can score either significantly higher or significantly lower than Group B.

Nondirectional research hypothesis   A specific prediction concerning the outcome of an experiment is not made.

Review the differences between directional and nondirectional hypotheses. How would you write a directional research hypothesis for the M&Ms and third-grade spelling experiment we described earlier? How would you write a nondirectional hypothesis for this same experiment?

A directional hypothesis might read as follows:

> If students in one group of third-graders receive an M&M each time they spell a word correctly, then their spelling performance *will be better* than that of a group of third-graders who do not receive an M&M for each correctly spelled word.

Of course, you might predict that receiving M&Ms would cause spelling performance to decrease and fall below that of the group that did not receive the M&Ms. In either instance, you would be using a directional hypothesis.

A nondirectional hypothesis would read as follows:

> If students in one group of third-graders receive an M&M each time they spell a word correctly, then their spelling performance *will differ* from that of a group of third-graders who do not receive an M&M for each correctly spelled word.

In this instance, we are simply predicting the two groups will perform differently.

Which type of hypothesis, directional or nondirectional, should you choose? If the theory you are testing calls for it, and you are *relatively certain* of your prediction, then you may want to use a directional hypothesis. For reasons we will discuss later, your chances of finding a statistically significant result are increased when you use a directional hypothesis. However, if you adopt a directional hypothesis, there is no changing your mind. If the results turn out exactly opposite to your prediction, the only thing you can say is that you were wrong and that nature doesn't operate as you thought it did. Because nature has a way of playing cruel tricks on our predictions, most researchers take a more conservative approach and state a nondirectional research hypothesis. Even though it may be slightly more difficult to achieve statistical significance, there is less potential for disappointment with the outcome of the research project when you use a nondirectional hypothesis.

REVIEW SUMMARY

1. The starting point for the research project is the **research idea** or identification of a gap in our current knowledge base.

2. Good research ideas should be testable and have a high likelihood of success (closely approximate nature).

3. **Nonsystematic sources** of research ideas give the impression that the idea simply appeared with little or no forethought. Inspiration, **serendipity** (looking for one phenomenon but finding another), and everyday occurrences are the major nonsystematic sources of research ideas.

4. Formal study and knowledge of a topic form the basis for **systematic sources** of research ideas. Past research and theories are the two main systematic sources of research ideas.

5. Developing a research question will help guide your research.

6. An organized approach is necessary to conduct a survey of the psychological literature. Such a search typically begins with the selection of index terms from the *Thesaurus of Psychological Index Terms*. Once you have selected these terms, you use them to access a computer database, such as PsycINFO, or the *Psychological Abstracts*. After you have identified and made copies of the relevant literature, you must integrate it in a meaningful manner.

7. Once the literature review is complete, the researcher is ready to develop a **research** or **experimental hypothesis**—the predicted outcome of the experiment.

8. The research hypothesis contains **synthetic statements** that can be either true or false and is stated in **general implication form** ("if . . . then").

9. The **principle of falsifiability** indicates that when an experiment does not turn out as predicted, the truthfulness of the research hypothesis is discredited. Because a research hypothesis is composed of synthetic statements, it can never be absolutely proved; it can only be disproved.

10. The development of the research hypothesis involves the use of **deductive logic** in which we reason from general principles to specific cases.

11. A **directional research hypothesis** is used when the *specific* direction or nature of the outcome of an experiment is predicted. When the experimenter does not predict the specific nature of the group differences, only that they *will differ*, a **nondirectional research hypothesis** is used.

CHECK YOUR PROGRESS

1. Matching

   1. research idea   A. look for one thing, find another
   2. serendipity   B. computer search of the literature
   3. *Psychological Abstracts*   C. identification of a gap in the knowledge base
   4. PsycLIT/PsycINFO   D. manual search of the literature
   5. experimental hypothesis   E. always true
   6. synthetic statement   F. either true or false
   7. analytic statement   G. experimenter's predicted answer to research

2. Good research ideas must be _____ and have a high _____ _____
   _____.

3. Distinguish between nonsystematic and systematic sources of research ideas. What are
   the specific ways each general source may be shown?

4. When we find something unexpected that is important in our research, what has occurred?

   a. inspiration   b. everyday occurrences
   c. serendipity   d. theory

5. _____ are always true.

   a. Synthetic statements   b. Contradictory statements
   c. Statements presented in general implication form   d. Analytic statements

6. Why are synthetic statements used in the experimental hypothesis?

7. Describe general implication form. Be thorough.

8. Which of the following is *not* associated with the principle of falsifiability?

   a. synthetic statements   b. general implication form
   c. experimental hypothesis   d. analytic statements

9. The construction of theories involves _____ logic; the development of the experimental hypothesis involves _____ logic.

10. Concerning research hypotheses, most researchers

    a. state a directional research hypothesis
    b. state a nondirectional research hypothesis
    c. do not use a research hypothesis
    d. use a research hypothesis that makes no prediction

KEY TERMS

Research idea, 24
Nonsystematic sources, 25
Serendipity, 26
Systematic sources, 27
Research or experimental
   hypothesis, 39

Synthetic statement, 39
Analytic statement, 39
Contradictory statement, 39
General implication form, 40
Principle of falsifiability, 40
Inductive logic, 41

Deductive logic, 41
Directional research
   hypothesis, 43
Nondirectional research
   hypothesis, 44

LOOKING AHEAD

In Chapters 1 and 2 we looked at the general nature of research, saw what constitutes a good research question, and found out how to state a good research hypothesis. However, you should be aware that research does not occur in a vacuum. Researchers must take ethics into consideration when they conduct their projects. We examine the topic of research ethics in Chapter 3.

Ethics in Psychological Research

The Need for Ethical Principles

Although it may appear that we are ready to begin our research project once we have developed our research hypothesis, this simply is not the case. We still have one major issue to deal with before we finalize our research design and start gathering data: We must consider the ethical nature of our research. The days of beating a confession out of a suspect with a rubber hose are gone for the detective. Likewise, psychologists must ask and answer such questions as "Are we putting our participants at risk?" "Is our experimental treatment harmful?" "Is the information we will gather from our experiment worth the potential risk and harm to participants that is involved?" Despite older views to the contrary, science does not operate in a moral vacuum (Kimmel, 1988).

Under the 1974 National Health Research Act, the United States government demands assurance that federally funded projects have been reviewed and approved by a group of the proposing scientist's peers and that human participants have given informed consent concerning research participation. Since that time, seeking approval for a project from a group such as a Human Subjects Review Panel, an Animal Care and Utilization Committee, or an Institutional Review Board has become standard practice.

What has prompted such concern with ethics? Although we could cite many unethical practices, we will describe four instances that created major concern: the medical atrocities of World War II, the Tuskegee syphilis project, the Willowbrook hepatitis project, and Stanley Milgram's obedience studies of the 1960s.

During World War II, Nazi doctors conducted a lengthy series of experiments on civilian prisoners of war to determine the effects of various viruses, toxic agents, and drugs. The prisoners had no choice concerning whether they wanted to participate. After World War II many of these doctors were tried in courts for the unethical practices they had inflicted on their unwilling participants. Many were found guilty and either hanged or given long prison sentences. The Nuremberg War Tribunal was responsible for developing a code of medical and research ethics (Sasson & Nelson, 1969). Among other things, the Nuremberg Code stressed consideration of the following ethical aspects of research:

1. Participants should consent to participate in research.
2. Participants should be fully informed of the nature of the research project.
3. Risks should be avoided whenever possible.
4. Participants should be protected against risks to the greatest extent possible.
5. Projects should be conducted by scientifically qualified personnel.
6. Participants have the right to discontinue participation at any time.

As we will see, the Nuremberg Code has had a major impact on the American Psychological Association (APA) code of ethics to which psychologists adhere.

In 1956 an outbreak of hepatitis at Willowbrook, a mental retardation facility, prompted doctors to begin *purposely* infecting newly admitted patients in order to study the disease's development under controlled conditions. Approximately 10% of the new admissions were infected, placed in a separate ward, and not given treatment (Beauchamp & Childress, 1979). Even though the patients' parents agreed to this procedure, a number of parents felt they had agreed under pressure. Although considerable information that improved the future treatment of hepatitis was gained from this project, it involved a major ethical problem. The ethical problem involved the use of the patients for research purposes not related to mental disability. It is difficult to envision a relation between mental disability and the investigation of hepatitis.

The Tuskegee syphilis study began in 1932 and continued into the early 1970s. The purpose of the study was to observe the course of the syphilis disease in untreated individuals. To accomplish this goal, 399 African-American men living in the area around Tuskegee, Alabama, who were infected with syphilis were recruited as participants. Doctors told the men they were being treated for syphilis by the U.S. Public Health Service (USPHS). The men were not told the real purpose of the study, nor did they ever receive any treatment for syphilis. Moreover, local physicians were told not to treat these men for syphilis, and the participants were told their USPHS treatment would be discontinued if they sought any sort of additional treatment for the disease. Although information about the course of syphilis may have been gained from this project, it was done at the expense of the unknowing participants (Jones, 1981).

Review the points of research concern from the Nuremberg Code. Which of these principles did the Tuskegee syphilis study violate? How did the study violate these principles?

It would appear that, with the exception of the principle concerning the conduct of the project by a qualified scientist, all of the principles of the Nuremberg Code were violated. The men did not consent to participate, nor were they fully informed about the project. The participants were not protected against risks, and they certainly did not appear to have the right to decline to participate.

In Milgram's (1963) obedience-to-authority study, each participant was assigned the role of "teacher" in what was portrayed as a "learning experiment." Another "participant" (actually an accomplice of the experimenter) played the role of "learner." The teacher's task was to teach the learner a series of words. The teacher was told the purpose of the experiment was to determine the effects of punishment on memory. Every time the learner, who was in an adjacent room, made a mistake, the teacher was to correct the learner by administering an electric shock. Even though no shocks were actually administered, the teacher (true participant) did not know it, and the learner always acted as if a shock had been administered.

Once the experimental session began, the learner purposely made mistakes so the teacher would have to administer shocks. With each mistake the experimenter instructed the teacher to increase the voltage level of the shock. As the mistakes (and voltage level) increased, the learner began to moan and complain and finally refused to answer any questions. The experimenter told the teacher to treat no response as a mistake and continue administering shocks. The session ended when the teacher (participant) reached the maximum level of shock or refused to administer any more shocks. Contrary to Milgram's initial prediction, the participants administered many shocks at what they assumed were *very high* voltage levels.

Although this research contributed to our understanding of obedience to authority, it was not without ethical problems. For example, rather than protecting the rights of the participants, the experimenter purposely made them feel discomfort and emotional distress by ordering them to continue administering the electrical shocks (Baumrind, 1964). Moreover, Milgram (1964) was not prepared for the amount of emotional upset his participants experienced. Even though this high level of discomfort was noted, Milgram made the decision to continue the research. To Milgram's credit, all participants received a debriefing session after they completed the experiment. During this session the researcher explained the purpose of the experiment and the "learner" talked with the real participant. Subsequently, all participants received a follow-up report describing the results of the experiment. Such debriefing and follow-up procedures were not mandatory in the early 1960s.

APA Principles in the Conduct of Research with Humans

Experiments such as the Tuskegee syphilis project and Milgram's study have led to the development of ethical guidelines by the APA. The APA adopted and published the original code of ethics in 1973; it was revised in 1982 and again in 2002.

The current ethical standards that pertain to Research and Publication appear in Table 3-1.

Those standards dealing with (a) securing "informed consent" from the participants (Standard 8.02), and (b) using "deception" in research (Standard 8.07) have proved to be controversial.

Why do you think these principles have proved to be controversial in conducting psychological research?

Much psychological research, especially in the area of social psychology, has involved deception. Researchers believe that in many cases they can obtain honest and unbiased responses only when the participants are unaware of the true nature of the research. Hence, researchers find it difficult to give their participants a complete and accurate description of the experiment and to secure informed consent before the research is conducted.

Is Deception in Research Necessary?

Ideally, the researcher should be able to explain the purpose of a research project to the participants and enlist their cooperation. However, providing a *complete* explanation or description of the project may influence the participants' responses. Consider, for example, the research conducted by Kim Driggers and Tasha Helms (2000) on salary and willingness to date or by Naomi Freeman and Diana Punzo (2001) on the relative importance of DNA evidence and eyewitness testimony in relation to jurors' verdicts (see Chapter 1). Had the participants in these two studies known they were to evaluate the effect of salary on dating or the relative importance of DNA and eyewitness testimony, respectively, then their behavior could easily have been influenced by what they believed their responses were supposed to

TABLE 3-1   APA Ethical Standard 8 for the Conduct of Research

8.01 Institutional Approval
When institutional approval is required, psychologists provide accurate information about their research proposals and obtain approval prior to conducting the research. They conduct the research in accordance with the approved research protocol.

8.02 Informed Consent to Research
(a) When obtaining informed consent as required in Standard 3.10, Informed Consent, psychologists inform participants about (1) the purpose of the research, expected duration, and procedures; (2) their right to decline to participate and to withdraw from the research once participation has begun; (3) the foreseeable consequences of declining or withdrawing; (4) reasonably foreseeable factors that may be expected to influence their willingness to participate such as potential risks, discomfort, or adverse effects; (5) any prospective research benefits; (6) limits of confidentiality; (7) incentives for participation; and (8) whom to contact for questions about the research and research participants' rights. They provide opportunity for the prospective participants to ask questions and receive answers.

(b) Psychologists conducting intervention research involving the use of experimental treatments clarify to participants at the outset of the research (1) the experimental nature of the treatment; (2) the services that will or will not be available to the control group(s) if appropriate; (3) the means by which assignment to treatment and control groups will be made; (4) available treatment alternatives if an individual does not wish to participate in the research or wishes to withdraw once a study has begun; and (5) compensation for or monetary costs of participating including, if appropriate, whether reimbursement from the participant or a third-party payor will be sought.

8.03 Informed Consent for Recording Voices and Images in Research
Psychologists obtain informed consent from research participants prior to recording their voices or images for data collection unless (1) the research consists solely of naturalistic observations in public places, and it is not anticipated that the recording will be used in a manner that could cause personal identification or harm, or (2) the research design includes deception, and consent for the use of the recording is obtained during debriefing.

8.04 Client/Patient, Student, and Subordinate Research Participants
(a) When psychologists conduct research with clients/patients, students, or subordinates as participants, psychologists take steps to protect the prospective participants from adverse consequences of declining or withdrawing from participation.

(b) When research participation is a course requirement or an opportunity for extra credit, the prospective participant is given the choice of equitable alternative activities.

8.05 Dispensing with Informed Consent for Research
Psychologists may dispense with informed consent only (1) where research would not reasonably be assumed to create distress or harm and involves (a) the study of normal educational practices, curricula, or classroom management methods conducted in educational settings; (b) only anonymous questionnaires, naturalistic observations, or archival research for which disclosure of responses would not place participants at risk of criminal or civil liability or damage their financial standing, employability, or reputation, and confidentiality is protected; or (c) the study of factors related to job or organization effectiveness conducted in organizational settings for which there is no risk to participants' employability, and confidentiality is protected or (2) where otherwise permitted by law or federal or institutional regulations.

8.06 Offering Inducements for Research Participation
(a) Psychologists make reasonable efforts to avoid offering excessive or inappropriate financial or other inducements for research participation when such inducements are likely to coerce participation.

(continued)

TABLE 3-1	APA Ethical Standard 8 for the Conduct of Research (continued)

(b) When offering professional services as an inducement for research participation, psychologists clarify the nature of the services, as well as the risks, obligations, and limitations.

8.07 Deception in Research

(a) Psychologists do not conduct a study involving deception unless they have determined that the use of deceptive techniques is justified by the study's significant prospective scientific, educational, or applied value and that effective nondeceptive alternative procedures are not feasible.

(b) Psychologists do not deceive prospective participants about research that is reasonably expected to cause physical pain or severe emotional distress.

(c) Psychologists explain any deception that is an integral feature of the design and conduct of an experiment to participants as early as is feasible, preferably at the conclusion of their participation, but no later than at the conclusion of the data collection, and permit participants to withdraw their data. (See also Standard 8.08, Debriefing.)

8.08 Debriefing

(a) Psychologists provide a prompt opportunity for participants to obtain appropriate information about the nature, results, and conclusions of the research, and they take reasonable steps to correct any misconceptions that participants may have of which the psychologists are aware.

(b) If scientific or humane values justify delaying or withholding this information, psychologists take reasonable measures to reduce the risk of harm.

(c) When psychologists become aware that research procedures have harmed a participant, they take reasonable steps to minimize the harm.

Source: American Psychological Association (2002). Ethical principles of psychologist and code of conduct. *American Psychologist, 57,* 1060–1073. Reprinted with permission.

be. As we will see, it is very important in psychological research with human participants to try to ensure that the participants are not responding simply because (a) they have "figured out" the experiment and know how they are supposed to act or (b) they think the experimenter expects them to respond in a certain manner (see Rosenthal, 1966, 1985).

Hence, it is arguable that deception may be justified in some cases if our results are to be unbiased or uncontaminated by knowledge of the experiment and the expectancies that such knowledge may bring. If researchers use deception, how do they deal with obtaining informed consent for participation?

Informed Consent

Standard 8.02 indicates that the participants should give informed consent regarding their participation in a research project. Informed consent frequently takes the form of a statement concerning the research that the participants sign before taking part in the research project. An example of an informed consent form appears in Figure 3-1 on the next page. As you can see, this document gives the participants a general description of the project they are going to participate in and informs them that no penalties will be invoked if they choose not to participate. Also, it clearly states that the participants have the right to withdraw their participation at any time they desire.

 Even though it may not be readily apparent, the process of informed consent has given researchers a new variable to evaluate. What is this variable?

The informed consent process itself and the information provided through this process have stimulated some interesting research. For example, Edward Burkley III, Shawn McFarland, Wendy Walker, and Jennifer Young, students at Southern Illinois University Edwardsville, evaluated the effect of having the "right to withdraw from the experiment" statement printed on the informed consent form. Two groups of students solved anagrams. One group of participants had the right to withdraw statement printed on their informed consent document, whereas the informed consent document for the second group did not

---

Informed Consent Document

Read this consent form. If you have any questions ask the experimenter and he/she will answer the question.

The Department of Psychology supports the practice of protection for human participants participating in research and related activities. The following information is provided so that you can decide whether you wish to participate in the present study. You should be aware that even if you agree to participate, you are free to withdraw at any time, and that if you do withdraw from the study, you will not be subjected to reprimand or any other form of reproach.

In order to help determine the relationship between numerous personality characteristics, you are being asked to complete several questionnaires. It should not take more than 30 minutes for you to complete these materials. These questionnaires will be completed anonymously.

"I have read the above statement and have been fully advised of the procedures to be used in this project. I have been given sufficient opportunity to ask any questions I had concerning the procedures and possible risks involved. I understand the potential risks involved and I assume them voluntarily. I likewise understand that I can withdraw from the study at any time without being subjected to reproach."

_____   _____

Participant and/or authorized representative   Date

FIGURE 3-1   An Example of an Informed Consent Document.

contain this statement. Burkley et al. (2000) found that the students who had the statement printed on their form solved significantly *more* anagrams than students whose form did not contain this statement. Clearly, the informed consent process can have an impact on the results of an experiment. The influence of ethical procedures likely will offer researchers rich experimental opportunities for years to come.

Although the objectives of Standard 8.02 may not seem difficult to satisfy, there is one group of participants that creates special problems—children. For example, if you want to conduct a project using first-graders, your research proposal initially has to be approved by a college or university committee. (We will discuss Institutional Review Boards at the end of this chapter.) Once you secure this approval, then you need to contact the school system for approval. This approval may need to be granted at several levels—teacher, principal, superintendent, and school board. Each of these individuals will scrutinize your proposal thoroughly to safeguard the rights of the children. Once you have successfully cleared these hurdles, then you must secure permission from the parent or legal guardian of each child. The parent or legal guardian is the individual who will sign the informed consent form.

The more general the statement of the research project, the more room there is for the possible use of deception or for not completely explaining the project. For example, the informed consent document shown in Figure 3-1 does not explicitly tell the participants that they are taking part in a study that will examine the relationship between interpersonal flexibility, self-esteem, and fear of death (Hayes, Miller, & Davis, 1993).

By deceiving participants about the true purpose of an experiment or not providing complete information about the experiment, the experimenter may take the chance of placing some participants "at risk." Who is to say that completing a particular survey or questionnaire will not provoke an intense emotional reaction in a given participant? Perhaps one of the participants in an investigation of child abuse was sexually molested as a preschooler and completing your questionnaire will reawaken those terrifying memories. You need to carefully consider all the possible reactions and evaluate their seriousness.

Participants at Risk and Participants at Minimal Risk

Participants at risk are participants who, by virtue of their participation in the research project, are placed under some emotional or physical risk. Certainly, the participants in the Tuskegee syphilis study and Milgram's obedience studies were participants at risk. Securing informed consent from participants at risk is a mandatory condition.

Participants at minimal risk are participants who will experience no harmful effects through taking part in the research project. For example, Anastasia Gibson, Kristie Smith, and Aurora Torres (2000) observed the glancing behavior of customers at ATM machines (see Chapter 4). In this research the participants were at minimal risk; the recording of their glancing behaviors did not influence their physical or emotional well-being. Although desirable, it is not mandatory to secure informed consent from participants at minimal risk. In fact, Gibson et al. (2000) indicated, "Because this study was a systematic naturalistic observation, participants did not complete a consent form" (p. 149).

Participants at risk By participating in an experiment, the participants are placed under some type of physical or emotional risk.

Participants at minimal risk Participation in an experiment does not place the participants under physical or emotional risk.

But what about those participants at risk who are participating in a study involving deception? How do we satisfy the ethical guidelines in such a case?

First, the researcher should tell the participants about all aspects of the research that are potentially harmful. If the researcher uses deception, the participants should not be deceived about some potentially harmful aspect of the research. For example, it would not be acceptable to tell participants they will be taking a vitamin tablet when the drug they are to consume is a hallucinogen. When participants are informed about all potentially harmful aspects of a research project, then they are able to give valid informed consent about participating.

The second procedure used to satisfy the ethical guidelines when using deception is to thoroughly debrief the participants once the experiment is completed. We turn to that topic after considering the needs of certain special populations.

Vulnerable Populations

What the researcher considers to be a risky or potentially harmful situation may depend on the type of participants chosen for a project. For example, experiments involving physical exertion, such as testing the effects of exercise on subsequent memory tasks, which pose no risk to healthy participants, may constitute a significant risk for persons in poor health. Likewise, the age of the participant may be a relevant consideration in determining potential emotional harm or distress in studies involving the selection of liked and disliked peers.

Researchers must exercise special care when the research participants may not be capable of fully understanding what participation in a project may entail. Such participant groups might include children, patients with physical or mental disorders, or persons with lower intelligence, low literacy, or English as a second language. In these instances the researcher must take special care to ensure that these individuals or their parents or legal guardians understand fully what is expected of them and any risks they may encounter in the research project. To understand the importance of taking these potentially vulnerable populations into account, imagine how you would feel if you were a college student in a foreign country where you didn't speak the language very well and you agreed to participate in a potentially hazardous research project without understanding the risks involved. In some instances professional organizations have developed specific guidelines for the treatment of such vulnerable populations. For example, the Society for Research in Child Development (SRCD) has developed a set of 16 guidelines for research with children. You can access these guidelines on the Internet at http://www.srcd.org/about.html#standards.

The Debriefing Session

Debriefing session The nature and purpose of an experiment are explained at its conclusion.

The **debriefing session**, usually the final step in conducting the research project, involves explaining to the participants the nature and purpose of the project. Debriefing can be very important and should not be taken lightly by the researcher. Eliot Aronson and J. M. Carlsmith (1968) proposed several excellent guidelines for effective debriefing:

1. The researcher's integrity as a scientist must be conveyed to the participants. The researcher's personal belief in the scientific method is the foundation for explaining why deception was necessary and how it was employed in the research project.

2. If deception was used, the researcher should reassure the participants that it was not wrong or a reflection on their integrity or intelligence to feel that they have been tricked or fooled. Such feelings indicate that the deception used in the project was effective.

3. Because debriefing is usually the last step in the conduct of the research project, there may be a tendency to try to rush through it. This approach is not advisable. The participants have a lot of information to digest and try to understand; therefore, the debriefing session should progress slowly. The explanations should be clear and understandable.

4. The researcher should be sensitive to indications that the participants' discomfort is not being alleviated by the debriefing session and strive to correct this situation. The goal of the debriefing session is to return the participants to the same (or close to the same) mental and emotional state they were in at the beginning of the project.

5. The researcher should repeat all guarantees of confidentiality and anonymity that were made at the beginning of the project. For such assurances to be seen as believable, the researcher must have clearly established his or her integrity as a scientist.

6. Do not try to satisfy debriefing requirements by saying that you will send an explanation and the results of the project at a later date. For maximum effectiveness, you should conduct the debriefing session immediately following the experimental session; there are no "easier" ways to satisfy this obligation.

These guidelines define the ideal debriefing situation, and they should be followed as closely as possible. However, in most instances the debriefing session will not be overly time consuming. For example, Elvo Kuai-Long Sou, a student at Washington State University at Vancouver, and his faculty advisor, Lori Irving, surveyed the attitudes of U.S. and Macao college students toward mental illness. The researchers indicated, "Once the participants finished the survey, each of them received a debriefing sheet that explained the purpose of the study and provided basic information regarding mental illness and how to seek help for a mental health issue" (Sou & Irving, 2002, p. 18).

Review the discussion of debriefing. What is the main goal of the debriefing session?

The main purpose of the debriefing session is to explain the nature of the experiment, remove or alleviate any undesirable consequences the participants may be experiencing, and generally try to return them to the same state of mind they were in prior to the experiment. For example, Milgram was sensitive to the emotional state of his participants. After the research was complete, he sent the participants a five-page report that described the results and their meaning. The participants also completed a questionnaire; 84% indicated that they were glad they participated. In a one-year examination of 40 participants, a psychiatrist reported there was "no evidence . . . of any traumatic reactions" (Milgram, 1974, p. 197).

The debriefing session also can provide the experimenter with valuable feedback concerning the conduct of the experiment from the participants' viewpoint. Was the IV manipulation successful? If deception was used, was it successful? Were the instructions clear? The answers to these and other relevant questions can be obtained during the debriefing session.

The Ethical Use of Animals in Psychological Research

Up to this point our ethical considerations have dealt with research in which humans are the participants. Since Willard S. Small (1901) used the first rat maze at Clark University in 1900, considerable psychological research has involved the use of animals. The use of animals in psychological research has created considerable controversy, debate, and even violence in recent years. Supporters of animal research point to the numerous accomplishments and scientific breakthroughs that are based on the results of animal studies (e.g., Kalat, 1992; Miller, 1985). For example, such medical procedures as blood transfusions, anesthesia, painkillers, antibiotics, insulin, vaccines, chemotherapy, CPR, coronary bypass surgery, and reconstructive surgery are based on animal studies. For over 100 years psychologists have used animals in studies of learning, psychopathology, brain and nervous system functioning, and physiology. It is undeniable that animal research has yielded numerous important and beneficial results.

However, animal activists argue that the price we have paid for such progress is too high. They point to problems with housing conditions, as well as the pain and suffering that research animals endure, and insist such treatment must stop (Miller & Williams, 1983; Reagan, 1983; Singer, 1975).

Although the debate between researchers and animal activists is likely to continue for some time, our present concern is with the ethical conduct of animal research. In addition to the concern over the ethics of human experiments, the 1960s also witnessed an increase in the concern for the ethical treatment of animals. For example, the Animal Welfare Act of 1966 was national legislation specifically passed to protect research animals. The APA has also established ethical standards for the use of animals in psychological research (APA, 2002). Table 3-2 presents these standards. These standards are designed to ensure humane treatment of animals used in research and for educational purposes. They have resulted in improved care and housing of animals.

Now that we have considered the ethical treatment of human and animal participants, let's examine the group that decides whether the proposed research should or should not be conducted. For the detective, the jury will make such decisions; in the case of the psychologist, our attention turns to the Institutional Review Board.

Institutional Review Board (IRB)   The university committee that is responsible for determining whether a proposed research project conforms to accepted ethical standards.

The Institutional Review Board

At some institutions the review panel for the use of human participants may be the Human Subjects Review Panel, whereas the Animal Care and Utilization Committee reviews proposals for animal research. At other institutions the **Institutional Review Board (IRB)** reviews both types of proposals. Although the exact name of the group may vary from institution to institution, its composition and functions are quite similar.

The typical IRB is composed of a cross-section of individuals. For example, if we examine a college or university IRB, we might find that it consists of faculty

TABLE 3-2   **APA Ethical Standard 8.09—Humane Care and Use of Animals in Research**

(a) Psychologists acquire, care for, use, and dispose of animals in compliance with current federal, state, and local laws and regulations, and with professional standards.

(b) Psychologists trained in research methods and experienced in the care of laboratory animals supervise all procedures involving animals and are responsible for ensuring appropriate consideration of their comfort, health, and humane treatment.

(c) Psychologists ensure that all individuals under their supervision who are using animals have received instruction in research methods and in the care, maintenance, and handling of the species being used, to the extent appropriate to their role. (See also Standard 2.05, Delegation of Work to Others.)

(d) Psychologists make reasonable efforts to minimize the discomfort, infection, illness, and pain of animal subjects.

(e) Psychologists use a procedure subjecting animals to pain, stress, or privation only when an alternative procedure is unavailable and the goal is justified by its prospective scientific, educational, or applied value.

(f) Psychologists perform surgical procedures under appropriate anesthesia and follow techniques to avoid infection and minimize pain during and after surgery.

(g) When it is appropriate that an animal's life be terminated, psychologists proceed rapidly, with an effort to minimize pain and in accordance with accepted procedures.

Source: American Psychological Association (2002). Ethical principles of psychologists and code of conduct. *American Psychologist, 57,* 1060–1073. Reprinted with permission.

members from history, biology, education, psychology, and economics. Additionally, there will probably be one or two individuals who are not associated with the institution. A veterinarian must be a member of the panel that reviews animal research proposals.

The task of this group is not to decide on the scientific merits of the proposed research; the scientist proposing the research is the expert in that area. The IRB's responsibility is to examine the proposed procedures, any psychological tests or questionnaires that will be used, the informed consent document, plans for debriefing the participants, the use of painful procedures in animal research, procedures for disposing of animals humanely, and so forth. If participants are at risk, will they be made aware of this risk before the experiment is conducted? Do participants have the ability to terminate participation at any time? Will debriefing counteract the effects of deception if it has been used? Is it possible that a particular questionnaire or survey may evoke a strong emotional reaction? In short, the IRB serves to ensure that the experimenter treats research participants, whether they are humans or animals, according to the established ethical guidelines. If the IRB determines that a proposed project does not meet ethical standards, the IRB can request that changes be made to bring the project in line with standards.

The Experimenter's Responsibility

Ultimately the experimenter is the single individual who is accountable for the ethical conduct of the research project. In accepting this responsibility, the researcher carefully weighs the *benefits* and *costs* of the project and then decides whether to conduct it. The new knowledge produced by the project represents the benefit. What about costs? Such factors as time and expense clearly are costs and must be considered. Whether the research will place the participants at risk is another major cost to deal with.

Students doing research as part of the requirements of a course also are responsible for conducting their projects in an ethical manner. Applications to use human or animal participants must be submitted to and approved by the appropriate IRB. In most cases the supervising faculty member signs such submissions.

The Participants' Responsibility

Clearly, research participants have numerous, important rights. Let's turn the situation around.

Do participants also have ethical responsibilities? What should researchers be able to expect from their participants?

Korn (1988) indicated that the research participant has the following responsibilities:

1. *Be on time for the research appointment.* The researcher and other participants are inconvenienced when participants are late for an appointment.

2. *Participants have the responsibility to listen carefully to the experimenter and ask questions in order to understand the research.* Such attention and questions are important for the participants to give informed consent and "receive the maximum education benefit from participation" (p. 77).

3. *Participants should take the research seriously and cooperate with the experimenter.* Regardless of the appearance of the research task, participants should take their role seriously and assume the researcher will provide an explanation later.

4. *When the study has been completed, participants share the responsibility for understanding what happened.* "Participants should ask questions that help to clarify the situation and enable them to learn more about the topic and method of research. Participants can be of great help by telling the researcher anything they think might be of interest" (p. 77).

5. *Participants have the responsibility for honoring the researcher's request that they not discuss the study with anyone else who might be a participant.* "Confidentiality works both ways" (p. 77). As part of the debriefing session, the researcher may ask the participants not to discuss the experiment with their friends. The participants are ethically responsible to honor this request; the disclosure of such information can invalidate the results of a research project (see Chapter 6).

Clearly, participants' responsibilities also must be factored into the ethical makeup of a research project. Unfortunately, participants' responsibilities usually receive the least amount of attention. Why? Many students become research participants because they are enrolled in introductory psychology and completion of the course carries some type of research participation requirement. The use of sign-up sheets posted on a "research participant" bulletin board or some other equally impersonal manner of contacting potential participants makes a discussion of participant responsibilities most difficult. The solution appears to rest with the class instructor's obligation to explain and discuss these responsibilities and benefits with his or her students.

Researchers' Ethical Obligations Once the Research Is Completed

The experimenter's ethical responsibilities do not end when the data are collected and the participants are debriefed. Experimenters are responsible for presenting the results of their research in an ethical manner. The two main problems encountered in this regard are plagiarism and fabrication of data.

Plagiarism

Plagiarism refers to using someone else's work without giving credit to the original author. Certainly, plagiarism is an obvious violation of the ethical standards of psychologists. Although it is difficult to believe that plagiarism occurs among established professionals, it does (Broad, 1980). Unfortunately, plagiarism is not an uncommon occurrence in colleges and universities. Although some students may view plagiarism as an easy way to complete an assignment or term paper, many students have told us that no one had ever explained plagiarism to them. The Department of Psychology at Bishop's University (1994) has clearly summarized what you need to do to avoid plagiarism. The guidelines suggest the following:

> **Plagiarism**   Using someone else's work without giving credit to the original source.

1. Any part of your paper that contains the exact words of an author must appear in quotation marks, with the author's name, and the date of publication and page number(s) of the source attached.
2. You should not adapt material with only minor changes, such as combining sentences, omitting phrases, changing a few words, or inverting sentence order.
3. If what you have to say is substantially your own words, but you took the facts or ideas from a particular author, then omit the quotation marks and reference with a parenthetical citation like this: (Jones, 1949).
4. Always acknowledge secondary sources. (See p. 64.)
5. You must reference every statement of fact and every idea or opinion not your own unless the item is part of common knowledge.
6. Do not hand in for credit a paper that is the same as or similar to one you have handed in elsewhere.
7. It is permissible to ask someone to criticize a completed paper before you submit it and to bring to your attention errors in logic, grammar, punctuation, spelling, and expression. However, it is not permissible to have another person rewrite any portion of your paper

"These days, it's publish or perish."

or to have another person translate into English for you a paper that you have written in another language.

8. Keep rough notes and drafts of your work and photocopies of material not available in your college or university library.

In our experience, Guideline 2 is most problematic for students. If you reread this guideline, you will find that even paraphrasing an author's words is considered plagiarism. It is a good idea to read your sources thoroughly but to put them away when you write so you are not tempted to copy or paraphrase. For example, if you paraphrased the last sentence as "It is good to read your sources carefully but to put them away when you write so you will not be tempted to copy," you would be guilty of plagiarism.

Why would a scientist engage in plagiarism? Although the specific reason(s) will vary from individual to individual, the pressure to publish one's research findings probably represents the single greatest cause (Mahoney, 1987). Because one's job security (tenure) or salary increases are often directly tied to the publication record, research and publication may become the central focus in the professional career. In haste to prepare articles and build an impressive publication record, it may seem easier and quicker to "borrow" a paragraph here and a paragraph there, especially if writing is not an easy and enjoyable task.

Fabrication of data
Those instances where the experimenter either deliberately alters or creates research data.

Fabrication of Data

Fabrication of data refers to those instances in which the experimenter either deliberately changes or alters data that were already gathered or simply makes up data to suit his or her needs. As with plagiarism, fabrication of data is an obvious ethical violation. Possibly the most famous instance of *apparent* data fabrication involved the famous British psychologist Cyril Burt (1883–1971). Burt's research on twins was influential in supporting the view that children's intelligence is largely inherited from their parents. His data went unchallenged for a number of years until researchers began to notice that he reported exactly the same results in different studies. Critics contended that it was very unlikely that exactly the same results would be produced in several different studies. Burt's supporters argued that Burt was elderly and likely forgot which data to present in which report. Unfortunately, scholars will not be able to resolve this debate because Burt's data were discarded shortly after his death. Researchers now agree that Burt's publications have little scientific value.

What would cause a scientist to fabricate data?

Again, we can point to the pressure to "publish or perish." Remember, we use synthetic statements in our research hypothesis; hence, there is always a chance that a project will not turn out as we predicted. When the data do not turn out as we had hoped, there may be a temptation to "fix" the data in order to bring them in line with our predictions and theory. Certainly, it is much easier (and quicker) to change a few numbers here and there than it is to redo an entire experiment. It does not seem to be a very great step to go from changing a few numbers to eliminating the experiment altogether and fabricating all the data.

The consequences of having false information in the body of scientific knowledge should be obvious to you. By falsifying a research finding, a psychologist actually encourages other researchers to conduct projects on a topic that is doomed to failure! The expenditures in time, effort, participants, and money can be enormous. And because much research is supported by federal grants, the costs to the taxpayers can be substantial. Because data form the cornerstone of research reports, ethical conduct is of vital importance.

Lying with Statistics

In addition to the sanctions against plagiarism and the fabrication of data, researchers have a responsibility to present their results in an unbiased manner. On first glance, this responsibility may seem rather straightforward and inconsequential. After all, results are results, aren't they? The answer to that question is yes and no. Yes, the basic results are not going to change; however, researchers exercise a great deal of individual choice and creativity in deciding what to present and how to present it. For example, a researcher could choose to selectively leave out important data and highlight other, possibly inconsequential data. The researcher's choice of what to present and how to present it is so important in determining the conclusion your intended audience reaches, that Darrell Huff (1954) published a book titled *How to Lie with Statistics* in which he described numerous "questionable" statistical practices designed to influence the consumer of this information. We will have more to say about the presentation of statistical results throughout the rest of this book. For now, you should be aware that researchers have the responsibility to present their results in an unbiased manner. Like a good detective, you need to be sensitive to those instances in which evidence may be misleading or missing.

Citing Your References Correctly

When other people read your research report and note the references you used to support the research idea, the hypothesis you are testing, and your interpretation of the data, they assume that you have actually read each reference that you cite. This assumption makes good sense; if you design a research project to test a theoretical prediction, then you should read about that theory firsthand.

On the other hand, there may be occasions when you *read about* an interesting and relevant piece of research but you simply cannot acquire a copy of the original report. Perhaps your library does not carry the journal in which this article was published, and you cannot obtain the paper on interlibrary loan. Lacking the author's address, you are at a standstill. Perhaps the research has not been published. What should you do when you cannot obtain a copy of the original report? If the paper is from a journal to which you do not have access, it may be tempting to cite and list this reference *as if* you had actually read the original. We caution you against adopting this practice; it is the researcher's ethical responsibility to cite and list *only* those works that have been read. Instead, you should cite the *secondary source* you are using.

Don't despair; there is a way you can include those unobtainable references in your research report. Here's how it works. Assume that you read a 1999 article by Smith and Davis that *described and referenced* a research project that Brown conducted in 1984. You would like to cite the paper by Brown, but you are unable to obtain it. In this instance you cite the reference as follows:

Brown (as cited in Smith & Davis, 1999) found that . . .

In the reference section you would list only the Smith and Davis reference (the one you actually read). The appropriate way to cite and list references is covered in detail in Chapter 14. We encourage you to examine this material now. We agree that there are a lot of details to master when it comes to citing and listing references; please work hard on this skill. Sherlock Holmes's comment "It has long been an axiom of mine that the little things are infinitely the most important" (Doyle, 1927, p. 194) is most appropriate in this context.

These, and other, APA ethical standards that are related to the presentation and publication of research data are shown in Table 3-3.

Now, we do not want to leave you with the impression that plagiarism, fabrication of data, and misrepresentation of results and references characterize all or even many scientists; they do not. The vast majority of scientists enjoy designing and conducting their own research projects to see if they can unlock nature's secrets. However, it takes only a few unethical individuals to give science a bad name. We hope you will not be among the ranks of the unethical.

TABLE 3-3	APA Ethical Standards 8.10–8.15–Reporting and Publishing Your Research

8.10 Reporting Research Results
(a) Psychologists do not fabricate data.

(b) If psychologists discover significant errors in their published data, they take reasonable steps to correct such errors in a correction, retraction, erratum, or other appropriate publication means.

8.11 Plagiarism
Psychologists do not present portions of another's work or data as their own, even if the other work or data source is cited occasionally.

8.12 Publication Credit
(a) Psychologists take responsibility and credit, including authorship credit, only for work they have actually performed or to which they have substantially contributed.

(b) Principal authorship and other publication credits accurately reflect the relative scientific or professional contributions of the individuals involved, regardless of their relative status. Mere possession of an institutional position, such as department chair, does not justify authorship credit. Minor contributions to the research or to the writing for publications are acknowledged appropriately, such as in footnotes or in an introductory statement.

(c) Except under exceptional circumstances, a student is listed as principal author on any multiple-authored article that is substantially based on the student's doctoral dissertation. Faculty advisors discuss publication credit with students as early as feasible and throughout the research and publication process as appropriate.

8.13 Duplicate Publication of Data
Psychologists do not publish, as original data, data that have been previously published. This does not preclude republishing data when they are accompanied by proper acknowledgment.

8.14 Sharing Research Data for Verification
(a) After research results are published, psychologists do not withhold the data on which their conclusions are based from other competent professionals who seek to verify the substantive claims through reanalysis and who intend to use such data only for that purpose, provided that the confidentiality of the participants can be protected and unless legal rights concerning proprietary data preclude their release. This does not preclude psychologists from requiring that such individuals or groups be responsible for costs associated with the provision of such information.

(b) Psychologists who request data from other psychologists to verify the substantive claims through reanalysis may use shared data only for the declared purpose. Requesting psychologists obtain prior written agreement for all other uses of the data.

8.15 Reviewers
Psychologists who review material submitted for presentation, publication, grant, or research proposal review respect the confidentiality of and the proprietary rights in such information of those who submitted it.

Source: American Psychological Association (2002). Ethical principles of psychologists and code of conduct. *American Psychologist, 57,* 1060–1073. Reprinted with permission.

1. It is the experimenter's responsibility to ensure that a research project is conducted in an ethical manner.

2. The World War II atrocities perpetrated by Nazi doctors, the Willowbrook hepatitis project, the Tuskegee syphilis project, and psychological research such as Milgram's obedience studies have increased ethical concerns and awareness.

3. The American Psychological Association (APA) has developed a set of ethical standards for the conduct of research with human participants.

4. Although the researcher should try to avoid it, using deception may be justified in order to yield unbiased responses.

5. Informed consent is a signed statement indicating that participants understand the nature of the experiment and agree to participate in it.

6. **Participants at risk** are individuals whose participation in an experiment places them under some emotional and/or physical risk. **Participants at minimal risk** are individuals whose participation in an experiment results in no harmful consequences.

7. The experimenter explains the nature and purpose of the experiment to the participants during the **debriefing session**. Although the debriefing session is designed to counteract any negative effects of research participation, it also can provide the experimenter with valuable information about the research procedures that were employed.

8. Ethical standards also exist for the conduct of research using animals.

9. The **Institutional Review Board (IRB)** is a group of the researcher's scientific and nonscientific peers who evaluate research proposals for adherence to ethical guidelines and procedures.

10. In addition to their rights and protection, participants also have several responsibilities.

11. Researchers have a responsibility to present their findings in an ethical manner. **Plagiarism** (the use of another's work without giving proper credit) and **fabrication of data** are the chief ethical infractions encountered in the presentation of research results.

1. Describe the three projects that raised concern about the ethical conduct of research.

2. What aspects of the research endeavor did the Nuremberg Code stress?

3. In what types of research situations might the use of deception be justified? If deception is used, how can the need to provide informed consent be satisfied?

4. Participants in a research project who are placed under some emotional or physical risk are classified as
   a. participants at risk
   b. participants at minimal risk
   c. volunteer participants
   d. participants at no risk

5. The main purpose of the _____ is to explain the nature of an experiment and re-move any undesirable consequences.
   a. informed consent form
   b. Institutional Review Board
   c. Ethical Principles of Research with Human Participants
   d. debriefing session

6. Describe the guidelines for the ethical use of animals in psychological research.

7. What is an IRB? Describe the composition of the typical IRB. What responsibility does an IRB have?

8. With regard to the conduct of research, what is the ethical responsibility of the experimenter?

9. Distinguish between plagiarism and fabrication of data. What sets of pressures are responsible for these unethical actions?

KEY TERMS

Participants at risk, 55
Participants at minimal
  risk, 55

Debriefing session, 56
Institutional Review Board
  (IRB), 58

Plagiarism, 61
Fabrication of data, 62

LOOKING AHEAD

Now that we have discussed the sources of research problems, conduct of an effective literature review, and development of an experimental hypothesis, we turn our attention to actual techniques for gathering data. In the next chapter you will learn about nonexperimental research methods. These descriptive and observational techniques provide ways to gather data in situations where it may not be possible or desirable to conduct a scientific experiment.

CHAPTER

4

Nonexperimental Methods I: Descriptive Methods, Qualitative Research, and Correlational Studies

Descriptive Methods
Archival and Previously Recorded Sources of Data
Observational Techniques

Qualitative Research
Grounded Theory

Correlational Studies
The Nature of Correlations
Correlational Research

Not all research projects use the experimental method. In fact, researchers have developed a large number of nonexperimental strategies. Although they are classified as nonexperimental, these methods do not necessarily produce inferior results. As you will see, the choice of a nonexperimental research strategy depends on the type of problem being investigated, where it is being investigated, and the nature of the data the researcher gathers.

Descriptive Methods

Because several of these methods do not involve the manipulation of an independent variable (IV), they are called **descriptive research methods**. When we use descriptive methods, we can only speculate about causation that may be involved.

> **Descriptive research methods**   Research methods that do not involve the manipulation of an independent variable (IV).

Archival and Previously Recorded Sources of Data

In some instances researchers may not gather their own data; they may answer their research question by using data recorded by other individuals for other purposes. For example, public health and census data may be analyzed years later to answer questions about socioeconomic status, religion, or political party affiliation. In some instances the records and data you need to consult are stored in a central location. The Archives of the History of American Psychology were established at the University of Akron in 1974 for conducting research on the history of psychology. Although the letters, documents, and photographs contained in this collection were originally produced for numerous reasons, they are now used by researchers interested in answering questions about the history of our discipline.

You also can access several archival sources online. For example, the General Social Survey (GSS) has been conducted almost annually since 1972 by the National Opinion Research Center. The responses of more than 35,000 respondents to a wide range of socially relevant questions are available at http://www.icpsr.umich.edu/gss/home.htm. The number of research questions that can be addressed with this huge body of information seems endless. There is no charge for accessing this site; we encourage you to peruse it.

Not all sources of previously recorded data are stored in an archive or library or are available online for our use. There are numerous real-life sources. For example, if you are interested in differences in sexual preoccupation between men and women, you might choose to examine graffiti on the walls of public restrooms.

The use of archival and previously recorded data is certainly in line with being a psychological detective. You are putting together bits and pieces of data to answer research questions. Unfortunately, there are several problems associated with this approach to gathering information. Consider conducting this type of research and see what problems you can discover.

Potential Problems   There are several potential problems associated with using archival and previously recorded sources of data. First, unless you are dealing with the papers and documents of a few clearly identified individuals, you will not know exactly who left the data you are investigating. Not knowing the participants who comprise your sample will make it difficult to understand and generalize your results. Consider the graffiti example. You may choose to record graffiti from restrooms on your campus. Who created the graffiti? Was it created by a representative sample of students? Although common sense may tell you that the sample of graffiti writers is not representative of students on your campus, let alone college students in general, you do not know. Your ability to make statements other than those that merely describe your data is severely limited.

Second, the participants may have been selective in *what* they chose to write. Clearly, this consideration may be important in our graffiti example, particularly if we are evaluating the presence of sexual comments. What others chose to record may drastically influence our conclusions in other instances. For example, until recently what we knew about Wilhelm Wundt, the founder of scientific psychology, was provided by E. B. Titchener, who originally translated Wundt's books and papers from German into English. Unfortunately, Titchener chose to misrepresent Wundt on several occasions; hence, our impression of Wundt may be severely distorted (Goodwin, 1999). Fortunately, Wundt's original writings are still available for retranslation and examination. Even if his works are retranslated, we will still face the possible problem that Wundt may have omitted things from his own writings that he did not want to share with others. Whenever archival or previously recorded sources are used, you cannot avoid this problem of *selective deposit*.

A third problem with this type of data concerns the survival of such records. In our study of graffiti it will be important to know something about the cleaning schedule for the restroom(s) we are observing. Are they scrubbed clean each day, or are graffiti allowed to accumulate? In this example the data in which you are interested will probably not have a very high survival rate. Printed materials may not fare much better. During the 1920s John Watson and his call to behaviorism made psychology immensely popular in the United States; the number of journal articles and books written during this period attest to its popularity. It was only recently, however, that researchers discovered a very popular magazine, *Psychology: Health, Happiness, and Success*, which was published from 1923 to 1938 (Benjamin, 1992). Why the mystery surrounding this once-popular magazine? The problem had to do with the type of paper on which the magazine was printed. The high acid content of the paper led to rapid disintegration of these magazines; hence, only a precious few have survived.

Comparisons with the Experimental Method   Certainly, the researcher can gain valuable information from archival and prerecorded sources. However, we must be aware of the problems of a nonrepresentative sample, data that are purposely not recorded, and data that have been lost. A comparison of using this technique with conducting an experiment reveals other weaknesses in addition to these limitations. Because we examined data and documents that were produced at another time under potentially unknown circumstances, we are not able to exercise any control with regard to gathering these data. Hence, we are unable to make any type of cause-and-effect statement; the best we can do is speculate about what might have occurred.

These concerns notwithstanding, this type of research can yield interesting and valuable results. For example, much of what you read in a history of psychology text is the product of archival research. In the next section we examine methods in which we observe the phenomenon of interest firsthand.

Observational Techniques

Even though the techniques described in this section involve the direct observation of the phenomenon or behavior of interest, they do not involve the direct manipulation of any variables by the experimenter. Being able to specify which responses we will observe is as close to control as we come with these methods. Among the most common observational techniques are case studies, naturalistic observation, and the use of surveys or questionnaires.

Case Studies   When we conduct **case studies**, we intensively observe and record the behavior of one or sometimes two participants over an extended period of time. Because there are no guidelines for conducting a case study, the procedures employed, behaviors observed, and reports produced may vary substantially.

> **Case study**   The intensive observing and recording of the behavior of (usually) a single participant.

Frequently, case studies are used in clinical settings to help formulate hypotheses and ideas for further research. For example, the French physician Paul Broca (1824–1880) reported the case study of a patient nicknamed "Tan" because he said nothing except the word *tan* and an occasional obscenity when he was frustrated or annoyed (Howard, 1997). On the basis of his observations, Broca hypothesized that the center controlling the production of speech was located in the frontal lobe of the left hemisphere of the brain and that this area was damaged in the patient's brain. An autopsy indicated that Broca's hypothesis was correct. This case study provided the inspiration for numerous subsequent studies that yielded considerable information concerning the neurological system that is responsible for the comprehension and production of speech. Other case studies might involve the observation of a rare animal in the wild or at a zoological park, a specific type of mental patient in a hospital, or a gifted child at school.

Although case studies often provide interesting data, their results may be applicable only to the individual participant who was observed. In other words, when using the case study method, the researcher should not generalize beyond the participant who was studied. Additionally, because the researcher manipulates no variables, use of the case study method precludes establishing cause-and-effect relations. Yet, if your research goal is to understand the behavior of one individual (such as Broca's study of Tan), the case study may be the perfect research procedure. Your understanding of the behavior of one individual may lead to more general predictions.

Naturalistic Observation   **Naturalistic observation** involves seeking answers to research questions by observing behavior in the real world. For example, each spring, animal psychologists interested in the behavior of migrating sandhill cranes conceal themselves in camouflage blinds to observe the roosting behavior of these birds on the Platte River in central Nebraska. For another example, a researcher who is interested in the behavior of preschool children might go to a day-care center to observe the children.

> **Naturalistic observation**   Seeking answers to research questions by observing behavior in the real world.

The possibilities for conducting studies using naturalistic observation are limited only by our insight into a potential area of research. Regardless of the situation we choose, we have two goals in using naturalistic observation. The first goal should be obvious from the name of the technique: to describe behavior as it occurs in the natural setting without the artificiality of the laboratory. If the goal of research is to understand behavior in the real world, what better place to gather research data than in a natural setting? The second goal of naturalistic observation is to describe the variables that are present and the relations among them. Returning to our sandhill crane example, naturalistic observation may provide clues concerning why the birds migrate at particular times of the year and those factors that seem to determine the length of stay in a certain area.

In a naturalistic observation study, it is important that the researcher not interfere with or intervene in the behavior being studied. For example, in our study of preschoolers, the observer should be as inconspicuous as possible. For this reason, the use of one-way mirrors that allow researchers to observe without being observed is popular.

Why should the researcher be concealed or unobtrusive in a study using naturalistic observation?

The main reason the researcher must be unobtrusive in studies using naturalistic observation is to avoid influencing or changing the behavior of the participants being observed. The presence of an observer is not part of the natural setting for sandhill cranes or preschoolers; they may well behave differently in the presence of observers.

Reactance or **reactivity effect** The finding that participants respond differently when they know they are being observed.

The **reactance** or **reactivity effect** refers to the biasing of the participants' responses because they know they are being observed. Perhaps the most famous example of a reactivity effect occurred in a study conducted at the Western Electric Company's Hawthorne plant located on the boundary between Chicago and Cicero, Illinois, in the late 1930s (Roethlisberger & Dickson, 1939). The purpose of the research was to determine the effects of factors such as working hours and lighting on productivity. When researchers compared productivity of the test participants to that of the general plant, an unusual finding emerged. The test participants produced at a higher rate, often under test conditions that were inferior to those normally experienced. For example, when the room lighting was reduced well below normal levels, productivity increased. What caused these individuals to produce at such a high rate? The answer was simple: Because these workers knew they were research participants and that they were being observed, their productivity increased. Thus, the knowledge that one is participating in an experiment and is being observed may result in dramatic changes in behavior.

Hawthorne effect Another name for reactance or reactivity effect.

Because of the location of the original study, this reactivity phenomenon is often referred to as the **Hawthorne effect**. Having considered the general nature of naturalistic observation, we will examine a specific observational project more closely.

Anastasia Gibson and Kristie Smith, students at the University of Alabama in Huntsville, and their faculty advisor, Aurora Torres, conducted an interesting study that used naturalistic observation. They wanted to examine the relation between the glancing behavior of people using an automated teller machine (ATM) and the proximity of other customers. On the basis of previous studies of social distance and personal space, they predicted that other potential customers would not invade the personal space of the person using the ATM and that glancing behavior would decrease as other customers approached the 4-ft. radius that defined the personal-space boundary. The researchers were "in inconspicuous locations where [they] could view the ATM" (Gibson, Smith, & Torres, 2000, p. 150). Contrary to their predictions, the results indicated that glancing behavior *increased* as proximity between the person using the ATM and other potential customers *decreased*.

As you may have surmised by now, the main drawback with the use of naturalistic observation is, once again, the inability to make cause-and-effect statements. Because we do not manipulate any variables when we use this technique, such conclusions are not possible.

Why use naturalistic observation if it does not allow us to make cause-and-effect statements? The first reason is quite straightforward: Naturalistic observation may be our only choice of research techniques to study a particular type of behavior. Psychologists who are interested in reactions to natural disasters, such as earthquakes, tornadoes, and fires, cannot ethically create such life-threatening situations just to study behavior; they must make their observations under naturally occurring conditions. Conducting an experiment in which researchers manipulate variables is only one of many legitimate techniques used to gather data.

A second reason for using naturalistic observation is as an adjunct to the experimental method. For example, you might use naturalistic observation before conducting an experiment to get an idea of the relevant variables involved in the situation. Once you have an idea about which variables are (and are not) important, you can conduct systematic, controlled studies of these variables in the laboratory setting. After you have conducted laboratory experiments, you may want to return to the natural setting to see whether the insights gained in the laboratory are indeed mirrored in real life. Hence, psychologists may use naturalistic observation before and after an experimental research project to acquire further information concerning relevant variables.

Participant Observation   When using naturalistic observation, a researcher attempts to be as unobtrusive as possible. However, with **participant observation**, the researcher abandons his or her concealment and becomes part of the group being studied. Yes, the participant observer is just like the detective who goes undercover to acquire information.

> **Participant observation** A type of naturalistic observation in which the observer becomes part of the group being studied.

Researchers often use this research technique when the goal of the research project is to learn something about a specific culture or socioeconomic group. The investigator assumes the role of a member of the group and makes observations from this vantage point.

Participant observation is not limited to the study of human behavior; it can also be implemented in animal studies. Jane Goodall's study of chimpanzees in the Gombe Stream Reserve in Africa is a good example of the use of this technique with nonhumans. Goodall spent so much time observing the chimpanzees each day that they finally treated her more as a member of the chimpanzee group than as an outside observer. Such acceptance facilitated her observations. A researcher who is interested in observing an entire culture, as opposed to certain specific behaviors, uses **ethnography**, a research technique based on the anthropological tradition of research. In

> **Ethnography** A descriptive research approach that involves becoming a part of the culture being studied.

the ethnographic approach, the investigator becomes immersed in the "culture" of the population being studied. We enclosed the word *culture* in quotation marks because we do not refer to culture only in the cross-cultural sense of the word (e.g., different tribes, countries, continents). For example, you might use this approach to study an inner-city neighborhood or a teenage gang. As a researcher, you would become immersed in this culture for a long period of time, gathering data through participant observation and interviewing.

Glesne (1999) differentiated between two types of participant observation depending on the degree of participation. The *observer as participant* is a researcher who primarily observes a situation but also interacts with the others. Glesne used the example of Peshkin's semester-long study of a fundamentalist Christian school in which the researchers predominantly sat in the back of the classroom and took notes, with little interaction. The *participant as observer* is a researcher who becomes a part of the culture by working and interacting extensively with the others. Glesne spent a year in St. Vincent, where she socialized, assisted in farm work, and even became an intermediary with governmental agricultural agencies.

There is a cost-benefit relation with these two approaches. The more immersed in a culture you become, the more you stand to learn about it, but at the same time, you stand to lose your objectivity about a culture as you become more immersed in it. To be a good participant observer, you likely would have to fit Dr. Watson's description of Sherlock Holmes: "You really are an automaton—a calculating machine. There is something positively inhuman in you at times" (Doyle, 1927, p. 96). You can probably understand why strict experimentalists, by placing a premium on objectivity and control, shy away from ethnographic research.

The participant observer technique has considerable appeal as a research procedure; the researcher is actually a part of the situation under study. What better way to acquire the desired information! Despite such appeal, this procedure has its drawbacks and weaknesses. What are they?

There are two drawbacks to the use of participant observation. First, an extended period of time may be necessary before the participant observer is accepted as a member of the group that is under study. Has such an extended period been budgeted into the overall design of the project in terms of both cost and time? Moreover, just being part of the situation does not guarantee that the observer will be accepted. If such acceptance is not granted, the amount of information that can be acquired is severely limited. If the observer is accepted and becomes part of the group, then a loss of objectivity may result. Thus, time, finances, acceptance, and objectivity may pose severe problems for participant observer research.

As with the other observation techniques, the ability to make cause-and-effect statements is the second problem with participant observer research. Even though the participant observer may be close to the source of relevant information, no attempts are made to manipulate IVs or control extraneous variables.

Clinical perspective
A descriptive research approach aimed at understanding and correcting a particular behavioral problem.

Clinical Perspective   Although some people categorize the **clinical perspective** or model as a subcategory of participant observation, Schein (1987) argued convincingly that it should be considered separately. There are several key differences between the two approaches:

- A client typically chooses the clinician, whereas the participant observer chooses the others to be studied.
- Unlike participant observers, clinicians cannot be unobtrusive because they have been asked to participate in the situation.
- Although the participant observer can remain passive, clinicians must intervene in the situation.
- The participant observer's goal is understanding, whereas the clinician's goal is helping.

Thus, the participant observer is content to be inside a system far enough to develop a full understanding of the dynamics and interaction patterns. The clinician, however, wishes not only to develop this understanding but also to change the dynamics and interaction patterns. Often the clinician deals with only a narrow slice of the whole, wanting to get an in-depth understanding of the problem area. In contrast, the participant observer wants to develop a broad picture of the entire behavioral and interpersonal spectrum. The clinician can be compared to the detective who attempts to generate a psychological profile of a particular suspect.

An important question, of course, relates to both participant observation and the clinical perspective: How do researchers scientifically validate what they have found? According to Schein (1987), the key for participant observers is replication—if another participant observer studies the same culture, will the conclusions be the same? For clinicians, on the other hand, the key to validity is being able to predict the results of a given intervention—will this particular type of therapy help this patient?

In this section we have examined four observational research strategies—case studies, naturalistic observation, participant observation, and the clinical perspective. Once you have decided which type of observational research you will conduct, you will have to decide which behaviors to observe and how to record your observations.

Choosing Behaviors and Recording Techniques   It is one thing to say you are going to conduct an observational study, but it is another task to actually complete such a project. Even though the researcher does not manipulate the variables, a great deal of planning must take place. As is true with *any* research project, you must make several important decisions before beginning the project. Let's examine several of these decisions.

It seems simple enough to indicate that all behaviors will be observed; hence, everything of interest will be captured. Again, saying may be quite different from (and much easier than) doing. For example, observing and recording all behaviors may necessitate using video equipment, which may, in turn, make the observer identifiable. A participant observer with a video camera would probably not be especially effective. Had Anastasia Gibson and her colleagues (2000) used video equipment in their naturalistic study of glancing behavior at the ATM, their obvious presence could have influenced the behavior of their participants. Hence, they remained as inconspicuous as possible when they observed the customers.

Instead of observing at exactly the same time each afternoon, the ATM researchers used a procedure known as time sampling. **Time sampling** involves making observations at different time periods in

> **Time sampling**   Making observations at different time periods.

order to obtain a more representative sampling of the behavior of interest. The selection of time periods may be determined randomly or in a more systematic manner. Moreover, the use of time sampling may apply to the same or different participants. If you are observing a group of preschoolers, then using the time-sampling technique will allow you to describe the behavior of interest over a wide range of times in the same children. In addition, time sampling may permit the observation of different participants and increase the generality of your observations. Gibson et al. did not make any nighttime observations; hence, their results may not apply to *all* glancing behavior at ATMs. In fact, they said, "It would be interesting to see whether or not proximity or glancing behavior are influenced by the amount of sunlight at hand" (Gibson et al., 2000, p. 151).

It also is important to note that Gibson et al. (2000) observed customers at four different ATMs: two machines were located outside ("one outside a mall and one in an urban shopping area," p. 150), whereas "two indoor ATMs were inside discount department stores" (p. 150). Why did they make observations in these different locations? Had they limited their observations to one ATM in one location, they would not be able to generalize their results beyond that one machine to other ATMs. By observing four different ATMs, they used a technique known as **situation sampling**, which involves observing the same type of behavior in several different situations. This technique offers the researcher two advantages. First, by sampling behavior in several different situations, the investigator can determine whether the behavior in question changes as a function of the context in which it is observed. For example, a researcher might use situation sampling to determine whether the amount of personal space people prefer differs from one culture to another or from one geographic area of a country to another.

Situation sampling
Observing the same behavior in different situations.

The second advantage of the situation sampling technique involves the fact that researchers are likely to observe different participants in the different situations. Because different individuals are observed, the ability to generalize any behavioral consistencies seen in the various situations is increased. Because Gibson et al. (2000) made observations at four different ATMs and obtained the same results at each one, they could not attribute their findings to the customers at one specific machine.

Even if you have decided to time-sample or situation-sample, there is still another major decision you must make before you actually conduct your research project. You need to decide whether to present the results in a *qualitative* or *quantitative* manner. If you choose the qualitative approach, your report will consist of a description of the behavior in question (a *narrative record*) and the conclusions prompted by this description. A narrative record can be in the form of written or tape-recorded notes that you make during or immediately after observing the behavior. Video recordings also are frequently made. In all narrative records the language and terms used should be as clear and precise as possible, and the observer should avoid making speculative comments.

If your research plans call for a quantitative or numerical approach, then you will need to know how you are going to measure the behavior under investigation and how you will analyze these measurements. We will have more to say about measurement and analysis in Chapter 7.

Using More Than One Observer: Interobserver Reliability   Another consideration we must deal with in the case of observational research is whether we will use one or more observers. As the good detective knows, there are two main reasons for using more than one observer: One observer may miss or overlook a bit of behavior, and there may be some disagreement concerning exactly what was seen and how it should be rated or categorized. More than one observer may be needed even when videotape is used to preserve the complete behavioral sequence; someone has to watch the videotape and rate or categorize the behavior contained there.

When two individuals observe the same behavior, it is possible to see how well their observations agree. The extent to which the observers agree is called **interobserver reliability**. Low interobserver reliability indicates that the observers disagree about the behavior(s) they observed; high interobserver reliability indicates agreement. Such factors as fatigue, boredom, emotional and physical state, and experience can influence interobserver reliability. If two observers are well rested, interested in their task, and in good physical and emotional health, then high interobserver reliability should be obtained. An observer's physical, emotional, and attitudinal state can be monitored and dealt with easily. Additionally, the need for training observers should be considered. The importance of thorough training, especially when observing complex and subtle behaviors, cannot be stressed too much. Such training should include clear, precise definitions of the behavior(s) to be observed. If at all possible, the trainer should provide concrete examples of positive and negative instances of the behavior in question.

> **Interobserver reliability**
> The extent to which observers agree.

Even if researchers follow all of these guidelines, it may be difficult to obtain high interobserver reliability. In some instances the problem may reside in the type of behavior being observed and how the observers code the behaviors. For example, think of how difficult it is for two observers to agree on (1) instances of "empathy," "shame," and "self-consciousness" in 2-year-old children, (2) the difference between aggression and teasing in 10-year-olds, and (3) whether a 6-week-old infant has smiled. These examples point to the difficulty in obtaining, and the importance of having, interobserver reliability.

How can you measure interobserver reliability? A simple technique involves determining the number of agreements between the two observers and the number of opportunities the observers had to agree. Once these numbers have been determined, they are used in the following formula:

$$\frac{\text{number of times observers agree}}{\text{number of opportunities to agree}} \times 100 = \text{percentage of agreement}$$

The final calculation indicates the percentage of agreement.

Another method for obtaining interobserver reliability is to calculate the correlation (see Chapter 8) between the raters' judgments and then square the correlation and multiply by 100. The resulting figure tells us the percentage of variation that is due to observer agreement; the higher the percentage, the greater the agreement.

What is a good measure of interobserver reliability? Although there are no rules to follow, a review of articles published in the two most recent issues of several journals indicated that all articles reporting interobserver reliability had at least 85% agreement. This figure is a guideline that indicates what journal editors and reviewers consider an acceptable minimum level for interobserver reliability.

Qualitative Research

Qualitative research
Research conducted in a natural setting that seeks to understand a complex human behavior by developing a complete narrative description of that behavior.

Almost since its inception, the nature of research has evolved and changed; it continues this evolution today. One of the newer forms of research is **qualitative research**. According to Creswell (1994), qualitative research "is defined as an inquiry process of understanding a social or human problem, based on building a complex, holistic picture, formed with words, reporting detailed views of informants, and conducted in a natural setting" (p. 2). The qualitative research style is much less formal and impersonal, and the reader of a qualitative research report can expect to find such additions as "definitions that evolved during a study" (Creswell, 1994, p. 7).

The observation that definitions might evolve or develop during a study suggests that the vocabulary of the qualitative researcher may be quite different from that of the traditional experimental researcher. It is. In fact, qualitative researchers have developed a whole new language (Gubrium & Holstein, 1997). Most qualitative descriptions feature substantially less scientific jargon, and the reader is likely to encounter more personal, even emotional, words. The qualitative researcher believes that a full description of human behavior includes people's *feelings* in addition to what they are doing and how they are doing it. If the participant is the final judge of what constitutes an accurate account or description of a situation, then personal terms will be the order of the day.

As Creswell's definition suggests, the qualitative researcher is committed to studying *particular* people in *specific* settings. This commitment favors the reporting of details as opposed to generalities and promotes a concern for the quality of life by the qualitative researcher. The definition also indicates that qualitative researchers place a premium on naturalism. If the researcher wants to answer *what* and *how* questions about the behavior and interactions of people in their typical environment, then what better place to study people than in their natural environment?

The type of reasoning and logic used by qualitative researchers differs significantly from the reasoning and logic used by the typical experimental researcher. For years the accepted mode of reasoning has involved *deductive logic*, with hypotheses and theories that spawn specific experiments designed to evaluate them. However, as we noted in Chapter 2, Proctor and Capaldi (2001) pointed out that a growing number of professionals do not believe that theory-driven research is the best option open to researchers. Qualitative researchers prefer to use *inductive logic*, in which the data (information) provided by the participants are assimilated and a pattern or theory to explain the phenomenon of interest emerges from this growing body of information.

The nature of the problems studied by qualitative research differs significantly from the typical experimental investigation. Unlike the experimental research problem, which likely will be associated with a significant amount of previously reported research, qualitative research deals with problems for which little or no information exists. It is the researcher's task to ferret out and delineate the relevant variables and determine how these variables are related to each other.

Unlike traditional hypothesis-testing research, in which the researcher develops a specific, rather narrowly focused experimental hypothesis, qualitative research begins with a more global question. These more global issues are frequently called *guiding hypotheses* (Marshall & Rossman, 1989). A guiding hypothesis may be followed by several subquestions that reflect specific, more narrowed aspects of the research project. It is important that none of these research questions, whether they are global or subquestions, constrain the researcher.

Procedures for data analysis also differ greatly between traditional quantitative approaches and the newer qualitative research strategies. As we saw in Chapter 1, the time-honored procedure followed by generations of experimental researchers is to conduct the experiment (gather the research data), analyze the data, and then prepare a written report based on the results of the data analysis. In contrast, qualitative researchers typically analyze their data "*simultaneously* with data collection, data interpretation, and narrative reporting writing" (Creswell, 1994, p. 153). This logic makes sense in view of the ever-developing nature of the qualitative research project: The categories of responses are forever emerging and changing, and the nature of the explanation is continually being modified.

Grounded theory is one of the most popular examples of contemporary qualitative research. We briefly examine this approach in the next section.

Grounded Theory

Strauss and Corbin (1990) favored the **grounded theory** approach to qualitative research. As with participant observation and the clinical perspective, the primary tools of discovery are interviews and observations. However, grounded theory goes beyond the descriptive and interpretive goals of these two approaches and is aimed at building theories. The ultimate goal of this approach is to derive theories that are grounded in

> **Grounded theory** A descriptive research approach that attempts to develop theories of understanding based on data from the real world.

(based on) reality. A grounded theory is one that is uncovered, developed, and conditionally confirmed through collecting and making sense of data related to the issue at hand. The hope is that such theories will lead to a better understanding of the phenomenon of interest and to ideas for exerting some control over the phenomenon. Although grounded theory is designed to be a precise and rigorous process, creativity is also an important part of that process in that the researcher needs to ask innovative questions and come up with unique formulations of the data—"to create new order out of the old" (Strauss & Corbin, 1990, p. 27). The grounded theory approach is reminiscent of a detective's attempt to build a theory about why certain types of crimes are committed. For example, by interviewing a number of arsonists, you might develop a theory about why arson takes place.

Strauss and Corbin (1990) did not advocate using grounded theory for all types of questions. In fact, they maintained that certain types of questions support certain types of research. For instance, if someone wanted to know whether one drug is more effective than another, then a grounded theory study would not be appropriate. However, if someone wanted to know what it was like to be a participant in a drug study, then he or she might sensibly engage in a grounded theory project or some other type of qualitative study.

The use of literature also differs in the grounded theory approach. Strauss and Corbin (1990) recommended against knowing the research literature too well before using this approach because knowing the categories, classifications, and conclusions of previous researchers may constrain your creativity in finding new formulations. Instead, nontechnical materials such as letters, diaries, newspapers, biographies, and videotapes are essential to grounded theory studies.

The heart of the grounded theory approach occurs in its use of coding, which is analogous to data analysis in quantitative approaches. Three different types of coding are

Open coding The process of describing data through means such as examination, comparison, conceptualization, and categorization.

Axial coding The process of rearranging data after open coding so that new relations are formed between concepts.

Selective coding The process of selecting the main phenomenon (core category) around which all other phenomena (subsidiary categories) are grouped, arranging the groupings, studying the results, and rearranging where necessary.

Process The manner in which actions and interactions occur in a sequence or series.

Transactional system An analysis of how actions and interactions relate to their conditions and consequences.

Conditional matrix A diagram that helps the researcher consider the conditions and consequences related to the phenomenon under study.

Correlational study Determination of the relation between two variables.

Positive correlation As scores on one variable increase, scores on the second variable also increase.

Negative correlation As scores on one variable increase, scores on the second variable decrease.

used in a more or less sequential manner (Strauss & Corbin, 1990). **Open coding** is much like the description goal of science. During open coding the researcher labels and categorizes the phenomena being studied. **Axial coding** involves finding links between categories and subcategories from open coding. The final step in the process, **selective coding**, entails identifying a core category and relating the subsidiary categories to this core. From this last type of coding, the grounded theory researcher moves toward developing a model of **process** and a **transactional system**, which essentially tells the story of the outcome of the research. *Process* refers to a linking of actions and interactions that result in some outcome (see Figure 4-1 for a hypothetical process diagram). A transactional system is grounded theory's analytical method that allows an examination of the interactions of different events. The transactional system is depicted in a **conditional matrix** such as that shown in Figure 4-2. In the conditional matrix, the factors that are most pertinent to an event are shown at the interior, the least important factors on the exterior. Once the coding is completed and a model of process or a transactional system developed, the grounded theory procedure is complete. It then remains for the researcher to write a report about the findings (often a book rather than a journal article). Subsequent grounded theory research projects tend to focus on different cultures. Comparisons between the original project and subsequent projects shed light on whether the original project has generalizability to other cultures or whether it is specific only to the culture studied.

In the next section we consider an approach that directly examines the relation between two variables. Correlational studies are one of the most popular nonexperimental research strategies.

Correlational Studies

In its basic form a **correlational study** involves the measurement and determination of the relation between two variables (hence the term *co-relation*). In terms of control, empirical measurement, and statistical analysis, a correlational study is likely to be more rigorous than one of the descriptive methods we've just considered. In order to understand the intent and purpose of a correlational study, we need to review some basic facts about correlations.

The Nature of Correlations

One of three basic patterns may emerge when a correlation is calculated. The two variables may be **positively correlated**: as one variable *increases*, scores on the other variable also *increase*. For example, test scores are positively correlated if a student who makes a low score on Test 1 also scores low on Test 2, whereas a student who scores high on Test 1 also scores high on Test 2. Likewise, height and weight are positively related; in general, the taller a person is, the more he or she weighs.

Two variables may also be negatively related. A **negative correlation** indicates that an *increase* in one variable is accompanied by a *decrease* in the second variable. For example, drinking water on a hot day and thirst are negatively related; the more water consumed, the less intense the thirst. Likewise, increasing

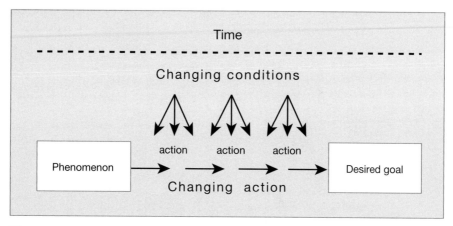

FIGURE 4-1   A Process Diagram from Grounded Theory Showing the Occurrence of Actions and Interactions in a Sequence.

FIGURE 4-2   A Transactional System Conditional Matrix from Grounded Theory.

"There's a significant NEGATIVE correlation between the number of mules and the number of academics in a state, but remember, correlation is not causation."
(Courtesy of Warren Street)

self-esteem scores might be accompanied by decreasing anxiety scores. Thus, an individual who scores high on a self-esteem scale would have a low score on an anxiety scale, whereas an individual who scores low on the self-esteem scale would score high on the anxiety scale.

Researchers use correlations to make predictions. For example, you probably took an entrance examination, such as the American College Test (ACT) or the Scholastic Aptitude Test (SAT), when you applied for admission to college. Previous research has shown that scores on such entrance examinations are positively correlated with first-semester grades in college. Thus, your entrance-exam score was used to predict how you would perform in your college classes. Obviously, the closer a correlation comes to being perfect, the better our predictions will be.

We have seen that correlations can be positive or negative in value. What has happened when we obtain a zero correlation?

Zero correlations indicate that the two variables under consideration are not related. High scores on one variable may be paired with low, high, or intermediate scores on the second variable, and vice versa. In other words, knowing the score on Variable 1 does not help us predict the score on Variable 2. A zero correlation may not be exactly 0. For example, a correlation of 0.03 would be considered a **zero correlation** by most researchers. It is important to remember that a correlation tells us only the extent to which two variables are related. Because these two variables are not

Zero correlation Two variables under consideration are not related.

under our direct control, we are still unable to make cause-and-effect statements. In short, *correlations do not imply causation*. It is possible that a third variable is involved. A rather far-fetched example illustrates this point quite well. In an introductory statistics class, a student told one of your authors about a correlational study that investigated the relation between the number of telephone poles erected in Australia each year for the 10 years following World War II and the yearly birth rate in the United States during the same time period. The result was a very high, positive correlation. The point of the example was to illustrate that correlation does not imply causation. It also illustrates the likely presence of a third variable. It is arguable that the increasingly better worldwide economic conditions that followed World War II encouraged both industrial development (the increase in telephone poles in Australia) and the desire to have a family (the higher birth rate in the United States).

Correlational Research

We agree that it is confusing when a type of mathematical analysis and a research technique have the same name. Because the common goal is to determine the relation between two variables or factors, more than coincidence is at work. Also, you should keep in mind that a correlational research project uses the correlational mathematical technique to analyze the data that the researcher gathers. Now that we have reviewed the nature and types of correlations, let's examine an example of correlational research. Scott Weaver, a student at the State University of New York in Plattsburgh, and his faculty supervisor, Katherine Dunham, were interested in determining what factors correlated with (*predicted*) different types of youth violence. They administered several questionnaires, including a survey that measured the participants' history of violence, to a sample of 131 male and female college students. Once they gathered the data, they correlated such factors as parenting style, affective empathy, academic performance, and father presence during childhood and adolescence with the scores on the history of violence questionnaire. Their data revealed several interesting correlations. For example, participants whose fathers were present during adolescence reported fewer violent acts (a *negative* correlation). Such "predictors have the potential to contribute to the design of violence prevention and intervention programs" (Weaver & Dunham, 2002, p. 3).

Researchers use correlational studies when data on two variables are available but they can only measure, rather than manipulate, either variable. Although investigators can determine the degree of relation that exists between these two variables, they are not able to offer a cause-and-effect statement concerning these variables.

REVIEW SUMMARY

1. **Descriptive research methods** are nonexperimental procedures for acquiring information. They do not involve the manipulation of variables.

2. Some researchers make use of archival and previously recorded sources of data. Although the use of such data avoids biasing participants' responses, this approach suffers from lack of generalizability, selective deposit, and selective survival.

3. Although observational techniques do not involve the direct manipulation of variables, they do allow the researcher to directly observe the behavior(s) of interest.

4. Case studies involve the intensive observation of a single participant over an extended period of time. They are often used in clinical settings.

5. **Naturalistic observation** involves directly observing behaviors in the natural environment. In these studies the observer should remain unobtrusive in order to avoid a **reactance** or **reactivity effect** on the part of the participants.

6. When the **participant observation** approach is used, the observer actually becomes a member of the group that is under study. An extensive time commitment may be required to conduct this type of study.

7. Because the observer may not be able to observe all behaviors at all times, decisions concerning which behaviors to observe, as well as when and where to observe them, must be made.

8. **Time sampling** involves making observations at different time periods, whereas **situation sampling** involves observing the same behavior(s) in several different situations.

9. The use of more than one observer may be desirable to avoid missing important observations and to help resolve disagreements concerning what was or was not observed. **Interobserver reliability** refers to the degree to which the observers agree.

10. **Qualitative research** is conducted in a natural setting. It seeks to understand a complex human behavior by developing a complete narrative description of that behavior.

11. A **correlational study** involves the measurement and determination of the relation between two variables.

12. Two variables are **positively correlated** when an increase in one variable is accompanied by an increase in the other variable.

13. Two variables are **negatively correlated** when an increase in one variable is accompanied by a decrease in the other variable.

14. A **zero correlation** exists when a change in one variable is unrelated to changes in the second variable.

CHECK YOUR PROGRESS

1. What is the reactance effect? How is it avoided by the use of archival sources of data?

2. Selective deposit is a problem associated with
   a. case studies
   b. naturalistic observation
   c. cause-and-effect research
   d. archival research

3. Matching

   1. case study
   2. naturalistic observation
   3. Hawthorne effect
   4. participant observation
   5. measurement

   A. behavior is observed in the real world
   B. establishes a set of rules to assign symbols
      to events
   C. behavior of a single individual is observed
      over a lengthy period of time
   D. observing participants influences their behavior
   E. experimenter joins the group being studied

4. Why are time sampling and situation sampling employed?
5. What is interobserver reliability? How is it calculated?
6. You decide to learn about a Pacific island culture by going to live there for a year. What approach does this exemplify?

   a. clinical perspective
   c. grounded theory

   b. ethnography
   d. ecological psychology

7. In which approach is the development of a theory the ultimate goal?

   a. clinical perspective
   c. grounded theory

   b. ethnography
   d. ecological psychology

KEY TERMS

Descriptive research methods, 69
Case study, 71
Naturalistic observation, 71
Reactance or reactivity effect, 72
Hawthorne effect, 72
Participant observation, 73
Ethnography, 73

Clinical perspective, 74
Time sampling, 75
Situation sampling, 76
Interobserver reliability, 77
Qualitative research, 78
Grounded theory, 79
Open coding, 80
Axial coding, 80
Selective coding, 80

Process, 80
Transactional system, 80
Conditional matrix, 80
Correlational study, 80
Positive correlation, 80
Negative correlation, 80
Zero correlation, 82

LOOKING AHEAD

In the next chapter we will examine another procedure in which the relevant variables are carefully selected and examined. What makes this procedure unique is that the variables are selected *after the fact* and the experimenter has no control over their administration. Then we will examine the nature of surveys, questionnaires, tests, and inventories. Finally, we will consider how to select research participants for several basic research strategies.

Nonexperimental Methods II: Ex Post Facto Studies, Surveys and Questionnaires, Sampling, and Basic Research Strategies

In this chapter we continue our presentation and evaluation of nonexperimental research methods. Specifically, we will examine ex post facto studies and the use of surveys, questionnaires, and tests; then, we will consider the proper methods for selecting a sample of research participants. Finally, we will look at some of the basic research strategies.

Ex Post Facto Studies

Can we conduct experimental research on variables that we cannot control or manipulate? Yes, we can conduct research on such variables, but we must be cautious in drawing conclusions. When we work with independent variables (IVs) that we cannot or do not manipulate, we are conducting an **ex post facto study**. (*Ex post facto* is a Latin phrase meaning "after the fact.") When we conduct an ex post facto study, we are using an IV "after the fact"—it has already varied before we arrived on the scene. A great deal of detective work would seem to fall into this category. Because the experimenter has no control over administering the IV, let alone determining who receives this variable and under what conditions it is administered, the ex post facto study clearly qualifies as a descriptive research technique. However, it does have some properties in common with experimental methods.

> **Ex post facto study**
> The variable(s) to be studied are selected after they have occurred.

Let's look at an example of student research using an ex post facto approach. Carolyn Licht of Marymount Manhattan College in New York City evaluated occupational stress as a function of the sex of the participants and whether the participants worked for a nonprofit or for-profit organization. Her results showed "that employees perceive more occupational stress in nonprofit than in for-profit organizations" and that "men report more stress than women in most situations" (Licht, 2000, p. 46).

What causes Licht's research to fall into the ex post facto category?

Because Licht had no control over sex of the participants or the type of organization a participant worked for, these variables put this project in the ex post facto category.

Surveys, Questionnaires, Tests, and Inventories

In both experimental and nonexperimental research, investigators frequently use surveys, questionnaires, tests, and inventories to assess attitudes, thoughts, and emotions or feelings. One reason surveys and questionnaires are popular is that they appear to be quite simple to conduct; when you want to know how a group of individuals feel about a particular issue, all you have to do is ask them or give them a test. As we will see, appearances can be quite deceptive; it is not as easy to use this technique as it appears. What type of instrument is best suited for our particular project? There are numerous choices available to us. We first consider surveys and questionnaires, then turn our attention to tests and inventories.

Surveys and Questionnaires

Surveys typically request our opinion on some topic or issue that is of interest to the researcher. There are two basic types of surveys: descriptive and analytic. Although we will discuss these types separately, you should keep in mind that some surveys can serve both purposes.

Descriptive survey
Seeks to determine the percentage of the population that has a certain characteristic, holds a particular opinion, or engages in a particular behavior.

Types of Surveys   The purpose of your research project will determine the type of survey you choose to administer. If you seek to determine what percentage of the population has a certain characteristic, holds a certain opinion, or engages in a particular behavior, then you will use a **descriptive survey**. The Gallup Poll that evaluates voter preferences and the Nielsen television ratings are examples of descriptive surveys. When a researcher uses this type of survey, no attempt is made to determine what the relevant variables are and how they may relate to the behavior in question. The end product is the description of a particular characteristic or behavior of a sample with the hope that this finding is representative of the population from which the sample was drawn.

Analytic survey   Seeks to determine the relevant variables and how they are related.

The **analytic survey** seeks to determine what the relevant variables are and how they might be related. For example, Amanda Gray, a student at Agnes Scott College in Decatur, Georgia, and her faculty supervisor, Jennifer Lucas, used the Subjective Impedence Scale (Novaco, Stokols, & Milanesi, 1990) to determine "automobile commuters' subjective perceptions of travel impedence and their driver stress" (Gray & Lucas, 2001, p. 79). They found that one of the key determinants of commuters' stress level is the *perception* of impedence, whether it actually occurs or not.

What about conducting research in areas without readily available surveys? To address the issues you are interested in, you may have to construct your own survey. In this case you will have to choose the questions for your analytic survey carefully before the survey is administered. In

fact, it will probably be necessary to do some pilot testing of the analytic survey before you use it in a full-scale investigation. **Pilot testing** refers to testing and evaluating that is done in advance of the complete research project. During this preliminary stage the researcher tests a small number of participants and may even use in-depth interviews to help determine the type of questions that should appear on the final survey instrument.

> **Pilot testing**
> Preliminary, exploratory testing that is done prior to the complete research project.

Developing a Good Survey or Questionnaire   A good survey or questionnaire, one that measures the attitudes and opinions of interest in an unbiased manner, is not developed overnight; considerable time and effort typically go into its construction. Once you have decided exactly what information your research project seeks to ascertain, there are several steps you should follow in order to develop a good survey or questionnaire. These steps are summarized in Table 5-1.

The first step is to determine how you will obtain the information you seek. Will you use a mail survey? Will your project involve the use of a questionnaire that is administered during a regular class session at your college or university? Will trained interviewers administer your questionnaire in person, or will a telephone interview be conducted? Decisions such as these will have a major impact on the type of survey or questionnaire you will develop.

Once you have made a decision concerning the type of instrument to be developed, in the second step you can give attention to the *nature* of the questions that will be used and the type of responses the participants will make to these questions. Among the types of questions that are frequently used in surveys and questionnaires are the following:

1. Yes-No Questions.   The respondent answers yes or no to the items.

EXAMPLE:

The thought of death seldom enters my mind.
(*Source:* Templer's Death Anxiety Scale; Templer, 1970)

2. Forced Alternative Questions.   The respondent must select between two alternative responses.

EXAMPLE:

A.   There are institutions in our society that have considerable control over me.
B.   Little in this world controls me. I usually do what I decide to do.
(*Source:* Reid-Ware Three-Factor Locus of Control Scale; Reid & Ware, 1973)

TABLE 5-1	Steps in Developing a Good Survey or Questionnaire
Step 1	Decide what type of instrument to use. How will the information be gathered?
Step 2	Identify the types of questions to use.
Step 3	Write the items: They should be clear, short, and specific.
Step 4	Pilot-test and seek opinions from knowledgeable others.
Step 5	Determine the relevant demographic data to be collected.
Step 6	Determine administration procedures and develop instructions.

3. *Multiple-Choice Questions.* The respondent must select the most suitable response from among several alternatives.

EXAMPLE:

Compared to the average student:
A. I give much more effort.
B. I give an average amount of effort.
C. I give less effort.
(*Source:* Modified Jenkins Activity Scale; Krantz, Glass, & Snyder, 1974)

4. *Likert-Type Scales.* The individual answers a question by selecting a response alternative from a designated scale. A typical scale might be the following: (5) strongly agree, (4) agree, (3) undecided, (2) disagree, or (1) strongly disagree.

EXAMPLE:

I enjoy social gatherings just to be with people.

1	2	3	4	5
Not at all characteristic of me	Not very	Slightly	Fairly	Very much characteristic of me

(*Source:* Texas Social Behavior Inventory; Helmreich & Stapp, 1974)

5. *Open-Ended Questions.* A question is asked to which the respondent must construct his or her own answer.

EXAMPLE:

How would you summarize your chief problems in your own words?
(*Source:* Mooney Problem Check List; Mooney, 1950)

Clearly, the questions you choose to use on your survey or questionnaire will directly influence the type of data you will gather and be able to analyze when your project is completed. If you choose the yes-no format, then you will be able to calculate the frequency or percentage of such responses for each question. The use of a Likert-type scale allows you to calculate an average or mean response to each question. Should you choose to use open-ended questions, you will have to either decide how to code or quantify the responses or establish a procedure for preparing a summary description of each participant's answers.

The third step is to actually write the items for your survey or questionnaire. As a general rule, these questions should be clear, short, and specific; use familiar vocabulary; and be at the reading level of the individuals you intend to test. In preparing your items, you should avoid questions that might constrain the respondents' answers. For example, you might ask your participants to rate the effectiveness of the President of the United States in dealing with "crises." Assuming that the President has dealt with several crises, it may not be clear whether the question is referring to one particular type of crisis or another. Hence, the respondents will have to interpret the item as best they can; their interpretation may not coincide with your intended meaning. Also, researchers should avoid using questions that might bias or prejudice the respondents' answers. A negatively worded question may result in a preponderance of negative answers, whereas a positively worded question may result in a preponderance of positive answers.

Consider this yes-no question: "Do you agree that wealthy professional athletes are overpaid?" What is wrong with this question, and how can it be improved?

By indicating that professional athletes are wealthy, you have created a mental set that suggests that they may be overpaid. Thus, your respondents may be biased to answer yes. Also, using the word *agree* in the question may encourage yes answers. If the researcher rewrites the question as follows, it is less likely to bias the respondents' answers: "Are professional athletes overpaid?"

The fourth step is to pilot-test your survey or questionnaire. It is important to ask others, especially professionals who have expertise in your area of research interest, to review your items. They may be able to detect biases and unintended wordings that you had not considered. It will also be helpful at this preliminary stage to administer your questionnaire to several individuals and then discuss the questions with them. Often there is nothing comparable to the insights of a participant who has actually completed a testing instrument. Such insights can be invaluable as you revise your questions. In fact, you may find it necessary to pretest and revise your survey in this manner several times before developing a final draft.

The fifth step involves a consideration of the other relevant information that you want your participants to provide. Frequently, such information falls under the heading of **demographic data**, which may include such items as age, sex, annual income, size of community, academic major, and academic classification. For example, recall the research by Robyn Scali and Sheila Brownlow discussed in Chapter 1. We saw that these researchers used six different sequences of task presentation to control for sequence effects (an extraneous variable) in their study of sex differences in spatial task performance. In addition, they considered demographic factors: "Because training and prior experience may have an effect on spatial ability, we assessed experience with art, math, sports, and similar tasks" (Scali & Brownlow, 2001, p. 6).

> **Demographic data**
> Information about participants' characteristics such as age, sex, income, and academic major.

Although the need for this step may seem obvious, it is important to review these items carefully to ensure that you have not forgotten to request a vital bit of information. (We cannot begin to tell you how many survey projects designed to evaluate male-female differences were less than successful because they failed to include an item that requested the participant's sex!)

The final step is to clearly specify the procedures that will be followed when the survey or questionnaire is administered. If the survey is self-administering, what constitutes the printed instructions? Are they clear, concise, and easy to follow? Who will distribute and collect the informed consent forms and deal with questions that may arise? If your survey or questionnaire is not self-administering, then you must prepare an instruction script. The wording of this set of instructions must be clear and easily understood. Whether these instructions are presented in a face-to-face interview, over the telephone, or in front of a large class of students, they must be thoroughly rehearsed by the individuals who will be giving them. The researcher in charge of the project must be sure that all interviewers present the instructions in the same manner on all occasions. Likewise, questions raised by the participants must also be dealt with in a consistent manner.

Because the administration procedures are crucial to the success of this type of research, we will examine the three basic options—mail surveys, personal interviews, and telephone interviews—in more detail.

Mail Surveys   Most likely you have been asked to complete a survey you received in the mail. This popular technique is used to gather data on issues that range from our opinions on environmental problems to the type of food we purchase.

One advantage of sending surveys through the mail is that the researcher does not have to be present while the survey is being completed. Thus, surveys can be sent to a much larger number of participants than a single researcher could ever hope to contact in person.

Although it is possible to put a survey in the hands of a large number of respondents, there are several disadvantages associated with this research strategy. First, the researcher cannot be sure who actually completes the survey. Perhaps the intended respondent was too busy to complete the survey and asked a family member or friend to finish it. Hence, the time and trouble spent in creating a random sample from the population of interest may be wasted.

Even if the intended respondent completes the survey, there is no guarantee that the respondent will answer the questions in the same order in which they appear on the survey. If the order of answering questions is relevant to the project, then this drawback may be a major obstacle to the use of mail surveys.

The low return rate associated with the use of mail surveys highlights another problem. In addition to disappointment and frustration, low return rates suggest a potential bias in the researcher's sample. What types of individuals returned the surveys? How did they differ from those individuals who did not return the surveys? Were they the least (most) busy? Were they the least (most) opinionated? We really do not know, and as the response rate drops lower, the possibility of having a biased sample increases. What constitutes a good response rate to a mail survey? It is not uncommon to have a response rate of 25% to 30% to a mail survey; response rates of 50% and higher are considered quite acceptable.

Assume that you are planning to conduct a mail survey project. You are concerned about the possibility of having a low response rate and want to do everything to ensure the return of your surveys. What can you do to increase your response rate?

Researchers have developed strategies such as these to increase the response rates of mail surveys:

1. The initial mailing should include a letter that clearly summarizes the nature and importance of the research project, how the respondents were selected, and the fact that all responses are confidential. You should include a prepaid envelope for the return of the completed survey.

2. It may be necessary to send an additional mailing to your respondents. Because the original survey may have been misplaced or lost, it is important to include a replacement.

One extra mailing may not be sufficient; you may find it necessary to send two or three requests before you achieve an acceptable response rate. These extra mailings are typically sent at two- to three-week intervals.

The use of mail surveys is not accepted by all researchers. Low response rates, incomplete surveys, and unclear answers are among the reasons that cause some researchers to use direct interviews to obtain data. These interviews may be done in person or over the telephone.

Personal Interviews   When a trained interviewer administers a survey in a respondent's home, the response rate climbs dramatically. It is not uncommon to have a 90% completion rate under these circumstances. In addition to simply increasing the response rate, the trained interviewer is able to cut down on the number of unusable surveys by clarifying ambiguous questions, making sure that all questions are answered in the proper sequence, and generally assisting with any problems that the respondents may experience.

Although this technique offers some advantages when compared to the mail survey, there are drawbacks. First, the interviews require an expenditure of time and money. Time has to be devoted to the training of the interviewers. Once trained, they will have to be paid for their time on the job. Second, the fact that the survey is being administered by an individual introduces the possibility of interviewer bias. Some interviewers may present some questions in a more positive (or negative) manner than do other interviewers. Only careful and extensive training of all interviewers to present all items in a consistent, neutral manner can overcome this potential difficulty. Finally, the prospect of administering surveys in the home is becoming less appealing and feasible. In many instances no one is at home during the day, and an increasing number of people are not willing to sacrifice their leisure evening hours to complete a survey. Additionally, the high crime rates in many urban areas discourage face-to-face interviewing; in its place many investigators have turned to telephone interviewing.

Telephone Interviews   In addition to overcoming several of the problems associated with personal interviews and mail surveys, telephone interviewing offers several other advantages. For example, the development of random-digit dialing allows researchers to establish a random sample with ease: The desired number of calls is specified and the computer does the rest. It is noteworthy that a random sample generated in this manner will contain both listed and unlisted telephone numbers because the digits in each number are selected randomly. With over 95% of all households in the United States currently having telephones, previous concerns about creating a biased sample consisting of only households having telephones seem largely unfounded.

Computer technology also has increased the desirability of conducting telephone interviews. For example, it is now possible to enter the participant's responses directly as they are being made. Hence, the data are stored directly in the computer and are ready for analysis at any time.

Despite these apparent advantages, telephone interviews do have potential drawbacks. Even though technology has assisted telephone researchers, it also has provided an obstacle. Many households are now equipped with answering machines or caller ID that allow incoming calls to be screened. Hence, potential respondents may be lost because they do not answer the phone. Even if the call is answered, it is easier to say no to an unseen interviewer on the telephone than to a person at your front door. These two situations lower the response rate and raise the possibility of a biased sample.

The use of the telephone also prohibits the use of visual aids that might serve to clarify certain questions. In addition, because the telephone interviewer cannot see the respondent, it is not possible to evaluate nonverbal cues such as facial expressions, gestures, and posture. Such cues might suggest that a certain question was not completely understood or that an answer is in need of clarification.

Not being in face-to-face contact with the respondent also makes it more difficult to establish rapport. Hence, telephone respondents may not be as willing to participate in the survey. This potential lack of willingness has led to the use of shorter survey instruments.

Although surveys and questionnaires are popular research tools with many investigators, there are other ways to gather data. Since the late 1800s when Sir Francis Galton (1822–1911) attempted to evaluate people's ability or intelligence by measuring physical attributes, such as reaction time or visual acuity, psychologists have developed a large number of tests and inventories for a wide variety of purposes.

Tests and Inventories

Unlike surveys and questionnaires, which evaluate opinions on some topic or issue, tests and inventories are designed to assess a specific attribute, ability, or characteristic possessed by the individual being tested. In this section we look at the characteristics of good tests and inventories and then discuss three general types of tests and inventories: achievement, aptitude, and personality.

Characteristics of Good Tests and Inventories   Unlike the case with surveys and questionnaires, the researcher is less likely to be directly involved with the development of a test or inventory. Because their development and pilot testing has already taken place, you can simply review reports concerning the development of each test or inventory you are considering. A good test or inventory should possess two characteristics: It should be valid, and it should be reliable.

Validity   A test or inventory has **validity** when it actually measures what it is supposed to measure. If your research calls for a test that measures spelling achievement, you want the instrument you select to measure that ability, not another accomplishment, such as mathematical proficiency.

There are several ways to establish the validity of a test or inventory. **Content validity** indicates that the test items actually represent the type of material they are supposed to test. A panel of expert judges is often used to assess the content validity of test items. Although the more subjective evaluation of such judges may not lend itself to a great deal of quantification, their degree of agreement, known as **interrater reliability**, can be calculated. Interrater reliability is similar to interobserver reliability. The main difference is that interrater reliability measures agreement between judgments concerning a test item, whereas interobserver reliability measures agreement between observations of behavior.

Concurrent validity can be established when we already have another measure of the desired trait or outcome and can compare the score on the test or inventory under consideration with this other measure. For example, the scores

---

Validity   The extent to which a test or inventory measures what it is supposed to measure.

Content validity   The extent to which test items actually represent the type of material they are supposed to.

Interrater reliability   Degree of agreement among judges concerning the content validity of test or inventory items.

Concurrent validity   Degree to which the score on a test or inventory corresponds with another measure of the designated trait.

made by a group of patients on a test designed to measure aggression might be compared with a diagnosis of their aggressive tendencies made by a clinical psychologist. If the test and the clinical psychologist rate the aggressiveness of the patients in a similar manner, then concurrent validity for the test has been established.

Often our second measure may not be immediately accessible. When the test score is to be compared with an outcome that will occur in the future, the researcher is attempting to establish the **criterion validity** of the test. Thus, criterion validity refers to the ability of the test or inventory to predict the outcome or criterion. For example, it is the desired outcome that college entrance examinations such as the SAT and ACT predict first-semester performance in college. To the extent that these tests are successful at predicting first-semester GPAs, their criterion validity has been established.

> **Criterion validity**
> Established by comparing the score on a test or inventory with a future score on another test or inventory.

Reliability   Once we have determined that a particular test is valid, we also want to make sure that it is reliable. **Reliability** refers to the extent to which the test or inventory is consistent in its evaluation of the same individuals over repeated administrations. For example, if we have developed a test to measure aptitude for social work, we would want individuals who score high (or low) on our test on its first administration to make essentially the same score when they take the test again. The greater the similarity between scores produced by the same individuals on repeated administrations, the greater the reliability of the test or inventory.

> **Reliability**   Extent to which a test or inventory is consistent in its evaluation of the same individuals.

Reliability is typically assessed through the test–retest or split-half procedures. When the **test–retest procedure** is used, the test is simply given a second time and the scores from the two tests are compared; the greater the similarity, the higher the reliability.

> **Test–retest procedure**
> Determination of reliability by repeatedly administering a test to the same participants.

On the surface, the test–retest procedure appears to be quite straightforward and reasonable. However, there may be a problem with establishing reliability in this manner. What is it?

The main problem with the test–retest procedure concerns the fact that the participants are repeatedly administered the same test or inventory. Having already taken the test or inventory, the individuals may remember the questions and answers the next time the instrument is administered. Therefore, their answers may be biased by the previous administration. If a lengthy time period is allowed to elapse between administrations, the participants might forget the questions and answers, and this familiarity problem might be overcome. However, this lengthy time period may influence reliability in yet another manner. An extended time period allows the participants to have numerous experiences and learning opportunities between administrations. These experiences, called *history effects* (see Chapter 6), may influence their scores when the participants take the test or inventory again.

Hence, the reliability measure may be influenced by the experiences that intervene between the two testing sessions.

It is possible to overcome the problems of test familiarity and lengthy time periods separating administrations by using the split-half approach. The **split-half technique** of establishing reliability involves dividing a test or inventory into two halves or subtests and then administering them to the same individuals on different occasions or by administering the entire test and then splitting it into two halves. Because the questions that comprise the two subtests came from the same test, it is assumed that they are highly related to each other if the test is reliable. Typically, the questions that comprise these two subtests are selected randomly or in some predetermined manner, such as odd–even. The higher the degree of correspondence between scores on the two subtests, the greater the reliability of the overall test from which they were selected.

Having determined that a test or inventory should be valid and reliable, we now examine several types of these instruments that are currently used for research and predictive purposes.

> **Split-half technique** Determination of reliability by dividing the test or inventory into two subtests and then comparing the scores made on the two halves.

Types of Tests and Inventories   **Achievement tests** are given when an evaluation of an individual's level of mastery or competence is desired. For example, doctors must pass a series of medical board examinations before they are allowed to practice medicine, and lawyers must pass the bar examination before they are allowed to practice law. The score that distinguishes passing from failing determines the minimum level of achievement that must be attained. You can probably think of many achievement tests you have taken during your life.

> **Achievement test** Designed to evaluate an individual's level of mastery or competence.

At many colleges and universities the counseling center or career development office offers students the opportunity to take an aptitude test to assist them in selecting a major or making a career choice. An **aptitude test** is used to assess an individual's ability or skill in a particular situation or job. For example, the Purdue Pegboard Test is often administered to determine aptitude for jobs that require manual dexterity. According to Anastasi (1988), "this test provides a measure of two types of activity, one requiring gross movements of hands, fingers, and arms, and the other involving tip-of-the-finger dexterity needed in small assembly work" (p. 461). Similarly, if you are planning to attend graduate school, you will probably be required to take the Graduate Record Examination (GRE). For most graduate schools, the two most important scores on the GRE are the verbal and quantitative subtests. These scores represent measures of your aptitude to successfully complete verbal and quantitative courses on the graduate level.

> **Aptitude test** Designed to assess an individual's potential ability or skill in a particular job.

The **personality test** or **inventory** measures a specific aspect of an individual's motivational state, interpersonal capability, or personality (Anastasi & Urbina, 1997). The use of a personality inventory in research is exemplified by a project reported by Dana Bodner and C. D. Cochran, students at Stetson University in DeLand, Florida, and their faculty advisor, Toni Blum (Bodner, Cochran, & Blum, 2000). The purpose of this study was to validate a scale, the General Unique Invulnerability Scale (GUI), that measures general optimism about unique invulnerability (the belief that you will not experience negative events or misfortunes). These researchers administered the GUI to a sample of 40 skydivers and a sample of 40 college

> **Personality test** or **inventory** Measures a specific aspect of the individual's motivational state, interpersonal capability, or personality.

students and found that skydivers had higher GUI scores than did the college students. It is not surprising that skydivers would have stronger belief in unique invulnerability than the typical college student who does not engage in this risky behavior.

Sampling Considerations and Basic Research Strategies

Having completed our review of surveys, questionnaires, tests, and inventories, we conclude this chapter with a consideration of two more issues in experimental or nonexperimental research: sampling and basic research strategies. Sampling deals with the question of who will participate in our research project and whether the participants are a representative group. Once we have dealt with sampling issues, then we must decide on our main research strategy. The main strategies used by researchers are the single-strata, cross-sectional, and longitudinal approaches.

Sampling

Assume that you want to determine which of two new titles for the college newspaper—*The Wilderbeast* (named after your school mascot) or *The Observer*—appeals most to the student body. You ask the 36 students in your senior-level biopsychology course and find that 24 prefer *The Observer* and 12 prefer *The Wilderbeast*. You report your findings to the publications advisory board and recommend that *The Observer* be chosen as the new title.

Should the publications board accept your recommendation? Are there some reasons to question your findings?

The publications advisory board should not accept your recommendation. Unlike Sherlock Holmes, who said, "I presume nothing" (Doyle, 1927, p. 745), you seem to have made some assumptions. The main problem with your data concerns the students you surveyed. Is your senior-level biopsychology class representative of the entire campus? The answer to this question must be a resounding no; only senior-level psychology majors take this class. Moreover, a quick check of the class roster indicates that the majority (67%) of the students in your class are women. Clearly, you should have selected a group of students more representative of the general student body at your college.

We shall designate the general student body as the **population** or complete set of individuals or events that we want to represent. The group that we select to represent the population is called the **sample**. When every member of the population has an equal likelihood of being selected for inclusion in the sample, we have created a **random sample**.

Population   The complete set of individuals or events.

Sample   A group that is selected to represent the population.

Random sample   A sample in which every member of the population has an equal likelihood of being included.

How would you obtain a random sample of students on your campus to take the newspaper title survey? Computer technology has made this task quite simple; you simply indicate the size of the sample you desire, and the computer can be programmed to randomly select a sample of that size from the names of all currently enrolled students. Because a name is not eligible to be chosen again once it has been selected, this technique is called **random sampling without replacement**. If the chosen item can be returned to the population and is eligible to be selected again, the procedure is termed **random sampling with replacement**. Because psychologists do not want the same participant to appear more than once in a group, random sampling without replacement is the preferred technique for creating a random research sample.

> **Random sampling without replacement**   Once chosen, a score, event, or participant cannot be returned to the population to be selected again.

> **Random sampling with replacement**   Once chosen, a score, event, or participant can be returned to the population to be selected again.

Suppose a sample of 80 students has been randomly selected from the entire student body by the computer and you are examining the printout. Even though you selected this sample randomly, it also has some apparent problems. Just by chance the majority of the students selected are freshmen and sophomores. Moreover, the majority of students in this sample are men. The views on the two newspaper titles held by this group of randomly selected students may not be much more representative than our original sample. What can we do to produce an even more representative sample?

There are two techniques that we can use to increase the representativeness of our sample. The first procedure is quite simple: We can select a larger sample. Generally speaking, the larger the sample, the more representative it will be of the population. If we randomly selected 240 students, this larger sample would be more representative of the general student body than our original sample of 80 students. Although larger samples may be more like the population from which they are drawn, there is a potential drawback. Larger samples mean that more participants will need to be tested. In our project dealing with the two newspaper titles, the testing of additional participants may not present any major problems. However, if we were administering a lengthy questionnaire or paying participants for their participation, increasing the number of participants might create unmanageable time or financial obstacles.

> **Stratified random sampling**   Random samples are drawn from specific subpopulations or strata of the general population.

If simply increasing the sample size does not offer a good solution to the problem of achieving a representative sample, the researcher may want to use the technique of **stratified random sampling**, which involves dividing the population into subpopulations or strata and then drawing a random sample from one or more of these strata. For example, one logical subdivision of a college student body would be by classes: freshmen, sophomores, juniors, and seniors. You could then draw a random sample from each class. How many students will be included in each stratum? One option would be for each stratum to contain an equal number of participants. Thus, in our newspaper title project we might include 20 participants from each academic classification. A second option would be to sample each stratum in proportion to its representation in the population. If freshmen comprise 30% of the student body, then our random sample would contain 30% first-year students. What about the number of men and women sampled in each stratum? We could have equal numbers, or we could sample in proportion to the percentage of men and women in each stratum. As you have probably surmised, the use of stratified random sampling indicates that you have considerable knowledge of the population in which you are interested. Once you have this knowledge, you can create a sample that is quite representative of the population of interest. A word of caution is in order, however. Although it may be tempting to specify a number of characteristics that your sample must possess, you can carry this process too far. If your sample becomes too highly specified, then you will be able to generalize or extend your results only to a population having those very specific characteristics.

One stratum that frequently appears in research reports is the subject or participant pool that many colleges and universities use. In these instances, students, typically enrolled in introductory psychology, have the option (among others) of participating in psychological research in order to fulfill a course requirement. Once students have volunteered to participate in a research project, they may be randomly assigned to specific groups or treatment conditions. For example, in the research on the wording of the informed consent document by Burkley et al. (2000) that we considered in Chapter 3, the authors stated:

> Twenty-five undergraduate university psychology students (2 men, 23 women) volunteered to participate. Participants were randomly assigned to either the control or experimental group. Participants received class credit for their involvement in the study. (p. 44)

Basic Research Strategies

Even though you have chosen your sample, you simply cannot rush out to start testing participants. You need to give some thought to the research question and how you can best conduct your project in order to answer that question. There are three basic approaches you can adopt: single-strata, cross-sectional, and longitudinal.

The **single-strata approach** seeks to acquire data from a single, specified segment of the population. For example, a particular Gallup Poll may be interested only in the voting preferences of blue-collar workers. Hence, a sample composed only of individuals from this stratum would be administered a voter-preference survey. This approach typically seeks to answer a rather specific research question.

When the single-strata approach is broadened to include samples from more than one stratum, a cross-sectional approach is being employed. **Cross-sectional research** involves the comparison of two or more groups of participants during the same, rather limited, time span. For example, a researcher may want to compare voter preferences of different age groups. To acquire this information, random samples of voters age 21, 31, 41, 51, 61, and 71 are obtained and their responses to a voter-preference survey are compared.

Perhaps the researcher wants to obtain information from a group of participants over an extended period of time. In this instance a **longitudinal research project** would be conducted. A random sample from the population of interest would be obtained; then this sample might be given an initial survey or test to complete. The same participants would then be contacted periodically to determine what, if any, changes had occurred during the ensuing time in the behavior of interest. This group of individuals that is born in the same time period and repeatedly surveyed or tested is called a **cohort**. For example, a researcher might be interested in the changes in the degree of support for environmental conservation that occur as individuals grow older. To evaluate such changes, a group of

Single-strata approach Gathering data from a single stratum of the population of interest.

Cross-sectional research Comparison of two or more groups during the same, rather limited, time period.

Longitudinal research project Obtaining research data from the same group of participants over an extended period of time.

Cohort A group of individuals born during the same time period.

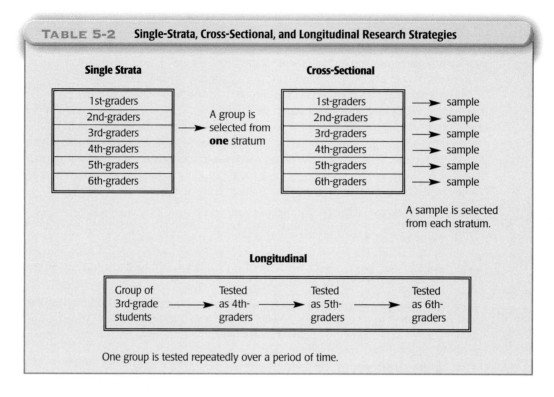

Table 5-2   Single-Strata, Cross-Sectional, and Longitudinal Research Strategies

Single Strata

| 1st-graders |
| 2nd-graders |
| 3rd-graders |
| 4th-graders |
| 5th-graders |
| 6th-graders |

A group is selected from **one** stratum

Cross-Sectional

1st-graders	→ sample
2nd-graders	→ sample
3rd-graders	→ sample
4th-graders	→ sample
5th-graders	→ sample
6th-graders	→ sample

A sample is selected from each stratum.

Longitudinal

| Group of 3rd-grade students | → | Tested as 4th-graders | → | Tested as 5th-graders | → | Tested as 6th-graders |

One group is tested repeatedly over a period of time.

grade-school children is randomly selected. Every five years all members of this cohort are contacted and administered an environmental conservation survey. These research strategies are compared in Table 5-2.

It is important that you remember that sampling concerns and decisions about your basic research strategy apply to both nonexperimental and experimental research projects. Moreover, our concerns with sampling and research strategy do not end at this point. For example, we will have more to say about the importance of randomization when we discuss experimental control in Chapter 6. Likewise, once we have decided on our basic research strategy, we will have to consider such details as how many groups of participants need to be tested to answer our research question. These topics fall under the general heading of experimental design; we begin our discussion of this topic in Chapter 9.

Review Summary

1. In an **ex post facto** study the variables have been experienced before they are examined by the researcher; thus, control and manipulation of variables cannot be accomplished.

2. Surveys, questionnaires, tests, and inventories are used to assess attitudes, thoughts, and emotions or feelings.

3. **Descriptive surveys** seek to determine the percentage of a population that has a certain characteristic, holds a certain opinion, or engages in a particular behavior. **Analytic surveys** seek to determine the variables that are relevant in a situation and their relation.

4. The steps to be completed in developing a good survey or questionnaire include considering the type of instrument to be developed, determining the types of questions to be used, writing the items, pilot testing, determining the relevant demographic data to be collected, and deciding on administration procedures.

5. **Demographic data** include relevant information, such as gender, age, income, and educational level, about the participants.

6. Mail surveys can be sent to a large number of potential respondents. However, the researcher cannot be sure who actually completed the survey or in what order they completed the questions. Low response rates for mail surveys can be improved by stressing the importance of the project and by sending additional mailings.

7. Personal interviews yield a higher rate of completed surveys but are costly in terms of time and money. The increase in the number of working families and the escalating crime rate in urban areas have made the use of personal interviews less desirable.

8. Telephone interviews allow the researcher to reach a large number of respondents more efficiently than personal interviews and mail surveys. However, answering machines and the inability to see nonverbal cues are drawbacks to this approach.

9. Tests and inventories should be **valid** (measure what they are supposed to measure) and **reliable** (be consistent in their evaluation).

10. Validity may be established by the **content**, **concurrent**, and **criterion** methods.

11. The **test–retest** and **split-half** procedures are used to establish reliability.

12. **Achievement tests** evaluate level of mastery or competence. **Aptitude tests** assess an individual's ability or skill in a particular situation or job. A **personality test** or **inventory** measures a specific aspect of the individual's motivational state, interpersonal capability, or personality.

13. The **sample** of individuals who complete a survey, questionnaire, test, or inventory should be representative of the **population** from which it is drawn.

14. When a **random sample** is selected, every member of the population has an equal likelihood of being selected. When **random sampling without replacement** is used, an item cannot be returned to the population once it has been selected. When **random sampling with replacement** is used, selected items can be returned to the population to be selected again.

15. **Stratified random sampling** involves dividing the population into subpopulations or strata and then drawing random samples from these strata.

16. Basic research strategies include investigating (a) a **single stratum** of a specified population, (b) samples from more than one stratum in a **cross-sectional project**, or (c) a single group of participants over an extended time period in a **longitudinal study**.

CHECK YOUR PROGRESS

1. Matching

    1. descriptive survey   A. defines participants born in the same time period

    2. analytic survey   B. affects ability to predict the outcome

    3. pilot testing   C. may include age, sex, and annual income

    4. demographic data   D. indicates the percentage having a certain characteristic

    5. cohort   E. compares scores on two separate measures

    6. concurrent validity   F. tries to determine what the relevant variables are

    7. criterion validity   G. does testing or evaluating in advance of the complete research project

2. Describe the steps involved in creating a good survey.

3. "Working with IVs that the experimenter does not manipulate" best describes

    a. a case study   b. naturalistic observation

    c. participant observation   d. an ex post facto study

4. How can the low return rate of mail surveys be improved?

5. Why is the use of personal interviews declining?

6. Distinguish between achievement and aptitude tests.

7. _____ are used to assess a specific attribute or ability.

    a. Surveys   b. Questionnaires   c. Pilot studies   d. Inventories

8. The general group of interest is the _____. The group that is selected to represent the general group is a _____.

9. A test can be _____ and not be _____.

    a. valid; accurate   b. reliable; valid   c. valid; reliable   d. split; halved

10. What is random sampling? With replacement? Without replacement?

11. What is stratified random sampling, and why is it used?

12. Distinguish among the single-strata, cross-sectional, and longitudinal approaches to research.

KEY TERMS

Ex post facto study, 87
Descriptive survey, 88
Analytic survey, 88
Pilot testing, 89
Demographic data, 91
Validity, 94
Content validity, 94
Interrater reliability, 94
Concurrent validity, 94
Criterion validity, 95
Reliability, 95

Test–retest procedure, 95
Split-half technique, 96
Achievement tests, 96
Aptitude test, 96
Personality test or inventory, 96
Population, 97
Sample, 97
Random sample, 97
Random sampling without replacement, 98

Random sampling with replacement, 98
Stratified random sampling, 98
Single-strata approach, 99
Cross-sectional research, 99
Longitudinal research project, 99
Cohort, 99

LOOKING AHEAD

In Chapters 4 and 5 we have considered approaches to gathering data that do not include the direct manipulation of an IV by the researcher. Hence, these approaches do not qualify as true experiments. In Chapter 6 we begin our consideration of experiments. First we carefully examine the variables involved in an experiment; then we consider procedures involved in the control of these variables.

The Basics
of Experimentation I:
Variables and Control

In this chapter we begin to examine methods and procedures that allow us to make cause-and-effect inferences. We begin by carefully examining the types of variables the researcher deals with: independent, extraneous, dependent, and nuisance variables. Recall from Chapter 2 that the experimenter directly manipulates *independent* variables; *dependent* variables change in response to the independent variable manipulation; and *extraneous* variables can invalidate our experimental results. As we will see, *nuisance* variables cause our results to be less clear. Once we have discussed these variables and made their relation to the experiment clear, we will consider the procedures that researchers have developed to keep unwanted, extraneous variables from influencing the results of our experiment.

The Nature of Variables

Before jumping into a discussion of independent variables, let's look at the nature of variables in general. A **variable** is an event or behavior that can assume at least two values. For example, temperature is a variable; it can assume a wide range of values. The same could be said for height, weight, lighting conditions, the noise level in an urban area, anxiety, confidence, and your responses to a test, as well as many other possibilities; each of these events can assume two or more values or levels.

> **Variable** An event or behavior that can assume two or more values.

So, when we discuss variables involved in a psychological experiment, we are talking about events or behaviors that have assumed at least two values. If the independent variable (IV) had only one level, we would have nothing to compare its effectiveness against. Assume you want to demonstrate that a new brand of toothpaste is the best on the market. You have a group of participants try the new toothpaste and then rate its effectiveness. Even though the entire group rates the toothpaste in question as "great," you still cannot claim that it is best; you do not have ratings from other groups using different brands.

Just as the IV must have at least two values, the dependent variable (DV) also must be able to assume two or more values. Your toothpaste study would be meaningless if the *only* response the participants can make is "great"; more than one response alternative is needed.

The same logic applies in the case of extraneous variables. If two or more values are not present, then the event in question is not an extraneous variable. If all the participants in our toothpaste study are women, then we do not have to be concerned with sex differences between the groups that we test. (This point will be important later in this chapter.) Notice that our concern about extraneous variables is quite different from our concern about IVs and DVs. Whereas we were concerned that the IV and DV have or are able to assume two or more values, we seek to limit the number of values an extraneous variable can assume to only one.

Operationally Defining Variables

As you will recall from Chapter 2, we suggested that replication of past research can be a valuable source of research ideas. Let's assume you have located a piece of research that you want to replicate. You carefully read how the experiment was conducted and find that each participant received a reward following every correct response. Assume this sentence is the only information you have concerning the *reward* and *response* involved in the experiment. If you asked 10 different researchers what reward they would use and what response they would record, how many different responses would you get? With this limited and vague information, chances are good that you would get as many different answers as people you asked. How valid will your replication be? If you use a totally different reward and a totally different response, have you even conducted a replication?

Problems and concerns such as these led a 1920s Harvard University physicist, Percy W. Bridgman, to propose a way to obtain clearer communication among researchers and thus achieve greater standardization and uniformity in experimental methodology (Goodwin, 1999). Bridgman's suggestion was simple: Researchers should define their variables in terms of the operations needed to produce them (Bridgman, 1927). If you define your variables in this manner, then other scientists can replicate your research by following the definitions you have given for the variables involved; such definitions are called **operational definitions**. Operational definitions have been a cornerstone of psychological research for nearly three quarters of a century because they allow researchers to communicate clearly and effectively with each other.

> **Operational definition**
> Defining the independent, dependent, and extraneous variables in terms of the operations needed to produce them.

To illustrate the use of operational definitions, let's return to the reward and response situation we described previously. If we define reward as a 45-mg Noyes Formula A food pellet, then other animal researchers can use the same reinforcer by ordering a supply of 45-mg Formula A pellets from the P. J. Noyes Company. Likewise, if we define the response as making a bar press in an operant conditioning chamber (Lafayette Model 81335), then another researcher can replicate our research setup by purchasing a similar piece of equipment from the Lafayette Instrument Company.

The experimenter must be able to clearly convey such information about all the variables involved in a research project. Hence, it is crucial to give operational definitions for the IV, DVs, and extraneous variables, as well as for nuisance variables.

Independent Variables

As you saw in Chapter 2, **independent variables (IVs)** are those variables that the experimenter purposely manipulates. The IV constitutes the reason the research is being conducted; the experimenter is interested in determining what effect the IV has. The term *independent* is used because the IV does not depend on other variables; it stands alone. A few examples of IVs that experimenters have used in psychological research are sleep deprivation, temperature, noise level, drug type (or dosage level), removal of a portion of the brain, and psychological context. Rather than attempting to list all possible IVs, it is easier to indicate that they tend to cluster in several general categories.

> **Independent variable (IV)**
> A stimulus or aspect of the environment that the experimenter directly manipulates to determine its influences on behavior.

Types of IVs

> **Physiological IV** A physiological state of the participant that the experimenter manipulates.

Physiological When the participants in an experiment are subjected to conditions that alter or change their normal biological state, a **physiological IV** is being used. For example, Susan Nash (1983), a student at Emporia State University in Emporia, Kansas, obtained several pregnant rats from an animal supplier. Upon their arrival at the laboratory, she randomly assigned half the rats to receive an alcohol–water mixture during gestation; the remainder received plain tap water. She switched the alcohol-exposed mothers to plain tap water when the pups were born. Thus, some rat pups were exposed to alcohol during gestation, whereas others were not. Nash tested all the pups for alcohol preference when they were adults and found that those animals that were exposed to alcohol (the physiological IV) during gestation drank more alcohol as adults. Nash received the 1983 J. P. Guilford–Psi Chi National Undergraduate Research Award for this experiment. Just as alcohol exposure was a physiological IV in Nash's experiment, administering a new drug to determine whether it is successful in alleviating schizophrenic symptoms also represents a physiological IV.

Experience   When the effects of amount or type of previous training or learning are the central focus of the research, the researcher is using an **experience IV**. A study conducted by Monica Boice, a student at Saint Joseph's University in Philadelphia, and her faculty advisor, Gary Gargano, illustrates the use of experience as an IV. Boice and Gargano (2001) studied memory for items in a list as a function of the number of related cues that were presented at the time of recall. Some participants received 0 cues, whereas other participants received 8 cues. The number of cues is an experience IV. The results of this study indicated that, under some conditions, receiving 8 related cues actually resulted in worse memory performance than did receiving no cues.

> **Experience IV** Manipulation of the amount or type of training or learning.

Stimulus   Some IVs fall into the category of **stimulus** or **environmental variables**. When researchers use this type of IV, they are manipulating some aspect of the environment. Kathy Walter, Sammi Ervin, and Nicole Williamson, students at Catawba College in Salisbury, North Carolina, conducted a study under the direction of Sheila Brownlow in which they used a stimulus IV (Walter, Brownlow, Ervin, & Williamson, 1998). They asked 144 college students to judge various traits of women who walked barefoot and in high heels. The stimulus variable was whether the person being judged was barefoot or wore heels. The results showed that when the women wore heels, student participants judged them as less sexy and more submissive than when they were barefoot.

> **Stimulus or environmental IV** An aspect of the environment that the experimenter manipulates.
>
> **Participant characteristics** Aspects of the participant, such as age, sex, or personality traits, that are treated as if they are IVs.

Participant   It is common to find **participant characteristics**, such as age, sex, personality traits, or academic major, being treated *as if* they are IVs.

> Although many researchers may treat participant characteristics as if they are IVs, they really are not. Why?

To be considered an IV, the behavior or event in question must be directly manipulated by the experimenter. Although experimenters can manipulate physiological, experience, and stimulus IVs, they are not able to directly manipulate participant characteristics. Thus, experimenters do not consider them to be true IVs. The experimenter does not create the participants' sex or cause participants to be a certain age. Participant characteristics or variables are best viewed as classification, not manipulation, variables. The categories for participant variables are created before the experiment is conducted, and the experimenter simply assigns the participants to these categories on the basis of the characteristics they display.

Extraneous Variables (Confounders)

> **Extraneous variables** Uncontrolled variables that can cause unintended changes between groups.

As we saw in Chapter 1, **extraneous variables** are those factors that can have an *unintended* influence on the results of our experiment. Extraneous variables influence the difference *between* groups. Figure 6-1A shows the relation of two groups without the influence of an extraneous variable; two possible effects of an extraneous variable are shown in Figures 6-1B and 6-1C. Thus, an extraneous variable can unintentionally cause groups to move closer together (Figure 6-1B) or farther apart (Figure 6-1C).

Review Figure 6-1 and the information we have presented about extraneous variables. The effect of an extraneous variable is similar to that of another major component of the experiment. What role does an extraneous variable appear to play in an experiment? How is the presence of an extraneous variable detrimental to the experiment?

The other component of an experiment that can influence the difference between groups is the IV. Thus, an extraneous variable can affect the outcome of an experiment. Just as other likely interpretations can damage a detective's case beyond repair, the presence of an extraneous variable is devastating to research; it is not possible to attribute the results of the experiment to the IV. Why? There are two variables that may have caused the groups to differ: the IV you manipulated *and* the unwanted extraneous variable. You have no way to determine which of these two variables caused the differences you observed. In such instances, when we can attribute the results either to an IV or to an extraneous variable, the experiment is **confounded**. (The terms *extraneous variable* and *confounder* are often used synonymously.) When an experiment is confounded, the best course of action is to discontinue the research and profit from your mistake. You can control the extraneous variable in the next experiment.

> **Confounding** A situation in which the results of an experiment can be attributed to either the operation of an IV or an extraneous variable.

To illustrate how confounding works, let's consider a reading comprehension study. We have first- and second-graders available to serve as participants. The researcher assigns all the first-graders to the standard method for teaching reading comprehension and all the second-graders to the new method. The experiment is conducted and we find that the comprehension scores for students using the new method are substantially better than those of students using the standard method (see Figure 6-1C). But what would have happened if the researcher had assigned the second-graders to the standard method and the first-graders to the new method? We might have seen results like those of Figure 6-1B. Why did these two sets of results occur? In each instance it is arguable that a preexisting difference in reading comprehension between the groups of children created differences

FIGURE 6-1
A. The difference
(A = standard method;
B = new method)
between two groups with
no confounder operating.

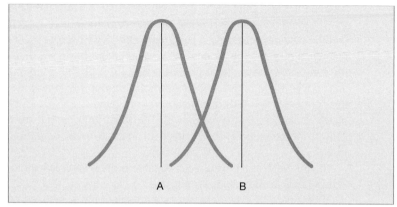

A

B. The difference between
two groups when a
confounder is present and
has moved the groups
closer together.

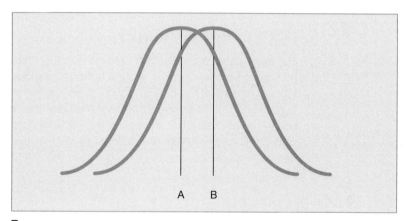

B

C. The difference between
two groups when a
confounder is present and
has moved the groups
farther apart.

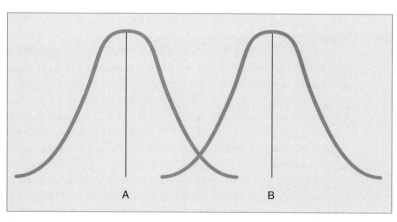

C

between the two groups (i.e., the preexisting difference acted *as if* it were an IV). Assuming the second-graders have superior reading comprehension, it seems reasonable to suggest that the new method seemed even more effective when the second-graders used it (i.e., the difference between the groups was exaggerated). However, when the second-graders used the standard method, the superior method used by the first-graders increased their scores and moved the groups closer together (i.e., group differences decreased). Certainly, all of this commentary is only speculation on our part. It is also possible that the IV created the group differences that we observed. The main point is that we really do not know what caused the differences—the IV (type of method used) or the extraneous variable (grade level).

The presence of an extraneous variable is often very difficult to spot; it may take several knowledgeable individuals scrutinizing an experiment from every possible angle to determine whether one is present. An experimenter who detects an extraneous variable before conducting an experiment can deal with the problem and proceed with the experiment. We present techniques for controlling unwanted variables later in this chapter.

Dependent Variables

Dependent variable (DV)
A response or behavior that is measured. It is desired that changes in the DV are directly related to manipulation of the IV.

The **dependent variable (DV)** changes as a function of the level of the IV the participant experiences; thus, the value the DV assumes *truly depends* on the IV. The DV consists of the data or results of our experiment. As with all aspects of psychological research, experimenters must give the DV appropriate consideration when they formulate an experiment. The experimenter must deal with such considerations as selecting the appropriate DV, deciding exactly which measure of the DV to use, and whether to record more than one DV.

Selecting the DV

Because psychology often is defined as the science of behavior, the DV typically consists of some type of behavior or response. However, when the researcher administers the IV, it is likely that several responses will occur. Which one should the researcher select as the DV? One answer to this question is to look carefully at the experimental hypothesis. If you have stated your hypothesis in general implication form ("if . . . then"—see Chapter 2), the "then" portion of the hypothesis will give you an idea of the general nature of your DV. For the Boice and Gargano (2001) memory study the choice was easy: "The dependent measure was the number of words correctly recalled" (p. 119).

What if your hypothesis is more general? Say that you want to study "spatial abilities." Where could you find information to help you choose a *specific* DV? We hope you are already a step ahead of us; our literature review (see Chapter 2) can provide valuable guidelines. If other researchers have used a particular response successfully as a DV in previous research, chances are that it will be a good choice again. Another reason for using a DV that researchers have previously used is that you will have a comparison for your own results. Although totally different DVs may provide exciting new information, the ability to relate the results of experiments using different responses is more difficult.

Recording or Measuring the DV

Once you have selected the DV, you will have to decide exactly how you will measure or record it. Several possibilities exist.

Correctness   Because they counted the number of words their participants remembered, Boice and Gargano (2001) used a correctness DV.

Rate or Frequency   If you are studying the lever-pressing performance of a rat or pigeon in an operant conditioning chamber (Skinner box), then your DV is likely to be the rate of responding that the animal shows. Rate of responding determines how rapidly responses are made during a specified time period. You can plot your data in the form of a cumulative record with steeper slopes representing higher rates (i.e., large numbers of responses being made in shorter periods of time). Figure 6-2 shows some different rates of responding.

If you are studying the number of social interactions among children during free play at a kindergarten, you may want to record the frequency, rather than the rate, of responding. Hence, your DV would simply be the number of responses shown during a specified time period without any concern for how rapidly the participant makes them.

Degree or Amount   Often researchers record the DV in terms of degree or amount. Research conducted by Amie McKibban and Shawn Nelson, students at Emporia State University in Emporia, Kansas, studied satisfaction with life among college students, using scores on a Satisfaction With Life scale (McKibban & Nelson, 2001).

Latency or Duration   In many situations, such as studies of learning and memory, how quickly participants make a response (latency) or how long the response lasts (duration) are of particular interest. For example, Rachel Ball, Erica Kargl, J. Davis Kimpel, and Shana Siewert, students at Wheaton College in Wheaton, Illinois, were interested in the relation between a participant's mood and his or her reaction time measured as a latency DV. They found that participants in sad and suspenseful moods had longer reaction times than participants in a neutral mood (Ball, Kargl, Kimpel, & Siewert, 2001).

Should You Record More than One DV?

If you have the measurement capabilities, there is nothing to prohibit the recording of more than one DV. Possibly additional data will strengthen your knowledge claim in the same way it might strengthen a detective's case. Should you record additional DVs? The answer to this question really boils down to deciding whether recording additional DVs is going to add appreciably to your understanding of the phenomenon under study. If recording an additional DV makes a meaningful contribution, then you should give it serious consideration. If measuring and recording another DV does not make a substantive contribution, then it is probably not worth the added time and trouble. Often you can use previous research as a guide concerning whether you should consider recording more than one DV.

FIGURE 6-2   Different Rates of Responding.

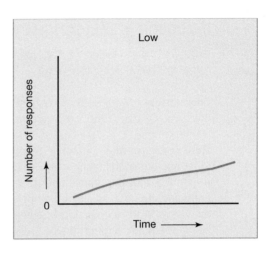

Low

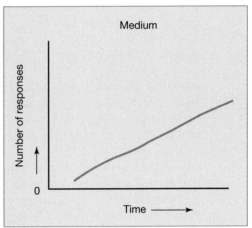

Medium

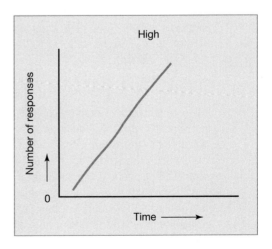

High

Consider a reversed eye–hand coordination (mirror tracing) experiment in which you record the time taken to complete the tracing of a star pattern (a latency DV) while looking in a mirror. Is this DV sufficient to give you a good, complete picture of the performance of this task, or should you also record another DV?

You probably should record a second DV. The latency DV indicates only how long it took to trace the star pattern. Hence, the experimenter has no record of the number of errors (going beyond the boundaries of the figure) that participants made. A second DV that measures the number of errors (a frequency DV) will make a significant contribution to this experiment.

The need for more than one DV was seen in an experiment conducted by Janet Luehring, a student at Washburn University in Topeka, Kansas, and her faculty advisor, Joanne Altman (Luehring & Altman, 2000). These investigators studied male–female differences in spatial ability performance. Their participants performed a mental rotation (visualizing what an object would look like after it was rotated in space). Because the participant's performance could be correct, incorrect, or (because the task was timed) uncompleted, Luehring and Altman recorded *both correct and incorrect responses.* The number of incorrect responses, which was *not* equal to the total number of responses minus the numer of correct responses, had the potential to provide additional, relevant information.

Characteristics of a Good DV

Although considerable thought may go into deciding exactly how the DV will be measured and recorded and whether more than one DV should be recorded, the experimenter still has no guarantee that a good DV has been selected. What constitutes a good DV? In Chapter 4 we saw that a good test or inventory must be valid and reliable. Because tests and inventories are designed to *measure* or *evaluate* some aspect of the participant, it should come as no surprise that the DV in an experiment shares the same characteristics. In other words, the DV is valid when it measures what the experimental hypothesis says it should measure. For example, assume you are interested in studying intelligence as a function of differences in regional diet. You believe the basic diet consumed by people living in different regions of the United States results in differences in intelligence. You devise a new intelligence test and set off to test your hypothesis. As the results of your project start to take shape, you notice that the scores from the Northeast are higher than those from other sections of the country; your hypothesis appears to be supported. However, a closer inspection of the results indicates that participants not living in the Northeast miss only certain questions. Are all the questions fair and unbiased, or do some favor Northeasterners? For example, you notice there are several questions about subways. How many individuals from Arizona are familiar with subways? Thus, your DV (scores on the intelligence test) may have a regional bias and may not measure the participants' intelligence consistently from region to region. A good DV must be directly related to the IV and must measure the effects of the IV manipulation as the experimental hypothesis predicts it will.

A good DV also is reliable. If the scores on an intelligence test are used as the DV, then we would expect to see similar scores when the test is again administered under the same IV conditions (test–retest procedure; see Chapter 5).

Nuisance Variables

Nuisance variables are either characteristics of the participants or unintended influences of the experimental situation that make the effects of the IV more difficult to see or determine. It is important to understand that nuisance variables influence all groups in an experiment; their influence is not limited just to one specific group. When they are present, nuisance variables result in greater variability in the DV; the scores *within* each group spread out more. For example,

> **Nuisance variable**
> Unwanted variables that can cause the variability of scores within groups to increase.

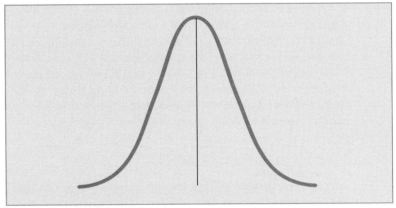

A. The spread of scores within a group when a nuisance variable is not operating.

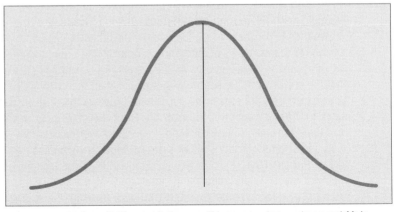

FIGURE 6-3   **B.** The spread of scores within a group when a nuisance variable is operating.

assume you are interested in studying reading comprehension. Can you think of a participant characteristic that might be related to reading comprehension? How about intelligence or IQ?

Figure 6-3A shows the spread of the reading comprehension scores within a group when there are not wide differences in intelligence among the participants within the group. In this instance a nuisance variable is not operating.

You can see how the majority of the comprehension scores are similar and cluster in the middle of the distribution; there are relatively few extremely low and extremely high scores. Figure 6-3B shows the distribution of comprehension scores when there are wider differences in intelligence (i.e., a nuisance variable is present). Notice that the scores are more spread out; there are fewer scores in the middle of the distribution and more scores in the extremes.

How does a nuisance variable influence the results of an experiment? To answer that question, we need to add another group of participants to our example and conduct a simple experiment. Imagine we are evaluating two methods for teaching reading comprehension—the standard method and a new method. In Figure 6-4A, we are comparing two groups that have not been influenced by the nuisance variable. The difference between these two groups is pronounced and clear; they overlap very little.

Let's add the effects of a nuisance variable, such as wide differences in verbal ability, to each group and then compare the groups. As you can see in Figure 6-4B, when the scores spread out more, there is greater overlap and the difference between the groups is not as distinct and clear as when the nuisance variable was not present. When a nuisance variable is present, our view of the experimental results is clouded; we are unable to see clearly the difference the IV may have created between the groups in our experiment. Notice that when the nuisance variable was added (Figure 6-4B), the *only* thing that happened was that the scores spread out in both extremes of each distribution—the relative location of the distributions did not change. *Nuisance variables increase the spread of scores within a distribution; they do not cause a distribution to change its location.*

For each example indicate the nuisance variable and its effect.
1. An experimenter measures reaction time in participants ranging in age from 12 to 78 years.
2. The ability of participants to recall a list of words is being studied in a room that is located by a noisy elevator.
3. The laboratory where participants are tested for manual dexterity has frequent, unpredictable changes in temperature.

In the first situation, the wide age range is the nuisance variable. The younger participants should display faster reaction times than the older participants. Thus, the scores will spread into both ends of the distributions. The change in noise level due to the operation of the elevator is the nuisance variable in the second example, whereas the frequent, unpredictable temperature changes are the nuisance variable in the third example; in both examples the change in environmental conditions is likely to increase the spread of scores. Our goal as researchers is to keep nuisance variables to a minimum so the effects of the IV are as clear as possible.

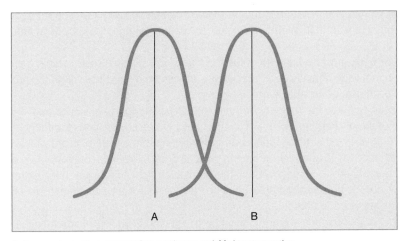

A. A comparison of two groups when a nuisance variable is not operating.

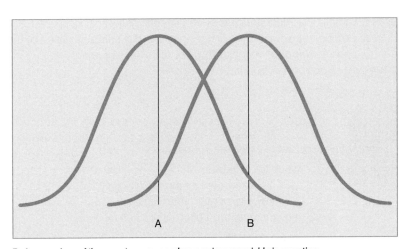

B. A comparison of the same two groups when a nuisance variable is operating.

FIGURE 6-4

1. A **variable** is an event or behavior that can assume at least two levels.
2. **Independent variables (IVs)** are purposely manipulated by the experimenter and form the core or purpose of the experiment. **Physiological IVs** refer to changes in the biological state of the participants, whereas **experience IVs** refer to manipulations of previous experience or learning. **Stimulus IVs** are manipulations in some aspect of the environment.
3. Although **participant characteristics** such as age, sex, or personality traits are often treated as IVs, technically they are not IVs because the experimenter does not directly manipulate them.
4. **Extraneous variables (confounders)** can have an unintended influence on the results of an experiment by changing the difference *between* the groups. When an extraneous variable is present, the experiment is confounded.
5. The **dependent variable (DV)** changes as a function of changes in the IV. The experimental hypothesis can provide possible guidelines concerning the selection of the DV. Past research also can assist the experimenter in selecting the DV.
6. The DV can be recorded in terms of correctness, rate or frequency, degree or amount, and latency or duration. If additional information will be gained, the experimenter should consider recording more than one DV. A good DV is directly related to the IV (valid) and reliable.
7. **Nuisance variables** are variables that increase the variability of scores *within all groups.* The presence of nuisance variables makes the results of an experiment less clear.

1. An event or behavior that can assume at least two values is a _____.
2. Matching

    1. DV   A. change in normal biological state
    2. extraneous variable   B. manipulation of environment
    3. physiological IV   C. can damage the experiment and its results
    4. experience IV   D. age
    5. stimulus IV   E. changes as a function of changes in IV
    6. participant variable   F. amount of previous learning

3. Your research involves determining the effects of persuasion on the strength of attitudes. You are using a _____ measurement of the DV.
   a. correctness   b. rate   c. degree   d. duration

4. A good DV has two primary qualities; it is both _____ and _____.
   a. easy to identify; easy to measure   b. dependent on the experimenter; identifiable
   c. valid; reliable   d. positively correlated; negatively correlated

5. Under what conditions should you record more than one DV?

6. Variables that result in greater within-group variability in the data are called
   a. independent variables   b. confounders
   c. nuisance variables   d. uncontrolled variables

Controlling Extraneous Variables

Care and precision are crucial when a detective attempts to solve a case; likewise, control forms an integral component of psychological research. The experimenter must exercise control over both extraneous variables and nuisance variables so the results of the experiment are as meaningful (no extraneous variables present) and clear (minimal influence of nuisance variables) as possible. When you are dealing with a variable that can be clearly specified and quantified (e.g., sex, age, educational level, temperature, lighting intensity, or noise level), then one of the five basic control techniques should be applicable. We describe these five basic control techniques—randomization, elimination, constancy, balancing, and counterbalancing—in the next section.

Basic Control Techniques

As we discuss the basic control techniques, it is important to keep in mind that their goals are to (1) produce groups that are equivalent prior to the introduction of the IV, thereby eliminating extraneous variables, and (2) reduce the effects of nuisance variables as much as possible.

Randomization A control technique that ensures that each participant has an equal chance of being assigned to any group in an experiment.

Randomization   We begin our discussion of control with randomization because it is the most widely used technique. **Randomization** guarantees that each participant has an equal chance of being assigned to any group in the experiment. For example, once the students had volunteered for the research on memory, Boice and Gargano (2001) noted: "The participants were placed randomly into one of the six experimental groups" (p. 120).

The logic behind using randomization is as follows. Because all participants have an equal likelihood of being selected for each group in an experiment, any unique characteristics associated with the participants should be equally distributed across all groups that are formed. Consider level of motivation, for example. Although it may not be feasible to measure each participant's level of motivation, this variable can still be controlled by randomly forming the groups in our experiment. Just by chance we would expect that *each* group would have some participants who are highly motivated, some participants who are moderately motivated, and some participants who are barely motivated. Thus, the groups should be equated with regard to the average level of motivation, as well as the myriad of other unknown and unsuspected extraneous variables that might be present.

Even though it is the most widely used control procedure, randomization has one major drawback. What is it?

Because we are never *fully* aware of the variables that randomization controls and thus do not know whether these variables are distributed evenly to all groups, we cannot be positive that this control technique is effective. It is possible that all the highly motivated participants will be randomly assigned to the same group. Also, you need to consider what is being controlled when randomization is employed. If you find yourself having some difficulty specifying exactly what is controlled by randomization, then you are on the right track. Randomization is used as a control technique for *all* variables that *might* be present that the experimenter is unaware of. If the experimenter is unaware of exactly which variables are being controlled and how effective the control is, then it should come as no surprise that the experimenter is never *completely* sure how effective randomization has been.

Elimination   When we know the extraneous variables or nuisance variables, our approach can be more direct. For example, we might choose to completely remove or **eliminate** the unwanted variable. This sounds easy, but in practice you may find it quite difficult to *completely* remove a variable.

> **Elimination**   A control technique whereby extraneous variables are completely removed from an experiment.

Shann Sagles, Sharon Coley, Germilina Espiritu, and Patricia Zahregian, students at Pace University in White Plains, New York, and their faculty advisor, Richard Velayo, used elimination as a control in their cross-cultural study of the identification of facial expressions. "The 35-mm photos of the target individuals, taken from the base of the chin to the top of the forehead, excluded their attire and body type. The rationale for this procedure was to *eliminate* [emphasis added] extraneous variables that may have influenced the participants' responses" (Sagles, Coley, Espiritu, Zahregian, & Velayo, 2002, p. 33). Thus, Sagles et al. guaranteed that clothing and weight did not affect their participants' responses.

When the variable in question consists of an entire category of events, such as noise, temperature, or lighting condition, it may be difficult, if not impossible, to eliminate. However, if the variable is a specific occurrence within one of these more general categories, such as temperatures above 80 degrees, then it may be possible to eliminate that *aspect* of the variable. In this situation, however, the experimenter is interested not just in eliminating a variable but also in producing and maintaining a constant condition under which the participants in the experiment are tested.

> **Constancy**   A control technique by which an extraneous variable is reduced to a single value that is experienced by all participants.

Constancy   When it is difficult or impossible to completely eliminate a variable, the experimenter may choose to exercise control by creating a uniform or constant condition that all participants experience. **Constancy** has become a standard control technique for many researchers. For example, experimental testing may take place in the same room, with the same lighting and temperature levels, and at the same time of day (if the experiment is conducted on more than one day). In this instance the location of the experiment, the temperature level, the lighting level, and the time of day have not been eliminated but, rather, have assumed a constant value.

Juan and Nancy are interested in determining which of two methods of teaching psychological statistics is best. Two statistics classes are available: Juan teaches one method to one class, and Nancy teaches the second method to the other class. This experiment is confounded because Juan and Nancy each teach one of the classes, so it is impossible to tell whether differences between the classes are due to the method or the teacher. How would you use constancy to control this extraneous variable?

The easiest approach would be to have only one of the experimenters, Juan or Nancy, teach both classes. Thus, the extraneous variable, the teacher, is the same for both classes and the experiment is no longer confounded.

By making sure the experimental testing conditions do not vary unpredictably, constancy can also control for nuisance variables. When the testing conditions are the same from testing session to testing session, there is greater likelihood that the scores within the groups will not spread out as much because of the constancy. Constancy can also control nuisance variable effects produced by participant variables such as age, sex, and educational level. For example, in a study of the effects of massage and touch on body dissatisfaction, Angela Larey, a student at Missouri Southern State College in Joplin, Missouri, "used only women [as participants] because they generally manifest greater body dissatisfaction than men" (Larey, 2001, p. 79). Recall that wide variations in such participant variables may result in greater spread of scores within the groups. If the technique of stratified random sampling (see Chapter 5) is employed, then the variability among the participants' scores should be smaller because the participants are more homogeneous. In such instances constancy is created by randomly sampling only a certain type of participant, such as first-year college women between the ages of 18 and 19.

Although constancy can be an effective control technique, there are situations in which the unwanted variable(s) cannot be reduced to a single value that all participants experienced in the experiment. What can be done when this variable assumes two or more values? The answer may lie in the control technique known as balancing.

Balancing   A control procedure that achieves group equality by distributing extraneous variables equally to all groups.

Balancing   **Balancing** represents a logical extension of control through constancy. Thus, the groups in our experiment are balanced or equivalent when each group experiences *all* unwanted variables or *levels* of unwanted variables in the same manner or to the same degree.

In the simplest example of balancing we would test two groups; one group (the experimental group) would receive the IV, whereas the second group (the

TABLE 6-1	Balanced Extraneous Variables

When the extraneous variables are experienced in the same manner, the groups are said to be balanced.

GROUP 1	GROUP 2
Treatment A	Treatment B
Ext. Var. 1	Ext. Var. 1
Ext. Var. 2	Ext. Var. 2
Ext. Var. 3	Ext. Var. 3
Ext. Var. 4	Ext. Var. 4

control or comparison group) would be treated identically but would not receive the IV. If the groups were balanced or equated with regard to extraneous variables, then we could tentatively conclude that differences between them were caused by the IV. This general situation is diagrammed in Table 6-1.

When the potential extraneous variables, such as various personality differences in human participants, are *unknown*, the experimenter uses randomization to form equivalent groups, and we assume that the respective extraneous variables are distributed equally to all groups. When the extraneous variables, such as sex of the experimenter, are known, then the experimenter can be more systematic in the use of the balancing technique to produce equivalent conditions.

Let's assume that all the students included in Juan and Nancy's experiment cannot be taught by one teacher; two are needed. How could balancing be used to remove the potential confounding due to a different teacher teaching each of the new methods?

As you can see in Table 6-2, an easy solution to their problem is to have Juan and Nancy each teach half the students under *each* method. Thus, the two teachers appear equally under each teaching method and the classes are balanced with regard to that potential

TABLE 6-2	Using Balancing to Eliminate Confounding in Teaching Two Methods of Psychological Statistics

Juan	Nancy
25 students → Method 1	25 students → Method 1
25 students → Method 2	25 students → Method 2

confounding variable. This teaching example illustrates the simplest situation in which balancing is used to control one extraneous variable. Balancing can also be used with several extraneous variables (see Table 6-1); the only requirement is that each extraneous variable appear equally in each group.

Although elimination, constancy, and balancing offer the experimenter powerful control techniques, they are not able to deal with all control problems. In the next section we examine one of these problem situations, sequencing or order, and how to control it through counterbalancing.

Counterbalancing   In some experiments, participants participate in more than one experimental condition. For example, you might want to conduct a cola taste test to determine which of two brands of cola is most preferred. As you set up your tasting booth at the local mall, you are sure you have taken all the right precautions: The tasting cups are all the same, the two colas will be poured from identical containers, the participants will consume the same amount of Cola A and then Cola B (in that order), and the participants will be blindfolded during the test so color differences will not influence their choice. Yes, your control seems to be perfect. Is it?

Review the experiment we have just described. What control procedures are being used? There is a problem that has been overlooked that needs to be controlled. What is this problem and how might it be controlled?

Constancy is achieved by ensuring that (a) the tasting cups are the same, (b) the colas are poured from similar containers, and (c) all participants consume the same amount of each cola. By blindfolding the participants, you have *eliminated* any problems that may be caused by differences in the visual appearance of the two colas. These are all relevant control procedures. The problem that is overlooked concerns the sequence or order for sampling the two colas. If Cola A is *always* sampled before Cola B and one cola is liked more, you cannot be sure the preference is due to its great flavor *or* the fact that the colas were always sampled in the same order and this order may have influenced the participants' reactions. The technique used when a sequence or order effect must be controlled is known as **counterbalancing**. There are two types of counterbalancing, within-subject and within-group. **Within-subject counterbalancing** attempts to control the sequence effect within each participant, whereas **within-group counterbalancing** attempts to control this problem by presenting different sequences to different participants.

Counterbalancing   A procedure for controlling order effects by presenting different treatment sequences.

Within-subject counterbalancing   Presentation of different treatment sequences to the same participant.

Within-group counterbalancing   Presentation of different treatment sequences to different participants.

Within-Subject Counterbalancing   Returning to the problem of sequence in our cola challenge, we could deal with this problem by having each participant sample the two colas in the following sequence: ABBA. By using within-subject counterbalancing, each participant will taste Cola A once before and once after tasting Cola B. Thus, the experience of having tasted Cola A first is counterbalanced by tasting Cola A last.

Although it may seem relatively easy to implement within-subject counterbalancing, there is one major drawback to its use: Each participant must experience each condition more than once. In some situations the experimenter may not want or be able to present the treatments more than once to each participant. For example, you may not have sufficient time to conduct your cola challenge and allow each participant the opportunity to sample *each* brand of cola more than once. In such instances within-group counterbalancing may offer a better control alternative.

Within-Group Counterbalancing   Another way to deal with the cola challenge sequencing problem is to randomly assign half the participants to experience the two colas in the Cola A → Cola B sequence and the remaining half of the participants to receive the Cola B → Cola A sequence. The preference of participants who tasted Cola A before Cola B could be compared with the preference of the participants who tasted Cola B first.

Assuming that we tested six participants, the within-group counterbalanced presentation of the two colas would be diagrammed as shown in Table 6-3.

As you can see, three participants receive the A → B sequence, whereas three participants receive the B → A sequence. This basic diagram illustrates the three requirements of within-subject counterbalancing:

1. Each treatment must be presented to each participant an equal number of times. In this example each participant tastes Cola A once and Cola B once.
2. Each treatment must occur an equal number of times at each testing or practice session. Cola A is sampled three times at Tasting 1 and three times at Tasting 2.
3. Each treatment must precede and follow each of the other treatments an equal number of times. In this example Cola A is tasted first three times and is tasted second three times.

Counterbalancing is not limited to two-treatment sequences. For example, let's assume that your cola challenge involves three colas instead of two. The within-group counterbalancing that will be needed in that situation is diagrammed in Table 6-4. Carefully examine this diagram. Does it satisfy the requirements for counterbalancing?

TABLE 6-3	Within-Group Counterbalancing for the Two-Cola Challenge When Six Participants Are Tested	
	Tasting 1	**Tasting 2**
Participant 1	A	B
Participant 2	A	B
Participant 3	A	B
Participant 4	B	A
Participant 5	B	A
Participant 6	B	A

TABLE 6-4	**Within-Group Counterbalancing for the Three-Cola Challenge When Six Participants Are Tested**

	Tasting Session		
	1	**2**	**3**
Participant 1	A	B	C
Participant 2	A	C	B
Participant 3	B	A	C
Participant 4	B	C	A
Participant 5	C	A	B
Participant 6	C	B	A

It appears that all the requirements have been met. Each cola is tasted an equal number of times (6), is tasted an equal number of times (2) at each tasting session, and precedes and follows each of the other colas an equal number of times (2). It is important to note that if we wanted to test more participants, they would have to be added in multiples of 6. The addition of any other number of participants violates the rules of counterbalancing by creating a situation in which one cola is tasted more than the others, appears more often at one tasting session than the others, and does not precede and follow the other colas an equal number of times. Try adding only 1 or 2 participants to Table 6-4 to see if you can satisfy the requirements for counterbalancing.

Table 6-4 also illustrates another consideration that must be taken into account when counterbalancing is used. When only a few treatments are used, the number of different sequences that will have to be administered remains relatively small and counterbalancing is manageable. When we tested 2 colas, only 2 sequences were involved (see Table 6-3); however, the addition of only 1 more cola resulted in the addition of 4 sequences (see Table 6-4). If we added an additional cola to our challenge (Colas A, B, C, and D), we would now have to administer a total of 24 different sequences, and our experiment would be much more complex to conduct! Our minimum number of participants would be 24, and if we wanted to test more than 1 participant per sequence, participants would have to be added in multiples of 24.

How do you know how many sequences will be required? Do you have to write down all the possible sequences to find out how many there are? No—you can calculate the total number of sequences by using the formula $n!$ (n factorial). All that is required is to take the number of treatments (n), factor or break that number down into its component parts, and then multiply these factors or components. Thus:

$$2! \text{ would be } 2 \times 1 = 2$$
$$3! \text{ would be } 3 \times 2 \times 1 = 6$$
$$4! \text{ would be } 4 \times 3 \times 2 \times 1 = 24$$

Complete counterbalancing All possible treatment sequences are presented.

and so forth. When you can administer all possible sequences, you are using **complete counterbalancing**. Although complete counterbalancing offers the best control for sequence or order effects, often it cannot be attained when several treatments are included in the experiment. As we just saw, the use of 4 colas would require a minimum of 24 participants ($4! = 4 \times 3 \times 2 \times 1 = 24$) for complete counterbalancing. Testing 5 colas would increase the number of sequences (and the minimum number of participants) to 120 ($5! = 5 \times 4 \times 3 \times 2 \times 1 = 120$). In situations requiring a large number of participants to implement complete counterbalancing, either you can reduce the number of treatments until your time, financial, and participant resources allow complete counterbalancing, or you can complete the experiment without completely counterbalancing.

Incomplete counterbalancing refers to the use of some, but not all, of the possible sequences. Which sequences are to be used, and which ones are to be excluded? Some experimenters randomly select the sequences they will employ. Once the number of participants to be tested has been determined, the experimenter randomly selects an equal number of sequences. For example, Table 6-5 illustrates a possible random selection of sequences for conducting the cola challenge with 4 colas and only 12 participants.

> **Incomplete counterbalancing** Only a portion of all possible sequences are presented.

Although random selection appears to be an easy approach to the use of incomplete counterbalancing, there is a problem. If you examine Table 6-5 carefully, you will see that although each participant receives each treatment an equal number of times, the other requirements for counterbalancing are not satisfied. Each treatment does not appear an equal number of times at each testing or practice session, and each treatment does not precede and follow each of the other treatments an equal number of times.

There are two approaches that can be adopted to resolve this problem, although neither one is completely satisfactory. We could randomly determine the treatment sequence for

TABLE 6-5   Randomly Selected Tasting Sequences for the Four-Cola Challenge Using 12 Participants

	Testing Session			
	1	2	3	4
Participant 1	A	B	C	D
Participant 2	A	B	D	C
Participant 3	A	C	D	B
Participant 4	A	D	C	B
Participant 5	B	A	C	D
Participant 6	B	C	D	A
Participant 7	B	C	A	D
Participant 8	C	A	B	D
Participant 9	C	B	A	D
Participant 10	C	D	B	A
Participant 11	D	B	C	A
Participant 12	D	C	B	A

the *first* participant and then systematically rotate the sequence for the remaining partici-pants. This approach is diagrammed in Table 6-6.

Thus, the first participant would taste the colas in the order B, D, A, C, whereas the sec-ond participant would experience them in the order D, A, C, B. We would continue systemat-ically rotating the sequence until each cola appears once in each row and each column. To test a total of 12 participants, 3 participants would be assigned to each of the 4 sequences. By ensuring that each treatment appears an equal number of times at each testing session, this approach comes close to satisfying the conditions for counterbalancing. It does not, however, ensure that the treatments precede and follow each other an equal number of times. A more complex procedure, the Latin square technique, is used to address this issue. Because of its complexity, this procedure is seldom used. If you are interested in reading about its use, Rosenthal and Rosnow (1991) offer a nice presentation of its particulars.

Now that we have examined the mechanics involved in implementing complete and in-complete counterbalancing, let's see exactly what counterbalancing can and cannot control. To simply say that counterbalancing controls for sequence or order effects does not tell the entire story. Although counterbalancing controls for sequence or order effects, as you will see, it also controls for *carryover effects*. It cannot, however, control for *differential carryover*.

Sequence or **order ef-fects**   The position of a treatment in a series de-termines, in part, the par-ticipants' response.

Sequence or Order Effects   **Sequence** or **order effects** are produced by the participant's being exposed to the sequential presentation of the treatments. For example, assume we are testing reaction time to three types of dashboard warn-ing lights: red (R), green (G), and flashing white (FW). As soon as the warning light comes on, the participant is to turn the engine off. To completely counterbalance this experiment would require 6 sequences and at least 6 participants ($3! = 3 \times 2 \times 1 = 6$). If we found the reaction time to the first warning light, regardless of type, was 10 seconds, and that improvements of 4 and 3 seconds were made to the second and third lights (regardless of type), respectively, we would be dealing with a sequence or order effect. This example is diagrammed in Table 6-7.

As you can see, the sequence or order effect depends on *where* in the sequential presentation of treatments the participant's performance is evaluated, *not* which treatment is experienced.

TABLE 6-6   An Incomplete Counterbalancing Approach

This approach involves randomly determining the sequence for the first participant and then systematically rotating the treatments for the following sequences.

	Tasting Sequence			
	1	2	3	4
Participant 1	B	D	A	C
Participant 2	D	A	C	B
Participant 3	A	C	B	D
Participant 4	C	B	D	A

TABLE 6-7   Example of Sequence or Order Effects in a Counterbalanced Experiment

The performance increase shown in parentheses below each sequence indicates the effect of testing reaction time to red (R), green (G), and flashing white (FW) lights on an instrument panel at that particular point in the sequence. Thus, second and third testings result in increases of 4 and 3, respectively, regardless of the experimental task.

	ORDER OF TASK PRESENTATION		
	R	G	FW
Performance Increase →	(0	4	3)
	R	FW	G
	(0	4	3)
	G	R	FW
	(0	4	3)
	G	FW	R
	(0	4	3)
	FW	R	G
	(0	4	3)
	FW	G	R
	(0	4	3)

Sequence or order effects will be experienced equally by all participants in counterbalanced situations because each treatment appears an equal number of times at each testing session. This consideration points to a major flaw in the use of randomized, incomplete counterbalancing: The treatments may not be presented an equal number of times at each testing session (see Table 6-5). Thus, sequence or order effects are not controlled in this situation.

Carryover Effects   When a **carryover effect** is present, the effects of one treatment persist to influence the participant's response to the next treatment. For example, let's assume that experiencing the green (G) warning light before the red (R) light always causes participants to *decrease* their reaction time by 2 seconds. Conversely, experiencing R before G causes participants to *increase* their reaction time by 2 seconds. Experiencing the flashing white (FW) warning light either before or after G has no effect on reaction time. However, experiencing R before FW increases reaction time by 3 seconds, and experiencing FW before R reduces reaction time by 3 seconds. In the R → G/G → R and R → FW/FW → R transitions, the previous treatment influences the participant's response to the subsequent treatment in a consistent and predictable manner. These effects are diagrammed in Table 6-8. Note that counterbalancing includes an equal

> **Carryover effect** The effects of one treatment persist or carry over and influence responses to the next treatment.

TABLE 6-8   Example of Carryover Effects in a Counterbalanced Experiment

Carryover effects occur when a specific preceding treatment influences the performance in a subsequent treatment. In this example, experiencing Treatment G prior to Treatment R results in a decrease of 2 (i.e., −2), whereas experiencing Treatment R prior to Treatment G results in an increase of 2 (i.e., +2). Experiencing Treatment G prior to FW or Treatment FW prior to G does not produce a unique effect. However, experiencing Treatment R prior to FW results in an increase of 3, whereas experiencing Treatment FW prior to R results in a decrease of 3.

	Sequence of Treatments		
	G	R	FW
Effect on Performance →	(0	−2	+3)
	G	FW	R
	(0	0	−3)
	R	G	FW
	(0	+2	0)
	R	FW	G
	(0	+3	0)
	FW	G	R
	(0	0	−2)
	FW	R	G
	(0	−3	+2)

number of each type of transition (e.g., R → G, G → R, R → FW, etc.). Thus the opposing carryover effects cancel each other.

Differential Carryover   Although counterbalancing can control many things, it offers no protection against differential carryover. **Differential carryover** occurs when the response to one treatment depends on *which* treatment is experienced previously. Consider an experiment investigating the effects of reward magnitude on reading comprehension in second-grade children. Each child reads three similar passages. After each passage is completed, a series of questions is asked. Each correct answer is rewarded by a certain number of M&M's (the IV). In the low-reward condition (A), children receive one M&M after each correct answer; three and five M&M's are received in the medium-reward (B) and high-reward (C) treatments, respectively.

Although this experiment might be viewed as another six-sequence example of counterbalancing (see Table 6-4), the effects may not be symmetrical as in the carryover example we just considered. The participant who receives the A → B → C sequence may be motivated to do well at all testing sessions because the reward progressively increases from session to session. What about the student who receives the B → C → A sequence? In this case the

> **Differential carryover** The response to one treatment depends on which treatment was administered previously.

TABLE 6-9	**Example of Differential Carryover in a Counterbalanced Experiment**

Differential carryover occurs when performance depends on which specific sequence occurs. In the following example, experiencing Treatment A prior to Treatment B results in an increase of 6 (i.e., +6), whereas all other sequences result in an increase of 2 (i.e., +2).

	Sequence of Treatments		
	A (1 M&M)	B (3 M&Ms)	C (5 M&Ms)
Effect on Performance →	(0	+6	+2)
	A	C	B
	(0	+2	+2)
	B	A	C
	(0	+2	+2)
	B	C	A
	(0	+2	+2)
	C	A	B
	(0	+2	+6)
	C	B	A
	(0	+2	+2)

reward rises from three M&M's (Session 1) to five M&M's (Session 2), but then is reduced to one M&M (Session 3). Will the decrease from five M&M's to one M&M produce a unique effect, such as the student's refusing to participate, that the other transitions do not produce? If so, differential carryover has occurred, and counterbalancing is not an effective control procedure. Some possible effects of differential carryover in the M&M study are shown in Table 6-9. As you can see, the drastic decrease in performance produced by the C-to-A (five M&M's to one M&M) transition is not canceled out by a comparable increase resulting from the A-to-C transition.

The potential for differential carryover exists whenever counterbalancing is employed. The experimenter must be sensitive to this possibility. A thorough review of the effects of the IV being used in your research can help sensitize you to the possibility of differential carryover. If this threat exists, it is advisable to employ a research procedure that does not involve presenting more than one treatment to each participant.

REVIEW SUMMARY

1. **Randomization** controls for extraneous variables by distributing them equally to all groups.
2. When experimenters use **elimination** as a control technique, they seek to completely remove the extraneous variable from the experiment.
3. **Constancy** controls an extraneous variable by creating a constant or uniform condition with regard to that variable.
4. **Balancing** achieves control of extraneous variables by ensuring that all groups receive the extraneous variables to the same extent.
5. **Counterbalancing** controls for sequence or order effects when participants receive more than one treatment. **Within-subject counterbalancing** involves the administration of more than one treatment sequence to each participant, whereas **within-group counterbalancing** involves the administration of a different treatment sequence to each participant.
6. The total number of treatment sequences can be determined by *n!* When all sequences are administered, **complete counterbalancing** is being used. **Incomplete counterbalancing** involves the administration of fewer than the total number of possible sequences.
7. The random selection of treatment sequences, systematic rotation, or the Latin square approaches can be used when incomplete counterbalancing is implemented.
8. Counterbalancing can control for **sequence** or **order** and **carryover effects**. It cannot control for **differential carryover**, in which the response to one treatment depends on which treatment was experienced previously.

CHECK YOUR PROGRESS

1. Matching
   1. randomization
   2. elimination
   3. constancy
   4. balancing
   5. counterbalancing

   A. complete removal of the extraneous variable
   B. extraneous variable is reduced to a single value
   C. most widely used control procedure
   D. used to control for order effects
   E. extraneous variable is distributed equally to all groups

2. The most widely used control technique is
   a. randomization   b. elimination   c. constancy   d. balancing   e. counterbalancing
3. Balancing is a logical extension of
   a. constancy   b. randomization   c. counterbalancing   d. elimination
4. Distinguish between within-subject and within-group counterbalancing.
5. What can *n!* be used for? Calculate the value of *4!*

6. _____ occurs when the response to one treatment depends on which treatment preceded it.

   a. Carryover

   b. Differential carryover

   c. A sequence or order effect

   d. Fault randomization

7. What is incomplete counterbalancing?

Internal Validity: Evaluating Your Experiment from the Inside

The concept of **internal validity** revolves around the question of whether your IV actually created any change that you observe in your DV. Researchers take many precautions aimed at increasing internal validity as they design and set up experiments. If you use adequate control techniques, your experiment should be free from confounding and you can, indeed, conclude that your IV caused the change in your DV.

> **Internal validity** A type of evaluation of your experiment; asks whether your IV is the only possible explanation of the results shown for your DV.

Threats to Internal Validity

In this section we will alert you to several categories of factors that can cause problems with the internal validity of an experiment. These factors are details that you should attend to when planning and evaluating your experiment and when scrutinizing research done by other investigators. Sherlock Holmes stressed the importance of details to his assistant, Dr. Watson: "Never trust to general impression, my boy, but concentrate yourself upon details" (Doyle, 1927, p. 196). The following list is drawn largely from the work of Donald T. Campbell (1957) and his associates (Campbell & Stanley, 1966; Cook & Campbell, 1979).

History We must beware of the possible extraneous variable of **history** when we test or measure experimental participants more than once. We might administer the IV between the DV measurements (pretest–posttest), or we may be interested in the time course of the IV effect—how participants react to the IV over time. In this case, history refers to any significant event, other than the IV, that occurs between DV measurements. Campbell and Stanley (1966) cited the example of a 1940 experiment concerning informational propaganda. Attitudes were measured, and then students read some Nazi propaganda. However, before the posttest was given, France fell to the Nazis. The subsequent attitude measurement was probably much more influenced by the historical event than by the propaganda. Obviously, this is an extreme example; historical events of this impact are rare. However, Campbell and Stanley also used the term to refer to less significant events that might occur during a lengthy experimental session. Noise or laughter or other similar events could occur during a session that might distract participants and cause them to react differently from participants who did not experience the same events. The distraction would then serve as an extraneous variable and the experiment would be confounded. One of our goals is to control or eliminate such distractions.

> **History** A threat to internal validity; refers to events that occur between the DV measurements in a repeated measures design.

Maturation   A threat to internal validity; refers to changes in participants that occur over time during an experiment; could include actual physical maturation or tiredness, boredom, hunger, and so on.

Maturation   This label seems to refer to experimental participants growing older during the course of an experiment, but that is somewhat misleading. Although true maturation is possible during a longitudinal study, Campbell (1957) used the term **maturation** to refer to systematic time-related changes, but mostly of a shorter duration than we would typically expect. Campbell and Stanley (1966) gave examples of participants growing tired, hungry, or bored through the course of an experiment. As you can see, maturation would be possible in an experiment that extends over some amount of time. How much time must occur before maturational changes can take place could vary widely, depending on the experiment's demands on the participants, the topic of the experiment, or many participant variables (e.g., the participants' motivation, how much sleep they got the night before, whether they have eaten recently, and so on). Maturational changes are more likely to occur in an experiment that uses repeated measurements of the DV because experimental participants are involved in the research for a longer period of time. You should attempt to safeguard against such changes if your experiment requires long sessions for your participants.

Testing   A threat to internal validity that occurs because measuring the DV causes a change in the DV.

Practice effect   A beneficial effect on a DV measurement caused by previous experience with the DV.

Testing   **Testing** is a definite threat to internal validity if you test participants more than once. As Campbell (1957) noted, if you take the same test more than once, scores on the second test may vary systematically from the first scores simply because you took the test a second time. This type of effect is often known as a **practice effect**—your score does not change because of anything you have done other than repeating the test.

For example, the people who run the testing services for the two major college entrance exams (ACT and SAT) acknowledge the existence of testing effects when they recommend that you take their tests two or three times in order to achieve your maximum possible score. It appears that there is some "learning to take a college entrance exam" behavior that contributes to your score on such tests. This factor is separate from what the test is designed to measure (your potential for doing college work). Thus, those in charge are not surprised when your scores increase a little when you take the exam a second time; they actually expect an increase simply because you are familiar with the test and how it is given. However, two points about this specific testing effect are important to note. First, the effect is short-lived. You can expect to gain some points on a second (and perhaps third) attempt, but you will not continue to gain points indefinitely just from the practice of taking the test. If improvement were constant, students could "max out" their scores merely by taking the test many times. Second, the expected improvement is small. Both the ACT and SAT administrators have a range of expected improvement that they consider normal. If you retake one of their tests and improve more than this normal range predicts, it is possible that your score will be questioned. You may be asked to provide documentation that accounts for your surprising improvement. If this documentation is not convincing, you may be asked to retake the test under their supervision. Unfortunately, the pressure to obtain scholarships (academic as well as athletic) has led some people to try to improve their scores through cheating or other unethical means.

Reactive measures   DV measurements that actually change the DV being measured.

In his discussion of testing effects, Campbell (1957) warned us against using **reactive measures** in our research. A measurement that is reactive changes the behavior in question simply by measuring it (see Chapter 4). Let us refresh your memory with an example. One popular topic for social psychology research is attitude change. If you are going to conduct an experiment on attitudes and attitude change, how will you measure your participants' attitudes? If you are like most people, you probably responded, "With an attitude questionnaire."

Although questionnaires are commonly used to measure attitudes, they have a significant drawback. Can you figure out what this drawback is? Hint: This problem is particularly evident when you want to use an IV designed to change people's attitudes. Can you think of a means for overcoming this difficulty?

Many attitude questionnaires are reactive measures. If we ask you a number of questions about how you feel about people of different racial groups, or about women's rights, or about the President's job performance, you can probably figure out that your attitude is being measured. The problem with knowing that your attitude is being measured is that you can alter your answers on a questionnaire in any way you wish. For example, if a woman administers a questionnaire to you, you may give answers that make you appear more sympathetic to women's issues. If the questioner is of a different race than you, you may guard against giving answers that would make you look prejudiced. This type of problem is particularly acute if we use an experimental manipulation designed to change your attitude. If we give you a questionnaire about women's rights, then show you a pro-women's rights movie, and finally give you the questionnaire again, it doesn't take a rocket scientist to figure out that we're interested in finding out how the movie changed your attitude toward women's rights! What can you do to avoid this problem in your research?

Campbell (1957) advocated using **nonreactive measures** that do not alter the participant's response by virtue of measuring it. Psychologists (and others) have devised many tools and techniques for nonreactive measures—one-way mirrors, hidden cameras and microphones, naturalistic observation, deception, and so on (see Chapter 4). If we are interested in your attitude about women's rights, perhaps we should see whether you attend women's rights lectures or donate money to women's issues, ask whether you voted for a political candidate who supports women's rights, or measure some other such behavior. In other words, if we can obtain some type of behavioral measure that is harder to fake than a questionnaire response, we may get a truer measure of your attitude. As a psychology student doing research, you should guard against using reactive measures, which are often appealing because they seem so easy to use.

> **Nonreactive measures**
> DV measurements that do not influence the DV being measured.

Instrumentation (Instrument Decay)   As with maturation, Campbell's category of instrumentation has a broader meaning than is implied by its name. Part of Campbell's (1957) description of **instrumentation** referred to changes in measurement by various apparatuses, although his list now seems quite outdated (e.g., "the fatiguing of a spring scales, or the condensation of water vapor in a cloud chamber," p. 299). However, he also included human observers, judges, raters, and

> **Instrumentation**   A threat to internal validity that occurs if the equipment or human measuring the DV changes the measuring criterion over time.

coders in this category. Thus, the broad definition of instrumentation refers to changes in measurement of the DV that are due to the measuring "device," whether that device is an actual piece of equipment or a human.

This measurement problem related to equipment is probably less of an issue today than it was in "the good old days." (By the way, "the good old days" are probably defined as whenever your professor was in school.) We're sure your instructor has a horror story about the time the equipment broke down in the middle of an important day of data collection. The reality of the situation is that even today equipment can break down or can develop flaws in measurement. You should always check out your equipment before using it to collect data each day. One of the drawbacks of modern equipment, such as computers, is that it may break down, but that fact will not be obvious to you. Although you can certainly tell whether or not a computer is working, you may not be able to tell if it appears to be working but actually has a bug or a virus. A careful experimenter checks out the equipment each day.

The same principle should govern your use of humans as monitors or scorers in your experiment. Often, you may serve as both the experimenter and the monitor or scorer for your experiment. This dual role places an extra obligation on you to be fair, impartial, and consistent in your behavior. For example, if you are scoring responses from your participants, you should have a set answer key with any judgment calls you might face worked out beforehand. So that you will not unconsciously favor one group over the other, you should score the responses blind as to which group a participant belongs to. If you have other persons scoring or monitoring your experiment, you should check their performance regularly to ensure that they remain consistent. Researchers often calculate interrater reliability (see Chapter 4) to determine if instrumentation is a problem in a research project.

Statistical Regression   You may remember the concept of statistical regression from your statistics course. When you deal with extreme scores, it is likely that you will see *regression to the mean*. This concept merely means that if you remeasure participants who have extreme scores (either high or low), their subsequent scores are likely to regress or move toward the mean. The subsequent scores are still likely to be extreme in the same direction, but not as extreme. For example, if you made a very high *A* (or very low *F*) on the first exam, your second exam score will probably not be as high (or as low). If a 7'0" basketball player has a son, the son will probably be tall but will probably be shorter than 7'0". If a 4'6" jockey has a son, the son will probably be short, but taller than 4'6". When you have extreme scores, it is simply difficult to maintain that high degree of extremity over repeated measures.

Statistical regression
A threat to internal validity that occurs when low scorers improve or high scorers fall on a second administration of a test due solely to statistical reasons.

How does **statistical regression** play a role in internal validity? It is fairly common to measure participants before an experiment in order to divide them into IV groups (based on whatever was measured). For example, imagine an experiment designed to test the effects of a study course for college entrance exams. As a preliminary measure, we give an ACT or SAT test to a large group of high school students. From this pool of students, we plan to select our experimental participants to take the study course. Which students are we likely to select? Why, of course, the ones who performed poorly on the test. After they take the study course, we have them retake the entrance exam. More than likely, we will find that their new scores are higher than the original scores. Why is this? Did the study course help the students improve their scores? It is certainly possible. However, isn't it also possible that regression to the mean is at work? When you score near the low end of a test's possible score, there's not room to do much except improve. Sometimes it is difficult for people to see this point—they are convinced that the study course must be responsible for the improvement. To help illustrate the power of statistical regression, imagine a similar experiment performed with students who made the highest scores on the entrance exams. We want them to take our study course also. After our study course, we find that their second test scores are actually lower than the first set! Did our study course lower their scores? We certainly hope not. Having made extremely high scores on the first test, students find it difficult to improve on the second.

The advice concerning statistical regression should be clear. If you select participants on the basis of extreme scores, you should beware of regression to the mean as a possible explanation for higher or lower scores on a repeated (or similar) test.

Selection   It should come as no surprise to you that **selection** can serve as a threat to internal validity. Before we conduct our experiment, it is imperative that we can assume that our selected groups are equivalent. Starting with equal groups, we treat them identically except for the IV. Then if the groups are no longer equal after the experiment, we can assume that the IV caused that difference.

> **Selection**   A threat to internal validity; if we choose participants in such a way that our groups are not equal before the experiment, we cannot be certain that our IV caused any difference we observe after the experiment.

Suppose, however, that when we select our participants, we do so in such a way that the groups are *not* equal before the experiment. In such a case, differences that we observe between our groups after the experiment may actually reflect differences that existed *before* the experiment began. On the other hand, differences after the experiment may reflect differences that existed *before* the experiment plus a treatment effect. Group differences that existed before the experiment are an extraneous variable, and the experiment is confounded.

Be careful not to confuse the selection problem with assignment of participants to groups. Selection typically refers to using participants who are already assigned to a particular group by virtue of their group membership. Campbell and Stanley (1966) cited the example of comparing people who watched a particular TV program to those who did not. People who choose to watch a program or not to watch a program probably differ in ways other than the knowledge of the program content. For example, it is likely that there are differences in people who watch and those who do not watch soap operas that are unrelated to the actual content of the soap operas. Thus, using soap opera viewers and non–soap opera viewers as groups to study the impact of a particular soap opera episode dealing with rape is probably not the best way to study the impact of that episode.

Mortality   As you might guess, "death" is the original meaning of *mortality* in this context. In research that exposes animals to stress, chemicals, or other toxic agents, mortality could actually occur in significant numbers. Mortality could become a threat to internal validity if a treatment were so severe that significant numbers of animals in the treatment group died. Simply because they had survived, the remaining animals in the treatment group would probably be different in some

> **Mortality**   A threat to internal validity that can occur if experimental participants from different groups drop out of the experiment at different rates.

"Today is the final session of our lab on rats, and Willy, I don't think I have to remind you that this time if you eat yours, I'm not giving you another one."

We certainly hope that you never experience this type of mortality in your research!

way from the animals in the other groups. Although the other groups would still represent random samples, those in the particular treatment group would not.

In human research, **mortality** typically refers to experimental dropouts. Remember the ethical principle from Chapter 3 that gives participants the right to withdraw from an experiment at any point without penalty. A situation somewhat analogous to the animal example in the preceding paragraph could occur if many participants from one group withdraw from the experiment compared to small numbers from other groups. If such a differential dropout rate occurs, it is doubtful that the groups of participants would still be equal, as they were before the experiment began.

If your experiment contains a treatment condition that is unpleasant, demanding, or noxious in any way, you should pay careful attention to the dropout rate for the various groups. Differential dropout rates could also be a significant problem in research that spans a long time (weeks or months, for example). If one group shows a higher rate, your experiment may lack internal validity. One final word of caution: It is possible that groups in your experiment will not show different rates of dropping out but will have previously experienced different rates that helped compose the groups. Campbell (1957) cited the example of a very common experiment in educational settings, namely, making comparisons of different classes. Suppose we wish to determine whether our college's values-based education actually affects the values of the students. We choose a sample of freshmen and a sample of seniors and give them a questionnaire to measure their values in order to see whether their values are in line with our general education curriculum's values goals.

How might previous dropout rates damage the internal validity of this experiment?

In this experiment it should not surprise you to find that the seniors' values are more in line with our college's stated values. Although this effect *could* be a result of taking our values-based curriculum, it could also represent the effect of mortality through dropouts. Most colleges bring in large numbers of freshmen and graduate only some percentage of those students a few years later. What types of students are more likely to leave? Probably students whose values are not in line with the college's values are more likely to drop out than those who agree with the college's values. Thus, when we assess seniors' values, we are measuring those students who did *not* drop out.

Interactions with Selection   **Interactions with selection** can occur when the groups we have selected show differences on another variable (i.e., maturation, history, or instrumentation) that vary systematically by groups. Let us give you an example for clarification. Suppose we are conducting a language development study in which we select our two groups from lower- and middle-class families. We wish to avoid selection as a threat to internal validity, so we pretest our children with a language test to ensure that our groups are equivalent beforehand. However, this pretesting could not account for the possibility that these two groups may show different maturation patterns, despite the fact that

> **Interactions with selection**   Threats to internal validity that can occur if there are systematic differences between or among selected treatment groups based on maturation, history, or instrumentation.

they are equal before the experiment begins. For example, if we look at children around the age of 1, we may find that the two classes of children show no language differences. However, by age 2, middle-class children might have larger vocabularies, talk more often, or have other linguistic advantages over lower-class children. Then if we look at children who are 6, these linguistic advantages may disappear. If this were the case, comparing lower- and middle-class children's language proficiency at age 2 would show a selection–maturation interaction that would pose a threat to internal validity. Although one group of children would show an advantage over another group, the difference would not be a reliable, lasting difference. Therefore, any conclusion we reached that implied the permanence of such an effect would be invalid because the difference would have been based on different maturation schedules of the two groups.

Similar interaction effects could occur between selection and history or between selection and instrumentation. A selection–history interaction that would jeopardize internal validity could occur if you chose your different groups from different settings—for example,

> **Diffusion** or **imitation of treatment** A threat to internal validity that can occur if participants in one treatment group become familiar with the treatment of another group and copy that treatment.

different countries, states, cities, or even schools within a city. This problem is especially acute in cross-cultural research (see Chapter 7). These different settings allow for different local histories (Cook & Campbell, 1979) that might affect the outcome variable(s). The selection and history are confounded together because the groups were selected on a basis that allows different histories. An example of a selection–instrumentation interaction (based on human "instrumentation") would be using different interpreters or scorers for participants that come from two different countries, assuming the IV was related to the country of origin.

Diffusion or Imitation of Treatments **Diffusion** or **imitation of treatments** creates a problem with internal validity by negating or minimizing the difference between the groups in your experiment. This problem can occur easily if your treatment involves providing some information to participants in one group but not to participants in another group. If the informed participants communicate the vital information to the supposedly uninformed participants, then the two groups may behave in identical manners.

If these two groups behave identically, what experimental conclusion would you draw? What would be wrong with this conclusion ?

If the participants behave identically, the experimental outcome would indicate no difference between the groups based on the IV. The problem with this conclusion is that in truth, there would actually be no IV in the experiment because the IV was supposed to have been the difference in information between groups. It is typical for experimenters to request that participants not discuss details of the experiment until it is completed.

Experiments dealing with learning and memory are particularly susceptible to the imitation of treatments. For example, suppose we want to teach students in our classes a new, more effective study strategy. To simplify the experiment, we will use our 9:00 A.M. general psychology class as a control group and our 10:00 A.M. general psychology class as the experimental group. We teach the 9:00 A.M. class as usual, saying nothing to the students about how they should study for their quizzes and exams. In the 10:00 A.M. class, however, we teach our new study technique. After the first few quizzes and the first major exam, the students in the 10:00 A.M. class are so convinced of the effectiveness of their new study approach that they talk to their friends in the 9:00 A.M. class about it. Soon everyone in the 9:00 A.M. class knows about the new study technique and is also using it faithfully. At this point, we have the problem of treatment diffusion. Our participants in both groups are now using the same study strategy, which effectively no longer gives us an IV. It should be obvious that if you cannot guarantee control over the IV, the hope of having an experiment with internal validity is not strong.

Protecting Internal Validity

There are two approaches you could take to fight the various threats to internal validity. First, you can (and should) implement the various control procedures that we have discussed in this chapter. These controls were specifically developed to deal with such problems. The second approach involves the use of a standard procedure. Just as detectives use standard police procedures to help them protect their cases, experimenters use standard research procedures, called experimental designs, to help ensure internal validity. We will have more to say about several experimental designs in subsequent chapters.

How important is internal validity? *It is the most important property of any experiment.* If you do not concern yourself with the internal validity of your experiment, you are wasting your time. Experiments are intended to derive cause-and-effect statements—to conclude that *X* causes *Y* to occur. You must take care to control any extraneous variables that might affect your dependent variable. You cannot count on your statistical tests to provide the necessary control functions for you. Statistical tests merely analyze the numbers you bring to the test—they do not have the ability to remove confounding effects (or even to discern that confounding has occurred) in your data.

REVIEW SUMMARY

1. For your experiment to have **internal validity**, it must be free from confounding due to extraneous variables.

2. There are nine specific threats to internal validity that we must guard against.

3. The **history** threat can occur if meaningful events that would affect the DV occur between two measurements of the DV (repeated measures).

4. The **maturation** threat may occur if experimental participants show some change due to time passage during an experiment.

5. The **testing** threat results if participants respond differently on the second measure of a DV simply because they have previously responded to the DV.

6. An **instrumentation** threat can refer to equipment changes or malfunctions or to human observers whose criteria change over time.

7. **Statistical regression** is a threat that can occur when participants are selected because of their extreme scores on some variable. Extreme scores are likely to regress toward the mean on a second measurement.

8. The **selection** threat results if we select groups of participants in such a way that our groups are not equal before the experiment.

9. **Mortality** becomes a threat if participants drop out of the experiment at different rates for different conditions.

10. **Interactions with selection** can occur for history, maturation, or instrumentation. If we select participants in such a way that they vary on these dimensions, then internal validity is threatened.

11. **Diffusion** or **imitation of treatments** is a threat if participants learn about treatments of other groups and copy them.

CHECK YOUR PROGRESS

1. Changing a behavior simply by measuring it refers to
   a. a reactive measure   b. a measured IV
   c. a manipulated IV   d. history

2. Comparing intact groups is likely to cause a problem because of
   a. mortality   b. selection   c. maturation   d. history

3. Why is it important to evaluate your experiment for internal validity?

4. Match the internal validity threat with the appropriate situation.

   1. history
   2. maturation
   3. testing
   4. instrumentation

   A. Your DV scorer gets sick and you recruit a new person to help you.
   B. You are conducting an experiment on racial prejudice and a race riot occurs between tests.
   C. Your participants grow bored and disinterested during your experimental sessions.
   D. You use a before-and-after DV measurement and the participants remember some of their answers.

5. Match the threat to internal validity with the correct situation.

   1. statistical regression
   2. mortality
   3. selection
   4. diffusion of treatments

   A. Many participants find one treatment condition very boring and quit.
   B. You select boys from lower-class homes and girls from upper-class environments.
   C. Students in your control group talk to students in the experimental group and imitate their treatment.
   D. You select the worst students in the class and try a new tutoring strategy.

6. You want to compare the formal education of college students and senior citizens. You select a group of each type of participant and give each a written test of math, social studies, and grammatical information. What threat of internal validity appears likely in this situation? Why?

7. Experimental dropouts are a problem linked to
   a. mortality   b. selection   c. maturation   d. history

KEY TERMS

LOOKING AHEAD

In this chapter we have explored the nature of variables in general and have seen the importance of selecting appropriate IVs and DVs. The potentially damaging effects of nuisance variables and confounders have led to the development of procedures for their control. We continue our examination of the basics of experimentation in the next chapter. There we will discuss the selection of appropriate types and numbers of participants and the actual collection of research data.

The Basics of Experimentation II: Final Considerations, Unanticipated Influences, and Cross-Cultural Issues

In the previous chapters we dealt with such topics as sources of research ideas, conducting a literature review, formulating the research hypothesis, the role of ethics in research, and the nature of variables and their control. In this chapter we continue our discussion of research basics by considering the type and number of participants to be used, the type of apparatus or testing equipment that will be employed, whether the experimenter or participants may be extraneous variables, and the cross-cultural implications of research.

Participants

Both the type and the number of participants to be used are important considerations in the formulation of an experiment.

Types of Participants

A moment's reflection will indicate a wide variety of organisms can serve as participants in a psychological experiment. For example, animal researchers might choose from bumblebees, flies, dolphins, chimpanzees, elephants, rats, and so on. Likewise, researchers dealing with humans might choose as their participants infants, young adults, the aged, the gifted, the handicapped, or the maladjusted, among many others. The range of participants for your research project may be overwhelming. Which one represents the best choice? Considering three things can help you answer this question: *precedent, availability*, and the *nature of the problem*.

Precedent   If your literature review indicates that a particular type of participant has been used successfully in prior research projects in your area of interest, then you may want to consider using this type of participant. For example, when Willard S. Small (1901) conducted the first rat

> **Precedent**   An established pattern.

study in the United States, he began a **precedent**, an established pattern, that continues to this day. Likewise, the precedent for using college students (especially those enrolled in introductory psychology) has a venerable history. For example, research in the area of human memory and cognitive processes relies heavily on projects conducted with college students. How strong is this reliance? We selected a copy of the *Journal of Experimental Psychology: Learning, Memory and Cognition* (Vol. 24, No. 4, July 1998) at random and examined it. There were 15 articles published in this issue, with 12 reporting results from experiments that used college students exclusively as participants, whereas 3 reported using paid volunteers/participants who may have been college students. It is noteworthy that in many of the articles using college students, the participants were drawn from a subject pool or participated in order to receive partial course credit.

Such precedents for the selection of participants have their advantages and disadvantages. What are they?

The fact that a particular type of participant has been used repeatedly in psychological research ensures that a body of knowledge exists about that type of participant. Researchers can take advantage of this wealth of knowledge as they plan their own research. They can implement already validated procedures without expending hours of exploratory testing and designing new equipment. Being able to draw on this body of already proven techniques means the *likelihood of success* (see Chapter 2) is increased.

However, the continual use of one type or species of participant can limit the generalizability of the information that is gathered (see the discussion of external validity in Chapter 13). For example, although the study of self-esteem in college students may tell us about this trait in that group, it may not tell us much about self-esteem in the general population. Likewise, although the choice to use white rats in an experiment may be prompted by the extensive literature that already exists on this animal, additional rat studies may not provide any useful information about other species.

Availability   The continued use of white rats and college students also stems from another source, their availability. White rats are relatively inexpensive, at least compared to many other animals, and are easy to maintain. Likewise, college students, especially those students enrolled in introductory psychology classes, constitute an easily accessible population from which to draw participants. For example, in his study of male and female differences in altruism (unselfishly helping another person), Nicholas Schroeppel, a student at the University of Nebraska in Lincoln, and his faculty advisor, Gustavo Carlo, administered questionnaires to college students (Schroeppel & Carlo, 2001). Likewise, college students served as participants in the study by Burkley et al. (2000) on the effect of the wording of the informed consent document (see Chapter 3). The researchers could have selected participants from the general population for both of these experiments; however, they used college students because they were available. In addition to their availability, college students are inexpensive participants because researchers do not usually pay them for their participation. At some institutions participation in a research project may be a course requirement, thus ensuring the ready availability of research participants. However, availability does not guarantee that the researcher selected the best or most appropriate participants.

Clearly, availability of one type of participant may discourage the use of others. In turn, we have seen that developing a large body of knowledge about a particular type of participant can result in pressures to use that participant in future research projects. Obviously, the problem can easily become circular. The precedent for using one type of participant is established and leads to the development of an extensive literature concerning that type of participant, which further encourages the use of that type of participant.

Type of Research Project   Often the nature of your research project will determine the type of participant you decide to use. For example, if you are interested in studying the visual ability of birds of prey, you are limited to studying birds such as eagles, vultures, hawks, and owls; ducks, geese, and songbirds are not predators. Likewise, if you want to study hallucinations and delusions, then you have limited your choice of potential participants to humans who are able to communicate and who experience those phenomena.

Consider the research project conducted by Molly Claus (2000), a student at Nebraska Wesleyan University in Lincoln. She was interested in studying the relation between toy preferences and assertiveness. The nature of this research question dictated that she use children as participants; she studied preschoolers. Her research indicated that children who played with masculine toys (e.g., trucks and blocks) were more assertive than children who chose to play with feminine toys (e.g., a tea set).

Number of Participants

Once you have decided what type of participant to use in your research project, you must then determine how many participants you are going to test. In making this decision, there are numerous factors that you must take into account:

1. **Finances.**   How much will it cost to test each participant? Animals must be purchased and cared for. It may be necessary to pay humans for their participation. Does the person who actually conducts the experiment need to be paid? If so, this cost also must be considered; it will rise as you test additional participants.

2. **Time.**   As you test additional participants, time requirements will increase, especially if you test participants individually.

3. **Availability.**   The sheer number of participants that are available may influence how many you choose to use in your experiment.

In addition to these more practical considerations, there is another factor that enters into our determination of the number of participants we will use. This factor is the amount of variability we expect to be present within each group. The less the *within-group* variability (i.e., the more homogeneous the participants), the fewer participants we will need. Conversely, the greater the *within-group* variability (i.e., the more heterogeneous the participants), the greater the number of participants we will need.

What is the reasoning behind these statements about variability and the number of participants to be tested in an experiment? In thinking about this question, you may want to review the material on nuisance variables (see Chapter 6).

When a nuisance variable, in this case the heterogeneous nature of the participants, is present, the scores within each group spread out considerably and the amount of group overlap is increased. The variability of the scores makes it more difficult to see absolute differences between the groups. One way to de-emphasize these extreme scores is to test more participants. By increasing the number of scores (i.e., participants), we should increase the number of scores that cluster in the center of the distribution and, therefore, decrease the impact of the extreme scores. When nuisance variables are not present (i.e., the groups are more homogeneous), there are fewer extreme scores and the differences between the groups can be seen more clearly.

As you saw in Chapter 5, another way to create more homogeneous groups is to use stratified random sampling. By sampling a more specific type of participant, we remove extremes from our sample. We will have more to say about the number of observations and variability in the next chapter.

The number of participants tested is related to the power of our statistical test. **Power** is the likelihood (probability) that the statistical test will be significant (i.e., the experimental hypothesis is accepted when it is true). Generally speaking, the greater the number of participants, the higher the power of your statistical test. So, it is to your advantage to use as many participants as possible under the specific constraints of your research. Statistics books routinely discuss power and present formulas and tables that will aid you in determining the number of participants you will need to test in order to achieve significance.

> **Power** The probability that a statistical test will be significant (i.e., the experimental hypothesis is accepted when it is true).

You should also use your literature review as a guideline concerning the number of participants you need to use in your experiment. If previous studies in your area have successfully employed a certain number of participants, then you can assume you will need to test a comparable number. For example, based on precedent, Kimberly Kiker (2001), a student at the University of Florida in Gainesville, chose to use 20 first-grade school children and 20 third-grade schoolchildren in her research on measurement errors in young children. However, if you are conducting a project in an area that has not received much research attention, then you will want to test as many participants as possible given your financial, time, and availability constraints.

Apparatus

While you are deciding on the number and type of participants to be used in your research, you also need to consider the type of apparatus, if any, you will be using. It is possible to use apparatus for both presenting the IV and recording the DV.

IV Presentation

Often the nature of the IV will influence the type of apparatus you choose to use. For example, Michael Jones (2001), a student at Lincoln Memorial University in Harrogate, Tennessee, was interested in studying the effects of noise and sex of participant on recall and spatial task (completing a block design) performance of children between 9 and 11 years old. He presented unstructured white noise (static) or a popular song to groups of children. His experiment dictated that he use audio equipment. He recorded the popular song on a continuous-loop tape that played the same song over and over. He presented the song and the white noise at exactly 74 decibels (dB), as measured by a digital sound meter. The results of this study indicated that participants in the white noise condition performed better on both tasks than did the group of children who heard the popular song.

The possible ways you can present the IV are limited by the type of IV you are manipulating, by finances, and by your own ingenuity. Clearly, the presentation of certain types of IVs requires specialized equipment. For example, the administration of a particular type of light will require a specialized projector. On the other hand, presenting food to a hungry rat that has learned to press a lever does not have to involve the purchase of an expensive Skinner box or a food-pellet dispenser. We have seen very effective handmade Skinner boxes and

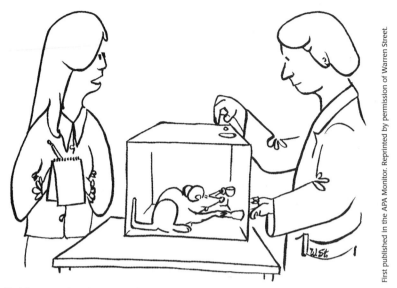

First published in the APA Monitor. Reprinted by permission of Warren Street.

"Besides operant equipment, Professor, have the federal cutbacks hurt you?"

Although large research laboratories may require extensive funds and elaborate equipment, you can conduct meaningful research on a limited budget with little or no fancy equipment.

food-delivery systems. For example, a sturdy cardboard box works just fine in place of a commercial Skinner box. What about the lever? No problem. Anything that protrudes into the box that the rat can learn to press or touch will work fine. In fact, some students have simply drawn a circle on one wall and required that the rat touch it with its nose before food is delivered. A piece of plastic tubing can serve as the food-delivery system. Simply fasten the tubing to the outside of the box so that one end is at the top and the other end enters the box near the bottom and is situated over a small dish. Dropping a piece of food down the tube results in a reinforcer being delivered into the food dish in the box. Some creative thought at this stage of planning can often save you substantial amounts of money.

DV Recording

Although recording evidence at the scene of a crime in great detail may be a major concern to the detective, recording the DV is such a fundamental task that it sometimes is taken for granted or overlooked by the psychologist. However, there are problems and options to be addressed. Recall the naturalistic observation research on glancing behavior at ATM machines that we discussed in Chapter 2. We noted that it was important for the observers to be inconspicuous, even when recording data. To accomplish this objective, the researchers constructed a special data sheet "to facilitate the recording of participant age, sex, ethnicity, and glancing behavior as well as the number of bystanders waiting behind the participant, the stop distance of the participant, and the occurrence of any verbal contact between the participant and the bystander" (Gibson et al., 2000, p. 150). Certainly the researchers would have had a more complete record to review if they had recorded the behaviors on video-tape; however, it is quite likely that the presence of video equipment would have changed the behaviors of the participants. An efficient data sheet that was the same for all participants met their needs perfectly.

Although technologically sophisticated equipment can be beneficial in conducting research, there are potential drawbacks associated with its use. What are some of these drawbacks?

Whether presenting the IV or recording the DV, the experimenter should not become a slave to the equipment that is available. Just because you have access to a certain piece of equipment does not mean that you must use it. If a handheld stopwatch provides data equivalent to or better than what can be obtained with an elaborate computer setup, the experimenter should prefer the less elaborate equipment. If researchers begin to rely too heavily on their equipment, the choice of research problems may start to be dictated by the equipment, not by the researchers' creativity. In such situations there is more concern for the stimuli that can be presented by the equipment than there is for the problem that is being investigated. Also, elaborate equipment requires the researcher to dedicate sufficient funds for appropriate maintenance. Consider the problems you would face if your research depended on a particular piece of equipment that was broken and you had no funds to pay for its repair.

In some instances a good pair of eyes may be your best equipment. Consider the following exchange between Sherlock Holmes and Dr. Watson:

> "What can you learn from this battered old felt?" Watson asks Holmes. "Here is my lens. You know the methods."
> "I can see nothing."
> "On the contrary, Watson, you can see everything." (Doyle, 1927, p. 246)

REVIEW SUMMARY

1. **Precedent**, availability, and the nature of the problem are factors that influence the choice of participants to use in psychological research.
2. The number of participants used in a research project will be determined by financial considerations, time constraints, and participant availability.
3. The use of homogeneous groups of participants allows the experimenter to test smaller groups, whereas heterogeneous groups dictate using more participants.
4. Automated equipment can be used for IV presentation and DV recording, but often quality data can be recorded with less sophisticated equipment.

1. Explain the relation between precedent and the type of participant used in a research project.
2. Why are white rats and college students the favorite participants in psychological research?
3. Group homogeneity is best associated with
   a. testing a larger number of participants
   b. testing a smaller number of participants
   c. multiple-strata sampling
   d. nonrandom sampling
4. One of the best guidelines for the number of participants to use in a successful research project is
   a. cost   b. availability   c. past research   d. type of IV presentation
5. You would like to assess the effects of trauma in people's lives but have ethical problems with causing traumatic events to occur to people. You have a problem with
   a. IV presentation   b. IV recording   c. DV presentation   d. DV recording
6. Describe the concern the experimenter must be aware of when using automated equipment to present the IV or the DV.

Although you may believe that you are ready to move forward with your research project, we still have some preliminary issues to deal with. Just as the good detective is careful, precise, and thorough, researchers cannot exercise too much care in developing their experiments. In the following sections we highlight two potential extraneous variables that often go overlooked: the experimenter and the participant. As the science of psychology has matured, researchers have paid increasing attention to these factors.

The Experimenter as an Extraneous Variable

Just as the characteristics of the detective can influence the responses of the suspects who are questioned, several aspects of the experimenter can influence the responses of the participant (Rosenthal, 1976). First we explore experimenter characteristics; then we will consider experimenter expectancies.

Experimenter Characteristics

Both physiological and psychological attributes of the experimenter can influence the outcome of your research. Physiological characteristics include such variables as age, sex, and race. Research has shown that each of these variables can have an influence on participants' responses. For example, Robert Rosenthal (1977) has shown that male experimenters are more friendly to their participants than female experimenters are.

If all participants in an experiment are tested by the same experimenter, then constancy (see Chapter 6) is established and this extraneous variable is controlled. If such control is exercised, why are experimenter characteristics, such as age, sex, and race, of potential concern?

Even though constancy is achieved by having one experimenter conduct the research project, it is possible the experimenter will influence the participants in a unique manner. Perhaps the friendliness of a male experimenter will encourage all participants to perform at a very high level, thus making the differences between the treatment groups less evident. Hence, problems can arise when one attempts to compare the results of similar research projects conducted by different experimenters. If these projects yield different results, you cannot be sure if the differences are attributable to differences in the IV or to effects created by the different experimenters.

Psychological attributes of the experimenter that can influence the results of an experiment include personality characteristics such as hostility, anxiety, and introversion or extraversion. An experiment conducted by an experimenter who is highly anxious is likely to yield different results than an experiment conducted by a confident, self-assured experimenter. The same is true for other personality characteristics.

Experimenter Expectancies

In addition to physiological and psychological characteristics, the experimenter's expectations concerning the participants' behavior can, and do, affect performance. The experimenter's expectations cause him or her to behave toward the participants in such a manner that the expected response is, indeed, more likely shown. The experimenter is literally a cause of the desired or expected response.

Are experimenter expectancies best categorized as extraneous variables that can confound the experiment, or are they simply nuisance variables that serve to obscure the effects of the IV?

If experimenter expectancy is operating in your experiment, you cannot tell whether your results are due to the influence of the IV or experimenter expectancy; hence they are best labeled as confounders.

Such effects have been demonstrated in both human and animal experiments. One of the most widely cited studies of the effects of human experimenter expectancy involved the IQ scores of grade-school children (Rosenthal & Jacobson, 1968). At the start of the school year all children in the classes that were studied took an IQ test. Then, several children in each class were randomly selected and their respective teachers were told that these children were "intellectual bloomers." Several months later, when all the children retook the IQ test, the IQ scores of the intellectual bloomers had increased more than those of the other children. Because the intellectual bloomers were randomly selected, it is doubtful that they were intellectually superior. However, they were perceived in this manner and were treated differently by the teachers. In turn, these students responded in accordance with the teachers' expectations.

Experimenter expectancy is not limited just to studies of humans; even rats will perform in accordance with what the experimenter anticipates. Rosenthal and Fode (1963) told half the students in a class that the rats they were going to train were "maze bright"; the remainder of the students were told that their rats were "maze dull." In actuality, there were no differences among the rats at the start of the project. However, the results were consistent with the students' expectations: The "smart" rats learned the maze better and more quickly than did the "dumb" rats. Because the rats did not differ at the start of training, this study clearly highlights the strong effects that experimenter expectancies can have on participants' performance. Because Rosenthal and his colleagues were among the first to systematically study experimenter expectations, the results of such expectations are often called **Rosenthal effects**.

> **Rosenthal effect** The experimenter's preconceived idea of appropriate responding influences the treatment of participants and their behavior.

Controlling Experimenter Effects

Physiological and Psychological Effects   The reason that experimenters have traditionally paid little attention to these variables may be clear by now: They are difficult to control. For example, to achieve constancy, *all* these characteristics would have to be measured in *all* potential experimenters and then the choice of experimenters would be determined by the level of each factor that was desired—a difficult, if not impossible, task. Likewise, we saw in Chapter 6 that balancing can be used to avoid confounding due to the sex of the experimenter. Although this control technique equates the groups for experimenter sex, it does not simultaneously control for other physiological and psychological characteristics. At present the most common procedures for controlling general experimenter characteristics are to (1) use standardized methods, (2) use careful training to a set standard when the experimenter administers procedures, and (3) standardize appearance, attitude, and so forth as much as possible. Replicating your research also provides a good check on possible experimenter effects; if you replicate the findings with a different experimenter, then experimenter effects are less likely to be a factor. A thorough literature review will help make you aware of any relevant experimenter variables in your area of research interest.

Experimenter Expectancies   There are several things that can be done to reduce, or possibly eliminate, experimenter expectancies. First, the instructions that the experimenter gives to the participants should be carefully prepared so their manner of presentation will not influence the participants' responses. Likewise, any instructions concerning scoring the participants' responses should be as objective and concrete as possible and established before the experiment is started. If these instructions are subjective, then there is room for experimenter expectancies to dictate how they will be scored.

A second method for controlling experimenter expectancies involves the use of instrumentation and automation. For example, instructions to participants may be tape-recorded prior to experimental testing in order to reduce any influences the experimenter might have. In many instances, potential influences of the experimenter are eliminated through the use of printed instructions or computer displays. Also, automated equipment can ensure the accurate recording and storage of response data. In some instances the participants' responses are entered directly at a computer terminal and thus are stored and ready for analysis at any time.

Single-blind experiment
An experiment in which the experimenter (or participants) is unaware of the treatment the participants are receiving.

A third method for minimizing experimenter expectancies is to conduct a single-blind experiment. The **single-blind experiment** keeps the experimenter in the dark regarding which participants receive which treatment(s). (As we will see, this procedure can be used to control participant effects as well.) For example, suppose you are conducting an experiment testing the effects of different descriptions of an individual's degree of altruism on the amount of warmth that individual is perceived to possess. Quite likely the different written descriptions will be printed in such a way that they all have the same appearance (constancy). If these different descriptions have the same demographic cover sheet, then all materials will appear to be identical. If another experimenter is in charge of determining which participants read which descriptions and arranging the order in which to distribute the testing materials to the participants, then the experimenter who actually conducts the research sessions will not know which descriptions are being read by which participants at any session, and therefore experimenter expectancies cannot influence the participants' responses. The single-blind procedure can also be used effectively when the IV consists of some type of chemical compound, whether it be in tablet or injection form. If all tablets or injections have the same physical appearance, the experimenter will be unaware of which participants are receiving the active compound and which participants are receiving a placebo. The experimenter truly does not know what treatment condition is being administered in single-blind experiments of this nature.

Participant Perceptions as Extraneous Variables

Just as the experimenter can unintentionally influence the results of an experiment, so can the participants. As you will see, there are numerous aspects of the participants' perception of the research project that can operate as extraneous variables and nuisance variables.

Demand Characteristics and Good Participants

Demand characteristics
Features of the experiment that inadvertently lead participants to respond in a particular manner.

If you have ever served as a participant in a psychological experiment, you know that most participants believe they are supposed to behave in a certain manner. As we have seen, the cues that participants use to guide their behavior may come from the experimenter; they may also be part of the experimental context or IV manipulation. When participants use these cues to determine what the experimenter's hypothesis is and how they are supposed to act, the cues are referred to as the **demand characteristics** of the experiment (Orne, 1962). In short, participants in psychological research may attempt to figure out how they are supposed to respond and then behave in this manner. The desire to cooperate and act as the

Reprinted from *The Chronicle of Higher Education*. By permission of Mischa Richter and Harold Bakken.

"Haven't we met in a previous experiment?"

It is important that participants not communicate about the nature of a psychological experiment.

participants believe the experimenter wants them to is called the **good participant effect** (Rosenthal & Rosnow, 1991).

> **Good participant effect**
> The tendency of participants to behave as they perceive the experimenter wants them to behave.

Allison Dickson, James Morris, and Keri Cass, students at Southwestern University in Georgetown, Texas, and their faculty advisor, Traci Giuliano, investigated race, stereotypes, and college students' perceptions of rap and country music performers. The "participants made judgments about either a Black or a White musician who performed either rap or country music" (Dickson, Giuliano, Morris, & Cass, 2001, p. 175). Rather than tell the participants that they were studying the effects of race and stereotypes, the researchers simply "asked them to contribute to an investigation exploring 'people's perceptions of music'" (Dickson et al., 2001, p. 177). Had they divulged the exact nature of their hypothesis, then the demand characteristics would have been quite strong and the participants might have tried to decide which group they were in and how they were expected to respond. These researchers found that the participants rated the black rap performer more favorably than the black country performer. The participants also rated the white country performer more favorably than the white rap performer.

Although experimenters have an ethical responsibility (see Chapter 3) to inform the participants about the general nature of the experiment, we have just seen that they usually do not want to reveal the exact nature of their experimental hypothesis. To do so can introduce strong demand characteristics that could influence the participants' behavior. Do demand characteristics operate as extraneous variables or nuisance variables?

Depending on how the demand characteristics are perceived, they can operate either as an extraneous or nuisance variable. If it is very clear to the participants which group they are in and how that group is expected to act, then the demand characteristics are functioning as an extraneous variable and the experiment is confounded. When the experiment is completed, the experimenter will not be able to tell whether the differences between the groups were due to the effects of the IV or the demand characteristics. If, however, the participants perceive the demand characteristics *but* are not sure which group they are in, then the demand characteristics may function as a nuisance variable. In this situation we would expect the demand characteristics to produce both increases and decreases in responding within all groups. Thus, the scores of *all* groups would spread out more.

Response Bias

Several factors can produce a response bias on the part of research participants. Here we examine such influences as yea-saying and response set.

Yea-Saying   You most likely know individuals who seem to agree with everything, even if agreeing sometimes means that they contradict themselves. We may never know whether these individuals agree because they truly believe what they are saying or because they are simply making a socially desirable response at the moment. Clearly, these individuals, known as **yea-sayers**, who say yes to all questions, pose a threat to psychological research. (Individuals who typically respond negatively to all questions are known as **nay-sayers**.) Contradicting one's own statements by answering yes (or no) to all items on a psychological inventory or test seriously threatens the validity of that participant's score.

> **Yea-sayers**   Participants who tend to answer yes to all questions.
>
> **Nay-sayers** Participants who tend to answer no to all questions.

Response Set   Sometimes the experimental context or situation in which the research is being conducted can cause participants to respond in a certain manner or have a **response set**. The effects of response set can be likened to going for a job interview: You take your cues from the interviewer and the surroundings. In some cases you will need to be highly professional, whereas in other interview situations you can be a bit more relaxed.

> **Response set**   The experimental context or testing situation influences the participants' responses.

Consider the two following descriptions of an experimenter and the testing room in which the research is being conducted. In the first instance the experimenter is wearing a tie and a white laboratory coat. The experiment is being conducted in a nicely carpeted room that has pleasing furnishings, several bookcases, and attractive plants; it looks more like an office than a research room. The second experimenter is dressed in jeans, a sweatshirt, and tennis shoes. In this case the research is being conducted in a classroom in a less-than-well-kept building. Have you already developed a response set for each of these situations? Will you be more formal and perhaps give more in-depth or scientific answers in the first situation? Even though the second situation may help put you at ease, does it seem less than scientific? Notice that our descriptions of these two situations did not make reference to the physiological or psychological characteristics of the experimenters or to the type of experiment being conducted. Hence, we are dealing with an effect that occurs in addition to experimenter and demand effects.

Likewise, the nature of the questions themselves may create a response set. For example, how questions are worded or their placement in the sequence of items may prompt a certain type of response; it may seem that a socially desirable answer is being called for. Also, it may seem that a particular alternative is called for. In such cases a response bias is developed. Clearly, response set can be a major influence on the participant's response.

Controlling Participant Effects

As we have seen, there are aspects of the participant that can affect the results of our research. Although such factors are rather difficult to control, several techniques have been developed.

Demand Characteristics   You will recall that one technique used to control for experimenter expectancies is to keep the experimenter in the dark by conducting a single-blind experiment. This same approach can be applied to the control of demand characteristics, only this time the participants will be unaware of such features as the experimental hypothesis, the true nature of the experiment, or which group they happen to be in.

> **Double-blind experiment**   An experiment in which both the experimenter and the participants are unaware of which treatment the participants are receiving.

It takes only a moment's thought to reach the conclusion that these two approaches can be combined; we can conduct an experiment in which both the experimenter and the participants are unaware of which treatment is being administered to which participants. Such experiments are known as **double-blind experiments**.

Regardless of whether a single- or double-blind experiment is conducted, it is likely that the participants will attempt to guess what the purpose of the experiment is and how they should respond. It is difficult to conceal the fact that they are participating in an experiment, and the information provided them prior to signing the informed consent document (see Chapter 3) may give the participants a general idea concerning the nature of the experiment.

Let's assume that you conduct a single- or double-blind experiment and leave your participants to their own devices to guess what the experiment is about. In this case you may be introducing an unwanted variable into your research project. Is this factor an extraneous variable or a nuisance variable? What effect(s) might it have?

It is almost certain that all participants will not correctly guess the true nature of the experiment and which group they are in. Those participants who make correct guesses may show improved performance; those participants who make incorrect guesses may have inferior performance. If the ability to correctly guess the nature of the experiment and which group one is in is comparable in all groups, then the scores within *all* groups will spread out. You have introduced a *nuisance variable* that will make it more difficult to see the differences that develop between the groups. Is there any way to avoid this problem? The answer is yes.

Another technique that can be used to control for demand characteristics is to give all participants incorrect information concerning the nature of the experiment. In short, the experimenter purposely deceives *all* the participants, thus disguising the true nature of the experiment and keeping the participants from guessing how they are supposed to respond. Although this procedure can be effective, it suffers from two drawbacks. First, we have already seen that the use of deception raises ethical problems with regard to the conduct of research. If deception is employed, a good IRB (see Chapter 3) will be careful to make sure it is a justifiable and necessary procedure. The second problem is that the information used to deceive the participants may result in erroneous guesses about the nature of the experiment; the participants are then responding to the demand characteristics created by the deception. Clearly, demand characteristics may be very difficult to control.

Yea-Saying   The most typical control for yea-saying (and nay-saying) is to rewrite some of the items so that a negative response represents agreement (control for yea-saying) or a positive response represents disagreement (control for nay-saying). Once some of the items have been rewritten, the experimenter needs to make a decision concerning the order for their presentation. All the rewritten items should not be presented as a group. One presentation strategy is to randomize the complete list, thereby presenting the original and rewritten items in an undetermined sequence. This approach works quite well with longer lists. If the list is smaller, within-subject counterbalancing can be used. Table 7-1 illustrates these two presentation styles and the use of within-subject counterbalancing.

TABLE 7-1   Controlling for Yea-Saying

The following yes-no items are based on the Type A scale developed by Friedman and Rosenman (1974). In Part A a "yes" answer is associated with the Type A personality. Yea-sayers, even though they are not Type A persons, would likely be assigned to this category with such questions. In Part B half of the items are rewritten so that a "no" answer is associated with Type A characteristics. Within-subject counterbalancing is also used with the items in Part B.

A. "Yes" answers are associated with Type A characteristics.
1. Do you play games like Monopoly to win?
2. Do you eat, speak, and walk rapidly?
3. Do you constantly schedule more activities than time allows?
4. Do you feel a sense of guilt if you try to relax?

B. Yes answers (Items 1 and 4) *and* "no" answers (Items 2 and 3) are associated with Type A characteristics. The 1(yes)−2(no)−3(no)−4(yes) sequence illustrates within-subject counterbalancing.
1. Do you play games like Monopoly to win?
2. Do you eat, speak, and walk slowly?
3. Do you constantly schedule just enough activities to fill the time available?
4. Do you feel a sense of guilt if you try to relax?

Response Set   The best safeguard against response set is to review all questions that are asked or items to be completed to see if a socially desired response is implied in any manner. The answer given or response made should reflect the participant's own feelings, attitudes, or motives rather than an attempt to appear intelligent or well-adjusted or otherwise "normal." Checking for response set offers excellent opportunities for pilot testing and interviewing of participants to determine whether the questions or behavioral tasks create a particular outlook. Additionally, you should carefully examine the nature of the experimental situation or context to avoid the presence of undesired cues.

REVIEW SUMMARY

1. Experimenter characteristics can affect the results of an experiment. Physiological experimenter characteristics include such aspects as age, sex, and race. Psychological experimenter attributes include such personality characteristics as hostility, anxiety, and introversion or extraversion.

2. Experimenter expectancies can produce behaviors in the experimenter that influence participants to make the desired response. Such experimenter expectancy effects are often called **Rosenthal effects**.

3. Because of their potential abundance, experimenter characteristics are difficult to control.

4. Experimenter expectancies can be controlled through the use of objective instructions and response-scoring procedures, as well as instrumentation and automation. A **single-blind experiment**, in which the experimenter does not know which participants are receiving which treatments, also can be used to control experimenter expectancies.

5. **Demand characteristics** refer to those aspects of the experiment that may provide the participants with cues concerning the experimenter's hypothesis and how they are supposed to act. Demand characteristics can be controlled through the use of single-blind and **double-blind experiments** (in which both the experimenter and the participants do not know which treatment the participants are to receive).

6. The desire to cooperate and act in accordance with the experimenter's expectation is called the **good participant effect**.

7. Response bias is caused by several factors. **Yea-saying** refers to the tendency to answer yes to all questions; **nay-saying** refers to the tendency to answer no to all questions. Yea- and nay-saying are controlled by writing some items in such a way that a negative response represents agreement (control for yea-saying) and a positive response represents disagreement (control for nay-saying).

8. When the experimental situation or context prompts a certain response, a **response set** has been created. The best safeguards against response set are careful scrutiny of the experimental situation, thorough review of all questions, pilot testing, and interviewing the participants.

CHECK YOUR PROGRESS

1. Explain how the experimenter can be an extraneous variable.
2. Matching

1. age, sex, race	A. psychological experimenter effects
2. hostility or anxiety	B. experimenter expectancies
3. Rosenthal effects	C. physiological experimenter effects
4. single-blind experiment	D. control for demand characteristics and experimenter expectancies
5. double-blind experiment	E. control for experimenter expectancies

3. An experiment in which the researcher doesn't know which treatment the participants are receiving
    a. is a blind experiment   b. is a confounded experiment
    c. cannot be replicated   d. is unable to employ randomization

4. Explain how instrumentation and automation can control experimenter expectancies.
5. Demand characteristics refer to
    a. demands the experimenter places on the participants
    b. cues that tell the participants how to act
    c. IRB requirements for conducting research
    d. the need to publish research in order to receive tenure and promotion

6. Which of the following is an example of response bias?
    a. demand characteristics   b. single-blind experiment
    c. nay-saying   d. balancing

The Interface Between Research and Culture

The recent and continuing explosion in information technology, coupled with the availability of inexpensive air travel, highlights the diverse, multicultural nature of our planet. For example, it is common to see live reports on the television evening news from countries on the other side of the world. In our own country the "information superhighway" instantly links diverse peoples in the farthest reaches of the United States.

As we complete the material on the basics of experimentation, it is important to keep such cultural differences in mind; they may influence how research is conceptualized, conducted, analyzed, and interpreted. To this end, cross-cultural psychology has grown dramatically in recent years. The goal of **cross-cultural psychology** is to determine whether research results and psychological phenomena are universal (found in individuals from different cultures) or specific to the culture in which they were reported. Before we examine cross-cultural research, a definition of culture is needed.

Cross-cultural psychology   A branch of psychology whose goal is to determine the universality of research results.

Rather than simply giving you a definition of culture, we would like you to spend a few minutes on this topic. Before reading further, decide which aspects or features should be included in a definition of culture.

You probably began thinking about culture with the word *similar*. After all, it's the similarities that help define our culture and distinguish it from other cultures. If you then started listing the important aspects that serve to distinguish cultures, you're on the right track. Among the important features that differentiate one culture from another are attitudes, values, and behaviors. Moreover, these culture-defining attitudes, values, and behaviors must be long-lasting or enduring. This enduring quality indicates that these attitudes, values, and behaviors are communicated or transmitted from one generation to the next. Putting these considerations together, we can tentatively define **culture** as the lasting values, attitudes, and behaviors that a group of people share and transmit to subsequent generations. It is important to note that our definition does not imply that race and nationality are synonymous with culture. Individuals can be of the same race or nationality and not share the same culture. Carrying this thought one step further, we can see that several cultures may exist within the same country or even in the same large city. Now, let's see how culture is related to what we consider to be truth.

> **Culture**   Lasting values, attitudes, and behaviors that are shared by a group and transmitted to subsequent generations.

Culture, Knowledge, and Truth

A finding that occurs across cultures is called an **etic**. You can think of an etic as a universal truth or principle. The finding that reinforcement increases the probability of the response it follows appears to be an etic; people of all cultures respond to reinforcement similarly. In contrast, an **emic** is a finding that is linked to a specific culture. The value placed on independence and individuality is an emic; it varies from culture to culture. Some cultures (e.g., the United States) are individualistic and place a premium on individual accomplishments. Other cultures (e.g., China) are collectivist and stress contributions to the welfare of the group. Emics represent truths that are relative to different cultures, whereas etics represent absolute truths. Given the great diversity of cultures, it should not surprise you to find that the number of emics is considerably greater than the number of etics.

> **Etic**   A finding that is the same in different cultures.
>
> **Emic**   A culture-specific finding.

At this point you may be wondering how this discussion relates to a course in research methods or experimental psychology. Consider this issue before reading further.

If the goal of your research project is to discover the effects of IV manipulations only within a certain culture, then this discussion may have little relevance. However, few researchers purposely set their research sights on only a single culture (also see Chapter 13). In fact, the question of culture may never enter the researcher's mind as a study is taking shape. Similarly, when the data are analyzed and conclusions reached, cultural considerations may not be addressed. The result is a project that one *assumes* is not culture dependent. In short, researchers often become **ethnocentric**—they view other cultures as an extension of their own. Hence, they interpret research results in accord with the values, attitudes, and behaviors that define their culture and assume that these findings are applicable in other cultures as well. For example, many researchers likely consider the *fundamental attribution error* (Ross, 1977) in which actions are attributed to the individual, even in the face of compelling situational cues, to be a universal finding. Although the fundamental attribution error is shown in individualistic, Western societies (Gilbert & Malone, 1995), situational cues are taken into account in collectivist societies, and this effect is appreciably smaller (Miller, 1984). Chapter 13 will have more to say about the generalizability of research findings when we consider the external validity of our research.

> **Ethnocentric**   Other cultures are viewed as an extension of one's own culture.

The Effect of Culture on Research

If you step back from your culture and try to put research in a more international perspective, it is clear that culture influences all aspects of the research process. We will consider cultural effects on the choice of the research problem, the nature of the experimental hypothesis, and the selection of the IV and the recording of the DV. In order to solve their respective problems, the detective and the research psychologist need a broad base of information that includes cultural information.

Choice of the Research Problem   In some cases there may be no doubt that the choice of your research problem is culture dependent. For example, let's assume you are interested in studying the nature of crowd interactions at a rock concert. Whereas this topic may represent a meaningful project in the United States, it has much less relevance to a psychologist conducting research in the bush country of Australia. In this example, culture clearly dictates the nature of the research project; some problems are important in one culture, but not in another. Likewise, whereas the study of individual achievement motivation is a topic of considerable interest and importance in an individualistic society like the United States, it would be a less important research topic in a collectivist society like China (Yang, 1982).

Nature of the Experimental Hypothesis   Once you have selected a problem that is relevant beyond your own culture, then you must deal with the experimental hypothesis. For example, even though the study of factors that determine one's personal space is relevant in a number of cultures, the creation of an experimental hypothesis that applies to all cultures will be most difficult. In some cultures very little personal space is the norm, whereas considerable personal space is expected in other cultures. For example, Italians typically interact within a smaller personal space (i.e., they prefer closer proximity) than either Germans or Americans (Shuter, 1977). Such cultural differences may lead to very different hypotheses.

Selection of the IV and the DV   Culture also can influence the selection of the IV and the DV. In technologically advanced cultures such as the United States, Japan, or Great

Britain, IV presentation may be accomplished via a computer. Likewise, DV measurement and recording also may be done by computer. Because such technology is not available in all cultures, the choice of the IV and the procedure for recording the DV may differ considerably. For example, handheld stopwatches, not digital electronic timers, may be used to record the time required to complete an experimental task. Similarly, the participants may read the stimulus items in booklet form, rather than having them presented at set intervals on a video screen by a computer. In fact, stimuli that have high (or low) meaning in one culture may not have the same meaning in another culture.

Methodology and Analysis Issues

In either conducting or evaluating cross-cultural research, a number of methodological issues will necessitate careful and thorough consideration. Among these issues are the participants and sampling procedures used, the survey or questionnaire employed, and the effects of cultural response set on data analysis.

Participants and Sampling Procedures   The basic question here is whether the sample of participants is representative of the culture from which they were drawn. Do sophomore college students represent the culture of the United States? What steps have been taken to ensure that the sample is representative of the culture in question? For example, extreme differences may exist between samples drawn from large urban centers and those drawn from rural areas.

Assuming you can satisfy the requirement that a sample is representative of its culture, you are likely to be faced with an equally difficult task: being able to ensure that samples from two or more cultures are equivalent before the research is conducted. We have stressed, and will continue to stress, the importance of establishing group equivalence before an IV is administered. Only when group equivalence is demonstrated can we have confidence in saying that our IV has had an effect in producing any differences we observe.

Let's assume you are reading research reports from three different cultures. All three investigations used freshman-level college students as participants. Can you assume that the requirements of group equivalence among these studies has been satisfied through the use of this common type of participant?

Even though the same *type* of participant, freshman college students, was used, you cannot assume the groups were equivalent before the research was conducted. Before you can make this assumption, you must be able to demonstrate that the same type of student attends college in all three cultures and that the "freshman" designation is equivalent across all three cultures. Perhaps the collegiate experience in one culture is quite different from the collegiate experience in another culture and therefore attracts students who differ from those in the culture with which it is being compared. For example, economics may dictate that only the wealthy attend college in some cultures. In short, assessing group equivalence will not be an easy task for cross-cultural research.

Type of Survey or Questionnaire Used   Although an existing survey or questionnaire may work in a few instances, most likely the researcher will not be able to use it for research in a different culture. The chances are good that the questionnaire or survey will have to be translated into a different language. Assuming the translation has been completed, how do you know that it is accurate and the correct meanings have been retained? The same word can have different meanings in different cultures. One technique for evaluating the accuracy of the translation is to have a *back translation* done. This procedure involves having another person translate the translated questionnaire back into its original language. If the back translation and the original version match, then the original translation was successful. The importance of the back translation is clearly reflected by Sou and Irving in their comments on the limitations of their research on student attitudes toward mental health in the United States and Macao (see Chapter 3). These researchers said, "the survey items created for this study did not receive a backward translation to ensure reliability between the Chinese and English versions; therefore, group differences may be due to inherent differences in the meaning of the survey items after translation" (Sou & Irving, 2002, p. 21).

Aside from these problems that are faced in translating the instrument into another language, there is the very real problem of whether the other cultures to be tested value the concept that is to be measured or evaluated. If they do not, then the survey or questionnaire is worthless.

Even if you determine that the concept or trait in question is valued in other cultures, there remains the problem of making sure that the *specific items* are equivalent when the survey or questionnaire is prepared for use in other cultures. Just translating the items into another language may not be sufficient. For example, a question about riding the subway that is appropriate for an industrialized society may have no meaning in less-developed cultures or in some parts of the industrialized society. Clearly, the same comment can be made for questions dealing with customs, values, and beliefs.

Cultural Response Set   Earlier in this chapter you learned that research participants may begin an experiment with a preexisting response set; some participants may be yea-sayers and others are nay-sayers. We have the same general concern, only on a larger scale, when conducting cross-cultural research.

> **Cultural response set**
> The tendency of a particular culture to respond in a certain manner.

In this instance it is the response of the entire culture, not individual participants, that concerns us. A **cultural response set**, or tendency of a particular culture to respond in a certain manner, may be operative. How often have individuals in another culture answered questions on a Likert-type rating scale like those commonly used in the United States? What reaction(s) will they have to being tested by such a scale? The fact that you use such scales effectively in your research does not mean participants in other cultures will find them easy to understand and answer. The same comments can be made about any survey or questionnaire that is used. Both the type of questionnaire (Likert-type scale, true-false, multiple choice, etc.) and the nature of the items themselves may intensify an already existing cultural response set.

How do you know whether a cultural response set is present? If differences exist among the groups tested in various cultures, a cultural response set may be operating.

The presence of a cultural response set is one possible cause for the differences among groups from various cultures. What other factor might cause such differences? What problem is created if you cannot distinguish between these two causes?

If you indicated that the influence of a manipulated IV or differences in the specific trait being measured could also be responsible for the differences among groups, you are absolutely correct. If you then indicated that an extraneous variable is present and the research would be confounded (see Chapter 6) if the researcher could not distinguish whether the scores on a questionnaire were caused by the trait or IV or the cultural response set, then you are correct again. Remember that our research results are worthless when a confounder is present. Hence, it is vitally important that cultural response set be accounted for whenever you are conducting or evaluating cross-cultural research.

The purpose of this section was not to teach all the fine points of cross-cultural research; it would take an entire book to accomplish that goal. Rather, we wanted to make you aware of these issues and problems before we began our discussion of statistics and research designs. Being acquainted with the issues involved in cross-cultural research will make you a better consumer of psychological research, regardless of where it is conducted.

REVIEW SUMMARY

1. The goal of **cross-cultural psychology** is to determine whether research findings are culture specific (i.e., **emics**) or universal (i.e., **etics**).
2. **Culture** can influence the choice of a research problem, the nature of the experimental hypothesis, and the selection of the IV and the DV.
3. In conducting or comparing cross-cultural research, the cultural representativeness of the participants and the sampling procedures used to acquire the participants must be carefully evaluated.
4. The appropriateness of a survey or questionnaire for cross-cultural research must be evaluated. Once the general trait or concept has been accepted, then the specific items must be examined and deemed acceptable for cross-cultural use.
5. The presence of a **cultural response set** must be considered in conducting cross-cultural research.

CHECK YOUR PROGRESS

1. The goal of cross-cultural psychology is best described as
   a. determining whether psychological findings are universal
   b. testing a variety of participants
   c. using a variety of test equipment
   d. conducting tests in a variety of locations

2. A finding linked to a specific culture best describes
   a. ethnocentrism   b. an ertic   c. an emic   d. an etic
3. Why is the goal of cross-cultural research incompatible with ethnocentrism?
4. In what ways can culture affect the conduct of psychological research?
5. The tendency of a culture to behave in a certain way best describes
   a. an etic   b. cultural response set   c. ethnocentrism   d. the just world stereotype

KEY TERMS

Precedent, 143	Yea-sayers, 154	Etic, 159
Power, 146	Nay-sayers, 154	Emic, 159
Rosenthal effect, 151	Response set, 154	Ethnocentric, 160
Single-blind experiment, 152	Double-blind experiment, 155	Cultural response set, 162
Demand characteristics, 152	Cross-cultural psychology, 158	
Good participant effect, 153	Culture, 159	

LOOKING AHEAD

So far, our view of research in psychology has been rather general. At this point in the book we are on the verge of discussing specific research designs. (Our consideration of research designs begins in Chapter 9.) Because statistics and data analysis are integral components of the various research designs, a brief statistical refresher appears to be in order. We turn to this topic in Chapter 8.

Using Statistics
to Answer Questions

Just as detectives seek out clues and leads and gather data to help solve a case, psychologists, too, gather data to help answer research questions. Once they gather the evidence, detectives need to determine whether it is real (meaningful). Likewise, in later chapters we will examine several statistical methods used to determine whether the results of an experiment are meaningful (significant). As we have seen, the term *significant* is used to describe those instances where the statistical results are likely to have been caused by our manipulation of the IV.

Statistics The branch of mathematics that involves the collection, analysis, and interpretation of data.

To better understand the nature of statistical significance, a closer look at statistics is in order. **Statistics** is a branch of mathematics that involves the collection, analysis, and interpretation of data. Various statistical techniques are used to aid the researcher in several ways during the decision-making processes that arise when conducting research.

Descriptive statistics Procedures used to summarize a set of data.

Inferential statistics Procedures used to analyze data after an experiment is completed; used to determine whether the independent variable has a significant effect.

The two main branches of statistics assist your decisions in different ways. **Descriptive statistics** are used to summarize any set of numbers so you can understand and talk about them more intelligibly. **Inferential statistics** are used to analyze data after you have conducted an experiment to determine whether your independent variable had a significant effect. Although we assume that you already have some familiarity with statistics, we have included several relevant formulas in Appendix B. We encourage you to review them at this time and as needed.

Descriptive Statistics

We use descriptive statistics when we want to summarize a set or distribution of numbers in order to communicate their essential characteristics. One of these essential characteristics is a measure of the typical or representative score, called a *measure of central tendency*. A second essential characteristic that we need to know about a distribution is how much *variability* or spread exists in the scores. However, before we discuss these measures of central tendency and variability, we need to examine the measurements on which they are based.

Scales of Measurement

Measurement The assignment of symbols to events according to a set of rules.

Scale of measurement A set of measurement rules.

Nominal scale A scale of measurement in which events are assigned to categories.

We can define **measurement** as the assignment of symbols to events according to a set of rules. Your grade on a test is a symbol that stands for your performance; it was assigned according to a particular set of rules (the instructor's grading standards). The *particular* set of rules used in assigning a symbol to the event in question is known as a **scale of measurement**. The four scales of measurement that are of interest to psychologists are nominal, ordinal, interval, and ratio scales. How you choose to measure the DV (i.e., which scale of measurement you use) directly determines the type of statistical test you can use to evaluate your data once you complete your research project.

Nominal Scale The **nominal scale** is a simple classification system. For example, if you are categorizing the furniture in a classroom as tables or chairs, you are using a nominal scale of measurement. Likewise, recording responses to an item on a questionnaire as "agree," "undecided," or "disagree" reflects the use of a nominal scale of measurement. The items being evaluated are assigned to mutually exclusive categories.

Ordinal Scale   When the events in question can be rank ordered, an **ordinal scale** of measurement is being used. Notice that we indicated *only* that the events under consideration could be rank ordered; we did not indicate that the intervals separating the units were comparable. Although we can rank the winners in a track meet (i.e., first, second, third, fourth), this rank ordering does not tell us anything concerning how far apart the winners were. Perhaps it was almost a dead heat for first and second; maybe the winner was far ahead of the second-place finisher.

> **Ordinal scale**   A scale of measurement that permits events to be rank ordered.
>
> **Interval scale**   A scale of measurement that permits rank ordering of events with the assumption of equal intervals between adjacent events.

Interval Scale   When the events in question can be rank ordered and equal intervals separate adjacent events, an **interval scale** is being used. For example, the temperatures on a Fahrenheit thermometer form an interval scale; rank ordering has been achieved *and* the difference between any two adjacent temperatures is the same, 1 degree. Notice that the interval scale does not have a true zero point, however. When you reach the "zero" point on a Fahrenheit thermometer, does temperature cease to exist? No, it's just very cold. Likewise, scores on tests such as the SAT and ACT are interval scale measures.

Assume you are on a college admissions committee and you are reviewing applications. Each applicant's ACT score forms an integral part of your review. You have just come across an applicant who scored 0 on the verbal subtest. What does this score tell you?

The score of 0 should not be interpreted as meaning that this individual has absolutely no verbal ability. Because ACT scores are interval scale measurements, there is no true zero. Hence, a score of 0 should be interpreted as meaning that the individual is very low in that ability. The same could be said for 0 scores on the wide variety of tests, questionnaires, and personality inventories that psychologists routinely use in personality research. The presence of a true zero is characteristic only of the ratio scale of measurement.

Ratio Scale   The **ratio scale** of measurement takes the interval scale one step further. Like the interval scale, the ratio scale permits the rank ordering of scores with the assumption of equal intervals between them, *but* it also assumes the presence of a true zero point. Physical measurements, such as the amplitude or intensity of sound or light, are ratio measurements. These measurements can be rank ordered, and there are equal intervals between adjacent scores. However, when a sensitive measuring device reads 0, there is nothing there. Because of the true zero point, the ratio scale allows you to make ratio comparisons, such as "twice as much" or "half as much."

> **Ratio scale**   A scale of measurement that permits rank ordering of events with the assumptions of equal intervals between adjacent events and a true zero point.

Our discussion of scales of measurement has progressed from the nominal scale, which provides the least amount of information, to the ratio scale, which provides the greatest amount of information. When psychologists evaluate changes in the DV, they try to use a scale of measurement that will provide the most information; frequently, they select interval scales because they often do not use measurements that have a true zero.

We now turn to the topic of central tendency. Keep in mind that the scales of measurement directly determine which measure of central tendency you will use.

Measures of Central Tendency

Measures of central tendency, such as the mode, median, and mean, tell us about the typical score in a distribution.

Mode   The score in a distribution that occurs most often.

Mode   The **mode** is the number or event that occurs most frequently in a distribution. If students reported the following work hours per week

$$12, 15, 20, 20, 20$$

the mode would be 20.

$$\textbf{Mode} = 20$$

Although the mode can be calculated for any scale of measurement, it is the only measure of central tendency that can be used for nominal data.

Median   The number that divides a distribution in half.

Median   The **median** is the number or score that divides the distribution into equal halves. To be able to calculate the median, you must first rank order the scores. Thus, if you started with the following scores

$$56, 15, 12, 20, 17$$

you would need to rank order them as follows:

$$12, 15, 17, 20, 56$$

Now, it's an easy task to determine that 17 is the median (*Mdn*):

$$\textbf{Mdn} = 17$$

What if you have an even number of scores, as in the following distribution?

$$1, 2, 3, 4, 5, 6$$

In this case the median lies halfway between the two middle scores (3 and 4). Thus, the median would be 3.5, halfway between 3 and 4. The median can be calculated for ordinal, interval, and ratio data.

Mean   The **mean** is defined as the arithmetic average. To find the mean we add all the scores in the distribution and then divide by the number of scores we added. For example, assume we start with

12, 15, 18, 19, 16

We use the Greek letter sigma, Σ, to indicate the sum. If X stands for the numbers in our distribution, then ΣX means to add the numbers in our distribution. Thus, $\Sigma X = 80$. If N stands for the number of scores in the distribution, then the mean would equal $\Sigma X/N$. For the previous example, $16 = 80/5$. The sum of these numbers is 80 and the mean is 16 (80/5). The mean is symbolized by M.

> **Mean**   The arithmetic average of a set of numbers; found by adding all the scores in a set and then dividing by the number of scores.

You may recall from your statistics class that $\overline{X}$ stood for the mean. We haven't arbitrarily changed symbols on you. Because M stands for the mean in APA-format papers (see Chapter 14), we chose to use it instead of $\overline{X}$. Thus, $M = 16$. The mean can be calculated for interval and ratio data, but not for nominal and ordinal data.

Choosing a Measure of Central Tendency   Which measure of central tendency should you choose? The answer to that question depends on the type of information you are seeking and the scale of measurement you are using. If you want to know which score occurred most often, then the mode is the choice. However, the mode may not be very representative of the other scores in your distribution. Consider the following distribution:

1, 2, 3, 4, 5, 11, 11

In this case the mode is 11. Because *all* the other scores are considerably smaller, the mode does not accurately describe the typical score.

The median may be a better choice to serve as the representative score because it takes into account all the data in the distribution. However, there are drawbacks with this choice. The median treats all scores alike; differences in magnitude are not taken into account. Thus, the median for *both* of the following distributions is 14:

Distribution 1: 11, 12, 13, **14**, 15, 16, 17   **Mdn** = 14
Distribution 2: 7, 8, 9, **14**, 23, 24, 25   **Mdn** = 14

When we calculate the mean, however, the *value* of each number is taken into account. Although the medians for the two distributions above are the same, the means are not:

Distribution 1: 11, 12, 13, 14, 15, 16, 17
$\Sigma X = 98$ $M = 98/7$ $M = 14$
Distribution 2: 7, 8, 9, 14, 23, 24, 25
$\Sigma X = 110$ $M = 110/7$ $M = 15.71$

The fact that the mean of Distribution 2 is larger than that of Distribution 1 indicates that the value of each individual score has been taken into account.

Because the mean takes the value of each score into account, it usually provides a more accurate picture of the typical score and is the measure of central tendency favored by psychologists. However, there are instances when the mean may be misleading. Consider the following distribution of charitable donations:

> *Charitable donations*: $1, $1, $1, $5, $10, $10, $100
> **Mode = $1**
> **Mdn = $5**
> **Mean = $128/7   *M* = $18.29**

If you wanted to report the "typical" gift, would it be the mode? Probably not. Even though $1 is the most frequent donation, this amount is *substantially* smaller than the other donations, and more people made contributions over $1 than made the $1 contribution. What about the median? You see that $5 appears to be more representative of the typical donation; there are an equal number of higher and lower donations. Would the mean be better? In this example the mean is substantially inflated by one large donation ($100); the mean is $18.29 even though six of the seven donations are $10 or under. Although reporting the mean in this case may look good on a report of giving, it does not reflect the typical donation.

The lesson to be learned from this example is that when you have only a limited number of scores in your distribution, the mean may be inflated (or deflated) by extremely large (or extremely small) scores. The median may be a better choice as your measure of central tendency in such instances. As the number of scores in your distribution increases, the influence of extremely large (or extremely small) scores on the mean decreases. Look what happens if we collect two additional $5 donations:

> *Charitable donations*: $1, $1, $1, $5, $5, $5, $10, $10, $100
> **Mode = $1 and $5**
> **Mdn = $5**
> **Mean = $138/9   *M* = $15.33**

Note we now have two values ($1 and $5) for the mode (i.e., a *bimodal distribution*). The median stays the same ($5). However, the mean has decreased from $18.29 to $15.33; the addition of only two more low scores moved the mean closer to the median.

Graphing Your Results

Once you have calculated a measure of central tendency, you can convey this information to others. If you have only one set of scores, the task is simple: You write down the value as part of your paper or report.

What if you are dealing with several groups or sets of numbers? Now the task is complicated, and the inclusion of several numbers in a paragraph of text might be confusing. In such cases a graph or figure can be used to your advantage; a picture may well be worth a thousand words. It is not uncommon to see a detective use a chart or graph to help make a point in the solution of a case. In preparing a research report, psychologists also use graphs effectively. There are several types of graphs for the researcher to choose from. Your choice of graphs will be determined by which one depicts your results most effectively *and* by the scale of measurement you used. For example, if you used a nominal scale of measurement, then you would likely use a pie chart, a histogram, a bar graph, or a frequency polygon.

Pie Chart If you are dealing with percentages that total 100%, then the familiar pie chart may be a good choice. The **pie chart** depicts the percentage represented by each alternative as a slice of a circular pie. The larger the slice, the greater the percentage. For example, if you surveyed college men to determine their TV viewing preferences, you might display your results as a pie chart (see Figure 8-1). From the hypothetical data presented in Figure 8-1 we can see that the mode is sports programs.

> **Pie chart** Graphical representation of the percentage allocated to each alternative as a slice of a circular pie.

Take another look at Figure 8-1. Why would it not be appropriate to describe a mean preference in this instance?

To answer this question, ask yourself what scores we would use to obtain the mean. We know there are four categories of TV preference and we know the percentage preferring each category. We could add the percentages for each category and then divide by the number of categories. The resulting number would tell us that there is an average of 25% per category; unfortunately, that number does not tell us much about the "mean preference." We would have to have individual scores, in the form of interval or ratio data, before we could calculate a mean preference. These data are simply not available.

Histogram We can use a **histogram** to present our data in terms of frequencies per category. When we study a *quantitative variable*, we construct a histogram. Quantitative categories are ones that can be numerically ordered. The levels or categories of a quantitative variable must be arranged in a numerical order. For example, we may choose to

> **Histogram** A graph in which the frequency for each category of a quantitative variable is represented as a vertical column that touches the adjacent column.

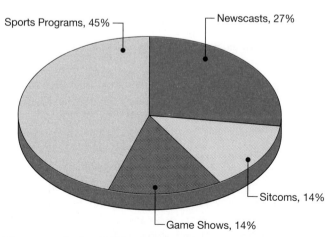

FIGURE 8-1   **TV Viewing Preferences of College Men.**

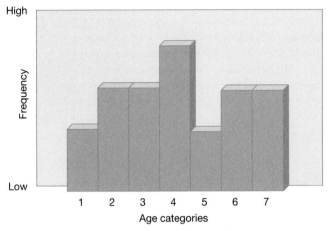

High

Frequency

Low

1   2   3   4   5   6   7

Age categories

**FIGURE 8-2   Histogram Depicting the Frequency of Partici-
pants in Various Age Categories in a Developmental Psychology Research Project.   Note that the sides of adjacent columns touch.**

arrange our categories from smallest to largest, or vice versa. Figure 8-2 shows a histogram
for the age categories of participants in a developmental psychology research project.

Bar Graph   The **bar graph** also presents data in terms of frequencies per category. However, we are using *qualitative categories* when a bar graph is constructed. Qualitative categories are ones that cannot be numerically ordered. For
example, single, married, divorced, and remarried are qualitative categories;
there is no way to numerically order them.

Figure 8-3 shows a bar graph for the sports and fitness preferences of men
and boys (Part A) and women and girls (Part B) who are frequent participants in
such activities. Placing a space between the bars lets the reader know that qualitative categories are being reported. You can see at a glance that the number per
category and type of activities differ dramatically between the two groups. Think
of how many words it would take to write about these results rather than present
them as a graph!

Frequency Polygon   If we mark the middle of the crosspiece of each bar in a
histogram (see Figure 8-4A) with a dot, connect the dots, and remove the bars,
we have constructed a **frequency polygon** (see Figure 8-4B).

The frequency polygon, like the histogram, displays the frequency of each
number or score. The only difference between the two is that we use bars in the
histogram and connected dots in the frequency polygon.

Line Graph   The results of psychological experiments are often presented as a
line graph. In constructing a line graph, we start with two axes or dimensions.
The vertical or *y* axis is known as the **ordinate**; the horizontal or *x* axis is known
as the **abscissa** (see Figure 8-5). Our scores or data (the DV) are plotted on the
ordinate. The values of the variable we manipulated (the IV) are plotted on the abscissa.

Bar graph A graph in
which the frequency for
each category of a quali-
tative variable is repre-
sented as a vertical
column. The columns of a
bar graph do not touch.

Frequency polygon A
graph that is constructed
by placing a dot in the
center of each bar of a histogram and then connect-
ing the dots.

Line graph A graph that
is frequently used to de-
pict the results of an experiment

Ordinate The vertical or
y axis of a graph.

Abscissa The horizontal
or *x* axis of a graph.

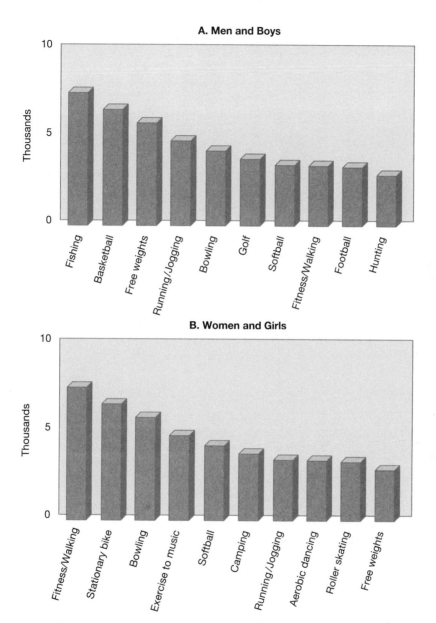

FIGURE 8-3 **Bar Graphs Depicting the Sports and Fitness Preferences of Men and Boys (A) and Women and Girls (B) Who Are Frequent Participants in Such Activities.** Because a bar graph depicts a qualitative variable, the bars do not touch.

(Source: *The American Enterprise,* September/October 1993, p. 101.)

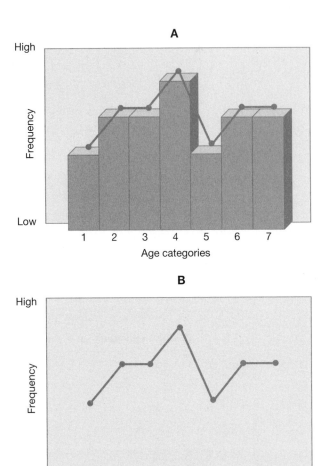

A

B

FIGURE 8-4   **The Frequency Polygon Is Constructed by Placing a Dot in the Center of Each Bar of a Histogram and Connecting the Dots (Part A) and Removing the Bars (Part B).**   The frequency polygon, like the histogram, displays the frequency of each score or number.

How tall should the *y* axis be? How long should the *x* axis be? A good rule of thumb is for the *y* axis to be approximately *two thirds* as tall as the *x* axis is long (see Figures 8-5 and 8-6). Other configurations will give a distorted picture of the data. For example, if the ordinate is considerably shorter, differences between groups or treatments will be obscured (see Figure 8-7A), whereas lengthening the ordinate tends to exaggerate differences (see Figure 8-7B).

In Figure 8-6 we have plotted the results of a hypothetical experiment that evaluated the effects of different levels of stress on making correct landing decisions by air traffic

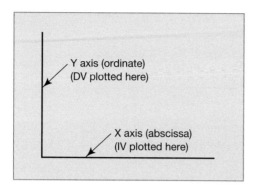

controllers. As you can see, as stress increased, the number of correct responses increased. What if we had tested two different groups of participants, college students and air traffic controllers? How would we display the results of both groups on the same graph? No problem. All we need to do is add the data points for the second group and a legend or box that identifies the groups (see Figure 8-8). Now, we can see at a glance that the air traffic controllers, whose occupation is very stressful, made more correct responses as stress levels increase, whereas the converse was true for the college students.

When you graph the results of an experiment in which more than one variable is employed, how do you know which IV to plot on the abscissa? Although there is no fixed rule, a good guideline is to plot the variable having the greatest number of levels on the abscissa. Thus, in Figure 8-8 the three levels of stress were plotted on the abscissa, rather than the two levels of participants.

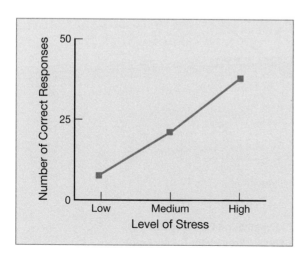

FIGURE 8-6 **Results of a Hypothetical Experiment Investigating the Effects of Stress on Correct Responding in Air Traffic Controllers.**

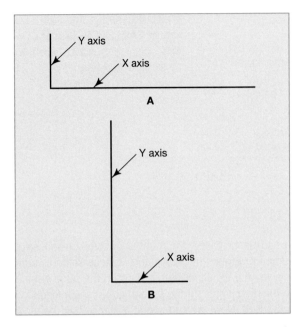

FIGURE 8-7   **Altering the *x* (Abscissa) or *y* (Ordinate) Axis Can Distort the Results of an Experiment.**   A. If the ordinate is considerably shorter than the abscissa, significant effects can be obscured. B. If the ordinate is considerably longer than the abscissa, very small effects can be exaggerated.

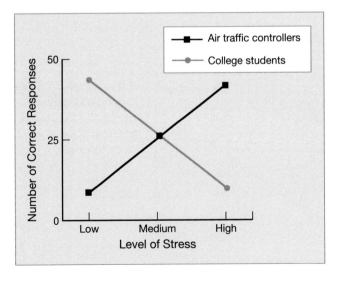

FIGURE 8-8   **Results of a Hypothetical Experiment Investigating the Effects of Stress on Correct Responding in Air Traffic Controllers *and* College Students.**

Why would you choose to plot the IV with the greatest number of levels on the abscissa?

By plotting the variable with the greatest number of levels on the abscissa, you reduce the number of lines that will appear on your graph. The fewer lines, the less difficulty you will have in interpreting your graph. For example, had we plotted the type of participants in our stress experiment on the abscissa, then Figure 8-8 would have had three lines, one for each level of stress. We will discuss the accepted APA format for preparing graphs and tables in Chapter 13.

Calculating and Computing Statistics

Remember, this is *not* a statistics text—we assume you have already taken a statistics course. Therefore, we will not review formulas for all the various statistical calculations and tests you will encounter in this book. You can find those formulas in Appendix B. Use them as needed. Your calculating skills may be a little rusty, but all statistical formulas merely require addition, subtraction, multiplication, division, and finding square roots—not all that challenging for a college student . . . especially a college student with a calculator!

By the same token, most psychologists (and probably psychology students) rarely use hand computation techniques for statistics after their initial statistics course; the vast majority use a computer package of some sort to analyze data they collect. Of course, these computer packages vary widely. You may have access to a large and powerful statistics package owned by your school or department (some standard packages are SPSS, SAS, Excel, and BMD). Alternatively, you may have access to a smaller statistics program; some schools even have students buy a statistics software program when they take the statistics course. In any case, you are likely to have access to a computerized statistical analysis program. We cannot begin to give instructions about how to operate the particular program you might have access to—there are simply too many programs. Throughout the chapters that deal with statistics, we will attempt to give you some *general* hints about how to interpret the output you receive from such programs.

Measures of Variability

Although measures of central tendency and graphs convey considerable information, there is still more we can learn about the numbers we have gathered. We also need to know about the variability in our data.

You just got your last psychology test returned in class; your score is 64. What does that number tell you? By itself it may not mean very much. You ask your professor for additional information and find that the class mean was 56. You feel better because you were above the mean. However, after a few moments of reflection you realize you need still more

Variability The extent to which scores spread out around the mean.

information. How were the other scores grouped? Were they all clustered close to the mean or did they spread out considerably? The amount of **variability** or spread in the other scores will have a bearing on the standing of your score. If most of the other scores are very close to the mean, then your score will be among the highest in the class. If the other scores are spread out widely around the mean, then your score will not be one of the strongest. Obviously, you need a measure of variability to provide a complete picture of these data. The range and standard deviation are two measures of variability frequently reported by psychologists.

Range A measure of variability that is computed by subtracting the smallest score from the largest score.

Range The **range** is the easiest measure of variability to calculate; you rank order the scores in your distribution and then subtract the smallest score from the largest to find the range. Consider the following distribution:

$$1, 1, 1, 1, 5, 6, 6, 8, 25$$

When we subtract 1 (the smallest score) from 25 (the largest score), we find that the range is 24:

Range: 25 − 1 = 24

However, other than telling us the difference between the largest and smallest scores, the range does not provide much information. Knowing the range is 24 does not tell us about the distribution of the scores we just considered. Consider Figure 8-9.

The range is the same in Parts A and B of Figure 8-9; however, the spread of the scores differs drastically between these two distributions. Most of the scores cluster in the center of the first distribution (Figure 8-9A), whereas the scores are spread out more evenly in the second distribution (Figure 8-9B). We must turn to another measure, the standard deviation, to provide additional information about how the scores are distributed.

Variance A single number that represents the total amount of variation in a distribution.

Variance and Standard Deviation In order to obtain the standard deviation, we must first calculate the variance. You can think of the **variance** as a single number that represents the total amount of variability in the distribution. The larger the number, the greater the total spread of the scores. The variance and standard deviation are based on how much each score in the distribution deviates from the mean.

When researchers conduct experiments, they use a sample of participants to provide information (an estimate) about an entire population. As an example we calculated the variance of the set of nine numbers for which we computed the range and found it to be 58.25. (See Appendix B for the formula to calculate the variance.) Once we have the variance, we can use it to find the standard deviation.

Standard deviation (SD) Square root of the variance; has important relations to the normal curve.

Interpreting the Standard Deviation To find the **standard deviation (SD)** all we have to do is take the square root of the variance. Using our variance of 58.25, then

$$\textbf{SD} = \sqrt{\text{variance}}$$
$$= \sqrt{58.25}$$
$$= 7.63$$

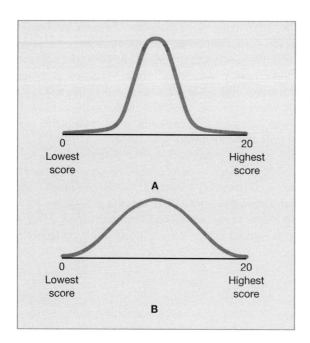

FIGURE 8-9   The Range Does Not Provide Much Information About the Distribution Under Consideration.   Even though the range is the same, these two distributions differ drastically.

As with the variance, the larger the standard deviation, the greater the variability or spread of scores.

A sample computer printout listing the mean, variance, and standard deviation for the nine scores we used when we calculated the range appears in Table 8-1. Rather than providing printouts from a specific statistics software package, we are using generic printouts in the text. Statistics packages provide slightly different information; we show you information you might reasonably expect to find on your printout. As you can see, the computer informs us that we entered nine numbers. The mean of these nine numbers is 6.00, whereas the variance is 58.25 and the standard deviation is 7.63.

Now that we have found the standard deviation, what does it tell us? To answer that question we must consider the normal distribution (also called the *normal curve*). The concept of the **normal distribution** is based on the finding that as we increase the number of scores in our sample, many distributions of interest to psychologists become symmetrical or bell-shaped. (Sometimes the normal distribution is called the *bell curve*.) The majority of the scores cluster around the measure of central tendency,

Normal distribution
A symmetrical, bell-shaped distribution having half the scores above the mean and half the scores below the mean.

TABLE 8-1	Computer Printout Showing Mean, Standard Deviation, and Variance				
	Mean	SD	Variance	Range	*N*
	6.00	7.63	58.25	24.00	9

with fewer and fewer scores occurring as we move away from it. As you can see from Figure 8-10, the mean, median, and mode of a normal distribution all have the same value.

Normal distributions and standard deviations are related in interesting ways. For example, distances from the mean of a normal distribution can be measured in standard deviation units (SD). Consider a distribution with an M of 56 and an SD of 4; a score of 60 falls 1 SD above the mean ($+1\ SD$), whereas a score of 48 is 2 SD below the mean ($-2\ SD$), and so on. As you can see from Figure 8-11, 34.13% of all the scores in *all* normal distributions occur between the mean and 1 SD *above* the mean.

Likewise, 34.13% of all the scores in a distribution occur between the mean and 1 SD *below* the mean. Another 13.59% of the scores occur between 1 and 2 SD *above* the mean; another 13.59% of the scores occur between 1 and 2 SD *below* the mean. Thus, slightly over 95% of all the scores in a normal distribution occur between 2 SD *below* the mean and 2 SD *above* the mean. Exactly 2.28% of the scores occur *beyond* 2 SD *above* the mean; another 2.28% of the scores occur beyond 2 SD *below* the mean. It is important to remember that these percentages hold true for *all* normal distributions.

Review Figure 8-11 for a moment. Why isn't the percentage of scores from 0 to 1 SD above (or below) the mean the same as the percentage of scores from 1 to 2 SD above (or below) the mean?

As we move away from the mean (either above or below), the scores become progressively different from the mean. Because larger scores occur less frequently and the scores between 1 and 2 SD are larger than those from 0 to 1 SD, the percentage of scores from 1 to 2 SD will be lower than the percentage of scores from 0 to 1 SD.

Now, let's return to your test score of 64. You know the mean of the class is 56. If the instructor also tells you that the $SD = 4$, what would your reaction be? Your score of 64 would be 2 SD above the mean; you should feel pretty good. Your score of 64 puts you in the top 2.28% of the class (100% minus 50% of the scores below the mean and minus 34.13% from the mean to 1 SD above the mean and minus 13.59% that occur between 1 and 2 SD above the mean)! (See Figure 8-12A.)

FIGURE 8-10   A Symmetrical or Bell-Shaped Normal Distribution.   Note that the mean, median, and mode coincide in a normal distribution.

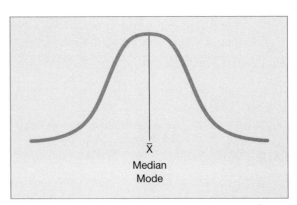

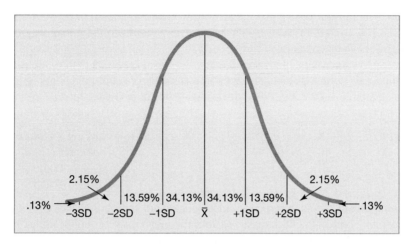

FIGURE 8-11   **The Relation of Standard Deviations and the Normal Distribution.**

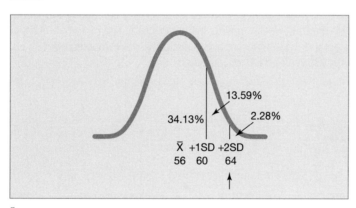

A

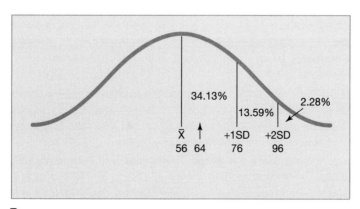

B

FIGURE 8-12   **A**. A score of 64 is exceptionally good when the mean is 56 and the SD is 4. **B**. The same score is not as highly regarded when the SD is 20.

What if your instructor told you the *SD* was 20? Now your score of 64 does not stand up as well as it did when the *SD* was 4. You are above the mean but a long way from being even 1 *SD* above the mean (see Figure 8-12B).

Because the percentage of the scores that occurs from the mean to the various *SD* units is the same for *all* normal distributions, we can compare scores from different distributions by discussing them in terms of standard deviations above or below the mean. Consider the following scores:

Test #	Your Score	*M*	*SD*	Relation of your score to the *M*
1	46	41	5	1 *SD* above
2	72	63	4	Over 2 *SD* above
3	93	71	15	Over 1 *SD* above

Even though your scores, the means, and the standard deviations differ considerably, we can determine how many *SD* units away from the mean each of your scores is. In turn, we can compare these differences. When these comparisons are made, we find that your scores are consistently 1 *SD* or more above the mean. Thus, you are consistently in at least the top 15.87% of the class (100% minus 50% of the scores below the mean and minus 34.13% of the scores from the mean to 1 *SD* above the mean). By comparing scores from various distributions in this manner, we are able to see patterns and suggest what might occur in the future. However, another type of descriptive statistic, the correlation coefficient, is often used for predictive purposes. We turn to this topic next.

REVIEW SUMMARY

1. **Statistics** involves the collection, analysis, and interpretation of data.
2. **Measurement** is the assignment of symbols to events according to a set of rules. A **scale of measurement** is a particular set of measurement rules.
3. A **nominal scale** is a simple classification system, whereas events can be rank ordered when an **ordinal scale** is used. Equal intervals separate rank-ordered events in an **interval scale**. The addition of a true zero to an interval scale results in a **ratio scale**.
4. **Descriptive statistics**, which summarize sets of numbers, include measures of central tendency and variability.
5. The **mode** is the most frequent score, whereas the **median** divides a distribution into two equal halves. The **mean** is the arithmetic average. Depending on the nature of the distribution, these measures of central tendency may not reflect the typical score equally well. They are, however, identical in a normal distribution.
6. Graphs, such as the **pie chart, bar graph, histogram**, and **frequency polygon**, are often used to depict frequencies or percentages.
7. The **line graph** is used to depict experimental results. The DV is plotted on the vertical (*y*) axis, and the IV is plotted on the horizontal (*x*) axis. A 2:3 relation of *y* to *x* axes produces a representative figure.

8. Measures of **variability** include the **range** (difference between high and low scores) and **standard deviation** *(SD)* (square root of the variance). The **variance** is a single number that represents the total amount of variability that is present.

9. The standard deviation conveys considerable information about the **normal distribution** that is under consideration.

CHECK YOUR PROGRESS

1. Matching
   1. inferential statistics   A. assignment of symbols to events
   2. descriptive statistics   B. rank order
   3. measurement   C. putting events into categories
   4. nominal scale   D. equal intervals plus a true zero
   5. ordinal scale   E. used to summarize a set of numbers
   6. interval scale   F. equal intervals
   7. ratio scale   G. used to analyze data after an experiment

2. The number that occurs most frequently is the
   a. mean   b. median   c. mode   d. harmonic

3. When you are dealing with a normal distribution of scores, which measure of central tendency is preferred? Why?

4. A _____ presents data in terms of frequencies per category.
   a. pie chart   b. line graph   c. bimodal distribution   d. histogram

5. You are constructing a line graph to depict the results of an experiment you just completed. What is the ordinate? What is the abscissa? What will be plotted on each of them?

6. Why does the range not convey much information about variability?

7. The _____ is a single number that represents the total amount of variability in a distribution.
   a. variance   b. standard deviation   c. range   d. mean

8. How does the standard deviation relate to the normal curve?

Correlation

Just as in the successful completion of a detective case, prediction plays an important role in psychology. Nowhere is this aspect of psychology more apparent than when moving from high school to college. You probably took a college entrance examination while you were in high school. Based on the results of this exam, a prediction about your grades in college was made. Similarly, should you plan to go on for graduate training after you complete your undergraduate degree, you probably will take another entrance examination. Depending upon your area of interest, you might take the GRE, the Law School Admission Test (LSAT), the Medical College Admission Test (MCAT), or some similar test.

Such predictions are based on the correlation coefficient. Sir Francis Galton (1822–1911) developed the basic ideas of correlation. Galton, who was independently wealthy, devoted his time to studying and investigating those things that interested him. According to E. G. Boring (1950), the eminent historian of psychology, Galton "was a free-lance and a gentleman scientist. He was forever seeing new relationships and working them out, either on paper or in practice. No field was beyond his possible interest, no domain was marked off in advance as being out of his province" (p. 461). For example, Galton studied such varied topics as the weather and fingerprints. He also proposed that a person's intelligence was directly related to the quality of the nervous system: The better the nervous system, the higher the intelligence. To be able to measure the predictive relation between these two variables, Galton's assistant, Karl Pearson (1857–1936), developed the correlation coefficient.

Correlation coefficient

A single number representing the degree of relation between two variables.

A **correlation coefficient** is a single number that represents the degree of relation (i.e., "co-relation") between two variables. The value of a correlation coefficient can range from −1 to +1.

A correlation coefficient of −1 indicates that there is a *perfect negative relation* (see Figure 8-13) between the two variables of interest.

That is, whenever we see an increase of 1 unit in one variable, there is always a proportional decrease in the other variable.

Consider the following scores on Tests X and Y:

	Test X	Test Y
Student 1	49	63
Student 2	50	61
Student 3	51	59
Student 4	52	57
Student 5	53	55

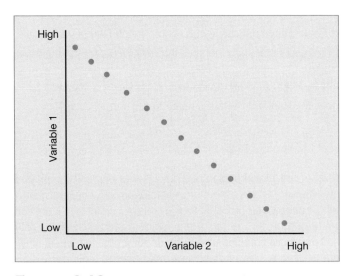

FIGURE 8-13   A Perfect Negative Correlation.

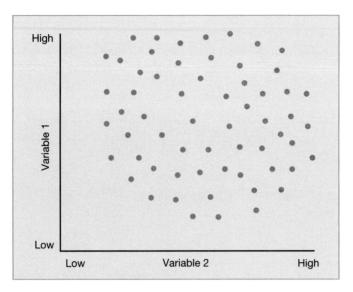

FIGURE 8-14 **A Zero Correlation.**

For each unit of increase in a score on Test X, there is a corresponding *decrease* of 2 units in the score on Test Y. Given this information, you are able to predict that if Student 6 scores 54 on Test X, that student's score on Test Y will be 53.

As you saw in Chapter 4, a zero correlation means that there is *little or no relation* between the two variables (see Figure 8-14). As scores on one variable increase, scores on the other variable may increase, decrease, or be the same. Hence, we are not able to predict how you will do on Test Y by knowing your score on Test X. A correlation coefficient does not have to be exactly 0 to be considered a zero correlation. The inability to make good predictions is the key consideration. Two sets of scores having a zero correlation might look like this:

	Test X	**Test Y**
Student 1	58	28
Student 2	59	97
Student 3	60	63
Student 4	61	60
Student 5	62	50

In this case the correlation between Test X and Test Y is 0.04. A correlation that small indicates that you will not be able to predict Test Y scores by knowing Test X scores; you are dealing with a zero correlation or no relation.

A correlation coefficient of +1 indicates that there is a *perfect positive relation* between the two sets of scores (see Figure 8-15). That is, when we see an increase of 1 unit in one variable, we always see a proportional increase in the other variable. Consider the following scores on Tests X and Y:

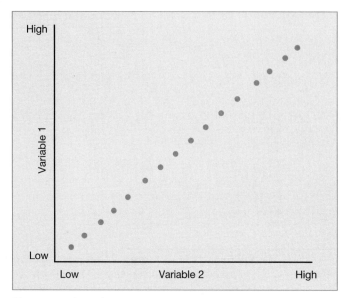

FIGURE 8-15   A Perfect Positive Correlation.

	Test X	Test Y
Student 1	25	40
Student 2	26	43
Student 3	27	46
Student 4	28	49
Student 5	29	52

In this example there is an *increase* of 3 units in the score on Test Y for every unit increase on Test X. The perfect positive correlation leads you to predict that if Student 6 scores 30 on Test X, then his or her score on Test Y will be 55.

Now that we have reviewed the basics of correlation, we would like you to think about the following question. Do perfect (either positive or negative) correlations occur frequently in the real world? Why or why not?

The existence of a perfect correlation indicates there are no other factors present that influence the relation we are measuring. This situation rarely occurs in real life. Think about correlating test scores. To obtain a perfect correlation, all of the participants would have to study and learn the same amount for each test. This situation is not likely to occur. Such factors as fatigue, illness, boredom, and distractions will likely have an effect and make the correlation less than perfect.

The Pearson Product–Moment Correlation Coefficient

The most common measure of correlation is the Pearson product–moment correlation coefficient (r), which Galton's assistant Karl Pearson developed. This type of correlation coefficient is calculated when both the X variable and the Y variable are interval or ratio scale measurements and the data appear to be linear. Other correlation coefficients can be calculated when one or both of the variables are not interval or ratio scale measurements or when the data do not fall on a straight line.

Examples of computer printouts for perfect positive and perfect negative correlations appear in Table 8-2. As you can see, the correlation of Tests X and Y with themselves is always 1.00; however, the correlation of Test X with Test Y is -1.00 (Table 8-2A) when the relation is perfect negative and 1 (Table 8-2B) when the relation is perfect positive. Because some computers do not provide a probability for correlations, you may have to consult a table of correlation probabilities to determine whether a particular correlation is significant (see Table A-3 in Appendix A).

Review Figures 8-13, 8-14, and 8-15; they will help you visualize the various correlations we discussed. Perfect positive and perfect negative correlations always fall on a straight line, whereas nonperfect correlations do not. You will find, however, that the more the scores cluster close together and form a straight line, the stronger (i.e., larger) the correlation coefficient. For positive correlations, the trend of the points is from lower left to upper right, whereas for negative correlations, the trend is from upper left to lower right. There is no consistent pattern for a zero correlation.

TABLE 8-2 **Computer Printout for (A) Perfect Negative Correlation and (B) Perfect Positive Correlation**

```
A. Perfect Negative Correlation

   PEARSON CORRELATION MATRIX

                TEST X          TEST Y

   TEST X       1.00

   TEST Y       -1.00           1.00

   NUMBER OF OBSERVATIONS: 5

B. Perfect Positive Correlation

   PEARSON CORRELATION MATRIX

                TEST X          TEST Y

   TEST X       1.00

   TEST Y       1.00            1.00

   NUMBER OF OBSERVATIONS: 5
```

Although descriptive statistics can tell us a great deal about the data we have collected, they cannot tell us everything. For example, when we conduct an experiment, descriptive statistics cannot tell us whether the IV we manipulated had a significant effect on the behavior of the participants we tested or whether the results we obtained would have occurred by chance. To make such determinations we must conduct an inferential statistical test.

Inferential Statistics

Once an experiment has been conducted, a statistical test is performed on the data that have been gathered. The results of this test will help you decide whether the IV was effective or not. In other words, we shall decide whether our statistical result is *significant* or not.

What Is Significant?

Null hypothesis   A hypothesis that says that all differences between groups are due to chance (i.e., not the operation of the IV).

An inferential statistical test can tell us whether the results of an experiment would occur frequently or rarely by chance. Inferential statistics with small values occur *frequently by chance*, whereas inferential statistics with large values occur *rarely by chance*. If the result occurs often by chance, we say that it is not significant and conclude that our IV did not affect the DV. In this case we would accept the **null hypothesis**, which says that the differences between groups are due to

Courtesy of Sidney Harris.

Unlike the warning on this truck, psychologists view data and statistical procedures as tools to help answer research questions.

chance (i.e., not the operation of the IV). However, if the result of our inferential statistical test occurs rarely by chance (i.e., it is significant), then we conclude that some factor other than chance is operative. If we have conducted our experiment properly and exercised good control (see Chapters 6 and 7), then our significant statistical result gives us reason to believe the IV we manipulated was effective (i.e., did not affect the DV scores).

When do we consider that an event occurs rarely by chance? Traditionally psychologists say that any event that occurs by chance alone 5 times or fewer in 100 occasions is a rare event. Thus, you will see frequent mention of the ".05 level of significance" in journal articles. This statement means that a result is considered significant if it would occur 5 or fewer times by chance in 100 replications of the experiment when the null hypothesis is true. As the experimenter, you decide on the level of significance before the experiment is conducted.

"I'm sorry, but you've been rejected at the .05 level."

Reprinted by permission of Warren Street.

You will encounter several significance tests in later chapters in this book. For the present we will use the *t* test to illustrate their use.

The *t* Test

For years you have heard the old saying that "clothes make the person." You decide to experimentally test this adage by determining whether type of clothing influences the time it takes a salesperson to wait on customers. You randomly select 16 students from an introductory psychology class and then randomly assign these students to two groups of 8 students each. Because you formed the groups randomly at the start of the experiment, you assume they are comparable before they are exposed to the IV.

The students in Group A wear dressy clothes to the shopping mall, whereas the students in Group B wear sloppy clothes to the shopping mall. Because the students in Group A have no relation to, or effect on, the students in Group B, these groups are *independent* of each other. Each student enters a store in the mall and uses a silent, inconspicuous stopwatch to measure the time (in seconds) it takes a salesperson to offer service. (Keep in mind that these data were *recorded* by the student shoppers; the salesclerks actually produced the data.) The "latency-to-service" scores (this is a latency DV—see Chapter 6) for the two groups appear below.

Group A (Dressy Clothes)	Group B (Sloppy Clothes)
37	50
38	46
44	62
47	52
49	74
49	69
54	77
69	76
$\Sigma X = 387$	$\Sigma Y = 506$
$M = 48.38$	$M = 63.25$

Do you think the students in dressy clothes were waited on more quickly? Just looking at the differences between the groups suggests this might be the case; the mean score of Group B is higher than that of Group A. (Higher scores reflect longer times before a salesperson offered service.) On the other hand, there is considerable overlap between the two groups; several of the latency-to-service scores were similar for students dressed in sloppy clothes and the students in the dressy clothes. Is the difference you obtained large enough to be genuine, or is it just a chance happening? Merely looking at the results will not answer that question.

t Test An inferential statistical test used to evaluate the difference between two means.

The **t test** is an inferential statistical test used to evaluate the difference between the means of *two groups* (see Chapter 9 for research designs using two groups). Because the two groups in our latency-to-service experiment were independent, we will use an independent-groups *t* test. (The correlated-groups *t* test is discussed in Chapter 9.) The computer printout for our *t* test appears in Table 8-3.

TABLE 8-3	**Computer Printout for Independent-Groups *t* Test**

```
Independent Groups t Test

GROUP      N      M         SD

Dressy     8     48.38      9.46

Sloppy     8     63.25     11.73

    t = 2.61        df = 14     p = .021
```

You can see that our *t* value is 2.61 and that the probability of this *t* value is .021. Because the probability of this result occurring by chance is less than .05, we can conclude that the two groups differ significantly.

If your computer program does not provide the probability of your result as part of the printout, then you will have to make this determination yourself. Here's how. Recall that our *t* value is 2.61. Once we have obtained our *t* value, we must follow several steps in order to interpret its meaning:

1. Determine the degrees of freedom (*df*) involved. (Because some statistical packages may not automatically print the degrees of freedom for you, it is important to keep this formula handy.) For our clothing problem:

$$df = (N_A - 1) + (N_B - 1)$$
$$= (8 - 1) + 8 - 1)$$
$$= 14$$

2. We use the degrees of freedom (we will discuss the meaning of degrees of freedom after we have completed the problem) to enter a *t* table (see Table A-1 in the Appendix). This table contains *t* values that occur by chance. We will compare our *t* value to these chance values. To be significant, the calculated *t* must be equal to or larger than the one in Table A-1.

3. We enter the *t* table on the row for 14 degrees of freedom. Reading across this row we find that a value of 2.145 occurs by chance 5% of the time (.05 level of significance). Because our value of 2.61 is larger than 2.145 (the .05 value in the table for 14 *df*), we can conclude that our result is significant (has a probability of occurring by chance less than .05). Thus, the type of clothing had a significant effect on latency to service. This result is one that occurs fewer than 5 times in 100 by chance. Had we chosen a different level of significance, such as once in 100 occurrences (.01), the table value would have been 2.977 and we would have concluded that our result is not significant. In many instances your computer program will print the probability of your *t* statistic automatically and you will not have to consult the *t* table.

Although it is easy to follow a formula to calculate the degrees of freedom, the meaning of this term may not be clear, even if you have already had an introductory statistics course. We will try to help you understand its meaning. By **degrees of freedom** we mean the ability of a number in a given set to assume any value. This ability is influenced by the restrictions imposed on the set of numbers. For every restriction, one number is determined and will assume a fixed or specified value. For example, assume we have a set of 10 numbers and we know the sum of these numbers to be 100. Knowing that the sum is 100 is a restriction; hence, one of the numbers will be determined or fixed. In Example 1 below, the last number must be 15 because the total of the first 9 numbers (which can assume any value) is 85. In Example 2, the first 9 numbers have assumed different values. What is the value of the last number?

> **Degrees of freedom**
> The ability of a number in a specified set to assume any value.

Numbers	1	2	3	4	5	6	7	8	9	10	Sum
Example 1	6	12	11	4	9	9	14	3	17	15	100
Example 2	21	2	9	7	3	18	6	4	5	?	100

As in the first example, the first nine numbers can assume any value. In this example the sum of the first nine numbers is 75. That means that the value of the last number is fixed at 25.

One-Tail Versus Two-Tail Tests of Significance

Recall from Chapter 2 that you state your experimental hypothesis in either a directional or a nondirectional manner. If you use the directional form, then you are specifying exactly how (i.e., the direction) the results will turn out. For the example we have been considering, an experimental hypothesis, stated in general implication form (see Chapter 2), might be as follows:

> If students wear dressy clothes to the shopping mall, then the time it takes a salesperson to offer to serve them will be shorter than the latency to service for students dressed in sloppy clothes.

Because we predict that the latency to service for the students wearing dressy clothes will be shorter than that for the students wearing sloppy clothes, we have a directional hypothesis. If we simply indicate that we expect a difference between the two groups and do not specify the exact nature of that difference, then we are using a nondirectional hypothesis.

Now, how do directional and nondirectional hypotheses relate to the *t* test? If you remember discussing one-tail and two-tail tests of significance in your statistics class, you're on the right track! A one-tail *t* test evaluates the probability of only one type of outcome, whereas the two-tail *t* test evaluates the probability of both possible outcomes. If you've associated directional hypotheses with one-tail tests and nondirectional hypotheses with two-tail tests, you're right again.

Figure 8-16 depicts the relation between the type of experimental hypothesis (directional versus nondirectional) and the type of *t* test used (one-tail versus two-tail). As you can see, the region of rejection is larger and only in one tail of the distribution when a one-tail test is conducted (Figure 8-16A). The probability of the result occurring by chance alone is split in half and distributed equally to the two tails of the distribution when a two-tail test is conducted (Figure 8-16B).

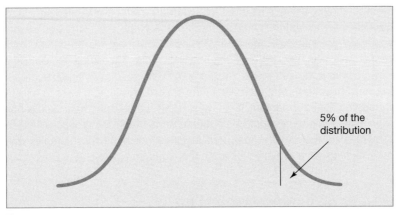

A

A. With a one-tail test the region of rejection of the null hypothesis is located in one tail of the distribution. Directional hypotheses, such as A > B, are associated with one-tail tests.

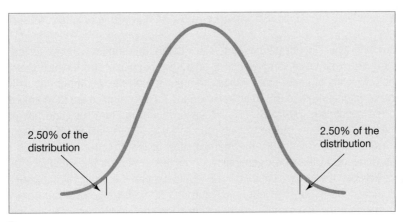

B

B. With a two-tail test the region of rejection of the null hypothesis is distributed evenly to both tails of the distribution. Nondirectional hypotheses, such as A ≠ B (A does not equal B), are associated with two-tail tests.

FIGURE 8-16   Regions of Rejection for (A) a One-Tail Test and (B) a Two-Tail Test.

Although the calculations for a one-tail test of significance and a two-tail test of significance are the same, you would consult different columns in the *t* table. For the shopping center example we conducted a two-tail test of significance; 2.145 was our critical value at the .05 level of significance. Hence, a *t* value equal to or greater than 2.145 is significant (see Table A-1 in the Appendix). Had we done a one-tail test, our critical value at the .05 level of significance would have been 1.761 (see Table A-1).

Because a lower value is required for significance with a one-tail test of significance, it is somewhat easier to find a significant result. If this is the case, why don't experimenters always state directional experimental hypotheses? The main reason is that researchers don't always know exactly how an experiment will turn out. If we knew the outcome of each experiment before it was conducted, there would be no need to do the experiment. If you state a directional hypothesis and then obtain the opposite result, you have to reject your hypothesis. Had you stated a nondirectional hypothesis, your experiment would have confirmed your prediction that there would be a difference between the groups. When conducting a *t* test, researchers are usually interested in either outcome; for example, what if casually dressed students were actually waited on more quickly?

The Logic of Significance Testing

Remember, we consider the result of an experiment to be statistically significant when it occurs rarely by chance. In such instances we assume that our IV produced the results. Although Sherlock Holmes wasn't speaking of a psychological experiment, he captured the intent of significance testing when he asked, "How often have I said to you that when you have eliminated the impossible, whatever remains, *however improbable*, must be the truth?" (Doyle, 1927, p. 111).

However, typically our ultimate interest is not in the samples we have tested in an experiment but in what these samples tell us about the population from which they were drawn. In short, we want to generalize, or *infer*, from our samples to the larger population.

We have diagrammed this logic in Figure 8-17. First, samples are randomly drawn from a specified population (Figure 8-17A). We assume that random selection has produced two equivalent groups: Any differences are due solely to chance factors. In Figure 8-17B we see the results of our experiment; the manipulation of the IV caused the groups to be significantly different. At this point generalization begins. Based on the significant difference that exists between the groups, we *infer* what would happen if our treatments were administered to all individuals in the population. In Figure 8-17C we have generalized from the results of our research using two samples to the entire population (see Chapter 13 for more on generalization). We are inferring that two separate groups would be created in the population due to the administration of our IV.

When Statistics Go Astray: Type I and Type II Errors

Unfortunately, not all our inferences will be correct. Recall that we have determined that an experimental result is significant when it occurs rarely by chance (i.e., 5 times or less in 100). There always is the chance that your experiment represents one of those 5 times in 100 when the results did occur *by chance*. Hence, the null hypothesis is true and you will make an error in accepting your experimental hypothesis. We call this faulty decision a **Type I error** (alpha, α). The experimenter directly controls the probability of making a Type I error by setting the significance level. For example, you are less likely to make a Type I error with a significance level of .01 than with a significance level of .05.

Type I error Accepting the experimental hypothesis when the null hypothesis is true.

However, the more extreme or critical you make the significance level (e.g., going from .05 to .01) to avoid a Type I error, the more likely you are to make a Type II or beta (β)

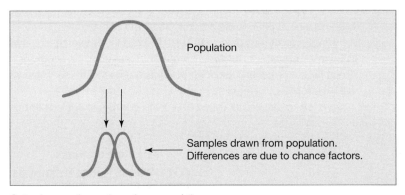

A. Random samples are drawn from a population.

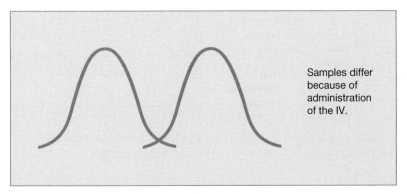

B. The administration of the IV causes the samples to differ significantly.

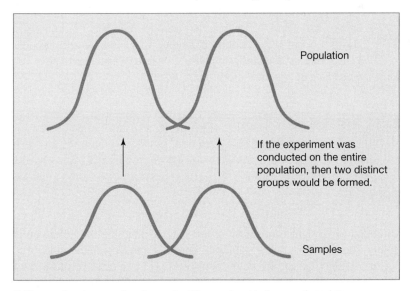

C. The experimenter generalizes the results of the experiment to the general population.

FIGURE 8-17

Type II error Accepting the null hypothesis when the experimental hypothesis is true.

error. A **Type II error** involves rejecting a *true* experimental hypothesis. Unlike Type I errors, Type II errors are not under the direct control of the experimenter. We can indirectly cut down on Type II errors by implementing techniques that will cause our groups to differ as much as possible. For example, the use of a strong IV and larger groups of participants are two techniques that will help avoid Type II errors.

We will have more to say about Type I and Type II errors in subsequent chapters. They are summarized as follows:

		True State of Affairs	
		EXPERIMENTAL HYPOTHESIS IS TRUE	**NULL HYPOTHESIS IS TRUE**
Your Decision	**Experimental Hypothesis Is True**	Correct Decision	Type I (α) Error
	Null Hypothesis Is True	Type II (β) Error	Correct Decision

You should keep in mind that the typical practice is to set the alpha level at .05 because it places the probability of Type I and II errors at acceptable levels.

Effect Size

Effect size The magnitude or size of the experimental treatment.

Before concluding this chapter, we want to introduce you to a statistical concept and procedure that currently is gaining in popularity and frequency of usage. **Effect size** is a statistical measure that conveys information concerning the *magnitude* of the effect produced by the IV.

Doesn't obtaining significance with an inferential test give us the same information? After all, significance indicates the IV had an effect, and that's what we are concerned with. So, why do we need anything else?

Unfortunately, a significant statistical test tells us only that the IV had an effect; it does not tell us about the size of the significant effect. Moreover, whether an effect is significant or not may depend on factors other than the IV. For example, you just saw that you are more likely to obtain significance (i.e., avoid a Type II error) when you use larger samples, even though the influence of the IV remains the same. The *Publication Manual of the American Psychological Association* (2001) indicates that "neither of the two types of probability values [your selected alpha level and the probability level associated with the inferential statistic you calculate] reflects the importance or magnitude of an effect because both depend on sample size" (p. 18).

Such considerations have encouraged researchers to report effect size in addition to inferential statistics that are used. In fact, some statisticians (e.g., Kirk, 1996) can envision a time when the reporting of effect size will be more common than significance testing. Indeed, the *APA Publication Manual* says, "You are encouraged to provide effect-size information" (p. 18) when you prepare your research report.

There are several different ways to calculate effect size. Here are two that should give you no problems. Cohen's *d* (Cohen, 1977) is computed easily when two groups are used and a *t* test is calculated. In these cases:

$$d = \frac{t(N_1 + N_2)}{\sqrt{df} \ \sqrt{N_1 N_2}}$$

or, when the two samples are of equal size:

$$d = \frac{2t}{\sqrt{df}}$$

Cohen (1977) indicated that $d = .20$ to $.50$ is a small effect size, $d = .50$ to $.80$ is a medium effect size, and *d* values greater than .80 reflect large effect sizes.

A second technique for determining effect size is appropriate when you calculate a Pearson product–moment correlation (*r*): r^2 gives you an estimate of the proportion of the variance accounted for by the correlation in question (Rosenthal & Rosnow, 1984). For example, even though $r = .30$ is significant ($p < .01$) with 90 pairs of scores, this correlation accounts for only 9% ($.30^2 = .09 = 9\%$) of the variance. This figure means that 91% of the variability in your research results is accounted for by *other* variables. This is a rather small effect size, indeed!

REVIEW SUMMARY

1. A **correlation coefficient** is a single number that represents the degree of relationship between two variables. Many predictions are based on correlations.

2. A perfect negative correlation (-1) exists when an increase of 1 unit in one variable is always accompanied by a proportional decrease in the other variable. A perfect positive correlation ($+1$) exists when an increase of 1 unit is always accompanied by a proportional increase in the other variable. A correlation of 0 indicates that there is no relation between the variables under consideration.

3. The Pearson product–moment correlation coefficient is calculated when both variables are interval scale measurements.

4. **Inferential statistics** help the experimenter decide whether the IV was effective. A significant inferential statistic is one that occurs rarely by chance.

5. The **t test** is an inferential statistic that is used to test the differences between two groups.

6. When results are significant, the experimenter hopes to be able to extend the results of the experiment to the more general population.

7. A one-tail *t* test is conducted when a directional hypothesis is stated, whereas a two-tail *t* test is conducted when a nondirectional hypothesis is stated.

8. Even though lower critical values are associated with one-tail tests, making it easier to attain significance, most experimental hypotheses are nondirectional because the researchers do not know exactly how the research will turn out.

9. Sometimes the results of an inferential statistical test produce an incorrect decision. An experimental hypothesis may be incorrectly accepted (**Type I error**) or incorrectly rejected (**Type II error**).

CHECK YOUR PROGRESS

1. Matching

   1. correlation coefficient
   2. perfect negative correlation
   3. perfect positive correlation
   4. significant
   5. inferential statistics
   6. Type I error
   7. Type II error
   8. one-tail test
   9. two-tail test

   A. nondirectional hypothesis
   B. result occurs infrequently by chance
   C. rejecting a true null hypothesis
   D. tests conducted to determine if the IV had an effect
   E. directional hypothesis
   F. represents the degree of relationship between two variables
   G. rejecting a true experimental hypothesis
   H. -1
   I. $+1$

2. Explain the difference between a positive correlation and a perfect positive correlation.

3. What does a zero correlation signify?

4. Explain the logic involved when an independent-groups *t* test is conducted.

5. What is meant by "level of significance?" How is the level of significance determined?

6. If it is easier to obtain a significant result with a one-tail test, why would an experimenter ever state a nondirectional experimental hypothesis and be forced to use a two-tail test?

7. A one-tail test of significance is associated with a

   a. directional hypothesis
   b. nondirectional hypothesis
   c. positive correlation
   d. negative correlation

8. The Type I error
   a. is under the direct control of the experimenter
   b. always occurs 5% of the time
   c. is specified by the experimental hypothesis
   d. all of the above
   e. none of the above

9. If you could compare all men and women in the world, you would find that men are significantly more aggressive. You conduct an experiment and find no difference in aggression between men and women. You have made a
   a. correct decision
   b. Type I error
   c. Type II error
   d. Type III error

KEY TERMS

Statistics, 166
Descriptive statistics, 166
Inferential statistics, 166
Measurement, 166
Scale of measurement, 166
Nominal scale, 166
Ordinal scale, 167
Interval scale, 167
Ratio scale, 167
Mode, 168
Median, 168

Mean, 169
Pie chart, 171
Histogram, 171
Bar graph, 172
Frequency polygon, 172
Line graph, 172
Ordinate, 172
Abscissa, 172
Variability, 178
Range, 178
Variance, 178

Standard deviation, 178
Normal distribution, 179
Correlation coefficient, 184
Null hypothesis, 188
t test, 190
Degrees of freedom, 192
Type I error, 194
Type II error, 196
Effect size, 196

LOOKING AHEAD

So far we have considered sources of researchable problems (Chapter 1), developed an experimental hypothesis (Chapter 2), considered the ethics involved in conducting research (Chapter 3), scrutinized our experiment for possible extraneous variables and nuisance variables (Chapter 5), and implemented control procedures to deal with these extraneous variables (Chapters 5 and 6). Now we are ready to combine all of these elements in an experimental design. In Chapter 9 experimental designs involving the use of two groups of participants are considered. We will consider more complex designs in subsequent chapters.

Designing, Conducting, Analyzing, and Interpreting Experiments with Two Groups

Experimental Design: The Basic Building Blocks

Now that the preliminaries are out of the way, we are ready to begin an experiment. Or are we? Although we have chosen a problem, read the relevant literature, developed a hypothesis, selected our variables, instituted control procedures, and considered the participants, we are still not ready to start the experiment. Before we can actually begin, we must select a blueprint. If you were about to design a house, you would be faced with an overwhelming variety of potential plans—you would have many choices and selections ahead of you. Fortunately, selecting a blueprint for your experiment is simpler than designing a house because there are a relatively small number of standard choices that experimenters are likely to use in designing experiments.

Selecting a blueprint for your experiment is just as important as doing so for a house. Can you imagine what a house would look like if you began building it without any plans? The result would be a disaster. The same is true of "building" an experiment. We refer to the research blueprint as our **experimental design**. In Chapter 1 you learned that an experimental design is the general plan for selecting participants, assigning those participants to experimental conditions, controlling extraneous variables, and gathering data. If you begin your experiment without a proper design, your experiment may "collapse" just as a house built without a blueprint might. How can an experiment collapse? We have seen students begin experiments without any direction only to end up with data that fit no known procedure for statistical analysis. We also have seen students collect data that have no bearing on their original question. Thus, we hope not only that you will use this text during your current course but also that you will keep the book and consult it as you design research projects in the future.

> **Experimental design**
> The general plan for selecting participants, assigning participants to experimental conditions, controlling extraneous variables, and gathering data.

In this chapter we will begin developing a series of questions in a flowchart to help you select the correct design for your experiment. As Charles Brewer, distinguished professor of psychology at Furman University, is fond of saying, "If you do not know where you are going, the likelihood that you will get there borders on randomness." If you don't design your experiment properly, the probability that it will answer your research question is slim. Sherlock Holmes knew this lesson well: "No, no: I never guess. It is a shocking habit—destructive to the logical faculty" (Doyle, 1927, p. 93).

When you were a child and played with Legos or Tinkertoys, you probably got a beginner's set first. This set was small and simple, but with it you learned the basics of building. As you got older, you could use larger sets that allowed you to build and create more complicated objects. The parallel between children's building sets and experimental design is striking. In both cases the beginner's set helps us learn about the processes involved so that we can use the advanced set later; the basic set forms the backbone of the more advanced set. In both cases combining simple models increases the possibilities for building, although more complex models must still conform to the basic rules of building.

The Two-Group Design

In this chapter we examine the most basic experimental design, the two-group design, and its variations. This design is the simplest possible one that can yield a valid experiment. In research situations, we typically follow the **principle of**

> **Principle of parsimony**
> The belief that explanations of phenomena and events should remain simple until the simple explanations are no longer valid.

parsimony, also known as Ockham's (or Occam's) razor. William of Ockham, a fourteenth-century philosopher, became famous for his dictum "Let us never introduce more than is required for an explanation" (McInerny, 1970, p. 370). In research, we apply the principle of parsimony to research questions, just as detectives apply the principle of parsimony to their investigations: Don't needlessly complicate the question that you are asking. The two-group design is the most parsimonious design available.

How Many IVs? Figure 9-1 shows the first question we must ask in order to select the appropriate design for our experiment: "How many **independent variables (IVs)** will our experiment have?" In this chapter and the next, we will deal with experimental designs that have one IV. You will remember (see Chapter 6) that an IV is a stimulus or aspect of the environment that the experimenter directly manipulates to determine its influences on behavior, which is the **dependent variable (DV)**. If you want to determine how anxiety affects test performance, for example, anxiety would be your IV. If you wish to study the effects of different therapies on depression, the different therapies would be your IV. The simplest experimental design has only one IV. We will look at research designs with more than one IV in Chapter 11.

> **Independent variable (IV)** A stimulus or aspect of the environment that the experimenter directly manipulates to determine its influences on behavior.
>
> **Dependent variable (DV)** A response or behavior that is measured. It is desired that changes in the DV be directly related to manipulation of the IV.

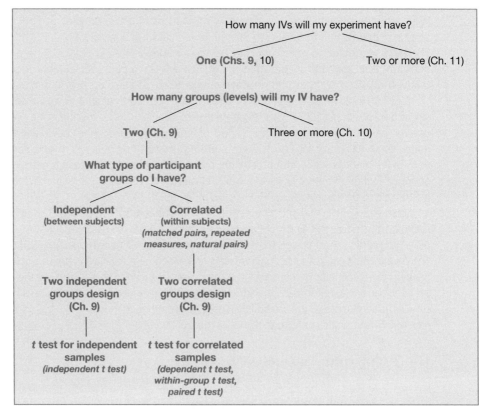

FIGURE 9-1   **Experimental Design Questions.**

A minority of the published research studies use one IV. Does that mean that experiments with one IV are somehow poor or deficient? No, there is nothing wrong with a one-IV design; however, such a design is simple and may not yield all the answers an experimenter desires. However, simple is not necessarily bad! Inexperienced researchers or researchers who are beginning to investigate new areas often prefer single-IV designs because they are easier to conduct than multiple-IV designs and it is simpler to institute the proper control procedures. Also, the results of several one-IV experiments, when combined in one report, can describe complex phenomena.

How Many Groups?   Assuming we have chosen to use a single-IV design, we then come to our second question (see Figure 9-1) in determining the proper experimental design: "How many groups will I use to test my IV?" In this chapter, the answer is two. Although an experiment can have a single IV, it must have at least two groups.

Why must we have two groups but only one IV?

The simplest way to find out whether our IV caused a change in behavior is to compare some research participants who have received our IV to some others who have not received the IV. If those two groups differ, and we are assured that we controlled potential **extraneous variables** (see Chapter 6), then we conclude that the IV caused the participants to differ. So, the way that we have two groups with only one IV is to make the two groups differ in the amount or the type of the IV that they receive. Note carefully that the last statement is *not* the same as saying that the groups have different IVs.

> **Extraneous variables**
> Undesired variables that may operate to influence the DV and, thus, invalidate an experiment.

The most common manner of creating two groups with one IV is to present some amount or type of IV to one group and to withhold that IV from the second group. Thus, the *presence* of the IV is contrasted with the *absence* of the IV. These differing amounts of the IV are referred to as the **levels** (also known as *treatment conditions*) of the IV. Thus, in the common two-group design, one level of the IV is none (its absence) and the other is some amount (its presence). Notice that the presence and absence of an IV is conceptualized as two differing levels of the same IV rather than as two different IVs. Now let's return to our earlier examples.

> **Levels** Differing amounts or types of an IV used in an experiment (also known as *treatment conditions*).

If you were interested in the effects of anxiety on test performance or the effects of therapy on depression, how would you implement an experimental design so that you could compare the presence of the IV to the absence of the IV?

In the first example, you would need to compare anxious test-takers (first level) to nonanxious test-takers (second level). In the second example, you would compare depressed people receiving therapy (first level) to depressed people who were not receiving therapy (second level).

Experimental group In a two-group design, the group of participants that receives the IV.

Control group In a two-group design, the group of participants that does not receive the IV.

In this presence–absence situation, the group of participants receiving the IV is typically referred to as the **experimental group**. It is as if we were conducting the experiment on them. The group that does not receive the IV is known as the **control group**. The members of this group serve a control function because they give us an indication of how people or animals behave under "normal" conditions—that is, without being exposed to our IV. They also serve as a comparison group for the experimental group. We will use statistics to compare performance scores on the DV for the two groups to determine whether the IV has had an effect. When our two groups differ significantly, we assume that the difference is due to the IV. If the groups do not differ significantly, we conclude that our IV had no effect.

Let's look at a research example using the two-group design. Kristen McClellan, a student at Madonna University in Livonia, Michigan, and her faculty advisor, Edie Woods, were interested in how salesclerks would react to customers with a disability. Their IV was the disability of hearing loss. Thus, their experimental group of salesclerks encountered pairs of customers who were deaf (easily identifiable because they entered the store conversing in sign language), and the control group of clerks had the chance to wait on hearing pairs of customers. McClellan and Woods (2001) randomly assigned 77 salesclerks to either the experimental or control group and had the confederates (customers) enter the store. The confederates timed how long it took a salesperson to approach and offer assistance after initial eye contact. McClellan and Woods found that the clerks in the experimental group took significantly longer on average (3.9 minutes) to wait on the deaf customers than the clerks in the control group, who took 1.3 minutes to wait on the hearing customers. This basic two-group design is depicted in Figure 9-2. Block diagrams such as the one in Figure 9-2 are commonly used to graphically portray the design of an experiment. Note that the IV

CONTROL GROUP   OUT OF CONTROL GROUP.

Fortunately, we deal with control groups and experimental groups in psychological research!

INDEPENDENT VARIABLE (CUSTOMER HEARING)
EXPERIMENTAL GROUP   CONTROL GROUP

Customers were deaf	Customers were not deaf

FIGURE 9-2   **The Basic Two-Group Design.**

(customer hearing) heads the entire block, with the two levels of the IV comprising the two subdivisions of the block. We will use this building-block notation throughout the three chapters concerning experimental design so that you can conceptualize the various designs more easily.

Assigning Participants to Groups   We have yet another question to face before we can select our experimental design: We must decide how we plan to assign our research participants to groups. (Before the 1994 edition, the *Publication Manual of the American Psychological Association* referred to research participants as "subjects." You are likely to read this term in older research studies; you may also hear the term for some time before the psychological language becomes standardized—it's hard to teach old psychologists new tricks!)

Random Assignment to Groups   As you saw in Chapter 6, an often-used approach for assigning participants to groups is **random assignment**. Given that we are dealing with only two groups, we could flip a coin and assign participants to one group or the other on the basis of heads or tails. As long as we flip a fair coin, our participants would have a 50-50 chance of ending up in either group. Remember that random assignment is *not* the same as **random selection**, which we also learned about in Chapter 6. Random assignment is concerned with control procedures in the experiment, whereas random selection influences the generality of the results. We will examine the generality issue more closely in Chapter 13.

When we randomly assign our participants to groups, we have created what are known as **independent groups**. The participants in one group have *absolutely no* ties or links to the participants in the other group; they are independent of each other. If you tried to relate or pair a participant in one group to one in the other group, there would be no logical way to do so. When we wish to compare the performance of participants in these two groups, we are making what is known as a **between-subjects comparison**. We are interested in the difference *between* these two groups of participants who have no ties or links to each other.

Terminology in experimental design can sometimes be confusing— for some reason, it has never been standardized. So, you may hear different people refer to *independent groups designs, randomized groups designs*, or *between-subjects designs*. All these names refer to the same basic strategy of randomly assigning participants to groups. The key to avoiding confusion is to understand the principle behind the strategy of random assignment; when you understand the basic ideas, the names will make sense. As you can see in

Random assignment   A method of assigning research participants to groups so that each participant has an equal chance of being in any group.

Random selection   A control technique that ensures that each member of the population has an equal chance of being chosen for an experiment.

Independent groups   Groups of participants that are formed by random assignment.

Between-subjects comparison   Refers to a contrast between groups of participants who were randomly assigned to groups.

Figure 9-1, when we have one IV with two levels and participants that are assigned to groups randomly, our experiment fits the two-independent-groups design.

Random assignment is important in experimental design as a control factor. When we randomly assign our research participants to groups, we can usually assume that our two groups will now be equal on a variety of variables (Spatz, 2001). Many of these variables could be extraneous variables that might confound our experiment if left uncontrolled (see Chapter 6). Random assignment is one of those statistical procedures that is *supposed* to work—in the long run. However, there are no guarantees that it will create the expected outcome if we select a small sample. For example, we would not be surprised to flip a coin 10 times and get 7 or 8 heads. On the other hand, if we flipped a coin 100 times, we would be quite surprised if we obtained 70 or 80 heads.

Thus, when we randomly assign participants to groups, we expect the two groups to be equal on a variety of variables that could affect the experiment's outcome. Think back to McClellan and Woods's (2001) experiment dealing with customers with and without hearing disability and salesclerks' response times. When we described their experiment, we were careful to point out that the researchers *randomly* assigned some clerks to wait on deaf customers and *randomly* assigned some clerks to wait on hearing customers. What if they had picked the most polite clerks to wait on the hearing customers (control group)? Putting the polite clerks in the control group would cause the clerks' politeness to vary systematically with levels of the IV (that is, polite clerks would wait on hearing customers, but less-polite clerks would not). Such assignment to groups would result in a **confounded experiment** (see Chapter 6). If the results showed that the control group clerks waited on the hearing customers faster than the experimental group clerks waited on deaf customers, we could not draw a definite conclusion about why that happened. They might have responded more quickly because they were more polite, because they were waiting on hearing customers, or because of the combination of these two factors. Unfortunately, with a confounded experiment, there is no way to determine which conclusion is appropriate. If McClellan and Woods had conducted their experiment in this manner, they would have wasted their time.

> **Confounded experiment**
> An experiment in which an extraneous variable varies systematically with the IV; makes drawing a cause-and-effect relation impossible.

Let us remind you of one more benefit of random assignment. In Chapter 6 you learned that random assignment is the only technique we have that will help us control unknown extraneous variables. For example, in McClellan and Woods's (2001) experiment, what extraneous variables might affect salesclerks' performance? We have already identified the clerks' politeness as a possibility. However, the researchers did not have access to any politeness measure for the clerks. Other variables that we do not even consider could also play a role in the clerks' performance; hence McClellan and Woods were careful to randomly assign their clerks to experimental and control groups. Random assignment should equate any differences between the two groups.

PSYCHO-LOGICAL DETECTIVE

Can you think of a flaw in McClellan and Woods's reasoning behind random assignment?

Random assignment is a technique that should work in the long run. Because McClellan and Woods assigned 77 clerks to the two groups, there is a good chance that random assignment made the groups perfectly equal. However, if they had measured only a few salesclerks, random assignment might not have created equal groups. If you thought of this potential problem, congratulations! What can we do when we conduct an experiment with small numbers of participants?

Nonrandom Assignment to Groups   In the previous section, we saw a potential pitfall of random assignment—the groups may not turn out equal after all. If we begin our experiment with unequal groups, we have a problem. Remember that random assignment should create equal groups in the long run. In other words, as our groups get larger, we can place more confidence in random assignment achieving what we want it to.

> **Correlated assignment**
> A method of assigning research participants to groups so that there is a relationship between small numbers of participants; these small groups are then randomly assigned to treatment conditions (also known as *paired* or *matched assignment*).

Suppose we are faced with a situation in which we have few potential research participants and we are worried that random assignment may not create equal groups. What can we do? In this type of situation, we can use a nonrandom method of assigning participants to groups. What we will do is either capitalize on an existing relationship between participants or create a relationship between them. In this manner, we know something important about our participants before the experiment and will use **correlated assignment** (also known as *matched* or *paired assignment*) to create equal groups. There are three common ways to use correlated assignment.

1. ***Matched Pairs.***   To create **matched pairs,** we must measure our participants on a variable (other than our IV) that could affect performance on our experiment's DV. Typically we measure a variable that could result in confounding if not controlled. After we have measured this variable, we create pairs of participants that are equal on this variable. After we have created our matched pairs, we then randomly assign participants from these pairs to the different treatment conditions.

> **Matched pairs**
> Research participants in a two-group design who are measured and equated on some variable before the experiment.

If this description seems confusing, an example should help clarify matters. Imagine that we wanted to replicate McClellan and Woods's salesclerk study because we were worried that random assignment may not have created equal groups. Suppose we suspect that female salesclerks tend to wait on customers faster than male clerks (a totally fictitious supposition, but it makes a good example). In this situation, we would be concerned if the ratio of female to male clerks differed between the groups. If we flip a coin to assign clerks to groups, the sex ratio of the groups might be higher in one group. Therefore, we decide to use matched assignment to groups. First, we create our matched pairs. The first pair consists of two clerks of the same sex; the second pair is another two clerks of the same sex. (We pair all the other clerks by sex also.) For each pair, we flip a coin to determine which clerk to assign to the experimental group and which clerk to assign to the control group. Then we repeat the procedure for our second pair, and so on. After we complete this matched assignment, we have an experimental group and a control group that are perfectly balanced in terms of sex. We have used matched assignment to create equal groups before our experiment begins. (Note: In this hypothetical example, if there were an odd number of clerks, one clerk would not have a match, and we could not use that clerk in the experiment.)

In what way is matched assignment guaranteed to create equal groups when random assignment is not?

The beauty of matched assignment is that we have measured our participants on a specific variable that could affect their performance in our experiment and have equated them on that variable. When we use random assignment, we are leaving this equating process to chance. Remember, we must match on a variable that could affect the outcome of our experiment. In the fictitious example we just used, you would need to be certain that sex was linked to salesclerks' performance. If you cannot measure your participants on a variable that is relevant to their performance in your experiment, then you should not use matched assignment. If you match your participants on a variable that is not relevant to their performance, then you have actually hurt your chances of finding a significant difference in your experiment (see "Statistical Issues" in the "Advantages of Correlated Group Designs" section later in this chapter).

Repeated measures An experimental procedure in which research participants are tested or measured more than once.

2. ***Repeated Measures.*** In **repeated measures**, we use the ultimate in matched pairs—we simply test or measure the same participants in both treatment conditions of our experiment. The matched pairs here are perfectly equal because they consist of the same people or animals tested across the entire experiment. No extraneous variables should be able to confound this situation because any difference between the participants' performance in the two treatment conditions is due to the IV. In this type of experiment, participants serve as their own controls.

Why is it not possible to use repeated measures in all experiments? Try to think of two reasons.

Thinking about using repeated measures for our groups forces us to consider some practical factors:
  a. Can we remove the effects of the IV? McClellan and Woods (2001) did not do anything to the salesclerks that had lasting effects—waiting on deaf customers should not affect how clerks respond to other customers in the future. However, in the study cited in Chapter 3, Burkley et al. (2000) could not use repeated measures in

their experiment because they could not remove the effects of reading a particular consent form on the students in their experiment. Think about it carefully—even though they could have allowed students to read the second form, they could not have removed the effects of reading the other form first. If the students remembered the previous form, giving them a new form would not remove its effects.

b. Can we measure our DV more than once? To this point, we have not focused on the DV in this chapter because it has little to do with the choice of an experimental design. However, when you consider using repeated measures, the DV is highly important. When you use repeated measures, the DV is measured multiple times (at least twice). McClellan and Woods could have used repeated measures by having each clerk wait on both a deaf and a hearing customer. However, in some cases, it is simply not possible to use the same DV more than once. In Burkley et al.'s (2000) experiment, once the students had solved the anagrams, solving the anagrams could not be used again as a DV. In other cases, we may be able to use a similar DV, but we must be cautious. To use repeated measures on solving anagrams in Burkley et al.'s experiment, we would need two different sets of anagrams, one for testing students with each type of consent form. If we use two different forms of our DV, we must ensure that they are comparable. Although we could use two sets of anagrams, they would have to be equally difficult, which might be hard to determine. The same would be true of many different DVs— mazes, tests, puzzles, computer programs, and so on. If we cannot assure comparability of two measures of the same DV, then we should not use repeated-measures designs.

c. Can our participants cope with repeated testing? This question relates at least to some degree to the ethics of research, which we covered in Chapter 3. Although no specific ethical principles speak to the use of repeated measures, we should realize that requiring extended participation in our experiment might affect participants' willingness to take part in the research. Also, in extreme cases, extended time in a strenuous or taxing experiment could raise concerns for physical or emotional well-being. Another of our worries in this area is whether human participants will agree to devote the amount of time that we request of them in a repeated-measures design.

It is important that we think about these practical considerations when weighing the possibility of a repeated-measures design. Although repeated-measures designs are one of our better control techniques, there are some experimental questions that simply do not allow the use of such a design.

3. ***Natural Pairs.*** **Natural pairs** is essentially a combination of matched pairs and repeated measures. In this technique, we create pairs of participants from naturally occurring pairs (e.g., biologically or socially related). For example, psychologists who study intelligence often use twins (natural pairs) as their research participants. This approach is similar to using the same participant more than once (repeated measures) but allows you to compose your pairs more easily than through matching. Thus, when you see an experiment that uses

> **Natural pairs** Research participants in a two-group design who are naturally related in some way (e.g., a biological or social relationship).

siblings, parents and children, husbands and wives, littermates, or some biological relationship between its participants, that experiment has used natural pairs.

In summary, whenever there is a relationship between participants in different groups, we are using a correlated-groups design. By looking at Figure 9-1, you can see that planning an experiment with (a) one IV that has (b) two levels, in which you plan to use (c) correlated assignment of participants to groups, results in the *two-correlated-groups design*. Participants who have been matched on some variable or who share some relationship would have scores that are related. When we wish to compare the performance of such participants, we are making what has traditionally been known as a **within-subjects comparison**. We are essentially comparing scores within the same participants (subjects). Although this direct comparison is literally true only for repeated-measures designs, participants in matched or natural pairs are the same with regard to the matching variable.

Within-subjects comparison   Refers to a contrast between groups of participants who were assigned to groups through matched pairs, natural pairs, or repeated measures.

Let's look at a student example of a two-correlated-groups design. A major area of study in psychology is the effect of stress on the body and the body's reactions. Rachel Wells (2001), a student from Nebraska Wesleyan University, found that previous researchers had used a mental arithmetic test to induce stress in participants. She wanted to determine the effects of such a test on college students' bodily reactions. She had students count backward from 715 by 13, telling them that most students could complete the task in 4 minutes. Immediately after counting for 4 minutes, she measured the participants' heart rate and blood pressure. Students then spent 10 minutes completing questionnaires as a nonstressful rest period. After the 10-minute period, Wells measured the participants' heart rate and blood pressure again. The students showed a decrease in both heart rate and blood pressure, demonstrating that the mental arithmetic was, indeed, stress provoking.

Because she used repeated measures, Wells's experiment is a good example of a correlated-groups design. She measured the students' body signs after a stressful event and then again after a rest period. The measurement after the stressor was a posttest; the measurement after rest served as the comparison period. Often in such research, the experimenter might measure the body reactions *before* inducing the stressor; this measurement would be a pretest. In Wells's experiment, the IV was the stress induced and the DV was the students' physiological reactions to the stress. Some of the particularly important participant (subject) variables that Wells controlled by the use of repeated measures were participants' ages (perhaps younger or older people have different reactions to stress), time of day (perhaps physiological indicators vary by the time of day), and students' intelligence (perhaps brighter students would find the task less stressful). All these extraneous variables (and others) were controlled because the *same* students took both the pretest and posttest.

What if Wells had wanted to use matched pairs rather than repeated measures? Remember that matching should occur on a relevant variable—one that could be an extraneous variable if left unchecked. Suppose that these students varied widely in their math ability. Wells might have wanted to create matched pairs based on that ability, thinking that math ability would likely affect performance on the counting task, which could determine the level of stress each student felt. Wells could have used other variables for matching as long as she felt certain that the variables were related to the students' physiological indicators.

Could Wells have run this experiment using natural pairs? Based on the information given you, there is no indication that natural pairs of students existed. If the students were sets of twins, then the experiment would be ideally suited for natural pairs. It seems unlikely that there was any factor that made these students natural pairs, so if pairing was important to Wells, she would have needed to create pairs by matching on some variable.

REVIEW SUMMARY

1. Psychologists plan their experiments beforehand using an **experimental design**, which serves as a blueprint for the experiment.
2. The **two-group design** applies to experimental situations in which you have one IV that has two levels or conditions.
3. Two-group designs often use an **experimental group**, which receives the IV, and a **control group**, which does not receive the IV.
4. **Randomly assigning** research participants to groups results in **independent groups** of participants.
5. **Correlated groups** of research participants are formed by creating **matched pairs**, using **natural pairs**, or by measuring the participants more than once (**repeated measures**).

CHECK YOUR PROGRESS

1. Why can't we conduct a valid experiment with only one group?
2. The differing amounts of your IV are known as the _____ of the IV.
3. How are independent groups and correlated groups different? Why is this difference important to experimental design questions?
4. Matching

   1. random assignment   A. brother and sister
   2. natural pairs   B. take the same test each month
   3. repeated measures   C. two people with the same IQ
   4. matched pairs   D. flipping a coin

5. In what type of situation do we need to be most careful about using random assignment as a control technique?
6. You are planning an experiment that could use either independent groups or correlated groups. Under what conditions should you use a correlated-groups design? When is it acceptable to use random assignment?

7. Random assignment is more likely to create equal groups when
   a. small samples are involved
   b. large samples are involved
   c. a directional hypothesis is being tested
   d. a nondirectional hypothesis is being tested

Comparing Two-Group Designs

Looking at Figure 9-1 again, you can see that the two-independent-groups design and the two-correlated-groups design are quite similar. Both designs describe experimental situations in which you use one IV with two groups. The only difference comes in how you assign your participants to groups. If you simply assign on a random basis, you use the two-independent-groups design. On the other hand, if you match your participants on some variable, if you test your participants twice, or if your participants share some relationship, you use the two-correlated-groups design.

Choosing a Two-Group Design   Now that you have two experimental designs that can handle very similar experimental situations, how can you choose between them? Should you use independent groups or should you use correlated groups of some sort?

You may remember we said that random assignment is supposed to "work" (i.e., create equal groups) in the long run. Therefore, if you are using large groups of participants, random assignment should equate your groups adequately. The next question, of course, is how large is large? Unfortunately, there is no specific answer to this question—the answer may vary from researcher to researcher. If you are using 20 or more participants per group, you can feel fairly safe that randomization will create equal groups. On the other hand, if you are using 5 or fewer participants in a group, randomization may not work. Part of the answer to the question of numbers boils down to what you feel comfortable with, what your research director feels comfortable with, or what you think you could defend to someone. In McClellan and Woods's (2001) study, there were 77 salesclerks to divide into two groups. Given our guidelines, this number is quite adequate to use random assignment to create independent groups. On the other hand, although Wells (2001) had 41 students to participate in the experiment, she may have decided to use repeated measures because she was worried about individual levels of stress that could have created a great deal of variability. Whatever you decide, it is critical to remember that the larger your samples, the more likely random assignment is to create equal groups.

Advantages of Correlated-Groups Designs   There are two primary advantages correlated-groups designs provide for researchers: control and statistical issues. Both advantages are important to you as an experimenter.

Control Issues   One basic assumption that we make before beginning our experiment is that the participants in our groups are equal with respect to the DV. When our groups are equal before the experiment begins and we observe differences between our groups on the DV after the experiment, then we can attribute those differences to the IV. Although randomization is designed to equate our groups, the three methods for creating correlated-groups designs give us greater certainty of equality; we have exerted control to create equal groups. Thus, in correlated designs, we have some "proof" that our participants are equated beforehand. This equality helps us reduce some of the error variation in our experiment, which brings us to the statistical issues.

Statistical Issues   Correlated-groups designs can actually benefit us statistically because they can help reduce error variation. You might be wondering, "What is error variation, anyhow?" In an experiment that involves one IV, you essentially have two sources of variability in your data. One source of variation is your IV—scores on the DV should vary due to the two different treatment groups you have in your experiment. This source of variation, referred to as **between-groups variability**, is what you are attempting to measure in the experiment. There are other factors that can cause variation in the DV, such as individual differences, measurement errors, and extraneous variation—collectively known as **error variability**. As you might guess, our goal in an experiment is to *maximize* the between-groups variability and *minimize* the error or within-groups variability.

> **Between-groups variability**   Variability in DV scores that is due to the effects of the IV.
>
> **Error variability**   Variability in DV scores that is due to factors other than the IV—individual differences, measurement error, and extraneous variation (also known as *within-groups variability*).

Why is it important to reduce error variability? Although formulas for different statistical tests vary widely, they all reduce to the following general formula:

$$\text{statistic} = \frac{\text{between-groups variability}}{\text{error variability}}$$

Remember that the probability of a result occurring by chance goes down as the value of your statistic increases. Thus, larger statistical values are more likely to show significant differences in your experiment. Your knowledge of math tells you that there are two ways to increase the value of your statistic: *increase* the between-groups variability or *decrease* the error variability. (Increasing between-groups variability is a function of your IV [see Chapter 6] and will not be discussed here.)

> Can you figure out why using a correlated-groups design can help reduce error variability?

Earlier in this section we listed individual differences as one source of error variability. Correlated-groups designs help reduce this source of error. If in our treatment groups we use the same participants or participants who share some important characteristic, either naturally or through matching, those participants will exhibit smaller individual differences between the groups than will randomly chosen participants. Imagine how dissimilar to you another participant would be if we chose that person at random. Imagine how similar to you another participant would be if that person was related to you, had the same intelligence as you, or (in the most obvious situation) was you! So, if we use a correlated design, error variability due to individual differences should decrease, our statistic should increase, and we should have a greater chance of finding a significant difference due to our IV.

Why did we use the hedge word *should* three times in the preceding sentence? Remember, when we discussed matched pairs earlier, we said that matching on an irrelevant variable could actually hurt your chances of finding a significant difference. If you match on an irrelevant variable, then the between-groups differences do not decrease. If the between-groups differences do not decrease, your error variability is the same as if you had used an independent-groups design, which results in identical statistical test results. When we use a statistical test for a correlated-groups design, we lose some of the degrees of freedom we would have if we conducted the same experiment with an independent-groups design. In the two-correlated-groups situation, the degrees of freedom are equal to $N - 1$, where N represents the number of *pairs* of participants. In the two-independent-groups situation, the degrees of freedom are $N - 2$, where N represents the *total* number of participants.

Suppose you ran an experiment with 10 participants in each group. How many degrees of freedom would you have if this were an independent-groups design? A correlated-groups design? Did you determine 18 for the independent-groups design and 9 for the correlated-groups design? Using the t table in the back of the book (see Table A-1), you will see that the critical t value at the .05 level with 18 df is 2.101, whereas it is 2.262 with 9 df.

These critical t values make it seem that it would be easier to reject the null hypothesis in the independent-samples situation (critical $t = 2.101$) than in the correlated-groups situation (critical $t = 2.262$). Yet we said earlier that the correlated-groups situation could benefit us statistically. What's going on?

The preceding numbers *do* support the first sentence of the paragraph—it *would* be easier to find a t of 2.101 than of 2.262. However, you must remember that a correlated-groups design should reduce the error variability and result in a larger statistic. Typically, the statistic is increased more than enough to make up for the lost degrees of freedom. Remember that this reasoning is based on the assumption that you have matched on a relevant variable. Matching on an irrelevant variable does not reduce the error variability and will not increase the statistic—in which case the lost degrees of freedom actually hurt your chances of finding significance. We will show you an actual statistical example of this point at the end of the statistical interpretation section later in this chapter.

Advantages of Independent-Groups Designs   The chief advantage of independent-groups designs is their simplicity. Once you have planned your experiment, choosing your participants is quite easy—you merely get a large number of participants and randomly assign them to groups. You don't need to worry about measuring your participants on some variable and then matching them; you don't need to worry about whether each participant can serve in all conditions of your experiment; you don't need to worry about establishing or determining a relationship between your participants—these concerns are relevant only to correlated-groups designs.

Does the statistical advantage of correlated-groups designs render independent-groups designs useless? We cannot argue about the statistical advantage—it is real. However, as you can tell by reviewing the critical t values mentioned earlier, the advantage is not overwhelming. As the number of experimental participants increases, the difference becomes smaller and smaller. For example, the significant t value with 60 df is 2.00, and with 30 df it is only 2.04. If you expect your IV to have a powerful effect, then the statistical advantage of a correlated-groups design will be lessened.

One final point should be made in favor of independent-groups designs. Remember that in some situations it is simply impossible to use a correlated-groups design. Some circumstances do not allow repeated measures (as we pointed out earlier in the chapter), some participant variables cannot be matched, and some participants cannot be related in any way to other participants.

So what is the elusive conclusion? As you might guess, there is no simple, all-purpose answer. A correlated-groups design provides you with additional control and a greater chance of finding statistical significance. On the other hand, independent-groups designs are simpler to set up and conduct and can overcome the statistical advantages of correlated-groups designs if you use large samples. So, if you have large numbers of participants and expect your IV to have a large effect, you are quite safe with an independent-groups design. Alternatively, if you have only a small number of experimental participants and you expect your IV to have a small effect, the advantages of a correlated-groups design would be important to you. For all those in-between cases, you need to weigh the alternatives and choose the type of design that seems to have the greatest advantage.

Variations on the Two-Group Design

To this point, we have described the two-group design as if all two-group designs were identical. This is not the case. Let's look at two variations on this design.

Comparing Different Amounts of an IV   Earlier we said that the most common use of two-group designs was to compare a group of participants receiving the IV (experimental group) to a group that does not receive the IV (control group). Although this is the most common type of two-group design, it is not the only type. The presence–absence manipulation of an IV allows you to determine whether or not the IV has an effect. For example, McClellan and Woods (2001) were able to determine that customers with a hearing disability received help from salesclerks slower than customers without such a disability; Wells (2001) found that her students did react to a mental arithmetic task in a stressful manner. An analogous situation to using the presence–absence manipulation in detective work is trying to sort out the clues that relate to the guilt or innocence of a single suspect.

However, a presence–absence IV manipulation does not allow you to determine the precise effects of the IV. McClellan and Woods did *not* discover whether having salesclerks wait on deaf customers caused a large or small delay in offering help, only that the clerks responded more slowly. Wells did not determine how stressful mental arithmetic was compared to other tasks, only that it did increase stress.

Typically, after we determine that a particular IV has an effect, we would like to have more specific information about that effect. Can we produce the effect with more (or less) of the IV? Will a different IV produce a stronger (or weaker) effect? What is the optimum amount (or type) of the IV? These are just a few of the possible questions that remain after determining that the IV had an effect. Thus, we can follow up on our IV presence–absence experiment with a new two-group experiment that compares different *amounts* or *types* of the IV to determine their effectiveness. Similarly, a detective may have two suspects and be faced with the task of sorting the evidence to decide which suspect is more likely the guilty party.

Some IVs simply cannot be contrasted through presence–absence manipulations. For example, Erin Vaughn (2002) of Ouachita Baptist University in Arkadelphia, Arkansas, was interested in the effects of stereotyping on "person perception." In her experiment, Vaughn wanted to assess the effects of the tendency to stereotype people on the basis of physical attractiveness (IV) on pairing pictures of men and women into dating couples (DV). This question would make little sense in an IV presence–absence situation—people could show more or less of a tendency to stereotype, but not zero or total tendency. Therefore, Vaughn compared differing amounts of this IV. Based on participants' answers to a survey, she formed "high tendency to stereotype" and "low tendency to stereotype" groups. When she compared these two groups' pairings of men and women, she found that people with a high tendency to stereotype created more pairings in which men and women were similar in physical attractiveness. Thus, the tendency to stereotype affected the way that participants believed that dating couples "paired up" in Vaughn's experiment.

The key point to notice when we conduct an experiment contrasting different amounts of our IV is that we no longer have a true control group. In other words, there is no group that receives a zero amount of the IV. Again, we are not trying to determine whether the IV has an effect—we already know that it does. We are merely attempting to find a difference between differing types or amounts of our IV.

Dealing with Measured IVs   To this point, every time we have mentioned IVs in this text, we have emphasized that they are factors that the experimenter *directly manipulates*. Technically, this statement is correct only for a **true experiment**. In a true experiment, the experimenter has total control over the IV and can assign participants to IV conditions. In other words, the experimenter can manipulate the IV. McClellan and Woods (2001) were able to assign their clerks to either the deaf-customer group or the hearing-customer group. If you wish to assess the effects of two different reading programs on teaching children to read, you can assign nonreading children to either program.

> **True experiment**   An experiment in which the experimenter directly manipulates the IV.

As you saw in Chapter 6, there are many IVs (participant IVs) that psychologists wish to study but cannot directly manipulate; we measure them instead. For example, Nicholas Schroeppel, a student at the University of Nebraska in Lincoln, and Gustavo Carlo, his faculty sponsor, examined sex differences in altruistic (helping) behaviors (2001). Because they were not able to directly manipulate the sex of their participants (of course!), Schroeppel and Carlo conducted **ex post facto research** (see Chapter 5). In the context of the present chapter, they used a two-group design. The participants completed scales to measure sympathy, perspective taking, and social desirability; they also received $2 in payment for participation and had the chance to donate any amount of that money to one of four charities. Schroeppel and Carlo found that women scored higher on the sympathy scale and on average donated more money than men ($1.59 compared to $1.16). The men and women did not differ on the perspective-taking or social desirability scales. Based on what we know about sex differences in empathy, Schroeppel and Carlo's finding may not be surprising. We can even develop hypotheses about why women tend to be more empathetic. However, we must be cautious in our interpretation. Perhaps women are biologically predisposed to be more nurturant, or maybe society reinforces women more for behaving empathetically. In any case, although we do know from Schroeppel and Carlo's research that women scored higher than men on sympathy and donated more money than men, we are not certain why they scored higher.

> **Ex post facto research**   A research approach in which the experimenter cannot directly manipulate the IV but can only classify, categorize, or measure the IV because it is predetermined in the participants (e.g., IV = sex).

The drawback of ex post facto research is certainly a serious one. Conducting an experiment without being able to draw a cause-and-effect conclusion is limiting. Why would we want to conduct ex post facto research if we cannot draw definitive conclusions from it? As we mentioned earlier, some of the most interesting psychological variables do not lend themselves to any type of research other than ex post facto. If you wish to study the genesis of female–male differences, you have no option other than doing ex post facto studies. Also, as psychologists continue to conduct ex post facto research, they do make progress. Attempting to specify the determinants of intelligence involves ex post facto research—surely you remember the famous heredity-versus-environment debate over IQ. What we *think* we know today is that both factors affect IQ: Psychologists believe that heredity sets the limits of your possible IQ (i.e., your possible minimum and maximum IQs) and that your environment determines where you fall within that range (Weinberg, 1989). Thus, it seems clear that we should not abandon ex post facto research despite its major drawback. We do, however, need to remember to be extremely cautious in drawing conclusions from ex post facto studies. Detectives, of course, are always faced with ex post facto evidence—it is impossible to manipulate the variables *after* a crime has been committed.

REVIEW SUMMARY

1. **Correlated-groups designs** provide more control because they guarantee equality of the two groups.
2. Correlated-groups designs generally reduce error variability and are more likely to achieve statistically significant results.
3. An advantage of **independent-groups designs** is that they are simple to conduct. With large numbers of research participants, they are also strong designs.
4. Researchers often use two-group designs to compare different amounts (or types) of IVs.
5. We cannot manipulate some IVs, so we must resort to measuring them and conducting **ex post facto research**, which cannot demonstrate cause-and-effect relations.

CHECK YOUR PROGRESS

1. Why is it important that our two groups be equal before the experiment begins?
2. The variability in DV scores that can be attributed to our experimental treatments is called _____ _____; variability from other sources is labeled _____ _____.
3. Which three factors cause variation in DV scores (error variability)?
   a. nonrandom assignment, random assignment, and mixed assignment
   b. individual differences, measurement errors, and extraneous variables
   c. placebo effects, measurement errors, and the IV
   d. variance, standard deviation, and the mean

4. Compare and contrast the advantages and disadvantages of independent and correlated-groups designs.

5. Other than the consent form and mental arithmetic IV examples given in the chapter, give two examples of IVs for which you might wish to compare differing amounts.

6. List three examples of IVs not in the text that you would have to study with ex post facto experiments.

Statistical Analysis: What Do Your Data Show?

After you have used your experimental design to conduct an experiment and gather data, you are ready to use your statistical tools to analyze the data. Let's pause for a moment to see how your experimental design and statistical tests are integrated.

The Relation Between Experimental Design and Statistics

At the beginning of this chapter we compared experimental design to a blueprint and said that you needed a design to know where you were headed. When you carefully plan your experiment and choose the correct experimental design, you also accomplish another big step. Selecting the appropriate experimental design determines the particular statistical test you will use to analyze your data. Because experimental design and statistics are intimately linked, you should determine your experimental design *before* you begin collecting data to ensure there will be an appropriate statistical test you can use to analyze your data. Remember, you don't want to be a professor's classroom example of a student who collected data only to find out there was no way to analyze the data!

Analyzing Two-Group Designs

In this chapter we have looked at one-IV, two-group designs. You may remember from your statistics course, as well as from Chapter 8, that this type of experimental design requires a *t* test to analyze the resulting data (assuming you have interval- or ratio-level data). You may also remember learning about two different types of *t* tests in your statistics class. For a two-independent-groups design, you would use a *t* test for independent samples (also known as an independent *t* test) to analyze your data. For a two-correlated-groups design, you would analyze your data with a *t* test for correlated samples (also called a dependent *t* test, a within-groups *t* test, or a paired *t* test).

Let's make certain that the relation between experimental design and statistics is clear. A *t* test is indicated as the appropriate statistical test because you conducted an experiment with one IV that has two levels (treatment conditions). The decision of *which t* test to use is based on how you assigned your participants to their groups. If you used random assignment, then you will use the *t* test for independent samples. If you used repeated measures, matched pairs, or natural pairs, then you would use the *t* test for correlated samples.

Calculating Your Statistics

In Chapter 8 we provided the computer analysis of a *t* test. The research example involved a comparison of how long it took salespeople to wait on customers who were dressed in sloppy or dressy clothes. In this chapter, we will examine those data more completely. To help set the stage for the remainder of the chapter, let's review some details of the hypothetical experiment behind the data. We wondered whether the clothes students wore actually make any difference in how quickly salesclerks would wait on them. We collected data from 16 different clerks, randomly assigning 8 to wait on customers wearing dressy clothes and 8 to wait on customers wearing sloppy clothes.

Which statistical test would you use to analyze data from this experiment, and why?

The simplest way to answer these questions is to use our chart in Figure 9-1. There is only one IV, the type of clothing worn. That IV has two levels, dressy and sloppy. We randomly assigned the participants to their groups. Thus, this design represents a two-independent-groups design and should be analyzed with an independent *t* test.

Interpretation: Making Sense of Your Statistics

We hope that your statistics instructor taught you an important lesson about statistics: Statistics are not something to fear and avoid; they are a tool to help you understand the data from your experiment. Because of today's focus on computerized statistical analyses, calculating statistics is becoming secondary to interpreting them. Just as having a sewing machine is useless if you don't know how to operate it, statistics are useless if you don't know how to interpret them. Detectives must learn the skills necessary to interpret the reports they receive from the police scientific labs. We will focus on two types of interpretation in this section: interpreting computer statistical output and translating statistical information into experimental outcomes.

Interpreting Computer Statistical Output

There may be hundreds of computer packages available for analyzing data. Thus, it would be impossible (and inefficient) to show output from every different package and teach you how to interpret each one. Remember that we will show you generic computer statistical output and present interpretations of those analyses. We believe that the similarity among statistical packages will allow you to generalize from our examples to the specific package that you may use. (Computerized statistical packages vary widely in the number of decimal places they report for statistical results. To be consistent with APA format, we will round the computerized output and use only two decimal places in the text.)

The *t* Test for Independent Samples Let's return to our statistical example from Chapter 8. Remember, we randomly assigned clerks to one of two groups, a sloppily dressed group of customers or a dressy-clothing group. We sent the customers to stores and obtained the time-to-service scores you saw in Chapter 8. If we analyzed these data using a computer package, what might the output look like? We presented an abbreviated version of the output in Chapter 8 for simplicity's sake; the complete printout appears in Table 9-1.

We usually examine the descriptive statistics first. The descriptive statistics are at the top of the printout. We see that GROUP 1 (defined at the top of the printout as "Dressy Clothing") had 8 cases, a mean salesperson response time of 48.38 seconds, a standard deviation of 10.11 seconds, and a standard error of 3.58 seconds. GROUP 2 (the "Sloppy Clothing" group) had 8 cases, a mean salesperson response time of 63.25 seconds, a standard deviation of 12.54 seconds, and a standard error of 4.44 seconds. Be cautious at this point—an old saying we learned regarding computers is "Garbage in, garbage out." This saying simply means that if you enter incorrect numbers into a computer, you will get incorrect numbers out of the computer. You should always verify any numbers you enter and, as much as possible, double-check the output. "Wait a minute," you may be saying. "What's the use of using a computer if I have to check its work?" We're not suggesting that you check up on the computer but that you check up on yourself! For example, suppose the computer information for GROUP 1 or GROUP 2 showed the number of cases to be seven. You would know that the computer didn't read one number—perhaps you entered only seven scores, or perhaps you mislabeled one score. With only eight scores, it is simple enough to calculate the mean for each group yourself. Why should you do that? If you find the same mean that the computer displays, you can be reasonably certain that you entered the data correctly and, therefore, can go on to interpret your statistics.

The second set of statistics provided contains only two statistical values: F and p. These values represent the results of a test known as F_{max}, a statistic used to test the assumption of

---

TABLE 9–1   Computer Output for *t* Test for Independent Groups

```
GROUP 1 = Dressy clothing
GROUP 2 = Sloppy clothing
Variable = Salesclerks' response time
```

GROUP	N	Mean	SD	Standard Error
GROUP 1	8	48.38	10.113	3.575
GROUP 2	8	63.25	12.544	4.435

F_{max} test F = 1.634 p = 0.222

Equal Variances Assumed

t = 2.61 df = 14 p = 0.021   Cohen's d = 0.92

Equal Variances Not Assumed

t = 2.61 df = 13.4 p = 0.021   Cohen's d = 0.92

homogeneity of variance for the two groups (Kirk, 1968). Homogeneity of variance simply means that the variability of the scores of the two groups is similar. To use a t test, we must assume that the variances are similar. In this particular example, our assumption is justified because the probability of chance for the F value is .22, well above the standard .05 cutoff. Because we have homogeneity of variance, we will use the third block of information ("Equal Variances Assumed") to interpret our test.

> **Homogeneity of variance**   The assumption that the variances are equal for two (or more) groups you plan to compare statistically.
>
> **Heterogeneity of variance**   Occurs when we do not have homogeneity of variance; this means that our two (or more) groups' variances are not equivalent.

In the second set of information, if our p value was less than .05, we would have found **heterogeneity of variance**, meaning that the variability of the scores of the two groups was *not* comparable. Thus, we would be violating a mathematical assumption for using the t test. Fortunately, statisticians have developed a procedure that allows us to interpret our statistics despite heterogeneity. In such a case, we would use the fourth block of information ("Equal Variances Not Assumed") rather than the third block. If the variances of the two groups are equivalent, we can pool or combine those estimates. However, if the variances are not equivalent, we must keep them separate. Again, in our current example, because the F_{max} statistic is not significant ($p = .22$), we will use the statistical results under the "Equal Variances Assumed" heading.

Generally speaking, t tests are **robust** with regard to the assumption of homogeneity (Kirk, 1968). A robust test is one that can tolerate violations of its assumptions and still provide accurate answers. Kirk noted that the t test is so robust that the homogeneity assumption is often not even tested. Therefore, the statistics package you use may not provide information about the F_{max} statistic (and thus probably will not give you equal and unequal variance estimates).

> **Robust**   Refers to a statistical test that can tolerate violation of its assumptions (e.g., homogeneity of variances) and still yield results that are valid.

Looking at the third set of information, we find that our t value (calculated by the computer) is 2.61. We have 14 degrees of freedom ($N_1 + N_2 - 2$). Rather than having to locate these values in a t table to determine significance, we can use the significance level provided by the computer: The probability (two-tail) is .021. Thus, the probability that two means as different as these could have come from the same population by chance is less than 3 in 100. This probability is less than the magical .05 cutoff, so we conclude that these two means are significantly different (i.e., the difference between them is *not* due to chance). In addition, the computer output shows that Cohen's d is 0.92. We learned in Chapter 8 that a d of 0.8 or larger is considered a large effect size. This information helps to confirm that customers' attire plays a major role in determining salesclerks' speed of helping. This decision completes the process of interpreting the computer output. Our next task is describing our statistical information in terms of the experiment we conducted.

Translating Statistics into Words   Think back to the logic of an experiment: We start an experiment with two equal groups and treat them identically (for control purposes) with one exception (our IV); we measure the two groups (on our DV) in order to compare them. At this point, based on our statistical analyses, we know that we have a significant difference (i.e., not due to chance) between our two means. If two equal groups began the experiment and they are now *un*equal, to what can we attribute that difference? If our controls have been adequate, our only choice is to assume that the difference between the groups is due to the IV.

Looking at our example, we have decided that the groups of students dressed in two different types of clothing received help from clerks in different amounts of time. Many students stop at this point, thinking that they have drawn a complete conclusion from their experiment.

Why would this conclusion be incomplete? Can you develop a complete conclusion before proceeding?

Saying that students who are dressed differently get waited on in different amounts of time is an incomplete conclusion because it specifies only a difference, not the *direction* of that difference. Whenever we compare treatments and find a difference, we want to know which group has performed "better." In a two-group experiment, this interpretation is quite simple. Because we have only two groups and we have concluded that they differed significantly, we can further conclude that the group with the higher mean score has outscored the group with the lower mean score (remember that high scores do not always indicate superior performance, as in this case).

To fully interpret the results from this experiment, we examine our descriptive statistics and find that the salespeople waiting on students dressed in sloppy clothes had a mean response time of 63.25 seconds, whereas the salespeople waiting on well-dressed students averaged 48.38 seconds. Thus, we can conclude that salesclerks waiting on nicely dressed customers responded more quickly than those waiting on sloppily dressed customers. Notice that this statement includes both the notion of a difference *and* the direction of that difference.

When we draw conclusions from our research, we want to communicate those results clearly and concisely in our experimental report. To accomplish these two objectives, we use both words and numbers in our communication. This communication pattern is part of the APA style for preparing research reports that we will consider in Chapter 14 (APA, 2001). We will introduce the form for statistical results here. Bear in mind that you are trying to communicate—to tell what you found in words and provide statistical information to support those words. For example, if you were writing an interpretation of the results from our sample experiment, you might write something like the following:

> Salesclerks who waited on well-dressed customers ($M = 48.38$, $SD = 10.11$) took significantly less time, $t(14) = 2.61$, $p = .021$, to respond to customers than salespeople who waited on customers dressed in sloppy clothing ($M = 63.25$, $SD = 12.54$). The effect size, estimated with Cohen's d, was .92.

Notice that the words alone give a clear account of the findings—a person who has never taken a statistics course could understand this conclusion. The inferential statistics regarding the test findings support the conclusion. The descriptive statistics (M = mean, SD = standard deviation) given for each group allow the reader to see how the groups actually performed and to see how variable the data were. This standard format allows us to communicate our statistical results clearly and concisely.

The *t* Test for Correlated Samples   Remember that we have covered two different two-group designs in this chapter. Now we will examine the computer output for analysis of the two-correlated-groups design. Our experiment concerning the salespeople was an example of the two-independent-groups design, which would *not* require a *t* test for correlated samples.

How could you modify this experiment so that it used correlated groups rather than independent groups?

You should remember that there are three methods for creating correlated groups: matched pairs, repeated measures, or natural pairs. If your modified experiment used one of these techniques, you made a correct change. As an example, let's assume that we were worried about the difference between salesclerks confounding our experiment. To better equate the clerks in our two groups, we decided to use the repeated-measures approach. We decide to measure each salesclerk's time to respond to two customers—once for a dressed-up customer and once for a sloppily dressed customer. Before beginning our experiment, we know that the salespeople are identical for the two groups, thus removing individual differences as a potential confounding variable.

Next, we conduct our experiment. We measure the response time of each of the eight clerks waiting on both types of customers (based on dress). Given this hypothetical example, the scores from Chapter 8 would now represent repeated-measures time scores rather than independent scores. After analyzing the data with our computer package, we find the output in Table 9-2. (Please note that it is *not* legitimate to analyze the same data with two different statistical tests. We are doing so in this chapter merely for example's sake. If you tested real-world data multiple times, you would increase the probability of making a Type I error; see Chapter 8.)

Look at Table 9-2. Again, we first look for the descriptive statistics and find them at the top of the printout. Of course, because we used the same data, we have the same descriptive statistics as for the independent-samples test. Salesclerks waiting on the students wearing sloppy clothing responded in an average of 63.25 seconds with a standard deviation of 12.54 and a standard error of 4.44. The students who wore dressy clothes received help in 48.38 seconds with a standard deviation of 10.11 and a standard error of 3.58. Remember that there are 8 *pairs* of scores (representing the 8 clerks) rather than 16 individual scores. This difference between the two *t* tests will be important when we consider the degrees of freedom.

The second block of information shows us the size of the difference between the two means, as well as its standard deviation and standard error. (This information is rarely used and may not appear in your computer output.) The third block gives you some information about the relation between the pairs of participants (or the same participant for repeated

---

TABLE 9-2   Computer Output for *t* Test for Correlated Groups

```
GROUP 1 = Dressy clothing
GROUP 2 = Sloppy clothing
Variable = Salesclerks' response time

              N       Mean      SD      Standard Error

GROUP 1       8       48.38    10.113       3.575
GROUP 2       8       63.25    12.544       4.435

Mean difference = 14.875 SD = 7.699   Std Error = 2.722

Corr. = 0.790        p = 0.020

t = 5.465      df = 7      p = 0.001      Cohen's d = 1.93
```

---

measures). Here you can determine whether the paired scores were correlated. Remember that we want them to be correlated so that we will gain the additional statistical control available by using the correlated-groups design. As you can see in this example, the scores were highly positively correlated (see Chapters 5 and 8). In our example, this result implies that if a salesclerk waited on one student quickly, he or she tended to also wait on the other student quickly.

In the fourth block we find the results of our inferential test. We obtained a *t* value of 5.47 with 7 degrees of freedom.

We have 16 data points (8 clerks measured twice each) in our experiment but only 7 degrees of freedom. In our earlier example, we had 16 participants and 14 degrees of freedom. What is the difference in this case?

You may remember that our degrees of freedom for correlated samples cases are equal to the *number of pairs of participants minus 1*. If this is fuzzy in your memory, refer to "Statistical Issues" earlier in the chapter.

The computer tells us that the probability of a *t* of 5.47 with 7 *df* is .001. With such a low probability of chance for our results, we would conclude that there is a significant difference between the clerks' response times to differently dressed students. In other words, we believe that it is highly unlikely that the difference between our groups could have occurred by chance and that, instead, the difference must be due to our IV. The effect size information, Cohen's *d*, provides ample support for our conclusion as *d* is 1.93. Remember that 0.8 represents a large effect size, so the effect of the IV is quite substantial in this analysis.

Translating Statistics into Words   Our experimental logic is exactly the same for this experiment as it was for the independent samples case. The only difference is that with our matched participants, we are more certain that the two groups are equal before the experiment begins. We still treat our groups equally (control) with the one exception (our IV) and measure their performance (our DV) so that we can compare them statistically.

To translate our statistics into words, it is important to say more than the fact that we found a significant difference. We must know what form or direction that significant difference takes. With the *t* test for correlated samples, we are again comparing two groups, so it is a simple matter of looking at the group means to determine which group outperformed the other. Of course, because we are using the same data, our results are identical: The sloppily dressed students received help in a mean of 63.25 seconds compared to 48.38 seconds for the well-dressed students.

How would you write the results of this experiment in words and numbers for your experimental report?

Did you find yourself flipping back in the book to look at our earlier conclusion? If so, that's a good strategy because this conclusion should be quite similar to the earlier conclusion. In fact, you could almost copy the earlier conclusion as long as you made several important changes. Did you catch those changes? Here's an adaptation of our earlier conclusion:

> Salespeople who waited on well-dressed customers ($M = 48.38$, $SD = 10.11$) took significantly less time, $t(7) = 5.47$, $p = .001$, to respond to the customers than when they waited on customers dressed in sloppy clothes ($M = 63.25$, $SD = 12.54$). The effect size, estimated with Cohen's *d*, was 1.93.

As you can see, four numbers in the sentences changed: We had fewer degrees of freedom, our *t* value was larger, our probability of chance was lower, and our effect size was much larger. In this *purely hypothetical* example in which we analyzed the same data twice (a clear violation of assumptions if you were to do this in the real world), you can see the advantage of correlated-groups designs. Although we lost degrees of freedom compared to the independent-samples case earlier in the chapter, the probability that our results were due to chance actually decreased and our effect size increased dramatically. Again, we gained these advantages because our matching of the participants helped to decrease the variability in the data.

You can see a vivid illustration of what we gained through matching by examining Table 9-3. In this example, we have used the same data from Chapter 8 but shuffled the scores for the second group before we ran a *t* test for correlated samples. Such a situation would occur if you matched your participants on an irrelevant variable (remember that we mentioned this possibility earlier in the chapter). As you can see by comparing Tables 9-3 and 9-2, the descriptive statistics remained the same because the scores in each group did not change. However, in Table 9-3, the correlation between the two sets of scores is now $-.88$. Because

TABLE 9-3   Computer Output for *t* Test for Correlated Groups (Shuffled Data)

```
GROUP 1 = Dressy clothing
GROUP 2 = Sloppy clothing
Variable = Salesclerks' response time

Group       N       Mean      SD        Standard Error
GROUP 1     8       48.38     10.113        3.575
GROUP 2     8       63.25     12.544        4.435

Mean difference = 14.88      SD = 21.977     Std Error = 7.770

Corr. = -.880        p = 0.004

t = 1.91         df = 7          p = 0.097      Cohen's d = 0.68
```

there is a negative correlation between our scores, the *t* value is 1.91, even lower than it was in our *t* test for independent groups (see Table 9-1). The marked change comes when we compare the inferential statistics in Tables 9-2 and 9-3. The original analysis showed a *t* of 5.47 with $p = .001$. In contrast, with a negative correlation between the pairs of scores, the new analysis shows a *t* of 1.91 with $p = .097$ and an effect size of 0.68 (the smallest of our three analyses). Thus, these results did not remain significant when the correlation between the participants disappeared. Again, the key point to remember is that when using a correlated-groups design, the groups should actually be positively correlated.

The Continuing Research Problem

Research is a cyclical, ongoing process. It would be rare for a psychologist to conduct a single research project and stop at that point because that one project had answered all the questions about the particular topic. Instead, one experiment usually answers some of your questions, does not answer others, and raises new ones for your consideration. As you have studied the work of famous psychologists, you may have noticed that many of them established a research area early in their careers and continued working in that area for the duration of their professional lives. We're not trying to say that the research area you choose as an undergraduate will shape your future as a psychologist—although it could! Rather, we are merely pointing out that one good experiment often leads to another.

We want to show you how research is an ongoing process as we move through the next two chapters with our continuing research problem. We sketched out a research problem in Chapter 8 (comparing how customers' style of dress affects salespeople's performance) and asked you to help us solve the problem through experimentation. We will continue to examine this problem throughout the next two chapters so that you can see how different questions we ask about the same problem may require different research designs. This research problem is purely hypothetical, but it has an applied slant to it. We hope the continuing research problem helps you see how a single question can be asked in many different ways *and* that a single question often leads to many new questions.

To make certain you understood the logical series of steps we took in choosing a design, let's review those steps, paying particular attention to our experimental design questions shown in Figure 9-1:

1. After reviewing relevant research literature, we chose our IV (style of dress) and our DV (salesclerk response time).

2. Because we were conducting a preliminary investigation into the effects of clothing on salesclerks' reactions, we decided to test only one IV (the style of dress).

3. Because we wanted to determine only whether clothing style can affect the performance of salespeople, we chose to use only two levels of the IV (dressy clothing vs. sloppy clothing).

4a. If we have a large number of participants available, then we can use random assignment, which yields independent groups. In this case, we would use the two-independent-groups design and analyze the data with a *t* test for independent groups.

4b. If we expect to have a small number of participants and need to exert the maximum degree of control, we choose to use a design with repeated measures or matched groups, thus resulting in correlated groups. Therefore, we would use a two-correlated-groups design for the experiment and analyze the data with a *t* test for correlated groups.

5. We concluded that salespeople responded more quickly to customers in dressy clothes than to customers dressed in sloppy clothes.

REVIEW SUMMARY

1. The statistical test you use for analyzing your experimental data is related to the experimental design you choose.

2. When you have one IV with two groups and use randomly assigned research participants, the appropriate statistical test is the *t* test for *independent* samples.

3. When you have one IV with two groups and use matched pairs, natural pairs, or repeated measures with your participants, the appropriate statistical test is the *t* test for *correlated* samples.

4. Computer printouts of statistics typically give descriptive statistics (including means and standard deviations) and inferential statistics.

5. To communicate statistical results of an experiment, we use APA format for clarity and conciseness.

6. Research is a cyclical, ongoing process. Most experimental questions can be tested with different designs.

CHECK YOUR PROGRESS

1. Which statistical test would you use if you compared the stereotyping of a group of female executives to a group of male executives? Explain your reasoning.

2. Which statistical test would you use if you compared the stereotyping of a group of male executives before and after an antidiscrimination bill passed through Congress? Explain your reasoning.

3. Compared to the *t* test for independent groups, the *t* test for correlated samples has _____ degrees of freedom.

   a. fewer

   b. more

   c. exactly the same number

   d. none of these; it is impossible to compare degrees of freedom between statistical tests

4. What information do we usually look for first on a computer printout? Why?

5. If the variability of our two groups is similar, we have _____; if the variability of the groups is dissimilar, we have _____.

6. When we write a report of our experimental results, we explain the results in _____ and _____.

7. Interpret the following statistics:

   Group A ($M = 75$); Group B ($M = 70$); $t(14) = 2.53$, $p < 0.05$

8. Why do we describe research as a cyclical, ongoing process? Give an example of how this cycling might take place.

KEY TERMS

Experimental design, 201
Principle of parsimony, 201
Independent variable (IV), 202
Dependent variable (DV), 202
Extraneous variables, 203
Levels, 203
Experimental group, 204
Control group, 204
Random assignment, 205
Random selection, 205

Independent groups, 205
Between-subjects comparison, 205
Confounded experiment, 206
Correlated assignment, 207
Matched pairs, 207
Repeated measures, 208
Natural pairs, 209
Within-subjects comparison, 210

Between-groups variability, 213
Error variability, 213
True experiment, 216
Ex post facto research, 216
Homogeneity of variance, 221
Heterogeneity of variance, 221
Robust, 221

LOOKING AHEAD

In this chapter we have examined the notion of planning an experiment by selecting a research design. In particular we examined the basic building-block designs with one IV and two groups. In the next chapter we will enlarge this basic design by adding more groups to our one IV. This enlarged design will give us the capability to ask more penetrating questions about the effects of our IV and to obtain more specific information about those effects.

Designing, Conducting, Analyzing, and Interpreting Experiments with More than Two Groups

Experimental Design: Adding to the Basic Building Block

In Chapter 9 we learned many concepts and principles about **experimental design** that are basic to planning *any* experiment, not merely the basic two-group experiment. When we come to one of those topics in this chapter, we will briefly review it and refer you back to Chapter 9 for the original discussion.

In this chapter we will add to our basic building-block design. Consider our previous analogy: As a child you quickly mastered the beginner's set of Legos or Tinkertoys. You learned to build everything there was to build with that small set and wanted to go beyond those simple objects to build larger, more exciting creations. To satisfy this desire, you got a larger set of building materials that you could combine with the starter set in order to build more complicated objects. Despite the fact you were using a larger set of materials, the basic principles you learned with your starter set still applied.

Experimental design works in much the same way. Researchers typically want to move beyond two-group designs so they can ask more complicated and interesting questions. Fortunately, they don't have to start from scratch—that's why we referred to the two-group design as the basic building-block design in the previous chapter. Every experimental design is based on the two-group design. Although the questions you ask may become more complicated or sophisticated, your experimental design principles will remain constant. In the same way, when they are faced with a more difficult case, detectives continue to use the basic investigative procedures they have learned.

It is still appropriate to think of your experimental design as the blueprint of your experiment. We hope the following analogy convinces you of the need for having an experimental design. Although you *might* be able to get by without a blueprint if you're building a doghouse, it is unlikely you would want to build your *house* without a blueprint. Think of building a small house as being equivalent to using the two-group design from Chapter 9. If you need a blueprint to build a house, imagine how much more you would need a blueprint to build an apartment building or a skyscraper. We will work toward the skyscrapers of experimental design in Chapter 11.

> **Experimental design**
> The general plan for selecting participants, assigning participants to experimental conditions, controlling extraneous variables, and gathering data.

> **Independent variable (IV)** A stimulus or aspect of the environment that the experimenter directly manipulates to determine its influence on behavior.

> **Principle of parsimony** The belief that explanations of phenomena and events should remain simple until the simple explanations are no longer valid.

The Multiple-Group Design

Here, we will consider an extension of the two-group design. Turn back to Figure 9-2 for just a moment. What would be the next logical step to add to this design so that we could ask (and answer) slightly more complex questions?

How Many IVs? The first question that we ask when considering any experimental design is the same: "How many **independent variables (IVs)** will I use in my experiment?" (see Figure 10-1). In this chapter, we will continue to consider experiments that use only one IV. We should remember that although one-IV experiments may be simpler than experiments that use multiple IVs (Chapter 11), they are not inferior in any way. Many students who are designing their first research study decide to throw in everything except the kitchen sink as an IV. A well-designed experiment with one IV is vastly preferable to a sloppy experiment with many variables thrown together. Remember the **principle of parsimony**

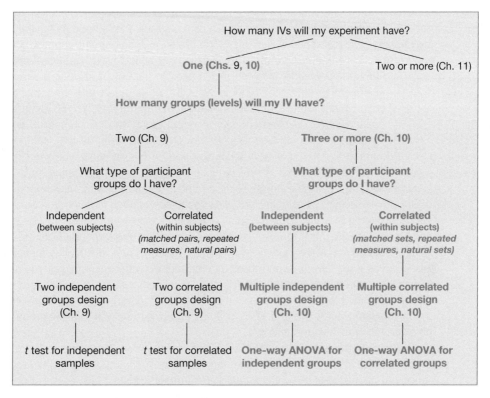

FIGURE 10-1   **Experimental Design Questions.**

from Chapter 9—if a one-IV experiment can answer your questions, use it and don't complicate things needlessly.

How Many Groups?   Once we have chosen to conduct a one-IV experiment, our second question (see Figure 10-1) revolves around how many groups we will use to test the IV. This question marks the difference between the multiple-group design and the two-group design. As their names imply, a two-group design compares two **levels** of an IV, whereas a multiple-group design compares three or more levels of a single IV. Thus, we could compare three, four, five, or even more differing levels of amounts of an IV. This experimental situation is similar to that experienced by a detective faced with multiple suspects. Instead of merely investigating two people, the detective must conduct simultaneous investigations of several individuals.

> **Levels**   Differing amounts or types of an IV used in an experiment (also known as *treatment conditions*).

In Chapter 9 we learned that the most common type of two-group design uses experimental and control groups. How will the multiple-group design differ from that common two-group design?

Actually, there are two answers to that question—if you got either, pat yourself on the back. (a) A multiple-group design *can* have a control group. But rather than having an experimental and a control group, a multiple-group design with a control group would also have two or more experimental groups. This combination allows us to condense several two-group experiments into one experiment. Instead of conducting a two-group experiment to determine whether your IV has an effect and a second two-group experiment to determine the optimum amount of your IV, you could conduct a multiple-group experiment with a control group and the number of **treatment groups** you would like to assess. (b) A multiple-group design does not have to have a control group. If you already know that your IV has an effect, you can simply compare as many treatment groups as you would like in your multiple-group design.

Treatment groups
Groups of participants that receive the IV.

Let's look at a research example using the multiple-group design. Michael Jones (2001) of Lincoln Memorial University in Harrogate, Tennessee, wanted to determine whether noise affected children's performance on recall and spatial tasks (see Chapter 7). He used white noise (static), music, and no noise conditions. Why does this experiment fit the multiple-group design? First, it has one IV—the type of noise. Second, the IV has more than two levels—it has three, based on the three different noise conditions. Thus, as you can see in Figure 10-1, with one IV and three levels, this experiment requires a multiple-group design. We can draw the block diagram depicted in Figure 10-2 to portray this experimental design. If you compare Figures 9-2 and 10-2, you can easily see how the multiple-group design is an extension of the two-group design.

Two of the groups in Figure 10-2 are experimental groups. Does this experiment use a control group? Yes, the no noise condition served as a control group. In this experiment, Jones was interested in the various differences among the three groups based on their differing types of noise. He found that children in the white noise condition performed better than children in the music condition; children in the no noise condition scored between the two noise conditions but were not significantly different from either group. In statistical terminology, then, Jones found results that supported the experimental hypothesis (i.e., that there was a difference between the performance of the groups as a function of noise condition). However, support for the experimental hypothesis is not the same as *proving* the experimental hypothesis. Did Jones *prove* that noise affects children's performance on recall and spatial performance? No, he merely demonstrated that there was a difference that was unlikely to have occurred by chance for the noise conditions he used and for his groups of participants. What about using different sounds? What about using different research participants—musicians or adults, for example? File away this clue for future exploration—in Chapter 13 we will talk about how to generalize our results beyond the specific participants in our experiment.

INDEPENDENT VARIABLE (Type of Noise)

EXPERIMENTAL GROUP 1	EXPERIMENTAL GROUP 2	EXPERIMENTAL GROUP 3
White noise	Music	No Noise

FIGURE 10-2   **The Multiple-Group Design Used by Jones (2001).**

Suppose you wished to test more than three noise conditions. Could you use a multiple-group design in such a case? Why or why not? If so, what would happen to the block design in Figure 10-2?

Yes, you could use the multiple-group design if you had four or five noises to assess. In fact, it could be used if there were 10, 20, or 100 sounds. The only requirement for using the multiple-group design is an experiment with one IV and more than two groups (see Figure 10-1). Practically speaking, it is rare that multiple-group designs are used with more than four or five groups. If we did use such a design with more than three groups, we would merely extend our block diagram, as shown in Figure 10-3.

Assigning Participants to Groups   After we decide to conduct a multiple-group experiment, we must decide about assignment of research participants to groups (see Figure 10-1). Just as in Chapter 9, we choose between using **independent groups** or **correlated groups**.

Independent Samples (Random Assignment to Groups)   Remember that with **random assignment** each participant has an equal chance of being assigned to any group. In his experiment on the effects of noise on performance, Jones (2001) used random assignment when he assigned children to groups—all 60 children had a 1 in 3 chance of being in the no noise, white noise, or music group. When we use large groups of participants, random assignment should create groups that are equal on potential extraneous variables such as personality, age, and sex. Recall from Chapter 9 that random assignment allows us to control extraneous variables about which we are unaware. Thus, random assignment serves as an important **control procedure**. For example, we would not want to use music with only boys or girls. We want to spread the different levels of the IV across all types of participants in order to avoid a **confounded experiment**. Suppose we put all girls in the music condition and all boys in the white noise condition. When we tabulated our results, we would not be able to draw a clear conclusion about the effects of noise because noise was confounded with participant sex.

Independent groups
Groups of participants that are formed by random assignment.

Correlated groups
Groups of research participants that are related in some way—through matching, repeated measures, or natural sets.

Random assignment
A method of assigning research participants to groups so that each participant has an equal chance of being in any group.

Control procedure
One of several steps experimenters take to ensure that potential extraneous variables are controlled. Examples include random assignment, matching, and so on.

Confounded experiment
An experiment in which an extraneous variable varies systematically with the IV; makes drawing a cause-and-effect relation impossible.

INDEPENDENT VARIABLE (Type of Noise)

EXPL GROUP 1	EXPL GROUP 2	EXPL GROUP 3	EXPL GROUP 4	EXPL GROUP 5
Noise 1	Noise 2	Noise 3	Noise 4	Noise 5

FIGURE 10-3   **Hypothetical Multiple-Group Design with Five Groups.**

cathy® by Cathy Guisewite

Is Cathy using random assignment or random selection in this cartoon? You may want to look back at Chapters 4 and 5.

Because she is tasting chocolate Santas in a nonsystematic way (rather than assigning Santas to groups), Cathy's gluttony illustrates random selection.

Random assignment results in participants who have no relation to participants in other groups; in other words, the groups are independent of each other. We are interested in comparing differences between the various independent groups. As shown in Figure 10-1, when we use random assignment in this design, we end up with a multiple-independent-groups design.

Correlated Samples (Nonrandom Assignment to Groups) In the multiple-group design, we have the same concern about random assignment that we did with the two-group design: What if the random assignment does not work and we begin our experiment with unequal groups? We know that random assignment *should* create equal groups, but that it is most likely to work in the long run—that is, when we have many participants. If we have few participants or if we expect only small differences due to our IV, we may want more control than random assignment affords us. In such situations, we often resort to using nonrandom methods of assigning participants to groups and thus end up with correlated groups. Let's examine our three ways of creating correlated groups and see how they differ from the strategies discussed in Chapter 9.

1. ***Matched Sets.*** Matched *pairs* are not appropriate for the multiple-group design because we have at least three groups, so we must use matched *sets*. The principle for forming matched sets is the same as that for forming matched pairs. Before our experiment, we measure our participants on some variable that will affect their performance on the DV. Then we create sets of participants who are essentially the same on this measured variable, often known as the **matching variable**. The size of the sets will, of course, depend on how many levels our IV has. If our IV has five levels, for example, then each set would have five participants equated on the matching variable. After we create our matched sets, we then randomly assign the participants within each set to the different groups (treatments).

> **Matching variable** A potential extraneous variable on which we measure our research participants and from which we form sets of participants who are equal on the variable.

Returning to Jones's experiment, suppose we believed that participant sex would be an extraneous variable because we were playing Britney Spears's music (which Jones did). To ensure equality of his groups on sex, Jones could have used sets of three participants who were matched on sex, with each participant then randomly assigned to one of the three groups. In this manner, he would have assured that the distribution of participant sex was uniform across all three groups. If all three of his groups had the same sex composition (regardless of whether it was 50–50), then participant sex could not be an extraneous variable.

One final caution is in order. We should remember that the potential extraneous variable must actually affect performance on the DV or else we have hurt our chances of finding a significant difference.

2. ***Repeated Measures.*** Other than the fact that participants perform in three or more conditions rather than only two, repeated measures in the multiple-group design are identical to repeated measures in the two-group design. When you use repeated measures in the multiple-group design, each participant must take part in *all* the various treatment conditions. Thus, for Jones to have used repeated measures, each child would have participated in the no noise, white noise, and music conditions.

Can you see any possible flaws in conducting Jones's experiment using a repeated-measures design? (Hint: Consider some of the practical issues from Chapter 9 about using repeated measures.)

Several problems could occur if we attempted the noise experiment with a repeated-measures design. Would you have one child perform the same task three different times? This approach would not seem to make any sense. The children might become suspicious about the differing noises; they would probably be able to figure out what the IV was. Or they might get tired from performing the task three times and not try hard on the third attempt. What about using three different tasks? Again, this approach could be problematic. Could we logically assume that children performed differently because of the noise? Not necessarily, because different tasks would have to cover different skills or knowledge. Students would be more likely to perform well on a task that dealt with a skill they enjoyed or had previously learned. Thus, we might be measuring the response rate to different tasks rather than to different types of noises! It seems that this experiment simply would not work well as a repeated-measures design. Remember that we mentioned this possible problem in Chapter 9—not all experiments can be conducted using repeated measures.

3. ***Natural Sets.*** Using natural sets is analogous to using natural pairs except that our sets must include more than two research participants. Using multiple groups takes away our ability to use some interesting natural pairs such as twins or husbands and wives, but other possibilities for using natural sets do exist. For example, many animal researchers use littermates as natural sets, assuming that their shared heredity makes them more

similar than randomly selected animals. In a similar fashion, if your research participants were siblings from families with three (or more) children, natural sets would be a possibility. Most natural pairs or sets involve biological relationships.

We create multiple-correlated-groups designs when we use matched sets, repeated measures, or natural sets. The critical distinction is that the participants in these types of groups are related to each other in some way—we are comparing differences *within* groups (or within subjects, to use the old terminology). On the other hand, in independent-groups designs, the participants have no common relationship. Thus, we compare differences *between* differing groups of subjects.

Kimberly Walker and her faculty advisors James Arruda and Keegan Greenier (1999) of Mercer University in Macon, Georgia, conducted an experiment that used a multiple-correlated-groups design. They were interested in measuring how accurately people respond on the Visual Analogue Scale (VAS). The VAS is a self-report scale used for people to indicate internal states such as mood, hunger, or pain. Participants respond on the VAS by making a mark somewhere along a line, typically 100 millimeters (mm) in length, that has marks at the ends designating extreme low and high values of the internal state. Walker et al. asked participants to make marks at distances of 10, 20, 30, 40, 50, 60, 70, 80, and 90 mm along the line. They calculated participants' errors by subtracting the difference between the actual distance and the marked distance. By measuring the errors over nine distances, Walker et al. could compare data to determine whether errors were more likely at different points along the line.

Why does the Walker, Arruda, and Greenier experiment illustrate a correlated-groups design? Which particular correlated-groups technique did they use? Why do you think they used a correlated-groups design?

In this experiment, the IV was distance, measured in mm. Thus, there were nine levels of the IV. They measured each participant on each different distance, so the correlated groups were a result of using repeated measures. Walker et al. probably used a repeated-measures design because it would take an enormous number of participants if they had each participant serve in only one distance group (nine groups of people needed). Also, it would have been an inefficient use of participants to use nine different groups. Finally, by having people participate in all levels of the IV, Walker et al. did not have to worry about the assumption that the groups were equivalent before the experiment began. By using each person as his or her own control across the nine measurements, the question of group equality was answered. The use of repeated measures helped control many subject variables that *might* have affected participants' performance on the VAS—factors such as motivation, spatial ability, and sex.

Walker et al. (1999) found that the participants were more accurate in making marks at the beginning and end of the VAS line than in the middle of the line. They explained their results as being due to a perceptual phenomenon—the law of visual angle. Further, they recommended adding depth cues to the VAS to increase accuracy on the task.

Comparing the Multiple-Group and Two-Group Designs

The multiple-group design is highly similar to the two-group design. As a matter of fact, all you have to do to change your two-group design into a multiple-group design is add another level (or more) to your IV. Given this high degree of similarity, how would we compare these two designs?

In choosing a design for your experiment, your paramount concern is your experimental question. Does your question require only two groups to find an answer, or does it necessitate three or more groups? This question almost seems like a "no-brainer," but it cannot be taken for granted. Following the principle of parsimony from Chapter 9, we want to select the simplest design possible that will answer our question.

In Chapter 9 we provided you with an ideal situation for a two-group design—an experiment in which we merely wish to determine whether or not our IV has an effect. Often such an experiment is not necessary because that information already exists in the literature. You should never conduct an experiment to determine whether a particular IV has an effect or not without first conducting a thorough literature search (see Chapter 2). If you find no answer in a library search, then you should consider conducting a two-group (presence–absence) study. If, however, you find the answer to that basic question and wish to go further, then a multiple-group design might be appropriate.

After these considerations, what do you do when you face a situation in which either a two-group design or a multiple-group design is appropriate? Although this answer may sound odd, you should think about your (future) results. What will they look like? What will they mean? Most critically, what will the addition of any group(s) beyond the basic two tell you? If the information that you expect to find by adding a group or groups is important and meaningful, then by all means add the groups. If, however, you're not really certain what you might learn by adding to the two groups, then you may be complicating your life needlessly to do so.

Think back to the two student examples cited in this chapter. Did the researchers learn important information by adding an extra group to their two groups? Jones (2001) found that task performance differed with three different types of noise (no noise, white noise, and music). Some people would probably wish for more levels in this experiment rather than for fewer. In fact, one of your first thoughts when you read about Jones's experiment earlier may have been, "I wonder how students would respond to _____?" (fill in the blank with a sound that bothers you or that you enjoy). You may believe that his experiment was not a fair test of the question about performance based on noise level, especially if you disagree with his noise choices. So it appears that Jones made a wise decision in using a multiple-group design rather than a two-group design. In fact, it might have been more informative had he used an even larger multiple-group design.

Walker et al. (1999) measured peoples' responses on the VAS to nine different distances. They clearly benefited by using a multiple-group design. If they had simply measured the responses on short or long distances, they would have found little error in the responses.

Suppose Walker et al. (1999) wanted to use a smaller or larger multiple-group design—say measuring people's responses over 5 or 15 distances rather than 9. Would it be possible to use such a small or large multiple-group design?

Could you use a multiple-group design with 5 or 15 groups or measurements? Sure you could. The only limitation would be a practical consideration—could you secure enough participants to take part (for matched sets or natural sets), or can the participants cope with being measured so many times (for repeated measures)? The Walker et al. experiment used repeated measures, so our concern would be for the experimental participants. In this case, all that would happen to the participants is that they would be measured either fewer or more times. So this experiment would be no problem to run over 5 measurement distances; participants would have fewer responses to make. The question is whether 5 distances would give the experimenters all the information they needed. On the other hand, using 15 measurements might make the task extremely difficult for the participants to discriminate; it would require more of the experimenters' time. Using 9 levels of an IV for repeated measures is quite unusual, so it is much more likely that other experimenters would use smaller, rather than larger, experimental designs.

In summary, the multiple-group and two-group designs are quite similar. However, there are important differences between them that you should consider when choosing an experimental design for your research project.

Comparing Multiple-Group Designs

As you might guess, our comparison of the multiple-independent-groups design to the multiple-correlated-groups design is going to be fairly similar to our comparison of the two-group designs in Chapter 9. However, practical considerations become somewhat more important in the multiple-group designs, so our conclusions will be somewhat different.

Choosing a Multiple-Group Design   Again, your first consideration in choosing an experimental design should always be your experimental question. Once you have decided on an experiment with one IV and three or more groups, you must determine whether you should use independent or correlated groups. If only one of those choices is viable, you have no further considerations to make. If, however, you could use either independent or correlated groups, you must make that decision before proceeding.

Control Issues   As with the two-group designs discussed in Chapter 9, your decision to use the multiple-independent-groups design versus the multiple-correlated-groups design revolves around control issues. The multiple-independent-groups design uses the control technique of randomly assigning participants to groups. If you have a substantial number of research participants (at least 10 per group), you can be fairly confident that random assignment will create equal groups. Multiple-correlated-groups designs use the control techniques of matching, repeated measures, or natural pairs to assure equality of groups and to reduce error variability. Recall the equation that represents the general formula for a statistical test:

$$\text{statistic} = \frac{\text{between-groups variability}}{\text{error variability}}$$

Reducing the error variability in the denominator of the equation will result in a larger computed statistical value, thereby making it easier to reject the null hypothesis. You may remember from Chapter 9 that using a correlated-groups design reduces your degrees of freedom, which makes it somewhat more difficult to achieve statistical significance and reject the null hypothesis. However, the reduced error variability typically more than offsets the loss of degrees of freedom. Therefore, correlated designs often produce stronger tests for finding statistical significance.

Practical Considerations   Matters of practicality become quite important when we contemplate using a multiple-correlated-groups design. Let's think about each type of correlated design in turn. If we intend to use *matched sets*, we must consider the potential difficulty of finding three (or more) participants to match on the extraneous variable we choose. Suppose we conduct a learning experiment and thus wish to match our participants on IQ. How difficult will it be to find three, four, five, or more participants (depending on the number of levels we use) with the same IQ? If we cannot find enough to make a complete set of matches, then we cannot use those participants in our experiment. Therefore, we may lose potential research participants through the requirement of large matched sets. We may be limited in our use of *natural sets* by set size also. How much chance would you have of running an experiment on triplets, quadruplets, or quintuplets? Using animal littermates is probably the most common use of natural sets in multiple-group designs. When we use *repeated measures* in a multiple-group design, we are requiring each participant to be measured at least three times. This requirement necessitates more time for each participant or multiple trips to the laboratory, conditions the participants may not be willing to meet. We hope this message is clear: If you intend to use a multiple-correlated-groups design, plan it very carefully so that these basic practical considerations do not sabotage your experiment.

What about practical considerations in multiple-independent-groups designs? The multiple-independent-groups design is simpler than the correlated version. The practical factor you must take into account is the large number of research participants you will need to make random assignment feasible *and* to fill the multiple groups. If participants are not available in large numbers, you need to consider using a correlated design.

Drawing a definite conclusion about running independent versus correlated multiple-group designs is not simple. The correlated designs have some statistical advantages, but they also require you to take into account several practical matters that may make using such a design difficult. Independent designs are simple to implement, but they force you to recruit or obtain many research participants to assure equality of your groups. The best advice we can provide is to remind you that each experiment presents you with unique problems, opportunities, and questions. You need to be aware of the factors we have presented and to weigh them carefully in conjunction with your experimental question when you choose a specific research design for your experiment.

Variations on the Multiple-Group Design

In Chapter 9 we discussed two variations on the two-group design. Those same two variations are also possible with the multiple-group design.

Comparing Different Amounts of an IV   This "variation" on the multiple-group design is not actually a variation at all—it is part of the basic design. Because the smallest possible multiple-group design would consist of three treatment groups, every multiple-group design must compare different amounts (or types) of an IV. Even if a multiple-group design has a control group, there are at least two different treatment groups in addition.

If we already know that a particular IV has an effect, then we can use a multiple-group design to help us define the limits of that effect. In this type of experiment, we often add an important control in order to account for a possible **placebo effect**. For example, is it possible that some of the effects of coffee on our alertness are due to what we *expect* the coffee to do? If so, a proper control group would consist of people who drink decaffeinated coffee. These participants would be blind to the fact that their coffee does not contain caffeine. This group, without any caffeine, would show us whether there are any placebo effects of coffee.

Dealing with Measured IVs   All the research examples we have cited in this chapter deal with manipulated IVs. It is also possible to use measured IVs in a multiple-group design. In Chapter 9 you learned that research we conduct with a measured rather than manipulated IV is termed **ex post facto research**. We cannot draw cause-and-effect relations from such an experiment because we do not directly control and manipulate the IV ourselves. Still, an ex post facto design can yield interesting information. Let's look at a student example of an ex post facto design with a measured IV.

Amanda Gray and her advisor Jennifer Lucas (2001) used an ex post facto approach in their study of commuters' perceptions of travel impedance and driver stress (see Chapter 5). They used Novaco, Kliewer, and Broquet's (1990) Subjective Impedance Scale to classify their participants' perceptions of travel impedance as high, average, or low. Why does this experimental design fit the multiple-group format? Does it have one IV? Yes, perception of travel impedance. Does it have three or more levels of that one IV? Yes, the high, average, or low perception. These perceptions were their measured IV—the researchers could not assign commuters to one of the different perception groups; they could only measure which level of perception was exhibited.

Gray and Lucas (2001) found that the high-perceived-impedance group reported the highest level of driver stress and the average group reported more driver stress than the low-perceived-impedance group. Notice that the multiple-group design allowed Gray and Lucas to detect a difference between one group versus the two other groups *and* a difference that occurred among all three groups. These types of findings show the advantage of the multiple-group design over the two-group design. Remember these various types of differences because we will return to them in the "Statistical Analysis" section of the chapter, next.

> **Placebo effect**   An experimental effect that is due to expectation or suggestion rather than the IV.
>
> **Ex post facto research**   A research approach in which the experimenter cannot directly manipulate the IV but can only classify, categorize, or measure the IV because it is predetermined in the participants (e.g., IV = sex).

REVIEW SUMMARY

1. Psychologists plan their experiments beforehand using an **experimental design**, which serves as a blueprint for the experiment.

2. You use the **multiple-group design** for experimental situations in which you have one **independent variable (IV)** that has three or more levels or conditions. A **control group** may or may not be used.

3. You form **independent groups** of research participants by **randomly assigning** them to treatment groups.

4. You form **correlated groups** of research participants by creating matched sets, using natural sets, or measuring each participant more than once (repeated measures).

5. **Multiple-correlated-groups designs** provide extra advantages for experimental control relative to **multiple-independent-groups designs**.

6. Practical considerations in dealing with research participants make the multiple-correlated-groups designs considerably more complicated than multiple-independent-groups designs.

7. Measured IVs can be used in multiple-group designs, resulting in **ex post facto studies**.

CHECK YOUR PROGRESS

1. Why is the two-group design the building block for the multiple-group design?

2. The simplest possible multiple-group design would have _____ IV(s) and _____ treatment group(s).

3. What advantage(s) can you see in using a multiple-group design rather than a two-group design?

4. Devise an experimental question that could be answered with a multiple-group design that you could not answer with a two-group design.

5. Why are matched sets, repeated measures, and natural sets all considered *correlated-groups* designs?

6. What is the real limit on the number of groups that can be included in a multiple-group design? What is the practical limit?

7. Make a list of the factors you would consider in choosing between a multiple-group design and a two-group design.

8. Correlated-groups designs are often advantageous to use because they _____.

9. Why are practical considerations of using a multiple-correlated-groups design more demanding than for using a two-correlated-groups design or a multiple-independent-groups design?

10. If we wished to compare personality traits of firstborn, lastborn, and only children, what type of design would we use? Would this represent a true experiment or an ex post facto study? Why?

Statistical Analysis: What Do Your Data Show?

We will remind you from the previous chapter that experimental design and statistical analysis are intimately linked. You *must* go through the decision-making process we have outlined before you begin your experiment in order to avoid the possibility that you will run your experiment and collect your data only to find out that there is no statistical test that you can use to analyze your data.

Analyzing Multiple-Group Designs

In this chapter we have looked at designs that have one IV with three (or more) groups. In your introductory statistics course you probably learned that these multiple-group designs are analyzed with the *analysis of variance* (ANOVA) statistical procedure. As you will see, we will also use ANOVA to analyze our designs that include more than one IV (see Chapter 11), so we need some way to distinguish between these types of ANOVA. In this chapter, we are looking at an ANOVA for one IV; researchers typically refer to this procedure as a **one-way ANOVA**.

You remember that we have looked at both multiple-independent-groups and multiple-correlated-groups designs in this chapter. We need two different types of one-way ANOVA to analyze these two types of designs, just as we needed different *t* tests in Chapter 9. As you can see from Figure 10-1, when we assign our participants to multiple groups randomly, we will analyze our data with a one-way ANOVA for independent groups (also known as a **completely randomized ANOVA**). On the other hand, if we use matched sets, natural sets, or repeated measures, we will use a one-way ANOVA for correlated groups (also known as a **repeated-measures ANOVA**) to evaluate our data.

> **One-way ANOVA** A statistical test used to analyze data from an experimental design with one independent variable that has three or more groups (levels).
>
> **Completely randomized ANOVA** A one-way ANOVA that uses independent groups of participants.
>
> **Repeated-measures ANOVA** A one-way ANOVA that uses correlated groups of participants.

Calculating Your Statistics

In Chapter 9 we featured the statistical analysis of data from an experiment designed to compare the response time of saleclerks as a function of their customers' clothing (also see Chapter 8). That example, of course, cannot serve as a data analysis example for this chapter because it represents a two-group design.

Suppose we have already conducted the sample experiment covered in Chapters 8 and 9. How could we conduct a similar experiment using a multiple-groups design?

The *most* similar experiment would be one in which students in the introductory class dressed in three different types of clothing rather than just two. Suppose that we decide to investigate further because we found (in Chapter 8) that salesclerks responded more quickly to customers in dressy clothes than to those dressed in sloppy clothes. We decide to add an intermediate clothing group—we choose to add casual clothing as our third group. Again, we need to consider the **operational definition** of our new IV group. We define casual clothing as slacks and shirts (e.g., khakis and polo shirts) for both male and female customers. We have 24 students in the class, so we have 8 students as "stimuli" in each of the three groups (one group for each type of clothing). We have the students go to the same store on the same day and randomly choose a department to browse in. The store is large and employs many clerks, so there is no problem with finding a different clerk for each student. This ran-

> **Operational definition** Defining the independent, dependent, and extraneous variables in terms of the operations needed to produce them.

TABLE 10-1	Salesclerks' Response Times for Hypothetical Clothing Style Experiment	
	CLOTHING STYLES	
Dressy	**Sloppy**	**Casual**
37	50	39
38	46	38
44	62	47
47	52	44
49	74	50
49	69	48
54	77	70
69	76	55
Mean = 48.38	Mean = 63.25	Mean = 48.88

dom choice will allow the salesclerks to be randomly assigned to the three groups (a requirement to create independent groups). An observer goes with the students to unobtrusively time the salesclerks' response time to each student, which is the DV. You can see the clerks' response times in Table 10-1. Let's discuss the basis behind the ANOVA procedure before we look at our statistical analyses.

Rationale of ANOVA

We expect that you learned something about ANOVA in your statistics course. We introduced a closely related concept in the "Control Issues" section in Chapter 9; you may wish to refer back to that section. You will remember that variability in your data can be divided into two sources—**between-groups variability** and **error variability** (also known as **within-groups variability**). The between-groups variability represents the variation in the DV that is due to the IV, whereas the error variability is due to factors such as individual differences, errors in measurement, and extraneous variation. Look at Table 10-2, which is a slightly altered version of Table 10-1.

Between-groups variability   Variability in DV scores that is due to the effects of the IV.

Error variability   Variability in DV scores that is due to factors other than the IV—individual differences, measurement error, and extraneous variation.

Within-groups variability   Same as error variability.

PSYCHO-
LOGICAL
DETECTIVE

What type of variability do you think is represented by the arrows in Table 10-2? What type of variability do you think is shown in the circled columns? If you have trouble with these questions, reread the previous paragraph.

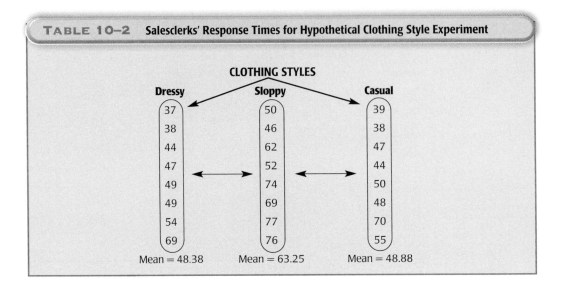

TABLE 10–2   Salesclerks' Response Times for Hypothetical Clothing Style Experiment

CLOTHING STYLES

Dressy	Sloppy	Casual
37	50	39
38	46	38
44	62	47
47	52	44
49	74	50
49	69	48
54	77	70
69	76	55
Mean = 48.38	Mean = 63.25	Mean = 48.88

The variability *between* the groups' response times represents the variability caused by the IV (the different types of clothing). Therefore, the arrows represent the between-groups variability. If the times differ among the three groups of clerks, the clothes should be responsible for the difference (assuming we have controlled extraneous variables). On the other hand, error variability should occur among the participants *within* each particular group (thus its name, *within-groups variability*); this is the variability represented by the circled columns.

"Wait a minute," you may say. "What we have just described as within-groups variability—individual differences, measurement errors, extraneous variation—can occur between the groups just as easily as within the groups." This thought represents very good thinking on your part. Your point is correct and is well taken. Thus, we must change the formula that we reviewed just a few pages ago:

$$\text{statistic} = \frac{\text{between-groups variability}}{\text{error variability}}$$

The fact that we can find error between our groups as well as within our groups forces us to alter this formula to the general formula shown below for ANOVA. The *F* symbol is used for ANOVA in honor of Sir Ronald A. Fisher (1890–1962), who developed the ANOVA (Spatz, 2001).

$$F = \frac{\text{variability due to IV + error variability}}{\text{error variability}}$$

If our IV has a strong treatment effect and creates much more variability than all the error variability, we should find that the numerator of this equation is considerably larger than the denominator (see Figure 10-4A). The result, then, would be a large *F* ratio. If, on the other hand, the IV has absolutely no effect, there would be no variability due to the IV, meaning

A Between groups — | — Within groups

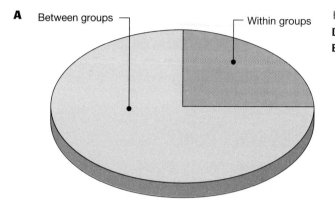

FIGURE 10-4 Possible
**Distributions of Variability in an
Experiment.**

B Between groups — | — Within groups

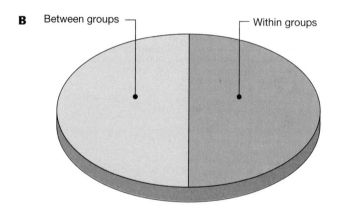

we would add 0 for that factor in the equation. In such a case, our *F* ratio should be close to 1 because the error variability between groups should approximately equal the error variability within groups. This situation is depicted in Figure 10-4B.

The notion that has evolved for the ANOVA is that we are comparing the ratio of between-groups variability to within-groups variability. Thus, the *F* ratio is conceptualized (and computed) with the following formula:

$$F = \frac{\text{between-groups variability}}{\text{within-groups variability}}$$

A simple way to think of ANOVA is that you are dividing the treatment effect by the error. When the IV has a significant effect on the DV, the *F* ratio will be large; when the IV has no effect or only a small effect, the *F* ratio will be small (near 1). You may wish to place a bookmark at this page—we will refer back to it shortly.

Interpretation: Making Sense of Your Statistics

With the addition of a third group, our experimental design has become slightly more complicated than the two-group design of Chapter 9. As you will see, adding a third group (or more) creates an interesting statistical problem for us so that we often need to compute an extra statistical test to explore significant findings.

Interpreting Computer Statistical Output

Once again we will look at generic computer output to give you experience with typical output so that you can better generalize your knowledge to the particular statistical package that is available to you. The results appear in Table 10-3.

TABLE 10–3   Computer Output for One-Way ANOVA for Independent Samples

GROUP	N	MEAN	STD DEV	STD ERR	95% CONF INT
1 (dressy)	8	48.38	10.11	3.57	39.92–56.83
2 (sloppy)	8	63.25	12.54	4.44	52.76–73.74
3 (casual)	8	48.88	10.20	3.61	40.34–57.41

ONEWAY ANOVA: RESPTIME by CLOTHING

SOURCE	SUM OF SQUARES	DF	MEAN SQUARES	F RATIO	PROB.
BETWEEN GROUPS	1141.75	2	570.88	4.71	.02
WITHIN GROUPS	2546.25	21	121.25		
TOTAL	3688.00	23			

POST HOC TEST: Tukey-HSD with significance level .05

* Indicates significant differences shown for pairings

Mean	CLOTHING	G r p 1	G r p 2	G r p 3
48.38	Grp 1			
63.25	Grp 2	*		*
48.88	Grp 3			

One-Way ANOVA for Independent Samples   We are examining results from a one-way ANOVA because we have one IV with three groups. We used the ANOVA for independent samples because we randomly assigned salesclerks to the three different clothing conditions. The DV scores represent the clerks' response times to differently attired customers.

As usual, we look for information about descriptive statistics first. You will find the descriptive statistics in the top portion of Table 10-3. Before going on, remember that we recommended that you make sure you have entered your data correctly in the computer by checking the means using a calculator. It will take only a few minutes but will spare you from using an incorrect set of results if you somehow goofed when you put the numbers in the computer. We can see that Group 1 (clerks responding to customers in dressy clothes) had a mean response time of 48.38 seconds, Group 2 (sloppy clothing) had a mean of 63.25 seconds, and Group 3 (casual clothes) responded in 48.88 seconds on the average. So, we do see numerical differences among these means, but we do not know if the differences are large enough to be significant until we examine the inferential statistics. We also see the standard deviation and standard error (standard deviation divided by $\sqrt{n}$) for each group (the times for group 2 are more variable than those of the other two groups), as well as 95% confidence intervals. You may remember that confidence intervals provide a range of scores between which μ (the true population mean) should fall. Thus, we are 95% confident that the interval of 40.34 to 57.41 seconds contains the population mean for all clerks responding to customers in casual clothing.

The inferential statistics appear immediately below the descriptive statistics. We see the heading "ONEWAY ANOVA," which lets us know that we have actually computed a one-way ANOVA. The subheading shows us that we have analyzed the variable "RESPTIME" in relation to the "CLOTHING" variable. This label simply means that we have analyzed our DV (RESPTIME, the clerks' response times) by our IV (CLOTHING, the three styles of dress).

The output from ANOVA is typically referred to as a **source table**. In looking at the table, you will see "SOURCE" printed on the left side of the page. Source tables get their name because they isolate and highlight the different *sources* of variation in the data. In the one-way ANOVA table, you see two sources of variation: between groups and within groups. Do you remember what these two terms refer to? *Between groups* is synonymous with our treatment (IV) effect, and *within groups* is our error variance.

The **sum of squares**, the sum of the squared deviations around the mean, is used to represent the variability of the DV in the experiment (Kirk, 1968). We use ANOVA to divide (partition) the variability into its respective components, in this case between-groups and within-groups variability. In Table 10-3, you see that the total sum of squares (variability in the entire experiment) is 3688, which is partitioned into between-groups sum of squares (1141.75) and within-groups sum of squares (2546.25). The between-groups sum of squares added to the within-group sum of squares should always be equal to the total sum of squares (1141.75 + 2546.25 = 3688).

If we formed a ratio of the between-groups variability and the within-groups variability based on the sums of squares, we would obtain a ratio of less than 1. However, we cannot use the sums of squares for this ratio because each sum of squares is based on a different number of deviations from the mean (Keppel, Saufley, & Tokunaga, 1992). Think about this

> **Source table**   A table that contains the results of ANOVA. *Source* refers to the source of the different types of variation.
>
> **Sum of squares**   The amount of variability in the DV attributable to each source.

Mean square The "averaged" variability for each source; computed by dividing each source's sum of squares by its degrees of freedom.

idea for a moment—there are only three groups that can contribute to the be-tween-groups variability, but there are many participants who can contribute to the within-groups variability. Thus, to put them on an equal footing, we need to transform our sums of squares to **mean squares**. We make this transformation by dividing each sum of squares by its respective degrees of freedom. Because we have three groups, our between-groups degrees of freedom are 2 (number of groups minus 1). Because we have 24 participants, our within-groups degrees of freedom are 21 (number of participants minus the number of groups). Our total degrees of freedom are equal to the total number of participants minus 1, or 23 in this case. As with the sums of squares, the between-groups degrees of freedom added to the within-groups degrees of freedom must equal the total degrees of freedom (2 + 21 = 23). Again, our mean squares are equal to each sum of squares divided by its degrees of freedom. Thus, our between-groups mean square is 570.9 (1141.75/2) and our within-groups mean square is 121.3 (2546.25/21).

Variance A single number that represents the total amount of variation in a distribution; also, the square of the standard deviation, σ^2.

We should note at this point that a mean square is analogous to an estimate of the **variance**, which you may remember from statistics as the square of the standard deviation (σ^2). Once we have the mean squares, we can then create our distribution of variation. Rather than drawing pie charts like those shown in Figure 10-4, we compute an F ratio to compare the two sources of variation. Referring to the bookmark we advised you to use a few pages back, we find that the F ratio is equal to the between-groups variability divided by the within-groups variability. Because we are using mean squares as our estimates of variability, the equation for our F ratio becomes

$$F = \frac{\text{mean square between groups}}{\text{mean square within groups}}$$

Thus, our F ratio of 4.71, as shown in Table 10-3, was derived by dividing 570.9 by 121.3. This result means that the variability between our groups is almost 5 times larger than the variability within the groups. Or, perhaps more clearly, the variability due to the IV is almost 5 times larger than the variability due to error. If we drew a pie chart for these results, it would look like Figure 10-5.

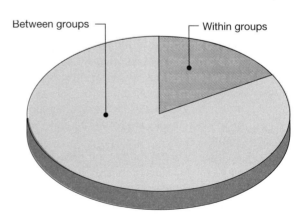

FIGURE 10-5 **Distribution of Variability for Different Clothing Experiment.**

Finally, we come to the conclusion (or so we think!). Did the different clothing styles have a significant effect? Next to "F RATIO" in Table 10-3 you see the "PROB" entry, .02. This probability of chance of these data (if the null hypothesis is true) is certainly lower than .05, so we did find a significant difference. The difference in the response times among the three groups of salesclerks probably did not occur by chance. Although the computer printed the probability of chance for you, you should know how to use a printed F table just in case your computer program does not calculate probabilities. This activity is somewhat different than using a printed t table because in ANOVA we have two values for degrees of freedom. In this case, our degrees of freedom are 2 (between groups, in the numerator) and 21 (within groups, in the denominator). When we look in the F table (see Table A-2), the column will show the numerator df and the row will show the denominator df. In this case, you must find 2 in the numerator column and 21 on the denominator line and locate the intersection of those two numbers. At that point you will see 3.47 as the .05 cutoff and 5.78 as the .01 cutoff. Because our F value of 4.71 is between these two numbers, the probability that it could have occurred by chance is less than .05 but greater than .01. Thus, if you were using a table rather than the computer output, you would have written $p < .05$ or $.01 < p < .05$ (to be as specific as possible). Sherlock Holmes stated, "I could only say what was the balance of probability" (Doyle, 1927, p. 93).

With the two-group design, we would be finished with our computer output at this point and could go on to interpreting our statistics in words. With significant findings in a two-group design, we merely note the higher mean and conclude that it is significantly higher than the other mean. However, this decision procedure is not correct with the multiple-group design when we find a significant difference because we have more than two means. We know there is significance among our means because of our significant F ratio, but which one(s) is (are) different from which one(s)? From a significant F ratio, we cannot tell.

To discern where the significance lies in a multiple-group experiment, we must do additional statistical tests known as **post hoc comparisons** (also known as *follow-up tests*). These tests allow us to determine which groups differ significantly from each other once we have determined that there is overall significance (by finding a significant F ratio). Many different post hoc tests exist, and there is much debate over these tests that is beyond the scope of this text. Simply remember that you will need to conduct post hoc tests if you find overall significance in a one-way ANOVA.

> **Post hoc comparisons** Statistical comparisons made between group means after finding a significant F ratio.

At the bottom of Table 10-3, you see the results of a post hoc test known as the Tukey HSD (an abbreviation for *honestly significant difference*). The Tukey test allows you to test all pairwise comparisons, meaning that you can test the difference between all sets of two means (Keppel, Saufley, & Tokunaga, 1992). In looking at Table 10-3, we see that Group 2 is significantly different at the .05 level from both Group 1 and Group 3 according to the Tukey test. This result means that the clerks took significantly longer to wait on sloppily dressed students (63.25 seconds) than either those in casual (48.88 seconds) or those in dressy clothes (48.38 seconds). No other groups differed significantly from each other, meaning that there was no statistical difference in the time it took clerks to wait on students dressed well or casually.

As in the previous chapter, we hope that you are learning general principles about computer printouts rather than specific words or terms for which you will blindly search. If you understand the general principles, interchanging *between groups* with *clothing* (or the name of some other IV) should not be problematical for you—different statistical programs may simply use different ways of getting at the same thing (much like having slightly different names for the same test). For example, don't be surprised to see the label *error* rather than *within groups*—both terms mean the same thing. The important conclusion is that given the same data, any two programs should find the same results.

Translating Statistics into Words   Let us remind you, as we did in Chapter 9, that the results of any statistical test are only as good as your experimental procedures. In other words, if you have conducted a sloppy experiment, your statistical results will be meaningless. When we draw the conclusion that our IV has caused a difference in the DV scores, we are assuming that we conducted a well-controlled experiment and removed extraneous variables from the scene. If you find that extraneous variables have confounded your experiment, you should not interpret your statistics because they are now meaningless. This is the same reason detectives must learn specific ways to collect evidence in the field. If they collect contaminated evidence, all the lab tests in the world cannot yield a definitive conclusion.

Based on our inferential statistics, we can conclude that the clothing customers wear is important because clerks took differing amounts of time to wait on customers depending on how they were dressed.

Although this conclusion is technically correct, it is a poor conclusion. Why? How would you revise this conclusion to make it better?

This conclusion is poor because it is incomplete. Reread the sentence and decide what you learn from it. All you know is that students who wore some type of clothing were waited on more quickly than students who wore some other clothing. Thus, you know that clothes can make a difference, but you don't know which type of clothing led to faster responses. To write a good conclusion, we must go back to our inferential statistics, particularly the post hoc tests. In Table 10-3, we find that students wearing dressy clothes were waited on in 48.38 seconds, students wearing sloppy clothes received attention in 63.25 seconds, and students wearing casual clothes got help in 48.88 seconds. The significant *F* ratio lets us know that there is significance *somewhere* among those means. The Tukey post hoc comparison tests informed us that the differences between Group 2 and both Groups 1 and 3 were significant. To interpret this difference, we must examine our descriptive statistics. When we examine the means, we are able to conclude that students in shabby clothes got help significantly more slowly than the students in dressy or casual clothes. *No other mean differences were significant.*

We must determine how to communicate our statistical findings in APA format. We will use a combination of words and numbers. There are many different ways to write this set of findings in an experimental report. Here is one example:

The effect of different clothing on salesclerks' response time was significant, $F(2, 21) = 4.71$, $p = .02$. The proportion of variance accounted for by the clothing effect (η^2) was .31. Tukey tests indicated ($p < .05$) that clerks waiting on customers dressed in sloppy clothes ($M = 63.25$, $SD = 11.73$) responded more slowly than clerks waiting on customers in dressy ($M = 48.38$, $SD = 9.46$) or casual clothes ($M = 48.88$, $SD = 9.55$). The response times of clerks waiting on customers in dressy and casual clothes did not differ from each other.

The words alone should convey the meaning of our results. Could someone with no statistical background read and understand these sentences if we removed the numbers? We think so. The inferential test results explain our finding to readers with a statistical background. The descriptive statistics allow the reader to observe exactly how the groups performed and how variable that performance was. The effect size information reported here, η^2 (eta squared), is similar to r^2 because it tells you the proportion of variance in the DV (response times) accounted for by the IV (clothing). (An easy way to calculate η^2 is to divide the between-groups sum of squares by the total sum of squares.) The reader has an expectation about what information will be given because we write our results in this standard APA format. You will find this type of communication in results sections in experimental articles. As you read more results sections, this type of communication will become familiar to you.

One-Way ANOVA for Correlated Samples Now we will look at the one-way ANOVA for correlated samples. The sample experiment about clothing and clerks' response times we have used so far in the chapter fits the multiple-group design for independent samples and thus is not appropriate to analyze with the one-way ANOVA for correlated samples.

How could the experiment concerning salesclerks' reactions to customers' style of dress be modified so that it used correlated groups rather than independent groups?

To be correct, you should have proposed the use of matched sets, natural sets, or repeated measures in your modified experiment. The best choices would involve matched sets or repeated measures; we don't think that natural sets is feasible in this situation—you're not using littermates, and finding sets of triplets who are all salesclerks is most unlikely! If you chose matched sets, you must decide on a matching variable. It is difficult to know what variable on which you should match salesclerks that would be related to their reactions to different clothing styles. Matched sets would not be a good choice for forming correlated groups.

Imagine that you conduct your experiment at a small store that employs only a few salesclerks. In order to have enough data points, you decide to have each salesclerk respond to a customer in each of the three clothing groups. Because you would measure each clerk's response times to all three styles of dress, you would control possible individual differences between the clerks. (Another scenario that might lead you to use repeated measures would occur if you decided that it is likely that some variable in salesclerks, such as attitudes, might affect their response times to customers in different types of clothing. Using repeated measures would allow you to essentially cancel out differences between different clerks, because each clerk would wait on a customer in each clothing group.)

You are now ready to begin the experiment. The students each dress in one of the three styles and enter the store. Because we are using repeated measures, we know for certain that the clerks in the three groups are equated (because they are the same clerks in each group). Given this hypothetical example, the scores in Table 10-1 would now represent sets of response times from eight salesclerks. (Remember that in the real world, it is not legitimate to analyze the same data with two different statistical tests. This is a textbook, certainly not the real world, and we are doing this as an example only.)

You can see the results for the one-way ANOVA for correlated samples in Table 10-4. As usual, we are first interested in obtaining descriptive statistics. The descriptive output is shown at the top of Table 10-4. As you can see, we obtain the mean, standard deviation, sample size, and 95% confidence interval for each group. The descriptive statistics for the three groups match what we have previously seen in Table 10-3, which is certainly logical.

TABLE 10-4 **Computer Output for One-Way ANOVA for Correlated Samples**

GROUP	N	MEAN	STD DEV	STD ERR	95% CONF INT
1 (dressy)	8	48.38	10.11	3.57	39.92–56.83
2 (sloppy)	8	63.25	12.54	4.44	52.76–73.74
3 (casual)	8	48.88	10.20	3.61	40.34–57.41

ONEWAY ANOVA: RESPTIME by CLOTHING (CORR SAMP)

SOURCE	SUM OF SQUARES	DF	MEAN SQUARES	F RATIO	PROB.
CLOTHING	1141.75	2	570.88	19.71	.000
SUBJECTS	2140.65	7	305.81	10.56	.000
WITHIN CELLS	405.59	14	28.97		
TOTAL	3688.00	23			

POST HOC TEST: Tukey HSD with significance level .01

* Indicates significant differences shown for pairings

			G r p 1	G r p 2	G r p 3
Mean	CLOTHING				
48.38	Grp 1				
63.25	Grp 2		*		*
48.88	Grp 3				

Although we are now using a correlated-samples analysis, nothing has changed about the samples themselves. So, we see the same means, standard deviations, and confidence intervals that we have seen before.

The other information that we see in Table 10-4 is our source table. Once again, the entries in this particular source table vary slightly from the tables we've looked at earlier. Although you may begin to believe that this is some sinister plot hatched just to confuse you, you need to focus on the basic information, remembering that terms are used slightly differently in different situations. Here, our two sources of variance are labeled "within cells" and "clothing." Because you know that we are comparing different types of clothing as our IV, it should be clear that "clothing" represents the effect of our IV and "within cells" represents our source of error variation (refer back to Table 10-2 to see our within-cell variation pictorially represented by the circles). When we examine the source table, we find that the F ratio for the comparison of the clerks' response times to different clothing styles is 19.71, with 2 (numerator) and 14 (denominator) degrees of freedom, which results in a probability of chance of .000 according to the computer.

This situation illustrates one of our pet peeves with computerized statistical programs. When you studied distributions in your statistics class, what did you learn about the tails of those distributions? We hope you learned that the tails of distributions are **asymptotic**—that is, the tails extend into infinity and never touch the baseline. This fact means that the probability of a statistic is *never* .000 no matter how large the statistic gets—there is always some small amount of probability under the tails of the distribution. Unfortunately, people who design statistics software either have a limited number of columns to work with *or* they don't think about this issue, so they have the computer print

> **Asymptotic** Refers to tails of distributions that approach the baseline but never touch the baseline.

a probability of .000, implying that there is no uncertainty. In light of this problem, we advise you to list $p < .001$ if you ever find such a result on your computer printout.

Pardon the digression, but you know how pet peeves are! Back to the statistics. The overall effect of the clothing is significant, which leads us to wonder which clothing styles differ from each other. This source table looks different from the one in Table 10-3 because it shows the effects of two IVs—CLOTHING and SUBJECTS. Although the SUBJECTS effect is significant, it does not tell us anything very important: We simply learn that there were significant differences between the eight salesclerks' response times. In other words, we found individual differences between the salesclerks. This effect is an expected one and is not profound. Typically, you would ignore this effect. However, the SUBJECTS effect *is* important statistically. If you compare Tables 10-3 and 10-4, you will see that the correlated samples ANOVA has taken the SUBJECTS variability (mean square) out of the WITHIN CELLS (or error) variability compared to the WITHIN GROUPS (or error) term in the independent-samples ANOVA. This difference demonstrates the power of the correlated-samples analysis to reduce variability in the error term and create a larger F ratio.

As with the multiple-group design for independent samples, we used a Tukey test for post hoc comparisons. Again, we found that Group 2 (sloppy clothing) was significantly different ($p < .01$) from both Group 1 (dress clothes) and Group 3 (casual clothes). However, Groups 1 and 3 did not perform significantly differently. Notice that our significant differences are at the .01 level rather than .05 as with the independent-samples case. This change is another indication of the increased power of the correlated-samples analysis.

Translating Statistics into Words Our experimental logic is no different from that for the independent-samples ANOVA. The only difference is that we used a somewhat more stringent control procedure in this design—we used repeated measures with our participants rather than assigning them to groups randomly.

Our conclusions should combine our numbers with words to give the reader a clear indication of what we found. Remember to include information both about any difference that was found as well as the directionality of such a difference.

How would you write the results of this experiment in words and numbers for an experimental report?

Although the conclusion for the correlated-samples test is similar to that for the independent-groups test, it is different in some important ways. We hope you figured out those important differences. Here's a sample conclusion:

> The effect of three different clothing styles on clerks' response times was significant, $F(2, 14) = 19.71$, $p < .001$. The proportion of variance accounted for by the clothing effect (η^2) was .74. Tukey tests showed ($p < .01$) that clerks took longer to respond to customers dressed in sloppy clothes ($M = 63.25$, $SD = 11.73$) than to either customers in dressy clothes ($M = 48.38$, $SD = 9.46$) or customers in casual clothes ($M = 48.88$, $SD = 9.55$). Response times did not differ between the clerks waiting on customers in dressy or casual clothing.

Did your conclusion look something like this? Remember, the exact wording may not necessarily match—the important thing is that you have all the critical details covered.

There are five important differences between this conclusion and the conclusion for the independent groups ANOVA. Can you find them?

The *first* difference comes in the degrees of freedom. There are fewer degrees of freedom for the error term in the correlated-groups ANOVA (WITHIN CELLS) than for the independent-samples case (WITHIN GROUPS). *Second*, the F value for the correlated groups test is larger than for the independent situation. The larger F value is a result of reducing the variability in the denominator of the F equation. This difference in F values leads to the *third* difference, which is the probability of chance. Despite the fact that there are fewer degrees of freedom for the correlated-samples case, its probability of chance is lower. *Fourth*, the proportion of variance accounted for by the clothing effect (η^2) was considerably larger. *Fifth*, the post hoc tests show a lower probability of chance in the correlated-groups situation.

These last three differences most clearly show the advantage of a correlated-groups design. Because using repeated measures reduced some of the error variability, the probability of the difference coming about by chance is smaller than in the independent-samples case. Thus, the conclusion from the correlated-groups design yields the clearer finding (reducing the chance of a Type I error). We cannot promise that correlated-groups designs will always allow you to find a clearer difference than independent-groups designs. However, we can tell you that correlated-groups designs do increase your odds of detecting smaller significant differences because such designs reduce error variance.

The Continuing Research Problem

In Chapters 8 and 9 we began our continuing research project by looking at clerks' response times as a function of how customers were dressed. Clerks' times were significantly higher when they waited on customers in sloppy clothing than when they waited on well-dressed customers. Because of this result, we decided to pursue this research further and, in this chapter, compared the effects of three different styles of clothing to each other. On the basis of our results, we can state that salespeople wait on customers in dressy or casual clothing more quickly than they wait on customers in sloppy clothing.

Is our research project complete at this point? As you might have realized, we could compare an endless number of styles of dress. This research problem could go on forever! In all seriousness, you might have wondered about the effects of other possible IVs on salesclerks' response times. As we begin to ask more complicated questions, we must move to more complex designs to handle those questions. As we move to Chapter 11, we will be able to continue our research problem with an experiment using more than one IV at a time.

Let's review the logical steps we took in conducting this experiment. Refer back to Figure 10-1 to take note of our experimental design questions.

1. After conducting a preliminary experiment (Chapter 9) and determining that salesclerks wait on well-dressed customers more quickly, we decided to further test the effects of different clothing (IV) on clerks' response times (DV).
2. We chose to test only one IV (clothing) because our research is still preliminary.
3. We tested three different styles of dress because they seemed to be likely ways that customers might dress.
4a. With access to many salesclerks, we used random assignment to the three groups and, thus, a multiple-independent-groups design. We used a one-way ANOVA for independent groups and found that clerks responded more quickly to customers in dressy or casual clothes than to customers in sloppy clothes.
4b. With smaller numbers of clerks, we chose to use repeated measures. Thus, we used a multiple-within-group design and a one-way ANOVA for correlated groups. Clerks responded to sloppily dressed customers more slowly than to well-dressed or casually dressed customers.
5. We concluded (hypothetically) that customers should not dress in sloppy clothes if they desire quick help in a store.

1. When your experimental design consists of one IV with three or more groups and you have randomly assigned participants to groups, the proper statistical analysis is a one-way ANOVA for independent groups (**completely randomized ANOVA**).

2. When your experimental design has one IV with more than two groups and you have used matched sets, natural sets, or repeated measures, you should analyze your data with a one-way ANOVA for correlated groups (**repeated-measures ANOVA**).

3. ANOVA partitions the variability in your DV into **between-groups variance** (due to the IV) and **within-groups variance** (due to sources of error). We then compute a ratio between these two sources of variation known as the F ratio.

4. ANOVA results are typically shown in a **source table**, which lists each source of variance and displays the F ratio for the effect of the IV.

5. A significant F ratio merely indicates that there is a significant difference somewhere among your various groups. **Post hoc comparisons** are necessary to determine which groups differ from each other.

6. Using APA format for our statistical results allows us to convey our findings in both words and numbers in a clear and concise manner.

7. Previous experiments often lead to further questions and new experiments. The multiple-group design is an ideal design to follow up on the results from a two-group experiment.

1. Suppose you wish to compare the ACT or SAT scores of the freshman, sophomore, junior, and senior classes at your school to determine whether differences exist among those students. Draw a block diagram of this design. What design and statistical test would you use for this research?

2. You wonder whether students who take the ACT or SAT three times are able to significantly improve their scores. You select a sample of such students and obtain their three scores. What type of experimental design does this question represent? Draw a block diagram of it. What statistical test would you use to analyze the data?

3. When we look at our F ratio and its probability in a multiple-group design, why can't we examine the descriptive statistics directly to reach a conclusion about our experiment?

4. The variability that is due to our IV is termed the _____ variance, whereas the variability due to individual differences and error is the _____ variance.

5. Suppose you conducted the experiment summarized in Question 2 and found the following statistics: $F(2, 24) = 4.07$, $p < .05$. On the basis of this information, what could you conclude?

6. What additional information do you need in Question 5 to draw a full and complete conclusion?

7. In the continuing research problem from this chapter, why was it important to have the (hypothetical) knowledge from the similar study in Chapter 9?

8. You decide to test how people's moods vary by the four seasons. What type of experimental design would you use for this research project? Why?

9. You choose to test people's preferences for fast-food hamburgers, and you have McDonald's, Burger King, Wendy's, and White Castle franchises in your town. What type of experimental design would you use for this research project? Why?

KEY TERMS

Experimental design, 230
Independent variable (IV), 230
Principle of parsimony, 230
Levels, 231
Treatment groups, 232
Independent groups, 233
Correlated groups, 233
Random assignment, 233
Control procedure, 233
Confounded experiment, 233

Matching variable, 234
Placebo effect, 240
Ex post facto research, 240
One-way ANOVA, 242
Completely randomized ANOVA, 242
Repeated-measures ANOVA, 242
Operational definition, 242

Between-groups variability, 243
Error variability, 243
Within-groups variability, 243
Source table, 247
Sum of squares, 247
Mean square, 248
Variance, 248
Post hoc comparisons, 249
Asymptotic, 253

LOOKING AHEAD

In this chapter, we furthered our knowledge about research design and how it fits with particular experimental questions. Specifically, we looked at an extension of the basic building-block design by using one IV and three or more groups. In the next chapter, we will make a significant alteration in our basic design by adding a second IV. This expanded design will give us the ability to ask much more sophisticated questions about behavior because most behaviors are affected by more than one variable at a time.

Designing, Conducting, Analyzing, and Interpreting Experiments with Multiple Independent Variables

Experimental Design: Doubling the Basic Building Block

This chapter will continue building on the experimental design material that we first encountered in Chapter 9. We will see many familiar concepts from the two previous chapters, as well as from earlier in the text (e.g., IVs, DVs, extraneous variables, control, and so on). So you can expect some of this chapter to be a review of familiar concepts. However, we will apply those concepts in a new and different framework—the factorial experimental design.

Let's return to our analogy for experimental design that we first saw in Chapter 9—that of building objects with Legos or Tinkertoys. Chapters 9 and 10 presented the beginner's set and a slightly larger version of that beginner's set, respectively. Now, with the factorial design, we encounter the top-of-the-line, advanced set that has all the possible options. When you bought the largest set of building materials, you could build anything from very simple objects to extremely complicated structures; the same is true of experimental design. Using a factorial design gives us the power we need to devise an investigation of several **factors** or **independent variables (IVs)** in a single experiment. Factorial designs are the lifeblood of experimental psychology because they allow us to look at *combinations* of IVs at the same time, a situation that is quite similar to the real world. A factorial design is more like the real world because there are probably few, if any, situations in which your behavior is affected by only a single factor at a time. Imagine trying to isolate only one factor that affected your ACT or SAT scores! What about intelligence, motivation, courses you had taken, a test time of 8:00 on Saturday morning, health, and so on?

> **Factors** Synonymous with IVs.
>
> **Independent variables** Stimuli or aspects of the environment that are directly manipulated by the experimenter to determine their influences on behavior.

In Chapter 10 we used another analogy for our experimental designs—we compared the two-group design to a house, the multiple-group design to an apartment building, and the factorial design to a skyscraper. The idea behind this analogy was not to frighten you into worrying about how complex factorial designs are, but instead to make two points. First, as we have already mentioned, even complex designs are based on principles that you encountered previously with simple designs. As you move from building a house to a skyscraper, most of the principles of building remain the same—they are merely used on a larger scale. This formula is true also for experimental design: Although we will be dealing with more complex designs in this chapter, you already have the majority of the background you need from Chapters 9 and 10. Second, just as building larger buildings gives you more decisions and options, designing larger experiments gives you more decisions and options. Decisions, of course, imply responsibility. You will have to take on additional responsibility with a factorial design. Rather than planning an experiment with only one IV, you will be planning for two or three (or possibly even more) IVs. Additional IVs mean that you have more factors to choose and control. By taking on additional responsibilities, you also gain additional information. By moving from a one-IV experiment to a two-IV experiment, you will gain information about a second IV *and* the interaction between the two IVs. We will discuss interactions in depth soon. Let's examine the factorial design first.

The Factorial Design

In this chapter, we will expand the basic two-group design by doubling it. Look back at Figure 9-2 and imagine what would happen if you doubled it. Of course, one possible result of doubling Figure 9-2 would be a design that we have already covered in Chapter 10—a multiple-group design with four levels. That design would result in an experiment similar to the continuing research problem of Chapter 10 if we planned an experiment contrasting the effects of four different styles of clothing rather than three. However, this type of doubling would be an extension rather than an expansion. We would take one IV with two levels (dressy clothes and shabby clothes) in Chapter 9 and extend it from two to four levels.

What would an *expansion* (rather than an extension) of Figure 9-2 look like? You may wish to draw a sketch of your answer.

Does your drawing resemble Figure 11-1? Contrast Figure 11-1 with Figures 10-2 and 10-3. Do you see the difference? To what can you attribute this difference? You'll find the answer in the next section.

How Many IVs? In the preceding two chapters the first question we have faced when considering the choice of experimental designs has dealt with how many IVs our experiment will have. Nothing has changed in Chapter 11—we still begin with "How many independent variables will I use in my experiment?" (see Figure 11-2). For the first time, though, we have a different answer. We are moving into more complex designs that use at least two IVs. We refer to any design that uses at least two IVs as a **factorial design**. The factorial design gets its name because we refer to each IV as a factor; multiple IVs, then, yield a factorial design. Theoretically, there is no limit to the number of IVs that can be used in an experiment. Practically speaking, however, it is unlikely that you would want to design an experiment with more than two or three IVs. After that point, the increased complexity is such that it would tax your ability to conduct the

> **Factorial design** An experimental design with more than one IV.

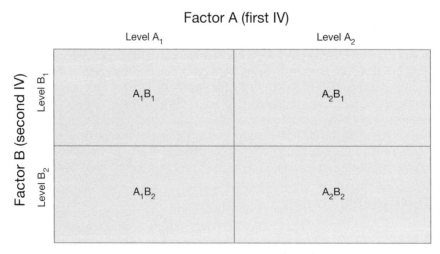

FIGURE 11-1 **Simplest Possible Factorial Design (2 × 2).**

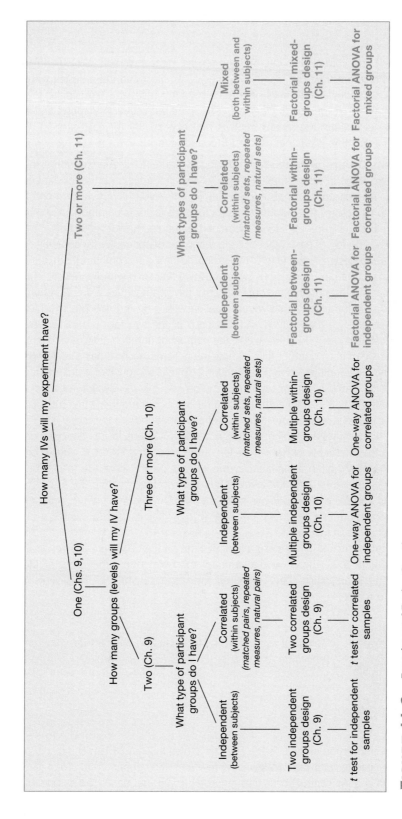

FIGURE 11-2 Experimental Design Questions.

261

experiment and your skill to interpret the results. Hence, we will use experimental designs with two IVs to illustrate our points (we give you an illustration of a design with three IVs in Appendix C). Real-life detectives often face complex cases that are similar to factorial designs. Imagine that you are a detective confronted with several suspects and that you are faced with evaluating the means, motive, and opportunity for each suspect. Can you see how such a situation is analogous to a factorial design?

How Many Groups or Levels?   In looking at Figure 11-2 you will notice that this question that we asked in both Chapters 9 and 10 does not appear on the relevant portion of the flowchart. The reason for its absence is simple: Once you have two (or more) IVs, you will use a factorial design. The number of levels for each factor is unimportant at this point.

Let's return to Figure 11-1 for a moment. Do you see how it represents 2 two-group designs stacked on top of each other? That is what we meant earlier by doubling or expanding the two-group design. If we take 2 two-group designs and combine them, we end up with the design pictured in Figure 11-1, which has two IVs, each with two levels. This figure represents the simplest possible factorial design, which is known as a *2 × 2 design*. This 2 × 2 shorthand notation tells us that we are dealing with a design that has two factors (IVs) because there are two digits given and that each of the two factors has two levels because each digit shown is a 2. In other words, the *number* of numbers tells us how many IVs there are; the *value* of each number tells us how many levels each IV has. Finally, when we complete the implied multiplication, this notation also tells us how many unique treatment combinations (or groups) our experiment requires. A 2 × 2 design requires 4 treatment combinations (2 times 2), whereas a 3 × 3 design would require 9 treatment combinations, and a 2 × 4 design would have 8 treatment combinations.

Figure 11-1 shows an additional design notation. Various factors are often designated by letters, so the first factor is labeled Factor A, the second as Factor B, and so on. The levels within a factor are often designated by the letter that corresponds to the factor *and* a number to differentiate the different levels. Thus, the two levels within the first factor would be labeled A_1 and A_2. If the factor has more than two levels, we continue numbering them in similar fashion until we reach the last level (e.g., A_1, A_2, A_3, . . . A_n), where *n* represents the number of levels of the factor.

What might such a 2 × 2 design look like in real life? To begin answering this question, refer to Figure 9-2, where we diagrammed the two-group experiment of McClellan and Woods (2001), in which they compared the response times of salesclerks to deaf and hearing customers.

How could you expand McClellan and Woods's (2001) experiment so it becomes a 2 × 2 factorial? Draw a diagram.

First, we hope you drew a design like that shown in Figure 11-3. The first IV (A) should be customer hearing, with the two levels representing the experimental group (customers who were deaf) and the control group (customers who were not deaf). The second IV (B) could be

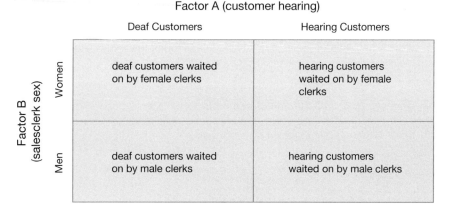

Factor A (customer hearing)

FIGURE 11-3 **Expansion of McClellan and Woods's (2001) Hearing Disability Study.**

any possible variable, as long as the two groups differ on that IV. For example, let's say that you are interested in determining whether the effects of the customers' hearing status vary due to the salesclerks' sex (as we mentioned in Chapter 9). Therefore, your second IV (a measured rather than manipulated IV) would be the sex of the clerks, with your two groups composed of women versus men. This particular experimental design appears in Figure 11-3. Four treatment groups are required, one for each possible combination of the two levels of the two treatments. Thus, we would have a group of female salesclerks who wait on deaf customers, a group of female salesclerks who wait on hearing customers, a group of male salesclerks who wait on deaf customers, and a group of male salesclerks who wait on hearing customers.

We hope it is clear to you that this 2 × 2 design is composed of 2 two-group designs. One two-group design contrasts the effects of customers' hearing, and the second two-group design contrasts the effects of salesclerks' sex. At this point, you might ask, "Wouldn't it be simpler to run two separate experiments rather than combining them both into one experiment?" Although it might be somewhat easier to run two experiments, there are two disadvantages of conducting separate experiments. First, it is not as time efficient as running one experiment. Even if you used the same number of participants in the experiment(s), two experiments will simply take longer to complete than one; there are fewer details to deal with in one experiment than in two. Imagine how inefficient it would be for a detective to complete an investigation of one suspect before even beginning the investigation of a second suspect! Second, by running two experiments, you would lose the advantage that you gain by conducting a factorial experiment—the interaction.

When we jointly combine two IVs in one experiment, we get all the information we would get from two experiments, plus a bonus. In the example using McClellan and Woods's (2001) experiment, we will still determine the solitary effect of customer hearing *and* the solitary effect of salesclerk sex. In a factorial experiment, these outcomes from the IVs are termed the **main effects**.

> **Main effect** Refers to the sole effect of one IV in a factorial design.

Interaction The joint, simultaneous effect on the DV of more than one IV.

The bonus that we get from a factorial experiment is the **interaction** of the two IVs. We will discuss interactions at length later in the chapter, but let us provide you a preview at this point. Suppose we ran the customer hearing/salesclerk sex study and found the results shown in Figure 11-4.

Can you interpret the main effects in Figure 11-4? Did the customer hearing have any effect? Did salesclerk sex have any effect? Study the graph carefully to answer these questions.

It does appear that the customer hearing factor had an effect on clerks' response times. Both groups of clerks (men and women) seemed to respond more slowly when the customer was deaf; notice how the lines for both groups go down as they move from left (deaf customers) to right (hearing customers). On the other hand, sex of the salesclerks seems to have made no *overall* difference in their time to help. It appears that both men and women waited on customers in approximately the same amount of time. If you average the two points on the women's line and average the two points on the men's line, the two means are virtually identical.

The crossing pattern you see graphically portrayed in Figure 11-4 illustrates an interaction effect. We find significant interactions when the effects of one IV change as the level(s) of the other IV changes. Another common way of describing interactions is that *the effects of one IV depend on the particular level of another IV*. If these descriptions are difficult for you to understand, look at Figure 11-4 and ask yourself whether the effects of the customer's hearing are the same for both groups of salesclerks. Although the response times of both sexes increased when they waited on customers who were deaf, it is clear that this effect is much more pronounced for the male clerks, who were much slower waiting on deaf customers

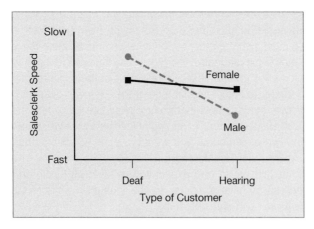

FIGURE 11-4 Hypothetical Results of Customer Hearing/Salesclerk Sex Experiment.

than hearing customers. On the other hand, the female clerks responded similarly to both deaf and hearing customers, although they were slightly slower in waiting on customers who were deaf. This difference for female clerks might not even be significant. If you were describing these results to someone, would it be correct to say merely that salesclerks were slower when they waited on deaf customers? Or should you note that the effect of customer hearing seemed to vary as a function of the sex of the clerks—that the customer's hearing greatly affected the response time in men but had only a small or nonexistent effect for women? It is apparent that the second conclusion, although more complex, paints a much clearer and more accurate picture of the results. Thus, it seems that the effects of customer hearing depend on the sex of the salesclerks; the effect of one IV depends on the specific level of the other IV. We will return to interactions later in this chapter to make certain that you understand them fully.

Let's look at an actual student example of a factorial design. Vania Gauthreaux (2000), a student at Tulane University in New Orleans, Louisiana, was interested in studying the effects of pretrial publicity and judicial instructions on jury decisions. Half of Gauthreaux's participants read a fictitious prejudicial article that was relevant to a particular crime (armed robbery of a dry-cleaning business), and half read a fictitious article about a crime (an arson that killed two people) that was irrelevant to the particular crime. The participants then served as mock jurors—they read a transcript of the armed-robbery trial. Also, Gauthreaux told half the participants, after they had read the article and transcript, that they had read the article in error and should disregard it (similar to a judge's admonition to ignore illegal testimony). Then, the participants rated the guilt of the defendant. This combination of treatments is shown in Figure 11-5. As you can see, there are two IVs (type of article read and "judicial" instructions), each with two levels.

Participants began the experiment by completing forms and reading the article (relevant or irrelevant). Afterward, the experimenter told half the participants that the article had been in their packet by mistake and asked them to disregard it. Then, participants read the

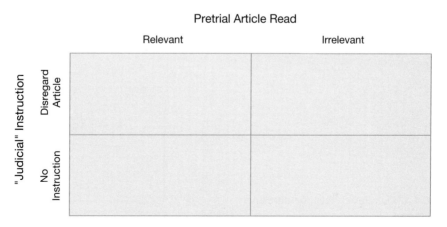

FIGURE 11-5   **Diagram of Gauthreaux's (2000) Experiment.**

Source: Adapted from V. M. Gauthreaux, 2000, Relating pretrial publicity, judicial instruction, and thought suppression with guilt ratings, *Psi Chi Journal of Undergraduate Research, 5,* 21–28.

fictitious trial transcript and rated the guilt of the defendant, as well as the strength of the prosecution's and defense's case. Gauthreaux's results appear in Figure 11-6. The graph shows that the type of article the participants read affected the guilt ratings of the defendant. Participants who read articles relevant to the trial story rated the defendant as being more guilty than participants who read an irrelevant article. The instruction had no effect on guilt ratings—the participants told to disregard the article thought the defendant was just as guilty as participants who were not told to disregard the article. Thus, a judicial instruction to disregard testimony in a legal case may have no effect. Both of these results are relatively straightforward; there was no interaction between the two IVs. Although the two lines on the graph are not perfectly parallel, they do not deviate significantly from that orientation. Therefore, we can conclude that reading a relevant article before judging guilt caused higher ratings of guilt, regardless of "judicial" instructions.

Independent groups
Groups of participants that are formed by random assignment.

Correlated groups
Groups of participants formed by matching, natural pairs, or repeated measures.

Mixed assignment A factorial design that has a mixture of independent groups for one IV and correlated groups for another IV. In larger factorial designs, at least one IV has independent groups and at least one has correlated groups (also known as *mixed groups*).

Assigning Participants to Groups As in Chapters 9 and 10, the matter of how we assign our research participants to groups is important. Again, we have two options for this assignment—**independent groups** or **correlated groups**. However, this question is not answered in such a simple manner as in the two-group and multiple-group designs, each of which had only one IV. Matters can become more complicated in a factorial design because we have two (or more) IVs to deal with. All IVs could have participants assigned randomly or in a correlated fashion, or we could have one IV with independent groups and one IV with correlated groups. We refer to this last possibility as **mixed assignment** (or mixed groups).

Random Assignment to Groups Factorial designs in which *both* IVs involve random assignment may be called *between-subjects factorial designs* or *completely randomized designs* (see Figure 11-2). These labels should make sense from our discussion of between- and within-groups variance in Chapter 10. Between-groups variance refers to variability between independent groups of participants, which results from random assignment.

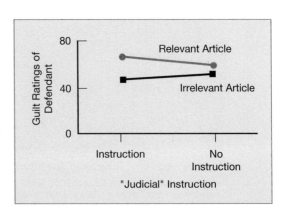

FIGURE 11-6 **Results from Gauthreaux's (2000) Experiment.**

Source: Adapted from V. M. Gauthreaux, 2000, Relating pretrial publicity, judicial instruction, and thought suppression with guilt ratings, *Psi Chi Journal of Undergraduate Research, 5,* 21–28 (Table 1).

Gauthreaux (2000) used a completely randomized design for her experiment dealing with judgments of guilt as a function of type of article and "judicial" instructions. She randomly assigned participants to one of the four possible treatment groups based on type of article (relevant/irrelevant) and instructions (presence/absence). Thus, her experiment required the use of four independent groups of participants; she used four groups ranging from 18 to 22 participants. Each group was independent of the others in the experiment.

After she collected the data, Gauthreaux compared the guilt ratings for defendants *between* those participants who read relevant and irrelevant articles and and *between* those participants who did and did not hear instructions to ignore the article they read. The comparisons were between-groups comparisons because Gauthreaux had randomly assigned the participants to article groups and the instruction groups.

Nonrandom Assignment to Groups   In this section, we deal with factorial designs in which participant groups for all IVs have been formed through nonrandom assignment. We refer to such designs as *completely within-groups* (or *within-subjects*) *designs*. We may want to resort to nonrandom assignment in order to assure the equality of participant groups before we conduct the experiment. It is important to remember, particularly in research with small numbers of participants or with small IV effects, that random assignment cannot guarantee equality of groups. Let's take a brief look at the three methods of creating correlated groups.

1. **Matched Pairs or Sets.** Matching can take place in either pairs or sets because factorial designs can use IVs with two or more levels. The more levels an IV has, the more work matching for that variable takes, simply because of having to form larger sets of participants that are equated on the matching variable. Also, the more precise the match that is necessary, the more difficult matching becomes. For example, matching on sex or educational level may be fairly simple. However, matching on college major or family background may be more difficult. Likewise, when more than one IV uses matching, the demand for a large number of a specific type of research participant may become overwhelming. For instance, using matched participants for both IVs in a 2 × 2 experiment requires 4 matched groups, a 2 × 3 requires 6 such groups, and a 3 × 3 design would necessitate 9 matched groups. Imagine what would happen in an experiment with three IVs! For this reason, factorial designs that use matching for all IVs are relatively rare.

2. **Repeated Measures.** You will remember that a repeated-measures design is one in which participants take part in all levels of an IV. In a completely within-groups experiment using repeated measures, participants would take part fully and completely; that is, they would participate in every possible treatment combination. As you might imagine, this requirement often makes it difficult or impossible to conduct an experiment with repeated measures on multiple IVs.

Would it have been possible to conduct Gauthreaux's (2000) experiment with repeated measures on both IVs? If it were possible, would it be wise to do so? Why or why not?

To answer the first question, you have to understand its implication. Look at Figure 11-5. To conduct this experiment using repeated measures on both IVs, each participant would experience each of the four possible conditions. Could a single participant read both relevant and irrelevant articles? Certainly yes, but not at the same time. Could a single participant get and not get instructions to ignore the article read? Yes, *if* the participant read two different articles. Thus, it would be possible to have repeated measures on both IVs.

Given that it is *possible* to use repeated measures on both variables, would it be wise to do so? "Being wise" is a little harder question to answer than "being possible" because it involves a value judgment. However, if you can think of a problem with a design, then it is probably *not* wise to use that design. There is a fairly obvious problem in using repeated measures on both factors in Gauthreaux's design. Isn't it logical to assume that participating in all four conditions would alert participants to the two independent variables in the experiment? If the participants can figure out what an experiment is about, then you have to worry about their expectancies and demand characteristics (see Chapter 7) affecting their responses in the experiment. So, although it would be possible to use repeated measures for the independent variables, it probably would not be wise to do so.

Of course, not all factorial experiments have these types of problems with using repeated measures. It is possible to design an experiment with multiple IVs in which you expose participants to all treatment combinations. As you have probably guessed by now, the smaller the design, the more feasible it is to include the same participants in all conditions of the experiment. Thus, a 2 × 2 design would be the most likely candidate for a totally repeated measures design.

3. ***Natural Pairs or Sets.*** Using natural groups in a totally within-subjects design has the same difficulties as the matched pairs or sets variation of this design, but it would be even harder. If it would be difficult to form matched pairs or sets to participate in a factorial design, imagine how much harder it would be to find an adequate number of naturally linked participants. At least when we match participants, we usually have a large number to measure in our attempt to make matches. To use natural sets, we would have to find substantial numbers of natural groups. As we noted in Chapter 10, experimenters rarely use this approach other than for animal littermates. We will not consider natural sets in this chapter because of their infrequent use.

Let's examine a student research project that used a factorial design with a totally within-subjects approach. Paula Selvidge (2000), a student at Wichita State University in Wichita, Kansas, was interested in the effects of type of recall task and serial position on location memory for visual stimuli. Selvidge used a computer to show her participants a 5 × 5 grid (i.e., 25 squares) that had a small triangle located in one square of the grid. She used serial position (where the triangle was located on which trial) as one IV because she showed participants five consecutive displays, so she could determine the level of memory for each of the five trials. She varied the recall task in one of three ways: free recall (participants could recall the five triangles' positions in any order), serial recall (participants had to recall the five triangles' positions in order of the trials), or probe recall (participants viewed a 5 × 5 grid with a circle in one position and had to tell whether they had seen a triangle in that position). Thus, Selvidge's design was a 3 (recall task) × 5 (serial position) design.

Draw a block diagram of Selvidge's experiment. Be sure to label it completely.

We hope you drew a diagram like that in Figure 11-7. If so, good job! If not, review the material earlier in this chapter concerning number of IVs and levels of IVs.

Participants in Selvidge's experiment saw 15 grids, 5 (for each of the 5 serial positions) in each of the 3 recall conditions (free, serial, probe). The fact that participants saw grids from all 15 possible treatment conditions means that repeated measures were used for both IVs; the participants used each recall strategy for all the serial positions. Selvidge found a significant interaction between recall task and serial position such that recall went down across serial position for free and serial recall but showed a *V*-shaped pattern (higher recall at beginning and end of the list) for probe recall. Had Selvidge conducted this experiment as two separate two-variable designs, she would never have gained the information about the interaction between recall task and serial position.

Mixed Assignment to Groups   Because factorial designs have at least two IVs, we have the opportunity for a new type of group assignment that we have not encountered in the single-IV designs. As we mentioned previously, mixed assignment designs involve a combination of random and nonrandom assignment, with at least one IV using each type of assignment to groups. In a two-IV factorial design, mixed assignment involves one IV with random assignment and one IV with nonrandom assignment. In such designs, the use of repeated measures is probably more likely than other types of nonrandom assignment. What we often end up with in a *mixed factorial design* is two independent groups that are measured more than once. Such an experimental plan allows us to measure a difference between our groups and then determine whether that difference remains constant over time or across different types of stimuli. Mixed designs combine the advantages of the two types of

Serial Position

		1	2	3	4	5
Recall Task	Free Recall					
	Serial Recall					
	Probe Recall					

FIGURE 11-7   **Block Diagram of Selvidge's (2000) Experiment.**

designs. The conservation of participants through the use of repeated measures for a be-tween-subjects variable makes for a popular and powerful design.

Let's consider a student research example using a mixed design. Jennifer Bonds-Raacke, Kendra Wright, and Jessica Lewin, students at Christian Brothers University in Memphis, Tennessee, and Elizabeth Nelson, their faculty advisor, conducted a study to examine students' attitudes toward animal behavior as a function of source and time. They had 85 undergraduates (41 men, 44 women) read an article about animal cognition from one of two sources (*Journal of Experimental Psychology* or *National Enquirer*); a control group read an article about gambling with no source cited. Bonds-Raacke et al. (2001) measured students' attitudes toward the locus of animals' behavior (instinctive vs. cognitive) immediately after reading the article and again a week later.

What are the two IVs in this experiment, and what are their respective levels? Which is the between-groups variable and which is the within-groups variable? How would you describe this experiment in shorthand notation? What is the DV in this experiment?

One IV is type of article, with three levels. The second IV is time of attitude measurement. Type of article is the between-groups variable because participants read only one article. The three groups were independent—there is no relationship or pairing among participants who read the different articles. Time is the within-groups variable—students participated in all conditions of this variable, as they gave attitude judgments immediately after reading the article and a week later. Because this experiment had two IVs, one (type of article) with three levels and one (time) with two levels, it was a 3 × 2 design (traditionally, in a mixed design, the between-subjects variable is listed first and the within-subjects variable listed second). Finally, the DV was the students' ratings of the animal behaviors. The experimenters compared students' ratings for the three types of articles and for the two different times of measurement.

In their experiment, Bonds-Raacke et al. (2001) found a significant main effect of article type, with no main effect of time and no interaction between the two variables. Students who read the article from *Journal of Experimental Psychology* rated animal behavior as more cognitive than students who read the same article from *The National Enquirer* or an unrelated article on gambling. Interestingly, the researchers found no effect for time, which they expected, based on attitudinal research on the sleeper effect. The *sleeper effect* shows that attitudes often show greater effect of a message after passage of time. Perhaps students found cognitive explanations for animal behavior to be unlikely, so that attitudes were unlikely to change over time. However, other potential hypotheses also exist, as Bonds-Raacke et al. (2001) noted: "There are many possible reasons why the sleeper effect was not replicated" (p. 35). They raised possible explanations of insufficient time for the sleeper effect to occur, difficulty in comprehending the articles, and apathy. The possible explanations for Bonds-Raacke et al.'s results should remind you to seek alternative explanations for your experimental results. Perhaps a follow-up experiment would help you find the correct explanation.

REVIEW SUMMARY

1. The plan by which psychologists guide their experiments is known as the **experimental design**.

2. If you have an experiment that consists of two (or more) IVs, you will use a **factorial design**. Each IV (individually) is considered a **main effect.**

3. The number of levels of each IV is not important in choosing the particular factorial design you will use.

4. Combining two IVs in an experiment allows you to test for **interactions**—that is, situations in which the effect of one IV depends on the specific level of another IV.

5. When you randomly assign research participants to their groups, you have **independent groups**. If all the IVs in your factorial design use independent groups, you are employing a **between-subjects factorial design**.

6. When you use matched pairs or sets, repeated measures, or natural pairs or sets, you have **correlated groups**. If all IVs in your experiment use correlated groups, you are using a **within-subjects factorial design**.

7. **Mixed factorial designs** result from using both independent groups and correlated groups in a factorial design. At least one IV must use independent groups and at least one must use correlated groups.

CHECK YOUR PROGRESS

1. How is the two-group design related to the factorial design? Draw a picture as part of your answer.

2. Why is there a practical limit to the number of IVs you could use in an experiment?

3. You have conducted a 2 × 2 experiment; what information will you obtain from the analysis?
   a. The effects of IV A
   b. The effects of IV B
   c. The effects of A × B
   d. All of the above

4. Matching
   1. mixed factorial design   A. fraternity members vs. nonmembers; men vs. women
   2. totally between-groups design   B. fraternity members matched for family income measured twice
   3. totally within-groups design   C. fraternity members vs. nonmembers measured twice

5. The simplest possible factorial design would have _____ IV(s) and _____ total treatment group(s).

6. Devise an original example of a factorial design that uses mixed assignment to groups.

Comparing the Factorial Design to Two-Group and Multiple-Group Designs

As we mentioned earlier, factorial designs are based on the basic building-block designs we encountered in the two previous chapters. We create factorial designs by combining two of our basic building-block designs into a single design. Again, detectives use basic investigative principles as their building blocks even in complex cases.

You may remember that we described two-group designs as being ideal for a preliminary investigation of a particular IV in a presence–absence format (refer back to Figure 9-2). In a similar fashion, 2 × 2 factorial designs may be used for preliminary investigations of two IVs. If you look at Figure 11-3, where we created a hypothetical expansion of McClellan and Woods's (2001) hearing study, you can see we used that design to make a preliminary investigation of salesclerks' responses based on customer hearing (deaf vs. hearing) and sex of the clerks (female vs. male). When we completed this experiment, we would have information about whether customer hearing and clerks' sex have any effects on clerks' response times. Suppose we wished to go further: What if we wanted to delve deeper into the effects of customer impairment or sex?

In Chapter 10 we found that the multiple-group design could be used to conduct more in-depth investigations of an IV that interests us. We took our basic two-group design and extended it to include more levels of our IV. We can make the same type of extension with factorial designs. Figure 11-8 shows an extension of Figure 11-3 to include three levels of one IV, thus creating a 3 × 2 factorial design (of course, there is no way to add a third level to salesclerks' sex!). Notice that Figure 11-8 is simply a three-level, multiple-group experiment and a two-group experiment combined into one design. From this hypothetical design, we get much more specific information about the effects of customer disability because we used three different types of customers rather than just the presence versus absence of a disability, as shown in Figure 11-3. Just as with the multiple-group design, there is no limit to the number of levels for any IV in a factorial design. Also, the number of levels of the IVs can be unequal (as in this case) or equal. Thus, we could create 2 × 5 factorial designs, 3 × 3 factorial designs, 3 × 6 factorial designs, and so on.

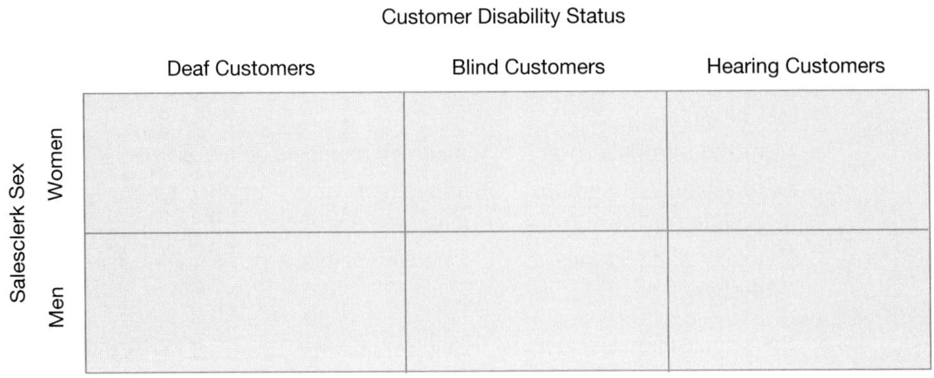

FIGURE 11-8   Combination of Two Multiple-Group Designs.

To this point, our discussion of Figure 11-8 has not added anything that we couldn't obtain by conducting two separate experiments. Whether we conduct one factorial experiment or two single-IV experiments, we will uncover information about the effects of our main effects or IVs. However, as we have already seen, the true advantage of factorial designs is that they measure interaction effects. We have mentioned several times that interaction effects enable us to better understand the complexities of the world in which we live.

Unfortunately, we frequently come across students who are not interested in learning about complex relations as characterized by interaction effects. Instead, they would prefer to conduct single-IV experiments because the results from such experiments are simpler to understand. We are not against simple research designs—they contribute a great deal to our ability to understand the world—but we are against the attitude that says, "I want to use simple research designs because they are easier." If your sole reason for choosing a research design is that it is simpler, we believe that you are making a choice for the wrong reason. Remember that we have cautioned you to choose the simplest research design that will *adequately test your hypothesis*. It is possible that the simplest research design available will *not* adequately test your hypothesis. For example, if we already have a great deal of information about a particular IV, then a presence-versus-absence manipulation of that IV is probably too simple. By the same token, if we already know that changes in a particular DV are caused by complex factors, then a simple design may not advance our knowledge any further. Let us provide you with an example in the following paragraph to illustrate what we're talking about.

Let's suppose that a friend, Joe, wishes to conduct research on why college students make the grades that they do. In this research grades will be the DV, and Joe wants to isolate the IV that causes those grades. One logical choice for a factor that causes grades is intelligence because it stands to reason that more intelligent students will make higher grades and less intelligent students will make lower grades. Joe knows that he cannot give intelligence tests to a large number of college students, so he decides to use ACT or SAT scores as a very rough measure of intelligence. Joe chooses a group of students with high ACT or SAT scores and a group of students with low ACT or SAT scores and compares their respective grades. Sure enough, Joe finds that the students in the high group have higher GPAs than those in the low group. Joe is excited because his hypothesis has been confirmed. He writes a report about his results and goes on his merry way, telling everyone he meets that intelligence causes differences in college students' grades.

Is there anything wrong with the scenario we have just sketched for you? Do you see any specific flaws in the research itself? Do you see any flaws in the reasoning or in the original design?

Is this research flawed? Not really—there are neither obvious violations of experimental guidelines nor obvious extraneous variables. A better answer is that the original reasoning is flawed, or at least too simplistic.

Think about the original question for a moment. Do you believe that ACT or SAT scores can be used to explain *everything* there is to know about college students' grades? If you are like most students, your answer will be a resounding no. We all know students who entered college with low test scores, perhaps even on probation, but who have gone on to make good grades. On the other hand, we know students who entered with academic scholarships and yet flunked out. Clearly, there must be more to grades than intelligence or whatever is measured by entrance exams. What about factors such as motivation and study skills? What about living in a dorm versus an apartment? What about being married versus being single? What about belonging to a sorority or fraternity versus being an independent? All these factoss could contribute to some of the variability in GPA that we observe among college students. Thus, if we decide to "put all our eggs in one basket" of entrance exam scores, we may be simplifying the question too much.

The problem with asking simple questions is that we get simple answers because that is all that we *can* get from a simple question. Again, there is nothing inherently wrong or bad about asking a simple question and getting a simple answer—*unless* we conclude that this simple answer tells us everything we need to know about our subject matter. In such a case, we would be guilty of what Sherlock Holmes criticized: "You see, but you do not observe" (Doyle, 1927, p. 162). Asking more complex questions may yield more complex answers, but those answers may give us a better idea of how the world actually works. Factorial designs give us the means to ask these more complex questions.

Choosing a Factorial Design

Three considerations are important when you choose a particular factorial design. At the heart of the choice are your experimental questions; factorial designs provide considerable flexibility in devising an experiment to answer your questions. Second, it will not surprise you that you should consider issues of control in your design choice because experimental design is primarily concerned with the notion of control. Third, due to the wide degree of experimental choices possible with factorial designs, considerations of a practical nature are also important.

Experimental Questions   The number of questions we can ask in a factorial experiment increases dramatically. Being able to ask additional questions is a great opportunity, but it also puts a burden on us. When we ask additional questions, we must make certain that the questions coordinate with each other. Just as many people would not want to wear clothes with colors that clash, we do not want to ask questions that "clash." By clashing questions, we refer to questions that do not make sense when put together. No doubt you have sat in class and heard a student ask a question that seemed to have no relation to what was being covered in class. Experimental questions that have no relevance to each other may seem to clash when combined in the same experiment. For example, suppose you heard of a proposed experiment to find the effects of self-esteem and eye color on test performance. Does that planned experiment jar you somewhat? We hope it does. Does it make sense to combine self-esteem and eye color in an experiment? Does it make sense to examine the effects of eye color on test performance? This factor sounds like an IV that was thrown in simply because it could be. Could eye color be a logical IV? Perhaps it could in another situation. For example, eye color might well influence people's judgments of a target person's attractiveness or even of his or her intelligence. It seems unlikely, though, that eye color might affect one's test performance. We hope that "off-the-wall" combinations of IVs will be minimized by a review of the existing psychological literature. When you base your experimental questions on previous research and theory, the odds of using strange combinations of IVs are decreased.

Control Issues   We hope that by now you are able to anticipate the topic of discussion when you see the "Control Issues" heading. A glance at Figure 11-2 will remind you that we do need to consider independent versus correlated groups in factorial designs. A complicating factor for factorial designs is that we have to make this decision for each IV we include in an experiment.

Research psychologists typically assume that random assignment to groups will adequately equate the groups if you have approximately 10 participants per group. On the other hand, a correlated assignment scheme (matching or repeated measures) will provide you with greater assurance of the equality of the groups. We hope that by now you fully understand the reasoning behind these two approaches. If you need a review, look back to Chapters 9 and 10.

Practical Considerations   As IVs multiply in experimental designs, some of the practical issues involved become more complex. Often when students find that they can ask more than one question in an experiment, they go wild, adding IVs left and right, throwing in everything but the proverbial kitchen sink. Although curiosity is a commendable virtue, it is necessary to keep your curiosity somewhat in check when designing an experiment. Remember the **principle of parsimony** that we encountered in Chapter 9: You are well advised to keep your experiment at the bare minimum necessary to answer the question(s) that most interest(s) you. We heard this principle cast in a slightly different light when a speaker was giving advice to graduate students about planning their theses and dissertations. This speaker advised students to follow the *KISS principle*—**K**eep **I**t **S**imple, **S**tupid. This

> **Principle of parsimony**
> The belief that explanations of phenomena and events should remain simple until the simple explanations are no longer valid.

piece of advice was not given as an insult or meant to be condescending. The speaker merely realized that there seems to be a natural tendency to want to answer too many questions in one brilliantly conceived and wonderfully designed experiment.

With a two-group or multiple-group design, there is an obvious limitation on how many questions you can ask because of the single IV in those designs. However, with a factorial design, the sky seems to be the limit—you can use as many IVs with as many levels as you wish. However, you should always bear in mind that you are complicating matters when you add IVs and levels. Remember the two problems we mentioned earlier in the chapter. One complication occurs in actually conducting the experiment: More participants are required, more experimental sessions are necessary, you have more chances for things to go wrong, and so on. A second complication can occur in your data interpretation: Interactions between four, five, six, or more IVs become nearly impossible to interpret. It is probably this reason that explains why most factorial designs are limited to two or three IVs. Wise detectives limit their investigations to a few leads at a time rather than trying to simultaneously chase down every lead they get.

Variations on Factorial Designs

In Chapters 9 and 10 we saw two variations that have carried with us to this chapter, comparing different amounts of an IV and using measured IVs. For factorial designs, we add to this list the use of more than two IVs. Let's look at the two carryovers before looking at the new variation.

Comparing Different Amounts of an IV   We have already mentioned this variation earlier in the chapter. When we created the hypothetical experiment diagrammed in Figure 11-8, we compared three different types (levels) of customers.

A caution is in order about adding levels to any IV in a factorial design. In the multiple-group design, when you used an additional level of your IV, you added only one group to your experiment. When you add a level to an IV in a factorial design, you add *several* groups to your experiment because each new level must be added under each level of your other independent variable(s). For example, expanding a 2×2 design to a 3×2 design requires 6 groups rather than 4. Enlarging a $2 \times 2 \times 2$ design to a $3 \times 2 \times 2$ design means using 12, rather than 8, groups. Adding levels in a factorial design increases groups in a multiplicative fashion.

Using Measured IVs   It will probably not surprise you to learn that we can use nonmanipulated IVs in factorial designs also. It is important to remember that using a measured rather than a manipulated IV results in **ex post facto research**. Without the control that comes from directly causing an IV to vary, we must exercise extreme caution in drawing conclusions from such studies. Still, ex post facto studies give us our only means of studying IVs such as sex or personality traits.

> **Ex post facto research**
> A research approach in which the experimenter cannot directly manipulate the IV but can only classify, categorize, or measure the IV because it is predetermined in the participants (e.g., IV = sex).

Because of the fact that factorial designs deal with more than one IV at a time, we can develop an experiment that uses one manipulated IV and one measured IV at the same time. Nicole Wolensky (2001), a student at Marquette University in Marquette, Wisconsin, conducted research that provides a good example of just such an experiment. She had elderly participants evaluate pictures of couples as a function of participant sex and age of the couples in the photographs.

After reading this one-sentence description of Wolensky's experiment, can you tell which IV was manipulated and which was measured?

If you decided that participant sex was the measured IV and that age of couples in photos was the manipulated IV, you are correct. Of course, participant sex is always a measured variable—we cannot "cause" our participants to be male or female! Thus, the age of couples in the photographs *had* to be the manipulated variable. Indeed, Wolensky showed half her participants pictures of young couples, and the other half of the participants saw pictures of elderly couples.

What are the implications for interpreting information from an experiment that uses both manipulated and measured IVs? We must still be cautious about interpreting information from the measured IV(s) because we did not cause the levels to vary. On the other hand, we are free to interpret information from manipulated IVs just as usual. Thus, Wolensky could be more certain about the results from viewing older or younger couples' photos than she could about why any effects due to participant sex occurred.

Dealing with More than Two IVs   Designing an experiment with more than two IVs is probably the most important variation of the factorial design. In this section we will discuss the use of factorial designs with three IVs. Larger designs with more than three IVs follow

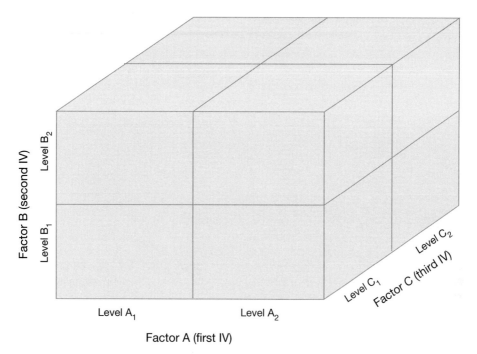

FIGURE 11-9   Simplest Possible Three-Way Factorial Design (2 × 2 × 2).

the same basic strategies that we outline here. Again, we must caution you against adding IVs to an experiment without a good reason.

Figure 11-9 depicts the simplest possible factorial design with three IVs (often referred to as a **three-way design**). As you can see, it is somewhat difficult to draw three-dimensional designs on a two-dimensional surface. This design has three IVs (A, B, and C), each with two levels. Thus, this design represents a 2 × 2 × 2 experiment. We could expand this design by adding levels to any of the IVs, but remember that the number of treatment combinations increases in a multiplicative rather than an additive fashion.

> **Three-way design** A factorial design with three IVs.

Let's look at a hypothetical example of a three-way design. If you look back at Figure 11-3, you will remember that we conceptualized an extension of McClellan and Woods's (2001) customer hearing study by adding a second IV, the sex of the salesclerks. Imagine that we were also interested in testing for the effects of the customers' sex, in testing whether male and female customers receive help from salesclerks more quickly. This change would transform the design in Figure 11-3 to the design shown in Figure 11-10. We have "exploded" the design so that you can easily see each of the eight treatment combinations. Notice that there is a group of participants specified for each of those different treatment combinations.

Figure 11-10 specifies eight different combinations of treatments (the three IVs). Would this design require eight different groups of customers? Why or why not?

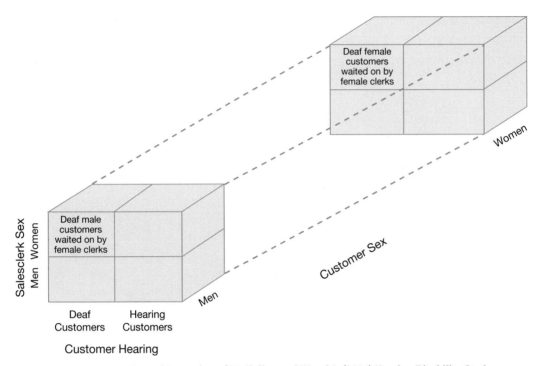

FIGURE 11-10   **Second Expansion of McClellan and Woods's (2001) Hearing Disability Study.**

This design would require eight different groups of clerks if it is planned as a completely between-groups design. In that case, you would need to create eight different groups of clerks through random assignment. The design would also require eight different groups if you used matched sets of clerks. One possibility that would reduce the number of clerks needed would be the use of repeated measures. Could any of the three IVs be used with repeated measures? Clearly, sex of the salesclerks *or* the customers is out—a person cannot be both male and female. Customer disability has the possibility of being used as a repeated measure, depending on how you chose the customer confederates. In McClellan and Woods's original experiment, they used confederates who were actually deaf. Such a situation would rule out its use as a repeated measure. However, if you had hearing confederates pretend to be deaf, the possibility of repeated measures does exist—the confederates would have to participate as both hearing and deaf customers.

One more consideration is necessary before you could advocate the use of repeated measures—the DV. Can the DV be used more than once with the same salesclerks? If we continue to use response time as the DV, the answer would be yes. There is nothing that would prevent us measuring a salesclerk's response time to more than one customer. On the other hand, some DVs cannot be used more than once. Again, remember the Burkeley et al. (2000) experiment in which participants solved anagrams. We cannot use the same anagrams in a repeated measures situation because the participants would have already solved them. Using repeated measures on anagram solving would require two different but equal sets of anagrams, which should be possible to design.

Thus, the answer to the short question in the previous Psychological Detective section is, "It depends." Although the design in Figure 11-10 specifies eight groups of salesclerks, it does not necessarily specify eight *different* groups of clerks. Our determination of the number of groups depends on whether we use independent groups or repeated measures.

One final point remains for us to cover about factorial designs with more than two IVs. We have mentioned interaction effects several times in this chapter. As we add IVs, we also add more interaction effects to our design. If we have three IVs (A, B, and C) we would obtain information about four interactions—AB, AC, BC, and ABC. To make these interactions more specific, let's use Figure 11-10 as our example. Given that our experiment diagrammed in Figure 11-10 has customer hearing, salesclerk sex, and customer sex as IVs, our statistical tests will evaluate interactions for customer hearing and clerk sex, customer hearing and customer sex, clerk sex and customer sex, and for all three variables simultaneously (customer hearing, salesclerk sex, and customer sex). You will find as many interaction effects as there are unique combinations of the treatments (see Appendix C).

Imagine that you had an experiment with four IVs—A, B, C, and D. List all the possible interactions.

Did you find that there are 11 possible interactions? Let's look at the possibilities:

Two-way (two IVs) interactions:	AB, AC, AD, BC, BD, CD
Three-way (three IVs) interactions:	ABC, ABD, ACD, BCD
Four-way (all four IVs) interactions:	ABCD

The idea of evaluating 11 different interactions, including one with a possibility of all four variables interacting at once, may be challenging enough for you to understand why we suggest that you limit your experiments to no more than three IVs.

REVIEW SUMMARY

1. **Factorial designs** are created by combining two-group or multiple-group designs.
2. We use factorial designs to test the effects of more than one IV on a particular DV at the same time. These designs allow us to test under conditions that are more like the real world than dealing with only one variable at a time.
3. In choosing a particular factorial design, you must consider your experimental questions, issues of control, and practical matters.
4. In a factorial design, we can deal with different types or amounts of an IV or with measured IVs, just as we can with a two-group or multiple-group design.
5. Factorial designs may consist of three or more IVs, although the statistical interpretation of such designs becomes more complicated because of an increasing number of interactions.

CHECK YOUR PROGRESS

1. Why are factorial designs merely combinations of what you learned about in Chapters 8 and 9? Drawing a picture may help you here.
2. Suppose a friend told you about her $2 \times 4 \times 3$ experimental design. Draw a diagram of this design. Explain its structure.
3. Describe (a) totally between-groups, (b) totally within-groups, and (c) mixed-groups designs. How are they similar? How are they different?
4. Why should your experimental questions be your first consideration in choosing a factorial design?
5. Suppose you wish to test children from two different racial groups. You would be dealing with a(n) _____ IV.
6. Your friend who plans to take experimental psychology next term tells you that she is very excited about taking the class because she already has her experiment planned. She wants to test the effects of parental divorce, socioeconomic status, geographical area of residence, parental education, type of preschool attended, and parents' political preference on the sex-role development of children. What advice would you offer this friend?
7. A 2×3 experiment has been conducted. How many interactions will be calculated?
   a. 1   b. 2   c. 3   d. 6

Statistical Analysis: What Do Your Data Show?

We are certain that you know this by now, but we will remind you that experimental design and statistical analysis go hand in hand. You must plan your experiment carefully, choosing the experimental design that best enables you to ask your questions of interest. Having selected your experimental design from the list of choices we are presenting guarantees that you will be able to analyze your data with a standard statistical test. Thus, you will be spared the "experimental fate worse than death"—collecting your data and finding no test with which to analyze the data.

Naming Factorial Designs

In this chapter we have covered designs with more than one IV. Depending on your statistics course, you may not have reached the point of analyzing data from these more complex designs. We analyze factorial designs with the same type of statistical test that we used for analyzing multiple-group designs—analysis of variance (ANOVA). As we mentioned in Chapter 10, we need to be able to distinguish among the various ANOVA approaches, so we often modify ANOVA with words that refer to the size of the design and the way we assign participants to groups. Labels you may hear that refer to the size of the design include *factorial ANOVA* as a general term or *two-way ANOVA* or *three-way ANOVA* for designs with two or three IVs, respectively. Alternatively, the size of the design may be indicated as *X by Y*, where *X* and *Y* represent the number of levels of the two factors, as we have noted several times in this chapter. Labels that describe how participants are assigned to groups might include *independent groups, completely randomized, completely between-subjects, completely between-groups, totally between-subjects,* or *totally between-groups* for designs that use random assignment for all IVs. Designs that use matching or repeated measures may be called *randomized block, completely within-subjects, completely within-groups, totally within-subjects,* or *totally within-groups.* Designs that use a mixture of "between" and "within" assignment procedures may be referred to as *mixed* or *split-plot factorial.* As you can see, the labels for factorial designs can get quite long. Again, if you understand the principles behind the designs, the names are usually not difficult to interpret. For example, you might hear about a *three-way totally between-groups design* or a *two-way mixed ANOVA.*

Can you "decode" the two examples given in the previous sentence? What types of designs do these two cases indicate?

The design indicated by the *three-way totally between-groups* label would include three IVs ("three-way") and would use random assignment of participants in all conditions. *Two-way mixed ANOVA* refers to an experiment with two IVs, one of which uses random assignment and one of which uses a correlated assignment technique (matching or repeated measures). Notice that these descriptions do not give us a full picture of the design because there is no numerical description that would allow us to know how many levels each IV has. To get the fullest amount of information, a label such as *a 2 × 3 × 2 completely between-groups design* is necessary. From this label, we know that there are three IVs, with two, three, and two levels, respectively. We also know that the experimenter assigned participants to each of the IVs in a random manner. Notice how much information about experimental design we can pack into a short descriptive label.

Planning the Statistical Analysis

In Chapter 10 we featured a hypothetical experiment to investigate the effects of dress on the time salesclerks took to wait on customers. That example used a multiple-group design because we compared three different styles of clothing to see how they affected clerks' responses. It should be clear to you that we must derive a new hypothetical experiment to use as an example because we are dealing with a new design.

How could we make a slight alteration in our clothing style experiment of Chapter 10 in order to make it appropriate for use as an example in this chapter? Give this question some careful thought— make the alteration as simple as possible. Draw a block diagram of your proposed experiment.

As is often the case when you are designing an experiment, there are many possible correct answers. The key feature that your altered experiment must contain is the *addition* of a second IV. Keeping the clothing difference as one IV and adding a second IV, your design should resemble Figure 11-1. Although you could have included more than two levels of either or both of your IVs, that would complicate the design. In asking you to keep your altered design simple, we also assumed you would not choose a three-IV design.

Our statistical example for this chapter will build on our example in Chapter 10. You will remember from Chapter 10 that we compared three different styles of clothing to determine whether the clothes made any difference in how quickly salesclerks responded. Indeed, we found that clerks responded more quickly to customers in dressy or casual clothes than to customers in sloppy clothes. Suppose you are examining the data from the previous experiment and you think you detected an oddity in the data: It appears to you that salesclerks may have responded differently to female and male customers in addition to the different styles of dress. You decide to investigate this question in order to find out whether both customer sex and dress affect salesclerks' response times to customers. Because there was no difference between responses to customers in dressy and casual clothing (see Chapter 10), you decide to use only casual and sloppy clothes. Thus, you have designed a 2 × 2 experiment (see Figure 11-11) in which the two IVs are clothing style (casual and sloppy) and customer sex (male and female).

Treatment variability
Variability in DV scores that is due to the effects of the IV (also known as *between-groups variability*).

Error variability
Variability in DV scores that is due to factors other than the IV—individual differences, measurement error, and extraneous variation (also known as *within-groups variability*).

Rationale of ANOVA

The rationale behind ANOVA for factorial designs is basically the same as we saw in Chapter 10, with one major modification. We still use ANOVA to partition (divide) the variability into two sources—**treatment variability** and **error vari-**

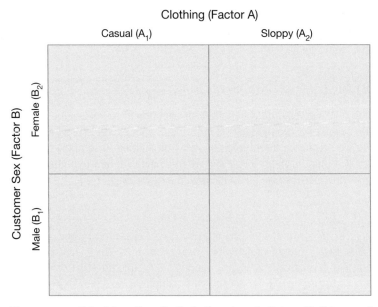

FIGURE **11-11** **Hypothetical Experiment Using Clothing and Customer Sex IVs.**

ability. However, with factorial designs, the sources of treatment variability increase. Instead of having one IV as the sole source of treatment variability, factorial designs have multiple IVs and their interactions as sources of treatment variability. Thus, rather than partitioning the variability as shown in Figure 10-4, we would divide the variability as shown in Figure 11-12. The actual distribution of the variance among the factors would depend, of course, on which effects were significant. If you used a factorial design with three IVs, the variability would be partitioned into even more components.

You might guess that we will add statistical formulas because we have added more components to the statistical analysis. You would be correct in this guess. You can turn back to Chapter 9 to review the general ANOVA equations for the one-IV situation. For a two-IV factorial design, we use the following equations:

$$F_A = \frac{\text{IV A variability}}{\text{error variability}} \qquad F_B = \frac{\text{IV B variability}}{\text{error variability}} \qquad F_{A \times B} = \frac{\text{interaction variability}}{\text{error variability}}$$

These equations allow us to separately evaluate the effects of each of the two IVs as well as their interaction. If we used a larger factorial design, we would end up with an *F* ratio for each of the IVs and each interaction.

Understanding Interactions

When two variables interact, their joint effect may not be obvious or predictable from examining their separate effects. Let us cite one of the most famous examples of an interaction effect. Many people find drinking a glass or two of wine to be a pleasurable experience. Many people find taking a drive to be relaxing. What happens if we combine these two activities—do we end up with an extremely pleasurable and relaxing experience? Of course not. We may end up with deadly consequences. Interaction effects often occur with different drugs. Hence, you often hear very strict guidelines and warnings about combining various drugs.

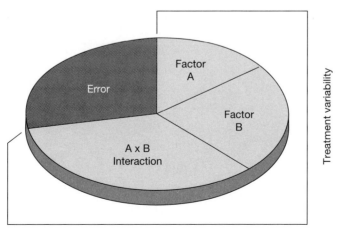

FIGURE 11-12   Partitioning the Variability in a Factorial Design with Two IVs.

Combinations of drugs, in particular, are likely to have synergistic effects so that a joint effect occurs that is not predictable from either drug alone. You may have seen interaction or **synergistic effects** when two particular children are together. Separately, the children are calm and well behaved. However, when they are put together, watch out! Detectives often face interaction effects in their work. A seemingly normal person, when confronted with a stressful day and an irritating situation, may react violently. Neither the stress nor the annoyance alone would have led to a violent crime, but their combination could turn deadly.

Synergistic effects
Dramatic consequences that occur when you combine two or more substances, conditions, or organisms. The effects are greater than what is individually possible.

Remember our earlier discussion of Figure 11-4 and the interaction pattern found there? In an experimental situation, we are concerned with how different levels of different IVs interact with respect to the DV. A significant interaction means that the effects of the various IVs are not straightforward and simple. For this reason, we virtually ignore our IV main effects when we find a significant interaction. Sometimes interactions are difficult to interpret, particularly when we have more than two IVs or many levels of an IV. A strategy that often helps us make sense of an interaction is to graph it. By graphing your DV on the *y* axis and one IV on the *x* axis, you can depict your other IV with lines on the graph (see Chapter 8). By studying such a graph, you can usually deduce what happened to cause a significant interaction. For example, by examining Figure 11-4 you can see that the results for the customers' disability are not constant based on the sex of the salesclerks. The disability affected the behavior of male clerks to a much greater degree than it affected the behavior of female clerks. Thus, the effects of a customer's hearing disability are not straightforward; they depend on whether you're talking about female or male

Reprinted from *The Chronicle of Higher Education*. By permission of Mischa Richter and Harald Bakken.

"On the other hand, if you're not interested in good and evil, this one would give you a good understanding of statistical probability."

A good background in statistics should keep you from becoming this desperate.

salesclerks. Remember that an interaction is present when the effect of one IV *depends on the specific level of the other IV.*

When you graph a significant interaction, you will often notice that the lines of the graph cross or converge. This pattern is a visual indication that the effects of one IV change as the second IV is varied. Nonsignificant interactions typically show lines that are close to parallel, as you saw in Figure 11-6. Gauthreaux (2000) found that reading an article relevant to a trial resulted in higher ratings of guilt than reading an irrelevant article. She also found that either hearing or not hearing an instruction to ignore the article made no difference in the guilt ratings. However, there was no interaction between the two IVs (the lines on her graph were nearly parallel). As we cover our statistical examples in the next few pages, we will pay special attention to the interaction effects.

Interpretation: Making Sense of Your Statistics

Our statistical analyses of factorial designs will provide us more information than we got from two-group or multiple-group designs. The analyses are not necessarily more complicated than those we saw in Chapters 9 and 10, but they do provide more information because we have multiple IVs and interaction effects to analyze.

Interpreting Computer Statistical Output

As in Chapters 9 and 10, we will examine generic computer printouts in this section. If you look back at Figure 11-2, you will see that we have three different ANOVAs to cover, based on how we assign the participants to groups. We will deal with 2 × 2 analyses in these three different categories to fit our clothing-by-customer-sex experiment.

Two-Way ANOVA for Independent Samples   The two-way ANOVA for independent samples requires that we have two IVs (clothing style and customer sex) with independent groups. To create this design we would use four different randomly assigned groups of salesclerks, one for each possible combination pictured in Figure 11-11. The DV scores (see Table 11-1) represent clerks' response times in waiting on customers.

Computer Results   The descriptive statistics appear at the top of Table 11-2. You can see that salesclerks took almost a minute on average to wait on the customers—the mean for the "total population" (all 24 clerks) was 53.50 seconds. The means for the clerks waiting on customers in casual and in shabby clothes were 46.92 and 60.08 seconds, respectively; for the female customers and the male customers, the means were 49.83 and 57.17 seconds, respectively. The last set of descriptive statistics shows the combination of the two clothing styles and the two sexes. Clerks waiting on the casually dressed women averaged 48.17 seconds; those waiting on casually dressed men averaged 45.67. For the sloppy clothing, clerks waiting on women had a mean of 51.50 seconds, whereas the clerks waiting on men took an average of 68.67 seconds. Again, to make sure you entered the data correctly, you could check these means with a hand calculator in a matter of minutes.

The **source table** for the completely randomized factorial design appears at the bottom of Table 11-2. In the body of the source table, we want to examine only the effects of the two IVs (clothing and customer

> **Source table**   A table that contains the results of ANOVA. "Source" refers to the source of different types of variation.

> ### TABLE 11-1   Hypothetical Sales Clerks' Response Times (in Seconds) for Comparing Clothing Styles and Sex of Customers

TYPE OF CLOTHING

		Casual	Sloppy	
CUSTOMER SEX	**Female**	46 39 50 52 48 54 $M = 48.17$	37 47 44 62 49 70 $M = 51.50$	Female $M = 49.83$
	Male	38 50 38 44 49 55 $M = 45.67$	47 69 69 74 77 76 $M = 68.67$	Male $M = 57.17$

Casual $M = 46.92$ Sloppy $M = 60.08$

Total Population $M = 53.50$

sex) and their interaction. The remaining source (w. cell or Within) is the error term and is used to test the IV effects. One important item to note is that different programs are likely to label the error term with a variety of different names. (If you need to review concepts like sum of squares or mean squares, refer back to Chapter 10.) When we examine the main effects, we find that "Clothes" produced an F ratio of 11.92, with a probability of occurring by chance of .003 (from rounding). The effect of sex shows an F ratio of 3.70, with a probability of .07. Can you verify these probabilities in the F table in the back of the book? You should find that the probability of "Clothes" falls below .01 level in the table. The sex IV shows **marginal significance**, which we usually attribute to probabilities of chance between 5% and 10%. Although marginal significance is not within the normal significance range, it is close enough that many experimenters discuss such results anyway. Keep in mind when you deal with higher and higher probabilities of chance that you are taking a greater risk of making a **Type I error** (see Chapter 8).

Our next step is to examine the interaction between the two IVs. Notice that we have one two-way interaction because we have just the two IVs. The interaction between clothing and customer sex produced an F ratio of 6.65 and has $p = .02$, therefore denoting significance. Remember that a significant interaction renders the main effects moot because those main effects are qualified by the in-

Marginal significance Refers to statistical results with a probability of chance between 5% and 10%—in other words, almost significant, but not quite. Researchers often talk about such results as if they reached the $p = .05$ level.

Type I error Accepting the experimental hypothesis when the null hypothesis is true.

TABLE 11-2   Computer Output for Two-Way ANOVA for Independent Samples

```
TABLE OF MEANS:
                              CLOTHES
                      CASUAL    SLOPPY    ROW M
Customer    Female    48.17     51.50     49.83
Sex           Male    45.67     68.67     57.17
          Column M    46.92     60.08
                              Pop. M = 53.50
```

SOURCE TABLE

SOURCE	SS	df	MS	F	p
Clothes	1040.17	1	1040.17	11.922	.0025
Customer Sex	322.67	1	322.67	3.698	.068
Clo × Cust Sex	580.17	1	580.17	6.649	.0179
W. Cell	1745.00	20	87.25		
Total	3688.00	23			

teraction and are not straightforward. Thus, to make sense out of these results, we must interpret the interaction. The first step in interpreting an interaction, as we saw, is to draw a graph of the results from the descriptive statistics. Figure 11-13 depicts this interaction.

Translating Statistics into Words   Remember that we are justified in drawing conclusions from our statistics *only if* we are certain that our experimental design and procedures had sufficient control to eliminate extraneous variables. Computers and statistical tests work only with the data you provide—they are not able to detect data from flawed experiments. To interpret our statistics, let's return to the graph of our significant interaction (Figure 11-13).

Study Figure 11-13 carefully. What do you think caused the significant interaction? In other words, why do the results of one IV depend on the particular level of the second IV?

You should remember that we described interactions as occurring when the lines on a graph cross or converge and that parallel lines indicate no interaction. The crossing lines of Figure 11-13, in conjunction with the low probability of chance for the interaction term, denote a significant interaction. When we examine the figure, the point that seems to differ most represents the clerks' response times to male customers in sloppy clothes. This mean is considerably higher than the others. Thus, we would conclude that clerks take longer to wait

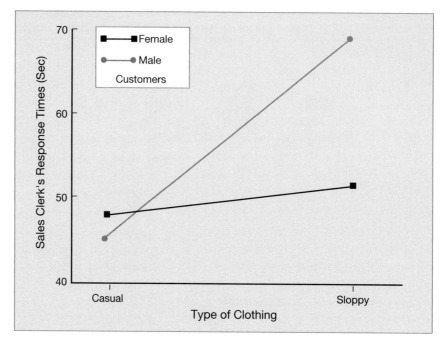

FIGURE 11-13   Interaction for Clothing and Customer Sex Experiment.

on men who are sloppily dressed than other customers. Notice that our explanation of an interaction effect *must* include a reference to both IVs in order to make sense—the previous sentence mentions the *male* customers in *sloppy* clothes.

From looking at Figure 11-13, can you figure out why this interaction qualifies the significant and marginally significant main effects?

If we had drawn conclusions from the main effects, we would have decided that clerks waiting on customers in casual clothes were faster (46.92 seconds) than clerks waiting on those in shabby clothes (60.08). Also, we would have concluded that clerks waiting on men took marginally longer (57.17) than those waiting on women (49.83). When you look at Figure 11-13, does it appear clerks actually waited on sloppily dressed customers more slowly than those in casual clothes? No, only clerks waiting on *men* in sloppy clothes had longer response times. Does it seem that men received assistance more slowly than women? No, only the men in *sloppy clothes* had clerks who responded slowly. If you attempt to interpret the main effects in a straightforward fashion when you have a significant interaction, you end up trying to make a gray situation into a black-and-white picture. In other words, you would be guilty of oversimplifying the results. Remember that an interaction occurs when the effect of one IV depends on the *specific* level of the other IV.

Our final step in interpreting the results is communicating our results to others. You will remember that we use a combination of statistical results and words to convey our findings in APA style. Here is one way you could present the results from this experiment:

> The effect of the clothing on clerks' response times was significant, $F(1, 20) = 11.92$, $p = .003$. The customer sex effect was marginally significant, $F(1, 20) = 3.70$, $p = .069$. However, the main effects were qualified by a significant interaction between clothing and customer sex, $F(1, 20) = 6.65$, $p = .018$, $\eta^2 = 0.25$. The results of the interaction are graphed in Figure 1 *[see Figure 11-13]*. Visual inspection of the graph shows that clerks' response times for the sloppy clothes–male customer condition were higher than the other conditions.

Once again, our goal is to communicate our results clearly with the words alone. Although the concept of interactions is somewhat complicated for readers with no statistical background, we hope that anyone could understand our explanation of the results. However, we should note that to fully understand the interaction, you should actually conduct further statistical tests. These tests are somewhat advanced—we suggest that you consult with your advisor if your research involves a significant interaction. (Be sure to remember this warning because you will see significant interactions again in this chapter.) Also, we remind you that η^2 is a measure of effect size (see Chapter 10). We included an effect size estimate only for the interaction because the significant interaction supersedes the main effects.

We want you to note two important points from this presentation of results. First, compared to the examples in Chapters 9 and 10, this written summary is longer. When you deal with factorial designs, you have more results to communicate, so your presentations will be longer. Second, although we presented the significance of the interaction and referred to a figure, we did not fully interpret the interaction. Results sections in experimental reports are only for presenting the results, not for full interpretation. As the APA *Publication Manual* (2001) notes in describing the results section, "discussing the implications of the results is not appropriate here" (p. 20).

Two-Way ANOVA for Correlated Samples   The two-way ANOVA for correlated samples requires that we have two IVs (here, clothing and customer sex) with correlated groups for both IVs. Most often these correlated groups would be formed by matching or by using repeated measures. In our example of the clothing–customer sex experiment, repeated measures on both IVs would be appropriate—we would merely get one sample of salesclerks and have them wait on customers of both sexes wearing each style of clothing.

Is there a flaw in the logic of having a single group of clerks waiting on all four types of customers?

There is no obvious flaw in using repeated measures in this experiment. Salesclerks are certainly used to waiting on a variety of different customers in a short time span, so there should not be a problem in creating such a condition for this experiment. On the other hand, there are many experimental situations in which it would not be appropriate to use repeated measures. For example, imagine a classroom experiment that involved students reading chapters on the same topic from two different textbooks and then taking a quiz over each chapter. This hypothetical experiment would result in an advantage for the second quiz on each topic. Specifically, when students took that quiz, they would have read *two* chapters about the same topic. On the other hand, when they took their first quiz on each topic, they would have read only one chapter on the topic. Clearly, repeated measures on this textbook variable would not be appropriate. Thus, we would have to form correlated groups by forming matched groups of students.

Computer Results   The means for the factorial repeated measures analysis appear in Table 11-3. You will note that the group means are identical to those in Table 11-2 (the ANOVA for independent samples). This result is to be expected; we are analyzing the same numbers from Table 11-1. However, we used a different strategy for composing the groups in the analysis, so our ANOVA results should be different.

The source table for the two-way ANOVA with correlated groups appears in the bottom portion of Table 11-3. The clothing effect is significant at the .001 level and the sex effect is significant at the .014 level. However, both of those effects are qualified by the significant clothing-by-sex interaction ($p = 0.001$). Remember that this interaction effect signifies that the results of the IVs are not consistent across each other. To make sense of the interaction, we must plot the means for the combinations of clothing and customer sex. This interaction was shown in Figure 11-13.

Translating Statistics into Words   One important lesson to learn from these different analyses of the same data deals with the power of designing experiments in different ways. For example, take a minute to compare the source table for this analysis (Table 11-3) to the source table for the completely randomized analysis (Table 11-2). You will notice in the cor-

---

TABLE 11-3   **Computer Output for Two-Way ANOVA for Correlated Samples**

Table of Means:

		CLOTHES		
		CASUAL	SLOPPY	ROW M
Customer	Female	48.17	51.50	49.83
Sex	Male	45.67	68.67	57.17
	Column M	46.92	60.08	
			Pop. M = 53.50	

SOURCE TABLE

SOURCE	SS	df	MS	F	p
Clothes	1040.17	1	1040.17	24.688	.001
Customer Sex	322.67	1	322.67	7.658	.014
Clo × Cust Sex	580.17	1	580.17	13.770	.001
Residual	632.00	15	42.13		

related-samples design that the F ratios are larger and the probabilities are smaller for both the IVs and their interaction. In the previous chapters we told you that using correlated samples helps to reduce error variability by reducing some of the between-subjects variability. The result is typically a stronger, more powerful test of the treatment effects, as is shown in this case.

To fully interpret the results of this experiment, we must explain the interaction shown in Figure 11-13. We will be briefer at this point because we have already carefully examined the interaction in the previous analysis section. Again, it is clear that the interaction occurred because salesclerks waiting on sloppily dressed male customers were slower than when waiting on other customers. However, the effect was specific to that type of clothing on that sex of customer. Salesclerks are not slower in waiting on men in general because the time to wait on casually dressed men is not higher. By the same token, clerks are not generally slower in waiting on sloppily dressed customers because they waited on sloppily dressed women in about the same time as casually dressed customers. Thus, we must confine our conclusion to slower responses to one mode of dress for one sex of customer. Notice that explaining an interaction forces us to refer to both IVs in the same explanatory sentence—we can't ignore one IV to focus on the other.

Of course, we must still communicate our results to other parties using APA style. We rely on our standard combination of words and numbers for the summary of the results—words to explain and numbers to document the findings. One possible way of summarizing these results follows:

> Both the main effects of clothing and customer sex were significant, $F(1, 5) = 24.69$, $p = .001$ and $F(1, 5) = 7.66$, $p = .014$, respectively. However, the interaction of clothing and customer sex was also significant, $F(1, 5) = 13.77$, $p = .001$, $\eta^2 = .78$. This interaction appears in Figure 1 *[see Figure 11-13]*. Salesclerks waiting on sloppily attired male customers were considerably slower than clerks with any other combination of customer sex and clothing.

You would provide a fuller explanation and interpretation of this interaction in the discussion section of your experimental report.

Two-Way ANOVA for Mixed Samples   The two-way ANOVA for mixed samples requires that we have two IVs (here, clothing and customer sex) with independent groups for one IV and correlated groups for the second IV. One possible way to create this design in our clothing–customer sex experiment would be to use a different randomly assigned group of salesclerks for each customer sex. Clerks waiting on each sex, however, would assist customers attired in both types of clothing. Thus, customer sex would be independent groups and constitute a between-subjects variable, whereas clothing would use repeated measures and be a within-subjects variable. Looking at Figure 11-11, note that different salesclerks would wait on men or women (looking down the diagram) and would wait on customers in both casual and sloppy clothes (across the top of the diagram). The DV scores (see Table 11-1) still represent response times of clerks to customers, but the same clerks produced the response times for each clothing type within the two customer sexes. This design is efficient because it requires fewer clerks to conduct the study and it minimizes the individual differences within the response times.

Computer Results   The descriptive statistics appear at the top of Table 11-4. Once again, the descriptive statistics did not change from our first and second analysis—we are still analyzing the same data (see Table 10-1) for demonstration purposes.

TABLE 11-4 **Computer Output for Two-Way ANOVA for Mixed Samples**

TABLE OF MEANS:

CLOTHES

		CASUAL	SLOPPY	ROW M
Customer	Female	48.17	51.50	49.83
Sex	Male	45.67	68.67	57.17
	Column M	46.92	60.08	
			Pop. M = 53.50	

SOURCE TABLE

SOURCE	SS	df	MS	F	p
Between subjects effects					
Cust Sex	322.67	1	322.67	2.422	.151
Error (Cust Sex)	1332.33	10	133.23		
Within subjects effects					
Clothes	1040.17	1	1040.17	25.206	.001
C to X Cust Sex	580.17	1	580.17	14.059	.004
Error	412.67	10	41.27		

The source table appears at the bottom of Table 11-4. As you can see from the headings, the between-subjects effects (independent groups) and the within-subjects effects (repeated measures) are divided in the source table. This division is necessary because the between-subjects effects and within-subjects effects use different error terms. The interaction appears in the within-subjects portion of the table because it involves repeated measures across one of the variables involved.

Which IV is the between-subjects variable, and why? Which IV is the within-subjects variable, and why?

No, that wasn't a trick question—it's just a simple review query to make sure you're paying attention. Customer sex is the between-subjects variable because different salesclerks wait on men or women. The clothing is the within-subjects variable because each salesclerk waits on customers in both sloppy and casual clothes (repeated measures).

The information for the customer sex IV showed an F ratio of 2.42 and a probability of chance of .15—therefore, the customers' sex made no significant difference in the sales-clerks' response times. The clothing effect yielded an F ratio of 25.21 with a probability of .001, a significant finding. However, we also notice that the interaction of clothing and customer sex is significant ($p = .004$), with an F ratio of 14.06. Because of this significant interaction, we will not interpret the significant clothing result. Once again, we need to graph the interaction in order to make sense of it (see Figure 11-13).

This set of ANOVA results differs from either of the other two analyses in this chapter, again demonstrating the importance of experimental design in determining significance. Interestingly, the customer sex effect was the weakest in this design. Kirk (1968) noted that tests of between-subjects factors are relatively weaker than tests of within-subjects factors in a mixed (split-plot) design. The results of this analysis, when compared to the previous analysis, demonstrate that point.

Translating Statistics into Words   We have already completed some of our interpretation in our coverage of the statistical results. We know that the customer sex effect was not significant and that the clothing variable was significant. However, because the interaction between customer sex and clothing was significant, we ignore the clothing results and interpret the interaction.

Figure 11-13 shows that clerks who waited on casually dressed women, casually dressed men, and sloppily dressed women responded more quickly than those who waited on sloppily dressed men. How can we communicate these findings in APA format? Here's one possibility:

> Results from the mixed factorial ANOVA showed no effect of the customer sex, $F(1, 10) = 2.42$, $p = .15$. The clothing effect was significant, $F(1, 10) = 25.21$, $p = .001$. This main effect, however, was qualified by a significant customer-sex-by-clothing interaction, $F(1, 10) = 14.06$, $p = .004$, $\eta^2 = .58$, which is shown in Figure 1 *[see Figure 11-13]*. This interaction shows that salesclerks who waited on sloppily dressed male customers were slower in responding than clerks who waited on casually dressed men or women dressed in either manner.

> Note the similarity for the clothing and interaction effects in this mixed analysis and the completely within-groups analysis in the previous section. Why do you think the findings are similar in each case?

To answer this difficult question, you have to be able to see the similarities between these last two analyses. Although they may seem rather different, there is one important similarity between them. Both of these analyses, because of the underlying experimental designs, treat the clothing and interaction effects as within-groups effects. Thus, the two ANOVAs are essentially analyzing the same data in the same manner.

As a final word about the analyses in this chapter, please remember that you cannot analyze the same data using several different analyses in the real world of experimentation. We have used the same data for instructional purposes *and* to demonstrate how you could take one experimental idea and put it in the context of several possible experimental designs.

A Final Note

For simplicity's sake, all the analyses we have shown in this chapter have dealt with IVs that had only two levels. You remember from Chapter 10 that we often wish to test IVs with more than two levels. In Figure 11-7 we showed you an example of a 3×3 design. That design had two IVs, each with three levels. Do you remember what happened in Chapter 10

Post hoc tests Statistical comparisons that are made between group means after finding a significant *F* ratio.

when we found significance for an IV with three levels? To determine what caused the significant findings, we carried out **post hoc tests**. These tests that we calculated after finding a significant IV allowed us to determine which levels of that IV differed significantly.

We hope that this issue has occurred to you at some point during this chapter. What should you do, in a factorial design, if an IV with more than two levels turns out to be significant? Assuming that this main effect is not qualified by an interaction, you need to calculate a set of post hoc tests to determine exactly where the significance of that IV occurred.

The Continuing Research Problem

In Chapters 8 and 9 we began this section about our hypothetical continuing research problem. Our early interest was in determining whether customers in dressy or sloppy clothing received faster assistance from salesclerks. When we found that dressy clothes were associated with faster responses, we enlarged our research question to include three different types of clothing (Chapter 10). Evidence showed that customers dressed in either casual or dressy clothes were helped by salesclerks more quickly than customers in shabby clothing.

As you saw in Chapter 9, we began our research problem with a fairly simple question, and we got a fairly simple answer. However, that research led to a slightly more complex

Programmatic research A series of research experiments that deal with a related topic or question.

question, and so on. You should expect your research problems to show a similar pattern. Although you may start with a simple question and expect one experiment to provide all the answers, that will rarely be the case. Keep your eyes open for new questions that arise after an experiment. Pursuing a line of **programmatic research** is challenging, invigorating, and interesting. Remember that pursuing such a line of research is how most famous psychologists have made names for themselves!

This chapter was more complex than either Chapter 9 or Chapter 10 because of the extra choice in experimental design. Let's review the steps we took in designing the experiments in this chapter. You may wish to refer to Figure 11-1 to follow each specific question.

1. After our preliminary research in Chapters 9 and 10, we decided to use two IVs (clothing and customer sex) in these experiments. Each IV had two levels (clothing → casual, sloppy; customer sex → men, women). This design allows us to determine the effects of the clothing, the effects of the customer sex, and the interaction between clothing and customer sex.

2. The DV was the time it took salesclerks to respond to customers.

3a. With large numbers of clerks, we randomly formed four groups of clerks, with each waiting on one sex of customer in one type of clothing, resulting in a factorial between-groups design. We analyzed the response times using a factorial ANOVA for independent groups and found that clerks were slower to wait on male customers in sloppy clothing than all other customers (see Table 11-2 and Figure 11-13).

3b. In a hypothetical situation with fewer clerks for the experiment, we used repeated measures on both IVs; that is, each salesclerk waited on both sexes of customers attired in both types of clothing, so that each clerk waited on four different customers. Thus, this experiment used a factorial within-groups design. We analyzed the data with a factorial ANOVA for correlated groups and found that clerks were slowest in waiting on sloppily dressed men (see Table 11-3 and Figure 11-13).

3c. In a third hypothetical situation, we randomly assigned salesclerks to the two customer sex groups but used repeated measures on the clothing IV so that clerks waited either on men in both types of clothing or women in both types of clothing. This arrangement resulted in a factorial mixed-groups design (one IV using independent groups, one using correlated groups). We analyzed the response times with a factorial ANOVA for mixed groups and found the slowest response times for clerks to male customers in sloppy clothes (see Table 11-4 and Figure 11-13).

4. We concluded that clothing and customer sex interacted to affect salesclerks' response times. Women received help quickly regardless of their attire, but men received help quickly only if they were not sloppily dressed. Men attired in sloppy clothes had to wait longer for help than the other three groups.

REVIEW SUMMARY

1. When you use an experimental design with two or more IVs and have only independent groups of participants, the proper statistical analysis is a factorial ANOVA for independent groups.

2. A factorial ANOVA for correlated groups is appropriate when your experimental design has two or more IVs and you used matched groups or repeated measures for all IVs.

3. If you have a design with two or more IVs and a mixture of independent and correlated groups for those IVs, you would use a factorial ANOVA for mixed groups to analyze your data.

4. ANOVA partitions the variability in the DV into separate sources for all IVs and their interactions and for error. *F* ratios show the ratio of the variation for the experimental effects to the error variation.

5. A significant *F* ratio for a main effect indicates that the particular IV caused a significant difference in the DV scores.

6. A significant interaction *F* ratio indicates that the two (or more) IVs involved had an interrelated effect on the DV scores. To make sense of an interaction, you should graph the DV scores.

7. We use APA format to communicate our statistical results clearly and concisely. Proper format includes a written explanation of the findings documented with statistical results.

CHECK YOUR PROGRESS

1. You wish to compare the ACT or SAT scores of the freshman, sophomore, junior, and senior classes at your school as a function of sex. Draw a block diagram of this design. What design and statistical test would you use for this project?

2. You wonder whether test-taking practice and study courses can actually affect SAT or ACT scores. You recruit one group of students to help you. They take the test three times. Then you give them a study course for the test. They take an alternative form of the same test, also three times. Thus, each student has taken two different tests three times (to study practice effects) and each student has taken the study course (to assess its effects). Draw a block diagram of this design. What design and statistical test would you use for this project?

3. You are interested in the same question as in Problem 2, but you recruit two groups of students to help you. One group takes the SAT or ACT three times; the other group has a study course and then takes the SAT or ACT three times. Draw a block diagram of this design. What design and statistical test would you use for this project?

4. What is an interaction effect? Why does a significant interaction render its associated main effects uninterpretable?

5. Suppose you are reading an experimental report. What would you know from the following sentence?

   Reading speed was affected by both print size and age, with younger participants reading large print faster and older participants reading small print faster.

   a. The interaction of print size and age was significant.

   b. The interaction of print size and age was not significant.

   c. The interaction of print size, age, and reading speed was significant.

   d. The main effects of print size and age were significant.

6. You wish to determine whether people's moods differ during the four seasons and by sex. What experimental design would you use for this research project? Why?

7. You choose to test people's preferences for fast-food hamburgers in three different restaurants (McDonald's, Burger King, Wendy's) among three different age groups (children ages 4–12, college students, senior citizens). What experimental design would you use for this project? Why?

KEY TERMS

Factors, 259
Independent variables, 259
Factorial design, 260
Main effect, 263
Interaction, 264
Independent groups, 266
Correlated groups, 266

Mixed assignment, 266
Principle of parsimony, 275
Ex post facto research, 276
Three-way design, 277
Treatment variability, 282
Error variability, 282

Synergistic effects, 284
Source table, 285
Marginal significance, 286
Type I error, 286
Post hoc tests, 294
Programmatic research, 294

LOOKING AHEAD

In this chapter, we have learned about the most sophisticated of all experimental designs—factorial designs that include multiple IVs. This material completes a three-chapter section on experimental design, data analysis, and interpretation. In the next chapter we will look at some alternative research approaches that you may need to use sometime.

Alternative Research Designs

Although you may think that, by now, we have covered every conceivable type of research design that psychologists might use to gather data, you would be wrong. There are many other types of research designs. In this chapter we will consider some designs that researchers developed with specific purposes in mind. We will first look at research designs that help us to protect the internal validity of our experiments.

Protecting Internal Validity Revisited

In Chapter 6, we introduced the concept of **internal validity**. The issue of internal validity revolves around **confounding** and **extraneous variables**. When you have an internally valid experiment, you are reasonably certain that your IV is responsible for the changes you observed in your DV. You have established a **cause-and-effect relation**, knowing that the IV *caused* the change in the DV. For example, after many years of painstaking research, medical scientists know that cigarette smoking *causes* lung cancer. Although there are other variables that can also affect cancer, we know that smoking is a causative agent. Our goal as experimenters is to establish similar cause-and-effect relations in psychology. Experiments that are internally valid allow us to make statements such as "X causes Y to occur" with confidence.

Internal validity A type of evaluation of your experiment; it asks the question of whether your IV is the only possible explanation of the results shown for your DV.

Confounding Caused by an uncontrolled extraneous variable that varies systematically with the IV.

Extraneous variables Variables that may unintentionally operate to influence the dependent variable.

Cause-and-effect relation Occurs when we know that a particular IV (cause) leads to specific changes in a DV (effect).

Examining Your Experiment from the Inside

In Chapter 6 we talked about the necessity for controlling extraneous variables in order to reach a clear-cut conclusion from our experiment. It is only when we have designed our experiment in such a way as to avoid the effects of potential extraneous variables that we can feel comfortable about making a cause-and-effect statement—that is, saying that Variable X (our IV) *caused* the change we observed in Variable Y (our DV). What we are trying to accomplish through our control techniques is to set up a buffer for our IV and DV so that they will not be affected by other variables. This reminds us of a cartoonlike toothpaste commercial we saw—perhaps you have seen it also. When the teeth brushed themselves with the particular brand of toothpaste being advertised, they developed a protective "invisible barrier" against tooth decay. In an analogous manner, our controls give our experiment a barrier against confounding (see Figure 12-1). Similarly, police detectives strive to make their case against a particular suspect airtight. If they have done their investigations well, the case against the accused should hold up well in court.

Dealing with the internal validity of an experiment is an interesting process. We take many precautions aimed at increasing internal validity as we design and set up our experiment, and we usually evaluate our experiment with regard to internal validity after we have completed the research. If this approach seems a little strange to you, don't be alarmed—it does seem odd at first. Internal validity revolves around the question of whether your IV actually created any change that you observe in your DV. As you can see in Figure 12-1, if

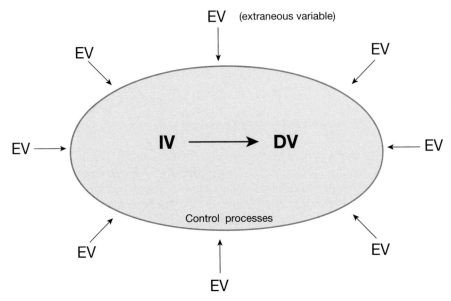

EV (extraneous variable)

EV

EV

IV ⟶ DV

EV ⟶ ⟵ EV

Control processes

EV

EV

EV

FIGURE 12-1 **The Role of Control Processes in Preventing Experimental Confounding.**

you learned your lessons from Chapter 6 well and used adequate control techniques, your experiment should be free from confounding and you can, indeed, conclude that your IV caused the change in your DV. Let's review briefly.

Imagine you have been given responsibility for conducting the famous Crest test—you are supposed to determine whether brushing with Crest actually does reduce cavities. Your boss wants you to use an experimental group (Crest) and a control group (Brand X) in the experiment. Write down at least *five* potential extraneous variables for this experiment before reading further.

Were you able to list five possible extraneous variables? The list could be quite long; you may have thought of some possibilities that we didn't come up with. (Although this exercise could easily have been an example dealing with confounding found in Chapter 6, it is also relevant to the issue of internal validity. If you fail to control an important extraneous variable, your experiment will not have internal validity.) Remember, any factor that systematically differs between the two groups (other than the type of toothpaste) could be an extraneous variable that could make it impossible to draw a definite conclusion about the effect of the toothpastes. Here's our (partial) list of possibilities:

number of times brushed per day
amount of time spent in brushing per day

how soon brushing occurs after meals

types of foods eaten

type of toothbrush used

dental genetics inherited from parents

degree of dental care received

different dentists' "operational definition" of what constitutes a cavity

whether the city's water is fluoridated

As we said, this list is not meant to be exhaustive—it merely gives you some ideas of factors that could be extraneous variables. To make certain you understand how an extraneous variable can undermine an experiment's internal validity, let's use an example from the previous list. In addition, we will discover why we take precautions aimed at internal validity *before* the experiment and assess the internal validity of an experiment *afterward*.

When you design the study, you want to make sure that people in the experimental and control groups brush their teeth an equivalent number of times per day. Thus, you would instruct the parents to have their children brush after each meal. Your goal is to have all children brush three times a day. Suppose that you conducted the experiment and gathered your data. When you analyzed the data, you found that the experimental group (Crest) had significantly fewer cavities than the control group (Brand X). Your conclusion seems straightforward at this point: Brushing with Crest reduces cavities compared to brushing with Brand X. However, as you dig deeper into your data, you look at the questionnaire that you had the parents complete and find that children in the experimental group averaged 2.72 brushings a day compared to 1.98 times per day for the control group. Now it is obvious that your two groups differ on two factors—the type of toothpaste used and the number of brushings per day. Which factor is responsible for the lower number of cavities in the experimental group? It is impossible to tell! There is no statistical test that can separate these two confounded factors. So, you attempted to control the brushing factor before the experiment to assure internal validity. You could not assess your control technique until after the experiment, when you found out that your experiment was not internally valid. A word to the wise should be sufficient: Good experimental control leads to internally valid experiments.

Remember that we listed nine threats to internal validity in Chapter 6. We also provided you with a variety of control strategies to deal with those threats. Now that you are familiar with research designs, we can explain how some research design strategies eliminate threats to internal validity. As you read about these strategies, you will see that some are a part of those designs from Chapters 9 through 11.

Protecting Internal Validity with Research Designs

There are two approaches you could take to fight the various threats to internal validity. In the first approach, you would attempt to come up with nine different answers, one for each threat. Although this approach would be effective in controlling the threats, it would be time consuming and, perhaps, difficult to institute that many different controls simultaneously. Perhaps the idea of controlling the threats through research design occurred to you, even if you could not come up with a specific recommendation. Detectives use standard police procedures to help them protect their cases; experimental design procedures can help us as psychological detectives.

In the three previous chapters we presented you with a variety of experimental designs, often noting various control aspects of those designs. However, we never mentioned the nine general threats to internal validity until this chapter. Can we apply experimental design to these problems? According to Campbell (1957) and Campbell and Stanley (1966), the answer is yes. Let's take a look at their recommendations.

Random Assignment   Although **random assignment** is not a specific experimental design, it is a technique that we can use within our experimental designs. Remember, with random assignment (see Chapter 5) we distribute the experimental participants into our various groups on a random (nonsystematic) basis. Thus, all participants have an equal chance of being assigned to *any* of our treatment groups. The purpose behind random assignment is to create different groups that are equal before beginning our experiment. According to Campbell and Stanley (1966), "the most adequate all-purpose assurance of lack of initial biases between groups is randomization" (p. 25). Thus, random assignment can be a powerful tool. The only drawback to random assignment is that we cannot *guarantee* equality through its use.

> **Random assignment**
> A control technique that ensures that each participant has an equal chance of being assigned to any group in an experiment.

One caution is in order at this point. Because *random* is a frequently used term when dealing with experimental design issues, it sometimes has slightly different meanings. For example, in Chapters 9 through 11, we repeatedly referred to *independent groups* to describe groups of participants that were not correlated in any way (through matching, repeated measures, or natural pairs or sets). It is not unusual to see or hear such independent groups referred to as *random groups*. Although this label makes sense because the groups are unrelated, it is also somewhat misleading. Remember back to Chapter 9 when we first talked about matching participants. At that point we stressed that after making your matched pairs of participants, you *randomly assigned* one member of each pair to each group. The same is true of naturally occurring pairs (or sets) of participants. These randomly assigned groups would clearly *not* be independent. Because of the power of random assignment to equate our groups, we should use it at every opportunity. Campbell and Stanley (1966) noted that "within the limits of confidence stated by the tests of significance, randomization can suffice without the pretest" (p. 25). Thus, according to Campbell and Stanley, it may not even be necessary to use matched groups because random assignment can be used to equate the groups.

What is the major exception to Campbell and Stanley's argument that randomization will create equal groups?

We hope that you remembered (from Chapters 9–11) that randomization is supposed to create equal groups *in the long run*. Therefore, you need to be aware of randomization's *possible* shortcoming if you conduct an experiment with small numbers of participants. Although randomization may create equal groups with few participants, we cannot be as confident about this possibility as when we use large groups.

Finally, you should remember from Chapter 5 that random assignment is *not* the same as **random selection**. Random assignment is related to the issue of internal validity, whereas the notion of random selection is more involved with external validity, a topic we will consider in the next chapter.

Experimental Design   Campbell and Stanley (1966) reviewed six experimental designs and evaluated them in terms of controlling for internal validity. They recommended three of the designs as being able to control the threats to internal validity we listed in Chapter 6. Let's examine their three recommended designs.

The Pretest–Posttest Control Group Design   The pretest–posttest control group design appears in Figure 12-2. As you can see, this design consists of two randomly assigned groups of participants, both of which are pretested, with one group receiving the IV.

The threats to internal validity that we summarized in Chapter 6 are controlled by one of two mechanisms in this design. The random assignment of participants to groups allows us to assume that the two groups are equated before the experiment, thus ruling out **selection** as a problem. Using a pretest and a posttest for *both* groups allows us to control the effects of **history**, **maturation**, and **testing** because they should affect both groups equally. If the control group shows a change between the pretests and posttests, then we know that some factor other than the IV is at work. **Statistical regression** is controlled as long as we assign our experimental and control groups from the same extreme pool of participants. If any of the **interactions with selection** occur, they should affect both groups equally, thus equalizing those effects on internal validity.

The other threats to internal validity are not controlled, but the pretest–posttest control group design does give us the ability to deter-

R O_1 O_2 (control group)
R O_3 X O_4 (experimental group)

KEY:
R = Random assignment
O = Pretest or posttest observation or measurement
X = Experimental variable or event
Each row represents a different group of participants.
Left-to-right dimension represents passage of time.
Any letters vertical to each other occur simultaneously.
(Note: This key also applies to Figures 12-3, 12-5, and 12-6.)

FIGURE 12-2   **The Pretest–Posttest Control-Group Design.**

Random selection
Choosing participants from a population in such a way that all possible participants have an equal opportunity to be chosen.

Selection   A threat to internal validity; if we choose participants in such a way that our groups are not equal before the experiment, we cannot be certain that our IV caused any difference we observe after the experiment.

History   A threat to internal validity; refers to events that occur between the DV measurements in a repeated measures design.

Maturation   An internal validity threat; refers to changes in participants that occur over time during an experiment; could include actual physical maturation or tiredness, boredom, hunger, and so on.

Testing   A threat to internal validity that occurs because measuring the DV causes a change in the DV.

Statistical regression
A threat to internal validity that occurs when low scorers improve or high scorers fall on a second administration of a test due solely to statistical reasons.

mine whether they were problematic in a given experiment. We can check to see whether **experimental mortality** was a problem because we measure both groups on two occasions. **Instrumentation** is measured if we are dealing with responses to a test, for example, but it could still remain a problem if human interviewers or observers are used. There is simply no substitute for pretraining when you use humans to record or score data for you. Finally, **diffusion** or **imitation of treatments** could still remain a problem if participants from the control group (or different experimental groups) learn about the treatments for other groups. Again, though, you do have the control group as a "yardstick" to determine whether their scores increase or decrease in similar fashion to the experimental group's scores. If you see similar changes, you can suspect that internal validity controls may have failed.

The Solomon Four-Group Design Figure 12-3 contains a diagram of the Solomon four-group design, first proposed by Solomon (1949). Notice that this design is identical to the pretest–posttest control-group design with the first two groups but adds an additional two groups—thus gaining the name *four-group design*. Because the Solomon four-group design has the same two groups as the pretest–posttest control-group design, it has the same protection against the threats to internal validity. As you will see in the next chapter, the main advantage gained by adding the two additional groups relates to external validity.

One problem with the Solomon design is statistical analysis of the data because there is no statistical test that can treat all six sets of data at the same time. Campbell and Stanley (1966) suggested treating the *posttest* scores as a factorial design, as shown in Figure 12-4. Unfortunately, this approach ignores all the pretest scores.

The Posttest-Only Control-Group Design Figure 12-5 shows the posttest-only control-group design. As you can see by comparing Figure 12-5 to Figures 12-2 and 12-3, the posttest-only control-group design is a copy of the pretest–posttest control-group design but without the pretests included and is a copy of the two added groups in the Solomon four-group design. Does the lack of pretests render the posttest-only control-group design less desirable than the other two designs that included them? No, because we can count on the random assignment to groups to equate the two groups. Thus, using random assignment of participants to groups and withholding the IV from one group to make it a control group is a powerful experimental design that controls the threats to internal validity we covered in Chapter 6.

Interactions with selection Threats to internal validity that can occur if there are systematic differences between or among selected treatment groups based on maturation, history, or instrumentation.

Experimental mortality A threat to internal validity that can occur if experimental participants from different groups drop out of the experiment at different rates.

Instrumentation A threat to internal validity that occurs if the equipment or human measuring the DV changes its measuring criterion over time.

Diffusion or imitation of treatment A threat to internal validity that can occur if participants in one treatment group become familiar with the treatment of another group and copy that treatment.

FIGURE 12-3 **The Solomon Four-Group Design.**
This design is used to protect internal validity.

$$
\begin{array}{llll}
R & O_1 & & O_2 \\
R & O_3 & X & O_4 \\
R & & & O_5 \\
R & & X & O_6
\end{array}
$$

	No IV	Receives IV
Pretested	O_2	O_4
Unpretested	O_5	O_6

FIGURE 12-4 **Factorial Treatment of Solomon Four-Group Design Posttest Scores.**

After examining Figure 12-5, what type of design (from Chapters 9–11) does this appear to be?

We hope that you identified Figure 12-5 as the two-group design from Chapter 9. However, we must point out that it is *not* critical to have only two groups in this design. The posttest-only control-group design could be extended by adding additional treatment groups, as shown in Figure 12-6. This extended design should remind you of the multiple-group design from Chapter 10. Finally, we could create a factorial design from the posttest-only control group by combining two of these designs simultaneously so that we ended up with a block diagram similar to those from Chapter 11.

It should be clear that the posttest-only design is not defined by the number of groups. What is (are) the defining feature(s) of this design? Take a moment to study Figures 12-5 and 12-6 before answering.

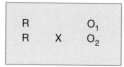

R		O_1
R	X	O_2

FIGURE 12-5 **Posttest-Only Control-Group Design.** This is a powerful design for protecting internal validity.

FIGURE 12-6   An Extension of the Posttest-Only Control-Group Design.   This design allows for testing multiple treatment groups.

The two features that are necessary to "make" a posttest-only control-group design are random assignment of participants to groups and the inclusion of a control (no-treatment) group. These features allow the design to derive cause-and-effect statements by equating the groups before the experiment and controlling the threats to internal validity.

We hope you can appreciate the amount of control that can be gained by the two simple principles of random assignment and experimental design. Although these principles are simple, they are quite elegant in the power they bring to the experimental situation. You would be wise not to underestimate their importance.

Conclusion

How important is internal validity? It is *the most important* property of any experiment. If you do not concern yourself with the internal validity of your experiment, you are wasting your time. Experiments are intended to produce cause-and-effect statements—to conclude that X causes Y to occur. If you merely wish to learn something about the association of two variables, you can use one of the nonexperimental methods for acquiring data summarized in Chapter 5 or calculate a correlation coefficient. However, if you wish to investigate the cause(s) of a phenomenon, you must take care to control any extraneous variables that might affect your dependent variable. You cannot count on your statistical tests to provide the necessary control functions for you. Statistical tests merely analyze the numbers you bring to the test—they do not have the ability to remove confounding effects (or even to discern that confounding has occurred) in the data you bring.

> **REVIEW SUMMARY**

1. One important control for internal validity is **random assignment** of participants to groups. This procedure assures us that the groups are equated before beginning the experiment.

2. **Random selection** refers to choosing our participants from a population so that all potential participants could be chosen. Random selection is important to external validity.

3. The *pretest–posttest control-group design* consists of two groups of participants that are randomly assigned to an experimental and control group, pretested and posttested, with the experimental group receiving the IV. This design controls for internal validity threats but has the problem of including a pretest.

4. The *Solomon four-group design* is a copy of the pretest–posttest control-group design except that it adds two groups that are not pretested. This design also controls for internal validity threats but there is no statistical test that can be used to analyze all six sets of data.

5. The *posttest-only control-group design* consists of two groups of participants that are randomly assigned to an experimental and control group with the experimental group receiving the IV treatment. Both groups are tested with a posttest. This design controls for internal validity threats and is free from other problems.

6. The posttest-only control-group design can be extended to include additional treatment groups or additional IVs.

7. It is essential for an experiment to be internally valid. Otherwise, no conclusion can be drawn from the experiment.

(CHECK YOUR PROGRESS)

1. The two general methods that we use to protect the internal validity of our experiment are _____ and _____.

2. Why is it essential to use random assignment of our participants to their groups?

3. Distinguish between random assignment and random selection.

4. What is the drawback of using the pretest–posttest control-group design to help with internal validity?

5. A friend tells you she was a participant in a psychology experiment and says, "It was crazy! We took a personality test, watched a film, and then took the same test again!" From this description, you could tell that she was in the

   a. control group of a posttest-only control-group design
   b. experimental group of a posttest-only control-group design
   c. control group of a pretest–posttest control-group design
   d. experimental group of a pretest–posttest control-group design

6. What is the drawback of using the Solomon four-group design as a control for internal validity?

7. Diagram the posttest-only control-group design. Why is it a good choice for controlling internal validity?

Single-Case Experimental Designs

In the case of a **single-case experimental design** (also known as an $N = 1$ design), the name says it all. This term simply refers to an experimental design with one participant. This approach, of course, is quite similar to the detective's strategy of pursuing a single suspect.

> **Single-case experimental design** An experiment that consists of one participant (also known as $N = 1$ designs).

The $N = 1$ approach probably sounds familiar to you. What data-gathering approach have we studied that involves one participant?

Case-study approach
An observational technique in which we compile a record of observations about a single participant.

We hope you remember the **case-study approach** from Chapter 4. In a case study, we conduct an intense observation of a single individual and compile a record of those observations. As we noted in Chapter 4, case studies are often used in clinical settings. If you have taken an abnormal psychology course, you probably remember reading case studies of people with various disorders. The case study is an excellent descriptive technique—if you read about an individual with a mental disorder, you get a vivid picture of what that disorder is like. However, a case study is *merely* a descriptive or observational approach; the researcher does not manipulate or control variables, but simply records observations. Thus, case studies do not allow us to draw cause-and-effect conclusions.

You will remember that we must institute control over the variables in an experiment in order to derive cause-and-effect statements. In a single-case design, we institute controls just as in a typical experiment—the only difference is that our experiment deals with only one participant. Also, just as in a typical experiment, we must take precautions dealing with the internal validity of a single-case design. We hope that the single-case design raises many questions for you. After all, it does go against the grain of some principles we have developed thus far. Let's take a quick look at this design's history and uses, which will help you understand its importance.

History of Single-Case Experimental Designs

The single-case experimental design has quite an illustrious past in experimental psychology (Hersen, 1982; Hersen & Barlow, 1976). In the 1860s Gustav Fechner explored sensory processes through the use of psychophysical methods. Fechner developed two concepts that you probably remember from your introductory psychology course: *sensory thresholds* and the *just noticeable difference* (*jnd*). Fechner conducted his work on an in-depth basis with a series of individuals. Wilhelm Wundt (founder of the first psychology laboratory) conducted his pioneering work on introspection with highly trained individual participants. Herman Ebbinghaus conducted perhaps the most famous examples of single-case designs in our discipline. Ebbinghaus was the pioneering researcher in the field of verbal learning and memory. His research was unique—not that he used the single-case design, but that he was the single participant in those designs. According to Dukes (1965), Ebbinghaus learned about 2,000 lists of nonsense syllables in his research over many years. Dukes provided several other examples of famous single-case designs with which you are probably familiar, such as Cannon's study of stomach contractions and hunger, Watson and Rayner's study of Little Albert's learned fears, and several researchers' work with language learning in individual apes.

Other than the ape-language studies that Dukes (1965) cited, all these single-case design examples date to the 1800s and early 1900s. Dukes found only 246 single-case examples

Reprinted with special permission of King Features Syndicate and Tom Cheney.

"Sooner or later he'll learn that when he presses the bar, he'll receive a salary."

Much psychological knowledge has been gained from single-case designs.

in the literature between 1939 and 1963. Clearly, there are fewer examples of single-case designs than group designs in the literature. Why is the difference so great? Hersen (1982) attributed the preference for group designs over single-case designs to statistical innovations made by Fisher. Sir Ronald A. Fisher was a pioneer of many statistical approaches and techniques. Most importantly for this discussion, in the 1920s, he developed ANOVA (Spatz, 2001), which we covered in some detail in Chapters 10 and 11. Combined with Gosset's early 1900s development of a test based on the *t* distribution (see Chapter 9), Fisher's work gave researchers a set of inferential statistical methods with which to analyze sets of data and draw conclusions. You may have taken these tests for granted and assumed that they had been around forever, but that is not the case. As these methods became popular and accessible to more researchers, the use of single-case designs declined. In today's research world, statistical analyses of incredibly complex designs can be completed in minutes (or even seconds) on computers that you can hold in your hand. The ease of these calculations has probably contributed to the popularity of group designs over single-case designs.

Uses of Single-Case Experimental Designs

There are still researchers who use single-case designs. Founded by B. F. Skinner, the **experimental analysis of behavior** approach continues to employ this technique. Skinner (1966) summarized his philosophy in

Experimental analysis of behavior   A research approach popularized by B. F. Skinner, in which a single participant is studied.

this manner: "Instead of studying a thousand rats for one hour each, or a hundred rats for ten hours each, the investigator is likely to study one rat for a thousand hours" (p. 21). The Society for the Experimental Analysis of Behavior was formed and began publishing its own journals, the *Journal of the Experimental Analysis of Behavior* (in 1958) and the *Journal of Applied Behavior Analysis* (in 1968). Thus, single-case designs are still used today. However, the number of users is small in comparison to group designs, as you could guess with only a handful of journal titles devoted to this approach.

One question that might occur to you is "Why use a single-case design in the first place?" Sherlock Holmes knew that "the world is full of obvious things which nobody by any chance ever observes" (Doyle, 1927, p. 745). Dukes (1965) provided a number of convincing arguments for and situations that require single-case designs. Let's look at several. First, a sample of one is all you can manage if that sample exhausts the population. If you have access to a participant that is unique, you simply cannot find other participants. Of course, this example is perhaps closer to a case study than to an experiment because there would be no larger population to which you could generalize your findings. Second, if you can assume perfect generalizability, then a sample of one is appropriate. If there is only inconsequential variability among members of the population on a particular variable, then measuring one participant should be sufficient. Third, a single-case design would be most appropriate when a single *negative* instance would refute a theory or an assumed universal relation. If the scientific community believes that "reinforcement always increases responding," then finding one instance in which reinforcement does *not* increase responding invalidates the thesis. Fourth, you may simply have limitations on your opportunity to observe a particular behavior. Behaviors in the real world (i.e., nonlaboratory behaviors) may be so rare that you can locate only one participant who exhibits the behavior. Dukes used examples of people who feel no pain, who are totally color-blind, or who exhibit multiple personality disorder (again, close to a case study). You may remember reading about H. M. when you studied memory in introductory psychology. Because of surgery for epilepsy that removed part of his brain, H. M. could no longer form new long-term memories. Researchers have studied H. M. for almost 50 years for clues about how the brain forms new memories (Corkin, 1984; Hilts, 1995). Fifth, when research is extremely time consuming and expensive, requires extensive training, or has difficulties with control, an investigator may choose to study only one participant. The studies in which researchers have attempted to teach apes to communicate through sign language, plastic symbols, or computers fall into this category. Thus, it is clear that there are instances in which a single-case design is totally appropriate.

General Procedures of Single-Case Experimental Designs

Hersen (1982) listed three procedures that are characteristic of single-case designs: repeated measures, baseline measurement, and changing one variable at a time. Let's see why each of these procedures is important.

Repeated Measures   When we deal with many participants, we often measure them only once and then average all our observations. However, when you are dealing with only one participant, it is important to make sure that the behavior you are measuring is consistent. Therefore, you would repeatedly measure the participant's behavior. Control during the measurement process is extremely important. Hersen and Barlow (1976) noted that the procedures for measurement "must be clearly specified, observable, public, and replicable in all respects" (p. 71). In addition, these repeated measurements "must be done under exacting and totally standardized conditions with respect to measurement devices used, personnel involved, time or times of day measurements are recorded, instructions to the subject, and the specific environmental conditions" (p. 71). Thus, conducting a single-case experiment and making repeated measurements do *not* remove the experimenter's need to control factors as carefully as possible.

Baseline Measurement   In most single-case designs, the initial experimental period is devoted to determining the **baseline** level of behavior. In essence, baseline measurement serves as the control condition against which to compare the behavior as affected by the IV. When you are collecting baseline data, you hope to find a stable pattern of behavior so that you can more easily see any change that occurs in the behavior after your intervention (IV). Barlow and Hersen (1973) recommended that you collect *at least* three observations during the baseline period in order to establish a trend in the data. Although you may not achieve a stable measurement, the more observations you have, the more confident you can be that you have determined the general trend

> **Baseline**   A measurement of a behavior that is made under normal conditions (i.e., no IV is present); a control condition.

of the observations. Figure 12-7 depicts a hypothetical stable baseline presented by Hersen and Barlow (1976). Notice that they increased their odds of finding a stable pattern by collecting data three times per day and averaging those data for the daily entry.

Changing One Variable at a Time   In a single-case design it is vital that as the experimenter, you change only one variable at a time when you move from one phase of the experiment to the next.

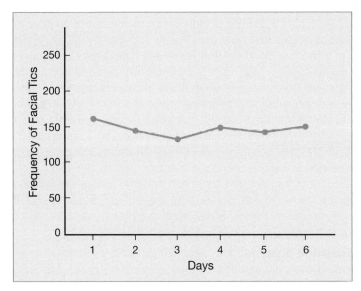

FIGURE 12-7   A Stable Baseline.   Hypothetical data for mean number of facial tics averaged over three daily 15-minute videotaped sessions.

Source: Figure 3-1 from Single-Case Experiemental Designs: Strategies for Studying Behavioral Change (p. 77) by M. Hersen and D. H. Barlow, 1976, New York: Pergamon Press. Used with permission of the publisher.

Why would it be important to change only one variable at a time in a single-case design?

We hope that the answer to this question came easily. Changing one variable at a time is a basic experimental control procedure that we have stressed many times. If you allow two variables to change simultaneously, then you have a confounded experiment and cannot tell which variable has caused the change in behavior that you observe. This situation is exactly the same in a single-case design. If you record your baseline measurement, change several aspects of the participant's environment, and then observe the behavior again, you have no way of knowing which changed aspect affected the behavior.

Statistics and Single-Case Experimental Designs

Traditionally, researchers have not computed statistical analyses of results from single-case designs. Not only has the development of statistical tests for such designs lagged behind multiple-case analyses, but there is also controversy about *whether* statistical analyses of single-case designs are even appropriate (Kazdin, 1976). Both Kazdin (1976) and Hersen (1982) summarized the arguments concerning statistical analyses. Let's take a quick look at this controversy.

The Case Against Statistical Analysis   As we mentioned, tradition and history say that statistical analyses are not necessary in single-case designs. The tradition has been to visually inspect ("eyeball") the data to determine whether or not change has taken place. Researchers who hold this position believe that treatments that do not produce visually apparent effects are either weak or ineffective. Skinner (1966) wrote that "rate of responding and changes in rate can be directly observed . . . [and] statistical methods are unnecessary" (p. 20).

Because many single-case studies involve clinical treatments, another argument against statistical analysis is that statistical significance is not always the same as clinical significance. A statistical demonstration of change may not be satisfying for practical application. "For example, an autistic child may hit himself in the head 100 times an hour. Treatment may reduce this to 50 times per hour. Even though change has been achieved, a much larger change is needed to eliminate behavior" (Kazdin, 1984, p. 89).

Finally, to the pro-statistics folks who argue that statistical analyses may help find effects that visual inspection would not (see next section), the anti-statistics camp makes the point that such subtle effects may not be replicable (Kazdin, 1976). As you will learn in the next chapter, if you cannot replicate a result, it has no external validity.

The Case for Statistical Analysis   The argument for using statistical analyses of single-case designs revolves primarily around increased accuracy of conclusions. Jones, Vaught, and Weinrott (1977) have provided the most persuasive appeal for such analyses. They reviewed a number of studies published in the *Journal of Applied Behavior Analysis* that used visual inspection of data to draw conclusions. Jones et al. found that analyses of these data showed that sometimes conclusions drawn from visual inspections were correct and that sometimes the conclusions were incorrect. In the latter category, both Type I and Type II errors (see Chapter 8) occurred. In other words, some statistical analyses showed *no* effect when the researchers had said there was an effect and some analyses showed significant effects when the researchers had said there were none. Kazdin (1976) pointed out that statistical analyses are particularly likely to uncover findings that do not show up in visual inspection when a stable baseline is not established, new areas of research are being investigated, or testing is done in the real world, which tends to increase extraneous variation.

As you can tell, there is no clear-cut answer concerning the use of statistics with single-case designs. Most researchers probably make their decision in such a situation based on a combination of personal preference, the audience for the information, and potential journal editors. Covering the various tests used to analyze single-case designs is beyond the scope of this text. Adaptations of *t* tests and ANOVA have been used, but these approaches have suffered some problems. For further information about such tests, see Kazdin (1976).

Representative Single-Case Experimental Designs

Researchers use standard notation for single-case designs that makes the information easier to present and conceptualize. In this notation, **A** refers to the baseline measurement and **B** refers to the measurement during or after treatment. We read the notation for single-case designs from left to right to denote the passage of time.

> **A** Refers to the baseline measurement in a single-case design.
>
> **B** Refers to the outcome (treatment) measurement in a single-case design.
>
> **A-B design** A single-case design in which you measure the baseline behavior, institute a treatment, and use a posttest.

A-B Design In the **A-B design**, the simplest of the single-case designs, we make baseline measurements, apply a treatment, and then take a second set of measurements. We compare the B (treatment) measurements to the A (baseline) measurements in order to determine whether a change has occurred. This design should remind you of a pretest–posttest design except for the absence of a control group. In the A-B design, the participant's A measurements serve as the control for the B measurements.

For example, Hall et al. (1971) used this approach in a special-education setting. A 10-year-old boy (Johnny) continually talked out and disrupted the class, which led other children to imitate him. The researchers had the teacher measure Johnny's baseline talking-out behavior (A) for five 15-minute sessions under normal conditions. In implementing the treatment (B), the teacher ignored the talking out and paid more attention to Johnny's productive behavior (attention was *contingent* on the desired behavior), again for five 15-minute sessions. Johnny's talking out diminished noticeably.

Hersen (1982) rated the A-B design as one of the weakest for inferring causality and noted that it is often deemed correlational.

PSYCHO-LOGICAL DETECTIVE

Why do you think the A-B design is weak concerning causality?

The A-B design is poor for determining causality because of many of the threats to internal validity that we saw in Chapter 6. It is possible that another factor could vary along with the treatment. This possibility is especially strong for extraneous variables that could be linked to time passage, such as history, maturation, and instrumentation. If such a factor varied across time with the treatment, then any change in B could be due to *either* the treatment or the extraneous factor. Because there is no control group, we cannot rule out the extraneous variable as a causative factor.

Can you think of a solution to the causality problem inherent in the A-B design? Remember that you cannot add a control group *or* participants because this is a single-case design. Therefore, any control must occur with the single participant.

The solution to this causality problem requires us to examine our next single-case design.

A-B-A design   A single-case design consisting of a baseline measurement, a treatment, a posttest, and a return to the baseline condition. May not be recommended if the participant is left without a beneficial or necessary treatment in the second baseline.

A-B-A Design   In the **A-B-A design**, the treatment phase is followed by a return to the baseline condition. If a change in behavior during B is actually due to the experimental treatment, the change should disappear when B is removed and you return to the baseline condition. If, on the other hand, a change in B was due to some extraneous variable, the change will not disappear when B is removed. Thus, the A-B-A design allows a causal relation to be drawn.

In Hall et al.'s (1971) experiment, the teacher did return to the baseline condition with Johnny. When the teacher began again to pay attention to Johnny's talking-out behavior, that behavior increased considerably. This return to the previous behavior strengthened the researchers' claim that the treatment had caused the original decrease in Johnny's talking out.

There is one glaring drawback to the A-B-A design. Think about the implications of conducting a baseline–treatment–baseline experiment. Can you spot the drawback? How would you remedy this problem?

If you end your experiment on an A phase, this leaves the participant in a baseline condition. If the treatment is a beneficial one, the participant is "left hanging" without the treatment. The solution to this problem requires us to examine another single-case design.

A-B-A-B design   A single-case design consisting of a baseline, treatment, posttest, return to baseline, repeated treatment, and second posttest. This design gives the best chance of isolating causation.

A-B-A-B Design   As you can figure out by now, the **A-B-A-B design** begins with a baseline period followed by treatment, baseline, and treatment periods consecutively. This design adds a final treatment period to the A-B-A design, thereby completing the experimental cycle with the participant in a treatment phase. Hersen and Barlow (1976) pointed out that this design gives two transitions (B to A and A to B) that can demonstrate the effect of the treatment variable. Thus, our ability to draw a cause-and-effect conclusion is further strengthened.

Hall et al. (1971) actually used the A-B-A-B design in their experiment with Johnny. After measuring Johnny's baseline talking-out behavior (A) under normal conditions, the teacher implemented the treatment (B) by ignoring the talking out and paying attention only to Johnny's productive behavior. The teacher then repeated the A and B phases. Results from this study appear in Figure 12-8. This graph shows us several things. First, visual inspection of these results should be enough to convince us of the efficacy of the treatment—the difference between baseline and treatment conditions is dramatic. This graph is a good illustration of why many researchers who use single-case designs believe that statistics are unnecessary. Second, it is apparent that the treatment did work. When the teacher stopped attending to Johnny's talking-out behavior and paid attention to his productive behavior, the talking out decreased substantially. Third, we can determine that the increased productive behavior was caused by the contingent attention because of the rapid increase in talking out when the attention was removed (see Baseline$_2$ in Figure 12-8).

Design and the Real World   From the preceding sections it should be clear that the A-B-A-B design is the preferred design for single-case research. However, we must ask whether typical practice actually follows the recommended path. Hersen and Barlow (1976) acknowledged that researchers often use the A-B design despite its shortcomings in terms of demonstrating causality. The main reason the A-B design is used concerns either the inability or undesirability to return to the baseline in the third stage. In the real world, perfect experimental design cannot always be used. We must simply accept that our ability to draw definitive conclusions in such instances is limited. Let's look at three common situations that preclude using a design other than the A-B design.

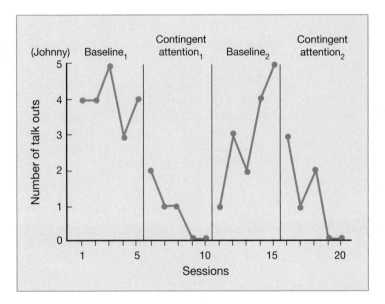

FIGURE   12-8   Talking-Out Behavior in a Mentally Retarded Student.   A record of talking-out behavior of an educable mentally retarded student. **Baseline1**—before experiemental conditions. **Contingent Attention1**—systematic ignoring of talking out and increased teacher attention to appropriate behavior. **Baseline2**—reinstatement of teacher attention to talking-out behavior. **Contingent Attention2**—return to systematic ignoring of talking out and increased attention to appropriate behavior.

Source: Figure 2 from "The Teacher as Observer and Experimenter in the Modification of Disrupting and Talking-out Behaviors" by R. V. Hall, R. Fox, D. Willard, L. Goldsmith, M. Emerson, M. Owen, F. Davis, and E. Porcia, 1971, *Journal of Applied Behavior Analysis*, 4, p. 143.

First, as is typical in many field experiments, it may be impractical to reverse a treatment. Campbell (1969, p. 410) urged politicians to conduct social reforms as experiments, proposing that they initiate a new policy on an experimental basis. If after five years there had been no significant improvement, he recommended that the politicians shift to a different policy. Political realities, of course, would not allow social change to be conducted experimentally. Campbell (1969) provided a good example of this problem. In 1955 Connecticut experienced a record number of traffic fatalities. The governor instituted a speeding crackdown in 1956, and traffic fatalities fell by more than 12%. Once this result occurred, it would have been politically stupid for the governor to announce, "We wish to determine whether the speeding crackdown actually caused the drop in auto deaths. Therefore, in 1957, we will relax our enforcement of speeding laws to find out whether fatalities increase once again." Yet this is what would be necessary in order to rule out rival hypotheses and draw a definitive cause-and-effect statement.

Second, it may be unethical to reverse a treatment. Lang and Melamed (1969) worked with a 9-month-old boy (see Figure 12–9) who had begun vomiting after meals when he was about 6 months old. Dietary changes had been implemented, medical tests had been conducted, exploratory surgery had been performed, but no organic cause could be found. The boy weighed 9pounds, 4 ounces at birth, had gained to 17 pounds at 6 months of age, but weighed only

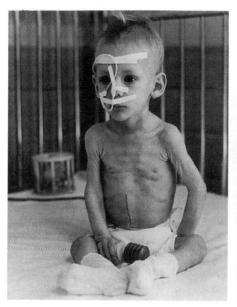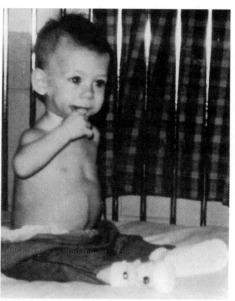

A   **B**

Figure 12-9   **Nine-Month-Old Boy Hospitalized for Frequent Vomiting (A) Before Treatment and (B) After Treatment (13 Days Later).**   The photograph at the left was taken during the observation period just prior to treatment. (It clearly illustrates the patient's debilitated condition—the lack of body fat, skin hanging in loose folds. The tape around the face holds tubing for the nasogastric pump. The photograph at the right was taken on the day of discharge from the hospital, 13 days after the first photo. The 26% increase in body weight already attained is easily seen in the full, more infantlike face, the rounded arms, and more substantial trunk.)

Source: Figure 1 from "Avoidance Conditioning Therapy of an Infant with Chronic Ruminative Vomiting" by P. J. Lang and B. G. Melamed, 1969, *Journal of Abnormal Psychology, 74,* pp. 1–8.

12 pounds at 9 months. The child was being fed through a nose tube and was in critical condition (see Figure 12-9A). Lang and Melamed instituted a treatment consisting of brief and repeated shocks applied to the boy's leg at the first signs of vomiting and ending when vomiting ceased. By the third treatment session, one or two brief shocks were enough to stop the vomiting. By the fourth day of treatment, vomiting stopped, so treatment was discontinued. Two days later, some vomiting occurred, so the procedure was reinstated for three sessions. Five days later, the child was dismissed from the hospital (see Figure 12-9B). A month later he weighed 21 pounds and 5 months later weighed over 26 pounds, with no recurrence of vomiting. Although this treatment bears some resemblance to an A-B-A-B design (because of the brief relapse), the additional session was not originally intended and was *not* conducted as an intentional removal of B to chart a new baseline—the researchers believed that the problem had been cured at the point treatment was discontinued. We are certain that you can see why ethical considerations would dictate an A-B design in this instance rather than the more experimentally rigorous A-B-A-B design.

Finally, it may be impossible, undesirable, or unethical to reverse a treatment if learning takes place during the treatment. Bobby Traffanstedt (1998), a student at the University of Central Arkansas in Conway, used an A-B design to modify a 10-year-old boy's TV watching and exercise behaviors. Traffanstedt wanted to teach the boy to spend less time watching TV and more time exercising. He used the operant procedures of shaping and reinforcement while working

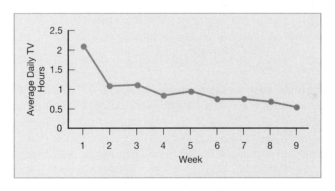

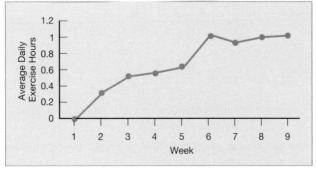

FIGURE 12-10   **Teaching a 10-Year-Old Boy to Decrease TV Viewing and Increase Exercise.**

Source: Adapted from "Weight Reduction using Behavior Modification" by B. Traffanstedt, 1998, *Journal of Psychological Inquiry*, 3, pp. 19–23.

with the child for several weeks. The baseline (Week 1) and posttest (Weeks 2–9) behavior measures appear in Figure 12-10. As you can see, visual inspection of these data is convincing.

Why did Traffanstedt (1998) *not* use the A-B-A-B design in this experiment?

Because Traffanstedt had successfully taught the child to spend less time watching TV and more time exercising, he did not want to "undo" this learning and return to the baseline condition. Traffanstedt had already attempted to gradually fade out the reinforcement over the course of Weeks 2 through 9, so going back to baseline was not really feasible. Having learned the new behaviors, it would make no sense to return the boy to the baseline condition.

The conclusion to this section is that you as an experimenter may find yourself caught in the middle. On the one hand, you have the knowledge of proper experimental design and what is necessary to yield cause-and-effect explanations. On the other hand, you have the realities of applied situations. The best rule of thumb for such situations is that you should use the most stringent experimental design you can, but you should not give up on an important project if you cannot use the absolute best design that exists. As a psychological detective, you have an edge on the real-life detective, who cannot apply a design even as rigorous as those we have presented in this section. The police detective must always work on a solution after the fact.

Additional Single-Case Designs   In presenting the A-B, A-B-A, and A-B-A-B designs, we have merely scratched the surface of single-case designs. We have covered the designs we think you might be likely to use in the near future. As our references show, entire books have been written about single-case designs. Hersen and Barlow (1976) covered many additional variations on single-case designs, including designs with multiple baselines, multiple schedules, and interactions. Thus, if you ever envision a single-case design that is more complicated than the ones we have presented in this text, we refer you to Hersen and Barlow (1976) or a similar book dealing with single-case designs.

REVIEW SUMMARY

1. **Single-case experimental designs** are experiments that deal with a single participant.
2. Single-case designs have several legitimate uses.
3. Single-case designs are characterized by repeated measures, **baseline** measurement, and changing one variable at a time.
4. There is controversy over the use of statistics with single-case designs. The traditional approach has been to draw conclusions by visually examining the data. Proponents of statistical analysis maintain that analysis yields more correct conclusions.

5. The **A-B-A-B** single-case design allows you the best chance to draw a cause-and-effect conclusion regarding a treatment. Realities of the real world often force the use of **A-B** designs, which are particularly prone to alternative explanations.

> ### CHECK YOUR PROGRESS

1. Why were single-case designs quite popular in psychology's early years but less popular today?
2. How can a single-case design be used to disprove a theory?
3. To come up with a comparison in the single-case design, we first measure behavior before the treatment during the _____ period. To get a stable measurement, we should make at least _____ observations.
4. In essence, _____ serve(s) as the control condition in the single-case design.
   a. baseline measurements
   b. repeated measures
   c. changing one variable at a time
   d. experimental analysis of behavior

5. Summarize two arguments for and two arguments against statistical analysis of single-case designs.
6. Match the design with the appropriate characteristic.
   1. A-B   a. leaves the participant in a baseline phase
   2. A-B-A   b. best single-case design for determining cause-and-effect relations
   3. A-B-A-B   c. has many threats to internal validity

7. Why might you be forced to use an A-B single-case design in the real world? Give an original example of such a situation.

Quasi-Experimental Designs

In this section, we will deal with designs that are virtually identical to true experimental designs with the *exception* of random assignment of participants to groups. When we are able to manipulate an IV and measure a DV but *cannot* randomly assign our participants to groups, we must use a **quasi-experimental design**. Similarly, police detectives sometimes face situations in which they must build their case on circumstantial evidence rather than using direct evidence.

> **Quasi-experimental design** A research design used when you cannot randomly assign your experimental participants to the groups but do manipulate an IV and measure a DV.

What problem results when we cannot randomly assign research participants to groups?

Not being able to randomly assign our participants to their groups has the effect of violating an important assumption that allows us to draw cause-and-effect conclusions from our experiments—the assumption of equal groups before the experiment. Even if we can randomly select participants from a larger group, we cannot make cause-and-effect statements without random assignment. For example, you could randomly *select* students from an introductory psychology course, but you could not randomly *assign* them to groups based on sex! As Campbell and Stanley (1966) pointed out, the assumption of random assignment has been an important part of statistics and experimental design since the time of Fisher. If we unknowingly began an experiment with unequal groups and our statistics showed a difference after the experiment, we would make a Type I error (see Chapter 8) by concluding that the IV caused the difference that was actually present from the outset. Clearly, this conclusion could be wrong.

It is likely that our description of quasi-experimental design reminds you of the ex post facto studies we covered in Chapter 5. Some writers categorize ex post facto and quasi-experimental designs together and some separate them. We will draw a small, but significant, distinction between the two. Remember in Chapter 5 we described the ex post facto study as having an IV that had *already* occurred and that we could not manipulate. Thus, if we wish to study sex differences on mathematics or English achievement, we are studying the IV of biological sex, which we cannot control or manipulate. Of course, because the IV is a preexisting condition, we also cannot randomly assign our participants to groups.

On the other hand, in a quasi-experimental design, our participants belong to preexisting groups that we cannot randomly assign, but we *do* have control over the IV—we can administer it when and to whom we wish. Thus, we could choose our participants on the basis of sex and *then* have some of them participate in a workshop designed to improve their math or English achievement. In this case, the workshop (or lack thereof) would serve as the IV for the preexisting groups of boys and girls, and the math or English achievement scores would be the DV. Obviously, random assignment is impossible in this case. Quasi-experimental designs are a step closer to true experimental designs than ex post facto studies because you, as the experimenter, are able to exert control over the IV and its administration. Being able to administer your own IV is preferable to having nature administer it for you, at least in terms of control.

The basic rationale for using quasi-experimental designs is the same as that for ex post facto studies—your inability to assign participants at random. According to Hedrick, Bickman, and Rog (1993), "a quasi-experimental design is not the method of choice, but rather a fallback strategy for situations in which random assignment is not possible" (p. 62). When dealing with selection variables that do not allow for random assignment, we have the choice of using a quasi-experimental design or simply ignoring an important or interesting experimental question. Instead of letting such questions go unasked, researchers resort to quasi-experimental research.

History of Quasi-Experimental Designs

It is difficult to trace the history of quasi-experimental designs. Although McGuigan (1960) did not include the term in the first edition of his classic experimental psychology text, Campbell and Stanley did use it in the title of their 1966 guide to experimental design. However, there is little doubt that researchers were tackling quasi-experimental design problems long before Campbell and Stanley's published work. Cook and Campbell (1979) noted that some researchers were writing about quasi-experiments in the 1950s, although the term did not originate until later. It is likely that Campbell and Stanley (1966) and Cook and Campbell (1979) are responsible for elevating quasi-experimental work to the respectable position it holds today.

Uses of Quasi-Experimental Designs

Hedrick et al. (1993) listed several specific situations that require quasi-experimental designs. Let's take a brief look at their list. First, there are many variables that simply make random assignment impossible. If we wish to study participants from certain groups (e.g., based on sex, age, previous life experiences, or personality characteristics), we must use quasi-experimental designs. Second, when you wish to evaluate an ongoing program or intervention (a retrospective study), you would need to use a quasi-experimental design. Because the program began before you decided to evaluate it, you would have been unable to use control procedures from the outset. Third, studies of social conditions demand quasi-experimental designs. You would not study the effects of poverty, race, unemployment, or other such social factors through random assignment. Fourth, it is sometimes the case that random assignment is not possible because of expense, time, or monitoring difficulties. For example, if you conducted a cross-cultural research project involving participants from several different countries, it would be nearly impossible to guarantee that the same random assignment procedures were used in each setting. Fifth, the ethics of an experimental situation, particularly with psychological research, may necessitate quasi-experimentation. For example, if you are conducting a research program to evaluate a certain treatment, you must worry about the ethics of withholding that treatment from people who could benefit from it. As you will see, quasi-experimentation provides a design that will work in such situations to remove this ethical dilemma.

Representative Quasi-Experimental Designs

Unlike the single-case design, we do not include sections covering general procedures and statistics of quasi-experimental designs. It is difficult to derive general principles because the representative designs we are about to introduce are so varied in nature. Because quasi-experimental designs resemble true experiments, the use of statistics for quasi-experimental designs is not an issue; the traditional statistical tests used with true experiments are also appropriate for quasi-experiments.

> **Nonequivalent group design**   A design involving two or more groups that are not randomly assigned; a comparison group (no treatment) is compared to one or more treatment groups.

Nonequivalent Group Design   The **nonequivalent group design** (Campbell & Stanley, 1966) appears in Figure 12-11.

The nonequivalent group design should remind you of a design that we covered in the section on research designs that protect internal validity. Which design does it resemble? How is it different? What is the implication of this difference?

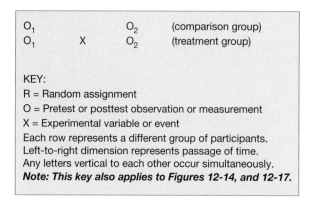

FIGURE 12-11   The Nonequivalent Group Design.

If you turn back to Figure 12-2, you will see that the nonequivalent group design bears a distinct resemblance to the pretest–posttest control-group design. However, the nonequivalent group design is missing the *R*s in front of the two groups; random assignment is *not* used in creating the groups. The lack of random assignment means that our groups may differ before the experiment—thus the name *nonequivalent group* design.

You also will notice that the two groups are labeled as the *comparison group* (rather than control group) and the *treatment group* (rather than experimental group [from Hedrick et al., 1993]). The *treatment* to *experimental* change is not particularly important; those terms could be used interchangeably. However, changing the name from *control* to *comparison* group is important and meaningful. In the nonequivalent group design, this group serves as the comparison to the treatment group but cannot truly be called a control group because of the lack of random assignment.

It is possible to extend the nonequivalent group design to include more than one treatment group if you wish to contrast two or more treatment groups with your comparison group. The key to the nonequivalent group design is creating a good comparison group. As far as is possible, we attempt to create an equal group through our selection criteria rather than through random assignment.

> Examples of procedures for creating such a group include using members of a waiting list for a program/service; using people who did not volunteer for a program, but were eligible; using students in classes that will receive the curriculum (treatment) at a later date; and matching individual characteristics. (Hedrick et al., 1993, p. 59)

Geronimus (1991) provided a good example of creating a strong comparison group. She and her colleagues completed several studies of long-term outcomes for teen mothers. As you are probably aware, the stereotypical outcome for teen mothers is quite dismal—younger mothers are more likely to have negative experiences such as poverty, high dropout rates, and higher rates of infant mortality. However, Geronimus believed that family factors such as socioeconomic status might be better predictors of these negative outcomes than the actual teen pregnancy. Random assignment for research on this topic would be impossible—you could not randomly assign teenage girls to become pregnant or not. Thus, quasi-experimentation was necessary. In looking for a comparison group that would be as similar as possible, Geronimus decided to use the teenage mothers' sisters who did not become pregnant until later in life. Thus, although the assignment to groups was not random, the groups were presumably very near to equivalence, particularly with respect to family background factors. Interestingly enough, when family background was controlled in this manner, many of the negative outcomes associated with teen pregnancy disappeared. For example, there was no longer any difference in the dropout rates of the two groups. "For indicators of infant health and children's sociocognitive development, at times the trends reversed direction (i.e., controlling for family background, the teen birth group did better than the postponers)" (Geronimus, 1991, p. 465).

In Geronimus's research, the "pretest" (actually a matching variable in this case) consisted of finding two women from the same family, one who first became pregnant as a teenager and one who did not get pregnant until after age 20. In this case the groups may still have been nonequivalent, but they were highly equivalent on family background. Sometimes it is impossible to begin with equivalent groups, and the pretest serves much like a baseline measure for comparison with the posttest. In this type of situation, the label *nonequivalent groups* seems quite appropriate.

Janet Luehring, a student at Washburn University in Topeka, Kansas, and Joanne Altman, her faculty advisor, used a nonequivalent group design in their research project (Luehring & Altman, 2000). They measured students' performance on the Mental Rotation Task (MRT; Vandenberg & Kuse, 1978). For each item on the MRT, participants saw 5 three-dimensional shapes, with the first shape being the test stimulus. Two of the other four shapes were matches of the test stimulus when rotated; participants had to identify the two that were the same as the test stimulus. The MRT consists of 20 such items and normally has a 6-minute time limit. The preponderance of evidence from psychological research indicates that men tend to perform better on spatial tasks than women (Luehring & Altman, 2000). Luehring and Altman compared the performance of female students on the MRT to that of male students. Thus, the groups were not equal before the experiment began. The IV in Luehring and Altman's experiment consisted of performing the MRT under timed or untimed conditions. They found that women who performed the MRT under timed conditions made as few errors as men under timed or untimed conditions—only the women under untimed conditions made more errors than the other three groups. Because the two gender groups began the experiment as nonequivalent, the appropriate question after the experiment was not whether a difference existed, but whether the difference was the same as before the experiment (see Figure 12-12A) or whether the difference had changed in some way. In Luehring and Altman's experiment the difference between the two groups had grown smaller in the timed condition (as in Figure 12-12B), thus supporting the hypothesis that the IV had an effect on MRT performance for women. Of course, there are several other possible outcomes that would also show some effect of the IV. More of Cook and Campbell's (1979) hypothetical outcomes appear in Figure 12-13. Can you interpret each set of findings pictured there?

Thus far, our discussion of this design has seemed similar to that of true experimental designs. What is different about quasi-experimental designs? The most important point to remember is that quasi-experimental designs are more plagued by threats to internal validity. Because you have not used random assignment, your interpretation of the findings must be cautious. Cook and Campbell (1979) isolated four threats to internal validity that are not controlled in the nonequivalent group design. We will list these only briefly because they

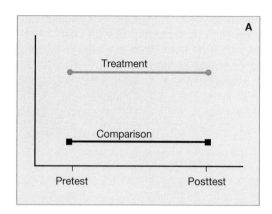
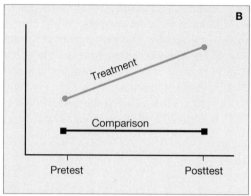

FIGURE 12-12   Two Possible Outcomes in a Nonequivalent Group Design.

Source: Thomas D. Cook and Donald T. Campbell, *Quasi-Experimentation: Design and Analysis.* Copyright © 1979 by Houghton-Mifflin Company. Reprinted by permission.

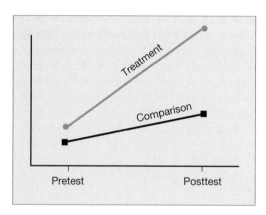
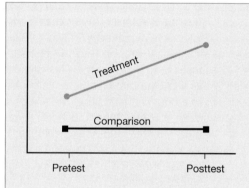
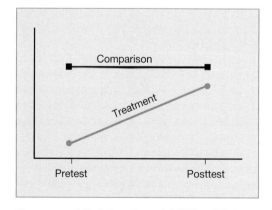
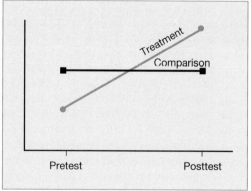

FIGURE 12-13   Several Additional Outcomes in a Nonequivalent Group Design.

Source: Thomas D. Cook and Donald T. Campbell, *Quasi-Experimentation: Design and Analysis.* Copyright © 1979 by Houghton-Mifflin and Company. Reprinted by permission.

appeared in Chapter 6. First, *maturation* is a potential problem. Because the groups begin as unequal, there is a greater potential that results such as those shown in Figure 12-12B might be due to differential maturation of the groups rather than to the IV. Second, we must consider *instrumentation* in the nonequivalent group design. For example, if we demonstrate nonequivalence of our participants by using a scale during the pretest, we must worry about whether the scale is uniform—are the units of measurement equal throughout the scale? *Statistical regression* is the third internal validity threat present in the nonequivalent group design. Regression is particularly likely to be a problem if we select extreme scorers on the basis of our pretest. Finally, we must consider the threat to internal validity of an *interaction between selection and history*. If some local event differentially affected our treatment and comparison groups, we would have a problem.

In conclusion, the nonequivalent group design is a strong quasi-experimental design. Its strength lies in the fact that "it provides an approximation to the experimental design and that, with care, it can support causal inference" (Hedrick et al., 1993, p. 62). However, we must be aware that the threat of confounds is higher than for the true experimental designs. Hedrick et al. (1993) warned that "throughout both the planning and execution phases of an applied research project, researchers must keep their eyes open to identify potential rival explanations for their results" (p. 64). Often researchers who use quasi-experimental designs must address potential alternative hypotheses in their research reports.

Interrupted Time-Series Design   Another quasi-experimental design, the **interrupted time-series design**, involves measuring a group of participants repeatedly over time (the time series), introducing a treatment (the interruption), and measuring the participants repeatedly again (more of the time series). Look at Figure 12-14 to see a graphic portrayal of an interrupted time-series design. We should make an important point about Figure 12-14: There is nothing magical about using five observations before (O1–O5) and after (O6–O10) the treatment. Any number of observations large enough to establish a pattern can be used (Campbell & Stanley [1966] showed four before and after; Cook & Campbell [1979] showed five; Hedrick et al. [1993] showed six before and five after). As you can probably guess, the idea behind an interrupted time-series design is to look for changes in the trend of the data before and after the treatment is applied. Thus, the interrupted time-series design is similar to an A-B design. A change in trend could be shown by a change in the *level* of the behavior (see Figure 12-15A), a change in the *rate* (slope) of the pattern of behavior (see Figure 12-15B), or both (see Figure 12-15C).

> **Interrupted time-series design**   A quasi-experimental design involving a single group of participants that includes repeated pretreatment measures, an applied treatment, and repeated posttreatment measures.

Interrupted time-series designs have been used for quite some time. Campbell and Stanley (1966) referred to their use in much of the classical research of nineteenth-century biology and physical science. Cook and Campbell (1979) cited a representative 1924 study dealing with the effects of moving from a 10-hour to an 8-hour workday in London. Hedrick

O_1 O_2 O_3 O_4 O_5 X O_6 O_7 O_8 O_9 O_{10}

FIGURE 12-14   **An Interrupted Time-Series Design.**

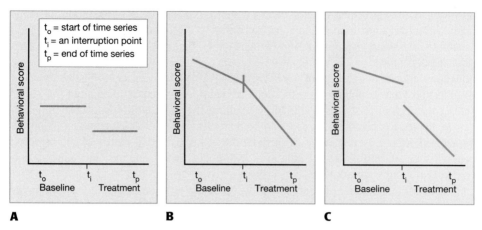

A **B** **C**

FIGURE 12-15 **Potential Changes in Trend in a Time-Series Design.** A. Change in level, no change in rate. B. No change in level, change in rate. C. Change in level, change in rate.

Source: Portions of Figure 1 from "Time-Series Analysis in Operant Research" by R. R. Jones, R. S. Vaught, and M. Weinrott, 1977, *Journal of Applied Behavior Analysis,* 10, pp. 151–166.

and Shipman (1988) used an interrupted time-series design to assess the impact of the 1981 Omnibus Budget Reconciliation Act (OBRA) that tightened eligibility requirements for Aid to Families with Dependent Children (AFDC) assistance. As shown in Figure 12-16, the

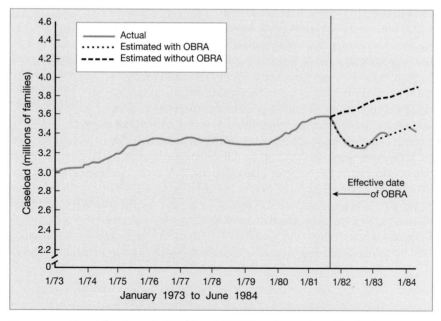

FIGURE 12-16 **Impact of Tightened AFDC Requirements on Caseload.**

Source: T. E. Hedrick and S. L. Shipman, "Multiple Questions Require Multiple Designs: An Evaluation of the 1981 Changes to the AFDC Program" *Evaluation Review, 12,* p. 438. Copyright © 1988 by Sage Publications, Inc. Reprinted by permission of Sage Publications, Inc.

immediate impact of this legislation was to lessen the number of cases handled by about 200,000. However, the number of cases after the change continued to climb at about the same slope it had before the change. Thus, the tightened eligibility requirements seemed to lower the *level* of the caseload but not its *rate*.

Review the threats to internal validity summarized in Chapter 6. Which threat would seem to create the greatest potential problem for the interrupted time-series design?

According to Cook and Campbell (1979), the main threat to most interrupted time-series designs is *history*. One of the primary features of the interrupted time-series design is the passage of time to allow for many different measurements. This time passage raises the possibility that changes in behavior *could* be due to some important event other than the treatment. Because of the time taken by repeated measurements, another potential threat to internal validity is *maturation*. However, the repeated pretesting does allow for the assessment of any maturational trends; thus, if scores change at the same rate before and after the treatment, the change is due to maturation. *Instrumentation* could be a problem if record-keeping or scoring procedures change over the course of time. Such a change, of course, would violate the principles of control in any experiment, not just an interrupted time-series design.

Although the interrupted time-series design can control for some of the internal validity threats, we still face the potential problem of history. This threat to internal validity is usually handled in one of three manners. First, Cook and Campbell (1979) advised frequent testing intervals. For example, if you test participants on a weekly rather than monthly, quarterly, or yearly basis, the probability of a major event occurring during the time period between the last pretest and the treatment is low. In addition, if you keep careful records of any possible effect-causing events during the quasi-experiment, it would be a simple matter to discern whether any occurred at the critical period when you administered the treatment. This first approach to controlling history is probably the most widely used because of its ease and the drawbacks of the other two solutions to be covered next.

A second solution to the history threat is to include a comparison (control) group that does not receive the treatment. Such a design appears in Figure 12-17. As you can see, the comparison group receives the same number of measurements at the same times as the treatment (experimental) group. Thus, if any important historical event occurs at the time the experimental group receives the treatment, the comparison group would have the same experience and show the same effect. The only problem with this solution is that the comparison group would most likely be a nonequivalent group because the groups were not

O_1	O_2	O_3	O_4	O_5	X	O_6	O_7	O_8	O_9	O_{10}
O_1	O_2	O_3	O_4	O_5		O_6	O_7	O_8	O_9	O_{10}

FIGURE 12-17   **An Interrupted Time-Series Design with Control Group.**

randomly assigned. This nonequivalence would put us back in the situation of attempting to control for that difference, with the associated problems we covered in the previous section of this chapter.

The third possible solution to the history problem is probably the best solution but is not always possible. In essence, this solution involves using an A-B-A format within the interrupted time-series design. The problems, of course, are those we mentioned earlier in the chapter when dealing with the A-B-A design. Most importantly, it may not be possible to "undo" the treatment. Once a treatment has been applied, it is not always reversible. Also, if we halt an experiment in the A stage, we are leaving our participants in a nontreatment stage, which may have negative consequences. Hedrick et al. (1993) presented the results of an unintentional interrupted time-series design in an A-B-A format. In 1966 the federal government passed the Highway Safety Act, including a provision that mandated helmets for motorcyclists. However, in the late 1970s states began to repeal helmet laws because of pressure concerning individuals' freedom of choice. Thus, if we examine motorcycle fatality rates over many years, we have an A (no restrictions), B (helmet laws), A (fewer restrictions) format for an interrupted time-series design. Figure 12-18 shows the graph Hedrick et al. (1993) presented. Because of the drop in fatalities after the law was passed and the rise in fatalities after the repeal of the law in some states, it seems straightforward to derive a cause-and-effect relation from these data. Although this type of design allows for a convincing conclusion, again we must point out that the circumstances that created it are unusual and would be difficult, if not impossible, to recreate in many typical quasi-experimental situations.

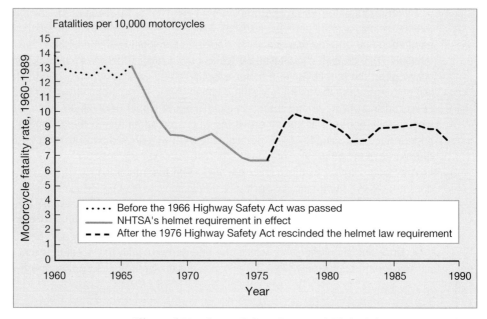

FIGURE 12-18   **Effects of Mandatory Helmet Laws and Their Subsequent Repeal on Motorcycle Fatalities.**

Source: Motocycle Helmet Laws Save Lives and Reduce Costs to Society (GAO/RCED-91-170, July), Washington, DC.

In summary, the interrupted time-series design has the ability to uncover cause-and-effect relations. You must be especially careful of history effects when using this design; however, frequent testing helps reduce this threat. The interrupted time-series design is particularly helpful when dealing with applied types of problems such as therapeutic treatment or in educational settings.

REVIEW SUMMARY

1. **Quasi-experimental designs** are identical to true experimental designs except that participants are not randomly assigned to groups. Thus, our research groups may not be equal before the experiment, causing problems in drawing clear conclusions.
2. Unlike the case in **ex post facto designs**, we are able to control the IV in a quasi-experimental design.
3. There are many situations in which the impossibility of random assignment makes quasi-experimentation necessary.
4. The **nonequivalent group design** involves comparing two groups—one receiving the IV and a comparison group that does not receive the IV. The groups are nonequivalent because of the lack of random assignment.
5. In the nonequivalent group design, it is imperative to select a comparison group that is as similar as possible to the treatment group.
6. **Maturation, instrumentation, statistical regression**, and **selection–history interactions** are all threats to internal validity in the nonequivalent group design.
7. An **interrupted time-series design** involves measuring participants several times, introducing an IV, and then measuring the participants several more times.
8. **History** is the main threat to internal validity in the interrupted time-series design. It can be controlled by testing frequently, including a comparison group, or removing the treatment after it has been applied (if possible).

CHECK YOUR PROGRESS

1. Differentiate between experimental designs, quasi-experimental designs, and ex post facto designs.
2. Give two reasons why you might choose to use a quasi-experimental design rather than an experimental design.
3. Match the design with the appropriate characteristics:

    1. Nonequivalent group design
    2. Interrupted time-series design

    A. typically has one group of participants
    B. has two groups of participants
    C. involves pretesting of participants
    D. does not involve pretesting participants
    E. is prone to the internal validity threat of history
    F. is prone to several internal validity threats

4. What was the key to Geronimus's (1991) research that allowed her to conclude that the effects of teenage pregnancy are not as negative as typically thought?

5. We summarized two interrupted time-series analyses in the text—one dealing with changing AFDC requirements (Figure 12-16) and one dealing with changing motorcycle helmet laws (Figure 12-18). Why are we more certain about our conclusion in the case of the helmet laws than with the AFDC requirements?

6. If Prohibition (the outlawing of alcoholic beverages in the 1920s) was treated as an experiment to determine its effects on alcohol consumption, what design would this represent?

a. nonequivalent group

b. single-case

c. interrupted time-series with control group

d. interrupted time-series

KEY TERMS

Confounding, 299
Extraneous variables, 299
Cause-and-effect relation, 299
Internal validity, 299
Random assignment, 302
Random selection, 303
Selection, 303
History, 303
Maturation, 303
Testing, 303
Statistical regression, 303

Interactions with selection, 304
Experimental mortality, 304
Instrumentation, 304
Diffusion or imitation of treatments, 304
Single-case experimental design, 307
Case-study approach, 308
Experimental analysis of behavior, 309
Baseline, 311

A, 313
B, 313
A-B design, 313
A-B-A design, 314
A-B-A-B design, 314
Quasi-experimental design, 319
Nonequivalent group design, 321
Interrupted time-series design, 325

LOOKING AHEAD

At this point in the text you have learned how to complete the majority of the steps that are necessary to complete a psychological experiment. In this chapter you have learned about more specialized research designs used to protect your experiment's internal validity, when you have only one participant, or when you cannot assign participants to groups randomly. Before we move on to completing your experimental report, we will discuss the concept of external validity—how you can generalize your experimental results beyond your specific experiment.

External Validity and Critiquing Experimental Research

External Validity: Generalizing Your Experiment to the Outside

Internal validity   A type of evaluation of your experiment; it asks the question of whether your IV is the only possible explanation of the results shown for your DV.

External validity   A type of evaluation of your experiment; do your experimental results apply to populations and situations that are different from those of your experiment?

Generalization Applying the results from an experiment to a different situation or population.

In Chapter 6, we covered the concept of **internal validity**, which is one way you must evaluate your experiment. As you will remember, internal validity concerns the question of whether your experiment is confounded—is your IV the only possible explanation for your finding? In this chapter, we will cover another type of validity you should assess in your experiment.

The second type of evaluation that you must make of your experiment involves **external validity**. When you consider external validity, you are asking a question about **generalization**. The root word of *generalization* is *general*. Of course, *general* is essentially the opposite of *specific*. So, when we want to generalize our experimental results, we wish to move away from the specific to the more general. In essence, we would like to take our results beyond the narrow confines of our specific experiment. Imagine that you have conducted an experiment using 20 college students as your participants. Did your experimental question apply only to those 20 college students, or were you attempting to ask a general question that might be applicable to a larger group of students at your school, or to college students in general, or perhaps even to people in general? Few experimenters gather data that they intend to apply only to the participants they actually use in their experiments. Instead, they hope for general findings that will apply more broadly. When you examine different definitions of psychology, you find that many include a phrase about psychology being the "science of behavior." We don't think you've ever seen a definition that referred to the "science of blondes' behavior," or "the science of Californians' behavior," or "the science of children's behavior"—probably not even "the science of human behavior." Psychologists attempt to discover information that applies to everyone and everything. As Sherlock Holmes said, "One's ideas must be as broad as Nature if they are to interpret Nature" (Doyle, 1927, p. 37). When we discover principles that apply broadly, then we have found behavior that is lawful. Finding such principles is a tall order, especially for a single experiment, but we keep this goal in mind as we do our research. We are ever mindful of the need and desire to extend our findings beyond our specific experiment.

Let us share with you a dilemma that this chapter posed for us. The dilemma revolved around where to put this chapter in the text. By placing it where we have, near the end of the book, you may get the idea that you need to worry about evaluating your experiment for external validity only after you complete your experiment. Nothing could be farther from the truth. Rather, we hope that you are constantly evaluating your experiment. Much of what we have written for this chapter is designed to help you evaluate your experiment from the day you begin planning your methodology. When designing their experiments, researchers take precautions that will allow them to increase the generalizability of their final results. So, our dilemma was whether to place this chapter near the beginning of the book or near the back. We chose to put it near the back because you do need to step back to take another look at your experiment after you have completed collecting, analyzing, and interpreting your data. It is here that you are about to write your experimental report (see Chapter 14). At this point, you must decide how far you can legitimately generalize your results.

After you have satisfied yourself that your experiment (or an experiment that you are evaluating) is internally valid, then you can focus on its potential for external validity. As we mentioned, the question of external validity revolves around whether you can take the results of a particular experiment and generalize them beyond that original experiment. Generalization is an important aspect for any science—there are very few occasions when scientists wish to restrict their conclusions to only the relevant conditions of their original experiment. Although police detectives are usually interested in a specific culprit, they are also interested in developing criminal profiles that describe general traits of a specific type of offender (e.g., the profile of mass murderers or of child molesters).

Population generalization Applying the results from an experiment to a group of participants that is different and more encompassing than those used in the original experiment.

There are three customary types of generalization in which we are interested. In **population generalization**, we are concerned about applying our findings to organisms beyond our actual experimental participants. When our students conduct research with fellow students from Emporia State University or Ouachita Baptist University as participants, they are not interested in applying their results only to students at their respective colleges. We doubt that many of you who do experimental projects will try to answer a question about students only at your school. Likewise, psychologists are not typically concerned with trying to discover truths only about the humans or animals who actually compose the participants in their studies. Instead, in all cases we have just mentioned, the researchers (including you) are usually trying to discover general principles about behavior that are applicable to people or animals as a whole. Thus, we must concern ourselves with whether our results will apply to a larger group than our experimental participants.

Environmental generalization refers to the question of whether our experimental results will apply to situations or environments that are different from those of our experiment. Again, it is doubtful that we are interested in finding results that are specific to the environment in which we tested our participants. Can we generalize our results from the college classroom or research lab in which we collected our data to other classrooms or labs or even the real-world environments in which behavior naturally occurs? For example, if students learn a list of words in a laboratory, does that behavior have any relevance to the real-world behavior of studying for an exam?

Environmental generalization Applying the results from an experiment to a situation or environment that differs from that of the original experiment.

Finally, **temporal generalization** describes our desire that our research findings apply at all times and not to only a certain time period. For example, the discovery of seasonal affective disorder (depression only during winter months) is an exception to generalized information about depressive disorders. Another example of research findings that might be specific to a certain time are the many findings of gender differences from research in the 1960s. Today, after several decades of progress on women's rights, we should wonder whether the 1960s findings are still applicable today. Such an issue raises thorny questions for the concept of temporal generalization.

Temporal generalization Applying the results from an experiment to a time that is different from that when the original experiment was conducted.

We must ask questions about the external validity of our research results because of the very property that we mentioned in the first paragraph of this chapter—*internal validity*. To achieve a high degree of internal validity, researchers seek to exert control over a large number of factors. The best way to exert control over factors is to conduct your experiment in a lab (or similar setting) with participants who are highly similar.

Reread the last sentence. Explain why this statement is true. Can you figure out why exerting control, which helps us in terms of internal validity, ends up weakening our external validity?

When we conduct our research in a laboratory, we can control many factors that might function as extraneous variables in the real world. For example, you can control factors such as temperature, lighting, outside noise, and so forth. In addition, you control the time at which your participants come to the experimental situation, as well as when and under what conditions they experience the IV. In short, the lab allows you to remove or hold constant the effects of many extraneous variables, which would be virtually impossible in the real world. In a similar fashion, using participants who are highly similar helps to reduce nuisance variation (see our discussion of nuisance variables in Chapter 6). For example, if you use only college students as participants, you will have an idea of their general reading ability if you have to compose a set of instructions for them to read. In the real world, potential participants would have a much wider range of reading abilities, thus adding nuisance variation to the experiment.

We hope that you can see that these advantages for internal validity become disadvantages for external validity. When we control so many factors so tightly, it is difficult to know if our results will apply to people or animals who are markedly different from our research participants and who encounter our research factors in the real world rather than in the artificial laboratory.

Threats to External Validity (Based on Methods)

Donald Campbell, who wrote extensively about internal validity, has also written widely about factors relating to external validity. We will summarize four factors affecting external validity from Campbell and Stanley (1966).

Interaction of Testing and Treatment When Campbell and Stanley (1966) rated the three experimental designs for internal validity that we previously summarized (pretest–posttest control group, Solomon four-group, posttest-only control group) in Chapter 12, they also attempted to rate them concerning external validity (although that task is much more difficult). We will make several references back to Chapter 12, so you may wish to turn back for a quick review. The **interaction of testing and treatment** is the most obvious threat to external validity, and it occurs for the pretest–posttest control group design (see Figure 13-1) that we discussed in Chapter 12. External validity is threatened because both groups of participants are pretested and there is no control to determine whether the pretesting has an effect. As Solomon (1949) pointed out, "There is a great possibility that merely taking a pretest changes the subjects' attitudes toward the training procedures" (p. 141).

Interaction of testing and treatment A threat to external validity that occurs when a pretest sensitizes participants to the treatment yet to come.

```
R     O₁              O₂        (control group)
R     O₃      X       O₄        (experimental group)

KEY:
R = Random assignment
O = Pretest or posttest observation or measurement
X = Experimental variable or event
Each row represents a different group of participants.
Left-to-right dimension represents passage of time.
Any letters vertical to each other occur simultaneously.
```

FIGURE 13-1   **The Pretest–Posttest Control Group Design.**

Imagine that you are working on an experiment dealing with prejudice toward people with mental disorders, specifically people with schizophrenia. You decide to test your participants by giving them a scale that measures their prejudice toward people with schizophrenia before showing them *A Beautiful Mind* (Grazer & Howard, 2001), a movie depicting John Nash's struggles with schizophrenia before he won a Nobel Prize for his work in mathematics. Does it seem likely that these people's responses to the movie will be different from those of a group of people who were not pretested? This question is the essence of an interaction between testing and treatment—because of a pretest, your participants' reaction to the treatment will be different. The pretest has a sensitizing effect on your participants; it is somewhat like giving a giant hint about the experiment's purpose before beginning the experiment. The pretesting effect is particularly troublesome for experiments that deal with attitudes and attitude change. This testing and treatment interaction is the reason that researchers developed nonpretesting designs such as the posttest-only control-group design. Also, although the Solomon four-group design does incorporate pretests for two groups, it includes no pretesting of the remaining two groups, thus allowing for a measurement of any pretesting effect.

Interaction of Selection and Treatment   You will remember we covered "interactions with selection" as a threat to internal validity in Chapter 12. In those cases, selection potentially interacted with other threats to internal validity such as history, maturation, and instrumentation. In this instance, however, the threat to external validity consists of an interaction between selection and treatments.

An **interaction of selection and treatment** occurs when the effects that you demonstrate hold true only for the particular groups that you selected for your experiment. Campbell and Stanley (1966) noted that the threat of a selection–treatment interaction becomes greater as it becomes more difficult to find participants for your experiment. As it becomes harder to get participants, it becomes more likely that the participants you do locate will be unique and not representative of the general population.

Interaction of selection and treatment   A threat to external validity that can occur when a treatment effect is found only for a specific sample of participants.

One of your authors ran into a selection–treatment interaction when he was attempting to complete his doctoral dissertation, in which he was testing a particular explanation of a common and easy-to-find phenomenon (better memory for material studied repeatedly at longer intervals rather than shorter intervals). Because of time pressures, he had to conduct his experiment during summer school. When he analyzed the data, the supposedly easy-to-find phenomenon was not evidenced by the statistics. Rather than concluding that the phenomenon did not exist (contrary to *much* published evidence), he decided that this finding was a result of a selection–treatment interaction. When he conducted his experiment a second time during the regular semester, the ubiquitous effect was found. It appears that for some reason, the summer school students were a unique population.

Reactive Arrangements   Reactive arrangements revolve around the artificial atmosphere of many psychological experiments. Because of our desire for control, we may create a highly contrived situation in a laboratory in which we attempt to measure a real-world behavior. There are some cases in which this type of arrangement is probably a dismal failure. As you saw in Chapter 7, experimental participants, particularly humans, seek clues about their environments. They may react to our experimental manipulations, but also to subtle cues that they find in the experimental situation. As Campbell and Stanley (1966) remarked, "The play-acting, outguessing, up-for-inspection, I'm-a-guinea-pig, or whatever attitudes so generated are unrepresentative of the school setting, and seem to be qualifiers of the effect of X, seriously hampering generalization" (p. 20). Although their comment was directed at educational research, if we substitute "real world" for "school setting," the quotation remains valid. Thus, **reactive arrangements** refer to those conditions of an experimental setting (other than the IV) that alter our participants' behavior. We cannot be sure that the behaviors we observe in the experiment will generalize outside that setting because these artificial conditions do not exist in the real world.

> **Reactive arrangements** A threat to external validity caused by an experimental situation that alters participants' behavior, regardless of the IV involved.

In Chapter 4 we mentioned a series of studies that are usually cited as classic examples of reactive arrangements, the Hawthorne studies. You recall that researchers studied productivity of a subset of plant workers over a period of time. This subset of workers tended to increase productivity regardless of the changes instituted in their environment. One of the representative experiments dealt with the level of illumination in a work area. A control group worked in a room with 10 foot-candles of light whereas the experimental group's illumination began at 10 foot-candles and was gradually decreased by 1 foot-candle at a time until it reached 3 foot-candles. At this point, "the operatives protested, saying that they were hardly able to see what they were doing, and the production rate decreased. The operatives could and did maintain their efficiency to this point in spite of the discomfort and handicap of insufficient illumination" (Roethlisberger & Dickson, 1939, p. 17).

> **Demand characteristics** Features from the experiment that inadvertently lead participants to respond in a particular manner.

In Chapter 7 we introduced the concept of **demand characteristics**. According to Orne (1962), demand characteristics can convey the experimental hypothesis to the participants and give them clues about how to behave. You (or your friends) may have experienced something similar to demand characteristics if you are a psychology major. When you tell people you are a psychology major, a common response is "Are you going to psychoanalyze me?" Rather than responding to you as an individual, people are responding to the demand characteristics of what they believe about psychology majors.

Orne said that it is impossible to design an experiment without demand characteristics. He also believed that demand characteristics make generalizations difficult because it is not clear from a set of research findings whether the participants are responding to an experiment's IV, its demand characteristics, or both. It seems that reactive arrangements tend to increase demand characteristics, thus creating further difficulties with generalization.

Multiple-Treatment Interference   As you can probably guess from the name of this threat to external validity, **multiple-treatment interference** can occur only in experiments that involve presenting more than one treatment to the same participants (repeated-measures designs). The potential problem that arises in repeated-measures designs is that the findings we obtain may be specific to situations in which the experimental participants experienced these multiple treatments. If they received only one treatment, then the experimental results may be different.

> **Multiple-treatment interference**   A threat to external validity that occurs when a set of findings results only when participants experience multiple treatments in the same experiment.

Campbell and Stanley (1966) cited Ebbinghaus's memory work as an example of multiple-treatment interference. Ebbinghaus was a pioneer in the field of verbal learning, conducting many experiments of learning lists of nonsense syllables by serving as his own experimental participant. He is responsible for giving us early versions of many common learning phenomena such as learning and forgetting curves. However, as it turns out, some of Ebbinghaus's findings are specific to people who have learned a large number of lists of nonsense syllables and do not apply to people learning a single list of nonsense syllables. Thus, Ebbinghaus's results show a clear failure to generalize, based on the concept of multiple-treatment interference.

In Chapter 10 we discussed the multiple-group design. Under what condition is multiple-treatment interference a concern in the multiple-group design? When should you not worry about multiple-treatment interference in the multiple-group design?

By definition, multiple-treatment interference can occur only when participants experience more than one treatment. Experiencing more than one treatment occurs in the multiple-group design *if* you use repeated measures. However, the remaining variations on the multiple-group design would not allow for multiple-treatment interference. Independent groups, matched sets, or natural sets require using different participants in each group.

This ends the list of four threats to external validity summarized by Campbell and Stanley (1966). Let's take a brief look at five additional threats to external validity that are based on our experimental participants.

Threats to External Validity (Based on Our Participants)

We must always remember that our experimental participants are unique individuals, just as the detective must remember that fact about each criminal. Certain unique traits may get in the way of our ability (or the detective's ability) to draw general conclusions.

The Infamous White Rat   In 1950, Frank Beach sounded the alarm about a distressing tendency he saw in **comparative psychology**. By charting the publication trends in that field from 1911 to 1947, he found

> **Comparative psychology**   The study of behavior in different species, including humans.

that more and more articles were being published but fewer species were being studied. The Norway rat became a popular research animal in the 1920s and began to dominate research in the 1930s. Beach examined 613 research articles and found that 50% of them dealt with the rat, despite the fact that the Norway rat represented only 0.001% of all living creatures that could be studied. In a follow-up study, Smith, Davis, and Burleson (1995) found that articles published between 1993 and 1995 showed attention to diversified species, but rats and pigeons accounted for over 75% of the studies published in *Journal of Experimental Psychology: Animal Behavior Processes* and *Animal Learning & Behavior* during those years.

Why should Beach's data (and the follow-up study) give us reason for concern regarding external validity?

There are two obvious concerns with external validity that arise from these data. First, if you are interested in the behavior of subhumans, generalizing from rats (and pigeons) to all other animals may be a stretch. Second, if you are interested in generalizing from animal to human behavior, there are certainly closer approximations to humans than rats (and pigeons) in the animal kingdom.

The Ubiquitous College Student   We hope that you have conducted a literature search at this point in your course. If you have, you should have noticed that experimental articles contain a "subjects" or "participants" subsection within the method section. (Remember that the label "participants" replaced "subjects" in the fourth edition of the APA *Publication Manual*, 1994).

First published in APA Monitor. Reprinted by permission of Warren Street.

"There's always an oddball subject that screws up your data."

Sometimes it's hard to tell which participants are more numerous in psychology experiments—lab rats or college students!

If your literature search involved human participants, you probably noticed that college students very likely served as participants in the research you reviewed. There is a simple explanation for this fact. Psychology departments that support animal research typically have animal lab facilities—often colonies of rats, as we saw in the preceding section. Psychologists who want to conduct human research have no such labs filled with participants, of course, so they turn to a ready, convenient source of human participants—students in introductory psychology courses (a technique referred to as **convenience sampling**). Often students may be required to fulfill a certain number of hours of experimental participation in order to pass their introductory class. As well as providing a large supply of participants for psychology experiments, this requirement should be an educational experience for the students. Such requirements have generated heated debates, some of which have focused on ethics. You will note in the ethical principles covered in Chapter 3 that coercion is not acceptable in finding experimental participants.

> **Convenience sampling** A researcher's sampling of participants based on ease of locating the participants; often does not involve true random selection.

We are including this section not to focus on the ethics of using students as research participants but, rather, to focus on the implications of this reliance. Sears (1986) raised this very issue with regard to social psychology. He pointed out that early social psychologists studied a variety of types of participants, including populations as diverse as radio listeners, voters, soldiers, veterans, residents of housing projects, industrial workers, union members, and PTA members. However, by the 1960s psychology had become entrenched in using laboratory experiments with college students as participants.

Is it a problem to rely almost exclusively on college students? Clearly, such reliance is similar to the reliance on the white rat by animal researchers. Sears (1986) cited evidence concerning the differences between adolescents and adults and between college students and other late adolescents. He worried that several notable social psychology findings might be the product of using college students as participants rather than the larger population in general.

Reread the last sentence. Can you identify Sears's position as consistent with one of Campbell and Stanley's threats to external validity?

Sears's hypothesis that some social psychology findings may be specific to college students fits into Campbell and Stanley's selection–treatment interaction. If Sears is correct, then a specific treatment might "work" only for college students. In addition, a particular IV might have a stronger (or weaker) effect for college students than for the general population.

As an example, Sears mentioned that much of social psychology revolves around attitudes and attitude change: Research often shows that people's attitudes are easily changed. However, developmental research shows that the attitudes of late adolescents and young adults are less crystallized than those of older adults. Thus, we have to wonder whether people's attitudes really are easily changed or whether this finding is merely an artifact of the population that is most often studied—the college student.

Although Sears concentrated on social psychology findings, it does not take much thought to see how similar problems might exist in other traditional research areas of psychology. For example, because college students are both students and above average in intelligence, might their learning and memory processes be a poor representation of those processes in the general population? Motivational patterns in adolescents are certainly different in some ways from those processes in adults. The stresses affecting college students differ from those facing adults—might their coping processes be different also? We know that some mental illnesses are age related and therefore strike older or younger people more often. Overall, we should be careful in generalizing to the general population from results derived only from college students.

The "Opposite" or "Weaker" or "Inferior" or "Second" Sex   All four derogatory labels—*opposite, weaker, inferior,* and *second*—have been applied to women at various points in time. As you took your school's required history, literature, and humanities classes, you probably noticed that famous women were in short supply. For many years (some would argue still now), women have simply not had the same opportunities as men in many situations.

This supposed inferiority of women carried over into psychological theories. For example, Freud's theories are biased toward men—remember castration anxiety and the Oedipus complex? The "parallel" concepts for women of penis envy and the Electra complex seem almost to be afterthoughts. Feminists have repeatedly attacked the concept of penis envy, supposedly part of equating Freud's theory for women and men. Erik Erikson labeled his theory of psychosocial crises the "Eight Stages of Man." Not only did the name not acknowledge women, but neither did the stages. Many women have not identified with Erikson's stages to the extent that men have. As Carol Tavris (1992) eloquently pointed out about developmental theories, "Theorists writing on adult development assumed that adults were male. Healthy 'adults' follow a single line from childhood to old age, a steady path of school, career, marriage, advancement, a child or two, retirement, and wisdom—in that order" (p. 37).

Tavris's thesis is that "despite women's gains in many fields in the last twenty years, the fundamental belief in the normalcy of men, and the corresponding abnormality of women, has remained virtually untouched" (p. 17). Tavris's ideas make us face an interesting question: Are we developing a body of knowledge that pertains to all organisms, regardless of sex? One detail we will emphasize about APA style in Chapter 14 is its requirement of non-sexist language in writing. Words carry hidden meanings, and sexist writing may lead to generalizations that are unwarranted. As psychology students, you should definitely be attuned to this issue. Surveys of psychology undergraduates across the country find that almost three quarters of all psychology majors are women. You may even encounter difficulty finding male participants for your future experiments. Without adequate male representation, the generality of your findings could be questioned.

Again, a word of caution is in order. When we generalize our findings, we typically generalize them to as large a segment of the population as we can. However, we should not generalize research conducted on only one sex to both sexes. Beware of drawing sexist conclusions from your research.

Even the Rats and Students Were White   This section's heading is an adaptation of the title of Robert Guthrie's thought-provoking book *Even the Rat Was White* (1976). In the book, Guthrie chronicled many of the "scientific" attempts to measure and categorize African

Americans as inferior to Caucasians, such as anthropometric measurements (e.g., skull size and cranial capacity), mental testing, and the eugenics movement (improvement of heredity through genetic control).

Some psychology students may believe that there were no African-American pioneers in psychology; that assumption is far from the truth. Guthrie (1976) provided a list of the 32 African Americans who earned doctorates in psychology and educational psychology in American universities between 1920 and 1950. He provided brief background and career sketches for 20 of these individuals. Let us give you a glimpse of two of these persons. Guthrie devoted a chapter to Francis Cecil Sumner, whom he labeled the "Father of black American psychology" (p. 175). Sumner, born in Pine Bluff, Arkansas, was the first African American to earn a Ph.D. in psychology in the Western Hemisphere. He earned his degree from Clark University in June 1920. His chief instructor was G. Stanley Hall; he also took courses from E. G. Boring. Sumner's dissertation title was "Psychoanalysis of Freud and Adler," which was published in *Pedagogical Seminary* (later renamed the *Journal of Genetic Psychology*). Sumner went on to teaching positions at Wilberforce University and West Virginia Collegiate Institute. In 1928 he accepted a position at Howard University, becoming chair of the newly established department of psychology in 1930. Under Sumner's leadership, Howard became one of the major producers of African-American Ph.D.s in psychology. Sumner remained at Howard until his death in 1954.

Ruth Winifred Howard was the first African-American woman to earn a doctorate in psychology, from the University of Minnesota in 1934. (Inez Beverly Prosser had earned a Ph.D. in *educational psychology* from the University of Cincinnati one year earlier.) Howard's dissertation, "A Study of the Development of Triplets," was one of the first studies to deal with a sizable group of triplets. She completed a clinical internship at the Illinois Institute for Juvenile Research and spent her career in private practice in clinical psychology.

Just as history has failed to record the accomplishments of many women throughout time, it has largely ignored the accomplishments of African Americans and other minority groups. Jones (1994) pointed out the inherent duality of being an African American—that one is separately considered an African and an American. Other writers have made similar points about and pointed out problems for members of other minority groups—for example Marín (1994) for Hispanics, Lee and Hall (1994) for Asians, and Bennett (1994) for American Indians. According to Lonner and Malpass (1994b), projections indicate that sometime in this century the United States will be 24% Hispanic, 15% African American, and 12% Asian. Thus, Caucasians will make up less than half the population for the first time in U.S. history. When we conduct research and make generalizations, we should be cautious that we do not exclude minority groups from our considerations.

Even the Rats, Students, Women, and Minorities Were American

Although experimental psychology's early roots are based in Europe, this aspect of the discipline quickly became Americanized, largely due to the influence of John B. Watson's behaviorism. For many years the study of human behavior was actually the study of *American* behavior. However, in the mid-1960s this imbalanced situation slowly began to change as psychologists started taking culture and ethnicity more seriously (Lonner & Malpass, 1994a). We mentioned this new emphasis on ethnicity in the previous section and wish to mention the notion of culture in this section.

The field of **cross-cultural psychology** has evolved from those changes that began in the 1960s. Today you can find textbooks and

Cross-cultural psychology   A branch of psychology whose goal is to determine the universality of research results.

courses devoted to this topic. We introduced you to cross-cultural research in Chapter 7. Because cross-cultural psychology "tests possible limitations of our traditional knowledge by studying people of different cultures" (Matsumoto, 2000, p. 10), it is closely intertwined with external validity. In fact, cross-cultural psychology tests the very limits of external validity. It asks the question of how far a set of experimental findings can be extended to other cultures. If psychology is made up of findings that are applicable only to Americans, then we should not claim that we know everything there is to know about *human* behavior! Making

> **Ethnocentric** Other cultures are viewed as an extension of one's own culture.

an **ethnocentric** claim such as that is akin to American professional baseball claiming to play the *World* Series, which actually began as a series of games sponsored by the *World* newspaper. What about the professional teams in Japan and other countries? Similarly, we shouldn't study maternal behaviors in the United States and claim that we know everything there is to know about mothering. Again, a word to the wise: Let's be careful about making grandiose claims about external validity when we don't have all the data. With our shrinking world of today, it is becoming easier and easier to conduct true cross-cultural research. The books by Lonner and Malpass (1994b) and Matsumoto (2000) will give you some good ideas about behavioral differences that exist as a function of culture.

The Devil's Advocate: Is External Validity Always Necessary?

Several years ago Douglas Mook (1983) published a thought-provoking article titled "In Defense of External Invalidity." In this article Mook attacked the idea that all experiments should be designed to generalize to the real world. He maintained that such generalization is not always intended or meaningful.

Mook cited as an example Harlow's work with baby rhesus monkeys and their wire-mesh and terry-cloth surrogate mothers. As you probably remember, the baby monkeys received nourishment from the mesh mothers and warmth and contact from the cloth mothers. Later, when faced with a threatening situation, the baby monkeys ran to the cloth mothers for comfort. As virtually all introductory psychology students learn, Harlow's work has been used to support the importance of contact comfort for the development of attachment. Was Harlow's research strong in external validity? Hardly! Harlow's monkeys could scarcely be considered representative of the monkey population because they were born in the lab and orphaned. Was the experimental setting lifelike? Hardly! How many baby monkeys (or human infants) will ever be faced with a choice between a wire or cloth "mother"?

Did these shortcomings in external validity negate Harlow's findings? As Mook pointed out, that depends on the conclusion that Harlow wished to draw. What if Harlow's conclusion had been, "Wild monkeys in the jungle probably would choose terry-cloth over wire mothers, too, if offered the choice" (Mook, 1983, p. 381)? Clearly, this conclusion could not be supported from Harlow's research because of the external validity problems mentioned in the previous paragraph.

On the other hand, Harlow *could* conclude that his experiment supported a theory of contact comfort for mother–infant attachment over a nourishment-based (drive-reduction) theory. Is there a problem with this conclusion? No, because Harlow did not attempt a generalization—he merely drew a conclusion about a theory, based on a prediction from that theory. Mook argued that our concern with external validity is necessary only when we are trying to "predict real-life behavior in the real world" (p. 381). However, there are reasons to conduct research that do not involve trying to predict behavior in the real world. Mook pointed out four alternative goals of research that do not stress external validity. First, we may merely want to find out if something *can* happen (not whether it usually happens). Second, we may be predicting from the real world to the lab—seeing a phenomenon in the real world, we think it will operate in a certain manner in the lab. Third, if we can demonstrate that a phenomenon occurs in a lab's unnatural setting, the validity of the phenomenon may actually be strengthened. Finally, we may study phenomena in the lab that don't even have a real-world analogy.

We do not mean to undermine the importance of external validity by presenting Mook's arguments. However, it is important to know that not all psychologists worship at the shrine of external validity. Being concerned with real-world applications is certainly important, but (unlike internal validity) it is not an absolute necessity for every experiment. By the same token, the detective does not attempt to generate a generalized criminal profile for each crime that is committed.

Just as with internal validity, we have looked at nine different threats to external validity. We hope you have been considering these threats in light of your potential experiment. What can you do in an attempt to avoid external validity problems?

This is probably the most difficult Psychological Detective question of this chapter; there is a sense in which this question is a trick. It *may* be impossible to conduct a single experiment that has perfect external validity. If you attempted to devise an experiment that answered every threat to external validity that we listed, you might be old and gray before you completed the experiment. Imagine trying to find a pool of human experimental participants that would satisfy sex, race, ethnicity, and cultural generalizability. You would need to find large numbers of participants from around the world—clearly an impossible situation.

Does the dismal conclusion of the previous paragraph mean that we should merely throw up our hands and quit? Are we justified in ignoring the problem of external validity? Of course not! The important question becomes one of what steps we can take to maximize our chances of achieving external validity. First, we recommend that you pay particular attention to the first four external validity threats that we listed. To a large extent, you do have control over interactions of testing or selection and treatment, reactive arrangements, and multiple-treatment interference. Careful experimental planning can usually allow you to avoid problems with those factors.

If you can control the methodological threats to external validity, that leaves you with the participant-related threats. It is unrealistic to expect any one experiment to be able to include all the various participants we would need to generalize our results across the world's population. Campbell and Stanley (1966) wrote that "the problems of external validity are not logically solvable in any neat, conclusive way" (p. 17). What is the solution?

It seems logical that the solution must involve an approach we discussed in Chapter 1—**replication**. When we replicate an experimental finding, we are able to place more confidence in that result. As we begin

Replication An additional scientific study that is conducted in exactly the same manner as the original research project.

to see the same result time after time, we become more comfortable with the idea that it is a predictable, regularly occurring result. However, it is shortsighted for us to continually test the same types of participants in every experiment we conduct, whether those participants are white rats or white American college students. Thus, we need to go beyond replication to experiments that involve replication with extension.

Replication with extension   An experiment that seeks to confirm (replicate) a previous finding but does so in a different setting or with different participants or under different conditions.

In a **replication with extension** experiment, we retest for a particular experimental finding, but we do so in a slightly (or even radically) different context. For example, if we think we know a great deal about how American college students learn lists of nonsense syllables, we should not try to generalize those results to all humans. Instead, we should broaden our participant population. Do the same rules apply when we test elderly people, children, and less-educated people? Do the same findings occur when we test Hispanic Americans, Asian Americans, and African Americans? Are the results similar in Japan, China, Peru, Australia, and so on? When we begin to collect data from experiments as indicated by the previous three sentences, then we truly start learning whether our findings are generally applicable.

There is another advantage to experiments that use replication with extension. Many times pure replication experiments are frowned on. Journals rarely, if ever, publish a straight replication study. Many undergraduates who complete required experimental projects are told that their projects must be original, that the project cannot be a replication study. Often, a replication with extension involves enough new work and produces enough new information that it will be acceptable either for a class requirement or for publication—or for both if you're extremely fortunate!

A 2001 research study by Carolyn Ann Licht, a student at Marymount Manhattan College in New York, and Linda Zener Solomon, her faculty advisor, illustrated a replication with extension experiment. Licht (2000) had previously compared stress levels of employees in two New York City organizations and found that stress levels were higher for employees of a nonprofit organization than for employees of a for-profit organization. Licht and Solomon extended the earlier study to include more organizations and more geographic areas. Their findings mirrored Licht's earlier findings, leading Licht and Solomon to conclude that the "results were consistent with previous findings and increased their external validity" (p. 14).

So what is the conclusion regarding external validity? We believe it is unrealistic to expect every (or any) experiment to be applicable to the entire world of animals or people. That type of external validity is probably a myth that exists only in fairy tales. However, we also believe that you should strive to make your experiment as externally valid as possible. That is, when you have choices, opt for the choices that will increase the external validity of your findings.

REVIEW SUMMARY

1. If your experiment is internally valid, then you can worry about **external validity**, which deals with applying your findings to new groups (**population generalization**), new situations (**environmental generalization**), and new times (**temporal generalization**).

2. There are many threats to external validity. The **interaction of testing and treatment** threat can occur if you pretest your participants and the pretest changes their reaction to the posttest.

3. The **interaction of selection and treatment** threat occurs if your findings apply only to the groups you selected for your experiment.

4. **Reactive arrangements** can threaten external validity if the experimental situation changes our participants' behavior.

5. **Multiple treatment interference** may threaten external validity if participants experience more than one treatment and this multiple participation causes a change in behavior.

6. Experimental psychology has been criticized for using only a narrow slice of possible types of participants in research. Animal research is particularly imbalanced by its overuse of white rats as participants.

7. Human research has tended to focus on white American college students as participants. Many theories seem to be aimed heavily or exclusively at men.

8. For reasons of external validity, there is currently a greater focus on research involving participants from the general population, women, ethnic minorities, and other cultures.

9. Mook has pointed out that there are occasional instances when the external validity question is not relevant to research.

10. It is nearly impossible to devise a single experiment that can answer all questions about external validity. Conducting experiments that involve replication with extension is a good way to simultaneously increase external validity and gather new information.

CHECK YOUR PROGRESS

1. What is external validity? Why is it important to psychology?

2. Generally speaking, as internal validity increases, external validity
   a. increases
   b. decreases
   c. remains the same
   d. fluctuates unpredictably

3. Distinguish among population, environmental, and temporal generalization.

4. Why should we be concerned about trying to use different types of participants (such as minorities and people who are not college students) in psychology studies?

5. What is cross-cultural psychology? Why is it of particular relevance to this section of the chapter?

6. Match the external validity threat with the proper description.

   1. testing–treatment interaction
   2. selection–treatment interaction
   3. reactive arrangements
   4. multiple-treatment interference

   A. An effect occurs only if participants experience all the experiment's treatment conditions.
   B. Women, but not men, demonstrate an experimental effect.
   C. Only participants who are pretested demonstrate an experimental effect.
   D. Demand characteristics provide cues to the participants about how they should respond.

7. Why did Mook argue that external validity is not always necessary?
8. Why is the notion of external validity for a single experiment virtually impossible to achieve?

Critiquing Experimental Research

The information we are about to introduce is another reason we chose to place this chapter near the end of the text. Although we present this information to help you evaluate your own research, it is a certainty that, in the future, you will evaluate more studies conducted by other researchers than you will ever complete yourself. As you do a literature search for background information, you may look at hundreds of other articles. You will carefully scrutinize only a subset of those hundreds, but you will still read a good number of experimental articles. It is imperative that you are able to inspect those articles as closely as you would your own research project. You must be able to spot any flaws that might exist in these other studies because you will be basing your research on previous work of other researchers. If you base your study on research that has some flaw, your research may well end up being flawed. As an analogy, suppose you were a detective and needed to have fingerprints from a crime scene compared to one of your suspects. When you went to the lab, you accidentally picked up the fingerprint report from a different crime scene. How accurate would the lab analysis be for the original suspect? Not very accurate at all! The parallel to designing your experiment is fairly close. If you begin your experiment with an incorrect premise or assumption, your experiment is probably doomed from its beginning. So, again, it is important to be able to evaluate other researchers' experiments before you begin your own.

If you are like many students, the last sentence of the previous paragraph may cause you some worry. You may wonder, "Who am *I* to be critiquing research conducted and *published* by psychologists?" If you find yourself saying something like this, you are selling yourself short. One of the behaviors our educational system fosters (sometimes too well) is respect for authorities. In school we learned that when we didn't have the answer for something, we could consult an authority. We could look up the answer in our book or in an encyclopedia, or we could ask a teacher. There is certainly nothing wrong with that approach—it helps make life much simpler. But this constant reliance on consulting authorities sometimes blinds us to the importance of questioning the answers we get (see our discussion of ways to acquire knowledge in Chapter 1). Although we are not encouraging you to become a cynic about everything you hear, we do believe that it is important as well as valuable to carry a little healthy skepticism around with you. Thus, not only is it acceptable, but we even encourage you to read research reports with a critical eye. *Do* think critically about the methods, the results, and the conclusions. *Do* question assumptions that researchers seem to make. *Do* wonder if there are other ways of defining and measuring the variables the experimenters used. In other words, don't merely be a passive recipient of experimental information—carefully sift it, weigh it, consider it before filing it away in your memory bank. Careful reading of and critical thinking about experimental reports has led many undergraduates (as well as graduate students and faculty members) to interesting and important research projects.

We present some guidelines to help you develop a critical eye when you read research reports (yours or those published by others) in Table 13-1. As you read these guidelines,

TABLE 13-1   Guidelines for Critiquing Psychological Research Literature

1. Does the literature review adequately describe the research area? Is this material consistent with the specific research question? (Chapters 2, 14)

2. Is the research question stated clearly? Do you have a clear idea concerning the research to be reported? (Chapter 2)

3. In view of the research area and research question, are the hypotheses appropriate, clearly stated, and able to be stated in general implication form? (Chapter 2)

4. Are the key terms operationally defined? (Chapter 6)

5. Are the IVs and their levels appropriate? (Chapter 6)

6. Is the DV appropriate for this research? Should the researcher have included more than one DV if only one was recorded? (Chapter 5)

7. Are the controls sufficient and appropriate? Are there any uncontrolled variables that could affect the results of the experiment? (Chapter 6)

8. Did the author(s) use an appropriate research design to test the specific hypotheses and answer the general research question? (Chapters 4, 9, 10, 11, 12)

9. Assuming you had access to the appropriate equipment and materials, could you replicate the research after reading the method section? (Chapters 6, 14)

10. Did the researcher(s) use appropriate sampling procedures to select the participants and assign them to groups? (Chapter 4)

11. What procedures were used to ensure group equivalence prior to the experiment? (Chapters 4, 9, 10, 11)

12. Did the research use a sufficient number of participants? (Chapter 7)

13. Were there any history, instrumentation, statistical regression, or mortality effects that might have influenced the results? (Chapter 6)

14. Were the appropriate statistical tests used, and are they reported correctly? (Chapters 8, 9, 10, 14)

15. Did the author(s) report means, standard deviations, and a measure of effect size? (Chapters 8, 9, 10, 11)

16. Are the tables and figures clearly and appropriately labeled and presented accurately? (Chapters 8, 14)

17. Does the author(s) correctly interpret the results? Does the discussion follow logically from the results? (Chapter 14)

18. Are the conclusions and generalizations valid and justified by the data? Did the author(s) consider other possible interpretations of the results? (Chapter 14)

19. Do all references cited in the text appear in the reference section, and vice versa? (Chapter 14)

20. Did the experimenter follow appropriate ethical procedures during all phases of the experiment? (Chapter 3)

you will be struck by their similarity to many of the concepts and topics you have read about in this book. Critiquing a completed manuscript or published article is similar to reviewing your entire experimental psychology or research methods course. Our discussion of each guideline that follows is brief—to help you refresh your memory for the location of the relevant material, we have listed a chapter(s) for each guideline.

1. *Does the literature review adequately describe the research area? Is this material consistent with the specific research question?*

   Typically, a student beginning the first research project is not sure where the research literature will lead. Similarly, the researcher has little idea of the methodology to be used at this point. Sometimes, as a research project evolves, the literature review and the actual experiment diverge somewhat over time. After you complete your project and work on the report, double-check to make certain that the actual project still shows a direct link with your research literature. It is possible that some additional library work will be necessary.

   This problem is less likely to occur for experienced researchers. Because most researchers carry out **programmatic research**, their new research ideas are likely to build directly on their (and others') previous research. As you conduct more research studies, reviewing the *relevant* literature will become second nature for you.

Programmatic research A series of research experiments that deal with a related topic or question.

Why is programmatic research important to psychology?

Programmatic research allows researchers to build on their previous findings in a narrow research area. Because they are specialists on a quite specific topic, they can often do research at a more penetrating depth than someone who does not know the area very well. Such a researcher would be akin to a detective who specializes in pursuing serial killers. Researchers who engage in programmatic research may advance our knowledge at a faster rate.

2. *Is the research question stated clearly? Do you have a clear idea concerning the research to be reported?*

   There are a variety of ways researchers can give you some information about the question(s) asked in their report. The title and abstract should give you an indication of the research's topic, although they may not contain the specific question per se. You will find the author's review of relevant literature in the article's introduction. As you read further into the introduction, the literature should apply more specifically to the particular research question. You will often find the research question in the last paragraph of the introduction—sometimes it will appear as a question; sometimes you may have to infer the actual question from the context at that point (e.g., the variables mentioned and the relationship hypothesized among them). Regardless of whether you find a literal question, there should be no confusion about the intent of the research when you finish reading the introduction.

3. *In view of the research area and research question, are the hypotheses appropriate, clearly stated, and able to be stated in general implication form?*

   The hypotheses, of course, are directly linked to the research question (as mentioned in the previous point). Thus, you should be clear about what the researcher's hypotheses are by the time you have read the introduction. Appropriate hypotheses are those that follow logically from the literature review. In other words, as you read the literature, you should be able to predict the hypotheses that are likely to follow. If you find a hypothesis that seems to come from nowhere and surprises you, it may be inappropriate—reread the introduction to make sure. A clearly stated hypothesis is one that you can easily understand without having to guess what the researcher is predicting. Remember that general implication form is the "if . . . then" format. *If* the researcher specifies a certain event (independent variable), *then* a certain outcome should occur (dependent variable). Although the researcher may not specifically use the general implication form, you should be able to restate the hypothesis using that form.

Why is the "if . . . then" approach of the general implication form important in phrasing a research hypothesis?

   It is the "if . . . then" approach to research questions that allows us to draw cause-and-effect conclusions—assuming that the researcher has done a good job in designing the experiment. As long as the internal validity of the research is strong, the researcher should be able to conclude that the IV caused the change in the DV.

4. *Are the key terms operationally defined?*

   The reader should not have to guess what a researcher means when he or she refers to a specific independent, dependent, or extraneous variable. Remember that operational definitions mean that you should define your variables in terms of the operations you use to manipulate, measure, or control them. For example, reading that rats ran a maze when they were hungry is too vague. The researcher should specify the number, type, and sex of the rats; provide a precise description (or a figure) of the maze; and describe "hunger" in terms of how it was manipulated (e.g., number of hours of food deprivation). Using operational definitions allows readers to compare and contrast different definitions of the same term by different researchers and to decide how they wish to manipulate, measure, or control similar variables in their experiments.

5. *Are the IVs and their levels appropriate?*

   In dealing with beginning research students, we are surprised at how often students say that they wish to study a certain variable's effects (the IV), but then propose an experiment that doesn't directly deal with or manipulate that variable. Be sure that you pick a manipulation that is actually appropriate to the IV—don't choose something merely because it is easy or convenient to use. For example, imagine that a student wishes to use the IV of caffeine intake but takes the easy way out and simply asks students how many cups of coffee they drank that morning. It is likely that self-reported caffeine intake will not be as accurate as bringing participants into the lab and actually manipulating how much caffeine they ingest. If the manipulation is not clearly a good example of the IV, then it may not be appropriate.

Similarly, be sure to choose the levels of your IV appropriately. Many researchers choose to use proportional amounts of their IV: for example, using 5, 10, and 15 milligrams of a drug rather than 5, 9, and 12 milligrams. Many beginning researchers make the mistake of trying to include too many IV levels in one experiment. Remember that you cannot answer all possible questions in one experiment—choose levels of the IV to answer your experimental question, but do so economically (remember the principle of parsimony in Chapter 9). Apply these same guidelines to research that you read to determine whether the researcher's IV and levels are appropriate.

6. *Is the DV appropriate for this research? Should the researcher have included more than one DV if only one was recorded?*

The first question here is similar to the previous one. If a researcher wishes to study a particular outcome, the behavior chosen for measuring (the dependent variable) should be a good indicator of that outcome. In other words, the operational definition of the DV should be one that other researchers would judge to be valid. This caution is a particularly important one for many student researchers who may wish to measure some type of clinical outcome (e.g., clinical depression, schizophrenia) in their research. Often, measuring such a DV is not feasible for undergraduates, so they settle for a different DV. If you follow a similar process, make sure that the DV you do choose is appropriate to the literature you reviewed and the hypothesis you generated. In similar fashion, as you read research reports, decide whether you think the DV adequately measures the concept in question. If you think that a different behavior would be a more valid DV, you may have generated a good idea for an experiment. For example, suppose other researchers have used GPA as a measure of academic achievement after teaching students a new study strategy. You might argue that GPA is too global a DV to measure the effects of study skills and therefore choose to use scores on a single test instead.

Sometimes a researcher's interest is so broad that a single DV will not adequately measure what the researcher wants. In such a case, the researcher should use multiple DVs to get a better sense of the concept she is measuring. Remember that we advised you to use multiple DVs *if* they added valuable information (see Chapter 6). This approach is economical—it is usually easier to give a smaller number of participants multiple measurements than to give a larger number of participants one measurement each. As you read research, look for DVs that you believe were measured in a "skimpy fashion." Again, enlarging the scope of the DV may give you a good experimental idea. Using the example from the previous paragraph, you might decide to measure the effects of the study skills on an entire semester's worth of tests rather than simply using one test.

7. *Are the controls sufficient and appropriate? Are there any uncontrolled variables that could affect the results of the experiment?*

This is one of the most critical questions you can ask of your experiment or those you read.

Why is the question regarding control such an important question?

As we hope you remember, leaving variables uncontrolled can result in a confounded experiment, which leaves the researcher unable to draw a conclusion. As you scrutinize research (whether yours or other researchers'), be extremely vigilant for variables other than the IV that differed between groups. However, a caution is in order at this point. As you look for possible extraneous variables, you should concentrate on variables that have a legitimate or reasonable chance to actually make a difference. For example, unless you are testing for sex differences, having one group composed of women and another group composed of men is an invitation for extraneous variation. On the other hand, having one group in which most people complete a questionnaire in pen and another group where most of the people use a pencil is unlikely to create a difference on the questionnaire results. So, look for extraneous variation, but don't go overboard and find variation that most researchers would consider negligible.

8. *Did the author(s) use an appropriate research design to test the specific hypotheses and answer the general research question?*

This question relates to the caution that we gave at the beginning of the first research design chapter (Chapter 9). Remember that, with poor planning, it is possible to gather data for which there is no appropriate research design and, thus, no appropriate statistical test. Your task with this guideline is to make sure that research reports use designs that match the question they sought to answer. Therefore, you will need to look at the introduction to find the question and the method or results section to determine the design used. For example, if the researcher asked a question involving multiple IVs, the experiment should involve a factorial design. The flowchart that recurs at the beginning of Chapters 9 through 11 will help you with this guideline.

9. *Assuming you had access to the appropriate equipment and materials, could you replicate the research after reading the method section?*

The method section (see Chapter 14) should contain enough detail about the variables and procedures of the experiment to enable a reader to replicate the experiment. The reader should not have to guess about any of the manipulations, measurements, or controls the researcher used. The reader must have all the vital details of the experiment in order to evaluate the operational definitions, the variables, and the procedures used in the experiment (see the previous five guidelines). Once again, knowing how other researchers conducted their experiments may help give you ideas about how you should plan your experiment.

10. *Did the researcher(s) use appropriate sampling procedures to select the participants and assign them to groups?*

Remember how often we have stressed the importance of random sampling and assignment in creating independent groups or the appropriate matching or repeated measures approach for correlated groups! This guideline is important for two different reasons—both internal and external validity. If a researcher uses sampling techniques that result in biased samples, the internal validity of the experiment is threatened because the groups are likely to be different before the experiment. Also, if poor sampling techniques are used, biased samples could threaten the external validity. If the samples are unique, then other samples may not show the same results.

As long as you use the proper techniques for creating independent or correlated groups, there should be no difference between the two approaches as far as internal or external validity are concerned. Remember—you create independent or correlated groups simply by the manner in which you assign participants to groups.

11. *What procedures were used to ensure group equivalence prior to the experiment?*

This guideline is related to the sampling guideline previously mentioned. Poor sampling techniques can result in biased samples. Biased samples are usually not equivalent before the experiment begins, so it would be impossible to draw valid conclusions about the effects of the IV. Thus, the internal validity of the experiment would be compromised. If you have reason to doubt the equivalence of your groups beforehand, you would be wise to use a pretest.

12. *Did the research use a sufficient number of participants?*

Many a student research project has been sabotaged by students who want to save a little time by running a small number of participants. In our view, this is a false economy. If you have spent weeks or months planning an experiment, the last thing you should do is try to save a few minutes or hours by running fewer participants. With small numbers of data points, statistical tests are simply less powerful to detect differences—the differences between groups have to be *quite large* for the difference to turn out significant. However, with reasonably sized groups (at least 10 participants per group), the tests become powerful enough to detect smaller differences. Don't back yourself into a corner so that you use the age-old student lament after your experiment: "If I had run more participants, my differences might have been significant."

13. *Were there any history, instrumentation, statistical regression, or mortality effects that might have influenced the results?*

These factors that we discussed in Chapter 6 can undermine the internal validity of experiments. For history, be alert to outside events that occur that could affect the results; remember, for example, that political and social events that are not part of your research could affect participants' responses to attitude questionnaires. Be sure to check the operation of your equipment before each session to avoid instrumentation effects. Choosing extreme high- or low-scoring participants can result in lower or higher scores, respectively, simply due to statistical regression. If many participants drop out of one condition in the experiment (i.e., mortality), the participants who are left in that condition may differ in some important way(s) from the participants in other conditions. Be vigilant about these problems both in your research and research that you read.

14. *Were the appropriate statistical tests used, and are they reported correctly?*

We have provided information in Chapters 9 through 11 that will help you evaluate this guideline for some experiments. However, remember that this text is not meant to give comprehensive coverage of all statistical tests that could be used in any experiment.

You may need to consult a statistics text or someone who teaches statistics to help you answer this question. On the other hand, this guideline points out the importance of becoming statistically knowledgeable so that you can evaluate this guideline on your own. Remember that statistics are merely a tool experimenters use to decipher the results they obtained—you should be well armed with the proper tools as you evaluate and conduct research.

15. *Did the author(s) report means, standard deviations, and a measure of effect size?*
    Although researchers use inferential statistics to determine whether their data show statistical significance, inferential statistics tell only part of the story. Descriptive statistics give the reader a chance to further evaluate the researcher's findings. For example, group means may allow the reader to compare participants' performance against existing norms. Also, extremely large samples can produce statistically significant results with only small differences between groups—differences that may seem negligible when you see the actual means. Standard deviations may allow the reader to determine that nonsignificant findings are due to extreme variability between groups rather than small differences between means. Effect sizes give standard comparison units so that readers can compare significant differences from several different experiments. These examples are only a small sample of the information you can obtain by looking at descriptive statistics, so be sure to include them in your experimental report and look for them in published reports.

16. *Are the tables and figures clearly and appropriately labeled and presented accurately?*
    Tables and figures exist to give a clearer and simpler presentation of data than is possible in writing. Thus, they usually present a large amount of data in a compact, concise mode. However, the data presentation will not be clear and simple if the author has done a poor job of composing the table or figure. Imagine trying to decipher a graph that had no legend—you would not know which line represented which group. Although you are unlikely to see tables or figures with such glaring problems, you may see ones that are poorly constructed or poorly labeled (see the discussion of graphing in Chapter 8). Just as paragraph after paragraph of statistical results can be confusing, a poorly constructed table or figure also can confuse the reader.

17. *Does the author(s) correctly interpret the results? Does the discussion follow logically from the results?*
    The first question has two possible interpretations. First, did the researcher correctly interpret $p < .05$ as significant and $p > .05$ as nonsignificant? Although you would be quite unlikely to see this type of error in a published report, some students still get confused and make such errors in their rough drafts. Second, and more relevant, did the researcher give a correct interpretation of his or her results in light of previous research? Interpreting one's results is a matter that is open to some difference of opinion, as the term *interpret* implies. As you are no doubt aware, there are famous and noteworthy examples in psychology's history of researchers interpreting the same data in different manners. For example, behaviorists and cognitive psychologists look at language and argue whether it develops because of conditioning or an innate mechanism. Thus, as we have highlighted several times in these guidelines, a difference of opinion or in ideas could lead you to a potential experiment.
    The second question of the guideline relates to whether the discussion "makes sense" given the data the researcher just presented. It seems obvious that the discussion should be

related to the data that were just presented, but there are many exceptions. For example, some researchers seem bent on drawing conclusions that go far beyond the data they have presented. Although there is some room in the discussion for conjecture and opinion, authors should make it clear when conclusions follow from data and when they are engaging in speculation. We have noticed that many student researchers seem to quickly gloss over their results in a rush to make excuses for nonsignificant findings. If you are careful to tie your discussion directly to the results you found, you are much less likely to run into such problems.

18. *Are the conclusions and generalizations valid and justified by the data? Did the author(s) consider other possible interpretations of the results?*

This guideline grows out of the previous one. This difficulty often comes when researchers have a favorite theory that they espouse. Sometimes, this theoretical leaning is so strong that it seems to blind them to any alternative explanations. You may remember sitting in class, hearing a theoretical interpretation of a set of results, and thinking to yourself that an alternative theory could also satisfactorily explain the results. Once more, alternative explanations for findings may provide you with the impetus for a new experiment.

How can you help yourself to consider alternative explanations for experimental findings?

Considering alternative explanations, particularly for published findings, is often difficult for novice researchers. Typically, when you read a study you will find the author's explanation for the results convincing. We have found two approaches that may help you. First, you are probably familiar with the role of "devil's advocate." As you read a study, try to put yourself in that role—look for any aspect of the author's explanation (no matter how small) that you disagree with. Second, particularly in cases of your research, have another person who is unfamiliar with your project read your report. Often, an unbiased eye can find weaknesses in your arguments that you overlooked.

19. *Do all references cited in the text appear in the reference section, and vice versa?*

This guideline is one of the simplest to follow, yet is often a problem in unpublished reports (it is highly unlikely that you would find this problem in a published study). There should be a one-to-one correspondence of the citations in the text and the references at the end of the study. Unlike some term papers you may have written, the reference section of an APA-format report consists only of material that you have read and included in the report—it is not a bibliography of everything you read in generating your experimental idea.

20. *Did the experimenter follow appropriate ethical procedures during all phases of the experiment?*

To evaluate this guideline, you may need to refresh your memory of the ethical principles that psychologists follow in conducting research. You can find these principles in

Chapter 3. Remember that there are ethical principles for both human and animal research, so you cannot avoid ethical responsibility through animal research. Because of the review process involved in published research, you should not find ethical violations in published research. However, some older research involves some procedures that have been hotly debated as far as their ethical nature is concerned—for example, we discussed the research by Milgram in Chapter 3 that involved considerable deception. Given the ethical principles in effect today, it is doubtful that such research studies would receive approval from institutional review boards.

REVIEW SUMMARY

1. You should read research reports with a critical eye, applying the guidelines for critiquing research.
2. When you read the introduction of a research report, you should scrutinize the literature review, the research question, the hypothesis or hypotheses, and the citations and references.
3. In the method section, you should focus your critique on the operational definitions, the independent and dependent variables, the control techniques, the research design, the experiment's replicability, the sampling procedures, group equivalence, the number of participants, and factors that could affect the internal validity of the research.
4. As you scrutinize the results section, pay particular attention to the descriptive and inferential statistics, as well as any visual data presentations.
5. When you read the discussion section, your critique should center on the interpretation of the results, the conclusions, and other potential explanations for the findings.
6. As you read the entire report, examine it carefully for ethical procedures.

CHECK YOUR PROGRESS

1. Why should students critically examine research reports, even those published by prominent psychologists?
2. How are the literature review and research question linked?
3. Why are control techniques necessary in experimentation?
4. Summarize three critique guidelines that deal with participants.
5. Describe how statistics are vital to research reports.
6. Researchers should present _____ in their research reports.
   a. only descriptive statistics
   b. only inferential statistics
   c. both descriptive and inferential statistics
   d. neither descriptive nor inferential statistics
7. How and why should the discussion be tied to the results in a research report?

KEY TERMS

Internal validity, 332
External validity, 332
Generalization, 332
Population generalization, 333
Environmental
  generalization, 333
Temporal generalization, 333

Interaction of testing and
  treatment, 334
Interaction of selection and
  treatment, 335
Reactive arrangements, 336
Demand characteristics, 336
Multiple-treatment
  interference, 337

Comparative psychology, 337
Convenience sampling, 339
Cross-cultural psychology, 341
Ethnocentric, 442
Replication, 343
Replication with
  extension, 344
Programmatic research, 348

LOOKING AHEAD

At this point, you may have finished planning, conducting, and analyzing your own research project. Still, one task lies ahead—writing the research report, which is the culmination of your research effort. In the next chapter, we will cover how researchers write their reports in APA style.

Writing and Assembling
an APA-Format Research Report

The final step in the scientific process is communicating your results to other people who are interested in your research topic. As you have seen in numerous police shows, detectives also have to spend time writing their reports. Their purpose is no different from ours—communicating what has happened to a particular audience. Sherlock Holmes knew the importance of communicating clearly when he said to Watson, "Never trust to general impressions, my boy, but concentrate yourself upon details" (Doyle, 1927, p. 197). We have hinted at writing and organizing various parts of a manuscript in APA format throughout several chapters of this book. In this chapter we will cover all the aspects of writing a research report in APA format. We will use a student research project as our example, tracing it from the research stage through manuscript preparation to publication. In this chapter, we will introduce Allison Dickson, Traci Giuliano, James Morris, and Keri Cass's (2001) research project concerning the effects of race of performer and type of music on ratings of a musical performer. Dickson, Morris, and Cass were students at Southwestern University in Georgetown, Texas, and Giuliano was their supervising professor. We include this research as an example not to intimidate you, but to show you what is possible at the undergraduate level.

What Is APA Format?

Although several styles exist for the preparation of reports in various academic disciplines, psychologists developed their own format to meet their specific needs. Because the American Psychological Association (APA) originally developed this style, it is often referred to as **APA format**. In Chapter 1 we saw that in the 1920s University of Wisconsin psychologist Joseph Jastrow found a need to bring uniformity to the publication of research articles in our field. The lack of a set model or pattern had resulted in published research reports that were nearly impossible to compare. In addition to the fact that there was no prescribed order for the presentation of information, there also was no consistent manner for describing one's methodology, procedure, or data analysis. In short, the order and manner of presentation varied from one article to the next. The development of the APA format for preparing papers was an attempt to bring order to this state of chaos.

> **APA format**   Accepted American Psychological Association (APA) form for preparing reports of psychological research.

The particular form for preparing APA format papers is found in the fifth edition of the *Publication Manual of the American Psychological Association* (American Psychological Association, 2001). The APA *Publication Manual* has changed and evolved since it was first published in 1952. Many of the changes that have occurred over the years, as well as much of the actual format itself, were implemented to assist printers—after all, APA format was adopted to help make the publication of journal articles more uniform. Although many earlier APA-format matters had the printer in mind, the latest edition of the APA *Publication Manual* clearly shows the influence and importance of the computer. For example, the earlier requirement of large 1½-inch margins has been replaced by more computer-friendly 1-inch margins. Likewise, the reference section has reverted back to hanging indentations (the first line begins at the margin and subsequent lines are indented) from the third edition because computers and word processing programs can easily deal with hanging indents. In addition to being computer friendly, the general layout and design of the APA-format paper are reader friendly. For example, using separate, specifically designated sections allows the reader to know exactly which part of the project is being dealt with. Authors use **headings** to divide the APA-format paper into sections and to help the reader understand the paper's organization.

> **Headings**   Titles for various sections of a psychology paper designed to help the reader understand the outline and importance of parts of the paper.

However, before we get started, we need to make an important point: This chapter is not meant to substitute for the *Publication Manual of the American Psychological Association* (APA, 2001). There is simply no way for us to condense a 439-page book into a single chapter for this text. You should buy a *Publication Manual* (*PM*) and think of it as an investment in your future. As well as using it in this class, you will use it when you write term papers in other psychology classes and for any writing you will do if you go to graduate school in psychology. In addition, other academic disciplines are beginning to adopt APA style for their writing assignments. One of your authors has had colleagues in education, political science, and speech pathology borrow his *PM*, for pointers on formatting and style.

Sections of the APA-Format Paper

The major components of an APA-format paper are, in order:

1. Title page
2. Abstract
3. Introduction
4. Method section
5. Results section
6. Discussion section
7. References
8. Appendixes (if any)
9. Author note
10. Tables (if any)
11. Figures (if any)

As we look at the various sections of the APA-format paper, we will refer to the Dickson, Giuliano, Morris, and Cass manuscript as an example (Figures 14-1 through 14-16; *M* indicates manuscript, and the number after *M* represents page order). In addition, you can refer to the published article (Dickson et al., 2001) displayed in Figures 14-17 through14-21 (*JA* indicates journal article) to see how a manuscript is reformatted as a journal article.

> **Title page** The first page of an APA-format paper. It includes the manuscript page header, the running head, the manuscript's title, and the name(s) of the author(s) and their affiliation(s).

Title Page

The title page of Dickson et al.'s manuscript appears in Figure 14-1. The *PM* contains information about the **title page** on pages 10–12 and

Eminem Versus Charley   1

Running head: RACE, STEREOTYPES, AND PERCEPTIONS OF PERFORMERS

Eminem Versus Charley Pride: Race, Stereotypes, and

Perceptions of Rap and Country Music Performers

Allison J. Dickson, Traci A. Giuliano, James C. Morris, and Keri L. Cass

Southwestern University

FIGURE 14-1   (M1). Title page

Manuscript page header
The first two or three words of the report's title. Appears with the page number on each page of the research report.

Running head   A condensed title that is printed at the top of alternate pages of a published article.

296–298. The important features are the manuscript page header, page number, running head, author(s), and affiliation(s). The **manuscript page header** consists of the first two or three words of the title and is used to identify pages of a particular manuscript should they become separated. It appears in the upper right-hand portion of each page two lines above the 1-inch margin. The page header appears either five spaces to the left of the page number or two lines above the page number. Neither the page number nor the page header should extend beyond the margin on the right side of the page. The manuscript page header and page number appear on *all* pages of the paper, *except* the figures.

Two lines below the manuscript page header, flush against the left margin, we find the **running head**. The running head is a condensed title that will be printed at the top of alternate pages when your paper is published in a journal. When you type the running head on the title page, it is in all-capital letters. Also, note that the *h* in running head is not capitalized. The running head "should be a maximum of 50 characters, including letters, punctuation, and spaces between words" (*Publication Manual*, 2001, p. 12). As you can see in Figure 14-1, Dickson et al. used different phrases for the manuscript page header and the running head. Although the same phrase might be a logical choice for both elements, APA style does not specify that they must be identical. The manuscript page header may not make sense, but the running head should communicate information about the contents of your manuscript because it will actually be printed with a published article (see Figure 14-18).

The title of the paper, which is centered, may begin six or eight lines below the page number. Capitalize the first word and all important words of the title. Your title should summarize clearly and simply the nature of the research you are reporting, but it should not be overly long. APA's recommended length for the title is 10 to 12 words. If your title is too long to fit on one line, then you can type it on two lines. You should be especially careful when you choose a title for your paper. Although it is often tempting to compose a title that is cute or catchy, such titles are often failures in communicating anything about the article's content. Keep in mind that many people will read your title and will use it to decide whether to read the entire paper. Dickson et al.'s title is slightly longer than APA's guideline; the subtitle fully communicates that the paper deals with the variables of race, stereotypes, and perceptions of musical performers. The title is slightly longer than the recommended length because of the four-word "main" title—although it does not communicate much about the content of the article, it is certainly attention-getting. Your instructor (or journal editor) may give you some leeway with the 10-to-12-word recommendation, as in this case.

The name of the author is double-spaced below the title. The author's institutional affiliation is double-spaced below the author's name. If there is more than one author, the authors' names appear in order of importance of their contributions to the research project. If authors are from the same institution, all the names are on one line, if they will fit. Dickson's final manuscript included an additional author. The class project was a group effort by Dickson, Morris, and Cass for their research methods course, so they were the original authors. Giuliano, the professor of the class, helped them develop their ideas, supervised the research project, assisted in the statistical analysis and interpretation, and participated with Dickson in cowriting the manuscript for submission after the class was finished. Morris and Cass did not participate in rewriting the manuscript after the class. Thus, although the research originated as a student group project, by the time it was published, it had become a team effort among three students and a faculty member. Sometimes it is difficult to decide whether an individual merits being listed as an author on a publication. According to the *PM*, "Authorship encompasses not only those who do the actual writing but also those who have made substantial scientific contributions to a study" (p. 6). This guideline is somewhat vague and results in people having to make judgment calls about authorship.

Abstract

Figure 14-2 shows the abstract page. Note, once again, the placement of the manuscript page header and page number. The word "Abstract" is centered and appears two lines below the page number. (A centered section title in which the first letters of major words are capitalized is designated as a **level 1 heading**. Remember that headings help to demarcate sections of the APA-format paper. (Full information explaining different levels of headings appears on pp. 388–389.)

> **Level 1 heading**   A centered section title in which the first letters of major words are capitalized. Occupies a line by itself.

Imagine that you have just picked up a journal issue and are skimming through it to see if you might be interested in reading any of the articles. What feature of an article will you use as a guide in deciding whether to read it? What information would you use in making this decision?

Eminem Versus Charley   2

Abstract

The present study explored the effects of stereotype deviation in the music industry on people's perceptions of performers. One hundred college students (48 men, 52 women) examined a profile of a fictitious performer containing a picture, a brief biography, and a lyric sample. As part of a 2-way between-subjects design, participants made judgments about either a Black or a White musician who performed either rap or country music. The results showed that a Black rap performer was rated more favorably than a Black country performer, and a White country performer was rated more favorably than a White rap performer. Consistent with predictions, people who violate societal expectations are judged more harshly than are people who conform to societal expectations, particularly in cases involving strong preexisting racial stereotypes.

FIGURE 14-2   (M2). Abstract.

Abstract A brief description of the research that is presented in an APA-format paper.

Of course, the title of this section answers the first question; you will use the abstract as a guide to determine whether you want to read the complete article. The **abstract** of an experimental report consists of a brief (up to 120 words), one-paragraph description of the research presented in your paper. In order to help you make an educated decision about pursuing an article in depth, the paragraph that comprises the abstract should include a description of the intent and conduct (including participants and method) of your project, the results you obtained, and the project's implications or applications. Also, it is important to note that the abstract is typed in block form; there is no indentation on the first line.

The *PM* states that an abstract for an experimental study should contain information about the problem, participants, experimental method, findings, and conclusions.

Can you find information about each of the five topics (problem, participants, method, findings, conclusion) in the abstract in Figure 14-2?

Here's where we found the relevant information:

Problem—lines 1–2

Participants—line 2

Experimental method—lines 2–5

Findings—lines 5–6

Conclusions—lines 6–8

Did you find all the necessary information? Writing a good abstract is challenging because of the large amount of information that must be covered in little space. You can find more information about abstracts on pages 12–15 and 298 of the *PM*.

Introduction

Introduction The first major section of the APA-format paper. Contains the thesis statement, review of relevant literature, and experimental hypothesis.

Your **introduction** section begins on page 3 of your report. Notice that the word *Introduction* does not appear as the level 1 heading that begins this section. Rather, you repeat the title from page 1. Be sure that the title is *exactly* the same in both places. Figure 14-3 shows the first page of Dickson et al.'s introduction section (Figure 14-4 shows the second page of the introduction); the concluding page of the introduction section appears in Figure 14-5.

We like to use the analogy of a funnel to describe a good introduction section. Like the introduction, a funnel starts off broad, then narrows to a specific focus. At the end the focus is very specific, and in the case of the introduction section it leads to a logical experimental question, your experiment. In our example, the first paragraph is broad, establishing the race and genre of musicians as the variables of interest. The second and third paragraphs provide basic background information about racial stereotypes. The fourth and

Eminem Versus Charley Pride: Race, Stereotypes, and

Perceptions of Rap and Country Music Performers

What do Eminem and Charley Pride have in common? Perhaps the connection these two performers share is subtle, but they are in fact quite similar in at least one aspect of their careers. Both Charley Pride, a Black country music performer, and Eminem, a White rap performer, deviate from social expectations that are a part of the music industry. Specifically, these two musicians defy cultural stereotypes by performing types of music that are not typically associated with their race.

Racial stereotypes exist in most individuals, and they can influence subsequent judgments made by a perceiver (Devine, 1989; Dovidio, Evans, & Tyler, 1986; Gaertner & McLaughlin, 1983). For example, Gaertner and McLaughlin (1983) studied the effect of racial stereotypes on perceptions and found that White students responded faster to positive stereotyped words (e.g., *smart*) when the words followed the race *White* rather than *Black*. In addition, Sagar and Schofield (1980) examined the perceptions made by sixth-grade boys about ambiguous behavior. They found that both Black and White boys construed ambiguously aggressive behaviors (such as one child bumping into another) as being more threatening if the actions were performed by a Black boy rather than a White boy. Most people today would not be likely to openly express racist beliefs, but the results of the above studies support the aversive racism perspective, which suggests that subtle and indirect forms of racism persist in society today (Dovidio & Gaertner, 1991; Gaertner & Dovidio, 1986). That is, although current cultural values emphasize fairness and racial equality, White individuals have a historic tradition of having negative beliefs concerning Blacks and other minority groups (Dovidio, Brigham, Johnson, & Gaertner, 1996). Consequently, racial stereotypes continue to exist and to influence interactions among individuals in society, but perhaps in more subtle ways.

Because stereotypes can influence the judgments and behaviors of perceivers, deviations from a stereotype should have similar effects. In general, the expectations of the perceiver and the extent to which these expectations are confirmed or disconfirmed can influence judgments. When behavior only slightly varies from expectations, the difference might not be noticed, but perceivers often magnify the discrepancy when actions differ significantly from expectations. This phenomenon is known as the contrast effect (Brehm, Kassin, & Fein, 1999). In fact, a person who displays behavior inconsistent with societal expectations is often evaluated more extremely than is a person who

FIGURE 14-3   (M3). **First page of introduction.**

behaves consistently with expectations (Knight, Giuliano, & Sanchez-Ross, 2001). Jackson, Sullivan, and Hodge (1993) examined the effects of describing stereotype-consistent or stereotype-inconsistent behavior of Black out-group targets and White in-group targets on social evaluations made by participants who assessed a college application. They found that people who deviate from a norm are judged more extremely than if they behave as the norm dictates. Specifically, stereotype-inconsistent Black applicants with strong credentials were evaluated more favorably than were strong White applicants, and stereotype-inconsistent White applicants with weak credentials were evaluated less favorably than were weak Black applicants.

Both stereotypes and stereotype-inconsistent behavior affect the evaluations individuals make about other people in a variety of social interactions. Fried (1996, 1999) studied biased reactions involving the music industry and found that individuals had very different reactions to music labeled as *rap* or *country* despite the fact that the song lyrics were exactly the same. In two studies, she found that people generally considered rap music to be more violent and more offensive than country music. Furthermore, a folk song that was presented as being performed by a Black artist was judged more negatively than the very same song when it was presented as being performed by a White artist (Fried, 1996). Fried (1999) attributed her results to stereotypes in that rap is usually associated with Black culture whereas country music is often thought of as being a part of White culture. By priming a Black stereotype with the use of the label *rap*, it is possible that individuals apply negative stereotypes that have been shown to be associated with African Americans (Brigham, 1971). Therefore, racial stereotypes can impact evaluations of music performers (Fried, 1996, 1999).

According to Fiske and Taylor (1991), long-held stereotypes are not easily altered, but modification of stereotypes may begin with a divergence by stereotyped individuals or groups. Previous research has examined the effects of stereotypes and stereotype deviation on people's evaluations of other individuals (Jackson et al., 1993; Knight et al., 2001). The present study attempted to integrate and expand on these concepts in relation to the music industry. Specifically, whereas Fried (1996, 1999) examined the effect of either the race of the performer or the - labeled genre of music of a song on evaluations about the music itself, the design of the present experiment explored the interactive effects of the race of the performer and the genre of music on participants' evaluations of the performer. In doing so, we explored the difference between perceptions of persons who adhere to social expectations versus persons who deviate from the stereotype.

FIGURE 14-4   **(M4). Second page of introduction.**

Consistent with previous research (Jackson et al., 1993; Knight et al., 2001), we expected that participants

would judge performers who behave consistently with social norms (i.e., Black rap artists and White country

performers) more favorably than performers who deviate from societal expectations (i.e., White rap artists and Black

country performers). That is, because country music is associated with White culture, a Black country performer

does not exhibit behavior consistent with this stereotype and, as a result, this performer should elicit negative

judgments. The same reaction should occur with a White rap artist because his or her behavior is inconsistent with

the stereotype that rap is predominantly a part of Black culture.

Method

Participants

Data were collected from 100 undergraduates (48 men, 52 women) at Southwestern University, a small

liberal arts college in the Southwest. Demographically, the university is composed primarily of White, middle- to

upper middle-class students; as such, the current sample (which was representative of the campus at large) consisted

almost exclusively of White students. Participant volunteers ranged in age from 18 to 26 years ($M = 19.77$ years).

Data from four participants were excluded from the analysis because these participants either failed to follow

instructions or they did not pass the manipulation check. Specifically, these participants were unable to identify the

race of the performer and genre of his music that was presented in the their survey packet.

Design and Procedure

The present study used a 2 (race of performer: Black or White) x 2 (genre of music: rap or country)

between-subjects design to explore the effect of the race of a performer and the genre of music on perceptions of the

performer. We recruited participants from various locations on campus and asked them to contribute to an

investigation exploring "people's perceptions of music." Once they agreed, participants viewed a picture of a male

performer, read a brief biography about him, and read a lyric sample of his music. Next, they completed a survey in

which they made judgments about the performer and his music, and they responded to filler questions concerning

their taste in music in general to corroborate the cover story. Each participant was randomly assigned to one of four

experimental conditions and read a profile of either a Black rap artist, a White rap artist, a Black country performer,

or a White country performer. Measures of the primary dependent variable (i.e., how favorably participants rated the

performers) were embedded among filler questions in the survey. Following completion of the survey and a brief

FIGURE 14-5   (M5). Last page of introduction; first two method subsections.

fifth paragraphs begin to narrow the funnel. Here, you read about some specific effects of stereotypes and race associated with music, as well as the effects of stereotype inconsistencies. Finally, the last paragraph lays out the specific experimental hypothesis of this research.

Can you identify the thesis statement in Dickson et al.'s introduction?

Thesis statement A statement of the general research topic of interest and the perceived relation of the relevant variables in that area.

The first sentence on page 5 (Figure 14-5) forms the thesis statement for the student manuscript. The **thesis statement** should indicate the general topic in which you are interested and your general view of the relation of the relevant variables in that area. Beginning with "we expected that," you see the specific predictions made for the performance of participants rating musical artists under stereotype-consistent conditions compared to stereotype-inconsistent conditions. Some writers prefer to present the thesis statement in the opening paragraph of the introduction. The exact location is not important as long as you include your thesis statement somewhere in the introduction. (The *PM* provides more information concerning introductions on pp. 15–17.)

Other than presenting the thesis statement, the introduction serves to report the results of previous research that support or refute your thesis statement. This material represents the outcome of your literature review. Give careful thought to its presentation; good organization and a logical flow of ideas are important ingredients. The introduction is similar to telling a story to someone who may not be familiar with what you are talking about; you must be clear and not make unwarranted assumptions. First, you establish the big picture. Then, you begin to fill in the details. Your ultimate goal is to lead the reader to a description of what you plan to do in your experiment. This description usually appears at the end of the introduction section. It is here that you will state your experimental hypothesis.

Citation A notation in text that a particular reference was used. The citation provides the name(s) of the author(s) and date of the work's publication.

Reference A full bibliographic record of any work cited in the text of a psychological paper.

Reference section A complete listing of all the references cited in a psychological paper.

Although we cannot teach you *how* to write in the limited space available, we can give you a few pointers that will assist you as you prepare your introduction section. Note that every fact-based statement is supported by a **citation** to a **reference**. If you wish to locate one of the references cited, you can find the necessary information in the **reference section** (also known as the *reference list*) at the end of the paper (see Figures 14-14 and 14-15). As you can see from Dickson et al.'s introduction, when citing references in the text of an APA-format paper, you use the last name of the author(s) and the year of publication. Such citations can take one of two forms. In the first form, the authors are either the subject or the object in a sentence in the text. In such cases only the date of the publication appears in parentheses. This type of citation takes the following form:

Jackson, Sullivan, and Hodge (1993) examined the effects . . .

In the second form of citation, you may wish to cite a reference only as support for a statement you have made. In this instance you would include the author(s) *and* the year of publication *inside* the parentheses. This type of citation takes the following form:

> This phenomenon is known as the contrast effect (Brehm, Kassin, & Fein, 1999).

There are two additional considerations for such references. When there are multiple authors, the name of the last author is preceded by the ampersand (&) sign, *not* the word *and*. When you cite more than one study within parentheses, you should arrange the references alphabetically by the first author's last name.

What if you are citing two papers published in the same year by exactly the same authors? How can you distinguish between these papers when you cite them in your research report?

To report papers published in the same year, simply place a lowercase *a* or *b* after the date of each reference in question. Thus, if you had two 2000 references by Smith and Jones, you would cite them as follows:

Smith and Jones (2000a, 2000b)

or

(Smith & Jones, 2000a, 2000b)

The *a* and *b* designations will *also* appear as part of the complete citation of the article in the reference section (see the section on references later in this chapter).

When a citation includes three to five authors, include each author's last name in the first citation, with subsequent citations using only the first author's name followed by et al. (Latin for "and others") and the date. As shown in paragraphs 3 and 5 of Dickson's introduction, this rule creates the following citations:

Jackson, Sullivan, and Hodge (1993) [first citation, paragraph 3]

(Jackson et al., 1993) [second citation, paragraph 5]

If a citation includes six or more authors, *all* citations (including the first) consist of the first author's last name followed by et al. and the date. However, in the reference section, you include all names. The *PM* provides more information about reference citations in text on pages 207–214.

A second pointer on writing in APA style is that the use of unbiased language is imperative. **Unbiased language** is language that does not state or imply a prejudice toward any individual or group. According to the *PM*:

> **Unbiased language**
> Language that does not display prejudice toward an individual or group.

> APA is committed both to science and to the fair treatment of individuals and groups, and policy requires authors of APA publications to avoid perpetuating demeaning attitudes and biased assumptions about people in their writing. Constructions that might imply

bias against persons on the basis of gender, sexual orientation, racial or ethnic group, disability, or age should be avoided. Scientific writing should be free of implied or irrelevant evaluation of the group or groups being studied.

Long-standing cultural practice can exert a powerful influence over even the most conscientious author. Just as you have learned to check what you write for spelling, grammar, and wordiness, practice reading over your work for bias. You can test your writing for implied evaluation by reading it while (a) substituting your own group for the group or groups you are discussing or (b) imagining you are a member of the group you are discussing (Maggio, 1991). (pp. 61–62)

Once you have presented your thesis statement, reviewed the relevant literature, and stated your experimental hypothesis, you are ready to tell the readers how you conducted your research. We turn to this topic next.

Method

Method section The second major section of the APA-format paper. Contains information about the participants; the apparatus, materials, and testing instrument(s); and the procedures used in the experiment.

The objective of the **method section** is to provide sufficient detail about your experiment to enable readers to evaluate its appropriateness or replicate your study should they desire. The method section is typically made up of three subsections: *participants, apparatus* (also designated *materials* or *testing instruments*), and *procedure*. Note that *Method* is a level 1 section head. You do not begin the method section on a new page if there is room on the previous page. There is no break between the introduction, method, results, and discussion sections of an APA-format paper. You begin on a new sheet of paper only if a heading falls on the last line of a page; if it does, move it to the next page and begin the section there.

Participants subsection The first subsection of the method section. Provides full information about the participants in the study.

Level 3 heading A section title that is left-margin-justified, underlined, and has the first letter of each major word capitalized. Occupies a line by itself.

Participants (Subjects) The **participants subsection** enumerates and describes the experimental participants. Figure 14-5 shows the first subsection of Dickson et al.'s method section; the *PM* (p. 19) indicates that *subjects* is a permissible label if an experimenter uses animals in the experiment. (Note that *Participants* is a **level 3 heading**.)

The subsection on participants answers three questions: Who participated in the study? How many participants were there? How were the participants selected? As you can see in Figure 14-5, Dickson et al. gathered data from 100 students at Southwestern University. The students were almost evenly divided by sex; we see their age range, average age, and racial composition. The researchers provided details about 4 participants who were excluded from the research for various reasons. Notice that the paper describes the participants (and their important characteristics) in sufficient detail to allow a replication of the study. The only missing information is any inducement the participants received for being in the study; Dickson et al. labeled them "volunteers," but we do not know if they received extra credit in a class, monetary payment, or anything else. See pages 18–19 of the *PM* for more information about this subsection.

If you use animal subjects, your description needs to be detailed enough to allow another investigator to replicate your samples. In addition to providing sample selection information, you need to indicate any special arrangements, such as housing conditions, dietary conditions, and so on. The following description of animal subjects, from a paper on evaluating rats' behavior in a startle paradigm by Megan Kazlauskas, a student at Saint Anslem College in Manchester, New Hampshire, and Mark Kelland, her faculty advisor, is a good example of the type of information to include:

> In this study we examined stargazer rats (homozygous stg/stg; stg group) and unaffected littermates (heterozygous stg/+; LM group) provided by Dr. Charles R. Ashby, Jr., of the Brookhaven National Laboratory (Upton, NY). Rat pups were bred in the vivarium and phenotyped at 14 days of age as stargazers or littermates, based upon the demonstration of stargazing behavior. After weaning, the rats were housed in pairs (stargazer with littermate), in rooms maintained at 25° C, 40% humidity, a 12-hr light/dark cycle (light, 0700–1900 hrs), with food and water available ad libitum. After being shipped to Saint Anselm College the rats were allowed to accommodate for 7 days, being maintained on a 12-hr light/dark cycle (light, 0800–2000 hrs), with food and water ad lib. All behavior measurements were performed during the light cycle, from 0800 to 1200 hrs. (Kazlauskas & Kelland, 1997, p. 92)

Apparatus, Materials, or Testing Instruments   Figure 14-6 shows the **materials subsection** of the method section. This subsection can have various names depending on what you use in your particular experiment; you should choose the term that best describes the elements you used in conducting your experiment. *Materials* is used here because the students created written information for their research. If you use items such as slides, pictures, videotapes, or paper-and-pencil tests that are not standardized, you would probably want to label this section *Materials*. For example, in a study of identifying facial expressions, Sagles, Coley, Espiritu, Zahregian, and Velayo (2002) indicated in this subsection, "The 35-mm photos of the target individuals, taken from the base of the chin to the top of the forehead, excluded their attire and body type" (p. 33). This project was done by students at Pace University in New York; Velayo was their faculty advisor.

> **Materials subsection**
> The second subsection of the method section. When appropriate, contains information about materials other than equipment used in the experiment.

If you use equipment in the experiment, you should label this subsection **Apparatus**. You should briefly describe the equipment used in the experiment and its function(s) in this subsection. If your equipment was commercially produced, mention the name of the manufacturer and the model number of the equipment. For example, Ball, Kargl, Kimpel, and Siewert (2001) used one piece of standard laboratory equipment labeled in this manner in their study of the effects of mood on reaction time: "Lafayette Instrument Multi-Choice Reaction Timers (Lafayette Instrument Co., Model #63014) measured participants' reactions times" (p. 23). Ball et al. were students at Wheaton College in Wheaton, Illinois. If your equipment was custom made, provide a more detailed description. In the case of complex equipment, you may want to include a diagram. If you report any physical measurements, such as height, weight, or distance, you must report them in metric units. The *PM* contains extensive sections describing the use of metric measurements and their correct abbreviations (see pp. 130–136).

> **Apparatus subsection**
> The second subsection of the method section. When appropriate, contains information about the equipment used in an experiment.

If your "equipment" consists of standardized psychological testing materials, then the label **Testing Instruments** (or **Measures**) would

> **Testing instrument(s) subsection**   The second subsection of the method section. When appropriate, contains information about standardized tests used in the experiment.

manipulation check that focused on the performer's race and the genre of music, we explained the purpose of the present study to the participants and asked them not to discuss it with anyone.

Materials

A three-page experimental packet, which ostensibly contained a survey about people's perceptions of music, was distributed along with an envelope. The first page contained a "performer profile" and included a color picture of a Black or White male performer, a brief biography about him indicating that he was either a rap or country performer, and a lyric sample from one of his songs. The subsequent pages contained the survey, which was used to measure participants' reactions to what they had seen and read on the previous page.

Each performer profile contained a biography that included the name of the performer (i.e., D.J. Jones), his hometown (Atlanta, Georgia), and a brief summary of his musical career (e.g., "D.J. has been singing since he was 14, and recently signed a record deal with a major country label. He will soon be on an international tour opening for a popular country artist"). To create the sample song lyrics, we slightly altered and combined two rock songs (May, 1973; May & Staffell, 1973). With the exception of the two manipulations, we used the same biography and song lyrics in each of the four experimental conditions. The first manipulation altered the genre of music (i.e., rap or country) that the artist performed. Specifically, the name of the performer and the type of music he performed was labeled beneath his picture, and this label coincided with the genre of music described in the biography. Next, a photograph manipulated the race of the performer so that each biography was accompanied by a picture of either a Black or a White man. To ensure that the only attribute differing between the Black and White performers was in fact race, we conducted a pilot test in a Research Methods class to match the Black and White performers on attractiveness and age. The participants in the pilot test were all White, which is representative of the ethnic composition of the participants in the present study. From a pool of 20 color photographs of nonfamous Black and White men selected from magazines, the two stimuli selected for the present study were most similar in perceived - attractiveness and age.

Following the performer profile were the questions that assessed perceptions of the performer and his music, as well as the musical tastes of the participants. Embedded among demographic questions (e.g., sex and age) and other filler questions (e.g., "On average, how many CDs and/or tapes do you buy a month?") were the items that examined participants' perceptions of the performer. Specifically, participants rated on 7-point scales with endpoints

FIGURE 14-6   (M6). Materials subsection of method section.

be appropriate. For example, Bruderick and Ernst (2000), a student and a faculty member from Hillsdale College in Hillsdale, Michigan, described the instruments they used in a study of college student drinking in the following manner:

> Positive and negative alcohol expectancies were measured using the CEOA questionnaire (Comprehensive Effects of Alcohol; Fromme, Stroot, & Kaplan, 1993). . . . We used Cahalan's Quantity–Frequency Index (CQFI; Cahalan, Cisin, & Crossley, 1969) to determine level of drinking. (pp. 62–63)

If your experiment entailed the use of more than one category, then you should combine the relevant names when labeling this subsection. The *PM* discusses this subsection on pages 19–20.

Procedure   The **procedure subsection** (see Figures 14-5 and 14-6) summarizes how you conducted the experiment. In addition to describing the steps that you followed, you need to include a description of the experimental manipulations and controls (see Chapter 6), such as randomization, balancing, constancy, or counterbalancing, that you employed. Summarize any instructions you used, unless they are unusual or complex. In the latter instance, you may want to present the instructions word for word.

> **Procedure subsection**
> The third subsection of the method section. Provides a step-by-step account of what the participants and experimenter did during the experiment.

If the experiment is involved and has several stages or phases, the procedure section can become lengthy. Dickson et al.'s procedure section is intermediate in length. In contrast, the procedure involved in the administration of a questionnaire may be straightforward and brief. For example, in their study of collegiate alcohol use, Bruderick and Ernst (2000) indicated:

> We tested the participants as a group in a classroom. The questionnaire packets were administered so that half of the participants completed the CEOA and the CQFI second (Packet A); the remaining participants completed the CQFI first and the CEOA second (Packet B). The abstainer sheet and the demographic sheet followed the CEOA and CQFI in each packet. Before the experimenter instructed the participants to begin, she read the instructions as the participants followed along in their questionnaire packet. The instructions assured the participants of their anonymity. (p. 64)

Your primary goal in the procedure subsection is to describe how you conducted your experiment. You should give enough information to allow a replication of your method, but do not include unnecessary details (e.g., note that you recorded times with a stopwatch—the brand and model number would be overkill).

PSYCHO-LOGICAL DETECTIVE

What critical methodological details do you find in Dickson et al.'s procedure subsection?

Critical details are pertinent points that another experimenter would need to copy in a replication study. We believe that the following details are critical:

2 × 2 design

between-subjects design

recruited participants from various locations on campus

order of presentation of materials

random assignment

DV questions embedded among filler questions

debriefing after participation

4 experimental conditions (type of artist: Black rap, White rap; Black country; White country)

Did we include any details that you left out? If so, reread the procedure subsection to see why we think that detail is absolutely necessary. For example, did you ignore the method of participant recruitment? We believe that this detail clarifies our earlier question about whether participants received any inducement to take part in the experiment—it appears unlikely from this statement.

The procedure subsection is typically the longest of the three components of the method section. Its length will vary depending on the complexity of your experiment. Dickson et al.'s procedure section is shorter than the materials section, but their procedure was rather simple, and they needed to include more detail about the materials used. To read more about the procedure subsection, check page 20 of the *PM*.

Finally, you should not be surprised to find variations in researchers' method sections. Sections with combined names (e.g., *Design and Procedure* in Dickson et al.'s case) or with subsections in different orders are not unusual (Dickson et al.'s *Materials* section came after *Procedure*). The key point is that experimenters should provide you with the information you need to understand what they did in their experiment and how they did it.

Results

Results section The third major section of the APA-format paper. Contains information about the statistical findings from the experiment.

We introduced the format for the **results section** in Chapter 9 and reinforced those ideas in Chapters 10 and 11 when we discussed the notion of translating statistics into words. We do not use the word *translating* lightly—to some people, statistics resembles a foreign language. It is your job in the results section to decode the meaning of your numbers into words for the reader. At the same time you must provide the factual, numerical basis to back your decoding. The *PM* covers the presentation of statistical results on pages 20–26 and 136–147. Figure 14-7 contains Dickson et al.'s results section. As you conduct your library research, you may notice that sometimes authors combine the results and discussion sections into one section in a published journal article. This combination is common for certain journals or for shorter experimental articles. It is likely that your instructor will want you to keep your sections separate.

Inferential Statistics As you write the results section, you should assume that your reader has a good understanding of statistics. Therefore, you do not review basic concepts labeled at 1 (*not at all*) and 7 (*very much*): (a) "Overall, how much do you like this performer?"; (b) "How talented do you think this performer is?"; (c) "How legitimate is this performer?"; and finally (d) "How successful do you predict this performer will be in the music industry?" Because these items were highly correlated, they were combined into an overall index reflecting participants' favorability of the performer (Cronbach's α = .80). The scores on the four items were averaged together, and consistent with the scales on the individual items, the overall index is on a 7-point scale with higher numbers representing a more favorable perception of the performer and lower numbers indicating an unfavorable perception.

Results

A 2 (race of performer: Black or White) x 2 (genre of music: rap or country) between-subjects analysis of variance (ANOVA) was performed on the index assessing the favorability of the performer (i.e., likability, perceived talent, perceived legitimacy, and predicted success). Data analysis revealed a significant main effect of race such that Black performers (M = 4.32, SD = .91) were rated more positively than were White performers (M = 3.76, SD = 1.00), $F(1, 92)$ = 10.42, p = .002, η^2 = .10. However, this main effect was qualified by the significant two-way interaction between race of performer and genre of music, which was consistent with predictions, $F(1, 92)$ = 26.72, p = .0001, η^2 = .23. An inspection of the means in Figure 1 shows that participants rated a Black rap artist (M = 4.79, SD = .68) more favorably than a Black country artist (M = 3.85, SD = .87), $t(46)$ = 4.17, p = .0001; however, they judged a White country artist (M = 4.19, SD = .92) more favorably than a White rap artist (M = 3.33, SD = .91), $t(46)$ = 3.24, p = .0001. There was no main effect of genre of music, $F < 1$, *ns*: Participants reported similar ratings for rap performers (M = 4.06, SD = 1.09) and country performers (M = 4.02, SD = .90).

Discussion

The present study integrated and expanded on two lines of research. First, it extended previous research (Fried, 1996, 1999) on stereotyping involving the music industry. Whereas Fried (1996, 1999) examined reactions to music lyrics based on either the genre label or the performer's race, our study considered the interactive effect of both the race of the performer and the genre of music on people's evaluations of performers. The current study also differs from previous research conducted by Fried (1996, 1999) in that the lyrics in our study did not attempt to convey negative images such as violence or aggression. That is, Fried (1996, 1999) asked participants specifically

FIGURE 14-7   (M7). Results section; portion of Discussion section.

such as how the null hypothesis is rejected. The most important information to report is the specific findings from your inferential statistics. In Dickson et al.'s paper, you see an example of how to report results from factorial ANOVA (*F* tests; see Chapter 11 for review) and post hoc *t* tests.

Why did Dickson and colleagues use a factorial ANOVA to analyze their data? What was or were their IV(s)? What was or were their DV(s)?

First, you should remember from Chapter 11 that a factorial ANOVA is appropriate when you have more than one IV—thus, you should look for more than one IV in the Dickson et al. experiment. One focus of the experiment was race of the performer, so one IV was race (Black vs. White). The other IV was the genre of music (rap vs. country).

In the procedure and materials subsections, you found out that participants rated the performers on four scales and the researchers averaged the scores on the four scales. Therefore, the experiment had one DV: the overall index rating of the performers.

In presenting inferential statistical results, you must present the test that was used, the degrees of freedom for the test, the test statistics, the probability level, and a measure of effect size. In looking at Dickson et al.'s results, the second sentence provides us a good example:

Data analysis revealed a significant main effect of race such that Black performers ($M = 4.32$, $SD = .91$) were rated more positively than were White performers ($M = 3.76$, $SD = 1.00$), $F(1, 92) = 10.42$, $p = .002$, $\eta^2 = .10$.

Notice that the statistical findings at the end of the sentence give us all five pieces of information: an *F* test (analysis of variance) was used, there were 1 and 92 degrees of freedom, the calculated test value was 10.42, the probability of these data occurring if the null hypothesis is true was 2 in 1,000, and the effect size was small (.10). You should present the same type of information for findings relevant to the experimental hypothesis even if you do not find statistical significance. Although information from different test statistics may appear in a slightly different fashion, these five basic pieces of information are always necessary. We presented a set of *t* test results in Chapter 9 to which you can refer. You can find examples of how to present other statistical test results on pages 138–139 of the *PM*.

Descriptive Statistics   In order to give a full picture of the data, it is customary to present descriptive statistics in addition to the inferential statistics. Means and standard deviations typically allow readers to get a good feel for the data. With a small number of groups, you can present the descriptive statistics in the text (as Dickson et al. did), as we showed you in Chapter 9. On the other hand, with many groups, it may be more efficient and clearer to present the descriptive statistics in either a table or a figure, which we will discuss next.

Complementary Information   In presenting your results, you must first decide how best to give the reader the necessary information. If your statistical information is relatively simple, merely reporting your findings in words and numbers is usually adequate. For more complex analyses or results, you may wish to include tables or figures to further explicate your words and numbers.

Figures   Because Dickson et al.'s DV showed a significant interaction, they used a **figure** to clarify the presentation of results (see Figure 14-8). Figures can take the form of graphs (line, bar, circle or pie, scatter, or pictorial graphs), charts, dot maps, drawings, or photographs.

> **Figure**   A pictorial representation of a set of results.

The *PM* presents information regarding figures on pages 176–201. As you can guess from the number of pages devoted to figures, they can be complex to deal with, but most of this information involves preparing figures for publication. Because you will probably be submitting your research paper as a class requirement, your instructor may not be a stickler for enforcing every APA requirement on figures you submit with your paper. For example, you can see from Figure 14-9 that figure caption(s) appear on a separate page

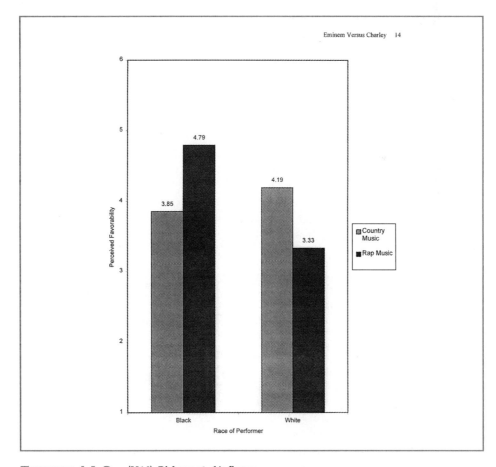

FIGURE 14-8   (M14). Dickson et al.'s figure.

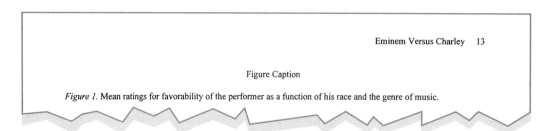

Eminem Versus Charley   13

Figure Caption

Figure 1. Mean ratings for favorability of the performer as a function of his race and the genre of music.

FIGURE 14-9   (M13) Caption for Dickson et al's figure.

in a manuscript prepared for publication. Your instructor may ask you to put your caption on the page with each figure.

It is likely that the majority of figures you use will be line graphs or bar graphs (see Chapter 8) that depict findings similar to Dickson et al's. Graphs are particularly good for showing interaction patterns. Because we showed interaction patterns in Chapter 11 with line graphs, we have reformatted Dickson et al.'s table as a line graph in Figure 14-10. It may be easier for you to see the interaction from the line graph than from the bar graph. Regardless of what type of figure you decide to use, you probably have access to a number of good software programs for graphing. For your class project, ask your instructor about his or her preference as to how you should produce a figure. Regardless of how you create your figures, one rule is constant: Be certain that you refer to your figures in the text at an appropriate place. This reference will cue the reader to look at the figure in order to process its meaning.

> **Table**   A chart containing an array of descriptive statistics.

Tables   A **table** consists of a display of data, usually in numerical form. Tables are an alternative to presenting data in pictorial form as a figure. To use a table, your data display should be large enough that it would be difficult or confusing to present it in the text.

You often have to decide between using a table or a figure to present your data. Notice that Dickson et al. presented their data only with a figure rather than a table. We have adapted the data from their Figure 1 into the format that you see in Figure 14-11

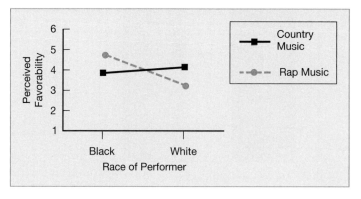

FIGURE 14-10   Adaption of Dickson et al.'s results to line graph.

Table 1
Perceived Favorability of Performance Based on Performer's Race and Music Genre

	Performer's Race	
Music Genre	Black	White
Rap		
M	3.85	4.19
SD	.87	.92
Country		
M	4.79	3.33
SD	.68	.91

Note: Favorability ratings made on a scale from 1 *(negative)* to 7 *(positive)*.

FIGURE 14-11   Adaption of Dickson et al.'s results to table.

(Dickson et al. would have included a manuscript page header and page number if this page were actually in their manuscript). The advantage of the table over the figure is that standard deviations can be included in the table. The advantage of the figure over the table is accessibility—the data, particularly the significant interaction, seem easier to understand and conceptualize in the pictorial presentation. Considering these advantages, the figure seemed a better choice in this situation. For your experimental report, your decision may be different. APA presents many guidelines for developing tables (see pp. 147–176 of the *PM*). You should check with your instructor to find out which guidelines you must follow in your paper. Because you will typically generate a table directly in your word-processing program (or on your typewriter), you may find a table easier to produce than a figure. However, you should make your choice of a table versus a figure on the quality of information provided to the reader rather than on ease of production. Again, if you use a table in your paper, be sure to refer to it at the appropriate point.

Can you think of a specific situation in which you would prefer a table over a figure?

The most obvious answer to this question is a situation in which you have a large number of means to present but for which there is not a significant interaction. We hope that a comparison of Figures 14-8 and 14-11 convinced you of the benefit of a figure for portraying interactions.

Discussion section   The fourth major section of the APA-format paper. Contains a summary of the experiment's results, a comparison of those results to previous research, and the conclusion(s) from the experiment.

Discussion

You can find Dickson et al.'s **discussion section** in Figures 14-7, 14-12, and 14-13. According to the *PM* (pp. 26–27), you can address issues such as problem choice, levels of analysis, and application and synthesis in the discussion section. We like the somewhat simpler and clearer guidelines laid out in the previous edition of the *PM* (APA, 1994, p. 19), which recommended that you be guided by three questions in the discussion section:

- *What have I contributed here?*
- *How has my study helped to resolve the original problem?*
- *What conclusions and theoretical implications can I draw from my study?*

Typically, authors answer these three questions by (a) briefly restating their findings, (b) comparing and contrasting their findings to previous research cited in the introduction, and (c) giving their interpretation of their findings.

Restating Results   Your first task in the discussion section is to recap your results as briefly as possible. Typically, you will summarize only your significant findings, unless a null finding is particularly meaningful. If you conducted a large study with many outcomes, you may wish to feature only the most important findings at this point—usually those findings that have some bearing on your experimental hypothesis. This summary ensures that the reader can extract the most important information from your results section.

If you examine Dickson et al.'s (2001) discussion section, you will find that the authors used the three techniques listed just before this section. In the first paragraph, they summarized the information from the results section in one sentence: "In our study, participants judged Black rap artists more favorably than Black country music performers, whereas they judged White country music performers more favorably than White rap artists" (p. 178). The sentence describes the significant interaction that Dickson et al. found rather than the main effect of race because the interaction qualified the race effect.

Comparing Results to Previous Research   It is important for you to evaluate how your results "stack up" against previous findings in your area of research you summarized in your introduction. The previous research studies will be related to, but not the same as, your experiment. Typically, you will have made a prediction before the experiment about your expected findings based on your survey of previous research. You should tell the reader how accurate your predictions were. This information will help the reader in drawing conclusions. For example, if you correctly predicted your results from previous research, the previous research and your study are both validated. On the other hand, if your prediction is not borne out, some doubt is cast—either your research or the previous research may be flawed in some way.

Looking at the first paragraph of Dickson et al.'s discussion section, you will see the comparison to previous research findings. In this case, the previous research studies were related to Dickson et al.'s study because they dealt with stereotyping and music. On the other hand, these studies were different because they did not specifically combine performer's race and genre of music. The Dickson et al. study demonstrated an interaction between those two variables, which was an important finding.

about their negative impressions of the song lyrics (e.g., its offensiveness, its threat to society, its need for warning labels), whereas the current study emphasized overall impressions of the performer. Rap may be more often associated with negative topics, but these topics can be found in both rap and country music. We chose to use neutral lyrics in the present study because we were not focusing on the relation between negative themes and music genre. Instead, the current study was based on findings that rap is associated with a Black culture that has both positive and negative attributes (Brigham, 1971). We examined the connection between music genre and the stereotype-consistent or stereotype-inconsistent race of the performer. In our study, participants judged Black rap artists more favorably than Black country music performers, whereas they judged White country music performers more favorably than White rap artists. These results support the hypothesis that individuals who deviate from societal expectations are judged more negatively than are individuals who adhere to social norms (Jackson et al., 1993; Knight et al., 2001). Manis, Nelson, and Shedler (1988) found that extreme stereotypes yielded contrast effects when behavior was discrepant from the established stereotype. In the present study, Black country music performers and White rap artists contrast from fairly ingrained societal expectations and thus received more negative judgments than the performers who adhere to societal norms.

The present study could be extended in a number of ways. For example, like Fried's (1996, 1999) research, the current study also presented the lyric sample to participants on paper. It would be interesting to explore whether an audio-recorded lyric sample would affect participants' evaluations of performers or the music. Perhaps auditory processing and visual processing of stereotype-consistent and stereotype-inconsistent information differ. In addition, the present study could broaden its scope by including a more varied sample of participants. That is, future studies could incorporate participants of different races and ages. The data in the current study were collected primarily from White undergraduate students at a liberal arts university, and the results from such a homogenous sample may not necessarily generalize to alternative populations or settings. Furthermore, exploring alternate stereotype violations could support the findings of the present study, and one area of interest could be the world of sports. For instance, Black hockey players violate societal expectations similar to the apparent violation made by Black country music performers and White rap performers. According to our findings, Black hockey players would receive more negative evaluations than would White hockey players because their behavior is inconsistent with societal expectations.

FIGURE 14-12   **(M8). Second page of discussion.**

Because the population of other minority groups (e.g., Latinos) is approaching that of the Black population in America, future research concerning racial stereotypes in the music industry could examine the impact of the increasing popularity of Latin music (Gonzales, 1990). Garcia and Zapatel (2000) recently examined how the labels *Black rap*, *Latino rap*, and *alternative music* influence perceptions made by both Anglo and Hispanic participants and found that participants' perceptions of music differed depending on their own race. Specifically, Hispanic participants judged music labeled *Latino rap* more positively than music labeled *alternative*, whereas Anglo participants rated music labeled *alternative* more favorably than music labeled *Latino rap*. Similar to previous findings (Jackson et al., 1993), out-group categories (i.e., *Latino rap* for Anglo participants and *alternative* music for Hispanic participants) were judged more negatively than were categories that corresponded to the participants' ethnicity. Extended to a more diverse sample, the present study could offer support for the idea that out-group categories are judged more negatively than in-group categories by examining the relation between participants' ethnicities and their evaluations of rap and country music. Thus, regardless of the race of the performer, Black participants would be expected to rate country music more negatively than rap music, whereas White participants would be expected to judge rap music more negatively than country music. Furthermore, it would be interesting to determine whether or not performers of Latin music will remain primarily Latin and to examine perceptions of stereotype-consistent and stereotype-inconsistent performers in this genre. If future performers do deviate from racial stereotypes, the present study suggests that non-Latino performers of Latin music would be perceived less favorably than would Latino performers.

In closing, Eminem and Charley Pride share a connection in that their actions deviate from widespread stereotypes that specific races are associated with certain types of music. Although people may recognize these two performers because of their musical talent, it is more likely that they are recognized because they were bold enough to defy stereotypes in the music industry. By being a White rap artist and a Black country music performer, Eminem and Charley Pride became forerunners for performers who do not adhere to social norms, and they may have possibly influenced numerous music fans to expect the unexpected.

FIGURE 14-13   (M9). Final page of discussion.

Interpreting the Results   This portion of the discussion section gives you more of a free hand to engage in conjecture and speculation than any other portion of the experimental writeup. It is here that you draw the "bottom line" to your study: What is your overall conclusion? What are the implications of your results for any psychological theories? How can your results be applied in various settings—the laboratory, the real world, our body of psychological knowledge? What new research should grow out of this study? As you can see, there are a variety of questions you can address in your discussion section. Not all these questions are appropriate for every study—pick the ones that are most important for your particular experiment.

The interpretation of Dickson et al.'s results appears in the last three sentences of the discussion section's first paragraph. The results of this study supported the notion that people who deviate from societal expectations are judged more harshly than people who conform to stereotypes.

The second and third paragraphs of Dickson et al.'s discussion section include possible directions for future research.

How many ideas for further research can you find in the second and third paragraphs of Dickson et al.'s (2001) discussion?

We see four possible experiments mentioned:

1. Using audio-recorded lyrics rather than printed lyrics
2. Using participants from populations other than White students
3. Exploring racial stereotype expectations in sports settings
4. Extending the music genre to include Latin music

You may wish to mentally file this example away for future reference. As you read discussion sections of published articles, you might find ideas for your own research projects.

References

There are two important reasons why it is your responsibility to provide a complete list of accurate references to any published works that you cite in your research report. First, you must give credit to the original author(s) for any ideas and information that you got from reading other works. If you take exact wordings, paraphrases, or even ideas from an author without giving credit for that source, you are guilty of **plagiarism** (see Chapter 3). Second, you are providing a historical account of the sources you used in the event that a reader wishes to read them in their entirety. Have you ever worked on a term paper and "lost" a good source that you had read because you didn't write down all the necessary bibliographic information and couldn't find it again? Most of us have had this

Plagiarism   Using someone else's work without giving credit to the original source.

experience, and it is quite frustrating. You can prevent that frustrating experience by providing your reader with a complete and accurate reference list. The *PM* describes the reference list on page 28 and provides general pointers about the list as well as examples of APA format for 95 different types of sources on pages 239–281. Reference formatting is so important that the *PM* now has a separate chapter (Chapter 4, pp. 215–281) devoted to this topic.

Before going further, we need to distinguish between a reference list and a bibliography that you might have learned about in English classes. The reference list is *not* a list of every source that you read when you were writing your introduction and planning your experiment. The only references that you list are those from which you actually obtained information and cited somewhere in your paper. If you do not cite a particular source, you should not reference it.

The list of references begins on a new page after the end of your discussion section. You will find Dickson et al.'s references in Figures 14-14 and 14-15.

Look at Figures 14-14 and 14-15. How many different types of reference formats can you find? Can you identify each type?

There are five different types of references represented in Dickson et al.'s list:

1. Book: Brehm, Kassin, & Fein; Fiske & Taylor; Gonzales
2. Journal article: Brigham; Devine; Dovidio, Evans, & Tyler; Fried (both); Gaertner & McLaughlin; Jackson, Sullivan, & Hodge; Knight, Giuliano, & Sanchez-Ross; Manis, Nelson, & Shedler; Sagar & Schofield
3. Chapter in edited book: Dovidio, Brigham, Johnson, & Gaertner; Dovidio & Gaertner; Gaertner & Dovidio
4. Conference presentation: Garcia & Zapatel
5. Music recording: May; May & Staffell

As you look at a reference, you will find that the information about author(s) and date is listed first. This location makes it easy for the reader to see an author and date citation in your text and then to find the corresponding reference in your reference list. The reference list is alphabetized by the surname of the first author. If you have more than one article by the same first author, you alphabetize by the name of the second author. If the author information for two or more articles is identical, you should arrange the references by date, with the earliest article listed first. If the author information and dates are identical, alphabetize by the first main word of the title, and add lowercase letters (*a*, *b*, etc.) to the date to differentiate the articles, as we previously mentioned.

The title of the scholarly work is the next piece of information, followed by supplementary information that helps a reader locate that work. As you can see, the supplementary information differs depending on the particular type of reference you are using. Let's take a look at the general format for the three different types of references you are most likely to use in your papers.

Eminem Versus Charley   10

References

Brehm, S. S., Kassin, S. M., & Fein, S. (1999). *Social psychology* (4th ed.). Boston: Houghton Mifflin.

Brigham, J. C. (1971). Ethnic stereotypes. *Psychological Bulletin, 76,* 15-38.

Devine, P. G. (1989). Stereotypes and prejudice: Their automatic and controlled components. *Journal of Personality and Social Psychology, 56,* 5-18.

Dovidio, J. F., Brigham, J. C., Johnson, B. T., & Gaertner, S. L. (1996). Stereotyping, prejudice, and discrimination: Another look. In N. C. Macrae, C. Stangor, & M. Hewstone (Eds.), *Stereotypes & stereotyping* (pp. 276-322). New York: Guilford Press.

Dovidio, J. F., Evans, N., & Tyler, R. B. (1986). Racial stereotypes: The contents of their cognitive representations. *Journal of Experimental Social Psychology, 22,* 22-37.

Dovidio, J. F., & Gaertner, S. L. (1991). Changes in the expression and assessment of racial prejudice. In H. R. Knopke, R. J. Norrell, & R. W. Rogers (Eds.), *Opening doors: Perspectives on race relations in contemporary America* (pp. 119-148). Tuscaloosa: University of Alabama Press.

Fiske, S. T., & Taylor, S. E. (1991). *Social cognition* (2nd ed.). New York: McGraw-Hill.

Fried, C. B. (1996). Bad rap for rap: Bias in reactions to music lyrics. *Journal of Applied Social Psychology, 26,* 2135-2146.

Fried, C. B. (1999). Who's afraid of rap: Differential reactions to music lyrics. *Journal of Applied Social Psychology, 29,* 705-721.

Gaertner, S. L., & Dovidio, J. F. (1986). The aversive form of racism. In J. F. Dovidio & S. L. Gaertner (Eds.), *Prejudice, discrimination, and racism: Theory and research* (pp. 61-89). Orlando, FL: Academic Press.

Gaertner, S. L., & McLaughlin, J. P. (1983). Racial stereotypes: Associations and ascriptions of positive and negative characteristics. *Social Psychology Quarterly, 46,* 23-30.

Garcia, S. D., & Zapatel, J. P. (2000, January). *Perceptions of lyrics as a function of ethnicity and music genre.* Paper presented at the annual meeting of the Social Psychologists in Texas, San Antonio.

Gonzales, J. L., Jr. (1990). *Racial and ethnic groups in America: A collection of readings.* Dubuque, IA: Kendall/Hunt.

FIGURE 14-14   (M10). First page of reference list.

Eminem Versus Charley   11

Jackson, L. A., Sullivan, L. A., & Hodge, C. N. (1993). Stereotype effects on attributions, predictions, and

evaluations: No two social judgments are quite alike. *Journal of Personality and Social Psychology, 65,* 69-

84.

Knight, J. L., Giuliano, T. A., & Sanchez-Ross, M. G. (2001). Famous or infamous? The influence of celebrity

status and race on perceptions of responsibility for rape. *Basic and Applied Social Psychology, 23,* 183-190.

Manis, M., Nelson, T. E., & Shedler, J. (1988). Stereotypes and social judgment: Extremity, assimilation, and

contrast. *Journal of Personality and Social Psychology, 55,* 28-36.

May, B. (1973). The night comes down. [Recorded by Queen]. On *Queen* [Record]. London: EMI Records.

May, B., & Staffell, T. (1973). Doing all right. [Recorded by Queen]. On *Queen* [Record]. London: EMI Records.

Sagar, H. A., & Schofield, J. W. (1980). Racial and behavioral cues in Black and White children's perceptions of

ambiguously aggressive acts. *Journal of Personality & Social Psychology, 39,* 590-598.

FIGURE 14-15   **(M11). Last page of reference list.**

Periodical Articles   The *PM* shows examples of 22 different types of references to periodicals on pages 240–247. Your most typical use of periodicals will probably be to reference articles in journals. The general format for periodicals is as follows:

Author, A. A., Author, B. B., & Author, C. C. (date). Title of article. *Title of Periodical, vol,* ppp–ppp.

For examples, you can examine the 10 references in Figures 14-14 and 14-15 that we listed as the answer to the last Psychological Detective question. The last names and initials of *all* authors appear in the same order as in the journal article. You will remember we mentioned using et al. for multiple-author works earlier in this chapter. You *do not* use et al. in the reference list—list all authors. The date refers to the year in which the particular journal issue containing the article was published. Be careful here—you may need to look at the front of the journal to get this information.

Type the title of the article with *only* the first word and any proper nouns (e.g., names, states, organizations, or test names) capitalized and *not* italicized. If the article title includes a colon, capitalize the first word after the colon also.

Type the journal title with all important words capitalized; words such as *a, and,* and *the* are not capitalized unless they are the first word or follow a colon. The journal title *is* italicized, as is the volume number of the journal (and its following comma) that immediately follows the journal title. Type only the volume number—do not precede it by *Vol.* or *V.* It is often the case that volumes of journals also have issue numbers. For example, volume 57 represents the 2002 issues of *American Psychologist;* each month's issue is represented by its own number. Thus, the January 2002 issue would be Volume 57, Number 1, and so on.

Most journals use continuous pagination throughout a volume. That is, the first issue of a new volume begins on page 1 and the pages run continuously until the next volume, which begins with page 1. In this case, the issue number is not needed to find the referenced article and does not appear in the reference. A few journals, however, repaginate; that is begin *each issue* with page 1. If this is the case, then the issue number is necessary to find the article and is included in the reference.

> Author, A. A., Author, B. B., & Author, C. C. (date). Title of article. *Title of Periodical, vol*(n), ppp–ppp.

Notice that the issue number (n) appears within parentheses (no space after the volume number) and is *not* italicized. Finally, give the inclusive page numbers of the article—numbers only, no *p.* or *pp.* preceding.

Books   The *PM* provides 11 examples of references to books on pages 248–251. This category consists of references to entire books rather than to chapters in edited books. The general format for book references is:

> Author, A. A. (date). *Title of work*. Location: Publisher.

We have used a one-author example here, but don't be misled by it. You should include all authors' names and initials (see Brehm, Kassin, & Fein in Dickson et al.'s reference list), just as in the journal examples given previously. Use the date of the original publication of the book, which usually appears at the front of the book facing the title page.

The book title's format is a combination of the styles seen earlier for article titles and journal titles. It follows the style for an article title in terms of capitalization—you should capitalize only the first word (and the first word after a colon or normally capitalized words). However, like a journal title, the book's title is italicized.

The location and the name of the publisher appear in the last portion of the reference. If the city, such as New York, is well known for publishing, you type it alone (see p. 217 of the *PM* for a complete list). Otherwise, you must give the city and state (two-letter postal abbreviation) or country. Many publishers now have offices in several locations—typically the first location listed is the one referenced. The name of the publisher is given in a brief form, omitting "superfluous terms, such as *Publishers, Co.,* or *Inc.,* which are not required to identify the publisher" (APA, 2001, p. 230). Many times you will find that a corporate author and publisher are the same, as with the *PM*. In such a case, rather than repeat the information for the publisher, you simply type "Author" after the location (e.g., see the reference to the *PM* in the reference list for this book). Dickson's manuscript has three examples of references to books.

Chapters from Edited Books   Most edited books contain chapters written by different authors. You can cite information from a single chapter within such a book. The *PM* gives seven examples of such references on pages 252–255.

> Author, A. A., & Author, B. B. (date). Title of chapter. In C. C. Editor, D. D. Editor, & E. E. Editor
>
> (Eds.), *Title of book* (pp. nnn–nnn). Location: Publisher.

As you can see, this type of reference is much like a journal article reference combined with a book reference. This example includes two authors and three editors, but any number of either is possible. You would provide the information concerning author(s) and date as we have previously discussed. The title of the chapter refers to the specific smaller work within the larger book. Capitalize the chapter title in the same manner as a journal article title— capitalize only the first word, the first word after a colon, and words that are normally capitalized.

List all the editors' names. Notice that you do not reverse the initials and surnames. After a comma, you list the book's title (italicized), with capitalization in the same fashion as mentioned previously for a book title. The inclusive pages of the chapter appear parenthetically after the book's title to make it easier for the reader to locate the specific chapter in the book. Finally, include the location and publisher information as for any book. Dickson et al.'s manuscript includes three examples of chapters in edited books, as listed previously.

World Wide Web Sources   Providing references for information that you obtain from the World Wide Web is just as important as providing references for written material—in fact, it may be even more important. Unlike journal articles or books, material on the Web can change quite rapidly. Authors can modify Web information from day to day, which can create a problem in keeping current. The *PM* has an extensive section dealing with electronic media references, which includes 25 examples of Internet and Web references on pages 268–281. Because there are so many different types of electronic media sources, it is impossible to cover them all. We will provide an example of a citation to information on a Web site; if you have a different type of source, be sure to consult the *PM*.

American Psychological Association. (2001). Electronic reference formats recommended by the

American Psychological Association. Retrieved September 6, 2002, from http://www.

apastyle.org/elecref.html

Note that this reference style is similar to a book reference. However, you include the actual retrieval site and date. This additional information allows a reader to find the site and to determine whether the information still exists (or perhaps has been updated) at that site. Providing an exact date of retrieval is extremely important for these reasons.

The relevant text citation for this reference would be the same for a book; in this case, it would be (American Psychological Association, 1999). If you wish to cite an entire Web site (rather than a specific document on the Web site), you can simply list the site in the text—no reference is necessary (e.g., http://www.apa.org for the APA site).

Other References   Although we expect that most of your references will be to periodicals, books, and chapters in edited books, the *PM* has 30 examples of other types of references you might use. These other references include technical and research reports, proceedings of meetings and symposia, doctoral dissertations and master's theses, unpublished works and publications of limited circulation, reviews, and audiovisual media. No matter what type of material you wish to reference, the *PM* will have a format for you.

A Disclaimer   The fourth edition of the *PM* (APA, 1994) used a different reference format. Although all the information included was the same, the appearance of the references was different. In the older format, the initial line of each reference was indented and subsequent lines begin at the left margin. However, when references were printed in journal articles, this margin situation was reversed—the first line began at the left margin and subsequent lines were indented (referred to as a "hanging indent"). With this type of formatting, the first authors' names stand out and are easier to locate. Under the new (2001) guidelines, manuscript references are formatted exactly as they are in publication.

We give you this explanation to alert you to the possibility that you might see an older student paper with references formatted in the old manner. It is not unusual for students to find previous copies of research papers to use as examples. If you copy that style of reference format, you will be in error. As you have examined the manuscript pages of Dickson et al.'s paper and the published product, you may have noted other differences.

 Can you figure out why an APA-formatted manuscript and a published article (or final copy) might differ in appearance?

APA format is intended to help authors and journal editors produce a product more easily. In a published article or final copy, however, the appearance of the document is the more important goal. Instructors have a difficult dilemma deciding whether to require strict APA format or to accept a more aesthetically appealing product.

Appendix

Most published articles do not contain an appendix because of space limitations; appendixes are more common in student papers (*PM*, 2001, p. 324). Typically you include information that might help readers understand some details of your study that would be distracting in the body of the paper. The *PM* gives examples such as a new computer program, an unpublished test that you used, a mathematical proof, a list of stimuli used, and the description of a complex piece of equipment (p. 28).

Dickson et al. included an appendix that contained the lyrics to the music used in their experiment. We have *not* included the appendix in the text because of space limitations (but the reference to the appendix appears in the "Materials" subsection in Figure 14-19).

Author Note

Your manuscript may or may not have an **author note**, depending on your instructor's preferences. If you do use an author note, begin it on a new page. As you can see from Dickson et al.'s author note in Figure 14-16, they acknowledged several people who helped on the project and provided a name and address for readers to contact for information or copies of the paper. Other information that might be included would be an acknowledgment of an earlier presentation of the paper (e.g., at a conference) or sources of financial support that made the study possible. The *PM* provides information about the author note on pages 29, 203–205, and 300.

> **Author note** A note at the end of an experimental report that contains information about the author or paper for readers' use.

Eminem Versus Charley   12

Author Note

We would like to thank Jennifer Knight for her advice and input on this study, Marie Helweg-Larsen for

her helpful comments on an earlier draft of this manuscript, Alan Swinkels for his assistance with graphic

illustrations, and Johnnie Dickson for her proofreading skills and patience.

Correspondence concerning this study should be addressed to Traci Giuliano at Southwestern University,

Georgetown, TX 78626-6144. Electronic mail may be sent to giuliant@southwestern.edu.

FIGURE 14-16   (M12). **Author note page.**

Headings

To recapitulate, APA-format papers use a different type of heading for each section of the report. The major sections of the report, such as the introduction, method, results, and discussion, are introduced by a level 1 heading. Subsections within these main sections are introduced by lower-level headings. For example, the participants, apparatus, and procedure subsections of the method section are generally introduced by a level 3 heading. Level 3 headings are left-margin-justified, are italicized, have the first letter of each major word capitalized, and occupy a line by themselves. Should you need to further subdivide these subsections, use a **level 4 heading**. Level 4 headings are indented five spaces and italicized, have only the first letter of the first word capitalized, and end with a period. You begin typing on the same line following the period that concludes a level 4 heading.

> **Level 4 heading**   A section title that is indented five spaces, underlined, has only the first word capitalized, and ends with a period; it does not occupy a separate line.

Table 14-1 summarizes the five types of section headings used in APA-format articles. Level 1 and level 3 headings are the ones most frequently used in preparing a research report that describes a single experiment (as in Dickson et al.'s example). As we have seen, however, the description of a single experiment may require the use of level 4 headings when the participants, apparatus, and procedure subsections are further subdivided (see Table 14-1). Likewise, when you are presenting more than one experiment, you will use level 1, 2, 3, and 4 headings as shown in Table 14-1.

**TABLE 14-1   Levels and Locations of Headings Used in an APA-Format Paper
Selecting the Levels of Heading**

Find the section of your paper that breaks into the finest level of subordinate categories. Then use the guidelines that follow to determine the level, position, and arrangement of headings. Few articles require all levels of heading. Note that each subheading must have at least one counterpart at the same level within a section; for brevity, the examples that follow do not include counterparts.

One level. For a short article, one level of heading may be sufficient. In such cases, use only centered uppercase and lowercase headings (Level 1).

Two levels. For many articles in APA journals, two levels of headings meet the requirements. Use Level 1 and Level 3 headings:

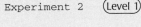

Procedure ◄——(Level 3)

If the material subordinate to the Level 1 headings is short or if many Level 3 headings are necessary, indented, italicized lowercase paragraph headings (Level 4) may be more appropriate than Level 3 headings. (A Level 4 heading should apply to all text between it and the next heading, regardless of the heading level of the next heading.)

Three levels. For many articles, three levels of headings are needed. Use Level 1, Level 3, and Level 4 headings.

In a single-experiment study, these three levels of headings may look like this:

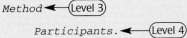

Apparatus and Procedure ◄——(Level 3)

  Pretraining period. ◄——(Level 4)

In a *multiexperiment study*, these three levels of headings may look like this:

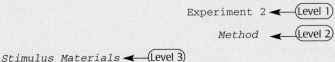

Method ◄——(Level 3)

  Participants. ◄——(Level 4)

Four levels. For some articles, particularly multiexperiment studies, monographs, and lengthy literature reviews, four levels of headings are needed. Use heading Levels 1 through 4:

Experiment 2 ◄——(Level 1)

  Method ◄——(Level 2)

Stimulus Materials ◄——(Level 3)

  Auditory stimuli. ◄——(Level 4)

Five levels. Occasionally, an article requires five levels of headings. In such cases, subordinate all four levels above by introducing a Level 5 heading—A CENTERED UPPERCASE HEADING—above the other four.

Eminem Versus Charley Pride: Race, Stereotypes, and Perceptions of Rap and Country Music Performers

ALLISON J. DICKSON

TRACI A. GIULIANO*

JAMES C. MORRIS

KERI L. CASS

Southwestern University

The present study explored the effects of stereotype deviation in the music industry on people's perceptions of performers. One hundred college students (48 men, 52 women) examined a profile of a fictitious performer containing a picture, a brief biography, and a lyric sample. As part of a 2-way between-subjects design, participants made judgments about either a Black or a White musician who performed either rap or country music. The results showed that a Black rap performer was rated more favorably than a Black country performer, and a White country performer was rated more favorably than a White rap performer. Consistent with predictions, people who violate societal expectations are judged more harshly than are people who conform to societal expectations, particularly in cases involving strong preexisting racial stereotypes.

WHAT DO EMINEM AND CHARLEY PRIDE HAVE in common? Perhaps the connection these two performers share is subtle, but they are in fact quite similar in at least one aspect of their careers. Both Charley Pride, a Black country music performer, and Eminem, a White rap performer, deviate from social expectations that are a part of the music industry. Specifically, these two musicians defy cultural stereotypes by performing types of music that are not typically associated with their race.

Racial stereotypes exist in most individuals, and they can influence subsequent judgments made by a perceiver (Devine, 1989; Dovidio, Evans, & Tyler, 1986; Gaertner & McLaughlin, 1983). For example, Gaertner and McLaughlin (1983) studied the effect of racial stereotypes on perceptions and found that White students responded faster to positive stereotyped words (e.g., *smart*) when the words followed race *White* rather than *Black*. In addition, Sagar and Schofield (1980) examined the perceptions made by sixth-grade boys about ambiguous behavior. They found that both Black and White boys construed ambiguously aggressive behaviors (such as one child bumping into another) as being more threatening if the actions were performed by a Black boy rather than a White boy. Most people today would not be likely to openly express racist beliefs, but the results of the above studies support the aversive racism perspective, which suggests that subtle and indirect forms of racism persist in society today (Dovidio & Gaertner, 1991; Gaertner & Dovidio, 1986). That is, although current cultural values emphasize fairness and racial equality, White individuals have a historic tradition of having negative beliefs concerning Blacks and other minority groups (Dovidio, Brigham, Johnson, & Gaertner, 1996). Consequently, racial stereotypes continue to exist and to influence interactions among individuals in society, but perhaps in more subtle ways.

Author note. We would like to thank Jennifer Knight for her advice and input on this study, Marie Helweg-Larsen for her helpful comments on an earlier draft of this manuscript, Alan Swinkels for his assistance with graphic illustrations, and Johnnie Dickson for her proofreading skills and patience.

Correspondence concerning this study should be addressed to Traci Giuliano at Southwestern University, Georgetown, TX 78626-6144. Electronic mail may be sent to giuliant@southwestern.edu.

FIGURE 14-17   (JA1).

Source: From "Eminem Versus Charley Pride: Race, Stereotypes, and Perceptions of Rap and Country Music Performers" by A. J. Dickson, T. A. Giuliano, J. C. Morris, and K. L. Cass, 2001, *Psi Chi Journal of Undergraduate Research, 6,* pp. 175–180. Used with permission of the publisher.

RACE, STEREOTYPES, AND PERCEPTIONS OF PERFORMERS ☐ *Dickson, Giuliano, Morris, and Cass*

Because stereotypes can influence the judgments and behaviors of perceivers, deviations from a stereotype should have similar effects. In general, the expectations of the perceiver and the extent to which these expectations are confirmed or disconfirmed can influence judgments. When behavior only slightly varies from expectations, the difference might not be noticed, but perceivers often magnify the discrepancy when actions differ significantly from expectations. This phenomenon is known as the contrast effect (Brehm, Kassin, & Fein, 1999). In fact, a person who displays behavior inconsistent with societal expectations is often evaluated more extremely than is a person who behaves consistently with expectations (Knight, Giuliano, & Sanchez-Ross, 2001). Jackson, Sullivan, and Hodge (1993) examined the effects of describing stereotype-consistent or stereotype-inconsistent behavior of Black out-group targets and White in-group targets on social evaluations made by participants who assessed a college application. They found that people who deviate from a norm are judged more extremely than if they behave as the norm dictates. Specifically, stereotype-inconsistent Black applicants with strong credentials were evaluated more favorably than were strong White applicants, and stereotype-inconsistent White applicants with weak credentials were evaluated less favorably than were weak Black applicants.

Both stereotypes and stereotype-inconsistent behavior affect the evaluations individuals make about other people in a variety of social interactions. Fried (1996, 1999) studied biased reactions involving the music industry and found that individuals had very different reactions to music labeled as *rap* or *country* despite the fact that the song lyrics were exactly the same. In two studies, she found that people generally considered rap music to be more violent and more offensive than country music. Furthermore, a folk song that was presented as being performed by a Black artist was judged more negatively than the very same song when it was presented as being performed by a White artist (Fried, 1996). Fried (1999) attributed her results to stereotypes in that rap is usually associated with Black culture whereas country music is often thought of as being a part of White culture. By priming a Black stereotype with the use of the label rap, it is possible that individuals apply negative stereotypes that have been shown to be associated with African Americans (Brigham, 1971). Therefore, racial stereotypes can impact evaluations of music performers (Fried, 1996, 1999).

According to Fiske and Taylor (1991), long-held stereotypes are not easily altered, but modification of stereotypes may begin with a divergence by stereotyped individuals or groups. Previous research has examined the effects of stereotypes and stereotype deviation on people's evaluations of other individuals (Jackson et al., 1993; Knight et al., 2001). The present study attempted to integrate and expand on these concepts in relation to the music industry. Specifically, whereas Fried (1996, 1999) examined the effect of either the race of the performer or the labeled genre of music of a song on evaluations about the music itself, the design of the present experiment explored the interactive effects of the race of the performer and the genre of music on participants' evaluations of the performer. In doing so, we explored the difference between perceptions of persons who adhere to social expectations versus persons who deviate from the stereotype.

Consistent with previous research (Jackson et al., 1993; Knight et al., 2001), we expected that participants would judge performers who behave consistently with social norms (i.e., Black rap artists and White country performers) more favorably than performers who deviate from societal expectations (i.e., White rap artists and Black country performers). That is, because country music is associated with White culture, a Black country performer does not exhibit behavior consistent with this stereotype and, as a result, this performer should elicit negative judgments. The same reaction should occur with a White rap artist because his or her behavior is inconsistent with the stereotype that rap is predominantly a part of Black culture.

Method

Participants

Data were collected from 100 undergraduates (48 men, 52 women) at Southwestern University, a small liberal arts college in the Southwest. Demographically, the university is composed primarily of White, middle- to upper middle-class students; as such, the current sample (which was representative of the campus at large) consisted almost exclusively of White students. Participant volunteers ranged in age from 18 to 26 years ($M = 19.77$ years). Data from four participants were excluded from the analysis because these participants either failed to follow instructions or they did not pass the manipulation check. Specifically, these participants were unable to identify the race of the performer and genre of his music that was presented in the their survey packet.

Design and Procedure

The present study used a 2 (race of performer: Black or White) × 2 (genre of music: rap or country) between-subjects design to explore the effect of the

176

FIGURE 14-18   (JA2).

race of a performer and the genre of music on perceptions of the performer. We recruited participants from various locations on campus and asked them to contribute to an investigation exploring "people's perceptions of music." Once they agreed, participants viewed a picture of a male performer, read a brief biography about him, and read a lyric sample of his music. Next, they completed a survey in which they made judgments about the performer and his music, and they responded to filler questions concerning their taste in music in general to corroborate the cover story. Each participant was randomly assigned to one of four experimental conditions and read a profile of either a Black rap artist, a White rap artist, a Black country performer, or a White country performer. Measures of the primary dependent variable (i.e., how favorably participants rated the performers) were embedded among filler questions in the survey. Following completion of the survey and a brief manipulation check that focused on the performer's race and the genre of music, we explained the purpose of the present study to the participants and asked them not to discuss it with anyone.

Materials

A three-page experimental packet, which ostensibly contained a survey about people's perceptions of music, was distributed along with an envelope. The first page contained a "performer profile" and included a color picture of a Black or White male performer, a brief biography about him indicating that he was either a rap or country performer, and a lyric sample from one of his songs. The subsequent pages contained the survey, which was used to measure participants' reactions to what they had seen and read on the previous page.

Each performer profile contained a biography that included the name of the performer (i.e., D.J. Jones), his hometown (Atlanta, Georgia), and a brief summary of his musical career (e.g., "D.J. has been singing since he was 14, and recently signed a record deal with a major country label. He will soon be on an international tour opening for a popular country artist"). To create the sample song lyrics, we slightly altered and combined two rock songs (May, 1973; May & Staffell, 1973; see Appendix A). With the exception of the two manipulations, we used the same biography and song lyrics in each of the four experimental conditions. The first manipulation altered the genre of music (i.e., rap or country) that the artist performed. Specifically, the name of the performer and the type of music he performed was labeled beneath his picture, and this label coincided with the genre of music described in the biography. Next, a

photograph manipulated the race of the performer so that each biography was accompanied by a picture of either a Black or a White man. To ensure that the only attribute differing between the Black and White performers was in fact race, we conducted a pilot test in a Research Methods class to match the Black and White performers on attractiveness and age. The participants in the pilot test were all White, which is representative of the ethnic composition of the participants in the present study. From a pool of 20 color photographs of nonfamous Black and White men selected from magazines, the two stimuli selected for the present study were most similar in perceived attractiveness and age.

Following the performer profile were the questions that assessed perceptions of the performer and his music, as well as the musical tastes of the participants. Embedded among demographic questions (e.g., sex and age) and other filler questions (e.g., "On average, how many CDs and/or tapes do you buy a month?") were the items that examined participants' perceptions of the performer. Specifically, participants rated on 7-point scales with endpoints labeled at 1 *(not at all)* and 7 *(very much)*: (a) "Overall, how much do you like this performer?"; (b) "How talented do you think this performer is?"; (c) "How legitimate is this performer?"; and finally (d) "How successful do you predict this performer will be in the music industry?" Because these items were highly correlated, they were combined into an overall index reflecting participants' favorability of the performer (Cronbach's $\alpha = .80$). The scores on the four items were averaged together, and consistent with the scales on the individual items, the overall index is on a 7-point scale with higher numbers representing a more favorable perception of the performer and lower numbers indicating an unfavorable perception.

Results

A 2 (race of performer: Black or White) × 2 (genre of music: rap or country) between-subjects analysis of variance (ANOVA) was performed on the index assessing the favorability of the performer (i.e., likability, perceived talent, perceived legitimacy, and predicted success). Data analysis revealed a significant main effect of race such that Black performers ($M = 4.32$, $SD = .91$) were rated more positively than were White performers ($M = 3.76$, $SD = 1.00$), $F(1, 92) = 10.42$, $p = .002$, $\eta^2 = .10$. However, this main effect was qualified by the significant two-way interaction between race of performer and genre of music, which was consistent with predictions, $F(1, 92) = 26.72$, $p = .0001$, $\eta^2 = .23$. An inspection of the means in Figure 1 shows that participants rated a Black rap artist ($M =$

FIGURE 14-19   **(JA3).**

RACE, STEREOTYPES, AND PERCEPTIONS OF PERFORMERS □ *Dickson, Giuliano, Morris, and Cass*

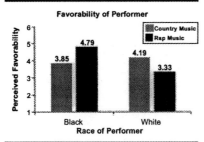

FIGURE 1

Mean ratings for favorability of the performer as a function of his race and the genre of music.

4.79, *SD* = .68) more favorably than a Black country artist (*M* = 3.85, *SD* = .87), *t*(46) = 4.17, *p* = .0001; however, they judged a White country artist (*M* = 4.19, *SD* = .92) more favorably than a White rap artist (*M* = 3.33, *SD* = .91), *t*(46) = 3.24, *p* = .0001. There was no main effect of genre of music, *F* < 1, *ns:* Participants reported similar ratings for rap performers (*M* = 4.06, *SD* = 1.09) and country performers (*M* = 4.02, *SD* = .90).

Discussion

The present study integrated and expanded on two lines of research. First, it extended previous research (Fried, 1996, 1999) on stereotyping involving the music industry. Whereas Fried (1996, 1999) examined reactions to music lyrics based on either the genre label or the performer's race, our study considered the interactive effect of both the race of the performer and the genre of music on people's evaluations of performers. The current study also differs from previous research conducted by Fried (1996, 1999) in that the lyrics in our study did not attempt to convey negative images such as violence or aggression. That is, Fried (1996, 1999) asked participants specifically about their negative impressions of the song lyrics (e.g., its offensiveness, its threat to society, its need for warning labels), whereas the current study emphasized overall impressions of the performer. Rap may be more often associated with negative topics, but these topics can be found in both rap and country music. We chose to use neutral lyrics in the present study because we were not focusing on the relation between negative themes and music genre. Instead, the current study was based on find-

ings that rap is associated with a Black culture that has both positive and negative attributes (Brigham, 1971). We examined the connection between music genre and the stereotype-consistent or stereotype-inconsistent race of the performer. In our study, participants judged Black rap artists more favorably than Black country music performers, whereas they judged White country music performers more favorably than White rap artists. These results support the hypothesis that individuals who deviate from societal expectations are judged more negatively than are individuals who adhere to social norms (Jackson et al., 1993; Knight et al., 2001). Manis, Nelson, and Shedler (1988) found that extreme stereotypes yielded contrast effects when behavior was discrepant from the established stereotype. In the present study, Black country music performers and White rap artists contrast from fairly ingrained societal expectations and thus received more negative judgments than did the performers who adhere to societal norms.

The present study could be extended in a number of ways. For example, like Fried's (1996, 1999) research, the current study also presented the lyric sample to participants on paper. It would be interesting to explore whether an audio-recorded lyric sample would affect participants' evaluations of performers or the music. Perhaps auditory processing and visual processing of stereotype-consistent and stereotype-inconsistent information differ. In addition, the present study could broaden its scope by including a more varied sample of participants. That is, future studies could incorporate participants of different races and ages. The data in the current study were collected primarily from White undergraduate students at a liberal arts university, and the results from such a homogenous sample may not necessarily generalize to alternative populations or settings. Furthermore, exploring alternate stereotype violations could support the findings of the present study, and one area of interest could be the world of sports. For instance, Black hockey players violate societal expectations similar to the apparent violation made by Black country music performers and White rap performers. According to our findings, Black hockey players would receive more negative evaluations than would White hockey players because their behavior is inconsistent with societal expectations.

Because the population of other minority groups (e.g., Latinos) is approaching that of the Black population in America, future research concerning racial stereotypes in the music industry could examine the impact of the increasing popularity of Latin music (Gonzales, 1990). Garcia and Zapatel (2000) recently examined how the labels *Black rap*, *Latino rap*, and

PSI CHI JOURNAL OF UNDERGRADUATE RESEARCH □ Winter 2001
Copyright 2001 by Psi Chi, The National Honor Society in Psychology (Vol. 6, No. 4, 175–180 / ISSN 1089-4136).

FIGURE 14-20   (JA4).

RACE, STEREOTYPES, AND PERCEPTIONS OF PERFORMERS □ *Dickson, Giuliano, Morris, and Cass*

alternative music influence perceptions made by both Anglo and Hispanic participants and found that participants' perceptions of music differed depending on their own race. Specifically, Hispanic participants judged music labeled *Latino rap* more positively than music labeled *alternative*, whereas Anglo participants rated music labeled *alternative* more favorably than music labeled *Latino rap*. Similar to previous findings (Jackson et al., 1993), out-group categories (i.e., *Latino rap* for Anglo participants and *alternative* music for Hispanic participants) were judged more negatively than were categories that corresponded to the participants' ethnicity. Extended to a more diverse sample, the present study could offer support for the idea that out-group categories are judged more negatively than in-group categories by examining the relation between participants' ethnicities and their evaluations of rap and country music. Thus, regardless of the race of the performer, Black participants would be expected to rate country music more negatively than rap music, whereas White participants would be expected to judge rap music more negatively than country music. Furthermore, it would be interesting to determine whether or not performers of Latin music will remain primarily Latin and to examine perceptions of stereotype-consistent and stereotype-inconsistent performers in this genre. If future performers do deviate from racial stereotypes, the present study suggests that non-Latino performers of Latin music would be perceived less favorably than would Latino performers.

In closing, Eminem and Charley Pride share a connection in that their actions deviate from widespread stereotypes that specific races are associated with certain types of music. Although people may recognize these two performers because of their musical talent, it is more likely that they are recognized because they were bold enough to defy stereotypes in the music industry. By being a White rap artist and a Black country music performer, Eminem and Charley Pride became forerunners for performers who do not adhere to social norms, and they may have possibly influenced numerous music fans to expect the unexpected.

References

Brehm, S. S., Kassin, S. M., & Fein, S. (1999). *Social psychology* (4th ed.). Boston: Houghton Mifflin.

Brigham, J. C. (1971). Ethnic stereotypes. *Psychological Bulletin, 76,* 15–38.

Devine, P. G. (1989). Stereotypes and prejudice: Their automatic and controlled components. *Journal of Personality and Social Psychology, 56,* 5–18.

Dovidio, J. F., Brigham, J. C., Johnson, B. T., & Gaertner, S. L. (1996). Stereotyping, prejudice, and discrimination: Another look. In N. C. Macrae, C. Stangor, & M. Hewstone (Eds.), *Stereotypes & stereotyping* (pp. 276–322). New York: Guilford Press.

Dovidio, J. F., Evans, N., & Tyler, R. B. (1986). Racial stereotypes: The contents of their cognitive representations. *Journal of Experimental Social Psychology, 22,* 22–37.

Dovidio, J. F., & Gaertner, S. L. (1991). Changes in the expression and assessment of racial prejudice. In H. R. Knopke, R. J. Norrell, & R. W. Rogers (Eds.), *Opening doors: Perspectives on race relations in contemporary America* (pp. 119–148). Tuscaloosa: University of Alabama Press.

Fiske, S. T., & Taylor, S. E. (1991). *Social cognition* (2nd ed.). New York: McGraw-Hill.

Fried, C. B. (1996). Bad rap for rap: Bias in reactions to music lyrics. *Journal of Applied Social Psychology, 26,* 2135–2146.

Fried, C. B. (1999). Who's afraid of rap: Differential reactions to music lyrics. *Journal of Applied Social Psychology, 29,* 705–721.

Gaertner, S. L., & Dovidio, J. F. (1986). The aversive form of racism. In J. F. Dovidio & S. L. Gaertner (Eds.), *Prejudice, discrimination, and racism: Theory and research* (pp. 61–89). Orlando, FL: Academic Press.

Gaertner, S. L., & McLaughlin, J. P. (1983). Racial stereotypes: Associations and ascriptions of positive and negative characteristics. *Social Psychology Quarterly, 46,* 23–30.

Garcia, S. D., & Zapatel, J. P. (2000, January). *Perceptions of lyrics as a function of ethnicity and music genre.* Paper presented at the annual meeting of the Social Psychologists in Texas, San Antonio.

Gonzales, J. L., Jr. (1990). *Racial and ethnic groups in America: A collection of readings.* Dubuque, IA: Kendall/Hunt.

Jackson, L. A., Sullivan, L. A., & Hodge, C. N. (1993). Stereotype effects on attributions, predictions, and evaluations: No two social judgments are quite alike. *Journal of Personality and Social Psychology, 65,* 69–84.

Knight, J. L., Giuliano, T. A., & Sanchez-Ross, M. G. (2001). Famous or infamous? The influence of celebrity status and race on perceptions of responsibility for rape. *Basic and Applied Social Psychology, 23,* 183–190.

Manis, M., Nelson, T. E., & Shedler, J. (1988). Stereotypes and social judgment: Extremity, assimilation, and contrast. *Journal of Personality and Social Psychology, 55,* 28–36.

May, B. (1973). The night comes down. [Recorded by Queen]. On *Queen* [Record]. London: EMI Records.

May, B., & Staffell, T. (1973). Doing all right. [Recorded by Queen]. On *Queen* [Record]. London: EMI Records.

Sagar, H. A., & Schofield, J. W. (1980). Racial and behavioral cues in Black and White children's perceptions of ambiguously aggressive acts. *Journal of Personality & Social Psychology, 39,* 590–598.

FIGURE 14-21 **(JA5).**

REVIEW SUMMARY

1. Psychologists have developed their own format, **APA style**, for the preparation of scientific reports.

2. The major sections of an APA paper include the title page, abstract, introduction, method, results, discussion, references, author note, tables, and figures.

3. The **title page** of a manuscript includes a manuscript page header and page number, the running head, the title, and author information.

4. The **abstract** provides a brief (100–120 words) summary of the contents of the paper.

5. The **introduction section** includes a thesis statement, literature review, and statement of the experimental hypothesis.

6. The **method section** contains a thorough description of the participants (**participants subsection**), the objects used in the experiment (**apparatus, materials, or testing instruments subsection**), and what took place during the study (**procedure subsection**).

7. The **results section** presents inferential and descriptive statistics to describe the experimental outcomes. **Figures** or **tables** may aid in presenting the statistical information.

8. In the **discussion section**, the researcher draws conclusions from the experiment by summarizing the results, comparing the results to previous research, and interpreting the results.

9. The **reference list** provides bibliographic information for any works cited in the paper. APA format includes different reference formats for periodical articles, books, chapters from edited books, and a host of other sources.

10. The **author note** allows the author to thank people for their help, cite a previous presentation of the findings, and designate a contact person for information about the experiment.

11. The specific sections of the APA-format paper are designated by various headings. **Level 1** and **level 3 headings** are most commonly used with experimental reports. For more complex papers, **level 4 headings** may need to be added.

CHECK YOUR PROGRESS

1. What is meant by the term *APA format*? Why was it developed?
2. Matching

   1. manuscript page header
   2. running head
   3. level 1 heading
   4. level 3 heading

   A. indicates the general topic you are interested in
   B. centered; upper- and lowercase letters
   C. first two or three words of the title
   D. left margin, underlined; upper- and lowercase letters

5. level 4 heading
6. thesis statement

E. condensed title

F. indented five spaces, underlined; only first word is capitalized; ends with period

3. Why is the abstract the most widely read section of most research reports?

4. How is the introduction section similar to what is found in a typical term paper? How is it different?

5. A citation includes three authors. The third citation of this study in the text should

   a. list all three authors

   b. list just the first author

   c. list the first author followed by et al.

   d. none of the above

6. List three different purposes of the method section. Which do you think is most important? Why?

7. We draw conclusions with _____ statistics and create a picture of our data with _____ statistics.

8. Could you use figures or tables as your sole information in a results section? Why or why not?

9. Some people believe that the discussion section is the most important section of an experiment report. Do you agree? Why or why not?

10. Why is the reference for a chapter from an edited book more complex than the reference for either a journal article or a book?

11. Matching:

   1. Title page
   2. Abstract
   3. Introduction
   4. Method
   5. Results
   6. Discussion
   7. References
   8. Author note

   A. presents statistical findings
   B. a short summary of the article
   C. includes full address of author
   D. reports the "bottom line" of the experiment
   E. includes manuscript page header and running head
   F. bibliographic information
   G. reviews previous research
   H. tells how the experiment was conducted

Writing in APA Style

We hope that you were a good student in your English composition classes because good writing is quite important in writing your research report. As we noted earlier, we do not want to attempt to teach writing, but we do want to provide some pointers you may find helpful. The topic of Chapter 2 in the *PM* is "expressing ideas." You should read that chapter carefully. In the next sections we will give you some general and specific guidelines that will assist you in writing your research report. As you will see, there are some differences between APA style and the way you learned to write in English classes. Scientific writing style is different in many ways from creative writing.

General Guidelines

The main objective of scientific writing is clear communication. It is your job to communicate your ideas as clearly as possible to the reader. The *PM* provides you with several hints about how to accomplish this goal; be sure to read pages 31–40 in the *PM* to supplement the following information.

Orderly Presentation of Ideas   The key idea here is continuity. From the beginning of your research report to the end, you are focusing on an idea or thought in which you tell the reader about your experiment. Do you remember sitting in class and getting lost in a lecture because you couldn't tell where the teacher was going (or where the teacher had been)? Those little side excursions in a lecture ("chasing rabbits") may be a delightful diversion in class, but they do tend to make you lose track of where you're going. Don't detour as you write your manuscript. Get on track and stay there with a singleminded purpose.

Smoothness of Expression   Writing in a continuous fashion will greatly aid your smoothness of expression. Creative writing is often not smooth because it uses literary devices to create tension or to conceal plot lines or to hide a surprise for later. Remember that scientific writing's goal is communication rather than escape and entertainment. One of the best things you can do to make your writing smooth is to work on transition sentences when you shift from one topic to another. Try to avoid abrupt shifts that make readers feel they have run into a wall.

Economy of Expression   Again, with your primary goal being communication, it is important to be direct and to the point in your writing. When journal editors work on submitted manuscripts, they have only a limited number of pages available for the printed journal; thus, it is to their advantage to have manuscripts that are short and communicative rather than long and unclear. Some people are surprised to find out that you can often shorten

"IN THE SOCIAL SCIENCES WE HARDLY USE NUMBERS, BUT WE CAN WRITE LONG, COMPLICATED SENTENCES."

Courtesy of Sidney Harris

We hope you recognize that both statements in this cartoon are incorrect. In psychology, we do use numbers and we work hard at communicating clearly.

your writing and make it clearer at the same time. The *PM* specifically advises you to avoid jargon, wordiness, and redundancy. Also, you should not repeat yourself. (Yes, that second sentence was there on purpose—did you catch the unnecessary repetition?)

Precision and Clarity   We encourage you to work on becoming a wordsmith rather than a wordmonger. As you probably know, a smith is someone who works with a particular material (e.g., a tinsmith, a goldsmith). A wordsmith works carefully with words, whereas a wordmonger uses words carelessly. Make sure the words you use fit the exact purpose and meaning that you have in mind. One of the major problems many of us have with writing is that we write in the same manner that we speak. Ambiguities may occur in speech, but we often clarify matters because we can interact directly with the speaker. Interaction is not possible when reading a text passage. Therefore, choose your words carefully so that you truly do say what you mean. Such clarity rarely occurs on a first attempt at writing—be sure that you reread and edit everything you write.

Strategies to Improve Writing Style   The *PM* (2001) suggests three approaches to becoming a more effective writer (p. 40).

1. ***Write from an outline.*** If you have a "road map" for your writing, you are more likely to arrive at your destination in a timely fashion.

2. ***Write your first draft, put it away, and reread it after a delay.*** If you attempt to cram your writing into a short time period, you will have difficulty editing your writing because you are likely to have the same thoughts you had a few minutes earlier. By giving yourself a time break, you are more likely to see the things you missed the first time—and it will be easier to think of ways to correct the problems.

3. ***Ask someone to evaluate your writing.*** It is usually quite helpful to have at least one other person read your papers before you submit them. It is easier for someone who is unfamiliar with the work to spot inconsistencies, weaknesses, ambiguities, and other flaws in your writing. Some instructors offer to critique rough drafts of your work—you should always take advantage of such an offer. Ask classmates to critique your writing and offer to do the same for them. You may learn a great deal both from their critiques and from reading and critiquing someone else's writing.

Grammatical Guidelines

The *PM* covers a variety of guidelines about grammar on pages 40–61. Most of these guidelines are standard conventions of grammar that you learned in grammar classes. We urge you to review these pages. Rather than turning this book into a grammar handbook at this point, we will cover only those conventions that are specific to APA style or with which students seem to have difficulty. Bellquist (1993) provided comprehensive guidelines for writing in psychology and other social sciences.

Passive Voice   According to the *PM*, as well as other style guides, you should use active voice rather than passive voice in writing your research report. In passive voice, the true object of the verb becomes the subject of the sentence and the true subject becomes the object. Passive voice often appears in methods sections because writers use the passivity to avoid personalizing that section. Let us give an example to clarify:

After viewing the slides, a recall test was given to participants.

This sentence is not direct and active; rather, it is indirect and passive. The test should be the object of the sentence, not the subject. Who did the acting? Presumably the experimenter did, but the experimenter is not even present in this sentence.

Reread the passive voice sentence. Can you recast it in active voice?

Actually, there are several ways you could change this sentence to make it active, depending on whether you want to include the experimenter. You could write

I gave the participants a recall test after they viewed the slides.

If you have coauthors for your experiment, the sentence could become this:

We gave the participants a recall test after they viewed the slides.

Although many experimenters seem to be uncomfortable using first person (*I, we*), the *PM* specifically permits it. In fact, the manual specifically says to avoid third-person references to yourself (e.g., "the experimenter," pp. 37–38). If you still wish to avoid first person, you could write

The participants took a recall test after viewing the slides.

In each of these sample sentences, you now have actors acting (active voice) rather than having something done to them (passive voice).

That* Versus *Which Clauses beginning with *that* are termed restrictive clauses and should be essential to the meaning of the sentence. Clauses beginning with *which* can be either restrictive or nonrestrictive (simply adding additional information). In APA style, you should confine yourself to using *which* for nonrestrictive clauses. Thus, *that* and *which* should not be used interchangeably. Using *which* is similar to making an "oh, by the way" addition to your sentence. To further help you distinguish the difference, remember that nonrestrictive clauses should be set off with commas. Let's look at an example:

The stimulus items *that* the participants did not recall were the more difficult items.

The phrase "that the participants did not recall" is essential to the sentence's meaning. Imagine the sentence without that phrase—it would make no sense. Let's look at another sentence:

The stimulus items, *which* were nouns, appeared on a computer monitor.

The phrase "which were nouns" is not essential to the meaning of this sentence. If we delete this phrase, the sentence retains its original meaning. The phrase does add some additional information about the stimulus items, but this information could be included elsewhere.

Words with Temporal Meaning The words *since* and *while* can cause difficulty in scientific writing because they have more than one meaning in everyday usage. Writers often use *since* interchangeably with *because* and use *while* to substitute for *although*. Some grammar books allow these multiple uses. APA style, however, does not. You should use *since* and *while* only for temporal purposes—in other words, to make time comparisons. Thus, use *while* to denote events that occur at the same time and *since* to denote that time has passed. Again, here are some examples:

> Many different IQ tests have evolved *since* Binet's original version.

Note that here *since* refers to time that has occurred after Binet's test; this sentence is acceptable.

> *Since* the XYZ group scored higher, we concluded that they learned the material better.

This use of *since* is incorrect—you should substitute *because* in its place.

> *While* the participants were studying the verbal items, they heard music.

Note that *while* in this sentence tells you that studying and music playing occurred simultaneously; this sentence is acceptable.

> *While* some psychologists believe in Skinner's ideas, many others have rejected his beliefs.

This use of *while* is incorrect—nothing is occurring at the same time. Instead, a contrast is being drawn. You should substitute *although* or *whereas* in this sentence.

Bias in Language   Remember that we stressed the use of unbiased language earlier in this chapter. We believe that this type of writing is important in helping maintain a neutral (unbiased) approach to science. Thus, we wish to remind you of the need for removing biased terms from your writing. The *PM* gives three guidelines that may be helpful in reducing bias in writing (pp. 61–76).

- *Describe at the appropriate level of specificity*. In other words, you should describe people as specifically as you can. When we use broad terms to describe people, we are more likely to include people who should not be included. For example, "Japanese Americans" is more specific than "Asian Americans."
- *Be sensitive to labels*. When we use stereotyped labels, we are likely using terms that contain bias. Basically, we should refer to groups as they wish to be referred to rather than imposing our own labels on them. When at all possible, it is better to avoid labels. As the *PM* points out, "people diagnosed with schizophrenia" is both more accurate and more preferred than "schizophrenics" (p. 64).
- *Acknowledge participation*. This guideline is generally aimed at experiments using human participants, although it would not hurt us to keep it in mind for animal studies also. The general idea of this guideline is to make sure you remember that the participants in your experiment are individuals. This idea formed the rationale for changing the label *subjects* to the label *participants*. Using active rather than passive voice also helps to personalize your participants.

A Disclaimer   Please remember that we could not possibly squeeze all the grammar guidelines from the *PM* into this section. Again, we chose to highlight the few that we did because they may differ from what you learned in English classes or because we know that students (and professors) tend to have trouble with these points of grammar and usage. We did not leave out the others because they are unimportant or even less important. We urge you to read pages 40–61 in the *PM* to review your knowledge of grammar.

APA Editorial Style

Chapter 3 of the *PM* addresses APA editorial style on pages 77–214—virtually a third of the book. This chapter gives writers a style guide to follow that will help create uniformity in writing by different authors in different publications. We have already covered the most important aspects of APA editorial style in this chapter—levels of headings, metrication, statistical copy in text, tables, figures, reference citations in text, and reference lists.

In addition to the important aspects of APA editorial style we have covered to this point, you should be aware that the *PM* gives you guidance on issues such as punctuation, spelling, capitalization, italics, abbreviations, seriation, quotations, numbers, footnotes, and appendixes. Again, we do not have the space it would take to address every possible concern in this chapter. When you have questions about any of these matters, consult Chapter 3 in the *PM*.

Preparing Your Manuscript

Chapter 5 of the *PM* (pp. 283–320) provides the guidelines you need in order to actually type your experimental paper. This is probably one of the most-used chapters in the manual because it includes three sample papers (pp. 306–320). These sample papers include notations of specific sections of the manual for each important component of the paper. We hope that the combination of the sample manuscript in this chapter and the sample papers in the *PM* make typing your paper a relatively simple matter.

Chapter 5 of the *PM* is primarily a reference chapter much like Chapters 3 and 4. You should consult it whenever you have a question about typing a specific portion of your manuscript. Let us provide you a short list of the highlights of the typing instructions:

- *Line spacing*. Double-space everything everywhere.
- *Margins*. Use at least 1-inch margins on all sides. Keep in mind that the top margin refers to the point at which the text begins (not the manuscript page header and number). Thus, you can set the top margin in your word processor to less than 1 inch so that the text begins at least 1 inch down from the top of the paper.
- *Lines*. Set your word processor to left justification. Your paper should have a ragged right edge throughout (i.e., the right margin should not line up down the page). Do not divide or hyphenate words between lines.
- *Pages*. Number all pages (including the title page, excepting figures) consecutively. The following sections should begin on new pages: title page, abstract, introduction (remember not to label it *Introduction*), references, appendixes, author note, footnotes, tables (a separate page for each), figure captions (all on one sheet), figures (each on a separate page).

- *Word spacing.* Space once after all punctuation, including plus and minus signs in equations. There is no spacing before or after hyphens (-) or dashes (– or —). Use a hyphen to denote a negative value; in this case, use a space before the hyphen but not after.
- *Quotations.* Enclose quotations that are shorter than 40 words in double quotation marks (" ") and write them as part of the text. You should block (indent) longer quotations from the left margin—be sure to double-space them.

Consult Table 14-2 for more comprehensive guidelines regarding APA formatting of your manuscript. If you have questions about other matters as you type your manuscript, consult Chapter 5 of the *PM*.

TABLE 14–2   Checklist for Correct APA Formatting

General Formatting and Typing

	Publication Manual Section
• There are 1-in. (2.54-cm) margins on all four sides of each page of the manuscript.	5.04
• The typeface is the correct size (12 points on a word processor) and the correct style (serif typefaces such as Courier or Times Roman).	5.02
• The manuscript is double-spaced throughout, including title page, references, tables, figure captions, author notes, and appendixes.	5.03
• The page header is the first two or three words of the title.	5.06
• The page number appears (a) on the same line with the page header and is five spaces to the right or (b) below the page header.	5.06
• The page header and page number are typed at the top of each page of the manuscript (except pages containing figures).	5.06
• The page header and figure number are handwritten on the back of figures (or on the front, outside the image area of the figure).	5.22
• There is only one space after these punctuation marks: commas, colons, semicolons, punctuation at the end of sentences, periods in citations, and all periods in the references section.	5.11
• Lowercase letters in parentheses have been used to indicate a series of events or items within a paragraph.	5.12
• Words are not broken (hyphenated) at the end of a line.	5.04
• All units of measurements have correct abbreviations.	3.25, 3.51

• Arabic numbers have been used correctly to express
    all numbers in the abstract
    numbers that are 10 or larger
    numbers that immediately precede a unit of measurement
	3.42

TABLE 14-2 Continued

	Publication Manual Section
numbers that represent fractions and percentages	
numbers that represent times, dates, ages, participants, samples, populations, scores, or points on a scale	
numbers less than 10 *only when* those numbers are compared to a number greater than 10 (e.g., "Participants included 15 humanities and 3 natural science majors.")	
Words have been correctly used to express	3.43
numbers less than 10	
numbers at the beginning of a title, sentence, or heading	

Title Page

The running head is aligned with the left margin and is equal to or less than 50 characters and spaces long.	5.15, 1.06
The author note *does not* appear on the title page; instead, the author note appears on a separate page after tables, figures, and appendixes (if included).	3.89, 5.20

Abstract

The word Abstract is typed at the top of the page.	5.16
The first line of the abstract is even with the left margin.	5.16
The abstract is not more than 120 words.	1.07, 5.16

Body of the Manuscript

There are *no* one-sentence paragraphs.	2.03
Gender-inclusive language is used through plural pronouns (e.g., *they, their*), by using nouns (e.g., *one, an individual, participant's*), sparse use of *he or she* or *she or he*, or by sparse use of alternating between gendered pronouns (e.g., *he . . . ; she . . .*).	2.13
The words *male* and *female* are used *only* as adjectives (e.g., *female* quail), whereas the words *men, women, boys,* and *girls* are used as nouns.	Table 2.1
Quotations are word-for-word accurate and page numbers are provided.	3.35, 3,39
The word *while* is used *only* to indicate events that take place simultaneously (alternatives: *although, whereas, and, but*).	2.10
The word *since* is used *only* to indicate the passage of time (alternative: *because*).	2.10
Terms that are abbreviated are written out completely the first time they are used, then always abbreviated thereafter.	3.21

(continued)

TABLE 14-2 Continued

	Publication Manual Section
Latin abbreviations are used sparingly and *only* in parenthetical material.	3.24
The word *and* is used in citations outside of parentheses.	3.95
The ampersand (*&*) is used in citations within parentheses.	3.07, 3.95
When two or more citations are in parentheses, the citations are typed in the same order in which they appear in the references section.	3.99
Each and every citation used in the manuscript is correctly typed in the references section.	4.01, 4.02
The phrase *et al.* is used with each citation that lists six or more authors, and with each citation that lists three to five authors *after* the first instance of that citation.	3.95
In the method section the word *participants* is consistently used (use *subjects* only with animals).	1.09, 2.12
In the results section all test statistics (e.g., *F, t, p*) are italicized.	3.19, 3.58
References Section	
All entries are typed in alphabetical order.	4.04
Each and every entry occurs in the body of the manuscript.	4.01
Authors' names are separated by commas.	4.08
The volume numbers of journals are italicized.	4.11
Each entry is typed in a "hanging indent" format, meaning that the first ine of each reference is flush with the left margin and subsequent lines are indented.	4.07, 5.18
The names of journals, book chapters, and books are correctly capitalized.	4.11

Source: Adapted from J. Dunn, K. Ford, K. L. Rewey, J. A. Juve, A. Weiser, and S. F. Davis, 2001, "A modified presubmission checklist," *Psi Chi Journal of Undergraduate Research, 6,* 142–144.

REVIEW SUMMARY

1. The primary goal of scientific writing is clear communication.
2. Goals that aid in clear communication are orderly presentation of ideas, smoothness of expression, economy of expression, and a striving for precision and clarity.

3. To improve your writing style you should write from an outline, put away your first draft before editing it, and have someone evaluate your writing.

4. You should use active voice whenever possible in writing your research report.

5. *That* should be used only with restrictive clauses, which include information that is essential to the meaning of a sentence. *Which* should be used in nonrestrictive clauses, which add information but are not essential to a sentence's meaning.

6. *Since* should not be used to substitute for *because*, nor should *while* substitute for *although*. Both *since* and *while* should be used only for temporal (time-related) meaning.

7. Psychologists strive to use unbiased language in their writing.

8. APA style includes guidelines on diverse matters such as punctuation, capitalization, quotations, numbers, appendixes, and typing guidelines.

9. The *Publication Manual of the American Psychological Association* (2001) is the stylebook for psychological writing. It contains a wealth of information about the writing process.

CHECK YOUR PROGRESS

1. What would be wrong with writing your research paper in the style of Twain, Hemingway, or Faulkner? Be as specific as possible in your answer.

2. What are the three strategies to improve your writing style? As you list each strategy, also tell what you would have to change about your writing style to incorporate the strategy.

3. Which of the following illustrates passive voice?
   a. The experimenter gave the memory test to the participants.
   b. The participants took the personality test after a rest period.
   c. The endurance test was given by the experimenter's assistant.
   d. All of the above.
   e. None of the above.

4. Change each of the following sentences in passive voice to active voice.
   a. An experiment was conducted by Jones (1995).
   b. The participants were seated in desks around the room.
   c. The stimulus items were projected from the rear of the cubicle.
   d. A significant interaction was found.

5. Choose the correct sentence from each pair below. Add punctuation if necessary. Explain your answers.
   a. The experimenter tested the animals which were older first.
      The experimenter tested the animals that were older first.
   b. A room which was a classroom was the testing environment.
      A room that was a classroom was the testing environment.

6. Decide whether each sentence below is correct or incorrect. If it is incorrect, correct it.

   a. Since you are older, you should go first.

   b. Since I began that class, I have learned much about statistics.

   c. While we are watching TV, we can also study.

   d. While you are older than I, I should still go first.

7. Use unbiased language to express each phrase.

Orientals	elderly
mankind	girls and men
mothering	chairman
homosexuals	depressives

8. Correct the following incorrect expressions.

a+b=c	trial - by - trial
− 1	Enter: Your name

KEY TERMS

LOOKING AHEAD

At this point we have reached the end of this text—there is no Chapter 15 to look ahead to. We do, however, look ahead to your research career. Perhaps your research career will be nonexistent; you may not be required to design, plan, and conduct an experiment as part of this course or another course. In this case, we hope you have learned something about research that will make you a critical consumer of research information in the future. Perhaps your research career will entail only one study—the one you conduct for this course. We believe this book will prove helpful for you in that endeavor. Finally, perhaps some of you now envision an ongoing research career for yourselves. We hope this book has opened your eyes to the powerful possibilities of experimental research in psychology and that you are eager to follow that path in the future.

   Regardless of what your future plans regarding research are, we hope we have made you think, challenged you to work, helped you contemplate conducting research, and perhaps entertained and amused you a little along the way. All of you will be faced with research in some fashion in your future. We wish you luck as you begin your journey.

 Statistical Tables

TABLE A-1 THE t DISTRIBUTION*

df	α LEVELS FOR TWO-TAILED TEST					
	.20	.10	.05	.02	.01	.001
	α LEVELS FOR ONE-TAILED TEST					
	.10	.05	.025	.01	.005	.0005
1	3.078	6.314	12.706	31.821	63.657	636.619
2	1.886	2.920	4.303	6.965	9.925	31.598
3	1.638	2.353	3.182	4.541	5.841	12.924
4	1.533	2.132	2.776	3.747	4.604	8.610
5	1.476	2.015	2.571	3.365	4.032	6.869
6	1.440	1.943	2.447	3.143	3.707	5.959
7	1.415	1.895	2.365	2.998	3.499	5.408
8	1.397	1.860	2.306	2.896	3.355	5.041
9	1.383	1.833	2.262	2.821	3.250	4.781
10	1.372	1.812	2.228	2.764	3.169	4.587
11	1.363	1.796	2.201	2.718	3.106	4.437
12	1.356	1.782	2.179	2.681	3.055	4.318
13	1.350	1.771	2.160	2.650	3.012	4.221
14	1.345	1.761	2.145	2.624	2.977	4.140
15	1.341	1.753	2.131	2.602	2.947	4.073
16	1.337	1.746	2.120	2.583	2.921	4.015
17	1.333	1.740	2.110	2.567	2.898	3.965
18	1.330	1.734	2.101	2.552	2.878	3.922
19	1.328	1.729	2.093	2.539	2.861	3.883
20	1.325	1.725	2.086	2.528	2.845	3.850
21	1.323	1.721	2.080	2.518	2.831	3.819
22	1.321	1.717	2.074	2.508	2.819	3.792
23	1.319	1.714	2.069	2.500	2.807	3.767
24	1.318	1.711	2.064	2.492	2.797	3.745
25	1.316	1.708	2.060	2.485	2.787	3.725
26	1.315	1.706	2.056	2.479	2.779	3.707
27	1.314	1.703	2.052	2.473	2.771	3.690
28	1.313	1.701	2.048	2.467	2.763	3.674
29	1.311	1.699	2.045	2.462	2.756	3.659
30	1.310	1.697	2.042	2.457	2.750	3.646
40	1.303	1.684	2.021	2.423	2.704	3.551
60	1.296	1.671	2.000	2.390	2.660	3.460
120	1.289	1.658	1.980	2.358	2.617	3.373
∞	1.282	1.645	1.960	2.326	2.576	3.291

*To be significant the t obtained from the data must be equal to or larger than the value shown in the table.

Source: Table A-1 is taken from Table III of Fisher and Yates, *Statistical Tables for Biological, Agricultural and Medical Research.* Published by Longman Group UK Ltd., 1974. We are grateful to the Longman Group UK Ltd., on behalf of the literary Executor of the late Sir Ronald A. Fisher, F.R.S. and Dr. Frank Yates F.R.S for permission to reproduce Table III from Statistical Tables for *Biological, Agricultural and Medical Research* 61E (1974).

.05 (ROMAN) AND .01 (BOLDFACE) α LEVELS FOR THE DISTRIBUTION OF F

DEGREES OF FREEDOM (FOR THE NUMERATOR)

Degrees of freedom (for the denominator)

df	1	2	3	4	5	6	7	8	9	10	11	12	14	16	20	24	30	40	50	75	100	200	500	∞
1	161	200	216	225	230	234	237	239	241	242	243	244	245	246	248	249	250	251	252	253	253	254	254	254
	4,052	**4,999**	**5,403**	**5,625**	**5,764**	**5,859**	**5,928**	**5,981**	**6,022**	**6,056**	**6,082**	**6,106**	**6,142**	**6,169**	**6,208**	**6,234**	**6,258**	**6,286**	**6,302**	**6,323**	**6,334**	**6,352**	**6,361**	**6,366**
2	18.51	19.00	19.16	19.25	19.30	19.33	19.36	19.37	19.38	19.39	19.40	19.41	19.42	19.43	19.44	19.45	19.46	19.47	19.47	19.48	19.49	19.49	19.50	19.50
	98.49	**99.00**	**99.17**	**99.25**	**99.30**	**99.33**	**99.34**	**99.36**	**99.38**	**99.40**	**99.41**	**99.42**	**99.43**	**99.44**	**99.45**	**99.46**	**99.47**	**99.48**	**99.48**	**99.49**	**99.49**	**99.49**	**99.50**	**99.50**
3	10.13	9.55	9.28	9.12	9.01	8.94	8.88	8.84	8.81	8.78	8.76	8.74	8.71	8.69	8.66	8.64	8.62	8.60	8.58	8.57	8.56	8.54	8.54	8.53
	34.12	**30.82**	**29.46**	**28.71**	**28.24**	**27.91**	**27.67**	**27.49**	**27.34**	**27.23**	**27.13**	**27.05**	**26.92**	**26.83**	**26.69**	**26.60**	**26.50**	**26.41**	**26.35**	**26.27**	**26.23**	**26.18**	**26.14**	**26.12**
4	7.71	6.94	6.59	6.39	6.26	6.16	6.09	6.04	6.00	5.96	5.93	5.91	5.87	5.84	5.80	5.77	5.74	5.71	5.70	5.68	5.66	5.65	5.64	5.63
	21.20	**18.00**	**16.69**	**15.98**	**15.52**	**15.21**	**14.98**	**14.80**	**14.66**	**14.54**	**14.45**	**14.37**	**14.24**	**14.15**	**14.02**	**13.93**	**13.83**	**13.74**	**13.69**	**13.61**	**13.57**	**13.52**	**13.48**	**13.46**
5	6.61	5.79	5.41	5.19	5.05	4.95	4.88	4.82	4.78	4.74	4.70	4.68	4.64	4.60	4.56	4.53	4.50	4.46	4.44	4.42	4.40	4.38	4.37	4.36
	16.26	**13.27**	**12.06**	**11.39**	**10.97**	**10.67**	**10.45**	**10.27**	**10.15**	**10.05**	**9.96**	**9.89**	**9.77**	**9.68**	**9.55**	**9.47**	**9.38**	**9.29**	**9.24**	**9.17**	**9.13**	**9.07**	**9.04**	**9.02**
6	5.99	5.14	4.76	4.53	4.39	4.28	4.21	4.15	4.10	4.06	4.03	4.00	3.96	3.92	3.87	3.84	3.81	3.77	3.75	3.72	3.71	3.69	3.68	3.67
	13.74	**10.92**	**9.78**	**9.15**	**8.75**	**8.47**	**8.26**	**8.10**	**7.98**	**7.87**	**7.79**	**7.72**	**7.60**	**7.52**	**7.39**	**7.31**	**7.23**	**7.14**	**7.09**	**7.02**	**6.99**	**6.94**	**6.90**	**6.88**
7	5.59	4.74	4.35	4.12	3.97	3.87	3.79	3.73	3.68	3.63	3.60	3.57	3.52	3.49	3.44	3.41	3.38	3.34	3.32	3.29	3.28	3.25	3.24	3.23
	12.25	**9.55**	**8.45**	**7.85**	**7.46**	**7.19**	**7.00**	**6.84**	**6.71**	**6.62**	**6.54**	**6.47**	**6.35**	**6.27**	**6.15**	**6.07**	**5.98**	**5.90**	**5.85**	**5.78**	**5.75**	**5.70**	**5.67**	**5.65**
8	5.32	4.46	4.07	3.84	3.69	3.58	3.50	3.44	3.39	3.34	3.31	3.28	3.23	3.20	3.15	3.12	3.08	3.05	3.03	3.00	2.98	2.96	2.94	2.93
	11.26	**8.65**	**7.59**	**7.01**	**6.63**	**6.37**	**6.19**	**6.03**	**5.91**	**5.82**	**5.74**	**5.67**	**5.56**	**5.48**	**5.36**	**5.28**	**5.20**	**5.11**	**5.06**	**5.00**	**4.96**	**4.91**	**4.88**	**4.86**
9	5.12	4.26	3.86	3.63	3.48	3.37	3.29	3.23	3.18	3.13	3.10	3.07	3.02	2.98	2.93	2.90	2.86	2.82	2.80	2.77	2.76	2.73	2.72	2.71
	10.56	**8.02**	**6.99**	**6.42**	**6.06**	**5.80**	**5.62**	**5.47**	**5.35**	**5.26**	**5.18**	**5.11**	**5.00**	**4.92**	**4.80**	**4.73**	**4.64**	**4.56**	**4.51**	**4.45**	**4.41**	**4.36**	**4.33**	**4.31**
10	4.96	4.10	3.71	3.48	3.33	3.22	3.14	3.07	3.02	2.97	2.94	2.91	2.86	2.82	2.77	2.74	2.70	2.67	2.64	2.61	2.59	2.56	2.55	2.54
	10.04	**7.56**	**6.55**	**5.99**	**5.64**	**5.39**	**5.21**	**5.06**	**4.95**	**4.85**	**4.78**	**4.71**	**4.60**	**4.52**	**4.41**	**4.33**	**4.25**	**4.17**	**4.12**	**4.05**	**4.01**	**3.96**	**3.93**	**3.91**
11	4.84	3.98	3.59	3.36	3.20	3.09	3.01	2.95	2.90	2.86	2.82	2.79	2.74	2.70	2.65	2.61	2.57	2.53	2.50	2.47	2.45	2.42	2.41	2.40
	9.65	**7.20**	**6.22**	**5.67**	**5.32**	**5.07**	**4.88**	**4.74**	**4.63**	**4.54**	**4.46**	**4.40**	**4.29**	**4.21**	**4.10**	**4.02**	**3.94**	**3.86**	**3.80**	**3.74**	**3.70**	**3.66**	**3.62**	**3.60**
12	4.75	3.88	3.49	3.26	3.11	3.00	2.92	2.85	2.80	2.76	2.72	2.69	2.64	2.60	2.54	2.50	2.46	2.42	2.40	2.36	2.35	2.32	2.31	2.30
	9.33	**6.93**	**5.95**	**5.41**	**5.06**	**4.82**	**4.65**	**4.50**	**4.39**	**4.30**	**4.22**	**4.16**	**4.05**	**3.98**	**3.86**	**3.78**	**3.70**	**3.61**	**3.56**	**3.49**	**3.46**	**3.41**	**3.38**	**3.36**
13	4.67	3.80	3.41	3.18	3.02	2.92	2.84	2.77	2.72	2.67	2.63	2.60	2.55	2.51	2.46	2.42	2.38	2.34	2.32	2.28	2.26	2.24	2.22	2.21
	9.07	**6.70**	**5.74**	**5.20**	**4.86**	**4.62**	**4.44**	**4.30**	**4.19**	**4.10**	**4.02**	**3.96**	**3.85**	**3.78**	**3.67**	**3.59**	**3.51**	**3.42**	**3.37**	**3.30**	**3.27**	**3.21**	**3.18**	**3.16**

408

*To be significant the F obtained from the data must be equal to or larger than the value shown in the table.

Source: Statistical Methods (6th ed.) by G. W. Snedecor and W. G. Cochran, 1967, Ames, Iowa: Iowa State University Press. Used by permission of the Iowa State University Press.

DEGREES OF FREEDOM (FOR THE NUMERATOR)

Degrees of freedom (for the denominator)

	1	2	3	4	5	6	7	8	9	10	11	12	14	16	20	24	30	40	50	75	100	200	500	∞	
14	4.60 / **8.86**	3.74 / **6.51**	3.34 / **5.56**	3.11 / **5.03**	2.96 / **4.69**	2.85 / **4.46**	2.77 / **4.28**	2.70 / **4.14**	2.65 / **4.03**	2.60 / **3.94**	2.56 / **3.86**	2.53 / **3.80**	2.48 / **3.70**	2.44 / **3.62**	2.39 / **3.51**	2.35 / **3.43**	2.31 / **3.34**	2.27 / **3.26**	2.24 / **3.21**	2.21 / **3.14**	2.19 / **3.11**	2.16 / **3.06**	2.14 / **3.02**	2.13 / **3.00**	14
15	4.54 / **8.68**	3.68 / **6.36**	3.29 / **5.42**	3.06 / **4.89**	2.90 / **4.56**	2.79 / **4.32**	2.70 / **4.14**	2.64 / **4.00**	2.59 / **3.89**	2.55 / **3.80**	2.51 / **3.73**	2.48 / **3.67**	2.43 / **3.56**	2.39 / **3.48**	2.33 / **3.36**	2.29 / **3.29**	2.25 / **3.20**	2.21 / **3.12**	2.18 / **3.07**	2.15 / **3.00**	2.12 / **2.97**	2.10 / **2.92**	2.08 / **2.89**	2.07 / **2.87**	15
16	4.49 / **8.53**	3.63 / **6.23**	3.24 / **5.29**	3.01 / **4.77**	2.85 / **4.44**	2.74 / **4.20**	2.66 / **4.03**	2.59 / **3.89**	2.54 / **3.78**	2.49 / **3.69**	2.45 / **3.61**	2.42 / **3.55**	2.37 / **3.45**	2.33 / **3.37**	2.28 / **3.25**	2.24 / **3.18**	2.20 / **3.10**	2.16 / **3.01**	2.13 / **2.96**	2.09 / **2.89**	2.07 / **2.86**	2.04 / **2.80**	2.02 / **2.77**	2.01 / **2.75**	16
17	4.45 / **8.40**	3.59 / **6.11**	3.20 / **5.18**	2.96 / **4.67**	2.81 / **4.34**	2.70 / **4.10**	2.62 / **3.93**	2.55 / **3.79**	2.50 / **3.68**	2.45 / **3.59**	2.41 / **3.52**	2.38 / **3.45**	2.33 / **3.35**	2.29 / **3.27**	2.23 / **3.16**	2.19 / **3.08**	2.15 / **3.00**	2.11 / **2.92**	2.08 / **2.86**	2.04 / **2.79**	2.02 / **2.76**	1.99 / **2.70**	1.97 / **2.67**	1.96 / **2.65**	17
18	4.41 / **8.28**	3.55 / **6.01**	3.16 / **5.09**	2.93 / **4.58**	2.77 / **4.25**	2.66 / **4.01**	2.58 / **3.85**	2.51 / **3.71**	2.46 / **3.60**	2.41 / **3.51**	2.37 / **3.44**	2.34 / **3.37**	2.29 / **3.27**	2.25 / **3.19**	2.19 / **3.07**	2.15 / **3.00**	2.11 / **2.91**	2.07 / **2.83**	2.04 / **2.78**	2.00 / **2.71**	1.98 / **2.68**	1.95 / **2.62**	1.93 / **2.59**	1.92 / **2.57**	18
19	4.38 / **8.18**	3.52 / **5.93**	3.13 / **5.01**	2.90 / **4.50**	2.74 / **4.17**	2.63 / **3.94**	2.55 / **3.77**	2.48 / **3.63**	2.43 / **3.52**	2.38 / **3.43**	2.34 / **3.36**	2.31 / **3.30**	2.26 / **3.19**	2.21 / **3.12**	2.15 / **3.00**	2.11 / **2.92**	2.07 / **2.84**	2.02 / **2.76**	2.00 / **2.70**	1.96 / **2.63**	1.94 / **2.60**	1.91 / **2.54**	1.90 / **2.51**	1.88 / **2.49**	19
20	4.35 / **8.10**	3.49 / **5.85**	3.10 / **4.94**	2.87 / **4.43**	2.71 / **4.10**	2.60 / **3.87**	2.52 / **3.71**	2.45 / **3.56**	2.40 / **3.45**	2.35 / **3.37**	2.31 / **3.30**	2.28 / **3.23**	2.23 / **3.13**	2.18 / **3.05**	2.12 / **2.94**	2.08 / **2.86**	2.04 / **2.77**	1.99 / **2.69**	1.96 / **2.63**	1.92 / **2.56**	1.90 / **2.53**	1.87 / **2.47**	1.85 / **2.44**	1.84 / **2.42**	20
21	4.32 / **8.02**	3.47 / **5.78**	3.07 / **4.87**	2.84 / **4.37**	2.68 / **4.04**	2.57 / **3.81**	2.49 / **3.65**	2.42 / **3.51**	2.37 / **3.40**	2.32 / **3.31**	2.28 / **3.24**	2.25 / **3.17**	2.20 / **3.07**	2.15 / **2.99**	2.09 / **2.88**	2.05 / **2.80**	2.00 / **2.72**	1.96 / **2.63**	1.93 / **2.58**	1.89 / **2.51**	1.87 / **2.47**	1.84 / **2.42**	1.82 / **2.38**	1.81 / **2.36**	21
22	4.30 / **7.94**	3.44 / **5.72**	3.05 / **4.82**	2.82 / **4.31**	2.66 / **3.99**	2.55 / **3.76**	2.47 / **3.59**	2.40 / **3.45**	2.35 / **3.35**	2.30 / **3.26**	2.26 / **3.18**	2.23 / **3.12**	2.18 / **3.02**	2.13 / **2.94**	2.07 / **2.83**	2.03 / **2.75**	1.98 / **2.67**	1.93 / **2.58**	1.91 / **2.53**	1.87 / **2.46**	1.84 / **2.42**	1.81 / **2.37**	1.80 / **2.33**	1.78 / **2.31**	22
23	4.28 / **7.88**	3.42 / **5.66**	3.03 / **4.76**	2.80 / **4.26**	2.64 / **3.94**	2.53 / **3.71**	2.45 / **3.54**	2.38 / **3.41**	2.32 / **3.30**	2.28 / **3.21**	2.24 / **3.14**	2.20 / **3.07**	2.14 / **2.97**	2.10 / **2.89**	2.04 / **2.78**	2.00 / **2.70**	1.96 / **2.62**	1.91 / **2.53**	1.89 / **2.48**	1.84 / **2.41**	1.82 / **2.37**	1.79 / **2.32**	1.77 / **2.28**	1.76 / **2.26**	23
24	4.26 / **7.82**	3.40 / **5.61**	3.01 / **4.72**	2.78 / **4.22**	2.62 / **3.90**	2.51 / **3.67**	2.43 / **3.50**	2.36 / **3.36**	2.30 / **3.25**	2.26 / **3.17**	2.22 / **3.09**	2.18 / **3.03**	2.13 / **2.93**	2.09 / **2.85**	2.02 / **2.74**	1.98 / **2.66**	1.94 / **2.58**	1.89 / **2.49**	1.86 / **2.44**	1.82 / **2.36**	1.80 / **2.33**	1.76 / **2.27**	1.74 / **2.23**	1.73 / **2.21**	24
25	4.24 / **7.77**	3.38 / **5.57**	2.99 / **4.68**	2.76 / **4.18**	2.60 / **3.86**	2.49 / **3.63**	2.41 / **3.46**	2.34 / **3.32**	2.28 / **3.21**	2.24 / **3.13**	2.20 / **3.05**	2.16 / **2.99**	2.11 / **2.89**	2.06 / **2.81**	2.00 / **2.70**	1.96 / **2.62**	1.92 / **2.54**	1.87 / **2.45**	1.84 / **2.40**	1.80 / **2.32**	1.77 / **2.29**	1.74 / **2.23**	1.72 / **2.19**	1.71 / **2.17**	25
26	4.22 / **7.72**	3.37 / **5.53**	2.98 / **4.64**	2.74 / **4.14**	2.59 / **3.82**	2.47 / **3.59**	2.39 / **3.42**	2.32 / **3.29**	2.27 / **3.17**	2.22 / **3.09**	2.18 / **3.02**	2.15 / **2.96**	2.10 / **2.86**	2.05 / **2.77**	1.99 / **2.66**	1.95 / **2.58**	1.90 / **2.50**	1.85 / **2.41**	1.82 / **2.36**	1.78 / **2.28**	1.76 / **2.25**	1.72 / **2.19**	1.70 / **2.15**	1.69 / **2.13**	26
27	4.21 / **7.68**	3.35 / **5.49**	2.96 / **4.60**	2.73 / **4.11**	2.57 / **3.79**	2.46 / **3.56**	2.37 / **3.39**	2.30 / **3.26**	2.25 / **3.14**	2.20 / **3.06**	2.16 / **2.98**	2.13 / **2.93**	2.08 / **2.83**	2.03 / **2.74**	1.97 / **2.63**	1.93 / **2.55**	1.88 / **2.47**	1.84 / **2.38**	1.80 / **2.33**	1.76 / **2.25**	1.74 / **2.21**	1.71 / **2.16**	1.68 / **2.12**	1.67 / **2.10**	27
28	4.20 / **7.64**	3.34 / **5.45**	2.95 / **4.57**	2.71 / **4.07**	2.56 / **3.76**	2.44 / **3.53**	2.36 / **3.36**	2.29 / **3.23**	2.24 / **3.11**	2.19 / **3.03**	2.15 / **2.95**	2.12 / **2.90**	2.06 / **2.80**	2.02 / **2.71**	1.96 / **2.60**	1.91 / **2.52**	1.87 / **2.44**	1.81 / **2.35**	1.78 / **2.30**	1.75 / **2.22**	1.72 / **2.18**	1.69 / **2.13**	1.67 / **2.09**	1.65 / **2.06**	28
29	4.18 / **7.60**	3.33 / **5.42**	2.93 / **4.54**	2.70 / **4.04**	2.54 / **3.73**	2.43 / **3.50**	2.35 / **3.33**	2.28 / **3.20**	2.22 / **3.08**	2.18 / **3.00**	2.14 / **2.92**	2.10 / **2.87**	2.05 / **2.77**	2.00 / **2.68**	1.94 / **2.57**	1.90 / **2.49**	1.85 / **2.41**	1.80 / **2.32**	1.77 / **2.27**	1.73 / **2.19**	1.71 / **2.15**	1.68 / **2.10**	1.65 / **2.06**	1.64 / **2.03**	29

DEGREES OF FREEDOM (FOR THE NUMERATOR)

Degrees of freedom (for the denominator)

df	1	2	3	4	5	6	7	8	9	10	11	12	14	16	20	24	30	40	50	75	100	200	500	∞	
30	4.17	3.32	2.92	2.69	2.53	2.42	2.34	2.27	2.21	2.16	2.12	2.09	2.04	1.99	1.93	1.89	1.84	1.79	1.76	1.72	1.69	1.66	1.64	1.62	14
	7.56	**5.39**	**4.51**	**4.02**	**3.70**	**3.47**	**3.30**	**3.17**	**3.06**	**2.98**	**2.90**	**2.84**	**2.74**	**2.66**	**2.55**	**2.47**	**2.38**	**2.29**	**2.24**	**2.16**	**2.13**	**2.07**	**2.03**	**2.01**	
32	4.15	3.30	2.90	2.67	2.51	2.40	2.32	2.25	2.19	2.14	2.10	2.07	2.02	1.97	1.91	1.86	1.82	1.76	1.74	1.69	1.67	1.64	1.61	1.59	15
	7.50	**5.34**	**4.46**	**3.97**	**3.66**	**3.42**	**3.25**	**3.12**	**3.01**	**2.94**	**2.86**	**2.80**	**2.70**	**2.62**	**2.51**	**2.42**	**2.34**	**2.25**	**2.20**	**2.12**	**2.08**	**2.02**	**1.98**	**1.96**	
34	4.13	3.28	2.88	2.65	2.49	2.38	2.30	2.23	2.17	2.12	2.08	2.05	2.00	1.95	1.89	1.84	1.80	1.74	1.71	1.67	1.64	1.61	1.59	1.57	16
	7.44	**5.29**	**4.42**	**3.93**	**3.61**	**3.38**	**3.21**	**3.08**	**2.97**	**2.89**	**2.82**	**2.76**	**2.66**	**2.58**	**2.47**	**2.38**	**2.30**	**2.21**	**2.15**	**2.08**	**2.04**	**1.98**	**1.94**	**1.91**	
36	4.11	3.26	2.86	2.63	2.48	2.36	2.28	2.21	2.15	2.10	2.06	2.03	1.98	1.93	1.87	1.82	1.78	1.72	1.69	1.65	1.62	1.59	1.56	1.55	17
	7.39	**5.25**	**4.38**	**3.89**	**3.58**	**3.35**	**3.18**	**3.04**	**2.94**	**2.86**	**2.78**	**2.72**	**2.62**	**2.54**	**2.43**	**2.35**	**2.26**	**2.17**	**2.12**	**2.04**	**2.00**	**1.94**	**1.90**	**1.87**	
38	4.10	3.25	2.85	2.62	2.46	2.35	2.26	2.19	2.14	2.09	2.05	2.02	1.96	1.92	1.85	1.80	1.76	1.71	1.67	1.63	1.60	1.57	1.54	1.53	18
	7.35	**5.21**	**4.34**	**3.86**	**3.54**	**3.32**	**3.15**	**3.02**	**2.91**	**2.82**	**2.75**	**2.69**	**2.59**	**2.51**	**2.40**	**2.32**	**2.22**	**2.14**	**2.08**	**2.00**	**1.97**	**1.90**	**1.86**	**1.84**	
40	4.08	3.23	2.84	2.61	2.45	2.34	2.25	2.18	2.12	2.07	2.04	2.00	1.95	1.90	1.84	1.79	1.74	1.69	1.66	1.61	1.59	1.55	1.53	1.51	19
	7.31	**5.18**	**4.31**	**3.83**	**3.51**	**3.29**	**3.12**	**2.99**	**2.88**	**2.80**	**2.73**	**2.66**	**2.56**	**2.49**	**2.37**	**2.29**	**2.20**	**2.11**	**2.05**	**1.97**	**1.94**	**1.88**	**1.84**	**1.81**	
42	4.07	3.22	2.83	2.59	2.44	2.32	2.24	2.17	2.11	2.06	2.02	1.99	1.94	1.89	1.82	1.78	1.73	1.68	1.64	1.60	1.57	1.54	1.51	1.49	20
	7.27	**5.15**	**4.29**	**3.80**	**3.49**	**3.26**	**3.10**	**2.96**	**2.86**	**2.77**	**2.70**	**2.64**	**2.54**	**2.46**	**2.35**	**2.26**	**2.17**	**2.08**	**2.02**	**1.94**	**1.91**	**1.85**	**1.80**	**1.78**	
44	4.06	3.21	2.82	2.58	2.43	2.31	2.23	2.16	2.10	2.05	2.01	1.98	1.92	1.88	1.81	1.76	1.72	1.66	1.63	1.58	1.56	1.52	1.50	1.48	21
	7.24	**5.12**	**4.26**	**3.78**	**3.46**	**3.24**	**3.07**	**2.94**	**2.84**	**2.75**	**2.68**	**2.62**	**2.52**	**2.44**	**2.32**	**2.24**	**2.15**	**2.06**	**2.00**	**1.92**	**1.88**	**1.82**	**1.78**	**1.75**	
46	4.05	3.20	2.81	2.57	2.42	2.30	2.22	2.14	2.09	2.04	2.00	1.97	1.91	1.87	1.80	1.75	1.71	1.65	1.62	1.57	1.54	1.51	1.48	1.46	22
	7.21	**5.10**	**4.24**	**3.76**	**3.44**	**3.22**	**3.05**	**2.92**	**2.82**	**2.73**	**2.66**	**2.60**	**2.50**	**2.42**	**2.30**	**2.22**	**2.13**	**2.04**	**1.98**	**1.90**	**1.86**	**1.80**	**1.76**	**1.72**	
48	4.04	3.19	2.80	2.56	2.41	2.30	2.21	2.14	2.08	2.03	1.99	1.96	1.90	1.86	1.79	1.74	1.70	1.64	1.61	1.56	1.53	1.50	1.47	1.45	23
	7.19	**5.08**	**4.22**	**3.74**	**3.42**	**3.20**	**3.04**	**2.90**	**2.80**	**2.71**	**2.64**	**2.58**	**2.48**	**2.40**	**2.28**	**2.20**	**2.11**	**2.02**	**1.96**	**1.88**	**1.84**	**1.78**	**1.73**	**1.70**	
50	4.03	3.18	2.79	2.56	2.40	2.29	2.20	2.13	2.07	2.02	1.98	1.95	1.90	1.85	1.78	1.74	1.69	1.63	1.60	1.55	1.52	1.48	1.46	1.44	24
	7.17	**5.06**	**4.20**	**3.72**	**3.41**	**3.18**	**3.02**	**2.88**	**2.78**	**2.70**	**2.62**	**2.56**	**2.46**	**2.39**	**2.26**	**2.18**	**2.10**	**2.00**	**1.94**	**1.86**	**1.82**	**1.76**	**1.71**	**1.68**	
55	4.02	3.17	2.78	2.54	2.38	2.27	2.18	2.11	2.05	2.00	1.97	1.93	1.88	1.83	1.76	1.72	1.67	1.61	1.58	1.52	1.50	1.46	1.43	1.41	25
	7.12	**5.01**	**4.16**	**3.68**	**3.37**	**3.15**	**2.98**	**2.85**	**2.75**	**2.66**	**2.59**	**2.53**	**2.43**	**2.35**	**2.23**	**2.15**	**2.06**	**1.96**	**1.90**	**1.82**	**1.78**	**1.71**	**1.66**	**1.64**	
60	4.00	3.15	2.76	2.52	2.37	2.25	2.17	2.10	2.04	1.99	1.95	1.92	1.86	1.81	1.75	1.70	1.65	1.59	1.56	1.50	1.48	1.44	1.41	1.39	26
	7.08	**4.98**	**4.13**	**3.65**	**3.34**	**3.12**	**2.95**	**2.82**	**2.72**	**2.63**	**2.56**	**2.50**	**2.40**	**2.32**	**2.20**	**2.12**	**2.03**	**1.93**	**1.87**	**1.79**	**1.74**	**1.68**	**1.63**	**1.60**	
65	3.99	3.14	2.75	2.51	2.36	2.24	2.15	2.08	2.02	1.98	1.94	1.90	1.85	1.80	1.73	1.68	1.63	1.57	1.54	1.49	1.46	1.42	1.39	1.37	27
	7.04	**4.95**	**4.10**	**3.62**	**3.31**	**3.09**	**2.93**	**2.79**	**2.70**	**2.61**	**2.54**	**2.47**	**2.37**	**2.30**	**2.18**	**2.09**	**2.00**	**1.90**	**1.84**	**1.76**	**1.71**	**1.64**	**1.60**	**1.56**	
70	3.98	3.13	2.74	2.50	2.35	2.23	2.14	2.07	2.01	1.97	1.93	1.89	1.84	1.79	1.72	1.67	1.62	1.56	1.53	1.47	1.45	1.40	1.37	1.35	28
	7.01	**4.92**	**4.08**	**3.60**	**3.29**	**3.07**	**2.91**	**2.77**	**2.67**	**2.59**	**2.51**	**2.45**	**2.35**	**2.28**	**2.15**	**2.07**	**1.98**	**1.88**	**1.82**	**1.74**	**1.69**	**1.62**	**1.56**	**1.53**	
80	3.96	3.11	2.72	2.48	2.33	2.21	2.12	2.05	1.99	1.95	1.91	1.88	1.82	1.77	1.70	1.65	1.60	1.54	1.51	1.45	1.42	1.38	1.35	1.32	29
	6.96	**4.88**	**4.04**	**3.56**	**3.25**	**3.04**	**2.87**	**2.74**	**2.64**	**2.55**	**2.48**	**2.41**	**2.32**	**2.24**	**2.11**	**2.03**	**1.94**	**1.84**	**1.78**	**1.70**	**1.65**	**1.57**	**1.52**	**1.49**	

DEGREES OF FREEDOM (FOR THE NUMERATOR)

Degrees of freedom (for the denominator)

	1	2	3	4	5	6	7	8	9	10	11	12	14	16	20	24	30	40	50	75	100	200	500	∞
100	3.94 **6.90**	3.09 **4.82**	2.70 **3.98**	2.46 **3.51**	2.30 **3.20**	2.19 **2.99**	2.10 **2.82**	2.03 **2.69**	1.97 **2.59**	1.92 **2.51**	1.88 **2.43**	1.85 **2.36**	1.79 **2.26**	1.75 **2.19**	1.68 **2.06**	1.63 **1.98**	1.57 **1.89**	1.51 **1.79**	1.48 **1.73**	1.42 **1.64**	1.39 **1.59**	1.34 **1.51**	1.30 **1.46**	1.28 **1.43**
125	3.92 **6.84**	3.07 **4.78**	2.68 **3.94**	2.44 **3.47**	2.29 **3.17**	2.17 **2.95**	2.08 **2.79**	2.01 **2.65**	1.95 **2.56**	1.90 **2.47**	1.86 **2.40**	1.83 **2.33**	1.77 **2.23**	1.72 **2.15**	1.65 **2.03**	1.60 **1.94**	1.55 **1.85**	1.49 **1.75**	1.45 **1.68**	1.39 **1.59**	1.36 **1.54**	1.31 **1.46**	1.27 **1.40**	1.25 **1.37**
150	3.91 **6.81**	3.06 **4.75**	2.67 **3.91**	2.43 **3.44**	2.27 **3.14**	2.16 **2.92**	2.07 **2.76**	2.00 **2.62**	1.94 **2.53**	1.89 **2.44**	1.85 **2.37**	1.82 **2.30**	1.76 **2.20**	1.71 **2.12**	1.64 **2.00**	1.59 **1.91**	1.54 **1.83**	1.47 **1.72**	1.44 **1.66**	1.37 **1.56**	1.34 **1.51**	1.29 **1.43**	1.25 **1.37**	1.22 **1.33**
200	3.89 **6.76**	3.04 **4.71**	2.65 **3.88**	2.41 **3.41**	2.26 **3.11**	2.14 **2.90**	2.05 **2.73**	1.98 **2.60**	1.92 **2.50**	1.87 **2.41**	1.83 **2.34**	1.80 **2.28**	1.74 **2.17**	1.69 **2.09**	1.62 **1.97**	1.57 **1.88**	1.52 **1.79**	1.45 **1.69**	1.42 **1.62**	1.35 **1.53**	1.32 **1.48**	1.26 **1.39**	1.22 **1.33**	1.19 **1.28**
400	3.86 **6.70**	3.02 **4.66**	2.62 **3.83**	2.39 **3.36**	2.23 **3.06**	2.12 **2.85**	2.03 **2.69**	1.96 **2.55**	1.90 **2.46**	1.85 **2.37**	1.81 **2.29**	1.78 **2.23**	1.72 **2.12**	1.67 **2.04**	1.60 **1.92**	1.54 **1.84**	1.49 **1.74**	1.42 **1.64**	1.38 **1.57**	1.32 **1.47**	1.28 **1.42**	1.22 **1.32**	1.16 **1.24**	1.13 **1.19**
1000	3.85 **6.66**	3.00 **4.62**	2.61 **3.80**	2.38 **3.34**	2.22 **3.04**	2.10 **2.82**	2.02 **2.66**	1.95 **2.53**	1.89 **2.43**	1.84 **2.34**	1.80 **2.26**	1.76 **2.20**	1.70 **2.09**	1.65 **2.01**	1.58 **1.89**	1.53 **1.81**	1.47 **1.71**	1.41 **1.61**	1.36 **1.54**	1.30 **1.44**	1.26 **1.38**	1.19 **1.28**	1.13 **1.19**	1.08 **1.11**
∞	3.84 **6.64**	2.99 **4.60**	2.60 **3.78**	2.37 **3.32**	2.21 **3.02**	2.09 **2.80**	2.01 **2.64**	1.94 **2.51**	1.88 **2.41**	1.83 **2.32**	1.79 **2.24**	1.75 **2.18**	1.69 **2.07**	1.64 **1.99**	1.57 **1.87**	1.52 **1.79**	1.46 **1.69**	1.40 **1.59**	1.35 **1.52**	1.28 **1.41**	1.24 **1.36**	1.17 **1.25**	1.11 **1.15**	1.00 **1.00**

TABLE A-3	CRITICAL VALUES FOR PEARSON PRODUCT-MOMENT CORRELATION COEFFICIENTS, r. TO BE SIGNIFICANT, THE OBTAINED r MUST BE EQUAL TO OR LARGER THAN THE TABLE VALUE.

	α LEVELS (TWO-TAILED TEST)				
df	.1	.05	.02	.01	.001
	α LEVELS (ONE-TAILED TEST)				
(df = N − 2)	.05	.025	.01	.005	.0005
1	.98769	.99692	.999507	.999877	.9999988
2	.90000	.95000	.98000	.990000	.99900
3	.8054	.8783	.93433	.95873	.99116
4	.7293	.8114	.8822	.91720	.97406
5	.6694	.7545	.8329	.8745	.95074
6	.6215	.7067	.7887	.8343	.92493
7	.5822	.6664	.7498	.7977	.8982
8	.5494	.6319	.7155	.7646	.8721
9	.5214	.6021	.6851	.7348	.8371
10	.4973	.5760	.6581	.7079	.8233
11	.4762	.5529	.6339	.6835	.8010
12	.4575	.5324	.6120	.6614	.7800
13	.4409	.5139	.5923	.6411	.7603
14	.4259	.4973	.5742	.6226	.7420
15	.4124	.4821	.5577	.6055	.7246
16	.4000	.4683	.5425	.5897	.7084
17	.3887	.4555	.5285	.5751	.6932
18	.3783	.4438	.5155	.5614	.6787
19	.3687	.4329	.5034	.5487	.6652
20	.3598	.4227	.4921	.5368	.6524
25	.3233	.3809	.4451	.4869	.5974
30	.2960	.3494	.4093	.4487	.5541
35	.2746	.3246	.3810	.4182	.5189
40	.2573	.3044	.3578	.3932	.4896
45	.2428	.2875	.3384	.3721	.4648
50	.2306	.2732	.3218	.3541	.4433
60	.2108	.2500	.2948	.3248	.4078
70	.1954	.2319	.2737	.3017	.3799
80	.1829	.2172	.2565	.2830	.3568
90	.1726	.2050	.2422	.2673	.3375
100	.1638	.1946	.2301	.2540	.3211

Source: Table VII of Fisher and Yates (1963), *Statistical Tables for Biological, Agricultural and Medical Research,* published by Longman Group, Ltd., London.

Appendix B

Selected Statistical Formulae

To help refresh your memory and understanding of the major statistical tests mentioned in the text, we have included complete formulae in this appendix. In all but one instance we present the raw-score formulae. (The one exception is the calculation of variance where we present the deviation-score formulae.)

In all instances, we have attempted to present the simplest formulae. If they look confusing or unfamiliar, consult your instructor, there are numerous ways to write these formulae. The meaning of statistical symbols and notations are presented where they might be confusing or unfamiliar. With these formulae you should be able to work any of the examples from the text by hand.

I. Variance and Standard Deviation

Sample

$$\text{Variance} = \frac{\Sigma (X - \overline{X})^2}{N - 1}$$

$$\text{Standard Deviation} = \sqrt{\text{variance}}$$

Population

$$\text{Variance} = \frac{\Sigma (X - \overline{X})^2}{N}$$

$$\text{Standard Deviation} = \sqrt{\text{variance}}$$

II. Pearson Product-Moment Correlation Coefficient

$$r = \frac{N\Sigma XY - (\Sigma X)(\Sigma Y)}{\sqrt{N\Sigma X^2 - (\Sigma X)^2][N\Sigma Y^2 - (\Sigma Y)^2]}}$$

Where N = The number of *pairs* of scores

III. t Test for Independent Samples

$$t = \frac{\overline{X}_1 - \overline{X}_2}{\sqrt{\frac{\left[\Sigma X_1^2 - \frac{(\Sigma X_1)^2}{N_1}\right] + \left[\Sigma X_2^2 - \frac{(\Sigma X_2)^2}{N_2}\right]}{(N_1 - 1) + (N_2 - 1)} \left(\frac{1}{N_1} + \frac{1}{N_2}\right)}}$$

IV.   *t* Test for Related Samples

$$t = \frac{\overline{X}_1 - \overline{X}_2}{\sqrt{\dfrac{\Sigma D^2 - \dfrac{(\Sigma D)^2}{N}}{N - 1}\left(\dfrac{1}{N}\right)}}$$

where: D = difference between measurement 1 and measurement 2

N = the number of *pairs* of scores

V.   One-Way Analysis of Variance

Between Groups Sum of Squares

$$SS_{BG} = \left[\frac{(\Sigma X_1)^2}{N_1} + \frac{(\Sigma X_2)^2}{N_2} + \ldots + \frac{(\Sigma X_j)^2}{N_j}\right] - \frac{(\Sigma X_{Total})^2}{N_{Total}}$$

Within Groups Sum of Squares

$$SS_{WG} = \left[\Sigma X_1^2 - \frac{(\Sigma X_1)^2}{N_1}\right] + \left[\Sigma X_2^2 - \frac{(\Sigma X_2)^2}{N_2}\right] + \ldots + \left[\Sigma X_j^2 - \frac{\Sigma X_j}{N_j}\right]$$

Total Sum of Squares

$$SS_{Total} = \Sigma X_{Total}^2 - \frac{(\Sigma X_{Total})^2}{N_{Total}}$$

Appendix C

Factorial Design with Three Independent Variables

Three-Way ANOVA for Independent Samples. As we mentioned in Chapter 11, the possibilities for factorial designs are almost limitless when you consider that you can vary the number of IVs, vary the number of levels for each IV, and vary how participants are assigned to groups for each IV. Thus, there is no way that we could cover every possible type of factorial design in Chapter 11. We concentrated on the simplest factorial designs (2×2) in order to provide a basic introduction. This Appendix gives an example of a factorial design involving three IVs. A three-way ANOVA for independent samples involves three IVs (thus the term *three-way*) that all use independent groups of participants.

To implement this design, we will make one final alteration to our first experiment involving clothing and customer sex in Chapter 11 (using the factorial between-groups design). Imagine that you are discussing your results from that experiment with a friend (remember that we found a significant interaction between clothing and customer sex such that men who were dressed in sloppy clothes received help from salesclerks most slowly). Your friend wonders aloud whether that result would hold true for all types of stores. (This is how experimental ideas develop sometimes!) That musing piques your curiosity, and you set out to test this new question. Trying to keep your design simple, you decide to contrast two different types of stores (a large discount store vs. an exclusive clothing store). Thus, your experimental design would now be a $2 \times 2 \times 2$ (clothing by customer sex by store type) completely randomized design (all groups composed of different participants). The general design for this experiment is depicted in Figure 11-9 on page 277. The response times of the clerks to the customers in the various treatment combinations appear in Table C-1. The means for the variables and their combinations also appear in Table C-1.

Computer Results. The source table for this analysis appears in Table C-2. As you can see, the table contains a wealth of information, neatly arranged by main effects, two-way interactions, and the three-way interaction. Remember we have talked many times about the notion that interactions qualify main effects. When we look at the three-way interaction, we find that it is significant ($p = .001$). If it had *not* been significant, then we would have examined and graphed the two-way interactions. (Although two of them—CLOTHES by STORE and CSEX by STORE—are significant, we do not interpret them because the three-way interaction supersedes them.) If the three-way interaction was not significant and none of the two-way interactions were significant, then we could have interpreted the main effects in a straightforward manner. Although CLOTHES and STORE show significance, we should not attempt to interpret them because the three-way interaction is significant. To interpret the CLOTHES by CSEX by STORE interaction, we must graph it (see Figure C-1).

Translating Statistics into Words. We found a significant three-way interaction. All other main effects and interactions are qualified because of this interaction. In Figure C-1, we see a classic interaction pattern as the lines on the graph cross.

From examining Figure C-1 carefully, it appears that salesclerks' response time to customers depended on the clothing and sex of the customer *and* the store in which the clerks

TABLE C–1   Clerk Response Time for Clothing by Customer Sex by Type of Store

EXCLUSIVE CLOTHING STORE

Customer Sex

	Women	Men
Casual	46 39 50 M = 48.17 52 48 54	38 50 38 M = 45.67 44 49 55
Sloppy	37 47 44 M = 51.50 62 49 70	47 69 69 M = 68.67 74 77 76

LARGE DISCOUNT STORE

Customer Sex

	Women	Men	
Casual	66 59 70 M = 61.50 72 48 54	58 70 58 M = 65.67 64 69 75	Casual M = 55.25
Sloppy	57 67 64 M = 71.50 82 69 90	61 52 54 M = 58.50 59 67 58	Casual M = 62.54

Women M = 58.17   Exclusive Clothing Store M = 53.50
Men M = 59.63   Large Discount Store M = 64.29

Total Population M = 58.90

TABLE C–2   Computer Output for Three-Way ANOVA for Independent Samples

SOURCE TABLE

SOURCE	SS	DF	MS	F	P
CLOTHES	638.02	1	638.02	7.69	.008
CSEX	25.52	1	25.52	.31	.582
STORE	1397.52	1	1397.52	16.85	.001
CLO × CSEX	4.69	1	4.69	.06	.813
CLO × STORE	414.19	1	414.19	4.99	.031
CSEX × STORE	414.19	1	414.19	4.99	.031
CLO × CSEX × STORE	1017.52	1	1017.52	12.27	.001
Residual	3316.83	40	82.92		
TOTAL	7228.48	47			

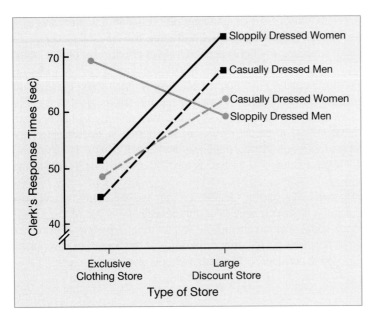

FIGURE C-1

worked. One line shows an obvious difference from the other three—the line for male customers in sloppy clothes. Notice that all three of the other groups (casually dressed men, casually dressed women, and sloppily dressed women) received slower service in the large discount store than in the exclusive clothing store. For sloppily dressed men, however, the pattern was reversed—they received faster attention in the discount store. We are not sure why these results occurred; we can only speculate. The pattern for the three similar groups probably depicts the experience most of us have had: It is far easier to find a salesclerk to help you in a "fancy" store than in a large discount store. On the other hand, perhaps clerks in the exclusive clothing store want nothing to do with a sloppily dressed man, so they ignore him for longer periods of time. In the large discount store, perhaps such a man gets help a little more quickly because the clerks are suspicious that he might be a shoplifter. Again, this is only conjecture—the type of hypothesizing we would save for our discussion section.

One last note about this design: We need to communicate our findings in APA style. You may shudder at the thought of writing such a large number of results in an APA-format paragraph. Fortunately, with larger designs such as this, researchers often take a shortcut when writing their results. Here's an example of a short way to communicate these findings.

The salesclerks' response times were analyzed with a three-way randomized ANOVA, using clothing, customer sex, and type of store as independent variables. The interaction of clothing by customer sex by store type was significant, $F(1, 40) = 12.27$, $p = .001$, $\eta^2 = .23$, and is graphed in Figure 1 [not shown]. All main effects and two-way interactions were qualified by the three-way interaction.

As you can see, we spent the bulk of our commentary on our significant effect and summarized the remaining six effects (three main effects and three two-way interactions) in a single sentence. This type of coverage is not only economical but also focuses on the important finding—the one that was significant and rendered the other significant effects moot. Remember in our discussion in Chapter 11 we pointed out how an interaction qualifies the main effects. Although our source table for this three-way ANOVA shows significant effects for both CLOTHES and STORE, neither makes sense by itself. We can't say that clerks react more quickly to customers dressed in casual clothes *or* that clerks in exclusive clothing stores respond to customers more quickly; the three-way interaction makes us realize that an explanation based solely on clothing or store type is too simplistic to describe the results that we found.

You may also remember that we said in Chapter 11 that factorial designs rarely use more than three or four IVs at a time. You have seen a three-way interaction in this Appendix; imagine adding a fourth variable to the interaction! Still, factorial experiments using two or three variables are quite popular with researchers because of the wealth of information they can provide. We urge you to consider such a design as you plan your research.

Appendix D

Check Your Progress Answers

Chapter 1

CHECK YOUR PROGRESS PAGE 12

1. tenacity

2. A

3. Your perception that the world may be altered and your knowledge base would not be accurate.

4. 1-C; 2-D; 3-A; 4-B; 5-E

5. The "self-correcting nature of science" refers to the fact that because scientific findings are open to public scrutiny, they can be replicated. Replications will reveal any errors and faulty logic.

6. B

7. The experimenter attempts to establish a cause-and-effect relation between the IV that is manipulated and the DV that is recorded.

8. B

CHECK YOUR PROGRESS PAGE 21

1. The steps involved in the research process include the following:

Finding a Problem. You detect a gap in the knowledge base.

Literature Review. Consulting previous reports determines what has been found in the research area of interest.

Theoretical Considerations. The literature review highlights theories that point to relevant research projects.

Hypothesis. The literature review also highlights hypotheses (statements of the relationship between variables in more restricted domains of the research area). Such hypotheses will assist in the development of the experimental hypothesis—the predicted outcome of your research project.

Research Design. You develop the general plan for conducting the research project.

Conduct the Experiment. You conduct the research project according to the experimental design.

Data Analysis and Statistical Decisions. Based upon the statistical analysis, you decide whether the independent variable exerted a significant effect upon the dependent variable.

Decisions in Terms of Past Research and Theory. The statistical results guide decisions concerning the relationship of the present research project to past research and theoretical considerations.

Preparation of the Research Report. You prepare a research report describing the rationale, conduct, and results of the experiment according to accepted American Psychological Association (APA) format.

Sharing Your Results: Presentation and Publication. You share your research report with colleagues at a professional society meeting and/or by publication in a professional journal.

Finding a New Problem. Your research results unearth another gap in our knowledge base and the research process begins again.

2. D

3. D

4. D

5. The reasons for taking a research methods or experimental psychology course include that they

    a. assist you in other psychology courses

    b. enable you to conduct a research project after graduation

    c. assist you in getting into graduate school

    d. help you to become a knowledgeable consumer of psychological research

Chapter 2

CHECK YOUR PROGRESS PAGE 46

1. 1-C; 2-A; 3-D; 4-B; 5-G; 6-F; 7-E

2. testable; likelihood of success

3. Nonsystematic sources of research ideas include those instances or occurrences that make us believe that the research idea was unplanned. These types of research ideas are shown through "inspiration," "serendipity," and "everyday occurrences." Systematic sources of research ideas are carefully organized and logically thought out. This source of research ideas may be found in "past research," "theory," and "classroom lectures."

4. C

5. D

6. Synthetic statements are used in the experimental hypothesis because they can be either true or false.

7. General implication form presents the experimental hypothesis as an "if . . . then" statement where the if portion of the statement refers to the IV manipulation and the then portion of the statement refers to the predicted changes in the DV.

8. D

9. inductive, deductive

10. B

Chapter 3

CHECK YOUR PROGRESS PAGES 66-67

1. The atrocities of World War II where prisoners of war were unwillingly subjected to experiments using drugs, viruses, and toxic agents. The Tuskegee syphilis study examined the course of untreated syphilis in a group of men who did not realize they were being studied. Doctors in the Willowbrook experiment purposely infected patients with hepatitis and did not give them treatment in order to study the development of the disease. Milgram's research on obedience studied the reaction to demands from an authority in participants who were being deceived.

2. The Nuremberg Code stressed the need to

    a. obtain participants' consent to participate in research

    b. inform participants about the nature of the research project

    c. avoid risks where possible

    d. protect participants against risks

    e. conduct research using qualified personnel

3. Deception may be needed if the results of a research project would be biased or contaminated by the participants knowing the nature of the experiment. A more general statement on the informed consent document in conjunction with a clear indication that the participants may terminate the project at any time might be used. Complete debriefing should follow the experiment.

4. A

5. D

6. The guidelines for the ethical use of animals in research involve attention to each of the following:

    I. *Justification of Research.* The research should have a clear scientific purpose.

    II. *Personnel.* Only trained personnel who are familiar with the animal care guidelines should be involved with the research. All procedures must conform to appropriate federal guidelines.

    III. *Care and Housing of Animals.* Animal housing areas must comply with current regulations.

    IV. *Acquisition of Animals.* If animals are not bred in the laboratory, they must be acquired in a lawful, humane manner.

    V. *Experimental Procedures.* "Humane consideration for the well-being of the animal should be incorporated into the design and conduct of all procedures involving animals, while keeping in mind the primary goal of experimental procedures—the acquisition of sound, replicable data."

    VI. *Field Research.* Field research must be approved by the appropriate review board. Investigators should take special precautions to disturb their research population(s) and the environment as little as possible.

    VII. *Educational Use of Animals.* The educational use of animals must be approved by the appropriate review board. Instruction in the ethics of animal research is encouraged.

7. The IRB is the Institutional Review Board. The typical IRB at a college or university is composed of faculty members from a variety of disciplines, members from the community, and a veterinarian if animal proposals are considered. The IRB examines proposed procedures, questionnaires, the informed consent document, debriefing plans, the use of pain in animals, and proposed procedures for animal disposal.

8. The experimenter is responsible for the ethical conduct of the research project and the ethical presentation of the research results.

9. Plagiarism refers to the use of someone else's work without giving credit to the original author. Fabrication of data involves the creation of fictitious research data. Pressures for job security (tenure), salary increases, and ego involvement in the research are factors that might lead to such unethical behaviors.

Chapter 4

CHECK YOUR PROGRESS PAGES 84–85

1. The reactance or reactivity effect refers to the biasing or influencing of the participants' scores or responses because they know they are being observed. Archival research avoids the reactance effect because the researcher does not observe the participants and the data of interest are recorded before they are used in the research project.

2. D

3. 1-C; 2-A; 3-D; 4-E; 5-B

4. Situation sampling and time sampling are used to provide greater generality for the research project.

5. The extent to which two observers agree is called interobserver reliability. It is calculated by dividing the number of times the observers agree by the number of opportunities for agreement and multiplying by 100. These calculations result in the percent agreement.

6. B

7. C

Chapter 5

CHECK YOUR PROGRESS PAGE 102

1. 1-D; 2-F; 3-G; 4-C; 5-A; 6-E; 7-B

2. The steps involved in developing a good survey include (a) determining how the information you seek is to be obtained and what type of instrument will you use, (b) determining the nature of the questions that will be used, (c) writing the items for your survey, (d) pilot testing your survey or questionnaire, (e) considering what demographic data are desired, and (f) specifying the procedures that will be followed in administering the survey or questionnaire.

3. D

4. The low return rate of mail surveys can be increased by (a) including a letter that clearly summarizes the nature and importance with the initial mailing (a self-addressed, prepaid return envelope should be included with the initial mailing) and (b) sending additional mailings at two- to three-week intervals.

5. The use of personal interviews is declining because (a) the expense involved in conducting them has increased greatly, (b) the fact that an individual administers the surveys increases the possibility for bias, and (c) the appeal of going from door to door is decreasing because of unavailability of respondents and high crime rates in large metropolitan areas.

6. Achievement tests are used to assess an individual's level of mastery or competence. Aptitude tests are used to assess an individual's skills or abilities.

7. D

8. population; sample

9. B

10. Random sampling occurs when every member of the population has an equal chance of being selected. Random sampling with replacement occurs when the chosen items are returned to the population and can be selected on future occasions. When random sampling without replacement is used, the chosen item is not returned to the population.

11. Stratified random sampling involves randomly selecting participants from a single layer or strata in the population (e.g., a limited age range). When stratified random sampling is used, group homogeneity is increased. The more homogeneous the sample, the less chances there are for nuisance variables to operate. The less the chance for nuisance variables to operate, the smaller the within-group variability.

12. The single-strata research approach attempts to secure research data from a single, specified segment of the population of interest. The cross-sectional research approach involves the comparison of two or more groups of participants during the same, rather limited, time span. The longitudinal research approach involves gathering information from a group of participants over an extended period of time.

Chapter 6

CHECK YOUR PROGRESS PAGES 117–118

1. variable

2. 1-E; 2-C; 3-A; 4-F; 5-B; 6-D

3. C

4. C

5. You should record more than one DV if the additional DV(s) add meaningful information.

6. C

CHECK YOUR PROGRESS PAGES 130–131

1. 1-C; 2-A; 3-B; 4-E; 5-D

2. A

3. A

4. When within-subject counterbalancing is used, each participant experiences more than one sequence of IV presentations. When within-group counterbalancing is used, each participant experiences a different sequence of IV presentations.

5. n! refers to factoring or breaking a number into its component parts and then multiplying these component parts. n! can be used to determine the number of sequences required for complete counterbalancing: $4! = 4 \times 3 \times 2 \times 1 = 24$.

6. B

7. The incomplete counterbalancing procedure refers to the use of some, but not all, of the possible sequences of treatment administration.

CHECK YOUR PROGRESS PAGE 140

1. A

2. B

3. It is important to evaluate your experiment for internal validity because you cannot place any confidence in your results if your experiment does not have internal validity. Cause-and-effect statements cannot be made without internal validity.

4. 1-B; 2-C; 3-D; 4-A

5. 1-D; 2-A; 3-B; 4-C

6. In this experiment the internal validity threat of selection is likely. Because we selected participants who are senior citizens, it is possible that they will have less formal education than college students of today. Obtaining a college education was not as common for today's senior citizens when they were young.

7. B

Chapter 7

CHECK YOUR PROGRESS PAGE 149

1. Once a precedent or established pattern for using a particular type of research participant is begun, it is likely that that type of participant will be used in experiments in the research area in question.

2. White rats and college students are the favorite participants in psychological research because of precedent and availability. An established pattern of research with these two populations has been established, and they are easy to obtain.

3. A

4. C

5. A

6. The experimenter must be careful not to become a slave to elaborate pieces of equipment. If this situation occurs, then it is likely that the equipment may begin dictating the type of research that is conducted and/or the type of DV that is recorded.

CHECK YOUR PROGRESS PAGE 158

1. The experimenter's physiological characteristics, psychological characteristics, and personal expectancies for the outcome of the experiment can operate as extraneous variables and influence the responses of the participants.

2. 1-C; 2-A; 3-B; 4-E; 5-D

3. A

4. Automated equipment and instruments to present instructions and record data are frequently used to control for experimenter expectancies because they help minimize experimenter contact with the participants. By minimizing contact with the participants, the experimenter is less likely to influence the outcome of the experiment.

5. B

6. C

CHECK YOUR PROGRESS PAGES 163–164

1. A

2. C

3. The goal of cross-cultural psychology is incompatible with ethnocentrism because ethnocentrism views other cultures as an extension of that culture. Hence, according to an ethnocentric view, there is no need for cross-cultural research.

4. Culture can influence the choice of the research problem, the nature of the experimental hypothesis, selection of the IV(s), selection of the DV(s), selection of participants, sampling procedures, and the type of questionnaire that is used.

5. B

Chapter 8

CHECK YOUR PROGRESS PAGE 183

1. 1-G; 2-E; 3-A; 4-C; 5-B; 6-F; 7-D

2. C

3. Because the three measures of central tendency (mean, median, and mode) are identical in a normal distribution, any one of them would serve as a representative measure of central tendency.

4. D

5. The ordinate is the vertical axis; it should be approximately two-thirds the size of the abscissa (horizontal axis). The DV is plotted on the ordinate, whereas the IV is plotted on the abscissa.

6. Because it takes into account only the highest and lowest scores and disregards the distribution of scores in between, the range does not convey much information.

7. A

8. Because the percentage of scores occurring between the mean and any standard deviation (e.g., 11, 12, −1, −2) away from the mean is constant, standard deviation scores from one distribution can be compared with standard deviation scores from other distributions.

CHECK YOUR PROGRESS PAGES 198–199

1. 1-F; 2-H; 3-I; 4-B; 5-D; 6-C; 7-G; 8-E; 9-A

2. A positive correlation indicates that as one variable increases, the other variable under consideration also increases, whereas a perfect positive correlation indicates that for every unit of increase in one variable there is a corresponding increase of one unit in the other variable.

3. A zero correlation indicates that changes in one variable are not systematically related to changes in the other variable.

4. When two independent groups are being compared, the t test compares the difference between the means of the two groups to the amount of variability (error) that exists within the two groups. Because the groups are assumed to be equivalent at the start of the experiment, larger t values indicate greater influence of the IV.

5. "Level of significance" refers to the point at which the experimenter feels that a result occurs rarely by chance. If an experimental result occurs rarely by chance, we conclude that it is significant. Although the experimenter arbitrarily sets the level of significance, tradition has established the .05 level as an accepted level of significance.

6. Because researchers don't always know how a research project is going to turn out, it is safer to state a nondirectional hypothesis and use a two-tail test. If a directional hypothesis is stated and the results turn out differently, then the researcher is forced to reject the experimental hypothesis even though differences may exist between the groups.

7. A

8. A

9. C

Chapter 9

CHECK YOUR PROGRESS PAGES 211–212

1. We cannot conduct a valid experiment with only one group because we have to have a second group for comparison purposes. We cannot tell whether our IV has any effect if we cannot compare the experimental group to a control group.

2. levels

3. Independent groups consist of participants who are totally unrelated to each other. Correlated groups are composed of pairs of participants who have some relationship to each other because (a) they have some natural relationship (natural pairs), (b) are matched with each other (matched pairs), or (c) are the same participants (repeated measures). This difference is important to experimental designs because it is one of the three questions we ask to choose an appropriate design for an experiment.

4. 1-D; 2-A; 3-B; 4-C

5. We must be cautious about the use of random assignment when we have small numbers of participants because the groups may end up being unequal before the experiment.

6. If your experiment could use either independent or correlated groups, you would most likely base your decision on the number of participants available to you. We often use correlated groups when we have a small number of participants so that we can be more confident about the equality of our groups. If you have many potential participants, independent groups will typically be equal.

7. b

CHECK YOUR PROGRESS PAGES 217–218

1. It is important for our groups to be equal before the experiment so that any difference we detect in our DV can be attributed to the IV.

2. between-groups variability; error variability

3. b

4. Correlated groups have the advantages of ensuring equality of the participants before the experiment and of reducing error variability. Independent groups are advantageous in that they are simpler than correlated groups and that they can be used in experimental situations that preclude correlated groups.

5. Many different answers are possible to the question about comparing differing amounts of an IV. Some representative examples include amount of study time or amount of reinforcement in a learning experiment, amount of pay or bonus on job performance, and length of therapy to treat a particular problem. As long as you chose a single IV and varied its amount (rather than presence vs. absence), your answer should be correct.

6. Again, many different answers are possible. Some possible answers include different types of life experiences, different majors, different musical preferences, and different hometowns. As long as you chose two levels of an IV that cannot be manipulated, your answer is correct.

CHECK YOUR PROGRESS PAGES 227–228

1. To compare the stereotyping of a group of female executives to the stereotyping of a group of male executives, you would use a *t* test for independent samples because men and women represent independent groups.

2. To compare the stereotyping of a group of male executives before and after the ERA, you would use a *t* test for correlated samples because this represents repeated measures.

3. a

4. We usually look for descriptive statistics first on a computer printout because this information helps us understand how the groups performed on the DV.

5. homogeneity of variance; heterogeneity of variance

6. words; numbers (statistical information)

7. Group A, with a mean of 75, scored significantly higher than Group B, which had a mean of 70.

8. Research is a cyclical, ongoing process because each experiment typically raises new questions. A multitude of examples of cyclical research could be given. For example, you might test a new antihyperactivity drug against a control group. If the drug is helpful, then you would need additional research to determine the most effective dosage. In the future, you would want to test this drug against new drugs that arrive on the market.

Chapter 10

CHECK YOUR PROGRESS PAGE 241

1. The two-group design is the building block for the multiple-group design because the multiple-group design essentially takes a two-group design and adds more groups to it. Thus, the multiple-group design is similar to changing a two-group design into a three-group design (or larger).

2. one; three

3. A multiple-group design allows you to ask and answer more questions than does a two-group design. You may be able to run only one experiment instead of two or three. Therefore, the multiple-group design is more efficient than the two-group design—you can save time, effort, participants, and so on.

4. There are many correct answers to this question. If you chose an IV that has more than two levels, your answer should be correct. For example, if you wished to test attendance in college students as a function of classification, you would use a multiple-group design with four groups (freshmen, sophomores, juniors, seniors).

5. Matched sets, repeated measures, and natural sets are all considered correlated groups because participants in such groups are related in some way.

6. There is no real limit on the number of groups in a multiple-group design. Practically speaking, it is rare to see more than four or five groups for a particular IV.

7. How many groups are required to adequately test your experimental hypothesis? Will you learn something important if you include more levels of your IV?

8. provide more control than independent groups designs

9. Practical considerations are more demanding in multiple correlated groups designs because there are simply more "equated" participants with which to deal. In repeated measures, participants must take part in more experimental sessions. Matched sets must include three (or more) matched participants. Natural sets require larger sets of participants.

10. To compare personality traits of firstborn, lastborn, and only children, we would use a multiple independent groups design (unless you matched participants on some variable). Repeated measures and natural sets are impossible (can you figure out why?). This would represent an ex post facto study because you cannot manipulate an individual's birth order.

CHECK YOUR PROGRESS PAGES 256–257

1.

CLASSIFICATION			
Freshman	Sophomore	Junior	Senior

This experiment would require a multiple independent groups design with four groups. The necessary statistical test would be a one-way ANOVA for independent groups (students could not be in more than one classification simultaneously).

2.   ACT/SAT ATTEMPTS
    1st Attempt   2nd Attempt   3rd Attempt

This question requires a multiple correlated groups design with three groups. The proper statistical test would be a one-way ANOVA for correlated groups because each student takes the test three times (repeated measures).

3. Because we have more than two groups, it is necessary to compute post hoc tests to tell which groups are significantly different from the others.

4. between groups; within groups

5. Given the statistical information shown, we can conclude that students perform differently on their three attempts at taking the ACT or SAT (i.e., there is a statistically significant difference).

6. To draw a full and complete conclusion from Question 5, you would need the results from post hoc tests comparing the three means. With this information you could conclude whether students improve over time in taking the entrance exam.

7. It was important to have the information from Chapter 9's continuing research problem so that we could begin a follow-up experiment with the knowledge that customers' clothing affects clerks' response times. The follow-up experiment, then, compared clerks' response times to three different clothing styles.

8. It depends. Do you want to measure the same people's moods across the four seasons (multiple correlated groups design) or four different groups of people in the four seasons (multiple independent groups)? Either approach is possible. Can you justify your answer? If you chose multiple correlated groups, your rationale should revolve around control issues. You should measure a large number of participants if you chose multiple independent groups.

9. It depends. Do you want the same people to eat at all four restaurants (multiple correlated groups) or to survey different people at each restaurant (multiple independent groups)? You could run the experiment either way. The rationale for your choice should be similar to that summarized in the answer to Question 8.

Chapter 11

CHECK YOUR PROGRESS PAGE 271

1. The two-group design is related to the factorial design because it forms the underlying basis of a factorial design. For example, a 2 × 2 factorial design is simply two two-group designs combined (see the shaded section below).

2. There is a practical limit to the number of IVs you can use in an experiment so that you will be able to interpret the results easily. Interactions involving many variables can be quite difficult to understand.

3. d

4. 1-C; 2-A; 3-B

5. two; four

6. Numerous correct answers are possible. Your answer should consist of an experiment with two IVs. One IV should be a between-subjects variable (no relationship between participants); one should be a within-subjects variable (repeated measures, matching, or natural groups). For example, you might assign students to either a group that takes an ACT or SAT preparation course or does not take such a course (between subjects). Each group would take the ACT or SAT twice (repeated measures).

CHECK YOUR PROGRESS PAGE 280

1. Factorial designs are combinations of the designs in Chapters 9 and 10 because a factorial design results from adding two (or more) simple designs (one IV each) together into a single design with two (or more) IVs; (e.g., see Figure 11-8).

2. A $2 \times 4 \times 3$ experimental design consists of three IVs; one has two levels, one has four levels, and one has three levels:

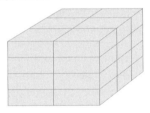

3. Totally between-groups designs use independent groups of participants for each IV. Totally within-groups designs use correlated groups of participants for all IVs. Mixed-groups designs have at least one IV that uses independent groups of participants and one that uses correlated groups. These designs are similar in that they are all factorial designs. They differ, of course, in the way that the experimenter assigns participants to groups.

4. Your experimental questions should be your first consideration in choosing a factorial design because the number of questions you ask will determine how many IVs your experiment will have.

5. measured

6. Your friend has listed six IVs that she wishes to include in her experiment. This is too ambitious for a beginning project, and the results could be incredibly difficult to interpret because of the many potential interactions.

7. a

CHECK YOUR PROGRESS PAGE 296

1. Your experimental design has two IVs, classification and sex. Both are between-subject variables because a participant cannot be in more than one group. You would use the

factorial between-group design and test the data with a factorial ANOVA for independent groups. Your block diagram would look like the following:

Freshman		
Sophomore		
Junior		
Senior		
	Male	Female

2. This experimental design has two IVs: test-taking practice and study course. Both are within-subject variables because each participant takes the tests repeatedly and takes the study course. You would use the factorial within-group design and use a factorial ANOVA for correlated groups to analyze the data. Your block diagram would be the following:

No study course			
With study course			
	1st Try	2nd Try	3rd Try

3. Again, you still have two IVs: the practice and the course. However, the study course is now a between-subject variable because some participants take it and some do not. Test-taking practice is a within-subject variable because each participant takes the test three times (repeated measures). Thus, you have factorial mixed-group design and would use a factorial ANOVA for mixed groups. Your block diagram would be the same as the one shown for Question 2—only the assignment of participants to groups differs.

4. An interaction effect is the simultaneous effect of two IVs in such a way that the effects of one IV depend on the particular level of the second IV. A significant interaction overrides any main effects because the interaction changes the meaning of the significant main effect.

5. a

6. This experiment has two IVs—the seasons and sex. Sex is always a between-subject variable, so you must choose between the factorial between-group design and the factorial mixed-groups design. Your decision rests upon how you wish to treat the participants with regard to the seasons. If you use different participants for each season, both IVs would be between subjects and you would use the factorial between-group design. If you wish to use the same participants for each season, you would use the factorial mixed-groups design. Your selection of a particular design would probably depend on how many participants you can find—with large numbers, using a between-subject manipulation is acceptable.

7. This experiment has two IVs—restaurant and age. Age must be between subjects; restaurant could be either between or within subjects based on whether the same or different people eat at each restaurant. Thus, your choices are the same as for Question 6.

Chapter 12

CHECK YOUR PROGRESS PAGE 307

1. random assignment; experimental design

2. It is essential to randomly assign participants to groups to help assure that the groups are equal before the experiment.

3. Random selection refers to choosing participants from a population in a nonsystematic manner. Random assignment refers to allocating those randomly selected participants to different groups in a nonsystematic manner.

4. It is problematic to use the pretest-posttest control group design to help with internal validity because this design cannot control all internal validity threats.

5. d

6. The drawback of using the Solomon four-group design to control for internal validity is that there is no statistical test to analyze all the data from this design.

7. The posttest-only control group design is a good choice for controlling internal validity because it seems to control the internal validity threats covered in Chapter 6.

Drawing a general diagram of the posttest-only control group design is not possible because the design can vary depending on the number of treatment groups in the experiment (e.g., see Figures 12-5 and 12-6).

CHECK YOUR PROGRESS PAGE 319

1. The use of single-case designs has decreased recently because of statistical innovations—an increase in both statistical tests and computerized analysis programs.

2. A single-case design can be used to disprove a theory because it takes only a single negative instance to invalidate a theory's general applicability.

3. baseline; three

4. a

5. For: Visual inspections of data may lead to incorrect conclusions. Statistical analysis gives increased accuracy.

Against: Treatments should produce effects that are visually apparent. Clinical significance is more important than statistical significance.

6. 1-C; 2-A; 3-B

7. You might be forced to use an A-B single-case design in the real world because it can be impractical or unethical to reverse a treatment. Many examples are possible. Suppose you work with an individual who suffers from anorexia or bulimia. You institute a treatment and the individual shows marked improvement. However, you fear that removing the treatment could result in a recurrence of the problem.

CHECK YOUR PROGRESS PAGE 329

1. Experimental designs involve manipulation of IVs, control of extraneous variables, and measurement of DVs so that cause-and-effect relationships can be determined. Ex post facto designs involve IVs that have already occurred or that are predetermined, such as sex. Quasi-experimental designs involve manipulating IVs with groups of participants that are predetermined, such as causing something to vary between men and women.

2. You might choose to use a quasi-experimental design rather than an experimental design in a situation when random assignment is impossible or if you wish to evaluate an ongoing program.

3. 1-B, C, F 2-A, D,* E

*Figure 12-14 gives the impression that the interrupted time-series design includes pretesting—in some cases, it may actually be pretesting. In many situations that use this design, however, the observations before the treatment are not true pretests because they were not made with an experiment in mind; rather, they may often simply represent data that were already available (e.g., sales records). This is a fine distinction, and it could easily be argued that both designs actually include pretesting.

4. The key element in Geronimus's research that allowed a more positive conclusion about teen pregnancy was the realization that finding a true control group would be impossible; hence the need for a strong comparison group.

5. We are more certain about our conclusion in the helmet law case because it simulated an A-B-A design, whereas the AFDC study was only an A-B design. If we can return to the baseline condition, we usually get a better reading of our results.

6. d

Chapter 13

CHECK YOUR PROGRESS PAGE 345

1. External validity is the ability to take your experimental findings and apply them beyond the experimental participants to the larger population. It is important to psychology so that we can develop general findings that apply to large groups of organisms.

2. b

3. Population generalization involves applying results from participants to the larger group. Environmental generalization involves applying your results to different settings than the original experiment. Temporal generalization involves applying experimental results to different times than in the experiment.

4. Using different types of participants helps increase the external validity of our findings.

5. Cross-cultural psychology involves testing psychological principles in different cultures to determine the generality of those principles. It is relevant to this chapter because it deals with external validity.

6. 1-C; 2-B; 3-D; 4-A

7. Mook thinks that external validity is necessary only when we are attempting to predict behavior in the real world. Much research in psychology is not aimed at such prediction, and Mook believes that external validity is not necessary in such situations.

8. It is almost impossible to achieve external validity in a single experiment because of the large number of threats to external validity. Usually an experiment can answer only one such threat at a time.

CHECK YOUR PROGRESS PAGE 355

1. Students should critically examine any research report for errors or faulty thinking. It is possible for anyone to make a mistake.

2. The literature review should lead directly to the research question. After reading the literature review, the research question is the next logical question to ask.

3. Control techniques are necessary in experimentation to prevent extraneous variables from affecting experimental results; these techniques allow for cause-and-effect explanations.

4. Three critique guidelines that deal with participants:

    a. Participants should be randomly selected from a population and randomly assigned to groups.

    b. Participant groups should be equal before the experiment.

    c. The research should use an adequate number of participants.

5. Statistics are vital to research reports because they provide the numerical evidence to support the author's claims.

6. c

7. The discussion should be tied to the results of a research report so that the researcher does not go beyond the data in drawing conclusions.

Chapter 14

CHECK YOUR PROGRESS PAGE 395

1. "APA format" refers to the accepted, standard form for preparing the results of psychological research that has been adopted by the American Psychological Association. APA format was developed in order to bring standardization and uniformity to the publication of research in the field of psychology.

2. 1-C; 2-E; 3-B; 4-D; 5-F; 6-A

3. The abstract is the most widely read section of most research reports because it is published in *Psychological Abstracts* and computerized indices such as PsycLIT.

4. The introduction is similar to a typical term paper because it summarizes a body of knowledge about a relatively narrow topic. It is different from a term paper because it provides a rationale and lead-in to a particular experiment.

5. c

6. The method section is designed to describe (a) the research participants, (b) the equipment or materials used in the research, and (c) the manner in which the experiment was conducted. Although all this information is important, the procedures are probably the most important because they allow other researchers to replicate the study. If different participants or equipment (materials) are used, external validity would simply be increased.

7. inferential; descriptive

8. No, you could not use figures or tables as your sole information in a results section. Figures and tables are meant to supplement descriptive and inferential statistics, not to replace them.

9. Although this answer involves opinion, you can make a strong argument that the discussion section is the most important section because it summarizes the experiment's evidence, ties that evidence into previous findings, and draws an overall conclusion.

10. The reference for a chapter from an edited book is more complex than a journal article or book reference because such a reference must include information about both the chapter and the book.

11. 1-E; 2-B; 3-G; 4-H; 5-A; 6-D; 7-F; 8-C

CHECK YOUR PROGRESS PAGES 405

1. You should not write your research paper in the style of a famous writer because your primary goal is communication rather than entertainment.

2. Three strategies used to improve writing style are (a) write from an outline, (b) write a draft and put it away for some time before rereading it, and (c) have another person read and evaluate your writing. You will have to answer for yourself what you need to change about your writing in order to incorporate these suggestions.

3. c

4. a. Jones (1995) conducted an experiment.

   b. The participants sat in desks around the room.

   c. I (or "The experimenter") projected the stimulus items from the rear of the cubicle.

   d. I found a significant interaction.   *or*   The data showed a significant interaction.

5. a. The participants that were older were tested first. (It is important to distinguish the older participants from the younger.)

   b. The room, which was a classroom, was used for testing. (The notation that the room is a classroom is probably merely a side comment that is not vital in describing the room.)

6. a. Because you are the oldest, you should go first. "Since" was incorrect because a justification was implied rather than a time reference.

   b. "Since" I began that class I have learned much about statistics. Correct because since denotes something has happened after beginning the class.

   c. "While" we are watching TV, we can also study. Correct because while denoted that watching TV and studying will occur at the same time.

   d. Although you are older than me, I should still go first. "While" was incorrect because a contrast was implied rather than a time reference.

7. Orientals–Asians mankind–humankind or humans mothering–parenting homosexuals–lesbian, gay

elderly–elderly people (or use specific age range) girls and men–women and men chairman–chair depressives–depressed patients

8. $a + b = c$ trial-by-trial
    -1 Enter: Your name

A Refers to the baseline measurement in a single-case design.

A-B design A single-case design in which you measure the baseline behavior, institute a treatment, and use a posttest.

A-B-A design A single-case design consisting of a baseline measurement, a treatment, a posttest, and a return to the baseline condition. May not be recommended if the participant is left without a beneficial or necessary treatment in the second baseline.

A-B-A-B design A single-case design consisting of a baseline, treatment, posttest, return to baseline, repeated treatment, and second posttest. This design gives the best chance of isolating causation.

Abscissa The horizontal or x axis of a graph.

Abstract A brief description of the research that is presented in an APA format paper.

Achievement test Designed to evaluate an individual's level of mastery or competence.

Analytic statement Statements that are always true.

Analytic survey Seeks to determine the relevant variables and how they are related.

APA format Accepted American Psychological Association (APA) form for preparing reports of psychological research.

Apparatus subsection The second subsection of the method section. When appropriate, contains information about the equipment used in an experiment.

Aptitude test Designed to assess an individual's potential ability or skill in a particular job.

Asymptotic Refers to tails of distributions that approach the baseline but never touch the baseline.

Author note A note at the end of an experimental report that contains information about the author or paper for readers' use.

Axial coding The process of rearranging data after open coding so that new relations are formed between concepts.

B Refers to the outcome (treatment) measurement in a single-case design.

Balancing A control procedure that achieves group equality by distributing extraneous variables equally to all groups.

Bar graph A graph in which the frequency for each category of a qualitative variable is represented as a vertical column. The columns of a bar graph do not touch.

Baseline A measurement of a behavior that is made under normal conditions (i.e., no IV is present); a control condition.

Between-groups variability Variability in DV scores that is due to the effects of the IV.

Between-subjects comparison Refers to a contrast between groups of participants who were randomly assigned to groups.

Carryover effect The effects of one treatment persist or carry over and influence responses to the next treatment.

Case study The intensive observing and recording of the behavior of (usually) a single participant.

Case-study approach An observational technique in which we compile a record of observations about a single participant.

Cause-and-effect relation Occurs when we know that a particular IV (cause) leads to specific changes in a DV (effect).

Citation A notation in text that a particular reference was used. The citation provides the name(s) of the author(s) and date of the work's publication.

Clinical perspective A descriptive research approach aimed at understanding and correcting a particular behavioral problem.

Cohort A group of individuals born during the same time period.

Comparative psychology The study of behavior in different species, including humans.

Complete counterbalancing All possible treatment sequences are presented.

Completely randomized ANOVA A one-way ANOVA that uses independent groups of participants.

Concurrent validity Degree to which the score on a test or inventory corresponds with another measure of the designated trait.

Conditional matrix A diagram that helps the researcher consider the conditions and consequences related to the phenomenon under study.

Confounded experiment An experiment in which an extraneous variable varies systematically with the IV; makes drawing a cause-and-effect relation impossible.

Confounding A situation in which the results of an experiment can be attributed to either the operation of an IV or an extraneous variable; caused by an uncontrolled variable that varies systematically with the IV.

Constancy A control technique by which an extraneous variable is reduced to a single value that is experienced by all participants.

Content validity The extent to which test items actually represent the type of material they are supposed to.

Contradictory statement Statements that are always false.

Control group In a two-group design, the group of participants that does not receive the IV.

Control procedure One of several steps experimenters take to ensure that potential extrane-

ous variables are controlled. Examples include random assignment, matching, and so on.

Control Two meanings: directly manipulating (1) a factor of interest in a research study to determine its effects or (2) other, unwanted variables that could influence the results of a research project.

Convenience sampling A researcher's sampling of participants based on ease of locating the participants; often does not involve true random selection.

Correlated assignment A method of assigning research participants to groups so that there is a relationship between small numbers of participants; these small groups are then randomly assigned to treatment conditions (also known as paired or matched assignment.

Correlated groups Groups of research participants that are related in some way—through matching, repeated measures, or natural sets.

Correlation coefficient A single number representing the degree of relation between two variables.

Correlational study Determination of the relation between two variables.

Counterbalancing A procedure for controlling order effects by presenting different treatment sequences.

Criterion validity Established by comparing the score on a test or inventory with a future score on another test or inventory.

Cross-cultural psychology A branch of psychology whose goal is to determine the universality of research results.

Cross-sectional research Comparison of two or more groups during the same, rather limited, time period.

Cultural response set The tendency of a particular culture to respond in a certain manner.

Culture Lasting values, attitudes, and behaviors that are shared by a group and transmitted to subsequent generations.

Debriefing session The nature and purpose of an experiment are explained at its conclusion.

Deductive logic Reasoning that proceeds from general theories to specific cases.

Degrees of freedom The ability of a number in a specified set to assume any value.

Demand characteristics Features of the experiment that inadvertently lead participants to respond in a particular manner.

Demographic data Information about participants' characteristics, such as age, sex, income, and academic major.

Dependent variable (DV) A response or behavior that the experimenter measures. Changes in the DV should be directly related to manipulation of the independent variable (IV).

Descriptive research methods Research methods that do not involve the manipulation of an independent variable (IV).

Descriptive statistics Procedures used to summarize a set of data.

Descriptive survey Seeks to determine the percentage of the population that has a certain characteristic, holds a particular opinion, or engages in a particular behavior.

Differential carryover The response to one treatment depends on which treatment was administered previously.

Diffusion or imitation of treatment A threat to internal validity that can occur if participants in one treatment group become familiar with the treatment of another group and copy that treatment.

Directional research hypothesis Prediction of the specific outcome of an experiment.

Discussion section The fourth major section of the APA-format paper. Contains a summary of the experiment's results, a comparison of those results to previous research, and the conclusion(s) from the experiment.

Double-blind experiment An experiment in which both the experimenter and the participants are unaware of which treatment the participants are receiving.

Effect size The magnitude or size of the experimental treatment.

Elimination A control technique whereby extraneous variables are completely removed from an experiment.

Emic A culture-specific finding.

Empirical Objectively quantifiable observations.

Environmental generalization Applying the results from an experiment to a situation or environment that differs from that of the original experiment.

Error variability Variability in DV scores that is due to factors other than the IV—individual differences, measurement error, and extraneous variation (also known as within-groups variability).

Ethnocentric Other cultures are viewed as an extension of one's own culture.

Ethnography A descriptive research approach that involves becoming a part of the culture being studied.

Etic A finding that is the same in different cultures.

Ex post facto research A research approach in which the experimenter cannot directly manipulate the IV but can only classify, categorize, or measure the IV because it is predetermined in the participants (e.g., IV = sex).

Ex post facto study The variable(s) to be studied are selected after they have occurred.

Experience IV Manipulation of the amount or type of training or learning.

Experiment An attempt to determine the cause-and-effect relations that exist in nature. Involves the manipulation of an independent variable (IV) recording of changes in a dependent variable (DV) and control of extraneous variables.

Experimental analysis of behavior A research approach popularized by B. F. Skinner, in which a single participant is studied.

Experimental design The general plan for selecting participants, assigning participants to experimental conditions, controlling extraneous variables, and gathering data.

Experimental group In a two-group design, the group of participants that receives the IV.

Experimental mortality A threat to internal validity that can occur if experimental participants from different groups drop out of the experiment at different rates.

External validity A type of evaluation of your experiment; do your experimental results apply to populations and situations that are different from those of your experiment?

Extraneous variable Undesired variables that may operate to influence the dependent variable (DV) and, thus, invalidate an experiment.

Fabrication of data Those instances where the experimenter either deliberately alters or creates research data.

Factorial design An experimental design with more than one IV.

Factors Synonymous with IVs.

Figure A pictorial representation of a set of results.

Frequency polygon A graph that is constructed by placing a dot in the center of each bar of a histogram and then connecting the dots.

General implication form Statement of the research hypothesis in an "if . . . then" form.

Generalization Applying the results from an experiment to a different situation or population.

Good participant effect The tendency of participants to behave as they perceive the experimenter wants them to behave.

Grounded theory A descriptive research approach that attempts to develop theories of understanding based on data from the real world.

Hawthorne effect Another name for reactance or reactivity effect.

Headings Titles for various sections of a psychology paper designed to help the reader understand the outline and importance of parts of the paper.

Heterogeneity of variance Occurs when we do not have homogeneity of variance; this means that our two (or more) groups' variances are not equivalent.

Histogram A graph in which the frequency for each category of a quantitative variable is represented as a vertical column that touches the adjacent column.

History A threat to internal validity; refers to events that occur between the DV measurements in a repeated measures design.

Homogeneity of variance The assumption that the variances are equal for two (or more) groups you plan to compare statistically.

Hypothesis An attempt to organize certain data and specific IV–DV relation within a specific portion of a larger, more comprehensive theory.

Incomplete counterbalancing Only a portion of all possible sequences are presented.

Independent groups Groups of participants that are formed by random assignment.

Independent variable (IV) A stimulus or aspect of the environment that the experimenter directly manipulates to determine its influences on behavior.

Inductive logic Reasoning that proceeds from specific cases to general conclusions or theories.

Inferential statistics Procedures used to analyze data after an experiment is completed; used to determine whether the independent variable has a significant effect.

Institutional Review Board (IRB) The university committee that is responsible for determining whether a proposed research project conforms to accepted ethical standards.

Instrumentation A threat to internal validity that occurs if the equipment or human measuring the DV changes the measuring criterion over time.

Interaction of selection and treatment A threat to external validity that occurs when a pretest sensitizes participants to the treatment yet to come.

Interaction of testing and treatment A threat to external validity that occurs when a pretest sensitizes participants to the treatment yet to come.

Interaction The joint, simultaneous effect on the DV of more than one IV.

Interactions with selection Threats to internal validity that can occur if there are systematic differences between or among selected treatment groups based on maturation, history, or instrumentation.

Internal validity A type of evaluation of your experiment; it asks the question of whether your IV is the only possible explanation of the results shown for your DV.

Interobserver reliability The extent to which observers agree.

Interrater reliability Degree of agreement among judges concerning the content validity of test or inventory items.

Interrupted time-series design A quasi-experimental design involving a single group of participants that includes repeated pretreatment measures, an applied treatment, and repeated posttreatment measures.

Interval scale A scale of measurement that permits rank ordering of events with the assumption of equal intervals between adjacent events.

Introduction The first major section of the APA-format paper. Contains the thesis statement, review of relevant literature, and experimental hypothesis.

Level 1 heading A centered section title in which the first letters of major words are capitalized. Occupies a line by itself.

Level 3 heading A section title that is left-margin justified, underlined, and has the first letter of each major word capitalized. Occupies a line by itself.

Level 4 heading A section title that is indented five spaces, underlined, has only the first word capitalized, and ends with a period; it does not occupy a separate line.

Levels Differing amounts or types of an IV used in an experiment (also known as treatment conditions).

Line graph A graph that is frequently used to depict the results of an experiment.

Logical syllogism A scheme of formal logic or argument consisting of a major premise, a minor premise, and a conclusion.

Longitudinal research project Obtaining research data from the same group of participants over an extended period of time.

Main effect Refers to the sole effect of one IV in a factorial design.

Manuscript page header The first two or three words of the report's title. Appears with the page number on each page of the research report.

Marginal significance Refers to statistical results with a probability of chance between 5% and 10%—in other words, almost significant, but not quite. Researchers often talk about such results as if they reached the .05 level.

Matched pairs Research participants in a two-group design who are measured and equated on some variable before the experiment.

Matching variable A potential extraneous variable on which we measure our research participants and from which we form sets of participants who are equal on the variable.

Materials subsection The second subsection of the method section. When appropriate, contains information about materials other than equipment used in the experiment.

Maturation A threat to internal validity; refers to changes in participants that occur over time during an experiment; could include actual physical maturation or tiredness, boredom, hunger, and so on.

Mean square The "averaged" variability for each source; computed by dividing each source's sum of squares by its degrees of freedom.

Mean The arithmetic average of a set of numbers; found by adding all the scores in a set and then dividing by the number of scores.

Measurement The assignment of symbols to events according to a set of rules.

Median The number that divides a distribution in half.

Method section The second major section of the APA-format paper. Contains information about the participants; the apparatus, materials, and testing instrument(s); and the procedures used in the experiment.

Mixed assignment A factorial design that has a mixture of independent groups for one IV and correlated groups for another IV. In larger factorial designs, at least one IV has independent groups and at least one has correlated groups (also known as mixed groups).

Mode The score in a distribution that occurs most often.

Mortality A threat to internal validity that can occur if experimental participants from different groups drop out of the experiment at different rates.

Multiple-treatment interference A threat to external validity that occurs when a set of findings results only when participants experience multiple treatments in the same experiment.

Natural pairs Research participants in a two-group design who are naturally related in some way (e.g., a biological or social relationship).

Naturalistic observation Seeking answers to research questions by observing behavior in the real world.

Nay-sayers Participants who tend to answer no to all questions.

Negative correlation As scores on one variable increase, scores on the second variable decrease.

Nominal scale A scale of measurement in which events are assigned to categories.

Nondirectional research hypothesis A specific prediction concerning the outcome of an experiment is not made.

Nonequivalent group design A design involving two or more groups that are not randomly assigned; a comparison group (no treatment) is compared to one or more treatment groups.

Nonreactive measures DV measurements that do not influence the DV being measured.

Nonsystematic sources Sources for research ideas that present themselves in an unpredictable manner; a concerted attempt to locate researchable ideas has not been made.

Normal distribution A symmetrical, bell-shaped distribution having half of the scores above the mean and half of the scores below the mean.

Nuisance variable Unwanted variables that can cause the variability of scores within groups to increase.

Null hypothesis A hypothesis that says that all differences between groups are due to chance (i.e., not the operation of the IV).

One-way ANOVA A statistical test used to analyze data from an experimental design with one independent variable that has three or more groups (levels).

Open coding The process of describing data through means such as examination, comparison, conceptualization, and categorization.

Operational definition Defining the independent, dependent, and extraneous variables in terms of the operations needed to produce them.

Ordinal scale A scale of measurement that permits events to be rank ordered.

Ordinate   The vertical or y axis of a graph.

Participant characteristics   Aspects of the participant, such as age, sex, or personality traits, that are treated as if they are IVs.

Participant observation   A type of naturalistic observation in which the observer becomes part of the group being studied.

Participants at minimal risk   Participation in an experiment does not place the participants under physical or emotional risk.

Participants at risk   By participating in an experiment, the participants are placed under some type of physical or emotional risk.

Participants subsection   The first subsection of the method section. Provides full information about the participants in the study.

Personality test or inventory   Measures a specific aspect of the individual's motivational state, interpersonal capability, or personality.

Physiological IV   A physiological state of the participant that the experimenter manipulates.

Pie chart   Graphical representation of the percentage allocated to each alternative as a slice of a circular pie.

Pilot testing   Preliminary, exploratory testing that is done prior to the complete research project.

Placebo effect   An experimental effect that is due to expectation or suggestion rather than the IV.

Plagiarism   Using someone else's work without giving credit to the original source.

Population   The complete set of individuals or events.

Population generalization   Applying the results from an experiment to a group of participants that is different and more encompassing than those used in the original experiment.

Positive correlation   As scores on one variable increase, scores on the second variable also increase.

Post hoc comparisons   Statistical comparisons made between group means after finding a significant F ratio.

Power   The probability that a statistical test will be significant (i.e., the experimental hypothesis is accepted when it is true).

Practice effect   A beneficial effect on a DV measurement caused by previous experience with the DV.

Precedent   An established pattern.

Principle of falsifiability   Results not in accord with the research hypothesis are taken as evidence that this hypothesis is false.

Principle of parsimony   The belief that explanations of phenomena and events should remain simple until the simple explanations are no longer valid.

Procedure subsection   The third subsection of the method section. Provides a step-by-step account of what the participants and experimenter did during the experiment.

Process   The manner in which actions and interactions occur in a sequence or series.

Programmatic research   A series of research experiments that deal with a related topic or question.

Qualitative research   Research conducted in a natural setting that seeks to understand a complex human behavior by developing a complete narrative description of that behavior.

Quasi-experimental design   A research design used when you cannot randomly assign your experimental participants to the groups but do manipulate an IV and measure a DV.

Random assignment   A control technique that ensures that each participant has an equal chance of being assigned to any group in an experiment.

Random sample   A sample in which every member of the population has an equal likelihood of being included.

Random sampling with replacement   Once chosen, a score, event, or participant can be returned to the population to be selected again.

Random selection A control technique that ensures that each member of the population has an equal chance of being chosen for an experiment.

Randomization A control technique that ensures that each participant has an equal chance of being assigned to any group in an experiment.

Range A measure of variability that is computed by subtracting the smallest score from the largest score.

Ratio scale A scale of measurement that permits rank ordering of events with the assumptions of equal intervals between adjacent events and a true zero point.

Reactance or reactivity effect The finding that participants respond differently when they know they are being observed.

Reactive arrangements A threat to external validity caused by an experimental situation that alters participants' behavior, regardless of the IV involved.

Reactive measures DV measurements that actually change the DV being measured.

Reference section A complete listing of all the references cited in a psychological paper.

Reference A full bibliographic record of any work cited in the text of a psychological paper.

Reliability Extent to which a test or inventory is consistent in its evaluation of the same individuals.

Repeated measures An experimental procedure in which research participants are tested or measured more than once.

Repeated-measures ANOVA A one-way ANOVA that uses correlated groups of participants.

Replication An additional scientific study that is conducted in exactly the same manner as the original research project.

Replication with extension An experiment that seeks to confirm (replicate) a previous finding but does so in a different setting or with different participants or under different conditions.

Research design The general plan for selecting participants, assigning participants to experimental conditions, controlling extraneous variables, and gathering data.

Research idea Identification of a gap in the knowledge base or an unanswered question in an area of interest.

Research or experimental hypothesis The experimenter's predicted outcome of a research project.

Response set The experimental context or testing situation influences the participants' responses.

Results section The third major section of the APA-format paper. Contains information about the statistical findings from the experiment.

Robust Refers to a statistical test that can tolerate violation of its assumptions (e.g., homogeneity of variances) and still yield results that are valid.

Rosenthal effect The experimenter's preconceived idea of appropriate responding influences the treatment of participants and their behavior.

Running head A condensed title that is printed at the top of alternate pages of a published article.

Sample A group that is selected to represent the population.

Scale of measurement A set of measurement rules.

Selection A threat to internal validity; if we choose participants in such a way that our groups are not equal before the experiment, we cannot be certain that our IV caused any difference we observe after the experiment.

Selective coding The process of selecting the main phenomenon (core category) around which all other phenomena (subsidiary categories) are grouped, arranging the groupings, studying the results, and rearranging where necessary.

Sequence or order effects The position of a treatment in a series determines, in part, the participants' response.

Serendipity Situations in which we look for one phenomenon but find something else.

Single-blind experiment An experiment in which the experimenter (or participants) is unaware of the treatment the participants are receiving.

Single-case experimental design An experiment that consists of one participant (also known as $N = 1$ designs).

Single-strata approach Gathering data from a single stratum of the population of interest.

Situation sampling Observing the same behavior in different situations.

Source table A table that contains the results of ANOVA. Source refers to the source of the different types of variation.

Split-half technique Determination of reliability by dividing the test or inventory into two subtests and then comparing the scores made on the two halves.

Standard deviation (SD) Square root of the variance; has important relations to the normal curve.

Statistical regression A threat to internal validity that occurs when low scorers improve or high scorers fall on a second administration of a test due solely to statistical reasons.

Statistics The branch of mathematics that involves the collection, analysis, and interpretation of data.

Stimulus or environmental IV An aspect of the environment that the experimenter manipulates.

Stratified random sampling Random samples are drawn from specific subpopulations or strata of the general population.

Sum of squares The amount of variability in the DV attributable to each source.

Synergistic effects Dramatic consequences that occur when you combine two or more substances, conditions, or organisms. The effects are greater than what is individually possible.

Synthetic statement Statements that can be either true or false.

Systematic sources Thoroughly examined, carefully thought-out sources for research topics.

t Test An inferential statistical test used to evaluate the difference between two means.

Table A chart containing an array of descriptive statistics.

Temporal generalization Applying the results from an experiment to a time that is different from that when the original experiment was conducted.

Tenacity Acceptance of knowledge or information simply because it has been presented repeatedly.

Testing instrument(s) subsection The second subsection of the method section. When appropriate, contains information about standardized tests used in the experiment.

Testing A threat to internal validity that occurs because measuring the DV causes a change in the DV.

Test–retest procedure Determination of reliability by repeatedly administering a test to the same participants.

Theory A formal statement of the relations among the IVs and DVs in a given area of research.

Thesis statement A statement of the general research topic of interest and the perceived relation of the relevant variables in that area.

Three-way design A factorial design with three IVs.

Time sampling Making observations at different time periods.

Title page   The first page of an APA-format paper. It includes the manuscript page header, the running head, the manuscript's title, and the name(s) of the author(s) and their affiliation(s).

Transactional system   An analysis of how actions and interactions relate to their conditions and consequences.

Treatment groups   Groups of participants that receive the IV.

Treatment variability   Variability in DV scores that is due to the effects of the IV (also known as between-groups variability).

True experiment   An experiment in which the experimenter directly manipulates the IV.

Type I error   Accepting the experimental hypothesis when the null hypothesis is true.

Type II error   Accepting the null hypothesis when the experimental hypothesis is true.

Unbiased language   Language that does not display prejudice toward an individual or group.

Validity   The degree to which a knowledge claim is accurate.

Validity   The extent to which a test or inventory measures what it is supposed to measure.

Variability   The extent to which scores spread out around the mean.

Variable   An event or behavior that can assume two or more values.

Variance   A single number that represents the total amount of variation in a distribution; also, the square of the standard deviation, s^2.

Within-group counterbalancing   Presentation of different treatment sequences to different participants.

Within-groups variability   Same as error variability.

Within-subject counterbalancing   Presentation of different treatment sequences to the same participant.

Within-subjects comparison   Refers to a contrast between groups of participants who were assigned to groups through matched pairs, natural pairs, or repeated measures.

Yea-sayers   Participants who tend to answer yes to all questions.

Zero correlation   Two variables under consideration are not related.

References

American Psychological Association. (1982). *Ethical principles in the conduct of research with human participants.* Washington, DC: Author.

American Psychological Association. (1985). *Guidelines for ethical conduct in the care and use of animals.* Washington, DC: Author.

American Psychological Association. (1992). *Guidelines for ethical conduct in the care and use of animals.* Washington, DC: Author.

American Psychological Association. (1994). *Publication manual of the American Psychological Association* (4th ed.). Washington, DC: Author.

American Psychological Association. (1999, August 9). *Electronic reference formats recommended by the American Psychological Association* [Announcement]. Washington, DC: Author. Retrieved September 6, 1999 from the World Wide Web.

American Psychological Association. (2001). *Publication manual of the American Psychological Association* (5th ed.). Washington, DC: Author

American Psychological Association (2001). *Thesaurus of psychological index terms* (9th ed.). Washington, DC: Author.

American Psychological Association. (2002). Ethical principles of psychologists and code of conduct. *American Psychologist, 57,* 1060-1073.

Anastasi, A. (1988). *Psychological testing* (6th ed.). New York: Macmillan.

Anastasi, A., & Urbina, S. (1997). *Psychological testing* (7th ed.). Upper Saddle River, NJ: Prentice Hall.

Aronson, E., & Carlsmith, J. M. (1968). Experimentation in social psychology. In G. Lindzey and E. Aronson (Eds.), *The handbook of social psychology* (2nd ed.). Reading, MA: Addison-Wesley.

Ball, R. M., Kargl, E. S., Kimpel, J. D., & Siewert, S. L. (2001). Effect of sad and suspenseful mood induction on reaction time. *Psi Chi Journal of Undergraduate Research, 6,* 21–27.

Barlow, D. H., & Hersen, M. (1973). Single-case experimental designs. *Archives of General Psychiatry, 29,* 319–325.

Baumrind, D. (1964). Some thoughts on the ethics of research: After reading Milgram's "Behavioral Study of Obedience." *American Psychologist, 19,* 421–423.

Beach, F. A. (1950). The snark was a boojum. *American Psychologist, 5,* 115–124.

Beauchamp, T. L., & Childress, J. F. (1979). *Principles of biomedical ethics.* New York: Oxford University Press.

Bellquist, J. E. (1993). *A guide to grammar and usage for psychology and related fields.* Hillsdale, NJ: Erlbaum.

Benjamin, L. T., Jr. (1992, April). *Health, Happiness, and Success: The popular psychology magazine of the 1920s.* Paper presented at the annual meeting of the Eastern Psychological Association, Boston, MA.

Bennett, S. K. (1994). The American Indian: A psychological overview. In W. J. Lonner & R. Malpass (Eds.), *Psychology and culture* (pp. 35–39). Boston: Allyn and Bacon.

Blumenthal, A. L. (1991). The intrepid Joseph Jastrow. In G. A. Kimble, M. Wertheimer, & C. L. White (Eds.), *Portraits of pioneers in psychology* (pp. 75–87). Washington, DC: American Psychological Association.

Bodner, D., Cochran, C. D., & Blum, T. L. (2000). Unique invulnerability measurement in skydivers: Scale validation. *Psi Chi Journal of Undergraduate Research, 5,* 104–108.

Boice, M. L., & Gargano, G. J. (2001). Part-set cuing is due to strong, not weak, list cues. *Psi Chi Journal of Undergraduate Research, 6,* 118–122.

Bonds-Raacke, J. M., Wright, K. L., Lewin, J. M., & Nelson, E. M. (2001). The sleeper effect on students' attitudes toward animal cognition. *Psi Chi Journal of Undergraduate Research, 6,* 32–36.

Boring, E. G. (1950). *A history of modern psychology* (2nd ed.). New York: Appleton-Century-Crofts.

Bridgman, P. W. (1927). *The logic of modern physics.* New York: Macmillan.

Broad, W. J. (1980). Imbroglio at Yale (I): Emergence of a fraud. *Science, 210,* 38–41.

Bruderick, J., & Ernst, D. (2000). The relation between positive and negative alcohol expectancies and alcohol use in college students. *Psi Chi Journal of Undergraduate Research, 5,* 60–67.

Burkley, E., III, McFarland, S., Walker, W., & Young, J. (2000). Informed consent: A methodological confound? *Psi Chi Journal of Undergraduate Research, 5,* 43–45.

Campbell, D. T. (1957). Factors relevant to the validity of experiments in social settings. *Psychological Bulletin, 54,* 297–312.

Campbell, D. T. (1969). Reforms as experiments. *American Psychologist, 24,* 409–429.

Campbell, D T., & Stanley, J. C. (1966). *Experimental and quasi-experimental designs for research.* Boston: Houghton Mifflin.

Claus, M. K. (2000). Gendered toy preferences and assertiveness in preschoolers. *Journal of Psychological Inquiry, 5,* 15–18.

Cohen, J. (1977). *Statistical power analysis for the behavioral sciences* (rev. ed.). New York: Academic Press.

Cook, T. D., & Campbell, D. T. (1979). *Quasi-experimentation: Design & analysis issues for field settings.* Boston: Houghton Mifflin.

Corkin, S. (1984). Lasting consequences of bilateral medial temporal lobectomy: Clinical course and experimental findings in H.M. *Seminars in Neurology, 4,* 249–259.

Creswell, J. W. (1994). *Research design: Qualitative and quantitative approaches.* Thousand Oaks, CA: Sage.

Darley, J. M., & Latané, D. (1968). Bystander intervention in emergencies: Diffusion of responsibility. *Journal of Personality and Social Psychology, 8,* 377–383.

Davis, S. F., Armstrong, S. L. W., & Huss, M. T. (1993). Shock-elicited aggression is influenced by lead and/or alcohol exposure. *Bulletin of the Psychonomic Society, 31,* 451–453.

Davis, S. F., Grover, C. A., & Erickson, C. A. (1987). A comparison of the aversiveness of denatonium saccharide and quinine in humans. *Bulletin of the Psychonomic Society, 25,* 462–463.

Davis, S. F., Grover, C. A., Erickson, C. A., Miller, L. A., & Bowman, J. A. (1987). Analyzing the aversiveness of denatonium saccharide. *Perceptual and Motor Skills, 64,* 1215–1222.

Department of Psychology, Bishop's University. *Plagiarism pamphlet.* Supplied December 23, 1994.

Dickson, A. J., Giuliano, T. A., Morris, J. C., & Cass, K. L. (2001). Eminem versus Charley Pride: Race, stereotypes, and perceptions of rap and country music performers. *Psi Chi Journal of Undergraduate Research, 6,* 175–180.

Dion, K. K., Berscheid, E., & Walster, E. (1972). What is beautiful is good. *Journal of Person-*

ality and Social Psychology, 24, 285–290.

Doyle, A. C. (1927). *The complete Sherlock Holmes.* Garden City, NY: Doubleday.

Driggers, K. J., & Helms, T. (2000). The effects of salary on willingness to date. *Psi Chi Journal of Undergraduate Research, 5,* 76–80.

Dukes, W. F. (1965) *N* = 1. *Psychological Bulletin, 64,* 74–79.

Dunn, J., Ford, K., Rewey, K. L., Juve, J. A., Weiser, A., & Davis, S. F. (2001). A modified presubmission checklist. *Psi Chi Journal of Undergraduate Research, 6,* 142–144.

Festinger, L. (1957). *A theory of cognitive dissonance.* Stanford, CA: Stanford University Press.

Freeman, N. J., & Punzo, D. L. D. (2001). Effects of DNA and eyewitness evidence on juror decisions. *Psi Chi Journal of Undergraduate Research, 6,* 109–117.

Friedman, M., & Rosenman, R. H. (1974). *Type A behavior and your heart.* New York: Knopf.

Gauthreaux, V. M. (2000). Relating pretrial publicity, judicial instruction, and thought suppression with guilt ratings. *Psi Chi Journal of Undergraduate Research, 5,* 21–28.

Geronimus, A. T. (1991). Teenage childbearing and social and reproductive disadvantage: The evolution of complex questions and the demise of simple answers. *Family Relations, 40,* 463–471.

Gibson, A. R., Smith, K., & Torres, A. (2000). Glancing behavior of participants using automated teller machines while bystanders approach. *Psi Chi Journal of Undergraduate Research, 5,* 148–151.

Gilbert, D. T., & Malone, P. S. (1995). The correspondence bias. *Psychological Bulletin, 117,* 21–38.

Glesne, C. (1999). *Becoming qualitative researchers: An introduction* (2nd ed.). New York: Longman.

Goodwin, C. J. (1999). *A history of modern psychology.* New York: Wiley.

Gray, A. D., & Lucas, J. L. (2001). Commuters' subjective perceptions of travel impedance and their stress levels. *Psi Chi Journal of Undergraduate Research, 6,* 79–83.

Grazer, B. (Producer), & Howard, R. (Producer/Director). 2001. *A beautiful mind* [Motion picture]. United States: Universal Studios.

Gubrium, J. F., & Holstein, J. A. (1997). *The new language of qualitative method.* New York: Oxford University Press.

Guerin, B. (1986). Mere presence effects in humans: A review. *Journal of Personality and Social Psychology, 22,* 38–77.

Guthrie, R. V. (1976). *Even the rat was white: A historical view of psychology.* New York: Harper & Row.

Hall, R. V., Fox, R., Willard, D., Goldsmith, L., Emerson, M., Owen, M., Davis, F., & Porcia, E. (1971). The teacher as observer and experimenter in the modification of disputing and talking-out behaviors. *Journal of Applied Behavior Analysis, 4,* 141–149.

Hayes, K. M., Miller, H. R., & Davis, S. F. (1993). *Examining the relationships between interpersonal flexibility, self-esteem, and death anxiety.* Paper presented at the annual meeting of the Southwestern Psychological Association, Corpus Christi, TX.

Hedrick, T. E., Bickman, L., & Rog, D. J. (1993). *Applied research design: A practical guide.* Newbury Park, CA: Sage.

Hedrick, T. E., & Shipman, S. L. (1988). Multiple questions require multiple designs: An evaluation of the 1981 changes to the AFDC program. *Evaluation Review, 12,* 427–448.

Helmreich, R., & Stapp, J. (1974). Short form of the Texas Social Behavior Inventory (TSBI), an objective measure of self-esteem. *Bulletin of the Psychonomic Society, 4,* 473–475.

Hersen, M. (1982). Single-case experimental designs. In A. S. Bellack, M. Hersen, &

A. E. Kazdin (Eds.), *International handbook of behavior modification and therapy* (pp. 167–203). New York: Plenum Press.

Hersen, M., & Barlow, D. H. (1976). *Single-case experimental designs: Strategies for studying behavioral change.* New York: Pergamon Press.

Hilts, P. J. (1995). *Memory's ghost: The strange tale of Mr. M and the nature of memory.* New York: Simon & Schuster.

Horvat, J., & Davis, S. F. (1998). *Doing psychological research.* Upper Saddle River, NJ: Prentice Hall.

Howard, D. (1997). Language in the human brain. In M. D. Rugg (Ed.), *Cognitive neuroscience* (pp. 277–304). Cambridge: MA: MIT Press.

Huff, D. (1954). *How to lie with statistics.* New York: Norton.

Jones, J. H. (1981). *Bad blood: The Tuskegee syphilis experiment.* New York: Free Press.

Jones, J. M. (1994). The African American: A duality dilemma? In W. J. Lonner & R. Malpass (Eds.), *Psychology and culture* (pp. 17–21). Boston: Allyn and Bacon.

Jones, M. D. (2001). The effects of noise and sex on children's performance on recall and spatial tasks. *Psi Chi Journal of Undergraduate Research, 6,* 63–67.

Jones, R. R., Vaught, R. S., & Weinrott, M. (1977). Time-series analysis in operant research. *Journal of Applied Behavior Analysis, 10,* 151–166.

Kalat, J. (2001). *Biological psychology* (7th ed.). Belmont, CA: Wadsworth.

Kazlauskas, M. A., & Kelland, M. D. (1997). Behavioral evaluation of the stargazer mutant rat in a tactile startle paradigm. *Psi Chi Journal of Undergraduate Research, 2,* 90–98.

Kazdin, A. E. (1976). Statistical analyses for single-case experimental designs. In M. Hersen, & D. H. Barlow (Eds.), *Single-case experimental designs: Strategies for studying behavioral change* (pp. 265–316). New York: Pergamon Press.

Kazdin, A. E. (1984). *Behavior modification in applied settings* (3rd ed.). Homewood, IL: Dorsey Press.

Keith-Spiegel, P. (1991). *The complete guide to graduate school admission: Psychology and related fields.* Hillsdale, NJ: Erlbaum.

Keith-Spiegel, P., & Wiederman, M. W. (2000). *The complete guide to graduate school admission: Psychology, counseling, and related professions* (2nd ed.). Mahwah, NJ: Erlbaum.

Keppel, G., Saufley, W. H., Jr., & Tokunaga, H. (1992). *Introduction to design & analysis: A student's handbook* (2nd ed.). New York: W. H. Freeman.

Kiker, K. (2001). Developmental changes in children's measurement errors. *Psi Chi Journal of Undergraduate Research, 6,* 68–74.

Kimmel, A. J. (1988). *Ethics and values in applied social research.* Beverly Hills, CA: Sage.

Kirk, R. E. (1968). *Experimental design: Procedures for the behavioral sciences.* Belmont, CA: Brooks/Cole.

Kirk, R. E. (1996, April). *Practical significance: A concept whose time has come.* Southwestern Psychological Association presidential address. Houston, TX.

Koestler, A. (1964). *The act of creation.* New York: Macmillan.

Korn, J. H. (1988). Students' roles, rights, and responsibilities as research participants. *Teaching of Psychology, 15,* 74–78.

Krantz, D. S., Glass, D. C., & Snyder, M. L. (1974). Helplessness, stress level, and the coronary-prone behavior pattern. *Journal of Experimental Social Psychology, 10,* 284–300.

Landrum, R. E., Davis, S. F., & Landrum, T. A. (2000). *The psychology major: Career options and strategies for success.* Upper Saddle River, NJ: Prentice Hall.

Lang, P. J., & Melamed, B. G. (1969). Avoidance conditioning therapy of an infant with chronic ruminative vomiting. *Journal of Abnormal Psychology, 74,* 1–8.

Langley, W. M., Theis, J., Davis, S. F., Richard, M. M., & Grover, C. A. (1987). Effects of denatonium sacccharide on the drinking behavior of the grasshopper mouse (Onychomys leucogaster). *Bulletin of the Psychonomic Society, 25,* 17–19.

Larey, A. (2001). Effect of massage and informal touch on body-dissatisfaction, anxiety, and obsessive-compulsiveness. *Journal of Psychological Inquiry, 6,* 78–83.

Lawson, T. J. (1995). An advisor update: Gaining admission into graduate programs in psychology. *Teaching of Psychology, 22,* 225–227.

Lee, D. J., & Hall, C. C. I. (1994). Being Asian in North America. In W. J. Lonner & R. Malpass (Eds.), *Psychology and culture* (pp. 29–33). Boston: Allyn and Bacon.

Licht, C. A. (2000). Occupational stress as a function of type of organization and sex of employee. *Psi Chi Journal of Undergraduate Research, 5,* 46–55.

Licht, C. A. (2001). Occupational stress as a function of type of organization and sex of employee: A reassessment. *Psi Chi Journal of Undergraduate Research, 6,* 14–20.

Loftus, E. F. (1979). *Eyewitness testimony.* Cambridge, MA: Harvard University Press.

Lonner, W. J., & Malpass, R. (1994a). Preface. In W. J. Lonner & R. Malpass (Eds.), *Psychology and culture* (pp. ix–xiii). Boston: Allyn and Bacon.

Lonner, W. J., & Malpass, R. (1994b). When psychology and culture meet: An introduction to cross-cultural psychology. In W. J. Lonner & R. Malpass (Eds.), *Psychology and culture* (pp. 1–12). Boston: Allyn and Bacon.

Losch, M. E., & Cacioppo, J. T. (1990). Cognitive dissonance may enhance sympathetic tonus, but attitudes are changed to reduce negative affect rather than arousal. *Journal of Experimental Social Psychology, 26,* 289–304.

Luehring, J., & Altman, J. D. (2000). Factors contributing to sex differences on the mental rotation task. *Psi Chi Journal of Undergraduate Research, 5,* 29–35.

Mack, D., & Rainey, D. (1990). Female applicants' grooming and personnel selection. *Journal of Social Behavior and Personality, 5,* 399–407.

Mahoney, M. J. (1987). Scientific publication and knowledge politics. *Journal of Social Behavior and Personality, 2,* 165–176.

Marín, G. (1994). The experience of being a Hispanic in the United States. In W. J. Lonner & R. Malpass (Eds.), *Psychology and culture* (pp. 23–27). Boston: Allyn and Bacon.

Marshall, C., & Rossman, G. B. (1989). *Designing qualitative research.* Newbury Park, CA: Sage.

Martin, K., Farruggia, S., & Yeske, K. (1993, May). *The effects of stress on reported state and trait anxiety.* Psi Chi paper presented at the annual meeting of the Midwestern Psychological Association, Chicago, IL.

Matsumoto, D. (1997). *Culture and modern life.* Pacific Grove, CA: Brooks/Cole Publishing Company.

Matsumoto, D. (2000). *Culture and psychology: People around the world* (2nd ed.). Belmont, CA: Wadsworth.

McClellan, K. S., & Woods, E. B. (2001). Disability and society: Appearance stigma results in discrimination toward deaf persons. *Psi Chi Journal of Undergraduate Research, 6,* 57–62.

McGuigan, F. J. (1960). *Experimental psychology.* Englewood Cliffs, NJ: Prentice Hall.

McInerny, R. M. (1970). *A history of Western philosophy.* Notre Dame, IN: University of Notre Dame Press.

McKibban, A. R., & Nelson, S. (2001). Subjective well-being: Are you busy enough to be happy? *Psi Chi Journal of Undergraduate Research, 6,* 51–56.

Medewar, P. B. (1979). *Advice to a young scientist.* New York: Harper & Row.

Milgram, S. (1963). Behavioral study of obedience. *Journal of Abnormal and Social Psychology, 67,* 371–378.

Milgram, S. (1964). Issues in the study of obedience: A reply to Baumrind. *American Psychologist, 19,* 848–852.

Milgram, S. (1974). *Obedience to authority: An experimental view.* New York: Harper & Row.

Miller, H. B., & Williams, W. H. (1983). *Ethics and animals.* Clifton, NJ: Humana Press.

Miller, J. G. (1984). Culture and the development of everyday social explanation. *Journal of Personality and Social Psychology, 46,* 961–978.

Miller, N. E. (1985). The value of behavioral research on animals. *American Psychologist, 40,* 423–440.

Montgomery, M. D., & Donovan, K. M. (2002, April). *The "Mozart effect" on cognitive and spatial task performance, revisited.* Poster presented at the annual meeting of the Southwestern Psychological Association, Corpus Christi, TX.

Mook, D. G. (1983). In defense of external invalidity. *American Psychologist, 38,* 379–387.

Mooney, R. L. (1950). *Mooney problem check list.* New York: The Psychological Corporation.

Nash, S. M. (1983). *The relationship between early ethanol exposure and adult taste preference.* Paper presented in J. P. Guilford/Psi Chi undergraduate research competition.

Novaco, R. W., Stokols, D., & Milanesi, L. (1990). Objective and subjective dimensions of travel impedance as determinants of commuting stress. *American Journal of Community Psychology, 18,* 231–257.

Orne, M. T. (1962). On the social psychology of the psychological experiment: With particular reference to demand characteristics and their implications. *American Psychologist, 17,* 776–783.

Pepperberg, I. M. (1994). Numerical competence in an African gray parrot (*Psittacus erithacus*). *Journal of Comparative Psychology, 108,* 36–44.

Proctor, R. W., & Capaldi, E. J. (2001). Improving the science education of psychology students: Better teaching of methodology. *Teaching of Psychology, 28,* 173–181.

Purdy, J. E., Reinehr, R. C., & Swartz, J. D. (1989). Graduate admissions criteria of leading psychology departments. *American Psychologist, 44,* 960–961.

Reagan, T. (1983). *The case for animal rights.* Berkeley, CA: University of California Press.

Reid, D. W., & Ware, E. E. (1973). Multidimensionality of internal-external control: Implications for past and future reserach. *Canadian Journal of Behavioural Research, 5,* 264–271.

Roethlisberger, F. J., & Dickson, W. J. (1939). *Management and the worker.* Cambridge, MA: Harvard University Press.

Rosenthal, R. (1966). *Experimenter effects in behavioral research.* New York: Appleton-Century-Crofts.

Rosenthal, R. (1976). *Experimenter effects in behavioral research* (enlarged ed.). New York: Irvington Press.

Rosenthal, R. (1977). Biasing effects of experimenters. *ETC: A review of general semantics, 34,* 253–264.

Rosenthal, R. (1985). From unconscious experimenter bias to teacher expectancy effects. In J. B. Dusek (Ed.), *Teacher expectancies.* Hillsdale, NJ: Lawrence Erlbaum Associates.

Rosenthal, R., & Fode, K. L. (1963). The effect of experimenter bias on the performance of the albino rat. *Behavioral Science, 8,* 183–189.

Rosenthal, R., & Jacobson, L. (1968). *Psychodynamics in the classroom.* New York: Holt.

Rosenthal, R., & Rosnow, R. L. (1984). *Essentials of behavioral research.* New York: McGraw-Hill.

Rosenthal, R., & Rosnow, R. (1991). *Essentials of behavioral research* (2nd ed.). New York: McGraw-Hill.

Ross, L. (1977). The intuitive psychologist and his shortcomings: Distortions in the attribution process. In L. Berkowitz (Ed.), *Advances in experimental social psychology* (Vol. 10, pp. 173–220). New York: Academic Press.

Sagles, S. E., Coley, S., Espiritu, G., Zahregian, P., & Velayo, R. (2002). Effects of racial background and sex on identifying facial expressions and person perception. *Psi Chi Journal of Undergraduate Research, 7,* 31–37.

Sasson, R., & Nelson, T. M. (1969). The human experimental subject in context. *Canadian Psychologist, 10,* 409–437.

Scali, R. M., & Brownlow, S. (2001). Impact of instructional manipulation and stereotype activation on sex differences in spatial task performance. *The Psi Chi Journal of Undergraduate Research, 6,* 3–13.

Schein, E. H. (1987). *The clinical perspective in fieldwork.* Newbury Park, CA: Sage.

Schroeppel, N., & Carlo, G. (2001). Sympathy and perspective taking as mediators of gender differences in altruism. *Journal of Psychological Inquiry, 6,* 7–11.

Sears, D. O. (1986). College sophomores in the laboratory: Influences of a narrow data base on social psychology's view of human nature. *Journal of Personality and Social Psychology, 51,* 515–530.

Selvidge, P. R. (2000). Effects of recall requirements on strategy selection in a visual-spatial span task. *Psi Chi Journal of Undergraduate Research, 5,* 68–72.

Shuter, R. (1977). A field study of nonverbal communication in Germany, Italy, and the United States. *Communication Monographs, 44,* 298–305.

Singer, P. (1975). *Animal liberation.* New York: Random House.

Skinner, B. F. (1961). *Cumulative record* (Expanded edition). New York: Appleton-Century-Crofts.

Skinner, B. F. (1966). Operant behavior. In W. K. Honig (Ed.), *Operant behavior: Areas of research and application* (pp. 12–32). New York: Appleton-Century-Crofts.

Small, W. S. (1901). An experimental study of the mental processes of the rat. *American Journal of Psychology, 11,* 133–165.

Smith, R. A. (1985). Advising beginning psychology majors for graduate school. *Teaching of Psychology, 12,* 194–198.

Smith, R. A., Davis, S. F., & Burleson, J. (1996). *Snark hunting revisited: The status of comparative psychology in the 1990s.* Paper presented at the meeting of the Southwestern Comparative Psychology Association, Houston, TX.

Solomon, R. L. (1949). An extension of control group design. *Psychological Bulletin, 46,* 137–150.

Sou, E. K., & Irving, L. M. (2002). Students' attitudes toward mental illness: A Macao-U.S. cross-cultural comparison. *Psi Chi Journal of Undergraduate Research, 7,* 13–22.

Spatz, C. (2001). *Basic statistics: Tales of distributions* (7th ed.). Belmont, CA: Wadsworth.

Steele, C. M., Southwick, L. L., & Critchlow, B. (1981). Dissonance and alcohol: Drinking your troubles away. *Journal of Personality and Social Psychology, 41,* 831–846.

Strauss, A., & Corbin, J. (1990). *Basics of qualitative research: Grounded theory procedures and techniques.* Newbury Park, CA: Sage.

Tavris, C. (1992). *The mismeasure of woman.* New York: Touchstone.

Templer, D. I. (1970). The construction and validation of a death anxiety scale. *Journal of General Psychology, 82,* 165–177.

Thomas, J., Rewey, K. L., & Davis, S. F. (2002). Professional development benefits of publishing in the *Psi Chi Journal of Undergraduate Research*. *Eye on Psi Chi, 6*(2), 30–35.

Traffanstedt, B. (1998). Weight reduction using behavior modification: Modifying sedentary behavior. *Journal of Psychological Inquiry, 3,* 19–23.

Vandenberg, S. G., & Kuse, A. R. (1978). Mental rotations, a group test of three-dimensional spatial visualization. *Perceptual and Motor Skills, 47,* 599–604.

Vaughn, E. J. (2002, April). *Matching hypothesis and physical attractiveness.* Paper presented at the Arkansas Symposium for Psychology Students, Arkadelphia.

Walker, K. A., Arruda, J. E., & Greenier, K. D. (1999). Assessment of perceptual biases extracted from the Visual Analogue Scale. *Psi Chi Journal of Undergraduate Research, 4,* 57–63.

Walter, K. D., Brownlow, S., Ervin, S. L., & Williamson, N. (1998). Something in the way she moves: The influence of shoe-altered gait on motion and trait impressions of women. *Psi Chi Journal of Undergraduate Research, 3,* 163–169.

Watson, L. (1998). The effects of noise volume on performance of a cognitive task. *Psi Chi Journal of Undergraduate Research, 3,* 99–104.

Weaver, S. R., & Dunham, K. (2002). Predictors of a new typology of youth violence. *Psi Chi Journal of Undergraduate Research, 7,* 3–12.

Weinberg, R. A. (1989). Intelligence and IQ: Landmark issues and great debates. *American Psychologist, 44,* 98–104.

Weintraub, D., Higgins, M., Beishline, M., Matchinsky, D., & Pierce, M. (1994, November). *Do impostors really hold irrational beliefs?* Paper presented at the annual meeting of the Association for Psychological and Educational Research in Kansas. Lawrence, KS.

Weiss, J., Gilbert, K., Giordano, P., & Davis, S. F. (1993). Academic dishonesty, Type A behavior, and classroom orientation. *Bulletin of the Psychonomic Society, 31,* 101–102.

Wells, R. (2001). Susceptibility to illness: The impact of cardiovascular reactivity and the reducer-augmenter construct. *Journal of Psychological Inquiry, 6,* 12–16.

Wolensky, N. H. (2001). The effects of society standards of physical attractiveness on body esteem in the elderly. *Psi Chi Journal of Undergraduate Research, 6,* 153–160.

Yang, K. S. (1982). Causal attributions of academic success and failure and their affective consequences. *Chinese Journal of Psychology, 24,* 65–83.

Zajonc, R. B. (1965). Social facilitation. *Science, 149,* 269–274.

Name Index

Subject Index